Education in West Africa

Available and forthcoming titles in the Education Around the World series

Series Editor: Colin Brock

Education Around the World: A Comparative Introduction,
Colin Brock and Nafsika Alexiadou
Education in Australia, New Zealand and the Pacific, edited
by Michael Crossley, Greg Hancock and Terra Sprague
*Education in the Commonwealth Caribbean and
Netherlands Antilles*, edited by Emel Thomas
Education in East and Central Africa, edited by Charl Wolhuter
Education in East Asia, edited by Pei-tseng Jenny Hsieh
Education in Eastern Europe and Eurasia, edited by Nadiya Ivanenko
*Education in the European Union: Pre-2003 Member
States*, edited by Trevor Corner
*Education in the European Union: Post-2003
Member States*, edited by Trevor Corner
*Education in Non-EU Countries in Western and
Southern Europe*, edited by Terra Sprague
Education in North America, edited by D. E.
Mulcahy, D. G. Mulcahy and Roger Saul
Education in South-East Asia, edited by Lorraine Pe Symaco
Education in Southern Africa, edited by Clive Harber
Education in South America, edited by Simon Schwartzman
Education in the United Kingdom, edited by Colin Brock
Education in West Central Asia, edited by Mah-E-Rukh Ahmed

Forthcoming volumes:

Education in Mexico, Central America and the Latin Caribbean,
edited by C. M. Posner, Christopher Martin and Colin Brock
Education in South Asia and the Indian Ocean Islands,
edited by Debotri Dhar and Hema Letchamanan
Education in the Arab World, edited by Serra Kirdar

Education in West Africa

Edited by Emefa Takyi-Amoako

Education Around the World

Bloomsbury Academic
An imprint of Bloomsbury Publishing Plc

B L O O M S B U R Y
LONDON • NEW DELHI • NEW YORK • SYDNEY

Bloomsbury Academic
An imprint of Bloomsbury Publishing Plc

50 Bedford Square	1385 Broadway
London	New York
WC1B 3DP	NY 10018
UK	USA

www.bloomsbury.com

BLOOMSBURY and the Diana logo are trademarks of Bloomsbury Publishing Plc

First published 2015 by Bloomsbury Academic
Paperback edition first published 2016 by Bloomsbury Academic

© Emefa Takyi-Amoako and Contributors, 2015

Emefa Takyi-Amoako and Contributors have asserted their right under the Copyright, Designs and Patents Act, 1988, to be identified as Author of this work.

All rights reserved. No part of this publication may be reproduced or transmitted in any form or by any means, electronic or mechanical, including photocopying, recording, or any information storage or retrieval system, without prior permission in writing from the publishers.

No responsibility for loss caused to any individual or organization acting on or refraining from action as a result of the material in this publication can be accepted by Bloomsbury or the author.

British Library Cataloguing-in-Publication Data
A catalogue record for this book is available from the British Library.

ISBN: HB: 978-1-4411-4251-1
PB: 978-1-4742-7061-8
ePub: 978-1-4411-7785-8
ePDF: 978-1-4411-9948-5

Library of Congress Cataloging-in-Publication Data
Education in West Africa / edited by Emefa Takyi-Amoako. pages cm.-- (Education around the world) Summary: "Education in West Africa is a comprehensive critical reference guide to education in the region. Written by regional experts, the book explores the education systems of Benin, Burkina Faso, Cameroon, Cape Verde, Chad, The Gambia, Ghana, Guinea, Guinea-Bissau, Ivory Coast, Liberia, Mali, Mauritania, Niger, Nigeria, Senegal, Sierra Leone and Togo. It critically examines the development of education provision in each country, whilst exploring both local and global contexts. Including a comparative introduction to the issues facing education in the region as a whole and guides to available online datasets, this handbook is an essential reference for researchers, scholars, international agencies and policy-makers at all levels"-- Provided by publisher.
 ISBN 978-1-4411-4251-1 (hardback) 1. Education–Africa, West. I. Amoako, Emefa.
 LA1611.E28 2015 370.966--dc23 2015004236

Series: Education Around the World

Typeset by Fakenham Prepress Solutions, Fakenham, Norfolk NR21 8NN
Printed and bound in Great Britain

Contents

Series Editor's Preface — vii
Notes on Contributors — viii

Introduction: Education in West Africa: A Regional Overview   *Emefa J. Takyi-Amoako* — 1

1 Benin: An Overview, Trends and Futures   *Mohamed Chérif Diarra* — 21
2 Burkina Faso: An Overview   *Martial Dembélé, Touorizou Hervé Somé and Fernand Ouédraogo* — 37
3 Burkina Faso: Trends and Futures   *Touorizou Hervé Somé, Martial Dembélé and Fernand Ouédraogo* — 53
4 Cameroon: An Overview   *Martha Beyang Egbe* — 67
5 Cameroon: Trends and Futures   *Willibroad Dze-Ngwa* — 85
6 Cape Verde: An Overview, Trends and Futures   *Jose Manuel Marques* — 101
7 Chad: An Overview, Trends and Futures   *Galy Panaïn Dibe and Mohamed Chérif Diarra* — 119
8 The Gambia: An Overview, Trends and Futures   *Makaireh A. Njie* — 135
9 Ghana: An Overview   *Ruby Selenu Avotri* — 151
10 Ghana: Trends and Futures   *Daniel Justin Eshun* — 167
11 Ghana: Education Financing   *Ato Essuman* — 183
12 Guinea: An Overview of Higher Education   *A. Tidjane Diallo, M. Kodiougou Diallo and Sékou Konate* — 199
13 Guinea-Bissau: An Overview, Trends and Futures   *Akemi Yonemura* — 217
14 Ivory Coast: An Overview, Trends and Futures   *François-Joseph Azoh* — 235
15 Ivory Coast: Evolving Gender Representation in Higher Education from Peace to the Era of Political Instability and Post-Conflict Reconstruction   *N'Dri Thérèse Assié-Lumumba* — 247
16 Liberia: Conflicts and Post-Conflict Trends   *Barbara G. Reynolds* — 265
17 Liberia: Citizenship Education in the Post-Conflict Era   *Laura Quaynor* — 283
18 Mali: An Overview, Trends and Futures   *Mohamed Chérif Diarra* — 297

19	Mauritania: An Overview, Trends and Futures *Akemi Yonemura and Mohamed Chérif Diarra*	311
20	Niger: An Overview *Nana Aicha Goza and Ibro Chekaraou*	329
21	Niger: Trends and Futures *Ibro Chekaraou and Nana Aicha Goza*	343
22	Nigeria: An Overview *Naomi A. Moland*	363
23	Nigeria: Technical, Vocational Education and Training *Benjamin Ogwo*	377
24	Nigeria: Financing Education *Mary Ogechi Esere*	393
25	Senegal: An Overview *Léa Salmon and Latif Dramani*	407
26	Senegal: Trends and Futures *Caroline Manion*	421
27	Sierra Leone: An Overview *Kingsley Banya*	435
28	Sierra Leone: Educational Trends and Futures *Kwabena Dei Ofori-Attah*	451
29	Togo: An Overview *Philippe Amevigbe*	465
30	Togo: Trends and Futures *Kossi Souley Gbeto and Koffi Nutéfe Tsigbé*	479

Index 493

Series Editor's Preface

This series will comprise nineteen volumes, between them looking at education in virtually every territory in the world. The initial volume, *Education Around the World: A Comparative Introduction,* aimed to provide an insight to the field of international and comparative education. It looked at its history and development and then examined a number of major themes at scales from local to regional to global. It is important to bear such scales of observation in mind because the remainder of the series is inevitably regionally and nationally based.

The identification of the eighteen regions within which to group countries has sometimes been a very simple task, elsewhere less so. Europe, for example, has four volumes and more than fifty countries. National statistics vary considerably in their availability and accuracy, and in any case date rapidly. Consequently the editors of each volume point the reader towards access to regional and international datasets, available on line, that are regularly updated. A key purpose of the series is to give some visibility to a large number of countries that, for various reasons rarely, if ever, have coverage in the literature of this field.

The region with which this book is concerned, West Africa, is probably the most difficult to deal with for a number of reasons. First, there are a very large number of countries to deal with. Second, at least four major official languages are involved and innumerable African vernaculars as well. Third, the region contains a larger proportion of the poorest countries in the world than any other, with correspondingly low levels of educational indices, including literacy rates and take-up of schooling.

Consequently the editor of this book, Dr Emefa Amoako, is to be highly commended on putting together what will be a most valuable resource, and addition to the literature of comparative and international education.

The majority of countries in this region have little or no visibility in that literature prior to the chapters in this book.

Colin Brock
Series Editor

Notes on Contributors

Philippe Amevigbe is the national co-ordinator of Educational Research Network for West and Central Africa. He holds a Doctorate in Science of Education and has written numerous publications.

N'Dri Thérèse Assié-Lumumba is Professor of African, African Diaspora and Comparative/International Education in the Africana Studies and Research Centre at Cornell University, USA. She is President-Elect of the Comparative and International Education Society (CIES), becoming President in 2015–16. She is a Fellow of the World Academy of Art and Science, Chercheur Associé at Université Félix Houphouët-Boigny, Ivory Coast, and Research Affiliate at the Institute for Higher Education Law and Governance of the University of Houston, USA. She is co-founder and Associate Director of the Centre PanAfricain d'Etudes et de Recherches en Relations Internationales et en Education pour le Développement (CEPARRED). She has served as Director of the Cornell programme on Gender and Global Change and Director of the graduate field of Africana Studies. She is a leading scholar with several published books, numerous articles in refereed journals, and major reports on various dimensions of education, especially higher education, gender and equity.

Ruby Selenu Avotri is a retired educationist and researcher who had worked at the Curriculum Research and Development Division (CRDD) of the Ghana Education Service as a curriculum developer and Head of the Research, Monitoring and Evaluation Unit. She holds a Doctorate degree in Education from the Murdoch University, Perth, Australia; a Master of Education (Educational Evaluation and Measurement) from the University of Ibadan, Nigeria; and a Bachelor of Arts and Diploma in Education from the University of Cape Coast, Ghana. She also has a Certificate in Public Administration from the Ghana Institute of Management and Public Administration (GIMPA). She coordinated the In-school Adolescent Sexual and Reproductive Health/HIV/AIDS Project of the African Youth Alliance and the Gender and Primary Schooling Research Project in Ghana for the Ministry of Education. Earlier in her career she taught at secondary school level in Ghana and Nigeria.

François Joseph Azoh is a social psychologist of education and teaches at Ecole Normale Supérieure of Abidjan, Ivory Coast. He is Lecturer in the Psychology Department at the University of Abidjan-Cocody, Ivory Coast, teaches at Centre Ivoirien d'Etudes et de Recherche en Psychologie Appliquée and collaborates with Senghor University, Egypt. He is the current Regional President of the Scientific Committee of Educational Research Network for West and Central African (ERNWACA). His research interests are social representations; citizenship and governance; and internal control of social and school performance.

Kingsley Banya is Professor of Curriculum Theory and Comparative and International Education. He has written extensively about development projects and educational reform in sub-Saharan Africa and has been published all over the world in various languages. Banya has made more than 165 refereed presentations at National and International Conferences. He has also served as external examiner of doctoral theses at many R-I institutions in Canada, USA and Australia. He holds a Ph.D. from the University of Toronto, Canada.

Ibro Chekaraou is Associate Professor of Education at the University Abdou Moumouni of Niamey, Niger, where he also chairs the Department of English Education. He received his Ph.D. in education from Indiana University, USA. He has taught Hausa language at Kansas University, Indiana University, the University of Memphis, Tennessee and at Michigan State University, where he also directed the African Languages Program. From 2004 to 2005 he worked for the HOPE Foundation in Indiana, helping to provide teachers and education leaders with leadership training throughout the USA. He has authored and co-authored online Hausa teaching materials, multiple journal articles and two books.

Martial Dembélé is Associate Professor in the Department of Educational Administration and Foundations at the Université de Montréal, Canada, which he joined in 2005 after co-directing for four years the Paul-Gérin-Lajoie Interuniversity Center for International Development in Education at the Université du Québec à Montreal, Canada. His teaching, research and consultancy have been in the areas of school improvement and teacher development; practitioner research; the comparative study of teacher education and management policies, programmes and practices; the qualitative aspects of educational planning; and more recently accountability policies and frameworks in education.

A. Tidjane Diallo is currently adviser for higher education at the Ministry of Higher Education and Scientific Research, Guinea. He holds a Ph.D. in mathematics from Babes-Bolyai University of Cluj Napoca, Romania, and a certificate for secondary inspectorate from the Ecole Normale Supérieure de Fontenay-Saint Cloud, France. He taught for many years at various higher education institutions in Guinea. He has been general director of the Institute of Education at Conakry, Guinea, national co-ordinator of the Guinean chapter of the Educational Research Network for West and Central Africa (ERNWACA) and general director of higher education at the Ministry of Higher Education. His research interests are in Bernstein type quasi-interpolants, mathematics education, teacher education and higher education governance.

M. Kodiougou Diallo is currently general director of Central University Library Project. He taught for many years at the University of Conakry, Guinea. He has been deputy vice-chancellor of Gamal Abdel Nasser University at Conakry, Guinea. He holds a Ph.D. in mathematics from University of Bucharest, Romania, and he spent one year at the National Institute for Informatics and Automatic, France. His research interests are in operational research and data analysis.

Mohamed Chérif Diarra is an education specialist. He holds a doctorate degree in Education Finance from Louisiana State University, USA. He has worked in various capacities for the Government of Mali; the United States Agency for International Development (USAID); the Association for the Development of Education in Africa (ADEA); and the United Nations Educational, Scientific and Cultural Organization (UNESCO). He has also served on various educational organizations' boards and scientific committees, including The African Network Campaign for Education for All (ANCEFA); the Educational Research Network for West and Central Africa (ERNWACA); E-Learning for Education and Sante for Africa (ELES4Africa); and Distance Education Africa (DEA). He has authored several book chapters and journal articles.

Galy Panaïn Dibe is an independent educational consultant. He holds a Master's degree from the University of Bourgogne, France. Formerly he was Director General of Planning and Administration at the Ministry of National Education, a Senior Technical Adviser for UNESCO in the Democratic Republic of Congo, an International Education Planning Expert at the Regional Bureau of Education in Africa, and an Education Program Specialist for UNESCO in Haiti.

Latif Dramani is Professor of Economics and Statistics at the University of Thies, Senegal, and Co-ordinator of the Centre for Research in Applied Economics and Finance (CREFAT). He also teaches at other universities in Africa and is associated with the University of Manchester, UK; the University of California, Berkeley, USA; the University of Parakou, Benin; and the University of Hawaii at Manoa, USA. He holds a Ph.D. in economics from the University Cheikh Anta Diop, Dakar and has worked at the National Agency of Statistics and Demography. His research is concentrated in Africa and focuses on national and regional economic integration; development issues and generational economy; and poverty dynamics.

Willibroad Dze-Ngwa is Senior Lecturer and Researcher at the University of Yaoundé I, Cameroon, in the areas of comparative education, geopolitics, leadership, human rights, political history, international relations and peace and conflict studies. He has taught extensively at universities in Cameroon, the School for International Training (SIT), USA, and at the Savannah State University, Georgia, USA, as a Senior Fulbright Scholar-In-Residence. He is the founding-President of Africa for Research in Comparative Education Society (AFRICE) and a member of the Publications Standing Committee of the World Council of Comparative Education (WCCES). He is also the Executive Director of the Africa Network Against Illiteracy, Conflict and Human Rights Abuse (ANICHRA). He currently serves as Consultant-Co-ordinator for Communication, Research and Publications at the Pan African Institute for Development.

Martha Beyang Egbe holds a Ph.D. from the University of Ibadan, Nigeria, and has over 15 years experience teaching mathematics in secondary schools. Formerly, she was the statistician of the African Development Bank 'Project Education 2' managed by the Ministry of Basic Education in Cameroon. Her research interests include the evaluation of projects sponsored by the World Bank and other funding agencies; and examining the reasons for poor performance of students in mathematics in the Cameroon Education System.

Mary Ogechi Esere is Senior Lecturer in the Department of Counsellor Education, University of Ilorin, Nigeria. She holds a BA Ed from the University of Calabar, Nigeria, and Ph.D. in Educational Guidance and Counselling from the University of Ilorin, Nigeria. She also holds a CLA degree from the Universitaire de Besançon, France. Her research focuses on sex, marriage, family counselling, gender issues, communication in marital therapy and general counselling-related issues. She has been involved in developing psychological support programmes for couples in conflict and implementation strategies for youth programming and young people. These efforts have resulted in well over 40 articles published in national and international peer-reviewed journals and two scholarly books.

Daniel Justice Eshun is University Chaplain and Senior Lecturer at the University of Roehampton, UK, and Associate Vicar at Holy Trinity Parish Church, UK. He has worked as a secondary teacher, a theological educator, Christian youth worker and parish priest in Africa, Asia and the United Kingdom. He was educated at the University of Cape Coast, Ghana; King's College, University of London, UK; St John's College, Durham University, UK; and Kellogg College, University of Oxford, UK. His research interests are in the areas of education; ethics; social and cultural anthropology; sociology of religions; theology; and mission studies.

Ato Essuman is Director of the Centre for Entrepreneurship Education Research and Training at the Methodist University College, Ghana. He holds a doctorate degree in education from the University of Sussex, UK. As a former Chief Director of Ghana's Ministry of Education, he championed the 2007 educational reforms and the education decentralization agenda, which in his view should be based on a deeper understanding of local contexts. His research interests cover fields in education policy and practice; education financing; decentralization; community-school relations; and school-age immigrants in Ghana. He has spoken widely on schooling reforms, both in Ghana and internationally, and was a member of a high-level panel on education at the World Economic Forum in Cape Town, South Africa in 2011.

Kossi Souley Gbeto is Senior Lecturer in French literature and in Francophone African literature at the University of Lomé-Togo, Togo. He is also a research fellow at the Educational Research Network for West and Central Africa (ERNWACA) in Togo. He is currently the chairman of the Togolese Association of French Teachers (APFT).

Nana Aicha Goza is Associate Professor of Education Psychology at Ecole Normale Supérieure (Education School) at the University Abdou Moumouni of Niamey, Niger, where she trains teachers and education leaders. In addition, she is currently serving her second term as Dean of Ecole Normale Supérieure in Niamey and has extensively worked on gender issues in education. She received her M.Ed. degree in education and teacher training from the University of Lyon, France, and her doctorate in education psychology from the University of Mons-Hainaut, Belgium. She has contributed many education book chapters, published articles in education journals and co-authored two books.

Sékou Konate is currently adviser for scientific research at the Ministry of Higher Education and Scientific Research, Guinea. He holds a Ph.D. in physics from the University of St. Petersburg, Russia, and taught for many years at the University of Conakry, Guinea, where he has been general director of the Scientific Centre of Conakry-Rogbane.

Caroline Manion is Instructor in Comparative, International and Development Education collaborative programme at the University of Toronto, Canada. Her research interests include gender and education; the politics of education; global governance and educational multilateralism; religion and education; and equity and social justice in and through education.

José Manuel Marques has worked for ten years in education planning, and in the last four years has worked in the management of the NGO Platform, under the programme for prevention and support for HIV victims in Cape Verde. He also teaches at the University of Cape Verde in the fields of Statistics, Education Planning and Information Systems. He graduated in Statistics and Information Management at the University of Nova Lisboa, Portugal, studied Education Planning at UNESCO's International Institute for Education Planning, France, and holds a Master's degree in information systems from the University of Aveiro, Portugal.

Naomi A. Moland is Postdoctoral Research Fellow at New York University, USA, where she obtained her Ph.D. in International Education. Her research interests include multicultural education, literacy, post-colonial nation building, anthropology of education, and the global diffusion (and localization) of liberal ideologies. Her doctoral research investigated the globalization of multicultural ideals via educational media. She conducted nine months of fieldwork in Nigeria researching how the Nigerian version of *Sesame Street* (funded by USAID) teaches about diversity and tolerance amidst escalating ethnic conflict.

She has conducted research on race, ethnicity, and education in the United States, Ghana, Zimbabwe, Spain and Nigeria. She has taught courses about globalization, international development, and sub-Saharan Africa at New York University, USA, The New School University, USA and Columbia University, USA.

Makaireh A. Njie is a specialist in Technical, Vocational Education and Training (TVET) and National Co-ordinator of the Educational Research Network for West and Central Africa in the Gambia. He has a Master's degree in Education from Sheffield University, UK, and an Advanced Diploma in further Education from the University of Leeds, UK. Njie has over 35 years of experience in the field of TVET, having been the National Director for Technical Education and Vocational Training in The Gambia and the Director of The Gambia Technical Training Institute.

Kwabena Dei Ofori-Attah teaches at Central State University, Wilberforce, Ohio, USA, as the Graduate Program Coordinator. He is Research Fellow of the African Educational Research Network (AERN) and the founder of an online journal, *The African Symposium* (*TAS*). He has over 15 years of online and on-ground teaching experience in Ghana, Nigeria and the United States. He holds a doctorate in Elementary Education from Ohio University, USA, and two master's degrees, one in International Affairs and the other in Public Administration. Over the years he has presented several papers at regional, national and international conferences and also published a number of articles in refereed journals, book chapters, and two articles in the *Encyclopedia of Education* (2004). He is the author of *Going to School in the Middle East and North Africa* (2008).

Benjamin Ogwo is Professor in Industrial Technical and Workforce Education and is affiliated with the State University of New York at Oswego, USA. He is a scholar and consultant with broad experiences in technical vocational education and training (TVET), e-learning, programme development, curriculum design, implementation and evaluation. He has been involved in training and development initiatives with agencies such as the World Bank, UNESCO, UNICEF, the African Devlopment Bank, USAID, the International Labour Organization, and the African Technology Policy Studies Network (ATPS). He has published more than 70 papers in various peer-reviewed journals and presented several international workshop papers.

Fernand Ouédraogo is a Ph.D. candidate in the Department of Educational Psychology and Adult Education in the Faculty of Education at the University of Montreal, Canada. His doctoral research focuses on the challenges faced by Burkina Faso's educational system, including issues related to school-family collaborative relationships, parents' educational styles, and their links with the academic achievement of elementary students. Prior to undertaking a Ph.D. study program, Ouédraogo worked as a psychologist at the National Center for Information, Academic and Vocational Counseling, and Scholarships (CIOSPB), Burkina Faso. He also taught at the University of Ouagadougou, Burkina Faso, in the Department of Philosophy and Psychology.

Laura Quaynor is Assistant Professor of Curriculum and Instruction in the School of Education at the University of South Carolina Aiken, USA. Her research focuses on the ways that schools and teachers prepare students as citizens in the context of disruptive change, with a particular emphasis on multilingual learners in the United States and students in transitional and post-conflict states. Her work with Liberian students stems from engagement with Liberian refugees in Ghana, and continued relationships with students and schools once they had repatriated to Liberia. She received funding from Emory University, USA, and the Open Society Institute, USA, to investigate citizenship education in Liberia.

Barbara G. Reynolds is currently Deputy Vice-Chancellor (Academic Affairs) at the University of Guyana. Prior to this, she was Head of Education for Save the Children UK and spent 22 years with UNICEF in a range of capacities, including representational and programme assignments in education, child protection and innovation. Reynolds has a keen interest in the development response to internally displaced persons, the role of the private sector in education, and the integration of computer technologies in education. She holds a BA in Education; an MA in Curriculum and Teaching from Howard University, USA; a Diploma in Distance Education from the University of London, UK; an EdD in International Education Development/Curriculum and Instruction from the University of Columbia, USA; and an MSt in International Human Rights Law from the University of Oxford, UK.

Léa Salmon is a sociologist specializing in developing countries. She holds a Ph.D. from Paris-X University, France, and her dissertation on *Street Children in Abidjan* was published in 2004. Since then, she has been involved in research programmes with the World Bank and the United Nations Development Programme. She has led and published research on poverty reduction, social exclusion, and vulnerable groups. In addition, she was involved in the management of World Bank projects supporting ex-combatants and their reintegration in Central Africa. She recently joined the Research Laboratory on Economic and Social Transformations in Dakar University, Senegal.

Touorizou Hervé Somé is a Fulbright scholar and Associate Professor at Ripon College, Wisconsin, USA. He teaches social and philosophical foundations of education; diversity in American education; issues in Africa and its diaspora; and English as a second language. He also supervises student teachers in their field placements. His research interests include comparative education, globalization, neoliberalism, the education of the African child in America, and gender bias in education. Prior to pursuing a Ph.D. at the University of New York at Buffalo, USA, Somé taught English as a Foreign Language in Burkina Faso, before being appointed as a teacher advisor in charge of pre-service and in-service teacher education at the Ministry of Secondary and Higher Education. He was also a faculty member of the Law and Political Science teaching and research unit at the University of Ouagadougou, Burkino Faso. He has published several peer-reviewed book chapters and journal articles addressing education policy and higher education finance in Africa. He is also the principal author of a forthcoming book about newcomer minority student school experiences in the USA.

Emefa J. Takyi-Amoako is Executive Director of Oxford ATP International Education and Education, Gender and Research Consultant, who holds a doctorate in Comparative and International Education from Oxford University, UK. Prior to this, she obtained her Bachelor's, and two Master's Degrees from University of Cape Coast, Ghana, and Oxford Universty's Wadham and St Anne's Colleges respectively. Her research interests are in the areas of education policy, globalization, foreign aid partnerships, power, gender, education and technology, as well as, pre-tertiary and higher education. She has published works and authored a number of reports on education including 'Comparing power spaces: the shaping of Ghana's Education Strategic Plan' (2012) in *COMPARE* and 'Developing nodes in leading networks of knowledge for leader and leadership development: Some African students' perspectives on their experience of doctoral education' (2014) in A. Taysum and S. Rayner, *Investing in Our Education: Leading, Learning, Researching and the Doctorate*. Emerald

Group Publishing Ltd. Emefa has taught at undergraduate and graduate levels and is also a Quality Assurance Expert in higher education.

Koffi Nutéfe Tsigbé is Senior Lecturer in History at the University of Lomé-Togo, Togo.

Akemi Yonemura has worked for UNESCO as an Education Program Specialist for more than a decade in Paris, New Delhi, Addis Ababa and Dakar. She holds a doctorate in education from Columbia University, USA, and her research interests include education finance and planning; policy-making process; education and migration; skills development; community college; and aid effectiveness.

Introduction: Education in West Africa: A Regional Overview

Emefa J. Takyi-Amoako

Rationale

A book that provides a comprehensive analysis of education in West Africa has long been overdue. Until now only fragmented and piecemeal analyses of education in the region have been done. Existing studies dedicated to West Africa as a region have been selective in the choice of countries. This book is significant at a time when the driving force towards economic, education/academic and other forms of integration in the region is accelerating due to the increasing need for a united front in engaging more effectively with: global trade and finance; knowledge economies; recent discoveries of more natural resources; educating and training the growing youthful populations that characterize the region; and the heightening necessity to grasp the complex nature of the issues that typify the region in general, along with the various sectors of the different countries, in particular. In this case, the education sectors of these countries seem even more crucial since their success has significant reverberations for manpower/skills development, job creation and their subsequent impact on the economies and overall progress of the region.

The West African region encompasses more nations than any other region on the continent, and central to the region's development in all spheres is education (World Bank 2013). Consequently, this book explores the education systems of each country in the region. With chapters on all the member countries of the Economic Community of West African States (ECOWAS) as well as Cameroon, Chad and Mauritania, the book critically examines the development of education provision in each country as well as local and global contexts. In this comparative introductory chapter, this important book is launched by providing a regional overview of education in West Africa within a global context.

In an attempt to set the context for the chapters, summarize them to offer a panoramic view of the state of education in the region, and define the structure of the book, I argue that the rising young national populations that characterize the region require universal access to quality education, relevant skills training and their prospects, because this phenomenon (of having over 60 per cent of national populations as youth) represents a tremendous and unique opportunity for the various national governments to comprehensively invest in capacity building, while 'thinking outside the box' with regards to how this could be achieved successfully. I contend that over the years, governments in West Africa have allowed their education sectors to be driven more externally by global policies, diktats and solutions than internally, by local/national/ regional home-grown resolutions. While this may not always necessarily be a disadvantage, and the situation may be due to historical factors and the economic and financial challenges faced by these countries, including the fact that international financial institutions (IFIs), bilateral and multilateral donors have been and still are inextricably linked to these national education sectors, it is crucial that countries decide through national leadership the trajectories their education sectors must take (Samoff and Carrol 2004). This step will provide the opportunity for countries to reconceptualize education with its objectives within the African context, and re-enact it in a more relevant and effective fashion for improved outcomes. At the moment, despite significant national and international funding as well as technical support of the education systems in Africa, and a few marginal gains, the educational outcomes are not encouraging and the future of education in sub-Saharan Africa in general, and West Africa in particular is nothing but bleak (UNESCO 2014).

Trends

According to the *Education for All Global Monitoring Report 2013/14: Teaching and Learning: Education Quality for All* (ibid.), which monitors the Education for All (EFA) goals, in early childhood care and education, sub-Saharan Africa was among the regions where three-quarters of children under five, some 162 million, remained malnourished, and enrolment rates in pre-primary education reached only 18 per cent while they increased globally from 33 per cent in 1999 to 50 per cent in 2011. According to the report, Africa continues to trail behind the rest of the world with 22 per cent of its primary school children still out of school as at 2011. While the number of out-of-school adolescents fell by 31 per cent globally since 1999 to 69 million, in sub-Saharan Africa, the number of out-of-school adolescents remained the same at 22 million between 1999 and 2011 due to the increase in population (ibid.).

Additionally, the lowest youth literacy rates in 2011 were in 18 countries, all of which were in West Africa. For instance, in Guinea (31 per cent), Niger (37 per cent), Burkina Faso (39 per cent), Benin (42 per cent), Mali (47 per cent), Chad (48 per cent) and Liberia (49 per cent), under half of the population between 15 and 24 years were literate (UNESCO 2013). While there have been rapid gains in adult literacy rates in other parts of the world since 1990, in sub-Saharan Africa, the number of illiterate adults has rather been on the ascendancy, reaching 182 million in 2011. It has actually been estimated that 26 per cent of adult illiterates worldwide will be living in sub-Saharan Africa after 2015, a rate rising from 15 per cent in 1990. Fifteen countries in West Africa are among those with the worst adult literacy rates in the world. They include the five countries with the world's lowest literacy rates, below 35 per cent. These same countries have the lowest female literacy rates, below 25 per cent in comparison with the sub-Saharan African average of 50 per cent. It is claimed that this situation will not recover any time soon. In fact, less than half of young women are literate in 12 of those 15 countries in West Africa (UNESCO 2014).

While most countries worldwide, that is 70 per cent, will have attained parity at both primary and secondary levels by 2015, and 10 per cent will edge towards it, 14 per cent will remain far from the goal, and 7 per cent will remain even farther away, and of this proportion, three-quarters are located in sub-Saharan Africa. A country on the verge of or attaining gender parity does not imply that all or more children are in school. Burkina Faso, which is scheduled to achieve gender parity at primary level by 2015, but continues to have the seventh lowest gross enrolment ratio is a case in point. In Senegal, where girls' enrolment has soared and gender parity has nearly been attained, enrolment rates of boys have stagnated (ibid.).

Moreover, quality of education, EFA Goal 6, which is the pivot and essence of education progress, is in crisis in sub-Saharan Africa. The absence of quality is the bane of any education system. Pupil/teacher ratio as a measure for evaluating this goal is crucial according to the report. Teacher recruitment lagging behind soaring enrolment rates in sub-Saharan Africa has culminated in pupil/teacher ratio stagnation, which is, currently, the most extreme globally at the pre-primary and primary levels. Out of the 162 countries with data in 2011, 26 had a pupil/teacher ratio in primary education surpassing 40:1, 23 of which are in sub-Saharan Africa. The pupil/teacher ratio in primary education rose by no less than 20 per cent in nine nations. It, however, declined by no less than 20 per cent in 60 states. For instance, primary-school enrolment increased twofold in Mali like in Congo and Ethiopia. Nevertheless, like both, its pupil/teacher ratio reduced by over ten pupils per teacher. While this may appear as progress, the problem is that the increase in teacher numbers occurred at the expense of education quality since most of the new teachers were employed without requisite training. In a third of countries with data, fewer than 75 per cent of teachers are qualified in keeping with national benchmarks. In 29 of the 98 nations, of which two-thirds are in sub-Saharan Africa, the pupil/trained teacher ratio outstrips the pupil/teacher ratio by ten pupils (ibid.).

Mamadou Ndoye, the past Executive Secretary of the Association for Development of Education in Africa (ADEA), emphasized secondary education as a leading concern in sub-Saharan Africa (Bregman and Bryner 2003).[1] By 2009, a pupil in the final class of primary school had at best a 75 per cent chance of transitioning to lower secondary school in nearly 20 countries globally. Most of these countries were in sub-Saharan Africa including Tanzania (36 per cent) and Nigeria (44 per cent) which recorded the lowest transition rates. The period between 1999 and 2009 witnessed the expansion of lower secondary education globally with a gross enrolment ratio (GER) rising from 72 per cent to 80 per cent. During this period, although sub-Saharan Africa saw the most remarkable growth with a GER increase from 28 per cent to 43 per cent, gender disparities persisted. Despite the increase in girls' enrolment (39 per cent) by 14 percentage points, the proportion of girls participating remained very low with 48 per cent as GER compared to their male counterparts. Moreover, in most of the countries, it was less likely for girls than boys to attain completion. Besides, sub-Saharan Africa had 21.6 million, that is, 30 per cent of out-of-school children globally. Forty per cent of all lower secondary school-age girls and 33 per cent of boys were out of school (UNESCO 2011). Bregman and Bryner (2003) noted the exclusive focus on expanding primary education instigated by donor policies over the years in sub-Saharan Africa, which has resulted in significant neglect of the demand to enhance quality and capacity in secondary education and caused acute difficulties in the region. Evidently, protracted and recent conflicts in sub-Saharan Africa in general and West Africa in particular have severely rendered the youth of secondary-school-going age in these countries vulnerable. The youth between the ages of 12 and 19 years in conflict-ridden countries such as Liberia, Ivory Coast and others represent the most vulnerable (Bregman and Bryner 2003).

Also, apart from North Africa with high enrolment in technical and vocational education and training (TVET) (22.95 per cent of total secondary school enrolment between 2001 and 2005), in sub-Saharan Africa in general, TVET is marginally positioned in school systems at 5.2 per cent between 2001 and 2005 with a declining trend since 2003. Consequently, sub-Saharan Africa lags behind the rest of the world. For instance, in 2006, the percentage of technical and vocational enrolment (PTVE) was significantly higher in the Organisation for Economic Co-operation and Development (OECD) countries of Australia (70 per cent), Austria (62 per cent), Belgium (68 per cent), Czech Republic (65 per cent), Finland (40 per cent), Italy (59 per cent) and Norway (49 per cent). Meanwhile, in 2005, the South East and East Asian nations of South Korea (19 per cent), China (18 per cent), Indonesia (16 per cent), Singapore (13 per cent), Thailand (18 per cent in 2006) recorded relatively high PTVE rates albeit lower than those of the OECD nations (but still higher than the rates in sub-Saharan Africa). The extremely low PTVE rates in sub-Saharan Africa suggest inertia and general low public funding and training potential. The sub-sector is unable to absorb the numerous primary school products due to lack of funds on the part of the youth to access formal TVET, under-funding of formal TVET, outmodedness of equipment, and feeble management capability, which undermine the quality of courses. Besides, the perception that students of TVET are the academically or intellectually unsuccessful and, therefore, the consideration of this type of education as low status also accounts for the low PTVE. The contradiction between its low standing and its real economic and social significance to national development needs to be addressed through sustainable policies and investment, while the connection between formal and informal TVET requires enhancement (African Economic Outlook 2008).

Furthermore, the picture painted by the higher education sector on the continent is even more depressing despite the efforts of revival. After very high levels of national commitment to this sector due to its perception as a 'public good' and provider of knowledge and skills for national and continental development of Africa in the immediate post-independence era of the 1950s, 1960s and early 1970s, decades of neglect and financial pressure compelled by the Bretton Woods Institutions (BWIs), the World Bank/International Monetary Fund (IMF) followed (Jegede 2012; Sawyerr 2004; Samoff and Carrol 2004; World Bank 1988). While the first phase (late 1950s to early 1970s) of the development of higher education in Africa could be described as the golden era, the second (mid-1970s to late 1980s) was characterized by deterioration: rapid expansion, tensions with national governments, steep decline in national and international funding assistance, sharp rise in student enrolments, staff attrition, infrastructural decay and national economic strife; and eventually the third phase (1990s to date), which has been termed a period of restoration (Mihyo 2008; Lindow 2011). From the 1990s, national governments in Africa began reforming their policies on higher education in order to enable the institutions to survive and innovate. Simultaneously, international donor agencies began re-evaluating their stance of abandonment after pressures from various angles not least from African nations (ibid.). According to Mihyo (2008), the period between 1995 and 2005 was the most significant as it represented the decade of African higher education institutions' taking advantage of the prospects emerging from increased national focus and international volte-face with regards to the sector by reclaiming their sense of agency and reinstating their dignity through extensive institutional and curriculum innovation and reforms. Yet, like the pre-tertiary education sector, there continues to be challenges plaguing higher education in Africa, an essential component of *African Union Commission (AUC) Agenda 2063* (Teferra 2013).

The missing link

Indeed, Africa seems to be constantly trailing behind the rest of the world despite the good will, leadership, significant financial commitments, and policy recommendations of external development partners (UNESCO 2014). It has become apparent that it is not prudent for Africa to continue leaving the development of its entire national/regional systems including the education sector to the leadership of external development partners. Over the years, international financial and donor institutions, particularly, the World Bank, have disseminated manifold and often ever-changing theoretical paradigms to shape education policies for Africa. It had deployed a discriminatory and limited pool of empirical studies and readings of the human capital and 'rates of return' theories to breed a profoundly disjointed and unequal education policy terrain, one that promoted basic or primary education, and yet repudiated and nearly decimated higher education in sub-Saharan Africa till the 1990s (Obamba 2013). But the advent of the millennium witnessed the World Bank, through its policy discourses, radically altering its stance by stressing the importance of higher education and a knowledge-based development framework, within which the generation, reworking and utilization of knowledge is the agent of continued economic progress and poverty alleviation for all globally (ibid.; World Bank 2014).

Attempts to render foreign aid effective signified by the High Level Fora on Aid Effectiveness in Rome, Paris, Accra and Busan in 2003, 2005, 2008 and 2011 respectively, and which culminated in the Busan Partnership Agreement ratified by over 100 countries as the plan for augmenting the impact of aid have been relevant (OECD 2013). The World Bank's current *Education Strategy 2020* may have theoretically shifted drastically and become more open to values embedded in global partnership, harmonization, and diversity in international development co-operation. It may now be promoting a multi-sectoral and systems approach to education development, a science-technology-innovation paradigm, learning for all instead of education for all discourses as Obamba (2013) argues. However, for African countries to simply avoid the 'yoyo' effect that this unending shifting policy position of external development partners engenders, which undermines the sustainability of Africa's educational development, they have to become the policy drivers and main funders of their own education systems. This requires their repositioning within the framework of this global partnership in a manner that they fully grasp, and will empower them to make the relevant choices that will benefit their countries. They have to understand how they engage with the wider world, and ensure the reactivation of their sense of agency, which includes not only creatively identifying alternative funding streams, but also fighting against corruption, financial mismanagement, and actively promoting practices linked to transparency, probity and accountability.

It is incumbent on national governments in sub-Saharan African countries to provide the leadership required for the African people who better understand or have the potential of understanding by virtue of their indigenous practical experiences of their education systems to fundamentally define the problem that plagues Africa's national education systems, and identify appropriate solutions. As Nsamenang and Tchombe (2011: xxvii) rightly point out:

> We have learned that no people entirely dislodged from their ancestral roots have ever made collective progress with development and that the era of outsiders deciding and 'supplying' what Africans need has not yielded hoped-for outcomes. We think the donor community and education partners can do much to support Africa in its quest for apt ... education, for funds and influence reside in them in disproportionate quantities. Their powers should not be used to 'show the way', but to support Africa's efforts to hear its own education theories and see its education practices, among others, and to seek its own way forward.

The confluence: Understanding the positioning of West/Africa globally

Consequently, I argue that to enhance the potential of West/African countries and national governments to effectively determine the appropriate paths that their education sectors should take in order to tackle the above challenges, there is the need to gain a deep understanding of how national policy contexts, processes and practices integrate the global (Lingard and Ozga 2007); how they often occur on the cusp of a nation state and global arena (Lingard 1996; Taylor et al. 1997; Vidovich 2001); and where the precise interconnectedness of the stages and milieus of policy are made manifest (Taylor 1997; Vidovich 2001). In fact, what needs to be grasped is the notion of education policy choices, processes and practices at the point where donors and recipients or external development partners and national agents meet, which I refer to as the *confluence*, situated on the cusp of the global and national (see Amoako 2009).[2] This is crucial because although generous percentages of African national gross domestic products (GDP) are devoted to the various education sectors of most of the countries analysed in this book, there remain funding gaps. These sectors continue to receive financial support from international/foreign aid donors, both bilateral and multilateral because funds of most African national governments often go towards recurrent costs, which leave none for service delivery. As a result, part of these gaps is financed with international aid and loans (ibid.).

It is important to note that although the BWIs lend huge sums of money to developing countries, it is not only their significant funding power but also their impact on other donors that counts (Moutsios 2008; Klein 2007; Harvey 2005). As a result, their political and economic integrity in a recipient country instils confidence in other donors to provide funding to that particular country. Strikingly, these loans and grants come with specific conditionalities, which explicitly or implicitly determine education policy directions in the said country (ibid.). A detailed quote from Jones (1992: xiv) indicates the significant policy influence of the World Bank and its transmission of developed-world ideas:

> The World Bank lies at the center of the major changes in global education of our time. Its financial power and influence have helped shape the economic and social policies of many governments, including policies that affect education. It has been an influential proponent of the rapid expansion of

formal education systems around the world, and has financed much of that expansion. It has been instrumental in forging those policies that see education as a precursor to modernisation. It has served as a purveyor of western ideas about how education and the economy are, or should be, connected. It has assumed a prominent role in educational research and policy analysis, and exercises a degree of leadership among those organisations committed to education.

The transnational character of the education policies, processes and practices in these African countries should not be underestimated. Substantial evidence is shown even in the structure and content of most of the chapters of this book. Countries' commitment to achieving the goals of global policy initiatives and macro-economic policies including World Declaration on Education for All of Jomtien 1990, the Dakar Framework of Action of the World Education Forum of 2000; the Millennium Development Goals (MDGs), poverty reduction strategies (PRSs) renders them credit worthy and eligible for international funding support. These global policies are non-negotiable if a national economy is foreign aid and loan dependent. Policy processes appear no longer only national or between nations, *'inter-national'* but also *'trans-national'* with the latter implying the blurring of the lines between national frontiers, their removal or amalgamation (Beck 2005; Amoako 2009). This engenders the surge of power from the global arena into the individual countries' domains of power. Transnational policy processes include those of the national, but, it is a nation state's policy processes that generate a space in which transnational policy is extended. In this regard international organizations are critical. It is deeply within the contexts of international institutions and not in national domains that the principles of the power game of global policies are agreed, shaped and reshaped (Beck 2005). These principles not only transform primarily the political and social processes of countries but are also ingrained within their body politic through the foreign aid system. Hence, national education policy processes are enmeshed in this revolution (Amoako 2009). As studies have shown, the BWIs emerged as the designers of national policies in Africa (Amoako 2009; Whitfield 2006; Hutchful 2002; 1996; Kraus 1991; Toye 1991; Callaghy 1990). The international aid structure is entrenched within African nation-states and societies because donors have customized and partially standardized the manner in which they relate with national entities, and in which they partake in the devising, execution and evaluation of national policies and processes (ibid.).

In spite of this, as Obanya (2011: xxv) observes, Africa is the only continent, which is:

> most lowly represented in international organizations, including the UN agencies, and about whom decisions for their situation and well-being are often taken without even token voices from their people's representatives.

However, it is important to point out that external influences are not necessarily always in disagreement with the local/national ones. It has been observed that remarkable intersections on standpoints and favoured practice, mirroring at any rate partly the internalized suppositions and perceptions that are themselves a key means of influence. Potent national/local forces also engage and sometimes converge with the external currents to form the dynamics at the confluence (Samoff and Carrol 2004). According to Samoff and Carrol (2004: 55),

> [t]o explore the nature of this convergence, its specific mechanisms and practices, and the relative balance between external, internal, and internalized factors we need much more detailed study at the local level, which for the most part has not yet been done.

Thus, a deep understanding of this confluence by African national governments, decision makers and agents of change in these African countries, and how they are positioned within this space on the cusp or in the nexus of the global and local is crucial. This clarity will bring about re-evaluation of priorities, active and innovative identification of alternative sources of funding, and forms of education practices that are relevant and compatible to Africa's development needs. Also, repositioning these countries at this confluence of the international and national in a manner that will scrutinize systems of accountability and transparency, partnership practices between African nation-states and external actors will create a productive awareness and sensitivity to tackle effectively the issues that are uniquely African. This is in no way suggesting that Africa isolates itself from the rest of the world since that will be to its detriment and will be impossible anyway. However, the strong implication here is that attaining a multi-layered appreciation of this confluence, and how national governments, actors, problems and solutions in these African countries are positioned within it in relation to external development partners and the wider world will: enable the leveraging of viable regional/continental/global networks; empower and grant the national/regional/continental self-confidence required to navigate and negotiate the current global village on their terms so as to become not only complete beneficiaries of it but also extensive contributors to its advancement (Obanya 2011).

The chapters in this book constitute one step in understanding the national/regional/continental peculiarities, and positioning of West Africa, in particular, and for that matter, Africa at this confluence, which encapsulates the global partnership for education development (OECD/UNDP 2014; United Nations 2013).

Book chapters: Description, approach, objective and main themes

The 30 chapters explore and discuss education in all the 15 member countries of ECOWAS in addition to Chad, Mauritania and Cameroon. They explore the history, current issues and futures of education in the countries in West Africa. The chapters examine themes that range from conflict and security, citizenship, gender, access and quality, financing, development, technology/ICT, to pre-primary, primary, secondary, TVET, religion and higher education.

The approaches the authors adopt for the chapters emphasize insightful knowledge based on notional, historical and contemporary expressions of the development of formal education in the various countries by methods ranging from participant observation, documentary analysis, to in-depth interviews, focused group interviews and surveys.

The book's objective is to provide very brief histories of the systems of education in the different countries in West Africa and show how they laid the foundation for current trends; identify the emerging trends in education in contemporary West Africa; map the futures of education in the various countries of the region; enable the reader to define and if possible, compare the educational systems in the Anglophone, Francophone and Lusophone contexts. Overall, the book aims to provide a comprehensive understanding of education in West Africa in relation to the world.

First, this book serves as an introductory book for readers who are interested in education in West Africa but have limited knowledge of it. Simultaneously, its Anglophone, Francophone and Lusophone perspectives give readers a comprehensive and sophisticated view of education in the region, which normally books on education in the region do not offer.

Second, the book offers a panoramic view of what constitutes education in the region by providing brief histories, the present state and future of education with regards to the youth and globalization in each of the 18 countries. Readers will benefit from the knowledge of the different dimensions that education is assuming in West Africa and their implications for the economies, politics and cultures of the countries in the region.

While all the chapters in this book raise very important issues including access and participation, education financing *inter alia*, the youthful nature of the various countries' populations and the dire need to improve the quality of education in order to maximize its benefits to young people cannot be overstated, as the success of this will no doubt determine the developmental prospects of West Africa, and for that matter, Africa in this and the next generations.

Futures, prospects and reflections: A commentary

Indeed, Africa's growing young population with a median age of 19 years presents either a huge challenge or risk if not managed effectively, or a substantial prospective labour force and human resource that would promote progress on the continent (Ata-Asamoah and Severino 2014). While the obvious goal one would prefer to attain is the latter, the questions to be asked are: Are the education systems in the various countries in West Africa enabling their graduates or beneficiaries with these considerations in mind? What choices are governments and decision makers making to ensure these conditions are fulfilled? What type and level of education quality is on offer to these growing young populations in the various countries? This book with all contributions from African education experts is an attempt to give voice to and draw on national histories, experiences, perspectives and knowledges to explore these questions, and help to understand the complex prospects and challenges that characterize education in West Africa. As indicated earlier, in doing so, the global or international is relevant since what signifies the local or national in the education sectors of these West African countries is increasingly being positioned on the cusp of the global and local. In other words, national education policies, plans and strategies are formulated and implemented within the nexus of the global and national. Whether the rising young populations of Africa would represent a potential or missed opportunity lies in: how these questions are addressed in practice; how national governments and other stakeholders adopt a systemic approach to the different levels of education and strengthen higher education on the continent; how willing nations are to critically evaluate the existing conditions, and take deliberate steps to innovatively 'think outside the box', and as agents of positive change, revolutionize their thought processes and actions in their bid to tackle the problems. In this sense, this book functions as an enlightening resource that aims to dialogue with national governments, countries, regional/continental bodies of Africa and other stakeholders, and enable them to reflect on their ongoing steps towards revolutionizing West Africa's, and for that matter, Africa's education systems for the better.

The educational component of the Strategic Plan 2011–2015 of the ECOWAS is to offer citizens increased access to quality education and training prospects existing in the region through synchronization of policies, strategies, programmes and activities, as well as academic curricula and qualifications (ECOWAS n.d.). For ECOWAS, higher education is perceived as an emerging strategy to actualize its *Vision 2020* (ECOWAS 2009; Biao 2011).

The AUC Agenda 2063, the 50-year-development strategy, which is currently being developed by the Africa Union Commission (AUC), positions education as one of its key pillars. Its first key strategic initiative is to strengthen African initiatives and strategies on a fast-tracked human capital development, science and technology and innovation: constructing a competent labour force, drawing on the digital revolution and global knowledge; appropriate conceptualization and engagement in African skills revolution rooted in the continent's uniqueness.

ADEA, a forum for policy dialogue, comprising all the 54 Ministers of Education in Africa and 16 development partners, is also reinforcing its comparative advantage in education development by executing its second medium-term strategic plan (2013–17) aimed at backing Ministries of Education to tackle key problems in education, and enact a paradigm shift and transformations in education that were recommended to African Heads of State during the ADEA Triennale in 2012. Indeed, the main thrusts of the Triennale are embodied in five strategic objectives, specifically to: (i) progress policies, strategies, practices, and programmes that stimulate analytic knowledge competences, and credentials; (ii) advance and cultivate African-led education and training resolutions to deal with national and regional needs; (iii) promote better use of pertinent ICT to hasten enhanced educational change and training reforms; (iv) leverage an assorted, viable collaborative network; and (v) reinforce institutional capability and efficiency (ADEA 2013).

Furthermore, the fast technological and economic advancement in the international market must be converted into tangible transformation and enhanced opportunities for Africa's youth. Investing in the education and training of present and future generations is the solitary means to sever the sequence of deprivation, discord and insularity. Vast post-conflict funding requirements necessitate a revision of strategy for secondary education (and other levels of education), and a reconsideration of its comparative precedence (Bregman and Bryner 2003). A deep knowledge of the confluence is critical since the regional/continental strategies for implementing the above initiatives include reaching out complementarily to global networks, strengthening African higher education through centres of excellence, and education systems in general with best practices from the continent and around the globe (AUC 2014 Outcomes of the Bahir Dar World Bank 2014).

Most of the chapters in this book make reference to the development of ICT policies and their implementation. There is an urgent need to look more critically at how technology could be deployed in a manner that will add value to and even reduce the cost of the process towards the goals of education access, quality and skills training. Unlike laptops and other electronic gadgets, the mobile phone is one piece of technological device that seems to have defied all the norms of technological limitations that constantly plague Africa. The mobile phone, which nearly everybody on the African continent in general and West Africa, in particular, owns is interesting and gives food for thought. Does this gadget, which seems to be playing the curious role of the 'great leveller' on the African continent, represent an opportunity for national governments in Africa to 'think outside the box' and creatively identify more sustainable means and solutions to crucial issues regarding education access and quality at all levels of the sector from basic to tertiary? Undoubtedly, this is one difficult challenge but an exciting opportunity for the continent! The new trends with regards to technology and others, which are latently shaping the future of the educational systems in the region, provide exciting prospects for research, investment, development, and quality assurance among others.

According to Castells (2005), three processes are essential for the occurrence of productivity growth. First, the creation and distribution of new digital technologies of information and communication, grounded in scientific enquiry and technological innovation; second, the transformation of the workforce, with an increase in a well-educated, independent workforce that has the ability to invent and adjust to a continually transforming global and local economy; and third, the dissemination of a novel type of arrangement around networking. It is only in the fulfilment of these conditions that a nation's productivity greatly increases, which in turn, would ultimately guarantee its regional or international competitiveness (ibid.). Like the East Asian countries, sub-Saharan Africa nations could effectively synchronize the development of education with an intensified and express conversion of their markets into more finished goods exports, enabling their markets to thrive within the modern international economy (ADB 2003).

Also, is the way in which poverty is analysed and tackled in West/African countries too simplistic and outmoded? Should national governments, continental and regional institutions with their development partners in Africa actively seek to consistently complement or supplant official income poverty strategies by adopting multidimensional poverty measures? These measures consider health, education and living standards with these three dimensions further broken down to multiple indicators that include nutrition, child mortality, years of schooling, school attendance, cooking fuel, improved sanitation, safe drinking water, electricity, flooring, asset ownership (Alkire and Foster 2011; Alkire 2013; UNDP 2014).[3] As Stiglitz (2014: 84) succinctly notes, '[i]f we are to formulate policies to reduce vulnerability, it is essential to take a broad view about what creates such vulnerability'.

In 2014, Africa's economy withstood both domestic and external shocks and growth is expected to expedite to 4.8 per cent and 5 to 6 per cent in 2015, heights unseen since the global economic meltdown of 2009. The sophisticated nature of the growth motivated by internal pressure, infrastructure and rise in trading finished products continentally must be blended with wise macro management. Investing in fresh and more lucrative sectors, developing skills of the youth to global standards, exporting labour, creating jobs and obtaining modern technology, knowledge and market information coupled with good public policies and entrepreneurship seem the way forward. According to predictions, West Africa is envisaged to maintain its fast growth. Following a slight restraint in 2013, growth is expected to exceed 7 per cent in 2014 and 2015 (African Economic Outlook 2014). Although strong economic growth is necessary for Africa and its countries, it is not sufficient, since it could/does engender or exacerbate inequalities (Sen 1992; 1993). However, if multidimensional poverty measures form part of development policies, both the incidence and intensity of deprivation could be measured and tackled in order to address the inequalities that occur during economic growth (Alkire 2013). The chapters in this book in exploring the state of education in the various countries lay the foundation for these questions to be addressed.

Some relevant databases updated regularly

A productive way to conclude this introductory chapter is to help advance the discourse and practice of knowledge and information networking by listing some relevant global/continental/regional databases. The education systems in

West Africa, and for that matter Africa, are in a constant state of flux. Readers will therefore find some of the frequently updated databases and sources below useful.

- Africa Economic Outlook (http://www.africaneconomicoutlook.org)
- Global Human Development Report published annually by the UNDP since 1990 (http://hdr.undp.org)
- ERIC (Education Resources Information Centre) (http://eric.ed.gov/?q=education+in+west+africa) http://eric.ed.gov/
- The World Bank EdStats (Education Statistics) – covers the whole world, 214 economies including those of West Africa and is updated quarterly (Coverage: 1970–2050): http://data.worldbank.org/data-catalog/ed-stats http://datatopics.worldbank.org/education/
- The UIS.Stat is UNESCO Institute for Statistics, which contains all the latest available data and indicators, for education, literacy, science, technology and innovation, culture, communication and information. http://data.uis.unesco.org/
- Educational Research Network for West and Central Africa (ERNWACA) http://www.ernwaca.org/web/spip.php?rubrique14
- Council for the Development of Social Science Research in Africa (CODESRIA) http://newebsite.codesria.org/spip.php?rubrique4#&panel1-1
- Association for Development of Education in Africa (ADEA) http://www.adeanet.org/portalv2/en/content/adea-publications-and documents#.VAmyzGPiuVo
- http://www.adeanet.org/portalv2/en/knowledge-sharing/adea-database#.VAnPL2PiuVo http://www.adeanet.org/min_conf_youth_skills_employment/en/content/documents
- The Global Multidimensional Poverty Index (MPI) Interactive Databank enables you to see at a glance results of OPHI's (Oxford Poverty and Human Development Initiative) 2014 analysis of acute poverty in 108 developing countries around the world. http://www.dataforall.org/dashboard/ophi/index.php/

Notes

1 In a keynote address at the First Regional Secondary Education in Africa (SEIA) Conference in Uganda in June 2003.
2 For comprehensive information on the notion of the confluence as a conceptual framework see Amoako, 2009 (full reference in the References section below).
3 Sen (1992).

References

African Economic Outlook (2008). *Developing Technical & Vocational Skills in Africa.* http://www.africaneconomicoutlook.org/theme/developing-technical-vocational-skills-in-africa/the-rationale-for-technical-and-vocational-skills-development/taking-stock-of-technical-and-vocational-skills-development/access-to-technical-and-vocational-education-in-africa/ (accessed 21 August 2014)

—(2014). *Global Value Chains and Africa's Industrialisation.* Tunis, Paris, New York: AfDB, OECD, UNDP .

African Union Commission (AUC) (2013). African Union Agenda 2063: A Shared Strategic Framework for Inclusive Growth and Sustainable Development Background Note. AUC.

—(2014). Outcomes of the Bahir Dar Ministerial Retreat of the Executive Council on Agenda 2063, 24–26 January 2014. As adopted by the 24th Ordinary Session of the Executive Council, 27–28 January 2014, Addis Ababa (Rev.1).

Alkire, S. (2013). Measuring Global Poverty: From maths and villages to Policy. A paper presented at Oxford Alumni Weekend, 20 September 2013.

Alkire, S. & Foster, J. E. (2011). Counting and multidimensional poverty measurement. *Journal of Public Economics* 95 (7–8), 476–87.

Amoako, E. J. A. (2009). Shaping policy at the confluence of the global and national: Ghana's Education Strategic Plan. DPhil thesis, University of Oxford.

Asian Development Bank (ADB) (2003). *Key Indicators*, vol. 34.

Association for the Development of Education in Africa (ADEA) (2013). *ADEA Medium Term Strategic Plan 2013-2017: Education, Skills and Qualifications for Sustainable Development in Africa.* Tunis: ADEA. http://www.adeanet.org/portalv2/sites/default/files/adea_medium-term_strategic_plan_2013-2017.pdf (accessed 3 August 2014)

Ata-Asamoah, A. and Severino, J. (2014). Head-to-head: Is Africa's young population a risk or an asset? BBC http://www.bbc.co.uk/news/world-africa-25869838 (accessed 4 April 2014)

Beck, U. (2005). *Power in the Global Age: A New Global Political Economy.* London: Polity.

Biao, I. (2011). 'Higher education as an emerging strategy for actualising the Vision

2020 of the Economic Community of West African States (ECOWAS)'. *Educational Research and Reviews* 6 (19): 961–8.

Bregman, J. and Bryner, K. (2003). Quality of Secondary Education in Africa (SEIA). Paris: Association for the Development of Education in Africa (ADEA).

Castells, M. (2005). 'The network society: from knowledge to policy'. In Castells, Manuel and Cardoso, Gustavo (eds), *The Network Society: from Knowledge to Policy*. Washington, DC: Johns Hopkins Center for Transatlantic Relations.

Callaghy, T. (1990). 'Lost between state and market: the politics of economic adjustment in Ghana, Zambia and Nigeria'. In J. Nelson (ed.), *Economic Crisis and Policy Choice: The Politics of Adjustment in the Third World*. Princeton: Princeton University Press, pp. 257–319.

ECOWAS. (n.d.). *Regional Strategic Plan (2011–2015): A Proactive Mechanism for Change*. Abuja: ECOWAS.

—(2009). *ECOWAS Vision 2020*. http//www.ecowasvision2020

Engberg-Pedersen, P., Gibbon, P., Raikes, P. and Udsholtt, L. (eds) (1996). *Limits of Adjustment in Africa: the Effects of Economic Liberalization*. Oxford: James Currey.

Harvey, D. (2005). *A Brief History of Neoliberalism*. Oxford: Oxford University Press.

Hutchful, E. (1996). 'Ghana 1983–94'. In P. Engberg-Pedersen, P. Gibbon; P. Raikes and L. Udsholtt (eds). *Limits of Adjustment in Africa: the Effects of Economic Liberalization*. Oxford: James Currey, pp. 141–214.

—(2002). *Ghana's Adjustment Experience: the Paradox of Reform*. Oxford: James Currey.

Jegede, O. (2012). Higher Education in Africa: Weaving Success. An Invited Contribution to the Panel Discussion on the Launch of *Weaving Success: Voices of Change in Higher Education* – A Project of the Partnership for Higher education in Africa (PHEA) Held at the Institute of International Education, 809 United Nations Plaza, New York, NY 10017, on Wednesday, 1 February, 2012.

Jones, P. W. (1992). *World Bank Financing of Education: Lending, Learning and Development*. London: Routledge.

Klein, N. (2007). *The Shock Doctrine: The Rise of Disaster Capitalism*. New York: Metropolitan Books.

Kraus, J. (1991). 'The Political Economy of Stabilization and Structural Adjustment in Ghana'. In D. Rothchild (ed.), *Ghana: The Political Economy of Recovery*. London: Lynne Rienner, pp. 119–55.

Lindow, M. (2011).*Weaving Success: Voices of Change in Higher Education*. New York: Institute of International Education.

Lingard, B. (1996). 'Review essay: educational policy making in a postmodern state. On Stephen J. Ball's education reform: a critical and post-structural approach'. *Australian Educational Researcher*, 23(1): 65–91.

Lingard, R. and Ozga, J. (2007). 'Reading Education Policy and Politics'. In R. Lingard and J. Ozga (eds), *The RoutledgeFalmer Reader in Education Policy and Politics*. London: Routledge pp. 1–8.

Mihyo, P. B. (2008). *Staff Retention in African Universities and Links with the Diaspora.* Accra: AAU.

Moutsios, S. (2008). 'International organisations and transnational education policy'. *Compare: A Journal of Comparative and International Education,* iFirst Article, 1–12. [Online]. Available from http://dx.doi.org/10.1080/03057920802156500 (accessed 4 July 2008).

Nsamenang, B. A. and Tchombe, T. M. S. (2011). *Handbook of African Educational Theories and Practices: A Generative Teacher Education Curriculum.* Cameroon: Human Development Resource Centre (HDRC).

Obamba, M. O. (2013). 'Uncommon knowledge: World Bank policy and the unmaking of the knowledge economy in Africa. *Higher Education Policy,* 26: 83–108.

Obanya, P. (2011). 'Foreword'. In B. A. Nsamenang and T. M. S. Tchombe, *Handbook of African Educational Theories and Practices: A Generative Teacher Education Curriculum.* Cameroon: Human Development Resource Centre (HDRC), pp. xxv–xxvi.

OECD (2013). 'Education at a glance 2013: OECD indicators', OECD Publishing. http://dx.doi.org/10.1787/eag-2013-en (accessed 19 August 2014)

—(no date). 'The high level fora on aid effectiveness: a history. OECD. http://www.oecd.org/dac/effectiveness/thehighlevelforaonaideffectivenessahistory.htm (accessed 19 August 2014)

OECD/UNDP (2014). *Making Development Co-operation More Effective: 2014 Progress Report,* OECD Publishing. http://dx.doi.org/10.1787/9789264209305-en (accessed 19 August 2014)

Samoff, J. and Carrol, B. (2004). 'Conditions, coalitions, and influence: the World Bank and higher education in Africa'. Prepared for presentation at the Annual Conference of the Comparative and International Education Society, Salt Lake City, 8–12 March 2004.

Sawyerr, A. (2004). 'Challenges facing african universities: Selected Issues'. *African Studies Review,* 47 (1): 1–59.

Sen, A. K. (1992). *Inequality Re-Examined.* Oxford: Clarendon Press.

—(1993). 'Capability and Well-being'. In Nussbaum, M. and Sen, A. K. (eds), *Quality of Life.* Oxford: Clarendon Press, pp. 30–53.

Stiglitz, J. (2014). 'Broadening our Thinking on Vulnerability. A Special Contribution'. In *Human Development Report: Sustaining Human Progress: Reducing Vulnerabilities and Building Resilience.* New York: UNDP.

Taylor, S. (1997). 'Critical policy analysis: exploring contexts, texts and consequences'. *Discourse,* 18(1): 23, 35.

Taylor, S., Rizvi, F., Lingard, B. and Henry, M. (1997). *Educational Policy and the Politics of Change.* London: Routledge.

Teferra, D. (2013). 'The African quest for nurturing doctoral education'. Center for International Higher Education. Available from http://www.insidehighered.com/

blogs/world-view/african-quest-nurturing-doctoral-education (accessed 4 March 2014).
Toye, J. (1991). 'Ghana'. In P. Mosley, J. Harrigan and J. Toye (eds), *Aid and Power: the World Bank and Policy-Based Lending*. London: Routledge pp. 150–200.
UNESCO (2011). *Global Education Digest 2011 Regional Profile: Sub-Saharan Africa*. Canada: UIS.
—(2013). *Adult and Youth Literacy National, Regional and Global Trends, 1985–2015*. Canada: UIS.
—(2014). *Education for All Global Monitoring Report 2013/14 Teaching and Learning: Education Quality for All*. Paris: UNESCO Publishing.
United Nations (2013). *Millennium Development Goal 8: The Global Partnership for Development: The Challenge We Face. MDG Gap Task Force Report 2013*. New York: United Nations.
United Nations Development Programme (2014). *Human Development Report: Sustaining Human Progress: Reducing Vulnerabilities and Building Resilience*. New York: UNDP.
Vidovich, L. (2001). 'A Conceptual framework for analysis of education policy and practices'. Paper proposed for presentation at the Australian Association for Research in Education, Fremantle, December 2001.
Whitfield, L. (2006). 'Aid's political consequences: The embedded aid system in Ghana', *GEG Working Paper 24*.
World Bank (1988). *A World Bank Policy Study: Education in Sub-Saharan Africa Policies for Adjustment, Revitalization, and Expansion*. Washington, DC: World Bank.
—(2013). 'Investing in higher education across West Africa'. World Bank. http://www.worldbank.org/en/news/feature/2013/07/29/investing-in-science-and-technology-across-west-africa (accessed 26 June 2014).
—(2014). 'World Bank to finance 19 centers of excellence to help transform science, technology, and higher education in Africa'. *Press Release*. World Bank. http://www.worldbank.org/en/news/press-release/2014/04/15/world-bank-centers-excellence-science-technology-education-africa (accessed 26 June 2014).

1

Benin: An Overview, Trends and Futures

Mohamed Chérif Diarra

Introduction

The aim of this chapter is to present an overview, the trends and the future prospects of Benin's educational system with specific reference to its history, the major reforms undertaken, its structure, organogram, funding and legal framework. The chapter further analyses the current trends and challenges facing the system and issues such as access, participation, quality, equity, relevance, the integration of the Information and Communication Technology (ICT) as well as regional integration and their bearings on teaching and learning.

The Republic of Benin (formerly Dahomey) is a French-speaking country in West Africa that stretches between the Bight of Benin in the Gulf of Guinea of the Atlantic Ocean in the south and the savannah in the north. It covers a surface area of 114,760 square kilometres (less than the size of England). Benin shares common borders with three former French colonies: Togo to the west, Burkina Faso to the north-west, and Niger to the north, as well as an Anglophone country, Nigeria to the east.

According to the 2013 general population census, the population of Benin was estimated to be 10 million, a significant increase of 3.2 million from the 6.7 million recorded in 2002 (RGPH4 2013). It has an annual increase rate of 3.5 per cent over a ten-year period. It is projected that Benin's population, at this inter-census increase rate, will reach 16 million by the year 2033, and 20 million by 2043. It is 51.2 per cent female and 48.8 per cent male which gives a gender parity index (GPI) of .95 per cent. Further, this population is extremely young. About 44.1 per cent is below the age of 14 years and 19.9 per cent is less than 24 years of age. About 60 per cent of this population lives in rural areas. In 2003, the population of Cotonou (the seat of government and the largest city of the country) was estimated to be 924,000 inhabitants whereas that of the capital city of Porto Novo was estimated to be 314,000. Benin has five major national languages; Fon (spoken by 50 per cent of the population), Yoruba, Mina, Bariba and Dendi. French is the official language and therefore the language of instruction. English is also used as a second language in Benin's secondary education. Benin is divided into 12 administrative departments.

Benin has been the seat of several kingdoms: Dahomey, Abomey and Bariba from the fifteenth century onwards. Dahomey became a French colony in 1872. It came under the influence of the Portuguese who founded Porto Novo in 1752. Between 1760 and 1885, the country remained under French rule which was officially confirmed by the 1885 Berlin Conference that portioned a big chunk of Africa between the French and the English. It marked the beginning of colonial rule in Africa. On 4 December 1958, the Republic was proclaimed Dahomey. It became independent on 1 August 1960. Her first government was overthrown by a military coup on 28 October 1963.

Between 1963 and 1972, Benin experienced a period of political instability and turmoil. The power struggle between the civilians and the military culminated, in 1972, in another military coup that brought to power General Mathieu Kerekou who ruled the country for 17 years. In 1975, Kerekou's regime adopted a hard line Marxist-Leninist orientation and ideology and Benin eventually became a People's Republic. Learning the lessons from 17 years of socialist regime and state ownership of the main means of production, Benin reverted to the market economy. A move to democracy began in 1989. Benin became the first African nation to initiate a Policy Dialogue Forum (PDF) known as the National Conference (NC) that brought together representatives from all the spectrum of the Benin nation. The NC became a reference and a model for many African nations emerging from the dark period of dictatorship and the one-party system that characterized the early phases of the post-independence era. The main purpose of the NC held in Cotonou, 19–28 February 1990, was to redefine the country's political orientation and reinvent its institutional framework in accordance with democratic principles. The NC made the following key recommendations with far-reaching consequences for Benin and perhaps the entire continent: i) abolition of the Marxist ideology as the State philosophy; ii) reversion to the genuine flag; iii) reversion to the multiparty system; iv) dissolution of all one-party structures; v) release of all political detainees and prisoners; and vi) respect of Human Rights. In 1991, free elections ushered in former Prime Minister Nicéphore Soglo as president making the successful transfer of power in Africa from a dictatorship to democracy. Kerekou was returned to power in 1996 and 2001 by elections.

The structure of the Beninese economy, which is poorly diversified and mainly agricultural, has not changed significantly over the past two decades. It is dominated by agricultural production, starting with cotton, its main export crop. Benin has enormous agricultural potential but is faced with numerous challenges to rationalize and modernize the sector. The absence of sound management and efficient governance principles along with the acute shortage of quality human resources constitute real impediments to economic growth. It should be noted that the contribution of cotton to the country's Gross Domestic Product (GDP) averages 8 per cent whereas that of the primary sector of the economy (agriculture) is close to 31 per cent. In the current economic context, its membership of the Economic Community of West African States (ECOWAS[1]) and the West African Economic and Monetary Union (WAEMU[2]) is an asset to capitalize on.

The methodology used in the chapter is basically qualitative. It consists of a desktop review of all the available sources of data, mainly secondary but also primary and others. Websites on Benin's educational system also provided useful information.

Overview

Benin's educational system is a legacy of French colonization. However, it has been, to a large extent, shaped by the context as well as several endogenous factors including but not limited to the local social traditions and values and politics.

Background and setting

According to Attanasso (2010), Benin's educational system went through three evolutionary phases aligned on the three distinct periods that characterize her post- independence political history: 1) 1960–75: an offspring of the colonial school; 2) 1975–90: the years of the socialist regime whose educational vision was captured in the new school model (école nouvelle); and 3) 1990 onward: the liberal type of school, a model that reflects the democratic renewal of the country.

Educational reforms

Conducting relevant educational reforms for a country like Benin emerging from colonial rule and struggling to build a new nation and to reinvent its educational system featuring new structures, objectives and contents focused on the national realities and values, was a challenge. Thus from 1960 to 1975, the colonial school model that retained the objectives, structures and contents of the French educational system was still in existence. In 1975, three years after the advent of the socialist regime, 'the new school model' was established. Thus, the objectives of education changed and the content of the curriculum reflected the national realities and values but no longer notions like the 'Gaulois'[3] our ancestors embedded in the school curriculum during colonization. However, after 15 years of implementation of this reform, although positive gains were made especially in access, the impact of the new school model was relatively limited (www.adobong.org). A key recommendation made by the NC was to upscale the reform based on the results of the evaluation of the new school model. Thus, the 'liberal school model' was adopted and it replaced the new school model. A National Forum also known as the 'Etats généraux de l'éducation' whose purpose was to define the contours of the new model was held in October 1990. The government adopted a new education policy framework featuring its vision of the new model that was to be translated into a strategy document along with an operational plan to facilitate its implementation. The impact of this reform was impressive for access indicators such as the Gross Enrolment Ratio (GER) that dramatically increased at all levels and for all types of education but disappointing for others such as the pupil/teacher ratio, etc.

Structure of Benin's educational system

Benin's educational system has five major layers (Attanasso 2010). Figure 1.1 illustrates the structural organization of the system. It is comprised, from bottom to top, of pre- primary, primary, secondary general, secondary technical and vocational and tertiary including higher education. Pre-primary education, the foundation of the pyramid, takes three years, primary, six, lower secondary, four, higher secondary, three, and higher education a minimum of four years. As for the technical and vocational schools, teachers' training institutions and colleges, the length of studies varies from a minimum of two to a maximum of four years. In a near future, Benin may revert from the current primary structure to the one recommended by the Basic Education in Africa Programme

Figure 1.1 Benin's educational system structure

	Universities and Private Institutions of higher learning		
	General Secondary Education	Technical and Vocational Education	
Second cycle of general secondary education	12th grade	Last Year	Second cycle of technical and vocational education 1
	11th grade	1st	
	10th grade	2nd	
First cycle of education	9th grade	3rd	First cycle of technical and vocational education
	8th grade	4th	
	7th grade →	1st year	
	6thgrade		
Primary education	5th grade		
	4th grade		
	3th grade		
	2nd grade		
	1st grade		
Pre primary education	Section of the old of kindergarten		
	Section of the young of kindergarten		

Source: Adapted from Attanasso (2010)

(BEAP),[4] an UNESCO initiative that advocates an uninterrupted nine to ten years of basic education. This section covers only formal education and excludes non-formal which is another ministry's responsibility.

Governance

The institutional architecture of Benin's educational system, as well as the number of ministries and their respective duties and responsibilities, have oftentimes been in sync with the political and historical phases of education transformation the country has experienced since its independence. Although the administrative structure of the system has been relatively unchanged over time, the number of Ministries of Education has fluctuated between one and four depending on the phase and the underlying education orientation and policies of the model. From 1975 to the NC of 1990, four ministries of education have been in charge. From a single Ministry of National Education and Scientific Research governance structure in 1990, Benin's educational system administration was split between four Ministries in 2001. They were as follows: 1) The Ministry of Primary and Secondary Education; 2) The Ministry of Technical Education and Vocational Training; 3) The Ministry of Higher Education and Scientific Research; and 4) The Ministry of Culture, Arts and Tourism. The typical organogram of a Ministry consists of the minister's office ('cabinet'), and national directorates. The directorates are comprised of divisions and sections. Other administrative entities report to the minister's office or the national directors. For example, institutions are governed by Heads who have assistants in charge of studies, finance and pupils' supervision.

Funding

The funding of education in Benin, as in other Francophone countries, is first and foremost the responsibility of the central government. This practice is a legacy of colonization (Diarra 1992). However, it should be noted that households spend a significant portion of their incomes to meet the cost of education of their siblings. For example, in 2009, the contribution made by households to the funding of primary education represented 25 per cent of the total funding whereas in higher education it amounted to only 12 per cent (Attanasso 2010). This relatively low contribution of households to the financing of higher education may be explained by the various cash transfers made by the government to the students in the form of bursaries, tuition waivers, housing and the like. In addition to these two major sources of funding, it is interesting to note that stakeholders such as development agencies and Non-Governmental Organizations (NGOs) are also major contributors to the funding of education in Benin. Local communities are also contributing their fair share to the costs of education across their own areas. Despite all these efforts, it appears that education in Benin is underfunded. This constitutes an impediment to its quality and the efficient and effective delivery of numerous educational services.

The private sector

The emergence of private schools in Benin goes as far back as the earlier years of colonization. The first schools, owned and operated by the Protestant church, were established in 1853, in Ouidah, Agoué and Grand Popo. This was followed by the creation of the first Roman Catholic school in 1881. These schools are the oldest of Dahomey. Therefore, the confessional school preceded the public school in this country. The government's role in the sector is to primarily be a regulatory body. It adopts laws, rules and regulations governing the establishment and operations of private schools in Benin. A case in point is the passing of Education Act 2003-17 of 11 November 2003 that authorizes the allocation of public funds to religious and confessional schools in Benin. In the final analysis, this issue raises the philosophical debate of whether public funds should be used to fund private institutions.

It is interesting to note that the proliferation of private schools in Benin has significantly improved the country's GER as well as the supply of all types of educational services. For example, it is especially at the pre-primary level that the contribution of the private sector to the provision of educational services in Benin is the most significant. The sector owns and operates most of the maternal schools. It provides support to the government regarding the funding of education and fills the gap created by the shortage of early childhood development centres (CESE) that have eventually become maternal schools. At the tertiary level, the private sector owns and operates many tertiary institutions such as professional, technical and vocational schools and higher education institutions (HEIs). In this respect, its contribution to the Licence-Master-Doctorate (LMD) reform has been remarkable. Compared to public schools, strikes are very limited in the private sector. However, the sector is faced with several challenges and there is a need to address them diligently with the assistance of the government and other actors, one challenge being the quality issue.

The legal and policy framework

The legal foundation of Benin's educational system rests on the new Constitution of 11 December 1990. In fact, the provisions of Article 13 of this constitution stipulate that 'schooling is compulsory and free till grade 6'. Besides, Benin has adopted and ratified many international legal instruments such as the African Charter for Human and People's Rights (ACHPR)[5] and the 1981 Arusha Convention on the recognition of degrees, diplomas, grades and other qualifications in Africa[6] that complete her legal arsenal regarding education. It should further be noted that the educational reform movement of the 1990s gained impetus in the early 2000s. This led, in 2003, to the adoption by the Parliament of the first Education Act, known as 'Loi d'Orientation Nationale'. This important piece of legislation constitutes the first regulatory document of the system. The Educational Act resulted, in 2006, in the formulation, adoption and implementation of a Ten-Year Development Plan of the Education Sector (2006–15), (PDDSE). It is interesting to note that the plan's lifespan coincides with the African Union Second Decade of Education for Africa Plan of Action and most of their components are the same.

The PDDSE encompasses all the levels and types of education and is articulated around several strategies, including but not limited to the following:

- Promoting girls' education;
- Improving school health;
- Raising awareness about early childhood care and education;
- Improving access and retention at all levels especially primary;
- Improving quality and equity at all levels; and
- Promoting scientific research in higher education.

Benin's ten-year educational policy framework is a key document articulated around six major pillars:

- Strengthening educational management capabilities and building human capacity;
- Improving the quality of learning and teaching;
- Increasing the provision of educational services;
- Improving the management of human resources;
- Addressing gender gap, urban/rural and rich/poor disparities; and
- Increasing the role of the private sector and local communities in the provision of education services.

Trends

As a matter of fact, numerous trends emerge from the above description of the educational system of Benin some of which constitute assets whereas others are impediments that need to be addressed to improve its performance. The section presents the trends likely to affect the system in the coming years.

Access and participation

As a general rule, access and participation in all types and levels of education have remarkably improved over the past two decades not only in Benin but in Africa as a whole. The democratization of education, the increase in educational opportunities, the value of education as perceived by the communities and the improvement in the supply of educational services have significantly contributed in boosting access to and participation in education. Nonetheless, there were still 30 million African school-age children not enroled in 2011 (UNESCO 2012). At the country level, Benin's performance in improving access has been outstanding. For example, according to the National Ministry of Education Statistics (2012), in primary education, the GER increased from 71 per cent in 1992 to 93 per cent in 2004 and peaked, in 2007, at 98.5 per cent. In secondary education, it more than doubled in just a period of 12 years. It rose from 12 per cent in 1992 to 27 per cent in 2004. It represented 35 per cent in lower secondary and 13 per cent in higher secondary. As for higher education, the increase has also been significant. There were 200 students for 100,000 inhabitants in 1992, 350 in 1999, and 565 in 2011.

The explosion of enrolments at all levels has resulted in numerous challenges for the government of Benin. Among these challenges, it is interesting to note the shortage of facilities and teachers as well as instructional materials and equipment. With specific reference to higher education, the number of students enroled in both public and private HEIs rose from 34,336 in 2001/2, to 64,910 in 2007/8, a 189 per cent increase in just a period of 7 years. During the same period of time, the number of institutions rose from 70 to 149, a 213 per cent increase. These two examples, on primary and higher education, illustrate the formidable task Benin has to face to alleviate the negative consequences in the explosion of enrolment. As her population continues to rise, the number of school-age children will also continue to increase as well as the number of secondary school graduates willing to attend HEIs. This situation is putting enormous pressure on Benin to build more facilities, purchase more instructional materials and recruit more teachers and more college professors at a time when the financial resources are scarce and education is competing with other priorities especially regarding development agencies.

Quality and equity

As access and participation continue to increase, the quality of education is deteriorating in all types and at all levels of education. Like in many other

African countries, Benin continues to grapple with the quality issue and the trend may not so easily be reversed in the near future. Indicators related to cohort survival analysis, repetition and primary cycle achievement provide powerful explanations to better understand the quality issue in the country. To illustrate the phenomenon, two examples come to mind: the grade repetition and the primary education completion rates. First of all, Attanasso (2010) posits that the grade repetition rate in primary education in Benin experienced ups and downs between 2003/4 and 2006/7.The rates decreased from 24 per cent in 2003/4 to 17 per cent in 2004/5 then to 8 per cent in 2005/6 and rose sharply to 11 per cent in 2006/7. With the exception of the 2003/4 school year, the repetition rate has been in double digits which is a clear indicator of the poor quality of learning. Second, after analysing further primary education, the primary cycle completion rate, although above 50 per cent in 2006/7, (the African average being 54 per cent) and having significantly improved since 2000/1, is still rather low. It increased from 37 per cent in 2000/1 to 66.32 per cent, in 2006/7, a significant jump in seven years. There is still a lot of room for improvement.

In terms of equity, it should be noted that there are still pronounced poor/rich, male/female (although the gender gap is gradually closing up) and urban/rural disparities in Benin's educational system. For example, significant disparities are observed between urban and rural departments as far as the GER between 1990 and 2009 is concerned. For example, in 1990, the GER in the Borgou/Alibori departments, (two rural departments in central and northern Benin), was only 34 per cent whereas in Ouémé/Plateau (two urban districts in coastal and southern Benin including the Cotonou Metropolitan Area), it was 67 per cent, the highest percentage point recorded in the country. In 2009, these GER were respectively 89 and 111 per cent (a gap of 21 per cent) during the same years.

Relevance

The relevance of education still continues to be a burning issue in Benin for a number of simple reasons. First of all, both the internal and external efficiency of the educational system are at stake. As highlighted in the previous section, evidence shows that both the internal and external efficiency rates of the system are relatively low. Available data show that graduate unemployment is rampant across the country. Its annual rate in Benin is estimated to be around 30 per cent and it continues to rise. For example, it is estimated that over two and a half million of Benin graduates (all types) are currently out of employment. Second, this situation raises, in the final analysis, the issue of the relevance of education and training programmes and negatively affects their credibility as well as the value of education and the credentials education confers. Third, this brings to the forefront the issue of the mismatch between training and employment. It is difficult to prove or disprove this claim, at this point, in the absence of valid research evidence on the real reasons why college graduates are unable to find jobs on the job market that are commensurate with their credentials and qualifications. Fourth, a major phenomenon that is down played, is the low level of job creation by the national economy. This situation is caused by the limited investments in the productive sector as the volume of foreign direct investments (FDI) continues to dwindle, resulting in limited impact on growth and job creation.

Decentralization and devolution

Many African countries, including Benin, embarked on a decentralization and devolution of powers initiative in the 1990s in the aftermath of the CN on the democratic rebirth. This type of reform was long overdue as the country, for decades, was run through a top-down centralized system inherited from the colonial period. Although the process started in 1999, it was only in 2002 that its implementation timidly got off the ground. Its main purpose was to design and implement a new governing model geared toward empowering the lower echelons of power and giving them more responsibility in the discharge of their duties and the decision-making process. This notion is referred to as the subsidiarity principle. Thus at the national level, 12 departments and several communes were established.

According to Hyden (1983), decentralization of responsibilities in African countries rose out of the rapid expansion of government activities. It was further argued that excessive central control stifles operations (of government) and reduces public accountability. Decentralization is the delegation of authority to lower levels of government, for example, states/departments, provinces, districts or as well as the creation of parastatal bodies to carry out public responsibilities for which government departments were ill equipped. At the local level, two governance structures of education were in existence: i) the Departmental Directorate of Education that is a regional government structure that constitutes a link between the higher and lower echelons of authority and ii) the school district, a decentralized government body close to school. As for devolution, it refers to an inter-organizational transfer of power to geographic units of the local government lying outside the command structure of the central government. The decentralization and devolution experience in Benin was not very successful because the transfer of the financial resources to the decentralized and devolved structures was not effective.

Human capacity

For post-independence Benin, the quantity and quality of the human capital in general and in the educational system in particular, has been a recurring issue. The supply and demand factors for the education personnel and mainly the teachers are the driving force behind the phenomenon. First, there is disequilibrium between the supply and demand for teachers at all levels especially primary. On the supply side, the imposition on Benin of the World Bank Structural Adjustment Policies (SAP) in 1986 led to the closure of all departmental teacher training colleges and early retirement of hundreds of experienced primary school teachers. On the demand side, the stock of teachers continued to decrease whereas the rapid expansion of access to education amplified teacher attrition. For example, in 1986, 13,452 primary school teachers were assigned to 12,403 classrooms, whereas in 1994, there were 12,924 teachers for 12,971 classrooms. Third, new categories of unqualified teachers (community, contractual) emerged. The pupil/teacher ratio increased from 39.8 in 1992 to 46.3 in 2008. This is a trend that will continue to dominate the human capacity landscape for years to come (Ministry of Education 2012).

Literacy

Although literacy is under the jurisdiction of the Ministry of Culture it is an integral part of education. Available literacy data indicate that in 2002, 70 per cent of the country's adult population (over 15 years of age) was literate which represented 50 per cent for male and 80 per cent for female. In 2011, the literacy rate among young males (15–24) was 66 per cent whereas for females it was 45 per cent (Ministry of Education 2012).

Integration of Information and Communication Technology (ICT)

The integration of ICT in Benin's educational system is in its infancy. Nonetheless, a national ICT strategy framework designed by the Ministry of ICT and a sector developed by the Ministry of Education are in existence. Furthermore, ICT initiatives are being experimented by pioneer institutions aware of the fact that its integration in the educational system opens up a window of opportunity, and makes it possible to upgrade teaching and increases the potential to facilitate marginalized groups' and communities' access to information and knowledge.

Despite the fact that Benin's e-readiness index is low and major constraints such as the six Cs: connectivity (lack of infrastructure/equipment and power supply), cost, contents, coverage, change management (resistance to change) and commitment (weak engagement of decision makers and ICT providers), are hampering the integration of ICT into the educational system, several promising initiatives are being experimented nationwide. This is the case of Globe Project, Introduction of ICT into Secondary Education Project (PIIES), CERCO Project, Francophone Distance Education: Project, Office of High School Diploma Web Portal Project, Higher Education Project and Non Formal Education ICT Project (Beheton 2012).

Private higher education and cross-border provision

With the diversification and differentiation of higher education, the advent of the knowledge economy and a more and more globalized world, private higher education and cross-border provision of higher education are gradually expanding in Benin. In 2012, there were 111 institutions of higher learning in the country, of which only 23 were fully accredited. Private higher education increases the supply of higher education services and also promotes student and academic mobility. At a time of expansion of the LMD reform, the cross-border provision of higher education is a trend to be reckoned with during the coming years.

Regional integration

Benin is a member of two West African sub-regional organizations; the WAEMU comprised of eight Francophone and one Lusophone countries and ECOWAS composed of eight Francophone, five Anglophone and two

Lusophone countries. WAEMU has embarked on an initiative to harmonize the secondary educational system of all its eight Member States with a view to having a common curriculum and a high school diploma. With ECOWAS, the experience of harmonizing the higher education system of its Member States would result in the mutual recognition of degrees, diplomas, grades and other qualifications in accordance with the provisions of the Arusha Conventions on the recognition of degrees, grades, diplomas and other qualifications on the African continent under the oversight of the African Union Commission (AUC).

Future prospects and conclusion

Benin's educational system, a legacy of French colonialism, has also been shaped by endogenous factors such as local traditions and values. It experienced several structural reforms aimed at redefining its contents, objectives, strategies, priorities, funding and philosophy – and at putting them in sync with the country's new vision in education. In the third decade of its existence, the system expanded rapidly as access and participation increased exponentially resulting in a constant deterioration in the quality of teaching and learning and causing challenges in terms of funding, facilities and instructional materials. The future prospects of Benin's education are promising but it is very likely to be affected by a number of key socio-economic and political factors in the near future.

First, population growth will affect schooling and try the government's ability to adequately fund education and fulfil its constitutional provisions of free and compulsory education.

Second, the human capital issue needs to be resolved in the long run. The labour quantity and quality are at stake. Benin will need more school personnel especially teachers at all levels including higher education. Thus, the system will continue to grapple with the dramatic shortage in teachers as well as their low level of qualification. No matter what measures the government of Benin takes between now and the end of 2015, the country will not reach any of the EFA and MDGs. Thus the country is at a crossroads and the post-2015 may be strategic for redefining and implementing new priorities for education.

Third, the funding of education will continue to dominate the future. The current economic growth is not strong enough to generate sufficient resources to combat poverty, and income inequality will hamper parents' ability to meet the costs of education of their children. There will be a gap in funding education and foreign aid may not provide the additional resources required.

Fourth, in developing a responsive, participatory and accountable system of educational governance and management Benin may be in a better position to efficiently utilize the resources allocated to education.

Notes

1. ECOWAS is one of the five major Regional Economic Communities (REC) of Africa. It covers West Africa and comprises the following 15 Member States: Benin, Burkina Faso, Cape Verde, Côte d'Ivoire, The Gambia, Ghana, Guinea Bissau, Guinea (Republic), Liberia, Mali, Niger, Nigeria, Senegal, Sierra Leone and Togo.
2. WAEMU is the West African Economic and Monetary Union comprising Benin, Burkina Faso, Côte d'Ivoire, Guinea Bissau, Mali, Niger, Senegal and Togo.
3. Gaulois are the peoples of Gaule (mostly of the present France) as defined by Julius Caesar. The term Gaulois is used ironically by Francophone Africans to refer to the French colonialists.
4. BEAP (Basic Education in Africa Program) was conceived and launched by UNESCO BREDA in Kigali (Rwanda) in 2004 and is so far being implemented by over 20 sub-Saharan African countries.
5. The African Charter for Human and People's Rights was adopted on 27 June 1981 by the former Organization of African Unity (OAU) to protect the rights and freedoms of Africans. It came into force on 21 October 1986.
6. The Arusha Convention on the Recognition of degrees, diplomas, grades and other qualifications in Africa is an instrument designed by UNESCO to harmonize higher education systems and promote faculty and staff mobility across Africa. It was launched in 1981 and was ratified by 19 member states including Benin.

References

Attanasso, M. O. (2010). Bénin: Presentation Efficace des Services Publics de l'Education.Une Etude d'AfriMAP et d'Open Society Initiative for West Africa.

Beheton, S. (2012). Introduction et Intégration des TIC dans l'Education au Bénin: Tome 1: Enseignement Primaire, Secondaire et Professionnel. Le Livre Blanc.

Diarra, M. C. (1992). 'Educational funding in Mali: past trends and contemporary issues'. Unpublished Master's Thesis. Baton Rouge: Louisiana State University.

Hyden, G. (1983). *No Shortcut to Progress: African Development Management in Perspective*. Berkeley and Los Angeles: University of California Press.
Ministry of Education (Ministère de l'Education) (2012). Lettre de Politique Educative. Benin.
Recensement Général de la Population et de l'Habitat (2013). Cotonou, Benin.
UNESCO (2012). Global Monitoring Report: Youth and Skills: Putting Education at Work. Paris, France.

Websites

www.beninsensis.net/vbenin_education
www.aedobong.org/index.php/
www.planipolis.iiep.unesco.org/

2

Burkina Faso: An Overview

Martial Dembélé, Touorizou Hervé Somé and Fernand Ouédraogo

Introduction

Like many sub-Saharan African countries, Burkina Faso became independent in 1960. Half a century later, it remains a developing country where virtually everything is a priority. Landlocked in the heart of West Africa, with a population of about 15 million people (INSD 2006), very few natural resources, a Poverty Index of 58.3 per cent (Statistiques Mondiales 2012), and a GDP around 600 US dollars per capita against $50,345 for Canada, for instance (Banque Mondiale 2011), it ranks 183rd out of 186 countries (PNUD 2012). This agrarian economy that relies on cotton, dairy products, gold, cattle, and leather, is highly dependent upon global changes in the prices of raw materials and on the vagaries of nature. External public debt is important and was as high as 23 per cent of the GDP in 2011, representing 85.3 per cent of the overall public debt against 14.7 per cent of the domestic debt (Perspectives économiques en Afrique 2012). The scarcity of resources has expectedly impinged upon the quality as well as the quantity of education provision at all levels.

In this chapter, we provide an overview of the development of education in this country. We review the strategies that have been deployed to widen access and ensure quality and equity, and discuss the challenges that threaten to undermine the attainment of EFA and education-related MDGs. As space is limited, we focus on primary education while acknowledging the systemic nature of any education and training arrangement. This focus is also justified by worldwide attention to primary education since the 1990 World Conference on EFA held in Jomtien.

Our analysis is rooted in a historical and critical perspective of educational development in countries in the periphery. Our main data sources are documents and statistics produced by the Ministry of Basic Education (MENA) and various non-governmental organizations. We also draw on scholarly publications, including our own, as well as relevant newspaper articles. In addition, we tap our individual educational and professional experiences to provide reflective insights nearly impossible to outsiders. As a matter of fact, we are, all three, citizens of Burkina Faso, and are privy to its educational system, having been students and having taught in this system. Our deep knowledge of the country and its educational policies, not forgetting the contextual factors that affect education outcomes, has allowed us to bring a fresh look to bear on our analysis of an educational system that is making great strides, but that is found wanting in many areas.

The first three post-independence decades: Twenty-three years of stagnation and a jump start in 1984

Burkina Faso has one of the lowest primary school enrolment rates in Africa and in the world (Pilon and Yaro 2007). In 1960, when the country gained independence from France, the gross enrolment rate (GER) was 6.5 per cent with 1,063 classrooms and a total of 55,598 students (Yaro 1994), for a population of 4,453,000 individuals. There are several reasons why the GER was so low at independence. A critical one is a colonial history marked by the dismantlement of the territory in 1932 (13 years after it became a colony following two decades of resistance); the reconstitution of the colony in 1947; and its use as a reservoir of cheap and reputably disciplined workers for the more viable coastal colony (Côte d'Ivoire), particularly, during the dismantlement period. All in all, this meant a minimal presence of the colonial administration and limited investments, especially in the education system; so much so that at reconstitution, the GER was an abysmally low 2 per cent.

In keeping with the commitments of the Conference of the African States' Education Ministers held in 1961 in Addis Ababa, the government decreed in August 1965, that universal schooling should be achieved by 1980. This decree stipulated, however, that this goal would take account of the availability of infrastructures, thus acknowledging the limit or the incapacity of the government to meet its own commitments. In 1967, a reform whose goal was to educate, primarily, rural adolescents who, for whatever reason, were on the fringe of the Western-type school system imported from France, was developed targeting the rural areas (Kaboré et al. 2001). Farming and other manual activities made up the staple of the curriculum. An evaluation of this reform in 1970 found it to be unsatisfactory and it was terminated.

In 1970, the GER was 11 per cent (Yaro 1994), which meant that thousands of children still did not attend school. Another reform was initiated in 1974 with the aim to broaden the base of knowledge as an intimation of democracy, and also to link school learning to real life and to develop national languages (Kaboré et al. 2001). In 1979, yet another reform introduced bilingual education in the primary school system. The goal was that by the time they reached 6th grade, the students in the 30 experimental schools would have the same level in French as those in French-only schools, with the added advantage of mastering their own mother tongues; the expectation being that such mastery would enhance their academic performance. The experimentation was scheduled to last four years (Madiéga and Nao 2003).

Came the revolution in 1983, and this reform was discarded without, unfortunately, any prior evaluation (Kaboré et al. 2001). This is not meant to disregard the breakthrough achieved by the National Revolutionary Council (NRC), whose political will to make education a public good accessible to all was very strong. This political will was channelled through the mobilization of grassroots, with slogans such as 'One Village, One School', and the use of the majority of National Service[1] recruits as primary school teachers. The actions undertaken by the NRC between 1984 and 1987 boosted educational provision remarkably, and therefore, access. Compared to the 1960s, the number of classrooms almost doubled under this regime and the GER doubled too, reaching 30 per cent (Kaboré et al. 2001).

The 1990s: The decade of the first major education policies

The 1990s were the decade when Burkina Faso first initiated major education policies, in the wake of the Jomtien Conference. For Burkina Faso, meeting the objectives set in Jomtien required a reorganization of its educational system and the implementation of new reforms and innovations. New organizational modes of teaching were introduced in 1992, namely double-shift classrooms (meaning two groups of students, one classroom and one teacher, or two groups of students, one classroom, and two teachers[2]) and multigrade classrooms (two grades, one classroom, one teacher). In September 1994, the State Generals of Education (SGEs) were convened for the first time. They concluded that the educational system was seriously lacking in internal efficiency, was ill-performing, and not responsive to the socio-economic and cultural environment. Reforms were thus recommended, of which: 1) the use of national languages in the formal educational system; 2) the creation of satellite schools[3] and nonformal basic education centres known by the French acronym CEBNF; 3) the modernization of French-Arabic schools; and 4) the promotion of private provision of education. Article 2 of the Education Act (Loi d'Orientation de l'Éducation), promulgated in 1996, provides that

> education is a national priority. Every citizen is entitled to education without any discrimination based on sex, social origin, race or religion. Schooling becomes mandatory for all children between the ages of 6 and 16 years, with the proviso that the infrastructure, physical and human resources and school regulation in force allow it. (Assemblée des Députés du Peuple 1996)

Article 4 of the law also specifies that 'languages of instruction are French and national languages', to meet the recommendations of the SGEs.

In September 1996, the government elevated the service for the promotion of girls' education to the level of a full-fledged directorate of girls' education. This move was meant to enhance the education of girls, with an enrolment rate of 35 per cent against 45 per cent for boys (Kaboré et al. 2001). The gender gap remained troubling four years later, however, as it hovered around 19 per cent in 1999–2000 (see Figure 2.1). As for the GER, it increased from 30 per cent in 1990 to 44.7 per cent in 2000 (MEBA 2000). Data show that despite the positive evolution of the school enrolment rate in the 1990s, the growth rate was still lower than what was recorded during the revolution. Moreover, the rate of 44.7 per cent in 2000 lagged far below the EFA objective set for that year. Barely more than one-third of children between 7 and 12 were enroled (Pilon 2004). The pass rate at the end of primary school certificate decreased slightly, from 48.6 per cent in 1998 to 48.2 per cent in 2000, and the completion rate increased from 23.7 per cent in 1996–7 to 26.2 per cent in 1999–2000 (MEBA 2000). Boys outperformed girls on both indicators, by 8.4 and 10.7 percentage points respectively.

In sum, the government of Burkina Faso launched multiple actions during the 1990s in order to meet its commitments to EFA as well as its domestic mandates through educational policies that favoured more justice and equity in primary education provision. Yet, on the ground, the results were a rather mixed picture. In defence of the government, we must bear in mind that the 1990s were etched with an economic recession. Burkina Faso, like other member countries of the WAEMU, was hard hit by the adverse effects of the

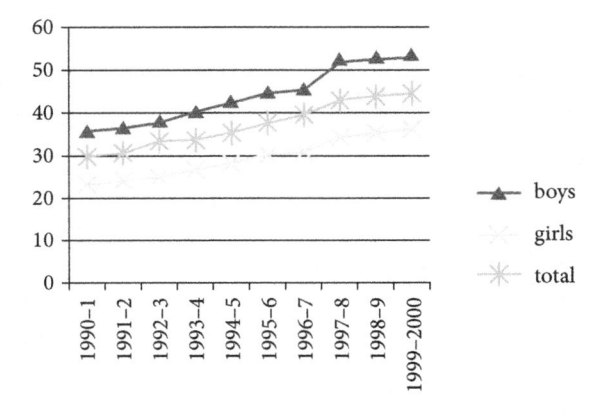

Figure 2.1 Gross Enrolment Rate by sex (1990–2000)

devaluation of the CFA franc. To make matters worse, the externally imposed Structural Adjustment Programs (SAPs) took a heavy toll on EFA progress, as they customarily mandated reductions in social services, with the education and healthcare sectors being the easy targets (Lange et al. 2002). As a whole, the period spanning 1960 and 2000 seems to be the harbinger of the massification of primary schooling, with new initatives introduced, especially during the revolutionary period and following the 1990 World EFA Conference.

Developments since the World Education Forum

The World Education Forum held in Dakar in 2000 prompted further developments. A year earlier, precisely in July 1999, the government had adopted the Ten-Year Basic Education Development Plan (known by its French acronym *PDDEB*), spanning the period 2001–10. As a powerful engine for the development of basic education, the PDDEB included three objectives related to primary education: 1) to achieve a GER of 70 per cent in 2009–10 and 100 per cent in 2015; 2) to achieve a GER of 65 per cent for girls in 2009–10; and 3) to bridge the gap among provinces. These objectives were translated into three programmes aimed at expanding basic education, improving its quality and relevance, and improving planning and management capacities. Between 2000 and 2012, besides implementing the PDDEB which ended technically in 2009, the government put forward several complementary policies and measures aimed at increasing educational access as well as improving quality.

Expanding access

As regards expansion of access, the PDDEB was guided by the 'One Village, One School' slogan coined during the revolution. It included building (or restoring) and equipping 2,013 new classrooms per year, with lodging for teachers, and completing 7,421 school wells (MEBA 1999, 2002). In order to bridge the gap between boys and girls, regions and socio-economic statuses of students, the government launched a major special priority programme to build, restore, and equip classrooms in the ten most underserved provinces in terms of GER. In addition to research and awareness-raising activities in favour of girls' education, and incentives designed to boost their enrolment and retention (e.g. 'positive discrimination' measures such as allocation of scholarships, free textbooks and school supplies [MEBA 1999, 2002]), a special campaign entitled 'priority enrolment for girls' was organized with a view to improving their educational trajectories. Other actions were undertaken as part of 'Initiative 25 by 2005', an international campaign that UNICEF launched in 2003, aimed at significantly increasing girls' participation in 25 developing countries (including 13 in Africa), in order to reach one of the aims of MDGs, namely gender parity in primary and secondary education by 2005 (UNICEF 2003).

Expectedly, the expansion of access implied a massive recruitment of teachers. As a matter of fact, the PDDEB included the recruitment and training of 20,670 new teachers, or 2,067 per year. Meeting this massive recruitment challenge required enhancing the preservice teacher education capacity. To this end, the creation of several new *Écoles nationales des enseignants du primare* (ENEP) and the shortening of the training to one year (from two) were envisaged; and so was a more active role for local communities, particularly in rural areas, in hiring and managing teachers, with government subsidy and support.

Still in the spirit of widening access, school fees were abolished in basic education and a fund supporting private entrepreneurship in education was set up, following the adoption of a new Education Act in 2007 (Assemblée Nationale 2007). The fund targeted underserved areas with respect to girls' education especially. Incentives to boost the creation of private schools and to support their smooth functioning included making land acquisition easier; reducing taxes and fees; equal access to teacher education programmes for both private and public school personnel; and new forms of association for the creation and management of private schools (MEBA 1999, 2002).

Finally, it is worth noting that the first cycle of secondary education was delinked and attached to primary education to constitute a 10-year basic education cycle (MENA 2012), in keeping with the 2007 Education Act. This welcome expanded vision of basic education poses new challenges that space does not permit discussing. Instead, we now turn to how the quality imperative has been addressed in Burkina Faso under the PDDEB.

Beyond expanding access

Several strategies were envisaged to improve internal efficiency, quality and relevance. These include, among others:

- the social promotion of students embodied in the cancellation in 2001 of grade repetition within sub-cycles (grades 1–2, grades 3–4 and grades 5–6);
- the revision of textbooks to take into account reforms and emerging issues;
- the production and distribution of textbooks and learning materials, as well as teacher guides and guides for head teachers, via a) the development of a blueprint of the school publishing press; b) the strengthening of the production capacities of the publication unit of the Pedagogic Institute of Burkina; and c) raising public awareness and training people about the maintenance of books;
- strengthening refresher courses for adjunct teachers (*Instituteurs Adjoints*), to prepare them towards certification;
- supporting continuing education by providing schools with teachers' kits and by building and equipping libraries;
- increasing the number of teacher supervisors, namely head teachers, inspectors, pedagogical advisors; and
- creating a permanent mechanism for evaluating quality (MEBA 1999, 2002).

In addition to the above, the PDDEB supported the continuation of most of the pedagogical innovations initiated during the 1990s, including the expansion of the linguistic and geographical coverage of bilingual education (Ilboudo 2009). The results-based teacher support and school improvement approach (*Nouvelle approche d'encadrement*) introduced in the late 1990s was also maintained; so were the teacher-led professional development groups (*Groupes d'animation pédagogique* or GAP).[4]

There is evidence that Burkina Faso has made remarkable progress towards universal schooling, given its starting point in 1960. But it is important not to see the forest for the trees. Indeed, major efforts are still needed in order to achieve quality universal primary education (UPE), let alone equitable access to quality universal basic education as the latter has expanded to include the first cycle of secondary education. The challenge is all the more daunting as there remain serious obstacles to achieving the UPE goal. We turn to these in the next section.

Challenges in primary education in Burkina Faso

Several factors have contributed to slowing down Burkina Faso's march towards universal schooling. These include, among others, a difficult passage from an elitist system to a mass system; a 6.69 per cent population growth and a 2.5 per cent growth rate between 1960 and 2000; economic hardships, including a chronically negative trade balance; political instability until the 1980s; the lack of an operational definition of what counts as quality; the absence of ownership of programmes by the grassroots and cultural barriers; poor governance; and ill-conceived notions of partnership with an unequal balance of power relations between donors and the Burkina Faso government. We discuss some of these factors below.

Socio-cultural challenges

The modern school is a foreign cyst (Ki-Zerbo 1992) lodged in the social fabric of a mosaic of multiple nationalities and cultures. Any national education development plan operates within a given society and culture. It sounds trite. Yet, Burkina Faso is characterized by the immense diversity of a population that counts at least 65 ethnic groups, all too aware of their cultural identity. No amount of financial investment in the building of modern facilities such as well-equipped classrooms will lead to universal education if the populations, at the grassroots level, do not adhere to the idea of sending their children to school, girls in particular. Several dozens of ethnic groups, all imbued with their own cultural practices often at loggerheads with modern ways of life (Kobiané and Pilon 2008) constitute obviously a potentially explosive cocktail. That the cultural dimension is one of the main culprits in the low school enrolment rate is not overstated. Most often, these cultural practices stem from beliefs handed down from generation to generation through socialization, eventually leading to a point where a generation may be repeating rituals without even knowing why. The only justification is that it is part of the *roog miki*, or what you find at birth (and perforce must pick up) in the *Mooré* language spoken by more than 50 per cent of the people in Burkina Faso. This is a slavish adherence to the authority of the eternal yesterday, otherwise called tradition. As Durkheim adeptly put it, each generation socializes itself based on the cultural templates handed down by the former generation (Lahaye, Pourtois and Desmet 2007).

Changes are hard to implement because, in part, they require people to call into question their beliefs and social representations and this process inevitably affects their stability, if not their self-concept and personality. Practices such as precocious marriages of girls are a check on school enrolment. Some parents are still adamant about the idea that a woman is best seen in the home rather than in public spaces, an enduring cultural outlook that has hurt girls' education for long. As Onochie (2010) ironized, the education of women ends in the kitchen. This mindset has a dampening effect on the enthusiasm of parents who may think twice before sending their daughters to school, and even on the aspirations of girls themselves. These practices, highly pervasive in rural areas, have prompted Lange, Zoungrana and Yaro (2002) to maintain that rural girls – compared to urban girls and those who hail from well-off families – have *de facto* no right to education.

Patriarchy remains the predominant form of social organization in most cultures in Burkina Faso. It is the social, cultural and symbolic domination of men over women, whereby the former are more valorized than the latter. This phenomenon can be observed when a baby child is born. The joy that shows through on the face of parents is 'correlated' with the child's sex. This behaviour affects the decision to send or not to send a child to school (Kaboré 1996; Paré-Kaboré 1998; Sanou 1996). Parents choose to enrol boys to the detriment of girls and rationalize their decision by invoking the imperative of heritage, performance, and safety. Girls are considered a potential loss of resources to their families (as they marry into another family), and prone to physiological hazards (risk of undesired pregnancies) during their schooling. Not so long ago, girls were dismissed from school for being pregnant; today it is more about self-dismissal, owing to the stigma attached to pregnant school girls and to the public obloquy – of their peers, and sometimes of insensitive teachers and the school authorities themselves.

Certain religious practices are also serious obstacles to the attainment of EFA goals. For example, some religious leaders would have children exposed to difficult situations in order to toughen their personality; hence, children are encouraged to take to the street to learn 'real-life' lessons. Many parents fall for this kind of education rather than for the Western-type education left by the French and that is reminiscent of colonization (Pilon 2004). We, however, do not mean to give the wrong impression that this cultural poverty is more determinant than the material poverty that besets several families in a country where more than 45 per cent of the population lives beneath the poverty threshold.

Poverty, the bedrock of illiteracy

Burkina Faso is one of the Highly Indebted Poor Countries (HIPCs). This means that most economic indicators are grim, notwithstanding visible efforts by the government to pull the country out of the squalor of an economic and social mal-development. This proverbial poverty poses real threats to EFA. The PDDEB was in need of 235 billion CFA francs, or 466,555,734 US$ for its implementation, three hundred times worth the national budget of the Year 2000. The situation today is hardly any better. It would cost 4,611,475 billion CFA francs, or approximately 9.3 billon US$ to implement the 2012–21 Basic Education Strategic Development Programme adopted in 2012 to consolidate the results of PDDEB, attain universal admission and a completion rate of 75.1 per cent in 2015, and reach UPE in 2020 (MENA 2012). Obviously the government alone will not make a dent in the struggle for mass education. It is obliged to hold out the begging bowl to foreign countries and international financial institutions. But it is known that foreign aid reinforces the dependence and the vulnerability of the receiving country. Ki-Zerbo (1992) rightly lamented the fact that living on such aid is no different from sleeping on somebody else's bed. Sooner or later, the bed owner is bound to re-appropriate her or his bed (Somé 2009), or to simply impose her or his diktat. The conundrum for Burkina Faso is to find a way to finance its education system on the national budget. A simple question is: Where is the government going to get this money? Taxation has its own limits in a country where fiscal evasion, and downright fiscal fraud are rife, and where revenues go unreported. Another challenge is to counter the crippling corruption that seriously affects the quality of public works and services. Financial management also cries out for more integrity and transparency. Effective control and monitoring procedures will help.

Poor parents make a cost-benefit analysis and decide to keep girls at home as they are valuable hands on the farms (Lange et al. 2002). In the same vein, some parents who are traders prefer to induct their children early on into commerce where the benefits are more concrete and quick, rather than enroling them in school where the outcomes are less obvious and to be reaped in the long term.

A reputational challenge

Another issue closely tied to poverty is what the people of Burkina Faso read of all the wonderful talk about EFA, a scheme spearheaded by the World Bank alongside other international organizations. The poor reputation of the Bretton Woods institutions in developing countries, especially in Africa, will remain for some time. Because the World Bank was one of the key players in the Jomtien Conference, there is a sense in which labour unions feel that EFA is just a skilful way to smuggle structural adjustment programmes into basic education. Teachers for instance saw the EFA program in Burkina Faso as the Trojan horse that will allow private providers to further clench their claws on and destroy a fledgling public education system. The fact that the PDDEB contained a clause about the expansion of private education fueled the highly emotional, ideological debate about whether education should be public or private. For teachers' unions, 'the disengagement of the state that shifts the financial, administrative, and pedagogical burden of the educational costs to the local authorities and communities in a country where more than 40 per cent of the population live on less than 200 CFA francs [40 US cents] a day' (Kongo 2005) is simply bothersome. Some teachers did not hesitate to say that the PDDEB was part of the vast plan to consolidate structural adjustment plans (SAPs), which means more disengagement of the government from the public sphere.

The SAPs have always tried to justify public cost cutting in social sectors such as education and healthcare, as part of the process of privatization. Teachers firmly believed that the PDDEB aimed to reduce the unit costs of education and to shift its real cost to the students and their parents along with reducing the number of teachers to contain the wage bill. That is what the SAPs were all about (Somé 2009). Workers have no sympathy for SAPs. The drastic measures adopted in the wake of multiple adjustments have reduced their quality of living. Teachers are among the most hit as their fringe benefits or material advantages accruing from their position have become insignificant. They have the sense that they are losing control of their profession, a sense magnified by the degradation of their material conditions. This has led to a situation where job seekers scramble for positions in the national customs, the internal revenue, the police, the treasury, etc., without any consideration for vocation. There is the risk that the Ministry of Basic Education will have to scrape the bottom of the barrel of job seekers if the main criterion for the 'attractiveness' of a job rests upon its capacity to make ends meet (ibid.). In the best of possible worlds, one would wish for schools to hire the brightest candidates for teachers. Unfortunately, pauperization of the teaching profession has induced this creaming of the most intelligent minds who, quite understandably, run for greener pastures. At the same time, higher education that has undergone a longstanding neglect by the World Bank and government alike, has fallen into crippling decrepitude that threatens to make the pristine mission of the university an impossibility (see Somé et al in this book).

Conclusion

The situation of education in Burkina Faso has evolved markedly since the push for EFA garnered renewed momentum following the Jomtien Conference. Results achieved in these last 12 years are far more impressive than those achieved in the preceding 40 years. Tremendous efforts have been made to make primary education accessible and equitable as shown by the GER of 79.6 per cent in 2012. The gender gap has also been narrowed down to 3 per cent in 2012. The number of trained teachers, available curriculum materials, infrastructures and equipment has also experienced an exponential increase. However, there are still area problems such as the insufficiency of seats and overpopulated classrooms. Access cannot be overemphasized, but it is of little use if it does not lead to opportunities to develop life-enhancing competencies and skills.

If quantitative gains are clearly observable, the question of quality remains a nagging one. This appears to be an institutional challenge. School attrition is still high in Burkina Faso. Students are not making steady progress in critical areas such as writing, reading, science, and maths. So while it is worth the while to strive for adequate classrooms and textbooks and other necessities germane to logistics, policy makers, decision-makers, parents and teachers need to pay attention to the actual school experiences of children.

Notes

1. The National Revolutionary Council instituted a National Service whereby all graduates of the education system had to spend one year working for the State (including several months of military training), with a very low stipend, before they could apply for any job.
2. These two organizational modes are respectively known as 2.1.1 and 2.1.2.
3. These are specific schools created in rural communities that are remote from a

classic primary school. They include three grades (Grade I, Grade II, and Grade III) and enrol children between 7 and 9. Gender parity is a key feature of these schools. After Grade III, students move to the nearest school that has all six grades, in order to complete the cycle of primary education. On average, 50 such schools were to be built and equipped every year in communities that expressed the need, with the aim to gradually generalize these successful innovations to the whole basic education system (MEBA 1999, 2002).

4 See Djibo (2010) for a critical analysis of the impact of teachers' continuing professional development activities on student achievement.

References

Assemblée des Députés du Peuple (1996). Loi 013/96/ADP portant loi d'orientation de l'éducation. Available from http://www.unesco.org/new/fileadmin/MULTIMEDIA/HQ/CLT/pdf/Conv2005_EU_Docs_BF_orientation.pdf (accessed October 2012).

Assemblée Nationale (2007). Loi n°013-2007/AN du 30 juillet 2007 portant loi d'orientation de l'éducation du Burkina Faso. Available from http://planipolis.iiep.unesco.org/upload/Burkina%20Faso/BurkinaFasoLoi_0132007.pdf (accessed October 2012).

Banque Mondiale (2011). PIB par habitant. Available from http://donnees.banquemondiale.org/indicateur/NY.GDP.PCAP.CD (accessed October 2012).

Djibo, F. (2010). *L' impact de la formation continue des enseignants sur la réussite scolaire: regard critique sur le cas du Burkina Faso*. Thèse de doctorat, Université Laval, Québec. Available from http://www.theses.ulaval.ca/2010/27048/27048

Ilboudo, P. T. (2009). *L'éducation bilingue au Burkina Faso. Une formule alternative pour une éducation de base de qualité*. Tunis: Secretariat de l'ADEA [Bilingual Education in Burkina Faso. An Alternative Approach for Quality Basic Education]. Available from http://www.adeanet.org/adeaPortal/includes/publications/PDF/experiencesafricaines_01_en.pdf (accessed October 2012).

INSD (2006). *Recensement général de la population et de l'habitation de 2006*. Available from http://www.insd.bf/fr/IMG/pdf/Resultats_definitifs_RGPH_2006.pdf

Kaboré, A. (1996). *Influence de la famille polygame ou monogame burkinabè sur la performance scolaire des filles et des garçons (cours moyen de quatre écoles primaires de Ouagadougou)*. Thèse de doctorat inédite, Université de Montréal, Québec.

Kaboré, I., Kobiané, J.-F., Pilon, M., Sanou, F. and Sanou, S. (2001). 'Politiques éducatives et système éducatif actuel au Burkina Faso'. In M. Pilon and Y. Yaro (eds), *La demande d'éducation en Afrique. État des connaissances et perspectives de Recherche*, Vol. 1, pp. 99–116. Dakar: UEPA/UAPS. Available from http://horizon.documentation.ird.fr/exl-doc/pleins_textes/pleins_textes_7/divers2/010029633.pdf (accessed October 2012).

Ki-Zerbo, J. (1992). *La natte des autres: Pour un développement endogène de l'afrique* [Other people's bed: Toward an endogenous development in Africa]. Paris: Karthala.

Kobiané, J. F. and Pilon, M. (2008). 'Appartenance ethnique et scolarisation au Burkina Faso: la dimension culturelle en question'. *Actes des coloques de l'AIDELF*, pp. 999–1014.

Kongo, E. (2005). 'Le PDDEB a bouffé Mathieu' [The PDDEB has eaten up Mathieu]. http://www.bendre.afdrica-web.org/article.php?id_article=1033 (accessed October 2012).

Lahaye, W., Pourtois, J. P. and Desmet, H. (2007). *Transmettre: d'une géneration à une autre*. Paris: PUF.

Lange, M. F., Zoungrana, C. M. and Yaro, Y. (2002). 'Éducation, enfants et sociétés de demain. Exemples africains'. *Actes des colloques de l'AIDELF*, pp. 1053–67.

Madiéga Y. G. and Nao, O. (2003). *Burkina Faso: cent ans d'histoire, 1895–1995*. Vols 1/2. Paris: Karthala.

MEBA (1999). *Plan décennal de développement de l'éducation de base 2000–2009*.

—(2000). *Annuaires statistiques de l'éducation nationale de 1990 à 2000*.

—(2002). 'Plan d'action national de l'éducation pour tous'. Available from http://planipolis.iiep.unesco.org/upload/Burkina%20Faso/Burkina%20PAN-EPT.pdf (accessed October 2012).

MENA. (2012). *Programme de développement stratégique de l'éducation de base (PDSEB) 2012-2021*. Repéré à http://www.mena.gov.bf/index.php/le-pdseb--2012--2021 (accessed November 2012).

Onochie, O. C. I. (2010). 'Guilty or not guilty? How Nigerian families impede the aspirations of nigerian girls for higher education'. Online submission. *US China Education Review*, 7 (6): 16–31.

Paré-Kaboré, A. (1998). 'Compétences littéraires et mathématiques selon le sexe et question de la discrimination éducative de la femme au Burkina Faso'. *Annales de l'Université de Ouagadougou*, 10 (série A), pp. 43–65.

Perspectives économiques en Afrique. (2012). 'Burkina Faso 2012'. Available from http://www.afdb.org/fileadmin/uploads/afdb/Documents/Publications/Burkina%20Faso%20Note%20de%20pays%20PDF.pdf (accessed November 2012).

Pilon, M. (2004). 'L'Évolution du champ scolaire au Burkina Faso: entre diversification et privatisation'. *Cahiers de la recherche sur l'éducation et les savoirs*, 1 (3): 143–65.

Pilon, M. and Yaro, Y. (2007). 'Le Burkina Faso à l'épreuve de l'éducation pour tous: Quel bilan des politiques au tournant des années 2000?' Available from http://uaps2007.princeton.edu/papers/70641 (accessed October 2012).

PNUD (2012). *Rapport Mondial sur le Développement humain. Indice de développement humain (IDH)*. Available from http://hdrstats.undp.org/fr/pays/profils/BFA.html (accessed October 2012).

Sanou, F. (1996). 'Étude sur la sous-scolarisation des filles au Burkina Faso'. *Annales de l'Université de Ouagadougou*, 10, pp. 103–45.

Somé, T. H. (2009). 'Global Forces and Neoliberal Forces at Work in Education in Burkina Faso: The Resistance of Education Workers'. In D. Hill and E. Rosskam, *The Developing World and State Education: Neoliberal Depradation and Egalitarian Alternatives*. New York: Routledge pp. 162–78.

Somé, T. H., Dembélé, M. and Ouédraogo, F. (2015). 'Education in Burkina Faso: trends and futures'. In E. Takyi-Amoako, *Education in West Africa*. London: Bloomsbury.

Statistiques mondiales. (2012). 'Burkina Faso: statistiques'. Available from http://www.statistiques-mondiales.com/burkina_faso.htm

UNICEF (2003). 'UNICEF launches girls' education initiative in western and central Africa'. Available from http://www.unicef.org/french/media/media_10944.html (accessed October 2012).

Yaro, Y. (1994). *Pourquoi l'expansion de l'enseignement primaire est-elle si difficile au Burkina Faso? Une analyse socio-démographique des déterminants et des perspectives scolaires de 1960 à nos jours*. (Thèse de doctorat, Université de Paris I, Paris).

Burkina Faso: Trends and Futures

Touorizou Hervé Somé, Martial Dembélé and Fernand Ouédraogo

Introduction

The post-1990 drive towards universal access to primary education has boosted the gross enrolment rate (GER) in Burkina Faso. Yet, as discussed in Chapter 3 in this book, the results invite caution. Several bottlenecks remain to be cleared: the lack of an operational definition of what counts as quality; the absence of ownership of programmes by the grassroots; cultural barriers; poor governance; and ill-conceived notions of partnership with an unequal balance of power relations between donors and the Burkina Faso government. To these, one must add the neglect of secondary education and even more so, of higher education. Taking a critical look at how EFA has been engineered in this country, we pry open the tension between global and local solutions that must be resolved for a truly universal schooling to materialize.

Just as in Chapter 2 in this book (see Dembélé et al.), dealing with an overview of education in Burkina Faso, we focus on primary education because of space limitation, using document analysis and heavily relying on government data mainly found in the sources of the Ministry of Basic Education (the MENA), our own publications, newspapers, websites, and sources of non-government organizations as well. Our individual perspectives and professional experiences were tapped to provide reflective insights nearly impossible to outsiders. As a matter of fact, we are, all three, citizens of Burkina Faso, and are privy to its educational system. We have taught in this system, which has allowed us to share here our unalloyed first-hand experience. Thanks to our deep knowledge of the country and its educational policies, not forgetting the contextual factors that affect education outcomes, we are able to bring a fresh look to bear on our analysis of an educational system that is making great strides, but that is found wanting in many areas. Our analysis is rooted in a critical perspective of educational development in countries in the periphery.

A critical look at the results of the national version of EFA in Burkina Faso

In all fairness to the efforts geared towards universal schooling in the wake of the Jomtien Conference in 1990, it is handy to start with the achievements of the Ten-Year Basic Education Development Plan (known by its French acronym PDDEB), the national EFA replica.

Infrastructural and material achievements

First, it is worth noting that there were 5,131 schools (of which 614 were private schools) for a total of 17,456 classrooms in 2000-1, the period when discussions about the PDDEB hit the public space. This number increased to 11,545 schools (of which 2,279 were private) for a total of 43,661 classrooms in 2011-12, representing quite an impressive three-fold increase in 12 years.

The number of schools with sufficient desks also increased, from 2,710 (522 in urban areas and 2,188 in rural areas) in 2000-1 to 4,544 (973 in urban areas and 3,571 in rural areas) in 2011-12. This is commendable even though the number of seats is still insufficient, with the number of schools missing desks increasing from 2,421 in 2000-1 to 7,001 in 2011-12. The consequence is that more than 483,324 students did not have seats in 2011-12, of which 81 per cent were in the rural areas. Thousands of students, thus, are obliged to stand or to sit on the floor to take classes. The adverse effects of this on learning need little elaboration. Nevertheless, the establishment of schools in many villages to advance the idea of 'One Village, One School' and the massive recruitment of teachers helped reduce the commuting distance for students. In 2011-12, 85.93 per cent of students in both urban and rural areas had less than 3 kilometers to cover to go to school; 11.5 per cent travelled between 3 and 5 kilometers; and 2.22 per cent travelled more than 5 kilometers, generally on foot. It goes without saying that efforts must be made in this area as it can have an impact on school persistence (PASEC 2009).

The number of teachers' housings also increased, from 9,749 in 2000-1 to 17,227 in 2011-12, alongside a remarkable increase in the number of curriculum materials (reading, maths, history, etc.), from 108,252 in 2000-1 to

359,454 in 2011-12, or an increase of more than 300 per cent. This obviously partakes in the improvement of teachers' living conditions and, as a whole, in the improvement of their work conditions (Kouraogo and Dianda 2008).

Expanding access with equity

As shown in Figure 3.1, the GER increased tremendously between 1999 and 2012, hitting 74.8 per cent (or 78.3 per cent for boys versus 71.2 per cent for girls) in 2009-10 and 79.6 per cent (81.1 per cent for boys versus 78.1 per cent for girls) in 2012, from 44.7 per cent (52.9 per cent for boys and 36.9 per cent for girls) in 2000.

These indicators speak volumes for the ability of Burkina Faso to take up the challenge of increasing the GER beyond the threshold of 70 per cent set for 2009-10, in excess of 4.8 per cent. No doubt, the combined effect of the infrastructural developments and improvements in learning conditions have been decisive factors. The other good news is that the gender gap has been narrowing, being only 3 per cent in 2012.

The evolution of the student population has been impressive. From 852,160 (504,383 boys versus 347,777 girls) in 1999-2000, the student population reached 1,906,279 (1,026,551 boys versus 879,728 girls) in 2008-9 and 2,344,031 (1,225,032 boys and 1,118,999 girls) in 2011-12. Within 12 years, Burkina Faso has nearly experienced a tripling of its student population. This has gone hand in hand with a significant reduction in the gap between boys and girls, as broached

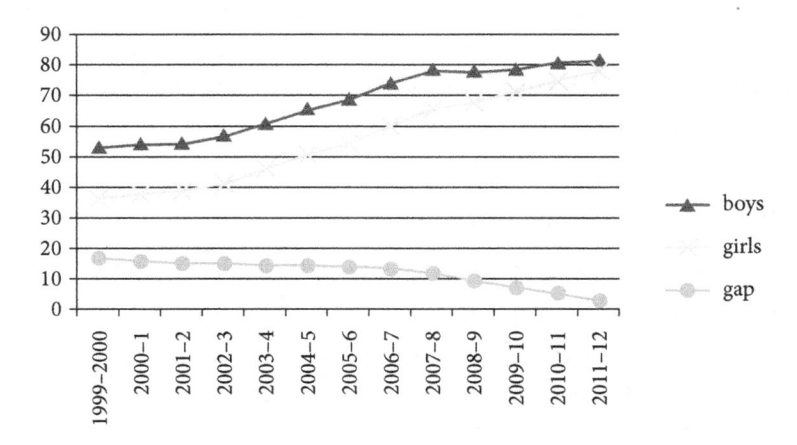

Figure 3.1 Gross Enrolment Rate by sex (2000-12)

earlier. Provinces where girls were the most underserved in terms of enrolment also saw an improvement in the girls' student populations and the GER had shown an upward trend until 2006–7. For both genders, it fell in 2007–8, then picked up in 2009–10. The last two years, 2010–12, also experienced a decrease. This latter decrease may be attributed in part to the food crisis caused by the severe 2011 drought and whose effects lingered well into 2012, thus leaving the government with no other solution than to enlist the support of the international community to eradicate pockets of famine. Another success story is the school completion rate that has increased from 27.4 per cent (33.3 per cent for boys and 21.5 per cent for girls) in 2000–1 to 55.1 per cent (56.6 per cent for boys and 53.7 per cent for girls) in 2011–12). A combined improvement of internal efficiency and student achievement has been instrumental in this performance.

The foregoing could lead to the facile conclusion that Burkina Faso is in good shape in its search for universal schooling. To assume that it could easily achieve a GER of 100 per cent by the Year 2015 is a little more than naïve. It could do so only if it could maintain a steady progress and if it could score a 6.8 per cent annual average in the run-up to 2015. This looks like a tall order given the observed growth rate of about 3 per cent. At the same pace, and considering population growth, the objective of 100 per cent enrolment rate could only be theoretically attained in the Year 2019–20, at best. The challenge may be more daunting if the quality imperative is factored into the picture.

The quality imperative, overshadowed by quantity

What has been achieved thus far in terms of access is, indeed, remarkable. Still, it is the case that grand actions are needed to achieve universal primary education, let alone basic education for all as it has expanded to include the first cycle of secondary education.

The tension between quality and quantity

There is a lingering tension between quality and quantity (Somé 2011a) in the pursuit of universal schooling. Kouraogo and Dianda (2008) contended that:

> The first phase of PDDEB seemed to have a superficial definition of quality. In most of its monthly reports for the joint government-technical partners evaluation meetings ..., the sections devoted to quality deal mostly with material inputs for improving teaching and learning conditions such as free distribution

of books, school meals, health and sanitation, teachers' housing, latrines and the likes. (p. 26)

The 2010 survey (DEP/MENA 2010) of the academic achievement of second and third graders showed that second graders exhibit more gaps in reading than in maths, while being fairly average in writing (see Table 3.1). As for fifth graders, their grades in maths, writing, and science were strikingly unsatisfactory. Their performance in reading, however, was very good. The survey points out that the results of past studies conducted, say, in 2006, were nearly similar to those of 2010. An analysis of the socio-demographic characteristics of students and their family environment shows that students who passed their test come mostly from urban areas and from private schools. It is to be feared that school achievement may be also unfortunately aligned with geographical origin, replicating the often stark development divide between the town and the countryside. Students who were using French at home, the language of instruction, had achieved good scores on these tests, too. Students with readers obtained higher scores in French.

This performance is a wake-up call for a (re)definition of quality beyond infrastructural and materials inputs. Hallak (1991) convincingly argued that the quality of education cannot be easily captured through just a better school environment, an adequate provision of books and more qualified teachers. In 2004, a few months after the PDDEB started off, the teachers' union voiced their disapproval about the direction the programme was heading. 'We see through the game. Thus, next year, they will be able to say that the GER has gone from X per cent to Y per cent, in other terms they prefer quantity to quality' (Sawadogo 2003: [cited in Somé 2011a], 176). In a rebuttal to this broadside attack, the then Minister of Basic Education, Mathieu Ouédraogo, put up a poor defence when

Table 3.1 Evaluation scores of Grade II and Grade V student learning, school year 2010

Tests	School Year 2010	
	Average Grades in Second Grade	Average Grades in Fifth Grade
French (writing)	51.1/100	43.3/100
Math	43/100	41.4/100
Sciences		48.4/100
Reading	30.6/100	67.2/100

Source: DEP/MENA (2010)

he said that he cared about quality, but that *only* (emphasis is ours), numbers could give an idea of the evolution of a country (Rouamba 2004).

Baux (2004) cautioned decision-makers and school managers against believing that the increase in infrastructure alone can be enough for equal educational opportunity. Rather, a partnership between school and home are crucial ingredients. The teaching and use of national languages in primary schools also can bridge the gap between home culture and school culture. As mentioned earlier, students whose home language is French have a leg-up in school, with the cultural capital of the home and that of the school showing little dissonance (Bourdieu and Passeron 1977).

Teacher education at the heart of the search for quality

The reduction of the length of preservice teacher education programmes has also taken its toll on the quality of education (Kouraogo and Dianda 2008; Sirois and Lesturgeon 2009). Indeed, initial teacher education due to last two years was reduced to one year under the pressure of the World Bank, as a way to contain the costs related to teacher training; or at least, this is what teachers and the general public read off it. Such strategies are ill-inspired. Quality of teachers matters and there is no quick fix to producing strong teachers. The government has done well as it has recently backtracked by reinstating the initial two years for the training of teachers (DEP/MENA 2012).

Seven years after unions took a dim view of EFA's lopsided efforts in Burkina Faso, a stand that could be dismissed as self-serving, coming from an organization rarely in agreement with the powers that be, King (2011), a World Bank employee privileged enough to take part in the World Education Conference of Jomtien, raised the red flag in her call, 'Jomtien, 20 Years Later: Global Education for All Partners Must Renew Commitment to Learning'. Her outcry comes from a deep sense that quantity has trumped quality and she makes no bones about it:

> When education for all has been reduced to schooling-for-all, success has been measured by the number of school-age students enroled in school as a proportion of the total number of children of that age, or even as the number of students who complete primary school. By these indicators alone, many developing countries have declared success in their progress towards reaching the EFA goals. [...] And it has to do with learning gains lagging far behind the rise in enrolment rates.

King acknowledges that the world has not weathered the longstanding crisis in education and that it would be foolhardy to claim victory. According to her, the world will be justified in celebrating victory when children and adults are in a position to meet their basic learning needs through relevant educational opportunities.

Local solutions, the missing link in the global search for universal schooling

Learning content in the form of knowledge skills, and attitudes and learning needs such as problem solving, education for democracy and human rights, oral expression, numeracy, literacy, etc., are certainly universals as King (2011) contends. Yet, 'the scope of basic learning needs and how they should be met varies with individual countries and cultures, and inevitably changes with the passage of time'. Burkina Faso may claim that the policies towards universal schooling have been customized to serve the specific needs of its children. The reality is that they smack of a global one-size-fits-all approach, an original sin inscribed in the very process of the development of EFA, with the several power asymmetries among the different actors who met at Jomtien. As we are mindful of King's admonition, universal schooling (in quantity and also in quality) may well be an elusive undertaking unless the goals and the indicators are revisited and re-examined seriously, alongside the process.

The policies and strategies for universal schooling have elicited much discontent from the teachers and the population at large, who have been little associated, or who have not always been genuinely associated to it in the few symbolic attempts to mobilize the wider society around the idea. The government is suspected of going 'through the motions of involving the civil society that comprises non-governmental organizations, trade unions, and parents' associations in the national debate around the PDDEB' (Somé 2011a). In plain terms, the PDDEB has been implemented without taking into account the concerns of all stakeholders as if the government had no choice but to have a reform tacked on to the educational system under an external constraint. Kéré (2002), a prominent activist in the NGOs milieu, observed that 'the surveys that helped to elaborate the PDDEB have literally ignored the opinion of the beneficiaries, parents, and students themselves' (p. 4). This speaks to the distrust for a scheme viewed rightly or wrongly as superimposed by global powers, with the risk of alienating critical stakeholders. Designing educational reforms and curricular revisions 'in vitro' and passing them down to supervisors, teachers, and students is impolitic at best, according to Kouraogo and Dianda (2008).

They may have a case to make. Indeed, 'no national policy in education can ever take place without teachers without taking into account their aspirations and their interests' (Lingani 2005). This is the place to acknowledge the fact that the solutions developed at Jomtien to solve the worldwide education crisis are, doubtless, a manifestation of global generosity. Yet, they are hardly in tune with local solutions to specific problems as they are written in broad terms, ignoring the specificity of 'real' countries in real time. Schaffer (1994), a staunch believer in local solutions, although not one to exclude partnership, maintains that

> basic learning needs are complex and diverse [and] meeting them requires multi-sectoral strategies and actions which are integral to overall development efforts. Many partners must join with education authorities, teachers, and other educational personnel in developing basic education ... (p. 6)

Arguably, teachers have smelled a rat with the reluctance of the government to open up the channels of communication on such an important reform that aims to overhaul the entire basic education system. Freeman and Faure (2003) castigated the exclusion of teachers from the policy formulation to its implementation and sternly warned that this 'has the effect of weakening the political legitimacy of many reform programs in basic education and tends to result in programs that lack relevance and practical application in such areas as teacher training, materials development and curriculum reform' (p. 6). Whither the umbilical link between the different levels of the education system, especially higher education, so crucial to teaching, the formation of community leaders, research, and service to the community?

The fate of higher education in the drive towards UPE

Burkina Faso, just like most African countries, has a dysfunctional higher education system. The bleak economic and financial crisis that has beleaguered several African countries is taking a heavy toll on the ability of universities to perform their pristine mission '... with rapidly expanding numbers, under conditions of limited or declining resources' (Court 1991: 330).

African universities have become contested arenas where students and police in riot gear fight pitched battles. The public university system in Burkina Faso that seemed to be an island of peace in the face of troubled higher education institutions in the subregion, at least before the 1990s, has morphed into a seething cauldron. It has joined the bandwagon of students' sit-ins, riots, voided academic years, and closure of campuses, etc. As the government is moving toward more cost sharing, a shift of the burden of the costs of higher education from government to all the stakeholders of the higher education system (Johnstone 2004), students have been fighting for the halcyon days of 'free' higher education.

Resistance to cost sharing on African campuses has been well documented in the literature (Ajayi et al. 1996; Balsvik 1998; Johnstone 2004; Experton and Fevre 2010; Somé 2010, 2011b). To implement cost sharing, Burkina Faso, as part of an agreement with the World Bank and the IMF, adopted structural adjustments, thus retreating from public sectors to contain the wage bill. Scholarships that were automatically granted to any high school graduate aged 23 are now rare. The government has drastically reduced the number of scholarships (Guenda 2003) and has set up a student loans programme.

External funding is the engine of higher education in Burkina Faso,[1] mainly because the university desperately remains an institution that is underfunded by the government. The lack of adequate funding coupled with poor governance has caused an accelerated dilapidation of higher education in Burkina Faso, with chaos being the rule rather than the exception. The multiple strikes launched by faculty and students over the past ten years or so to claim better pay, better work and living conditions, has led to a situation where several cohorts of students have found themselves repeating the same academic year two or three times in a row. With the paucity of facilities, due to lack of funding, classrooms are incredibly overpopulated. Some high-demand programmes such as law, economics and sociology enrol more than 1,500 new students every year (compared to the 1990s when class rosters were relatively much smaller), which further taxes the energy of an overworked and underpaid faculty and casts doubts on the overall quality of instruction and learning.

To remedy the confusion born out of the so many academic years to catch up with, the government has decided to void all incomplete years accumulated since 2008. In summer 2013, the government hunted out students from the residence halls on the grounds that residences should be vacated during the summer vacation. This caused students who claimed they had nowhere to go to burn down around 40 government vehicles. Whether there is going to be some quiescence on campuses nationwide during the academic year 2013–14 remains totally uncertain.

To hark back to the theme of the underfunding of the university, it is worth noting that the World Bank encouraged Burkina Faso to focus its meagre resources more on primary education, taking a dim view of higher education, seen as catering to the elite (World Bank 1988). Early on in 1985, Hinchcliffe stunningly made the case that higher education in sub-Saharan Africa was not sustainable, blaming high unit costs, overfunded students, underutilized facilities, the high non-teaching costs such as the salaries paid to faculty and employees. It was clear by then that higher education was off the priority list of the World Bank. The World Bank is now making amends. It has expressed its readiness to give more financial support to higher education (Bollag 2003). It is difficult to tell to what extent it influenced the participants in the Jomtien Conference, but higher education was not part of the agenda of this conference, which is a serious blemish to the EFA project.

The critique often levelled against the drive towards universal schooling is the sense in which EFA programmes lack a holistic approach to education. In most countries, EFA has been construed as concentrating efforts on basic education, as if secondary and higher education could be left to take care of themselves. This is strangely reminiscent of the debunked and discredited rate of returns to primary school education theorized by Psacharopoulos (1980). Psacharopoulos reasoned that primary education was worth more investment with regard to its rate of returns. It generated more profits for the individual and society than secondary education and, more so, higher education. For years, this has justified the withdrawal of the World Bank, or at least, its lackadaisical commitment to higher education, a stance that hurt cash-strapped African universities, precipitating them into further dilapidation. Many have become ghost universities with senior faculty and emerging scholars cutting loose for greener pastures. Burkina Faso's university has not been spared by this neglect.

Thus, a serious disservice has been done to African societies. The idea that Africa was in less need of universities is totally wrong, unconscionable, and indefensible. The opposite is rather true for the simple reason that good universities should be able to attend to teaching, research that adds to the body of knowledge and service to the local and global community. Universities are the place where basic education teachers are educated, or at least, where the latter are taught by professionals who are the product of a university. The circularity of this reasoning is a strong case for more commitment in favour of universities in developing countries by the global community. The rate of returns fallacy has not only hurt universities. Even secondary education has been disredarded, with EFA focusing mainly on basic (read formal primary) education. It strikes the observer as absurd to widen the base of enrolment in basic education without taking into consideration what is going to become of the graduates of this level of education.

As an example, out of 80,000 students who passed the primary school certificate in Burkina Faso in 2005, only 26,000 will access grade 7 in the public secondary schools. [...] The great majority, the 67.5 per cent, will have to repeat their classes, thus cramming them, or will go to private institutions because of limited seats in the public school system (Le Pays 2005).

It is troubling that a reform may be so narrowly focused on its goals that it fails to realize that, if anything, education is a system, and lacking a bird's-eye-view approach to policymaking will only result in a jammed, dysfunctional system as a whole.

Conclusion

Given its education indicators at independence, Burkina Faso has unquestionably come a long way in the drive towards EFA. The road is, however, still quite long, and there remain daunting challenges. In particular, the false dichotomy between primary education and secondary and higher education has been harmful. As long as education is not envisioned as a whole package, actions in basic education will be in disarray and will lack 'teeth'. Striving for universal schooling does not need to be a zero-sum game between primary and higher education, whereby the gains at one level are the losses at the other. In this respect, merging the primary and lower secondary cycles into an expanded ten-year basic education sub-system can be a laudable move. A number of challenges must, however, be addressed, including the lack of agreement among the different stakeholders of education, namely, the teachers' unions who remain distrustful of the implementation of the reform and the chances of its success.

The quality and well-being of teachers is another area that deserves more serious attention. As pointed out in Chapter 2, teachers feel that they are losing control of their profession. The de-professionalization of teachers as well as the degradation of their material conditions have the potential to blight the implementation of the 2012–21 basic education strategic development programme. It is, indeed, hard to imagine a successful educational reform that would not take into account the well-being of its frontliners.

Note

1 Between 1990 and 2003, the main funding sources of the University of Ouagadougou were the French Fund for Aid and Cooperation (FAC, $4,000,000), the Netherlands MHO ($12,000,000), the CIUF/CUD Project (Belgium, $3,200,000), against a total appropriation of $40,000,000 allocated by the government of Burkina Faso itself.

References

Ajayi, J. F. A., Goma, L. K. H. and Johnson, G. A. (1996). *The African Experience with Higher Education*. Accra: The Association of African Universities.

Balsvik, R. R. (1998). 'Student protest: University and state in Africa, 1960–1995'. *Forum for Development Studies*, 2: 301–25.

Baux, S. E. (2004). 'Les inégalités face à l'école au Burkina Faso: Analyse comparative des déterminants de la scolarisation en milieu urbain, semi urbain et rural'. Communication au Colloque International. Le Droit à l'Éducation: Quelles Effectivités aux Sud et au Nord? Université de Ouagadougou, 9–12 Mars, 2004. [Inequalities in Schooling in Burkina Faso: Comparative Analysis of determinants of schooling in urban, semi-urban, and rural areas. Paper presented at the International Symposium, The Right to Education: How Effective is it in the South and in the North? University of Ouagadougou, Burkina Faso, March 9–12, 2004].

Bollag, B. (2003). *Improving Tertiary Education in Sub-Saharan Africa: Things that Work*. Report of a Regional Training Conference, Accra, Ghana, 22–25 September 2003.

Bourdieu, P. and Passeron, J. C. (1977). *Reproduction in Education, Society and Culture*. London: Sage Publications.

Court, D. (1991). 'The Development of University Education in Sub Saharan Africa'. In P. G. Altbach, *International Higher Education: An Encyclopedia*, 1. New York: Garland Publishing, pp. 329–47.

DEP/MENA (2010). *Enquête 2010 sur les acquis au CP2 et au CM1. Rapport synthèse 2009-2010*.

—(2012). *Programme de developpement strategique de l'éducation de base (PDSEB) 2012-2021*. MENA, Ouagadougou, Burkina Faso.

Experton, W. and Fevre, C. (2010). *Financing Higher Education in Africa*. Washington, DC: The World Bank Group.

Freeman, T. and Faure, D. S. (2003). 'Local solutions to global challenges: Towards effective partnerships in basic education'. Paper presented at ADEA Biannual Meeting, Mauritius (3–6 December).

Guenda, W. (2003). 'Burkina Faso'. In D. Teferra and P. Altbach (eds), *African Higher Education*. Indianapolis: Indiana University Press, pp. 195–203.

Hallak, J. (1991). 'Education for all: High expectations or false hopes?' Paper presented at the Conference on Primary Education Pre-Jomtien on 7 May 1991, Institute of Education, University of London and International Institute for Educational Planning, UNESCO.

Hinchliffe, K. (1985). *Issues Related to Higher Education in Sub-Saharan Africa.* Washington, DC: World Bank.

Johnstone, D. B. (2004). 'Higher Education Finance and Accessibility and Student Loans in Subsaharan Africa'. *Journal of Higher Education in Africa,* 2, 2 (11): 11–36.

Kéré, M. (2002). 'L'expérience de la planification et de la mise en oeuvre de l'EPT au Burkina Faso' [The experience of planning and implementing of EFA in Burkina Faso]. Ouagadougou, Burkina Faso: CCEB. Available from http:www.unesco.org/education/efaglobal_co/working_group/rd_pros_maria_kere.pdf (accessed 10 July 2006).

King, E. (2011). 'Jomtien, 20 years later: Global education for all partners must renew commitment to learning'. Available from http://blogs.worldbank.org/education/what-s-new-Jomtien-20-years-later

Kouraogo, P. and Dianda, A. Y. (2008). 'Education in Burkina Faso at Horizon 2025'. *Journal of international Cooperation in Education,* 11 (1): 23–38.

Le Pays (2005). 'Journée Mondiale des enseignants: SNEAB et SNESS, main dans la main' [World Teachers' Day: SNEAB and SNESS: Hand in hand]. *Le Pays,* 3475, 5 October 2005. Available from http://www.lepays.bf/quotidiens/select.asp (accessed December 2005).

Lingani, S. (2005). 'Nous voulons renforcer l'unité syndicale dans l'enseignement', 25 December. [We intend to strengthen solidarity among education unions]. Available from http://www.sidwaya.bfsitesidwaya/Sidwaya_quotidiens/sid2005_24_12/rencontre.htm (accessed December 2005).

PASEC (2009). *Les apprentissages scolaires au Burkina Faso: Les effets du contexte, les facteurs pour agir.* Available from http://www.confemen.org/wp-content/uploads/2012/06/Rapport_Burkina_2009.pdf (accessed November 2012).

Psacharopoulos, G. (1980). 'Higher education in developing countries: A cost-benefit analysis'. Washington, DC: World Bank Staff Working Paper, 440.

Rouamba, A. L. G. (2004). 'Mathieu Ouédraogo: Je ne connais pas d'Enseignants PPTE'. [Mathieu Ouédraogo: I know not of HIPC teachers]. In *Le pays,* 3226, 7 October. http://www.lepays.bf/quotidien/lumières2php (accessed 10 July 2006).

Schaffer, S. (1994). *Participation for Educational Change. A Synthesis of Experience.* Paris: UNESCO.

Sirois, G. and Lesturgeon, N. (2009). *Mise en œuvre des politiques éducatives internationales et représentations des acteurs de l'éducation au Burkina Faso: vers la réalisation des objectifs de l'éducation pour tous?* Mémoire de maîtrise, Université du Québec à Montréal.

Somé, T. H. (2010). 'Understanding Student Resistance to Cost Sharing in a Resource-Poor Country: The Case of the University of Ouagadougou'. In C. Putcha,

Mathematic Formulation of Poverty Index: How We Measure Poverty in Different Nations around the World. New York: Mellen Edwin Press, pp. 109–26.

—(2011a). 'The magnificent elephant that was promised showed up lame: The Ten-Year Development Plan of Basic Education and Education for All in Burkina Faso'. In C. S. Malott and B. Porfilio (eds), *Critical Pedagogy in the Twenty-First Century: A New Generation of Scholars.* Charlotte, NC: Information Age Publishing.

—(2011b). 'In search of sources other than governmental in the financing of African Higher Education: A word of caution beyond the gains'. *Journal of Higher Education in Africa*, 9 (1): 73–98.

World Bank (1988). *Education in Sub-Saharan Africa: Policies for Adjustment, Revitalization, and Expansion.* Washington, DC: The World Bank.

4

Cameroon: An Overview

Martha Beyang Egbe

Introduction

In this chapter, the author has sought to outline a brief historical survey of the Cameroon unique education system as it obtains in the country today. The chapter features the descriptive research design of the ex-post facto type that influenced the present two sub-systems of education in the country; the Anglophone and the Francophone. The sources of material for the chapter included secondary data from the internet, information from national educationists' articles, government texts and decisions as well as relevant literature. This chapter has also portrayed the hybrid nature of the education system as an offspring of a bicultural colonial past with British and French overtones.

In retrospect, the Cameroon education system traces its evolution from the German occupation in 1884, through its partition between the British and the French after the fall of the Germans in the first World War (1914) by the League of Nations (1919). Thereafter, the territories were subjected to the education systems of their respective masters. Thus, the French applied a French-styled education system to East Cameroon and the English an English-styled education as it pertained in Nigeria to which Southern Cameroon was attached for purposes of administration.

At independence and upon the reunification of the two territories, it became necessary to harmonize the two sub-systems and proceed with reforms. At present, the harmonized structure of education runs through primary, secondary and higher education, and bilingualism, a characteristic feature of Cameroon, is mainstreamed in the system. Although the new system still embodies some old characteristics of the sub-systems, the duration of primary and secondary education has been harmonized to six and seven years respectively. Recent reforms in the university system have introduced the Bachelors, Master and Doctorate (BMD) programmes for all universities and higher institutions in the country.

Besides the historical overview, the author has also examined briefly the impact of the colonial cultures on the present system, the policies in place, some of the difficulties faced and the way forward. The report further underscores ICT, financing of education and Cameroon's bilingualism, a factor that characterizes her uniqueness in Africa.

Despite the ongoing challenges, Cameroon has developed sound and concrete policies which if properly implemented will lead the country to an emerging nation by 2035.

Cameroon: History

According to Amin (1999), the history of Cameroon started with the Portuguese who came to Cameroon in the 1500s but could not settle because of malaria fever that killed a number of them. Their major interest was in the slave trade that was carried out in the northern part of the country (Tambo 2003: 8). Later, in 1884, the Germans overtook Great Britain and annexed Cameroon which became a German territory called Kamerun (Cameroon Education 2010a).[1] After the first World War, under the 28 June 1919 League of Nations mandate, Cameroon was divided between the French (East Cameroon) and the British (West Cameroon). In 1961 the French Cameroon gained independence. The following year, two-thirds of the British northern Cameroon voted to join Nigeria while the southern one-third chose to join East Cameroon (Cameroon Education 2010b).[2] The Federal Republic of Cameroon was now born and it functioned with two distinct cultures, the French and the English.

The development of Western-type schools can be traced to the arrival of Christian missionaries in Cameroon. According to Tambo (2003: 7), the pioneer person in this venture was the British Reverend Joseph Merrick followed by Alfred Saker. Reverend Merrick opened the first primary school in Bimbia in 1844. Thereafter, there was the growth of many schools managed by the state, private individuals and the churches. To control this outburst, the Government enacted the 1910 education law regulating school activities. The German governor became the authority in educational policy (Tambo 2003: 9). A few government schools were created and run by the Germans and the

Table 4.1 Distribution of schools in Cameroon in 1930

	Public schools	Private primary schools	Private higher primary school	Public secondary schools	Private Secondary schools
French Cameroon Schools	137	1188	3	5	2
English Cameroon schools	1	2 (native Authority)	3 (assisted mission schools)	4 (unassisted mission)	5 (post primary)

Source: Cameroon National Education Policy since the 1995 Forum, tabulated by author

German language was used in the whole territory. The first World War (1914) brought an end to the German administration of Cameroon. As Tambo (2003: 21) again pointed out, this put an end to German educational activities. In 1916, the English and the French replaced the German language with the English and French languages respectively.

From 1922 to 1944, the British administered the Southern Cameroon as part of Nigeria, while the French administered East Cameroon as an integral part of France. The effect was that while East Cameroon schools received direct financial support from the French government those of Southern Cameroon were neglected. The number of schools in East Cameroon proportionately outnumbered those in Southern Cameroon (see Table 4.1 above).

Cameroon education

In October 1961, the two territories reunified to form the Federal Republic of Cameroon. Two education sub-systems prevailed: the English and the French sub-systems. In 1962, UNESCO recommended the harmonization of the two systems of education as the best strategy to solve the problems that had cropped up. In 1976, the government tried to merge the two sub-systems by creating bilingual schools and facilitating the teaching of both languages in schools. In this regard, in 1984 the Head of State convened a meeting of educational experts from the two cultures (English and French) to study the problems. The meeting failed to meet the targeted objective, thus delaying the harmonization of National Education policies (Shu 2000: 3). As such, the status quo remained in both cultural entities.

In 1993, following a popular uprising, the government affirmed the sub-systems by creating two examination Boards: the General Certificate of Education (GCE) Board for the Anglophone Cameroon and the Baccalaureate Board for French-speaking Cameroon (Tambo 2003: 16).

The school system

The Cameroon education system is structured into nursery, primary, secondary and higher education. Nursery education focuses on children aged 3 to 6 years and primary pupils aged 6 to 12. Secondary education targets children aged 11 to 18. Secondary education is divided into three, namely: secondary grammar schools, technical schools and vocational schools. In the French-sub-system, four years are spent at the lower-secondary and three at the upper secondary, while in the Anglophone sub-system, five years are spent at the lower-secondary and two at the upper level. There are many secondary high schools that are bilingual with lessons given in both French and English. Higher education teaches degree courses in different fields or disciplines. Bilingualism is given special focus in pilot centres spread over the national territory. There are specialized schools for training professionals like the School of Administration and Magistracy (ENAM), the School of Agriculture (ENSA), the Military Academy (EMIA), the Advanced School of Education (ENS), the school of Public Works, and others.

In June 2006, a technical team made up of members from different ministries including the author of this paper, elaborated, validated and presented the Cameroon Strategy of Education to financial partners to enable Cameroon to qualify for the 'Fast Track Initiative' programme which aimed at providing quality Education for All by 2015. This permitted Cameroon to revise her curricula to meet the economic challenges of the nation, recruit more teachers to cut down on class size, to meet the requirements of the Universalization of Primary Education and improve governance in the school system by the year 2015 (EFA-FTI 2002).

The 'Universalization of Primary Education' or 'Education for All' is a major policy option in the educational system of Cameroon. The 1996 constitution of Cameroon, (amended in 2008) provides that 'Primary Education shall be compulsory' (Law No 96–06, Art.17:43 [1996]). In effect, education at the primary level is 'obligatory' and 'free' (Decree No 2001/041, Art.41). This is to enable the beneficiaries to achieve a sustainable level of basic literacy and numeracy skills. The consequence of this measure was an explosion in school attendance and classrooms were overcrowded. This was not matched with an increase in staff and classrooms. It resulted in ineffective teaching and poor pass rates in class and official examinations (Amin 1999). Many studies (Amin 1999; UNICEF 2001; Fonkeng 2007) revealed high repetition rates (more than 40 per cent) at the level of primary schools. These shortcomings were addressed by the Education for All-Fast Track Initiative (EFA-FTI) programme. The objective was to increase the number of qualified teachers in the field so as to cut down on class size as recommended by the World Bank, that is, to have a ratio between 37:1 up to 40:1. The table below gives a picture of the situation before the implementation of the programme.

Furthermore, Adesina (1980) observed that lack of textbooks and teaching materials, poor and haphazard inspection of teachers point up to some of the causes of pupils' poor performance in schools. The advent of the economic crisis jeopardized the government's capacity to provide for adequate, qualified teachers and quality educational services. Since the government could not single-handedly finance the increasing cost of education, alternative financial sources were sought. The African Development Bank provided funding for the construction of classrooms, staff quarters, fences, water-points and toilets in some 150 primary schools from 2002 to 2004 (MINEDUC 2003; MINEDUC/PEII/CEP 2003). This was followed in 2007 by some financial assistance from the World Bank through the recruitment and payment of salaries for 37,200 qualified teachers recruited from 2007 to 2011 (MINEDUB 2011) (see Table

Table 4.2 School enrolment, pupil/teacher ratio, achievement rate and repeat rate in 2007

Region	School enrolment Urban	School enrolment Rural	Pupil/Teacher ratio Urban	Pupil/Teacher ratio Rural	Achievement rate Urban %	Achievement rate Rural%	Repeat rate
Adamawa	423,755	239,152	80	110	58	3.71	43%
Centre	1,053,557	1,094,229	60	80	67	16	30%
East	498,364	208,950	45	95	17	65	30%
Littoral	1,358,011	508,308	80	150	58	32	30%
Extreme North	1,930,355	475,392	80	156	30	11.3	58%
North	986,473	390,218	75	52	20	26.3	51%
North West	1,196,441	335,707	70	40	28	3.59	42%
South	314,941	121,438	40	15	33	66	41%
South West	761,060	340,300	60	45	18	80	17%
West	1,148,233	545,185	90	65	28	61	54%

Source: Cameroon School Enrolment: http://www.indexmundi.com/facts/cameroon/school-enrolment

Table 4.3 Statistics of Contract Grade One teachers recruited under the EFA-FTI Programme: MINEDUB (2007–11).

Region	2007 IC1	2008 IC2	2009 IC3	2010 IC4	2011 IC5	TOTAL
Adamawa	815	453	490	417	350	2,525
Centre	2,720	655	620	217	903	5,115
East	1,115	436	470	425	291	2,737
Extreme-North	1,681	666	590	1,336	1,411	5,684
Littoral	809	473	500	377	821	2,980
North	985	472	500	1,214	907	4,078
North-West	1,165	556	580	566	842	3,709
West	1,337	569	590	687	777	3,960
South	809	536	560	408	229	2,542
South-West	1,306	574	600	628	762	3,870
Total	**12,742**	**5,390**	**5,500**	**6,275**	**7,293**	**37,200**

Source: MINEDUB: Directorate of Human Resources; 'Contract Teachers (CT)' January, 2012

4.3 above) under the EFA-FTI programme to reduce Pupil/Teacher ratio (PTR) to ensure an accelerated progress towards achieving the Education Millennium Development Goal of 'Quality Education for all' by the year 2015 (Millennium Summit 2000).

Policy orientation

When the policies put in place such as the promotion of bilingualism and national harmonization of the two sub-systems among others were put in the dustbin (Shu 2000), the country portrayed certain insufficiencies and was no longer responsive to a fast-changing society. The sub-systems were not receiving proportionate attention, with poor legislation dealing with education, excessive centralization, shortage of qualified teachers and others. Consequently, the education offered was ill-adapted to the employment needs of the population and worse still, there was no follow-up of policies. This prompted the convening of an education General Assembly in 1995 to elaborate a new education policy blueprint.

The education General Assembly of 1995: The 1995 forum

This assembly that was held in Yaounde from 22 to 27 May, 1995 had as its main objective to establish a new education policy to meet the challenges of the twenty-first century. A working document was prepared and submitted to guide the deliberations at the forum. The document highlighted the following themes: The decentralization of powers, the development of a strong hierarchy and a thoughtful bureaucracy, harmonization of the duration of primary and secondary levels in the two sub-systems, defining the concept of bilingual schools and introducing democracy, tolerance and peace in the school programme (MINEDUC 1994: 9–26).

Thereafter, the Ministry of Education made recommendations for the reforms of nursery, primary, secondary and teacher education (Cameroon 1995). The objective was attained and the then minister of education submitted the report of the forum to the National Assembly. These recommendations were approved and passed into law in 1998. Since then government has progressively implemented some of the recommendations such as the control, management, training of teachers, and provision of didactic materials taking into consideration the linguistic and cultural leaning of the people. The forum also laid down rules for training and certification, selection and supply of teachers, thus, marking the turning point of the Cameroon education policy.

The 1998 Law of Educational Orientation

The 1998 law was the upshot of the 1995 education law. It harmonized the primary cycle to six years in both sub-systems, encouraged national integration, and instituted bilingualism at all levels. It also regulated the running of nursery, primary, secondary and teacher education (Law No 98/004 1998) (Cameroon 1998). Despite the talk on deployment of teachers, rural schools still remained understaffed and the urban schools overcrowded. Teachers' and students' rights and obligations are well defined in the law but the new statute for teachers designed to motivate them which was decreed in 2000 is yet to be implemented. Corporal punishment, prohibited in schools, still appears to be practised by some teachers. This law also includes the automatic promotion of students within each cycle to cut down on the repetition rate that stood at 40 per cent in 2002 (MINEDUC 2002).

New dispensation of primary and secondary education

As a result of the 1998 Education Law, all primary schools in the country now do six instead of seven years. The policy of compulsory and free education for public primary schools has been implemented. All secondary schools have an equal duration of seven years, that is a 5–2 years-system for Anglophone students, and a 4–3 years system for Francophone students. In 2002, secondary grammar was separated from secondary technical and vocational education. The new policy has also introduced non-formal education to permit illiterate adults to become literate.

Technical and vocational education in Cameroon

Ngundam and Tanyi (2000: 107) complained of the inadequate attention given to technical and vocational education in Cameroon in terms of quality and relevance of the system of training. Because the programme is overloaded with general courses (Mathematics, Science, English, French, Agriculture, Accounting, Administration, Legislation, Hygiene, Civics, History, Geography, Physical Education, Professional Calculation, General and Technical Drawing, Workshop Practice), the technical school student graduates with little technical know-how required to cope with industrial needs. Also, because technical workshops are expensive to equip, the available materials are old, and non-functional because the state does not provide money for new equipment nor does it make available maintenance budget or operational funds for technical schools. Because of the above reasons, only a few graduates pass the technical school final exams, very few continue to the technical high schools and then to the Advanced Technical Teachers' College (Technical University). That is why there are just a few trained technicians and training structures that can organize training and retraining of technicians to meet the changing industrial world (ibid.).

In Cameroon most children aged 10–11 years go to the grammar schools. Only drop-outs from grammar schools and the weak students of about 14 years old and above go to technical schools. Most of these students do not cope with studies in technical schools because they are academically, weak coupled with the fact that the programme is overloaded with too many general subjects. UNESCO reported that problems of incompetency in the technical field in Cameroon is attributed to a bizarre school programme, inadequate financing, structural and organizational problems, and problems of pedagogy (Ngundam and Tanyi 2000: 117). This translates into poor pass rates, and a high unemployment rate that compels the graduate to end up as a petty trader, a taxi or bike driver, or doing other menial jobs.

Higher education and quality assurance in Cameroon

In Cameroon, higher education includes: universities, polytechnics, higher training colleges and all post-secondary institutions. These institutions play a critical role in the economic, scientific, social and human development of the country. Other African countries including those of the Economic Community of Central Africa (CEMAC) zone require well-trained and knowledgeable human resources to meet the challenges that threaten development and growth in the region. Because some of these countries (Central African Republic, Chad, Cameroon etc.) have weak economies, they cannot afford strong education institutions capable of producing the quality of manpower necessary for their development needs. It is recommended that exchange educational programmes and technical co-operation among these countries could address these challenges.

Before independence in 1960, the government senior staff were trained in universities abroad. In 1961, the Cameroon government created the National Institute for University Studies to prepare students for degrees in Education, Law, Economics and the Arts. Professional training programmes were also developed through the School of Administration, the School of Agriculture and the Military Academy. In 1962 the National Institute for University Studies was transformed into the Federal University of Cameroon (Njeuma 2004), offering a generous system of student welfare whereby students paid no fees, had subsidized meals, lived in subsidized accommodation and received bursaries for other school requirements. As a result, student enrolment increased, thus reducing the number of students leaving the country to study abroad. Njeuma (2004) pointed out that graduates from the professional and technical institutes were readily employed into the public sector while those from the university were discriminated against as they were not given jobs on completion of their studies.

In 1992, Decree No 92/074 of 13 April 1992 raised the University of Buea to full-fledged status with the status of an English-speaking university (Tambo 2003: 26). In 1993, the University of Yaounde was decentralized and six new universities were created with the objectives of quality assurance in higher education including the promotion of national and international co-operation with other institutions with regards to quality control and the harmonization of university programmes in the CEMAC zone (MINESUP 2010).

Bomnsa (2012) pointed out that the university system was reformed and the Bachelor-Master-Doctorate degree programmes (BMD) instituted in all institutions of higher learning nationwide. The new programme uniformized learning in all these institutions with a view to producing competent and efficient manpower for the country.

The attainment of an emerging economy by 2035 as projected by the country will largely depend on the direct outcome of the new education programmes.

The integration of ICT in schools in Cameroon

The use of ICT in Cameroon schools

The Networked Readiness Index (NRI) framework is a major international assessment of countries' capacity to exploit the opportunities offered by ICTs. In 2004, Cameroon made its first appearance and was ranked 126th in the field of ICT, but with increased awareness and improved usage by government, it now occupies the 95th position. The use of computers in Cameroon schools is expanding progressively but there are concerns about the use to which students apply them. It is observed that rather than using the computers constructively, for useful purposes such as research, the students spend long hours before screens either watching fashion parades, playing games or chatting with friends on Facebook.

ICT policies

In 2004, key strategies on the use of ICTs in education were highlighted in the Cameroon National Information and Communication Infrastructure's (NICI) policy supported by the United Nations Development Programme (UNDP) and the United Nations Economic Commission for Africa (UNECA). The NICI plan document resolved to introduce ICTs in schools and universities, train teachers on the use of ICT facilities and equip centres with these facilities (Nangue 2010).

In June 2005, the Prime Minister signed a decree creating the national sub-committee for the integration of ICTs in education. The Sectorial Strategy document of Education was jointly drafted by the four Ministries of education

– MINEDUB, MINESEC, MINESUP and MINEFOP to use ICT in the teaching–learning educational situation (Cameroon 2006).

ICT infrastructure in schools

Students are required to pay a compulsory Parent Teacher Association (PTA) levy for ICT. Several private secondary schools and colleges have established partnerships with Western institutions to provide quality ICT infrastructure. Because of the partnership, Matchinda (2008) pointed out that more private than government schools are provided with ICT equipment thus having a low student/computer ratio.

The official ICT curriculum in secondary schools was released in 2003 by the Ministry of National Education and the subject made compulsory without adequate teaching materials and trained personnel for the course. However, ICT was introduced in the Higher Teacher's Training College in Yaounde in 2007 and the first batch of graduates from the Department of Computing Sciences and Instructional Technology was assigned to schools in March 2010 (MINEDUB 2010). Despite the efforts made in this sector, the high demand for ICT in Cameroon schools has yet not been met (Fluck 2003).

The language question in Cameroon

At reunification in 1961, English and French became the two official languages of Cameroon as the country opted for the policy of bilingualism (Echu 2004). Today, Cameroon operates under two official languages: French and English with equal importance, the heritage of Franco-British rule.

Bilingualism and bilingual education

Bilingualism constitutes the main core of Cameroon's language policy. Article 1, paragraph 3a of the Constitution of 18 January 1996 is clear in this regard:

> The official languages of the Republic of Cameroon shall be English and French, both languages having the same status. The State shall guarantee the promotion of bilingualism throughout the country.

Although all the Constitutions have always reiterated the policy of bilingualism, there is no well-defined language policy as to its implementation (Chumbow

1996). Moreover, English and French are said to be equal in status but French has a *de facto* dominance over English in administration and education. Indeed, French influence in language, culture and political policy prevails in all domains (Wolf 1997: 421). This has created an Anglophone/Francophone divide and caused disunity and conflict in the ideals of the two educational sub-systems. Thus, the Anglophones tend to unite to fight the hostile environment created by the Francophones (Wolf 1997). The story is different today.

Pilot centres have been created at some regional headquarters for the teaching of the two languages to promote bilingualism. Bilingual primary and secondary schools are also created throughout the national territory. There is a bilingual university located in Yaounde called the University of Yaounde 1 and an Anglo-Saxon-styled university in Buea (the South-West region). There are eight state universities where English and French are used as languages of instruction. The lecturer uses the language he/she is comfortable with and students take down notes, do assignments and examinations in the language of their choice. Despite this move, most lectures are delivered in French in universities in the Francophone regions in view of the numerical advantage of Francophone professors (Tambi 1973; Njeck 1992). This state of affairs contributes to the disgruntled attitude of Anglophones as even the correction of students' scripts tends to be biased when marked by a lecturer who lacks the linguistic competence of the language used by the student. That notwithstanding, most primary schools in urban centres have English and French as subjects on the timetable (Yembe 1991).

Both languages are compulsory in secondary schools. Another characteristic feature of secondary education is that different evaluation methods are applied in the two sub-systems: while the Anglophone student does four obligatory subjects with at least two others of his/her choice at the General Certificate of Education Ordinary Level (GCE O/L), the Francophone student does all the subjects in the curriculum including English and one other foreign language (Tambi 1973). This gives Francophones an edge over Anglophones in the mastery of foreign languages. In all, the implementation of the policy of bilingualism reveals total absence of language planning. With a stable political system, the government would have been able to implement a constructive language policy. Bilingualism needs to be properly addressed as it is gradually becoming a source of uneasiness amongst the two cultural linguistic groupings.

Financing of Education

In Cameroon there are several sources of education financing. These include:

- the Government that foots most of the bills for education including the construction of school buildings, staff houses, the purchase of furniture, equipment and teaching materials, the payment of teachers' salaries and subventions to public and private schools. The Government is supported in this regard by donor agencies/countries and international organizations such as the African Development Bank, the Islamic Bank, French corporation, Donations from Japan, the United Nation 'Educational Scientific and Cultural Organisation (UNESCO) and United Nations Children's Fund (UNICEF).
- the Parents Teachers Association (PTA), made up of teachers and parents of pupils/students of an institution. Pupils/students at the beginning of each school year, pay PTA levy which is used to pay contract teachers, build classrooms, and buy school materials including textbooks. All financial engagements are undertaken by school councils set up for that purpose.
- private individuals who construct their schools and provide equipment and didactic materials, employ and pay teachers and look forward to subventions that do not come regularly. This seems to be a very lucrative business as so many people, particularly retired teachers and private businessmen/women are engaged in it.
- private enterprises such as the National Social Insurance Fund owns primary schools throughout the country. They take charge of all their bills without expecting subvention from the government. The salaries they pay to teachers are better than salaries in the other private establishments.

Over the years, the budget for education has witnessed significant increases, occupying the first place in the country's yearly budget. Even though primary education is free, pupils are still required to pay building fees in schools where classrooms are inadequate. For secondary schools, the payment of fees is official but the amounts differ from school to school depending on whether the school is public, private or lay-private. The official fee paid to state-owned universities is 50,000frs, but the private and lay-private universities are paid more.

Education of girls

Amin (1999: 57) revealed that traditional beliefs, culture and religion particularly in the northern regions of Cameroon do not attach much value to girls' education. He recognized the fact that some parents, while waiting for their daughters to get ready for marriage, send their boys to school. Also, some parents keep their daughters at home for fear of sexual harassment by male teachers and professors because a significant number of teachers have demanded sexual favours of their female pupils and students. This dampens the girls' zeal to attend school and increases the unwillingness of family members to send their daughters to school.

Amin (1999) pointed out that early marriages are also a hindrance to girls' schooling while Amin and Fonkeng (2008) found that, the more parents are educated the more they encourage their children including girls to go to school. UNICEF (2007a) has tried to take girls out of their domestic chores at home such as carrying water and caring for their younger siblings and enable them to go to school by providing water to areas not far from their homes. To improve gender equality, UNICEF has adopted the system of providing a bag of rice or millet to any child that completes a semester in school. This move, including that of mothers' clubs (to encourage particularly girls), (UNICEF 2007b) and the World Bank, (1990) have increased school participation rates of girls in the northern regions of Cameroon.

Conclusion

For the ongoing reforms in the education system to take root and create visible encouraging impacts, government must invest huge sums in the training and retraining of teachers and in school infrastructures. This is not likely to be soon notwithstanding the sacrifices government is making through yearly budgetary allocations, for such sacrifices are inadequate in view of the magnitude of the problems. High levels of corruption and corrupt practices in the school system, though strongly addressed by government, continue to undermine meaningful reforms and progress. There are still problems on the way forward.

Notes

1 Cameroon Education (2010a), Unpublished manuscript available from http://www.mapsofworld.com/cameroon/history/ (accessed on 9 May 2010).
2 Cameroon Education (2010b), Unpublished manuscript available from http://www.cameroon50.cm/en/component/content/article/252–education-de-base-1960-2010 (accessed on 9 May 2010).

References

Adesina, S. (1980). 'The wastage factor in primary education: a case study of Lagos State primary school leavers'. *West African Journal of Education.* Volume 21 (1): 91–9.
Amin, M. E. (1999). *Trends in the Demand for Primary Education in Cameroon.* New York: New York University Press.
Amin, M. E. and Fonkeng, E. G. (2008). 'Gender and the Demand for Primary Education in Cameroon'. In V. Demos and M. T. Segal (eds), *Social Change for Women and Children.* Stanford: JAI Press.
Bomnsa, T. J. B. (2012). *Challenges and Prospects of Private Higher Education in Cameroon.* Bamenda: University of Science and Technology.
Cameroon Education (1995). *National Forum on Education: Final Report.* Yaounde: Ministry of National Education.
—(1998) *Law No 98/004 of 14 April 1998 to lay down guidelines for education in Cameroon.* Yaounde: Ministry of National Education.
—(2006) *ICT in Education in Cameroon.* Available from www.infodev.org/en/publication (accessed on 28 September 2012).
Chumbow, S. B. (1996). *The Role of National Languages within a Comprehensive Language Policy for Cameroon.* Academic Discourse presented at the University of Buea.
Echu, G. (2004). *The Language Question in Cameroon.* Available from http://www.linguistik-online.de/18_04/echu.htm (accessed on 25 September 2012). Yaounde: Bloomington.
EFA-FTI (2002). *A Global Partnership to Achieve the Education Millennium Development Goal of Universal Primary Education.* Available from www.worldbank.org/education/efafti
Fluck, A. E. (2003). *Integration or Transformation.* Available from UTas ePrints: eprints.utas.edu.au/232/1/01front.pdf (accessed 14 August 2009).
Fonkeng, E. G. (2007). *Strategies to Reduce Repetition in Cameroon Primary Schools.* Yaounde, Cameroon: The University of Yaounde I.
Matchinda, B. (2008). 'Guidelines for the Successful Integration of ICT in Schools in

Cameroon'. In C. R. Nangue 2010, *Factors that Impact on the Successful Integration of ICT in Schools in Cameroon*. South Africa: Nelson Mandela Metropolitan University.

Millennium Summit (2000). 'Dakar Framework for Action – Education for All: United Nations Millennium Declaration: Dakar, Senegal.' UNESCO. Available from http://www.edqual.org/publications/workingpaper/edqualwp3.pdf (assessed on 19 September 2012).

MINEDUB (2010). *Ministry of Basic Education Posting Decision, 2010.* Yaounde.

—(2011). *Current Situation of ICT in MINEDUB.* Yaounde: Ministry of Basic Education.

MINEDUC (1994). *Preparation for the National Forum of Education.* Yaounde: Ministry of National Education.

—(2002) *Compensatory Teaching and Automatic Promotion in Primary schools.* Yaounde: Ministry of National Education.

—(2003) *Education Sector Policy.* Yaounde: Ministry of Education. Available from www.mineduc.gov.rw/IMG/pdf/EDUCATION_POLICY.pdf (assessed on 28 September 2012).

MINEDUC/PEII/CEP (2003). *Expérience Pilote de Réduction des Redoublements.* Yaoundé: Ministry of Education.

MINESUP (2010). Éléments de reflexion pour l'harmonisation des cursus d'enseignement supérieur au Cameroun. *Rapport général du comité ad hoc de preparation scientifique des Assises des programmes Universitaire*, pp. 21–4.

Nangue, C. R. (2010). *Factors that Impact on the Successful Integration of ICT in Schools in Cameroon.* South Africa: Nelson Mandela Metropolitan University.

Ngundam, J. M. and Tanyi, S. A. (2000). 'Technical and Vocational Education in Cameroon'. In T. M. Ndongko and L. I. Tambo (eds), *Educational Development in Cameroon (1961-1999).* Platteville, WA: Nkemji Global Tech pp. 107–25.

Njeck, A. F. (1992). *Official Bilingualism in the University of Yaounde: Some Educational and Social Issues.* Mémoire de Maîtrise, Université de Yaoundé.

Njeuma, D. L. (2004). *Higher Education and Quality Assurance in Cameroon.* Yaounde: Federal University of Cameroon.

Shu, S. N. (2000). 'The National Education Forum of 1995'. In M. T. Ndongo and L. I. Tambo (eds), *Educational Development in Cameroon 1961-1999: Issues and Perspectives,* US: Nkemnji Global Tech, p. 3.

Tambi, J. (1973). *Received Language Bilingualism in Cameroon: A Study of Functions and Attitudes.* Mémoire du DES, Université de Yaoundé.

Tambo, L. I. (2000). 'The National Education Forum of 1995'. In T. M. Ndongko and L. I. Tambo (eds), *Educational Development in Cameroon (1961-1999).* Platteville, WA: Nkemnji Global Tech, pp. 257–65.

—(2003). *Cameroon National Education Policy since the 1995 Forum.* Cameroon, Limbe: Design House.

UNICEF (2001). *Évaluation des Formations Dispensées aux Enseignants et Directeurs*

d'écoles depuis 1998 dans les 12 Arrondissements du Programme d *'éducation*. Yaounde: Ministry of National Education.
—(2007a). 'Cameroon Education: Changing Attitude and Safe Water for Girls to Go to School.' http://www.unicef.org/infobycountry/cameroon_39992.html (accessed 26 September 2012.
—(2007b). 'Cameroon Education: More Girls to School through Mothers' club'. http://www.unicef.org/education/cameroon_39815.html (accessed 26 September 2012).
Wolf, H. G. (1997). 'Transcendence of ethnic boundaries: the case of the Anglophones in Cameroon'. *Journal of Sociolinguistics* 1 (3): 419–26.
World Bank (1990). 'World Declaration on Education for All: Meeting Basic Learning Needs'. *In World Conference on Education For All*. Jomtien, Thailand: UNESCO. Available from http://www.unesco.org/education/efa/wef_2000/regional_frameworks/frame_europe_north_america.shtml (assessed on 19 September 2012).
Yembe, O. W. (1991). 'Cameroon System of Education'. *Encyclopaedia of Education*, ENOFED 1243-22-07-93.

5

Cameroon: Trends and Futures

Willibroad Dze-Ngwa

Introduction

The trends of formal education in Cameroon have evolved over time and space with a gradual and continuous struggle for quality education. During the early days, religious bodies, (Islamic and Baptist) controlled the management of education in the territory. Initially, the trends of education reforms in Cameroon were either intended to ease evangelization or satisfy the needs of the colonial governments. With colonization, education largely remained in the hands of religious bodies, but with control from the Germans, and later, the British and French colonial authorities in their respective spheres of influence. At reunification in October 1961, two sub-systems of education – the Anglophone and the Francophone sub-systems were adopted. Education legislation initially concentrated powers in the hands of central government authorities, but the desire for quality education necessitated more reforms to ensure quality even in the remote areas. The current trend in Cameroon's educational system lays emphasis on quality, decentralization and professionalization.

Conceptual issues and methodology

To better understand this Chapter, it is important to provide a brief background; have a working definition for education before delving into its trends and futures in Cameroon. The methodology used in this paper will also be highlighted.

Cameroon is officially an English-French bilingual country which is reflected in the educational system. It is a very diverse country in terms of colonial backgrounds, ethnic cleavages, geographical, linguistic and religious differences (Grimes 1996: 185–215) alongside Arabic, Fulfulde, Latin and

German, which are also spoken in Cameroon (Chumbow 1980: 281). The country has a population of about 20 million people over a land surface area of about 475,000 square kilometres (Neba 1999: 1). The country is known as Africa in miniature and 'the racial and cultural cross-roads of the African continent' (Kofele 1980: 3). The country is a German creation, but was seized and partitioned by the combined Anglo-French forces in 1916 during the first World War. The British and French spheres became League of Nations Mandated Territories, and later, United Nations (UN) Trust Territories, which achieved independence separately. French Cameroon achieved independence on 1 January 1960 while British Southern Cameroons achieved independence through reunification with French Cameroon on 1 October 1961 (Dze-Ngwa 2014a: 292–3).

In an attempt to define education, I have simply considered education to mean, as Cardinal Tumi puts it:

> the deliberate and systematic influence of the mature upon the immature, through instructions, discipline and the harmonious development of all the faculties of the human being, with the aim to ensure, but of course, to philosophize and improve on the wellbeing of self and others (cited in Dze-Ngwa and Tamajong 2011: 55).

Education here is essentially done through teaching and training, or by inspiring the learner to reveal hidden ideas, knowledge and talents. The ultimate goal of education is for people to know and understand one another and undertake action for the good and development of society.

'Trends' in this chapter refer to the development or evolution of the education process in Cameroon over the years. 'Futures' will mean education perspectives or blueprints since the ultimate desire in education policies is to improve and develop the peoples and the country.

With the above definitions in mind, it is important to note that the trends of education in Cameroon have greatly been influenced by the logic of decentralization – with the intention to recognize and protect diversity, ensure equality, mutual respect and peaceful co-existence and, in fact, promote the traditions and customs of the diverse cleavages, with the desire to build a strong educational system.

In the attempt to carry out effective analyses on the trends and futures of education in Cameroon, the qualitative research method was adopted, academic literature and data on the current trends of education in Cameroon were consulted, and interviews and focus group discussions (FGDs) were conducted. Teachers, teacher-trainers, school heads, curriculum developers; and government and private individuals involved in the educational sector in Cameroon were interviewed. The study's method, therefore, was largely qualitative. These methods were adopted in order not to omit any important era of the trends of education in Cameroon.

Post-independence and current education trends in Cameroon

At independence and reunification, the education trend was coined to recognize and protect the inherited Anglo-Saxon and French values in the country and promote professionalism among learners. According to Ahmadou Ahidjo, the aim of education was to provide our young people or adults undergoing some sort of training with the knowledge working methods and attitudes necessary to ensure the efficient running of the nation's machinery (As quoted in the Political Bureau of the Cameroon National Union's *As Told by Ahmadou Ahidjo, 1958–1968*. 1968: 73). Articles 5 and 6 of the Federal Constitution stated that, 'the federal government was to organise and exercise control over higher education and scientific research, secondary general and technical education'. The Ministry of National Education provided 'a code for primary education and the encouragement of regional equality for educational opportunities in terms of enrolment and maintenance of standards' (Fonkeng 2007: 156).

While Decree No. 621F84 of 12 March 1962 placed the Ministry of Education under the direct control of the Minister, a Secretary of State for Education and Social Welfare was placed in East and West Cameroon respectively with a Regional Delegate for North Cameroon due to its distance and relative unawareness compared to the other regions (ibid.: 157). In 1965, decree No. 65DF350 of 5 August 1965, transformed the Ministry of National Education into the Ministry of National Education, Youth and Culture. Education was clearly decentralized under the Directorate of Higher Education, the Directorate of Secondary Education and the Directorate of Technical Education among others (ibid.: 157–8). Further decentralization was legislated by Decree No. 72/381 of 7 August 1973 which:

> provided for a Minister and Vice Minister of Education, a Secretary General with five services and a bureau directly under him; two technical services, three inspectors general of pedagogy and seven departments controlled each by a Director: General administration, Higher Education, Secondary Education, Technical and Vocational Training, Primary and Nursery

Education, Examinations and organisation and control of Private Education (ibid.: 180).

Teacher training was also considered important as President Ahmadou Ahidjo noted that, 'Cameroon must undertake the training *en masse* of teachers who are worthy of their vocation; such masters must be supplied both in the particular subject given and where they are wanted, in whatever part of the country that may be' (Political Bureau of the Cameroon National Union 1968: 72). For effective teacher education, the Higher Teacher Training College (ENS) was opened in Yaoundé with its annex in Bambili-Bamenda, to train secondary school teachers, counsellors and Pedagogic Inspectors in general education. For technical and vocational education, another Higher Teacher Training College (ENSET) was opened in Douala (Dze-Ngwa and Tamajong 2011: 58). This trend continued in the 1980s and many institutions were opened to train elementary school teachers, while in January 1999 a faculty of education was opened at the University of Buea with the Department of Curriculum Studies and Teaching, Department of Educational Administration and Department of Educational Psychology (Yuh 2006: 249). Although teacher training centres were temporarily closed down in 1987/8, they were reopened in 1995 for the training of Grade One teachers for the elementary schools. Today, state-owned teacher training colleges for Basic Education are found in nearly all of the 58 Divisions that make up the country, alongside privately-owned institutes. Despite the existence of the Higher Teachers' Training College in Yaoundé and Bambili, the government created another in Maroua, in October 2008. A Faculty of Education was also opened at the University of Yaoundé 1, during the 2013–14 academic year. In the Republic of Cameroon, teacher education and professional development is done through 'adequate doses of academics as well as practical training in the art of teaching' (Ngwo 2006: 3). This proliferation of teacher education centres probably explains the high literacy rate in Cameroon.

The Cameroon Government greatly improved on the educational system by taking education closer to the people especially in underserved areas. More primary and secondary schools were opened and the intention was to provide Universal Primary Education at the primary level, and train pupils at the secondary and higher institutions for the political, economic and socio-cultural development of the country. The Ministry of National Education (MINEDUC) in Cameroon was governed by Presidential decree no. 95/041 of 7 March 1995. To ensure quality education in Cameroon a National Forum on Education was held from 22–25 May 1995. By Law No. 98/004 of 14 April 1998, the general legal framework of education in Cameroon was laid down. This is the main document which guides nursery, primary, secondary and technical education and teacher training in Cameroon. Section 10 of its general provision states that, 'education shall be a top priority of the nation'. Decree No. 22–002/004 of 4 January 2002 further reorganized the ministry.

There also exist external services at the Regional, Divisional and Sub-Divisional levels. The Government of Cameroon, through Law No. 2004–19 of 22 July 2004 laying down rules applicable to regions, states in part that; 'regions shall devolve the powers to create, equip and maintain government high schools and colleges in the region; they shall also amongst others recruit and pay support staff of state high schools and secondary schools' (Fonkeng 2007: 204). These laws fall within the trend of decentralization, with the aim of achieving quality education through good governance.

In December 2004, the government of Cameroon increased the ministerial departments directly concerned with education in order to boost education and professionalization of the youth. The Ministries of National and Technical Education were dissolved and the Ministry of Basic Education and others were created. Education in Cameroon was now placed under seven different ministries including the Ministry of Basic Education, the Ministry of Secondary Education, the Ministry of Higher Education, the Ministry of Scientific Research and Innovations, the Ministry of Technical and Vocational Training, Sports and Physical Education and the Ministry of Youth and Civic Education. This has greatly improved on the trend of education and professionalization in the country, although finances within public institutions are still provided and controlled by the central government. The central government also provides subventions to private institutions. The decision on the school curriculum is, to a large extent, determined by the state.

Limitations of current trend of quality education in Cameroon

The trends of education in Cameroon have been to provide quality education for all, but Vernoz Munoz (n.d.) argues that there are 'a variety of issues revealing the lack of State commitment to education and the abysses between the rhetoric and the daily realities [of] millions of persons, whose human right to education is denied ...'. Generally, the level of education in Cameroon is high, but, the right to education in the country has had some shortcomings due to the manner in which stakeholders handle educational policies.

First of all, there is disconnection between words and actions. Although the education trend is decentralization for better output, decision-making in all the ministries of education is still influenced by the central government. As far as the Ministries of Basic and Secondary Education are concerned, the Ministries regulate all aspects of recruitment, appointments, postings, payments, curricula development and promotions in public (Government) schools. Although there are regional and divisional delegates of education, they do not take any major decisions affecting the school set-up in their areas of jurisdiction. This is so because of inadequate resources to ensure effective decentralization. Public schools also have School Managements Boards which unfortunately, are not powerful enough to generate revenue, receive and spend money from the government; and cannot sanction recalcitrant collaborators. The situation is, however, different in Lay Private and Denominational Schools where major decisions on recruitment, appointments, postings and payments are taken by the school owners, with the exception of public examinations where all candidates in both the Public and Private Schools take the same examinations (Dze-Ngwa and Tamajong 2011: 61). This proper follow-up within the private education sector probably explains why performance is better in private schools than in public schools. This situation is very similar in higher education.

An old trend in the education process in Cameroon is seen in the way schools are created. The government officials in Yaoundé decide on where, how and when to create public schools. Some of these schools are created as political compensation to areas, which are loyal to the politicians in power positions. In this reading, therefore, instead of providing schools to underserved areas, schools are rather seen as political compensations. This attitude has generated a great disparity between the number and quality of schools in the various regions of the country. Evidently, areas without influential elite are not provided with good schools and teachers. In higher education, the creation of public universities, professional schools and the appointment of its Rectors, Vice Rectors, Directors and Deans lie in the hands of the President of the Republic.

Again, the management of teachers in Cameroon is very inadequate as each teacher of the different ministries concerned is placed under at least three different ministries. Teachers are effectively recruited, disciplined and retired by the Ministry of Public Service and Administrative Reforms. Their salaries and allowances are paid by the Ministry of Finance, while the respective Ministries only post, transfer and appoint them in their respective ministries.

A school teacher may be recalcitrant and arrogant to the school head for the simple reason that the latter did not recruit the former. This situation however is only common with public schools. The co-ordination of the activities of such teachers becomes very cumbersome, and adversely affects education quality.

There is also very little interest in technical education. Quality technical education is the gateway for sustainable development in contemporary and emerging Africa. Unfortunately, after 50 years of independence, the Cameroon Government and stakeholders in the education sector have not departed from the old-fashioned general education mentality, which has continued to relegate technical education as sub-standard and meant for weak students. This probably explains why general education institutions have proliferated in the country as against technical schools. I argue that this situation has been largely responsible for the dependence of sub-Saharan Africa on Western technologies and the continuous exploitation and exportation of the continent's rich natural resources by foreign experts and with little transfer of technology.

There is equally class inequality in education. Education in Cameroon is divided between public schools and private schools. Private schools are further divided into denominational schools and lay private schools. Public schools are run by the state and the students virtually pay far lower fees because of state subventions. Their teachers are recruited, trained, transferred and paid by the state. Denominational schools are owned and run by religious bodies or churches, depending on their convictions. Meanwhile, lay private schools are owned and run by private individuals or groups of individuals interested in the education sector. Generally, public schools attract a large number of children because they are almost free, while the private schools, especially the denominational colleges, pay relatively very high fees. In terms of performances in public examinations, the denominational schools perform better. Due to the high fees and good results, only the children of parents who can afford such fees are admitted. Children from poor backgrounds are relegated to public or lay private schools. This creates a situation where the country, instead of progressing towards quality education for all, is rather progressing towards class inequality in education.

The problem of disparity in the deployment of staff within public schools in the rural and urban centres is also worrisome. There is a high concentration of teachers in urban areas with a few teaching hours per week. During field work, it was discovered that while French and English language teachers flood the cities of Yaoundé and Douala, rural areas like Assie in the Nyong et So'o Division of the Centre Region of Cameroon has only one community-recruited teacher, who teaches the English and German languages. In this same school, for the 2009/10 school year, there was only one trained teacher posted to teach three subjects: history, geography and citizenship education (Makoutsing: interviewed 2010).[1] The example of Assie is very common in rural areas. This disparity is explained by the fact that there are inadequate basic social amenities to attract teachers to rural areas and the government is doing very little to improve the situation. This fact is confirmed when 'the Regional Delegate of Secondary Education for the Centre region highlighted in an interview by indication that of the approximately 8000 teachers in the Centre Region, almost half of them are based in the town of Yaounde' (Yimga 2013: 1). This situation pushes rural communities to depend on untrained or unqualified persons in the name of teachers. The children in these rural areas do not enjoy the same basic right to education and have lost hope that, 'education was to be the Great Equaliser that would help reduce the wide disparities in conditions of living that existed between the rich and the poor and between those living in rural and in urban communities' (Bishop 1994: 1).

Another trend in the school system of Cameroon is the contradictions in the conditions of entry into public secondary schools in Cameroon. The first and most important certificate for a primary-school leaver in the country is the First School Leaving Certificate for Anglophones and the *Certificat d'études Primaire* for Francophones. Ironically these certificates do not automatically qualify the holder for secondary education. They are again subjected to other examinations, the Government Common Entrance Examination for Anglophones and the *Concours d'entrée en Sixième*, for Francophones. Candidates in the Anglophone sub-system are again classified under List 'A' and List 'B' passes. Only those who pass in List 'A' are supposed to benefit from public secondary schools. Unfortunately, these public schools cannot absorb all List 'A' candidates, so there is bound to be confusion and corruption in order to gain admission into such schools. Meanwhile, List 'B' children are supposed to attend the more expensive private schools. This policy simply deprives young children of the right to quality education as many poor children are forced to drop out from school at this level.

A very worrisome trend in Cameroon's educational system is the fact that children living with disabilities have inadequate rights to education, despite legislative dispositions to that effect. Apart from the fact that Cameroon is signatory to many international conventions and agreements protecting the rights of children living with disabilities, there are national legislative dispositions as well. Law No. 83/013 of 21 July 1983 and its Law of Application No. 90/156 of 26 November 1990 reads in part:

Families should provide their children with disabilities access to regular schools. In addition, an age waiver should be granted persons with disabilities to be admitted into various educational institutions on the request of the CWD and their guardians and the state should bear part of the charge by admitting them to educational institutions.

Part of this law suggests that building plans in such institutions and public buildings should have facilities to ease access by disabled persons and even prescribes punishments for school officials who discriminate against the admission of disabled children. Paradoxically, of all the teacher training colleges in Cameroon, only the Universities of Buea and Bamenda offer special needs education. There are no public schools with specialized teachers, structures and equipment to cater for the disabled, thereby abusing their rights to education. The very few private schools with such facilities are very expensive for children and their parents. This situation has caused many children living with disabilities to abandon school, with some becoming street beggars. This situation is compounded by the attitude of society, parents and teachers towards disabilities. There are also inadequate policies, structures and pedagogic tools in the teaching and learning process for the disabled.

More so, the use of information and communication technologies is a new trend of education in Cameroon. In this connection, there is a mad rush for computers by the various Ministries of Education, school authorities and other stakeholders to provide school computers 'without putting in place a policy environment and curriculum that supports the integration of technology into teaching and in ways that ensure equitable access' (Toure 2008: 1). The idea of computer labs is very common in the country, even in areas without electricity. Such technologies as:

> internet and computers are often introduced ... into schools in ways that do not enhance teaching and learning, that promote automated thinking instead of critical thinking, that encourage dependency rather than autonomy and independence, and that reinforce existing patterns of exclusion. Too often the emphasis is on equipment, on making profits from schools, or on promises of modernity than on opportunities for teachers to learn and experiment with effective uses of technologies to enhance teaching and learning processes (ibid.).

Many school authorities in Cameroon have been found to charge extra 'computer fees' even if their schools do not have electricity.

The way forward/futures for education in Cameroon

One of the most important futures of the educational system in Cameroon is the Vision 2035 strategy in which the government forecasts that:

> Cameroon will have a population of 40 million inhabitants in 2035 with a large number of youth. This population could be an important asset if only it is well trained, well-fed and in good health otherwise, it can become a burden. Therefore the stake in terms of human capital formation is to ensure that the population is in good health, is properly educated, skilled and professionally qualified on the one hand, and to facilitate its insertion on the job market and avert brain drain. *As concerns education, there is need to (i) ensure universal access to education, apprenticeship and vocational training; (ii) enhance internal efficiency and improve regulation of the whole education system (primary, secondary and higher education); (iii) enhance the value and relevance of vocational training given the requirements of the job market* (Vision 2035 2009: 9, emphasis mine).

This Vision 2035 dream summarizes the futures of education in Cameron. The country can attain the Vision 2035 goals, a year projected by the Cameroon Government as a year of emergence for the country only if there is real political will to transform words into concrete action. For a more effective education system, the government and various stakeholders in the education sector should respect the legislative dispositions that guarantee education decentralization in the country, such as the current constitution and the 1998 law on education. They should also provide the necessary resources for quality education. This will entail giving greater autonomy to the regions and local councils in the running of their schools.

In the same light, with the growing educational trend towards ICTs, education stakeholders in Cameroon should note that ICTs for the sake of it may be dangerous to the education system. Rather, it should be used for quality research by both the teachers and the learners. Kathryn Toure posits that:

> Creative and contextualised appropriation of new technologies contributes to more active and interactive pedagogies, increased motivation, updated teaching materials, discovery of self and others, and changed roles and relationships among teachers and students and with knowledge. Learning can become more dynamic as teachers and students become partners in accessing information, constructing relevant knowledge and representing self and others (Toure 2008: 1).

ICTs by themselves cannot guarantee quality education for the future. There is need for quality control and focus based on local needs and realities.

As regards the contradictory policies of gaining admission into public secondary schools, the government of Cameroon should adopt legislative dispositions which give students the right to attend any school of their choice, provided the basic qualifications are met. Instead of considering the Common Entrance Examination (for Anglophones) or the *Concours d'entrée en Sixieme* (for Francophones), as a precondition for gaining admission into public secondary schools, the government and education stakeholders should rather consider the First School Leaving Certificate for Anglophones and the *Certificat d'études Primaire* for Francophones. The argument here is that these latter qualifications are more important and less restrictive in determining the choice of the child's secondary school. It is equally the first recognized academic certificates that a child requires to complete primary school education in Cameroon.

In like manner, there should also be effective implementation of the legislative dispositions that protect the rights of learners with disabilities. The right to education is a fundamental right of existence. Children living with disabilities should be considered within the mainstream of government education policies. Such policies should be inclusive and all schools, public and private should be equipped with necessary specialized material and teachers to handle such children. The challenge should be change in attitudes, construction of relevant infrastructure for the disabled, designing of inclusive curricular in the school system, providing adapted training and learning materials for students and teachers and coining better strategies for evaluation (Mbibeh 2013: 52–65), based on the degree and type of disability.

To curb the problem of staff deployment, the recruitment and transfer of teachers and school administrators should be done at the regional and local levels to make them answerable to their local employers to ensure better performance. As far as the appointment of school heads is concerned, a strict career profile of the teachers should be put in place and respected so that principals are appointed based on well-defined criteria like longevity, assiduity and exemplary moral standing. Such appointments should be recommended by the management board or through democratic elections of specified duration. In this light, the principals will be accountable to the local communities rather than to those who appointed them at the centre. This situation will also check the underserved areas and limit the situation where teachers from one part of the country are recruited and posted to work in other parts of the country without adequate preparation and funding. Sometimes such postings and transfers are considered as punitive and teachers may be reluctant to take their positions. It will also check the quality and quantity of teachers transferred to rural and urban centres; and all schools will have teachers.

Another important feature to enhance improved education in Cameroon is teacher motivation, satisfaction and continuous capacity-building. Unfortunately, teachers are not sufficiently motivated in Cameroon. As a consequence, many teachers change their professions or seek appointments into different more rewarding ministerial departments. In order to change this trend, Yimga argues that, 'effective educational transformation relies on teachers' rate of motivation to bring about change, as well as their capability of being supported in doing so' (Yimga 2013: 2). This should be accompanied by training and re-training in order to boost the professional development of the teachers.

These notwithstanding, the future of education in Cameroon will rely on effective development research for quality education. To do this, the various stakeholders concerned with the education process in general should be more determined to move from theory to practice. There is need to eliminate the artificial divides between academic and policy researchers and promote adequate collaboration among the various education stakeholders, create a national syndicate for researchers in Cameroon, provide facilities for scientific publishing, network with other funding bodies, improve funding and implement research results by the various government departments, among other things (Dze-Ngwa 2014b: 51). Quality research, quality publication and dissemination of research results remain pivotal in improving the current trends of education in Cameroon.

The future of education in Cameroon is also dependent on the future of the education of the girl child in the country. While it is generally believed that in Cameroon both 'girls and boys have equal access to education, without discrimination at any level' (Ngomedje 2005: 15), with some areas having more girls than boys, cultural practices and customs in certain parts of the country still discriminate against the education of the girl child. In poor communities in general and in the Northern Regions of Cameroon in particular, the girl child is disadvantaged and regarded as commodity for early marriage, while the boy child is favoured for school. I join Ngomedje (2005) to argue that:

> The education of the girl child is related to the empowerment of the women, and through them to the development of society. A good quality education will enhance women's capacities and prepare them to seize opportunities in the public and private sectors. This is important to transform some of the societal attitudes and behaviours that discriminate against girls and women (p. 16).

The girl child, like any other child, has an absolute right to quality education, welfare and professional development.

Conclusion

In conclusion, it is clear that the trends of education in Cameroon have been a gradual movement towards effective education. This is evident in the high state budget allocated to all education ministries on a yearly base. Since 1990, there has been a steady movement towards education decentralization and good governance. The 1996 constitution of the country, the 1998 Laws on Education and the July 2004 Laws which give regions the power to run their own schools are some blueprints towards effective quality education in Cameroon. The truth is that, quality education is progressively being realized in Cameroon, but practically, there is still some degree of inadequacies in recruitment, staff deployment and payment, staff motivation, training and in determining school curricula. To enhance quality education in the country, the various stakeholders in the education sector should formulate and execute school policies and programmes whose trends are towards continuous improvement of the school system in Cameroon for better growth and development. While the Vision 2035 programme has laid a strong foundation for education quality in Cameroon, a much more focused political will is necessary to ensure its implementation for the effective development of the Cameroon.

Note

1   Makoutsing Marleine Flore was the lone trained teacher of History, Geography and Citizenship in the Government Secondary School, Assie for two years, 2009–11. She was interviewed on 5 March 2010 in Yaoundé. She was 32 years old.

References

Bishop, G. (1994). *Alternative Strategies For Education*. London: Macmillan Education Limited.
Chumbow, B. S. (1980). 'Language and language policy in Cameroon'. In N. Kofele Kale (ed.) *An African Experiment in Nation Building: The Bilingual Cameroon Republic since Reunification*. Boulder, CO: WestView Press.

Dze-Ngwa, W. (2014a). 'Educational Research and the Challenges to Quality Higher Education and in Africa: The case of Cameroon, 1974-2012'. In E. Kamdem and W. Dze-Ngwa (eds), *Pan-Africanism, Research, Peace and Concerted Development in Africa*. Geneva/Yaoundé: PAID Publishers, pp. 31-41.

—(2014b). 'Fiftieth Anniversaries of Independence/Reunification and the Challenges to Internal Cohesion in Cameroon: A Historical Analysis, 1960-2014'. In Habaru, *Revue Scientifique pluridisciplinaire du Département d'Histoire de la Faculté des Arts, Lettres et Science Humaines de l'Université de Yaoundé I, Volume 1, Numéro 2, Juin 2014*, pp. 291-307.

Dze-Ngwa, W. and Tamajong, E. V. (2011). 'Education decentralization and the rights to quality education in Cameroon'. In G. Pampanini (ed.), 1st *PA.RE.RE Pampanini Report on the Right to Education 2011: Comparing the Right to Education Policies, Methodological Issues*. Catania: Cooperativa Universitaria Editrice Catanese di Magistero, pp. 55-63.

Fonkeng, G. E. (2007). *The History of Education in Cameroon, 1844-2004*. Lewiston, NY: The Edwin Mellen Press.

Grimes, B. F. (1996). *Ethnologue: Languages of the World 13th Edition*. Dallas, TX: Summer Institute of Linguistics.

Kofele K. N. (1980). 'Reconciling the DualHeritage: Reflections on the "Kamerun Idea"'. In N. Kofele Kale (ed.) *An African Experiment in Nation Building: The Bilingual Cameroon Republic since Reunification*. Boulder, CO: West View Press.

Mbibeh, L. (2013). 'Implementing inclusive education in Cameroon: Evidence from the Cameroon Baptist Convention Health Board'. *International Journal of Education*, ISSN 1948-5476, 5 (1).

Munoz, V. (n.d.), 'Sex education, human rights. The wind on the stone, human right to holistic sexuality education'. *Preliminary Report by the United Nations Special Rapporteur on the Right to Education*.

Neba, A. (1999). *Modern Geography of the Republic of Cameroon*, 3rd edn. Bamenda: Neba Publishers.

Ngomedje, A. D. (2005). 'Education in the Context of Poverty and Inequality'. In *Devlopment in Context*. http://www.koed.hu/mozaik16/adele.pdf (accessed 20 July 2014)

Ngwo, A. S. (2006). 'Practice, Teacher Education, Training and Professionalism in Cameroon'. In T. M. Tchombe and P. Fonkoua (eds), *Professionalism et formation des Enseignants au Cameroun*. Therese M. Tchombe and Pierre Fonkoua (eds), *Les Cahiers de Terroires*, Number 1.

Political Bureau of the Cameroon National Union (1968). *As Told by Ahmadou Ahidjo, 1958-1968*. Monaco: Paul Bory Publishers.

Toure, K. (2008). 'Introduction: ICT and Changing Mindsets in Education'. In K. Toure, T. M. S. Tchombe and T. Karsenti (eds), *ICT and Changing Mindsets in Education*. Bamenda, Cameroon: Langhaa, Mali: ERNWACA/ROCARE.

Yimga, M. F. (2013). 'Education for sustainable development in Cameroon: Reflection on "A Call for Teachers"'. Foretia Foundation.

Yuh, E. (2006). 'Practicum: An Essential Component in Initial Teacher Education'. In T. M. Tchombe and P. Fonkoua (eds), *Professionalism et formation des Enseignants au Cameroun, Les Cahiers de Terroires*, Number 1.

6

Cape Verde: An Overview, Trends and Futures

Jose Manuel Marques

Introduction

Cape Verde is a small archipelago consisting of 10 islands that span 4,033 square miles of barren volcanic rock, most of it sterile. It had no indigenous population, and has been independent from Portugal since 1975. Cape Verde has left the list of least developed countries in 2008, the second country to achieve this result. According to the UNDAF report (2012–16), the country is on track to meet most of the MDGs by 2015, particularly, in education and health, and several of its development indicators are already exceptions in the region. However, despite advances, Cape Verde continues to face a structural vulnerability of the economy, and regional and urban/rural disparities persist for most of the MDG targets and indicators particularly in relation to poverty and access to water and sanitation.

According to estimates of the National Statistics Institute (INE), for the year 2012, the total resident population was 491,875 inhabitants, of which 54 per cent were under 24 years. The annual population growth is 1.2 per cent. In 2010, life expectancy at birth was estimated at 77 years for women and 69 years for men. The infant mortality rate fell from 57.9 per thousand in 1995 to 20.1 per thousand in 2009, but neonatal mortality is still 68 per cent of infant mortality.

The education level of the country has experienced a remarkable evolution. In ten years, according to the 2010 Census, the literacy rate increased from 74.8 per cent to 82.8 per cent; secondary education increased by 10.8 percentage points, covering 29.3 per cent of the population; and the population with higher education increased from 1.1 per cent to 5.5 per cent.

The tertiary sector employs most of the workforce (63.9 per cent), followed by the secondary sector (20.8 per cent) and the primary sector only 13.3 per cent. Unemployment, around 10.7 per cent, is a constant concern, especially for young people aged 15–24, with a significant imbalance between men and women (18.3 per cent for men and 25.5 per cent for women). There are wide disparities in unemployment between the islands and municipalities, with the highest incidence for the islands of São Vicente, Fogo and Brava.

Educational reform is in its fifth phase since 1910. Since gaining independence one of the country's main strategic challenges has been to improve the qualification of its population, placing education as a priority, within a broad framework of valuing human capital, recognizing education and training as essential factors for economic and technological development, social cohesion, personal development and the full exercise of citizenship.

The policy measures taken in the country for the development of education, so far, are primarily aimed at broadening and strengthening the quality of compulsory education, along the conclusions and recommendations of major international and world events on education, including the Conferences of Jomtien (1990) and Dakar (2000), and subsequent regional conferences on education and development.

The new Basic Law for Education adopted in 2010 became an important landmark for the transformation of the Cape Verde education system by introducing a set of fundamental measures to leverage the education system as a factor of development and competitive insertion of the country in the globalized world. Compared with the previous legislation, the new law puts emphasis on the modernization of the educational system at the national level, requiring qualitative structural adjustments for all subsystems and levels of education, including vocational training. It stresses the principle of inclusive education, enroling all children and young people with special educational needs. The present revision of the Education Act (LBSE) also advocates the strengthening of special education, implying a new, specific methodological approach to learning and teaching both in relation to students with disabilities and gifted learners, according to the international Salamanca Statement of 1994.

This legislation gives also special emphasis to the assertion of the Cape Verdean national language, 'crioulo', as the country's mother tongue and cultural heritage for its citizens, stressing the need of learning it more deeply and giving emphasis to its use both as a written national language and as the main language of oral communication.

General characteristics of the education system

Despite the approval of the new Basic Law of Education in 2010, the education system works in practice according to the old model, established by the Basic Law of 1990 (Law No. 103/111/90 of 29 December), according to which the education sector comprises the subsystems pre-school education, school and extracurricular education, complemented with cultural and sports activities in a perspective of integration

Additionally, the educational system includes a subsystem of school social action which, through a series of socio-educational programs, ensures food support (through a network of school canteens that benefits all students of basic education), the provision of teaching materials, uniforms, school transportation, student residence, school health grant tuition and scholarships, thus promoting the conditions for equity in access and success for students of all levels of education, regardless of the socio-economic conditions of their families.

The data show that 80.2 per cent of Cape Verde's population has six or more years of schooling, of which only 38.3 per cent had more than six years of basic education. Of these, only 6.1 per cent had secondary or higher education. Education inequality is visible at all levels, with the most remarkable differences in the rates of literacy between men and women, between urban and rural areas, as well as among various regions of the country. However, the disparity regarding women is being reduced, given the academic achievements observed in recent years, that show girls are more likely to complete education and less prone to school failure than boys.

In ten years, according to the 2010 Census, the level of education of the population aged 3 years and over has the following improvements: i) the literacy rate increased from 74.8 per cent in 2000 to 82.8 per cent in 2010; ii) secondary education went up 10.8 percentage points, comprising, in the year 2010, 31.2 per cent of the population; iii) the population with higher education increased from 1.1 per cent in 2000 to 5.1 per cent in 2010.

In summary, although the overall data on schooling of the population are not very strong, the educational level of Cape Verde has been improving thanks to the commitment of the country to ensure access to education for all Cape Verdeans, with a good prospect of substantial improvement in these indicators in the coming decades, considering the strong growth of higher education.

The organization of the education system and the resources available

The responsibility for education in Cape Verde is shared among the central government, local authorities and the private sector. The private sector has contributed particularly to the development of pre-school and secondary education, allowing a considerable section of the population outside school age to complete this level of education.

The public sector, through the Ministries of Education and Sports (MED), Higher Education Science and Innovation (MESCI) and the Institute of Employment and Vocational Training (IEFP) deal with primary, secondary, vocational training and higher education, while the municipalities are responsible for pre-school education, as well as for specific activities such as social support for poor households. The private sector is active in pre-school and secondary education, with strong participation in higher education, but relatively insignificant presence in basic education.

Public expenditure on education

The favourable macro-economic environment of the country in recent decades allowed for strong investments in education, reaching around 20 per cent of its annual budget. The state budget for education in 2012 stood at around 16.4 per cent including higher education and vocational training. This reduction is due to the progressive reduction of external financing as well as for the lower need to build more schools.

According to the estimates of overall education budget for the year 2012, the state is the largest investor, accounting for approximately 76 per cent of the resources allocated to education for the development of education, followed by proven industry that dispenses 14 per cent and families who pay 9.6 per cent of the cost of educating their students. The weight of the municipalities in education is still negligible at less than 1 per cent. This distribution of financial contributions reflects the importance to the educational system, of the roles played by different actions in the process of teaching and learning at different levels of education.

The public expenditures on education were distributed as follows, according to State Budget 2013 on MED, MESCI and training.

- Basic education: 31.3 per cent of current expenditures;

- Secondary education: 37.3 per cent, of which 35.5 per cent for general and 2.2 per cent for technical education;
- Preschool: just 0.1 per cent;
- 1.0 per cent for vocational training;
- Pedagogical Institute 1.2 per cent;
- Higher Education and Science: 10.0 per cent.

The operation of the school system eventually consumes almost all of the allocated resources, especially in terms of payment of teachers' salaries, a situation that leaves little room for investments such as rehabilitation of educational spaces, creating educational materials and media, which are important to provide better quality education at all levels.

Despite the global economic crisis, the percentage of public expenditure on education has remained close to 6 per cent, and in 2012 stood at 6.4 per cent of GDP, which shows the priority that education receives as a factor for the development of Cape Verde. However, investments in pre-school are negligible for the country's needs.

Sectors of the education and training system

Pre-school education

In the academic year 2012/13 year the pre-schools enroled a total of 22,052 children: 49.5 per cent girls and 50.5 per cent boys. 74.5 per cent were ages 4 and 5 in kindergarten, and 25.5 per cent ages 0 to 3, in nurseries. The public sector accounted for 43 per cent of the enrolment, against 57 per cent for the private sector.

There were 516 pre-schools, most of them working full-time, with 1,093 classes, and an average of 20 students per class. Municipal public institutions are concentrated in rural areas, while the community institutions (NGOs, associations and foundations) and the private sector concentrate in urban areas. Most of this provision comes from a wide range of municipal-based institutions (47 per cent), community (42 per cent) and private (11 per cent). Most staff do not have relevant training. Only the municipalities of the interior of Santiago (St. Michael, St. Dominic, St. Catherine and Santa Cruz) and Fogo have high levels of staff training. The situation is more critical elsewhere.

Despite the strong expansion of pre-school during recent decades it is still far from achieving universal access, at about 74 per cent overall. Some municipalities have less than 50 per cent enrolment in pre-school, including some of the most densely populated. This poor performance is due to urbanization largely related to serving increased tourist demand.

Basic education

Between the academic years 1993/4 to 1998/9, with the expansion of education reform, enrolment in basic education increased from 69,821 to 92,033. From 1998 we see a stabilization around 91,000, and from 2000 a downwards trend due to the falling birth rate. Consequently in the 2012/13 academic year, 66,665 students attended basic education in about 417 schools, 413 public and four private. Boys represent 52 per cent of basic school enrolment and girls 48 per cent. The situation is near universal, with a net enrolment rate of around 93.9 per cent. Some municipalities show universal basic enrolment, but others may be only up to 90 per cent.

The inclusion of children with special educational needs in mainstream or special schools is still very limited and this can become an obstacle to reach universal schooling in the country.

Teachers for basic education

The policies for teacher education in recent decades have produced 95 per cent of teachers with adequate certification for basic education in the academic year 2012/13. However, their geographic distribution is uneven, with some municipalities enjoying fully trained staff and others less so. Most teachers in this sector are relatively young (74.7 per cent under 44 years old), which shows some potential for pedagogic innovation. Classroom challenges are significant with a two-shifts-per-day operation and a high incidence of dropouts and repeaters. Despite the relative lack of specialist spaces such as libraries, laboratories and sports areas, all basic schools had 100 per cent energy and clean water supplies, most had bathrooms, kitchens and school vergers.

Basic school performance

Despite significant reforms in recent times including teacher education and ICT, signs that the quality of the teaching-learning process is improving are quite limited. The percentage of repeaters and dropouts in the year 2012/13, reached 11.23 per cent, more for boys (13.3 per cent) than girls (8.1 per cent). Repetition mainly affects the 2nd, 4th and 6th school years, in which students are to be examined. On average Cape Verdeans students take 6.5 years in school to complete primary education, representing a coefficient of efficiency of 82 per cent. Consequently most students can complete the basic education (8/10) and can proceed to secondary education. However there appear to be significant problems in Portuguese language and mathematics, where 6 out of 10 students got negative results. This may be due to the socio-economic conditions of the students, the lack of adequate equipment and educational materials.

Secondary education

With the near universalization of basic education, secondary education experienced a strong growth from the second half of the 1990s. Enrolment increased significantly between the academic years 1990/1 and 2006/7, from 9,568 to 62,124 students. There followed a period of stagnation between 2008 and 2012. From 2012/13 there was a decrease of 1,400 students, mostly in the private sector which decreased 24 per cent over the previous year. Nonetheless, there were 60,389 secondary school students in 2012/13, 53 per cent of which were girls, confirming a better performance and retention of girls both in basic and throughout secondary education.

Indeed the secondary sector has increased dramatically to accommodate the growing enrolment. Whereas in 1992 there were nine public secondary schools that enroled 12,511 students spread throughout seven counties in the country, in 2012/13 there were 74 secondary private, reaching all municipalities, thus fulfilling the aims of universalization of secondary schooling. This has been accompanied by a greater flow of better-educated and qualified teachers though there still remains a 'rump' of untrained staff.

Almost all (97 per cent) of the students in secondary education follow the general path, compared to only 3 per cent in technical education. There is also a growing tendency of students to choose the cycle that gives access to vocational education, rising from 13.8 per cent in 2006 to 15.7 per cent in 2012/13. However, it is noted that important measures for enhancement of professional technical education have recently been approved, such as the recognition and validation of professional competencies, and a forthcoming scheme of dual certification, allowing those students completing technical education to pursue higher education if they wish and according to their achievement. It is likely that, with these innovations, the demand for vocational education will increase, providing both a quick access to the labour market and opportunity for the pursuit of higher studies.

The subject areas of greatest demand remain the humanities and economics (69 per cent), showing a deficit in scientific and technological areas (30 per cent) and arts (1 per cent), which are of great importance to the development of the country, considering the expectations for 2030 which are:

> to build a competitive economy based on innovation and high productivity requiring good quality infrastructure, highly trained manpower and an institutional environment appropriate for the best business practices, based on the expansion of the economy and the creation of high value-added services – agribusiness, tourism, finance, business/ICT, outsourcing, and a cultural/creative industry (Concept Notes – Transformation Forum 2014).

Transition between basic and secondary education

The transition rate from basic to secondary education experienced a considerable improvement from 36.4 per cent in 1990/1 to 86.3 per cent in 2012/13, with girls arriving in greater numbers for secondary education: 89.6 per cent as against 83.1 per cent for boys. This is due to their better results in basic education. But despite a sharp increase in the number of secondary schools in all municipalities, there are still disparities in access. The best situations are predominantly in counties with lower population density (Boa Vista, Brava, Sal, Maio and São Miguel) as well as in Praia and São Vicente, places with the highest provision of education in the country, both public and private. In other municipalities, efforts are still needed to assure the universalization of eight years of schooling. Part of this improvement is due to a reduction in repetition. Today more than two-thirds of young people aged 12–17 are educated at the secondary level. This result, according to the Global EFA Monitoring Report is quite satisfactory, placing Cape Verde above the values achieved by developing countries in general (56.6 per cent)

However, there is still an age-grade distortion to be taken into account that also has gender implications and still a relatively poor academic performance in secondary education overall.

Education and teacher quality

In a succession of education reforms, a central component has been the qualification of teachers, to enable them to keep up with other changes taking place in the education system and therefore improve the quality of teaching. For basic education, teacher education used to take place in the School of Primary Teachers (*Escola de Magistério Primário*) established in 1970, and later at the

Pedagogical Institute, an entity created in 1994 to ensure the training of teachers adapted to the requirements of reform.

To this end, in 1988, the Pedagogical Institute was established in the cities of Praia and Mindelo, and in 1997/8 a new branch was established in Vila da Assomada, Santa Catarina. It had a major role in the retraining of educators through the completion of initial training courses, and continuing with a view to train practising and aspiring teachers. These actions helped increase the number of teachers with appropriate pedagogical training for different levels of education.

Faced with new challenges, in a society which is being rapidly transformed with technological developments that reflect a new culture and work relationships, Cape Verde, after 20 years, is introducing a new reform, with emphasis on ICT, social solidarity and the quality of higher education to compete and co-operate in the global market.

This led to a decision that all teachers need to have a higher education degree. So the Pedagogical Institute was closed and replaced by a new University Institute for Education (*Instituto Universitário de Educação* – IUE) in 2012.

Vocational education

The problem of unemployment in Cape Verde, whose incidence rate mainly affects young people, aged between 18 and 24 years, means that measures to combat unemployment must be taken, also promoting the integration of young people into working life, and consequently the socio-economic development of the country. To this end and in order to ensure a credible and sustainable system of vocational education in Cape Verde, the Institute of Employment and Vocational Training (*Instituto de Emprego e Formação Profissional*, IEFP), under the Ministry of Training and Employment, is implementing, through its regional training facilities, projects and employment and training programmes as a way to ensure socio-economic advance. IEFP has a network of public and private entities that work as training providers: Centres for Employment and Vocational Training, Private Training Centres, public and private Technical Schools, secondary schools with training units, universities, chambers of commerce, NGOs and training companies. Overall, this effort had involved over 250 training projects by 2010. Since then the government changed its policy and began to request more participation of the students in the financing of their education, as a result of which the number of graduates went down by 46 per cent, highlighting the need to revisit the issue of funding for education in general in the country.

The main areas of demand continue to be construction, tourism and hospitality, and information technologies. The government's priorities for vocational training include the reduction of training undertaken in tourism and some training in technical areas such as mechanics and mechatronics, energy and tourism as animation and heritage. Such demand has prioritized courses of greater integration into the labour market, such as construction, hospitality and catering and administration, management and information technology. The demand was mainly for short courses that do not confer professional certification. The strategic guidelines aim to adjust the training supply to the needs of the labour market, through courses that confers vocational certifications at levels III, IV and V.

Most of the supply is provided at the centres for employment and vocational education of IEFP that, together with the School of Hospitality and Tourism (*Escola de Hotelaria e Turismo*), accounted for 75 per cent of the education programmes in 2011. They are also concentrated in the Island of Santiago, which is the largest in terms of economic activity, employment and population.

In terms of infrastructure, the country has a network of schools of modern vocational training centres, some with well-defined areas of expertise. Of the 10 vocational training centres, only 70 per cent have the conditions of space and equipment necessary to ensure the quality of training they provide. Furthermore, most centres do not have enough qualified personnel, given their budgetary restrictions, and so they turn to the market for hiring trainers as needed. This is a problem for the centres located in less populated areas.

Higher education

Among the many social phenomena recorded in Cape Verdean society after independence, the democratization of education is one of the most evident.

This, together with the evolution of science and technology, the new market paradigm and globalizing world developments, led in 2004 to the National Commission for Installation of the University of Cape Verde (CNI-UniCV), created by Decree-Law No. 31/2004. The mission was completed in 2006 by the installation of the first public university in Cape Verde, bringing together the various institutions of public higher education, known as The Higher Institute of Education and the Institute of Engineering and Ocean Sciences, as associated units of the new University of Cape Verde (Uni-CV). In 2010, a second public university was created, through the transformation of the old Pedagogical Institute (PI) into the new Higher Education Institute (EUI).

Additionally, several private initiatives since 2000 have emerged. There are currently 10 higher education institutions, two public and eight private. That has brought a shift from a predominantly external demand for higher education, with most Cape Verdeans pursuing their studies abroad in countries like Portugal, the former USSR, Cuba and others, to an internal demand. From 2002 onwards, the demand for domestic higher education began to overcome the external demand. Indeed, the demand for higher education doubled in 12 years, becoming mostly domestic, both in public and private establishments.

Students in higher education in Cape Verde from 2001

The total number of students in higher education shows a growing trend, from 771 students in 2000/1 to 13,068 students in 2012/13, an average annual growth rate of 24 per cent. Students have become involved in more than a hundred courses, distributed as follows: 85.1 per cent in undergraduate courses (*licenciaturas*); 6.9 per cent in additional undergraduate courses (*Complemento de Licenciatura*); 3.5 per cent in vocational courses; 0.4 per cent in bachelor courses (*bacharelato*); 4.2 per cent in Masters courses, and 0.1 per cent in Ph.D. courses. The big challenge is to balance the levels of undergraduate and graduate programmes in order to promote research in the short to medium term.

In the academic year 2012/13, the total number of students enroled in higher education represented 22.9 per cent of the population aged 18–22 years, values that are close to the target suggested by the World Bank, and similar to the global trend. This trend brings new challenges related to the management of the new graduates' expectations and their employability.

During the last few years there has been a remarkable disparity in favour of women. In 2012/13 the parity index female/male was 1.41 which means that, for every 100 men in higher education, there were 141 women. This difference is explained by the fact that girls have better academic results than boys in basic and secondary schooling.

In the face of this demand, Cape Verde universities have begun to take important steps in terms of expanding physical and human resources. The country has now a total of 10 HEIs, concentrated in the three largest urban centres (Praia, Mindelo and Santa Catarina). There is also an ongoing development of distance education, in the modalities of E-learning/Blended-learning, as a way to reduce disparities in access in other parts of the country.

There is also a considerable improvement regarding the teaching staff. In 2011/12, about 64 per cent of the faculty had post-graduate qualifications, of which 8 per cent were doctors, 46 per cent teachers and 8 per cent with another kind of post-graduate education. This situation tends to improve every year, because the number of graduate students has been increasing, both internally, through masters and Ph.D. programmes, and externally, through our development partners that provide fellowships and admit our students in different areas of study which are relevant for to Cape Verde. It should be noted that one of the conditions for a career in public universities is to have a doctoral degree (in accordance with the Statute of the teaching staff). All this is leading towards a better system of Quality Assurance (QA) involving internal reviews, accreditation and the recognition of appropriate private institutions.

The faculty in higher education

There were 1,289 active faculty members in the 2012/13 academic year, of which 9 per cent were doctors, 46 per cent had master's degrees and 8 per cent had other kinds of post-graduate education. The public sector was slightly better, with 66.8 per cent of the faculty staff with required qualifications, compared to 48.6 per cent in the private sector. Most of the faculty are nationals, but there is a contractual problem leading to the need to hire teachers from secondary education or from other institutions on a part-time basis. These teachers seldom have the academic qualifications or the time to do research, and therefore the universities do not grow as research institutions as well as they should. All this makes it difficult to measure the effectiveness of higher education. It certainly cannot be correlated with qualifications achieved by either staff or students.

Non-formal education

Adult education, covering the components of literacy and post-literacy, is geared to promote personal and social development to provide: i) the acquisition of knowledge skills, values and behaviours that enable citizens to integrate into the community and contribute to its continued progress; ii) the elimination of illiteracy as its main task; iii) to contribute to safeguarding the country's cultural identity, as the basis for national consciousness and dignity, stimulating the harmonious development of society.

The activities of Literacy and Adult Education contributed to reducing the illiteracy rate in Cape Verde from 61.3 per cent in 1975 to 12.5 per cent in 2010. Links with the world of work are ensured by basic vocational education provided to many young people. The effort has been considerable, but: i) illiteracy remains very high among women, affecting about 23 per cent against

12.4 per cent of men. On average, 32.3 per cent of rural women are illiterate; ii) illiteracy in rural areas is 25 per cent or almost twice that of urban areas at 12.6 per cent; iii) illiteracy is distributed unevenly over the country, with some regions and municipalities with rates much higher than average, reaching 29 per cent; d) in general, illiteracy is associated with a greater propensity to poverty for women, especially in rural areas.

In the period 1975–2010, 44,198 persons achieved basic literacy in the first phase and 32,713 were advanced further in the second phase. The third phase began at the national level in 1996/8, and more than 15,000 persons received education equivalent to 6 years of compulsory education. Close to 15,000 young people also have successfully completed basic vocational education and over 250,000 attendances were recorded in community animation activities.

The DGEEA (Government) maintains fixed and mobile libraries that play an important role in the education of children, youngsters and adults, promoting public reading as a support for information, culture and leisure for the communities. Mobile libraries that began to be implemented through a pilot experiment in Praia in 1995, currently cover the six municipalities of Santiago: three in S. Antão, two in Fogo and one in S. Nicolau, with approximately 20,000 enroled and 239,439 requests. These libraries run along 179 routes and serve 75 rural locations.

These actions contributed to the reduction of the illiteracy rate in the age group of 15 and above to 12.5 per cent and 5 per cent in the age group of 15 to 49 years in 2010. The target is to reach an overall rate of adult literacy to 90 per cent by 2015, a goal considered by UNESCO as desirable to achieve under the plan of EFA.

Considerations and perspectives

Throughout this chapter, all levels and types of formal education in Cape Verde have been addressed, considering: i) the progress made in recent years in education; ii) some national limitations and asymmetries between regions of the country with regard to access, retention and quality of education. It is now important to highlight the major challenges to be faced in ensuring universal basic education as well as the expansion of secondary education, further education and higher education.

For the country as a whole, there has been a significant improvement in educational terms. The statistics of the last decade show a positive trend in the rate of population education with: i) reduction of the illiteracy rate of nearly 60 per cent in 1975 to 17.2 per cent in 2010 and its near elimination for young people aged between 15–24 years; ii) an increase in the population with secondary and higher education, with about 38 per cent of the population now having had 12 years of education or more; iii) a gradual reduction of gender and urban/rural inequalities. But in relation to pre-school, primary and secondary schooling, the results remain modest, despite the expansion seen in terms of resources, teacher qualifications and physical facilities.

This situation means for the country a huge challenge for the coming years, to achieve the goal of ensuring universal pre-school for children aged 4–5. Fundamental to achieving this is the need to continue to invest in teacher education, since the sector still operates with less than 50 per cent of professionals with adequate qualifications. This is not good enough to achieve an expectancy of schooling for all of 9.2 years.

On a more successful front there is vocational education where the gains consist of a strong increase of vocational training with over 20,000 being trained in one decade and the creation of various legal mechanisms for regulating training in order to meet demand with good quality responses.

Higher education has experienced expansion of levels of study, of facilities and relevant programmes. All this has helped to achieve a gross enrolment ratio of around 20 per cent. Another important gain worth mentioning is the creation of a single ministry dedicated to the development of higher education in the country.

This synthesis shows that Cape Verde has been able to expand its educational system over time, increasing educational opportunities at all levels of education, but has found great difficulties in improving its quality and efficiency. In this sense, the difficulties undergone by education are not very different from those that affect the country as a whole.

The challenges facing the education system

Enhancing the skills of Cape Verdeans is the main strategic challenge that guides priorities regarding education policy. These priorities fall within the framework of the new educational reform recognizing education and training as an irreplaceable factor of economic and technological development, social cohesion, personal development and the full exercise of citizenship. Such challenges point to a vision of creating a knowledge society capable of ensuring a competitive insertion of the country in the global market, following international trends such as: strengthening pre-school education, the gradual extension of compulsory education from 8th, 10th, and 12th grade by 2030. Each sector of formal education in Cape Verde exhibits its own challenges.

Pre-school is probably the most urgent, given its relatively poor profile as compared with subsequent stages. This is true of many countries and is becoming increasingly significant as ICT advances reach down to younger and younger age groups. So it is necessary to create stronger regulatory and organizational conditions for this sector.

For basic education the challenges are more to do with issues of access to schooling in all municipalities and retaining the pupils throughout the programme. There is also a need for improved teacher quality in this sector as well as much-improved physical facilities and resources.

Access and retention are also challenges for secondary education, especially in the more problematic municipalities. Developing sectors of employment in relation to the global market and tourism need appropriately educated school leavers. Areas such as mathematics, languages, including Portuguese, science and technology need attention.

Improved levels and qualities of teacher training are beginning to address these concerns. Closing the gap between academic and vocational education is a global problem, but urgently necessary in order to meet the human and environmental challenges of the twenty-first century, especially in a small country in a relatively remote maritime location. Connecting secondary schools with local companies in the interest of promoting entrepreneurship is an extremely important goal given that most secondary-school leavers will not likely proceed to higher education.

Finally, in higher education there seems to have been the most significant advance. Universities are at the forefront of meeting these upcoming challenges, and need to connect meaningfully with other sectors of education. This will involve more rigorous and relevant systems of quality assurance and considerable investment as this is the most expensive sector per capita in any country. The rapid emergence of private universities and colleges is both a necessary but potentially problematic development in many countries. Cape Verde must ensure that its new quality assurance and recognition systems enforce the same requirements as those in the public universities of the country.

References

Banco Mundial (World Bank) (2012). *Construindo o Futuro: Como é que o Ensino Superior Pode Contribuir Para a Agenda de Transformação Económica e Social de Cabo Verde* [Building the Future: How Can Higher Education Contribute to the Agenda of Economic and Social Transformation of Cape Verde].

Documento Orientador da Revisão Curricular (2006). Praia: Ministério da Educação e do Desporto (versão digital, não publicada) [Guidelines for Curriculum Review. (2006). Praia: Ministry of Education and Sports (digital version, unpublished)].

Dos Santos, Ana Cristina (2010). *Mise en place d'un système d'assurance qualité externe dans un petit pays: le cas du Cap-Vert.* Paris: Institut international pour la planification de l'éducation.

Ferreira, A. C. P. and Barros, C. (2014). *Estudo Para a Reorientação do Sistema de Educação e Formação Em Cabo Verde 2015–2030* [Study for Revising the System of Education and Training in Cape Verde 2015–2030]. Internal report of the Prime Minister's Office. Cape Verde: Policy Strategic Center – CPE.

Silva, T. (1999). *Documentos de identidade – uma introdução às teorias do currículo.* Belo Horizonte: Autêntica. [Identity Documents – an Introduction to Theories of Curriculum].

Transformation Forum (2014) 'Estudo para a Reorientação do Sistema de Educação e Formação Em Cabo Verde 2015–2030'. Internal report of the Prime Minister's Office. Cape Verde: Policy strategic Center.

UN (2009). *MDG Repports: 'Objectivos de Desenvolvimento do Milénio – 2009" Nações Unidas de Cabo Verde, 2009'.* [MDG Reports: 'Millennium Development – 2009']. Cabo Verde: Ministério das Finanças, Républic de Cabo Verde, UNDP, Nações Unidas.

UNDAF (2011–16). *Quadro de Assistência das Nações Unidas Para o Desenvolvimento Em Cabo Verde Nações Unidas de Cabo Verde, 2012.* [Framework for the United Nations Assistance to Cape Verde]. Cabo Verde: Ministério das Relações Exteriores, Nações Unidas.

UNESCO (2008). *Reforma da educação secundária: 'rumo à convergência entre a aquisição de conhecimento e o desenvolvimento de habilidade'.* Brasília. [Reform of Secondary Education: 'towards convergence between the acquisition of knowledge and skill development']. Brasil: UNESCO.

—(2006). 'Concepções, práxis e tendências de desenvolvimento curricular no ensino superior público em Cabo Verde. Um estudo de caso sobre a Universidade de Cabo Verde'. [Conceptions, practice and trends in curriculum development in public higher education in Cape Verde. A case study of the University of Cape Verde]. Available from http://bartvarela.wordpress.com/2012/07/19/concepcoes-praxis-e-tendencias-de-desenvolvimento-curriuclar-no-ensino-superior-publico-em-cabo-verde-um-estudo-de-caso-sobre-a-universidade-de-cabo-verde/ (accessed June 2014).

—(2012). 'Abordagem por competências no currículo escolar em Cabo Verde: desfazendo equívocos para uma mudança significativa nas políticas e práxis educacionais ['Competence-based approach in school curriculum in Cape Verde: dispelling misconceptions for a significant change in policies and educational praxis']. Available from http://bartvarela.files.wordpress.com/2012/12/abordagem-por-competencias-no-curriculo-escolar-em-cabo-verde1.pdf (accessed June 2014).

—(2013). 'Evolução do o ensino superior público em Cabo Verde'. ['Evolution of public higher education in Cape Verde'.] Available from https://bartvarela.files.wordpress.com/2013/08/evolucao_do_ensino_superior_publico_em_cv.pdf (accessed June 2014).

Varela, Bartolomeu. (2006). 'Manual da disciplina de estrutura e funcionamento do sistema educativo'. [Handbook of the discipline of structure and operation of the educational system]. Available from http://manuais-do-estudante.blogspot.com/2008/12/manual-da- disciplina-de-estutura-e.html (accessed February 2014).

Yearbooks, plans and guideline documents

Anuários MESCI 2010, 2011 e 2012 MESCI [Yearbooks 2010, 2011, 2012].

Constituição da República de Cabo Verde – Lei de Revisão Constitucional nº 1/VII/2010, de 3 de Maio, [Constitution of the Republic of Cape Verde – Constitutional Law Review No. 1/VII/2010, of 3 May].

Declaração de Salamanca – Sobre Princípios, Políticas e Práticas na Área das Necessidades Educativas Especiais, aprovada a 10 de Junho de 1994. [Salamanca Declaration – About Principles, Policies and Practices on Special Needs Education, adopted on 10 June 1994].

Decreto-Lei nº 17/2007, de 7 de Maio – *Aprova o Estatuto do Ensino Superior Privado*. [Decree-Law No. 17/2007 of 7 May – Approves the Statute of Private Higher Education].

Decreto-Lei nº 53/2006, de 20 de Novembro. *Aprova os Estatutos da Universidade de Cabo Verde*. [Decree-Law No. 53/2006, of 20 November. Approves the Statutes of the University of Cape Verde].

Decreto-Legislativo nº 2/2010, de 7 de Maio – *Revê a Lei de Bases do Sistema Educativo de Cabo Verde*. [Legislative Decree 2/2010 of 7 May – Revises Law on the Education System of Cape Verde].

Documento de Estratégia de Crescimento e Redução da Pobreza – (DECRP), 2004–7 Ministério das Finanças e Planeamento. [Strategy document for growth and poverty reduction].

Documento de Estratégia de Crescimento e Redução da Pobreza III (2012–16). [Document for Growth and Poverty Reduction Strategy III (2012–16)].

'Documento Orientador da Revisão Curricular' (2006). Praia: Ministério da Educação e Desporto (versão digital, não publicada). ['Guidelines for Curriculum Review, (2006). Praia: Ministry of Education and Sports (digital version, unpublished)].

2010 census available from http://www.INE.CV (accessed February 2014).

Lei de bases do sistema educativo, I – Série do B.O. n° 36 de 5 de Novembro de 2001. [Basic Law on the education system, I – Series BO # 36 of 5 November 2001].

Ministério da Educação. 'Plano estratégico da Educação (2003–2013). [Ministry of Education. 'Education Strategic Plan (2003–2013)'].

—'Anuário Estatístico 2009 a 2012'. [Ministry of Education and Sport. 'Statistical Yearbook 2009 to 2012')].

—'Principais indicadores 2011/2012' (MED 2011). [Ministry of Education and Sport. 'Key indicators 2011/2012'. (MED 2011)].

—(2011). *Relatório de diagnóstico do sistema educativo e perspecticas para 2020 – RESEN* [Ministry of Education and Sport (2011). Diagnostic report of the education system and perspectives for 2020 – RESEN].

—'Principais indicadores 2011/2012' (MED 2012). [Ministry of Education and Sport. 'Key indicators 2011/2012'. (MED 2012)].

—(2012). *Reforma educativa – Documento conceptualizador da ação no ensino não superior. Orientações 'para uma Educação de Qualidade'* (2012–16) [Ministry of Education and Sports, Educational reform – Concept document for action in non-higher education. Guidelines 'for a Quality Education' (2012–16)].

—'Principais indicadores 2012/2013' (MED 2012). [Ministry of Education and Sport. 'Key indicators 2012/2013'. (MED 2012)].

Ministério da Qualificação e Emprego. 'Plano estratégico da formação profissional (2006–10)'. [Ministry for Qualification and Employment. 'Strategic plan of vocational training (2006–10)'].

Plano Nacional de Educação para Todos (PN-EPT) – 2003–2010. [National Plan for Education for All (EFA-PN) – 2003–2010].

Plano Estratégico da Educação (PEE) 2003–2013. [Education Strategic Plan (ESSP) 2003–2013].

Plano estratégico de política integrada, Educação, Formação e Emprego (2013–2018). [Strategic plan for integrated policy, Education, Training and Employment (2013–2018)].

Programa do Governo 2011–2016 [Government Programme 2011–2016].

Quadro de Despesas Sectoriais a Médio Prazo (QDSMP). Gabinete de Estudos e Planeamento, MEVRH [Tables of Sector Medium Term Expenditure (QDSMP). Office of Research and Planning, MEVRH].

Chad: An Overview, Trends and Futures

Galy Panaïn Dibe and Mohamed Chérif Diarra

Introduction

This chapter presents the Chadian education system over three principal parts. It starts with general information on the country such as the political situation followed by the socio-demographic and macroeconomic contexts. The first part titled 'overview' provides information on the history of the education system as well as on policies and reforms since independence, education governance and funding.

The second part titled 'trends' covers the main challenges in the provision of basic education. It outlines issues regarding access and participation at all levels of the system including quality and relevance. The third part 'Future prospects' presents the future prospects the system is likely to face for achieving universal primary education.

The chapter ends with a conclusion that reflects on the government's capacity to implement the three-year Interim Strategic Plan for Education and Literacy.

Generality and political situation

The Republic of Chad is a landlocked country located in the centre of the African continent. It is bordered by Libya to the north, Sudan and South Sudan to the east, the Central African Republic to the south, Cameroon and Nigeria to the south-west and Niger to the west. The nearest seaports are at 1,500 km (seaport of Douala, Cameroun) and 1,700 km (seaport of Harcourt, Nigeria). The country's surface area is estimated to be 1,284,000 square kilometres (twice the size of France). Chad gained independence from France in 1960, and since this date, the country has suffered from instability and conflicts arising from tensions between different religious and ethnic factions. Instability and conflicts are sometimes fuelled by interference from neighbouring states. The country faced two recurrent conflicts over the last decade. This instability is caused by conflicts between Chadian armed political movements based in Sudanese Darfur area in the east and the actual Government of Chad. According to 'SIMONROUGHNEEN' 2008 review, the latest attack of 2008 was repelled by the government forces. In order to consolidate peace, the country pursues political dialogue with Sudan through the African Union mediation.

According to the Chadian constitution, the political system is presidential and the President is elected for two terms, each of five years' duration. President Idriss Déby Itno and his party, 'Mouvement Patriotique du Salut' have dominated Chadian politics since taking power in 1990. He won the 1996 (the first pluralist elections held in Chad), 2001, 2006 and 2011 elections successively. The electoral processes during these elections have, however, been controversial. The country also completed the legislative elections held in February 2011 when President's Deby's party won 118 out of the 188 seats. But these results were contested (opposition alleged irregularities and massive frauds). Main opposition leaders boycotted the presidential election held in April 2011, as in 2006. President Déby won 83.59 per cent against two marginal opponents, with a weak turnout rate of 55.71 per cent.

Socio-demographic context

According to the last General Population and Housing Census held in 1999, the population of Chad is estimated to be 11,039,873 inhabitants, 50.6 per cent are women and 49.4 per cent are men. The population annual growth rate is estimated to be 3.6 per cent. Thus, the population of Chad should potentially multiply by 2 in the next 20 years. It has been increasing rapidly and is expected to reach 14 million in 2015 (United Nations 2011). Ongoing civil unrest and food shortages have fuelled migration from rural to urban areas. In mid-2004, urban population accounted for 25 per cent of the total population, up from 16 per cent in 1975. More than 10 per cent of the population lives in or around the capital, N'Djamena. In the south, at least 1 million people earn incomes from cotton cultivation. Agriculture and livestock production are the major livelihoods of the majority of the population. Oil was discovered in the south east in 2003, but oil fields provide little employment and State revenues are controlled largely by minority groups originating in the east of the country (EIU 2008).

The population density increased from 4.9 in 1993 to 8.6 habitants in 2009. The population is young. The number of persons aged less than 25 years represents 67.2 per cent. The school age population (6–11) will double by 2030. As a consequence, Chadian educational system will be under strong pressure that could undermine the chances of achieving the MDGs. According to the 2009 census results, more than 200 different ethnic and linguistic groups exist in the country and more than 100 languages and dialects are spoken. French and Arabic are the official languages.

Many religions coexist in Chad. However, Islam and Christianity are the two most widely practised religions. Muslims represent 54 per cent of the population and Christians 40 per cent. Animists and other religion practitioners represent 6 per cent.

Chad is one of the poorest countries in the world and this poverty is both monetary and non-monetary. The third survey on Consumption and the Informal Sector in Chad (ECOSIT III) completed in 2011 reveals that a little less than half of the Chadian population (46.7 per cent) lives in a state of extreme monetary poverty compared to 55 per cent in 2003. The daily consumer-spending threshold is 652 FCFA (1€ = 655,955FCFA). A considerable gap exists between urban and rural areas: 25 per cent compared to 59 per cent.

Despite disparities between regions, Chad has made some progress towards poverty reduction. According to the 2011 household surveys held within the framework of ECOSIT by Chad National Institute of Statistics, Economic and Demographic Studies (INSEED), poverty headcount declined from 55 per cent in 2003 to 47 per cent in 2011. Thus, the percentage of Chadians living in poverty decreased between 2003 and 2011. The decline in poverty since 2003 can mostly be attributed to economic growth.

Chad has been among the countries ranked at the bottom of the Human Development Index (HDI) World Ranking with weak positive variations as shown in Table 7.1.

Table 7.1 HDI ranking 2008–12

Year	2008	2009	2010	2011	2012
Chad's HDI ranking	170/177	178/182	163/169	183/187	184/186

Source: UNDP 2008, 2009, 2010, 2011, 2012

Macro economic context

Chad integrated with the oil-producing countries in 2003. Consequently, its macro-economic trends have changed. Nonetheless the high annual population growth rate (3.5 per cent), negatively affects the country's per-capita GDP growth. According to the National Development Plan 2013-15, per capita GDP would double in 46 years on the basis of an average annual economic growth of 5 per cent.

Infrastructure and business environment should attract private and foreign investment. The investment growth is projected at an average rate of 6.7 per cent between 2012 and 2015.

Public finance

Despite the difficult international context, the growth recorded over the past decade has favoured generally satisfactory budgetary management. The budgetary cycle and cash flow management have been improved to ensure the quality of public investment and funding of social services. However, there are still weaknesses in mobilizing tax revenues, and in budget control.

In terms of budgetary resources, oil revenue accounts for an annual average of nearly 80 per cent of the government's budget revenue. Currently, non-oil revenue represents only 13 per cent of GDP and at most covers the wage bill. According to the World Bank report No. 78692-TD drawn on June 2013, the low tax burden, which is nearly 8 per cent, down ten points on the CEMAC (Central African Economic and Monetary Community) standard, explains this situation. Thus, foreign aid and other sources of funding growth have declined over the past three years.

According to OECD, the total net programmable ODA (Official Development Assistance) for Chad during the 2009-11 period is weak and represents an annual average of 221 million US dollars. In terms of amount by head of population, the total net programmable ODA is USD50/head compared to 112 in Ivory Coast and 128 in Sierra Leone. The limited number of technical and financial partners (TFPs) in Chad explains the low share of foreign funding in Chad. Consequently, the budgetary expansion enabled by oil explains the rapid growth of capital expenditure financed from domestic resources, which increased from 2.1 per cent of non-oil GDP in 2003 to 12.6 per cent in 2008-10.

Overview

History

According to Nomaye (1998), the first colonial and modern primary school was established in 1911 in the Kanem region. Pupils were trained by French military stationed there for ensuring country pacification. The scaling up of colonial schools has been, in general, slow. The colonial administration required that all instruction be in French, except for religion classes, which could be taught in local languages. In 1925, the state imposed a standard curriculum on all institutions wishing recognition and funding from the government. The majority of Chadian students attended private mission schools before the second World War. Education in Chad had focused on primary education, and until 1942, students who wanted to pursue a secondary education had to go to schools in Brazzaville, the capital of the French Equatorial Africa (AEF). There students received technical education rather than a liberal arts education in a 3-year programme designed to produce medical assistants, clerks or low-level technicians. State secondary schools were opened in Chad only in 1942 and its certificate programmes began in the mid-1950s. At independence in 1960, the government set a goal of universal primary education and school attendance became compulsory until age 12. Thus, from 1911–50, school was perceived to be destructive of ancestral values. Colonial administration relied on traditional leaders to govern and sensitize leaders and traditional chiefs to send their children to school.

From 1951 to 1970, schooling had moved to a phase of tolerance by the population due to visible results provided by education, notably, small jobs: elementary teachers, nurses, office clerk, etc. From 1971 onwards, interest in schooling was shown by almost all the Chad population, which finally accepted and considered education as a necessity for children and youth. Unfortunately, Chad faced a civil war early in the 1960s with political instability as a result. Therefore, the social and economic situation was deeply affected in general and education in particular.

A problem of the French curricula in Chadian schools at independence was that most students did not speak French when they entered school, and the teaching methods and materials were not suited to the rural settings, or did not prepare students for employment in Chad.

In the late 1960s, the government attempted to address these problems by modifying the teaching methods, adapted to their social and economic environments, and treated French as a foreign language. These new schools also introduced basic skills at the primary education level and those who could not go on to the secondary level were given the chance to attend agricultural training centers. In the 1970s and 1980s, Chad made considerable progress dealing with these problems. Unfortunately, the civil war in the late 1970s and early 1980s disrupted this progress. In the early 1980s, the Ministry of Education assumed responsibility for all formal education, but due to years of civil war, local communities had assumed many of the ministry's functions, such as the construction and maintenance of schools and payment of teachers' salaries. The major problems that hindered the development of an education system in Chad included: limited finance, lack of facilities and personnel, which led to overcrowded classes with more than 100 students, and the low qualifications of teachers.

Policies and educational reforms

Since 1962, several policies and educational reforms have been attempted:

- **1962–6**: 'Ruralisation' and 'tchadisation' of content to suit concept requirement for social, cultural and economic national development. Thus, agriculture and citizenship received a boost in the curriculum.
- **1970**: new reform based on practical work as a means of intellectual and children development was set up. This reform led to the creation of pilot schools in order to ensure the reform was implemented.
- **1982–9**: was the period of recovery activities to restart the Chadian educational system destroyed by war.
- **1989**: the Government set up in partnership with donors an educational strategy called 'Strategy of Education, Training in line with Employment'. This strategy aimed to promote human resources for increasing quantitatively and qualitatively the education and training system by 2000.
- **1993**: The National Consultation on Education (Etats Généraux de l'Education) was held.

Structure of the system

Based on the French model, the formal system begins at kindergarten followed by primary education, secondary education and higher education. The medium of instruction is French or Arabic.

- **Kindergarten:** Kindergarten attendance is not compulsory and has 3 levels. Young children begin kindergarten at age three or four and kindergartens exist only in major cities.
- **Primary Education:** According to the provisions of Article 35 of the Chadian constitution, citizens are entitled to free education and training which is compulsory for children starting at the age of six years for a period of 9 years. Primary education begins at age five or six and has six grades and is provided by public, private and community schools.
- **Secondary education:** Secondary education is provided by public, private and community schools, which are known as Lycées or Collèges with two tracks (technical education and general education). General Lycées include a lower division with four grades and the upper division with three. Collèges include only the lower divisions with four grades. Technical Lycées include three grades. Entrance into lower secondary requires examination (Concours d'entrée en 6ème) and obtaining the primary education completion certificate (Certificat d'Etudes Primaires et Elémentaires – Tchadien). Entrance into upper secondary requires the completion of the four grades of the lower division and obtaining the Brevet d'Etudes du Premier Cycle – Tchadien (BEPC/T). However, entrance into Technical Lycées requires in addition, a specific examination.
- **Higher education:** This is provided by universities and higher education institutions. They are limited in number and accessing higher education is subject to a selective application in addition to obtaining a baccalaureate degree. In higher education, the length of studies varies from 2–3 years (in institutes) to 6 years (in universities).

Governance of education sector

In addition to the Constitution, Education Act n° 16 March 2006 organizes Chad's educational system including the informal and non-formal. The Chad education sector went through many organizational changes. Thus, four different ministries are currently in charge:

- Ministry of Higher Education and Scientific Research;
- Ministry of Fundamental Education and Literacy;
- Ministry of Secondary Education Training and Vocational;
- Ministry of Social Action, National solidarity and Family.

Apart from the Ministry of Higher Education, which is highly centralized, the three other ministries are organized in regional, sub-regional and local structures. Each ministry has at different levels, Teacher Union Representation and a Parents' Association. Within the Parents' Association, we have a Management Committee of the School composed of a parents' representative, a teachers' union representative, and the head of the school. The Management Committee of the School is responsible for the management of financial, material and non-governmental human resources.

Funding

Education has always been the responsibility of Central Government. Thus, funding education is also its responsibility. However, due to the inadequacy of Government resources, the Chadian educational system is funded by other sources, notably by households, private providers and partners (Chang and Radi (2002).

- **Households funding**: During the civil war of the 1979s, Government structures stopped functioning. Since this date, households have to devote a share of their income to financing education. Households finance education through the Parents' Association, which is entirely responsible for resource management.
- **Partners funding:** Partners contribute to education development by financing Government capital expenditures in development programmes and project support. Through management units set up within the Ministries, partners support the implementation of programmes and projects in collaboration with Government teams.
- **Private funding** is provided by local enterprise/Non-Governmental Organizations (NGOs) /Individual providers. It aims to develop schools at the local level and is generally provided by Parents' Associations with management responsibility. Capital and current expenditures are generally covered.
- **Government funding** mostly finances the education system. It is largely centralized and made up of wages. Government funding goes to schools through decentralized educational structures: regional delegation, departmental delegation and local inspection.

Trends

The main challenge faced by the Chadian educational system is universal primary education. All statistical data provided in this section are from the 2010/11 Statistical Yearbook of the Primary and Secondary Education Ministry.

Access and participation

Pre-primary education

In Chad, only 356 pre-school institutions existed in 2009. Nationally, pre-primary education is owned and operated by private providers. 52 institutions are public preschools, 61, private and 243, community. The Gross Enrolment Rate (GER) is very low (2.5 per cent) in 2011.

Primary education

Like other sub-Saharan Africa countries, access to primary education has significantly improved over the last decade. The Gross Access Rate increased from 82 per cent in 2000 to 120 per cent in 2011. Education coverage has also significantly increased and the GER in primary education rose from 64 per cent in 2000 to 91 per cent in 2011.

Secondary education

Secondary institutions are mostly located in urban areas.

a. *Lower secondary.* The number of pupils at this level increased threefold from 119,103 in 2000/1 to 315,665 in the 2010/11 school year. The transition rate between primary and lower secondary was around 73 per cent (77 per cent for boys and 66 per cent for girls) and the GER in lower secondary was 29.2 per cent (41 per cent for boys and 18 per cent for girls) in 2010/11.
b. *Upper secondary.* At this level, pupils' population has also significantly increased. The number of pupils was 134,260 in 2010/11 compared to 44,000 in 2000/1. The transition rate between lower and upper secondary was estimated at 66 per cent (67 per cent for boys and 63 per cent for girls).
c. *Technical and vocational education* is behind compared to other segments of the education system. Its pupils' population represents only 1.4 per cent of enrolment in general secondary education. Lack of resources explains this

weakness although it has been on the rise over the past 20 years. However, the rate was gradually increasing. In 2009/10, technical and vocational education institutions numbered 33, (18 public and 15 private).

Higher education

Although universities are limited in number, we note a strong and positive evolution of student enrolments over the last decade. Student population increased from 6,730 in 2001 to 20,349 in 2010, of which 72 per cent were enroled in public institutions. Nevertheless, the major weakness is still that, in the public universities, arts and humanities studies as well as social studies and human sciences, legal and economic sciences attract the largest number of students (71 per cent). Nowadays, we note that the number of holders of a degree from these disciplines becomes more and more important although the capacity to meet the labour needs of the economy is weak. Moreover, Chadian universities do not offer various technology and science tracks. Thus, social studies and human sciences, legal and economic sciences are the unique alternative to get an advanced degree.

Quality and relevance

Many analyses and studies indicate that the problem of poor quality and the weak relevance of the Chadian educational system occurs at all levels, in all forms, particularly, in curricula, teaching and learning conditions, teacher training, teaching and evaluation methods, funding, et cetera.

Only 37 per cent of Chadian children complete primary school because of the lack of schools or the incomplete aspect of the cycle at the school to which they have access. This situation is partially explained by the high number of community schools throughout the country. Due to the weak completion rate, the primary education system generates high numbers of dropouts and repeaters. In 2011, repeaters represented 22 per cent of total enrolment. Thus, Chadian primary education is so far from the indicative framework of 10 per cent for repeaters in primary education. In general the date of starting school activities is largely delayed, reducing, in fact, school days mainly in rural areas due to the harvesting season, which corresponds to the period of starting school.

Students from technical and vocational education were mostly employed in the tertiary sector (bank, commerce, insurance, communication, education, health). In 2011, their number represented 66 per cent compared to 3 per cent in the primary sector (agriculture, fishing, forest exploitation, miner exploitation …). In higher education, the overwhelming majority of students are enroled in the arts and humanities, social sciences, and law studies at the expense of Math, technology and sciences (23 per cent) and health sciences (6 per cent). Thus, in secondary as well as in higher education, the capacity to meet the labour needs of the economy is weak. Nowadays, due to the inadequate relation between training and employment, graduates from higher education and from technical and vocational education are mostly unemployed or underemployed.

According to the 1993 general census, the percentage of the adult population aged 15 and over able to read and write was 11 per cent. This proportion has been increased to 34 per cent according to the 2009 general population and housing census. Out of this total, young people aged 15 to 24, who could read and write represented 46 per cent compared to 17 per cent in 1993. The main causes of this situation are the large number of children with no schooling, resulting from the high drop-out rate in secondary school and the low completion rate (37 per cent) in primary school.

Regarding teaching and learning conditions, school infrastructures are in decay and this hampers the quality of teaching and learning. The shortage and poor quality of infrastructure has generated problems of overcrowding in rural schools, some of which accommodate 100 to 200 students per class. At national level, the average classroom size is 61 and one teacher on average, taught some 63 children. In secondary education, some schools have no classrooms and students take their lessons on the floor in huts covered with millet stems.

At national level, there are three or four students sitting at each table and others are sitting around it or standing up. Textbooks are few. Textbooks in French and Mathematics books are shared between three children and Science textbooks between four children. In primary as well as in secondary education, the teaching staff lacks crucial resources for their work. In 2011 for example, five teachers in primary school shared one teaching guide, on average.

One of the education quality challenges is fundamentally the lack of qualified teachers. Despite efforts provided by Government and partners over the last decade, 66 per cent of primary school teachers were not qualified (community teachers) in 2011. At the secondary level, the lack of qualified teachers was also serious. In 2011, 45 per cent of teachers were temporary staff, volunteers or primary school teachers. Consequently, the chance of achieving universal primary education was slim.

The teaching method used by the Chadian educational system is inherited from colonization. It practices only the frontal principle and does not allow active participation of children. In class activities, the teacher is considered as the knowledge giver and the children as receptors. This method is nowadays considered classic and does not promote the intellectual development of children. Method evaluation is based on traditional principles. Children are graded to pass on the average of two or three examination results during the school year and factors such as participation in class activities and class attendance are not taken into account. The system does not have a standard test in order to determine regularly the level of achievement of students. However, in the spirit of international comparison, Chad participated in 2004 and 2010 in a PASSEC (Analysis Program of Education Systems of Francophone countries) study. According to the 2010 results, children's scholastic level in primary education was not improving. In the 2nd grade, the average scores (scores were over 100) in Mathematics decreased from 40.3 in 2004 to 37.8 in 2010 and those in French increased from 37.1 in 2004 to 39.1 in 2010. Nonetheless, in the 5th grade, the average scores increased from 34 in 2004 to 38.1 in 2010 in mathematics and from 32.1 in 2004 to 38 in 2010 in French. Furthermore, the baccalaureate examination of the 2012 academic year was disastrous. Only 9 per cent out of 69,919 candidates passed compared to other African countries such as Cameroon and Burkina Faso, which boast a pass rate of 53.50 per cent and 35.1 per cent respectively (Kagbe 2012).

Government spending on education represents just 2.8 per cent of national GDP, which is one of the lowest in the world. In addition only 10.4 per cent of the 2012 general budget was (Ministry of Finances, Initial Financial Law 2012) committed to education compared to the rate of 20 per cent of the State budget recommended by Fast Track.

The Chadian educational system has yet to be able to effectively engage and retain orphans and vulnerable children in the school system.

During 2012, the country sustained improved peace, security and stability. However, the region is still characterized by a protracted crisis, and Chad hosted 300,000 refugees over its territory (Executive Committee of the High Commissioner's Programme Standing Committee, 53rd Meeting, 13–15 March 2012). The humanitarian situation in Chad is characterized by chronic and cyclic emergencies. In addition to a severe food and nutrition crisis, Chad has faced meningitis, measles, yellow fever outbreaks and flooding.

Future prospects

To overcome these bottlenecks described above, the Government has placed the restoration and consolidation of the education system at the heart of the three-year Interim Strategic Plan for Education and Literacy (SIPEA), which emphasizes the promotion of more equitable access to improved basic education services for children. This SIPEA is partially funded by the Global Partnership for Education (GPE) and the Educate a Child Initiative of the Qatar Fund. The National Development Plan developed by the Ministry of Economy, Planning and International Cooperation in 2012, mainstreams SIPEA and has set a course for 2025. Through the National Development Plan, the President is determined to make Chad

> an emerging regional power by 2025, supported by diversified and sustainable sources of growth, creating added value and jobs and ensuring that every Chadian has adequate access to basic social services, decent housing and suitable educational provision" (National Development Plan 2013–15, April 2013: 49).

The 'development of human resources' is one of eight priority objectives that have been set. Through 'development of human resources', education is one of the strategic pillars.

The strategies chosen in education include:

- Increasing access to basic education
- Improving the quality of education and sector management and governance

SIPEA is an interim strategic plan, which covers three years and its measures, projects and programmes to be implemented include: universalization of primary education by addressing the bottlenecks such as the building of 1,500 classrooms annually over the next three years and 3,700 yearly by 2020, and by providing qualified teachers to relieve the financial burden to the communities.

It also includes the improvement of children's learning by: i) taking administrative actions in order to adapt calendar school to local context; ii) providing schools with adequate teachers at the beginning of school year; iii) fighting against and punishing unjustified absences of teachers; reduction of repetition rate (from 22 per cent to a maximum of 10 per cent by 2020); and education of children living in difficult contexts (children of nomadic, and island populations) and children with specific needs; enhancing the quality of training by improving teaching conditions in order to decrease pupil/teacher ratio from 60 in 2015 to 55 in 2020; providing enough textbooks and instructional materials as well as teaching guides; and improving qualification of inspectors, teaching advisers, and school managers by providing in-service training.

The strategic options of this segment aim to improve:

i. The diversification of literacy offer;
ii. the quality of learning to develop activities, aimed at improving the adaptation of literacy and post-literacy programmes;
iii. monitoring and management: develop national capacities in monitoring, supervision and evaluation of activities implemented.

Non-formal basic education aims to provide children aged 9 to 14 and who are out of school or have dropped out of school, a quality basic education by giving them competencies for an effective professional insertion or a quality education by improving the NFBE services, developing bridges between NFE and formal education and institutionalizing monitoring and evaluation.

Conclusion

Chad faces numerous challenges that hinder its ability to make progress towards achieving the Millennium Development Goals. Years of political instability and structural socio-economic weaknesses have had a lasting impact on development outcomes for children. Despite effort provided by the government in improving peace, security and stability, the country is still characterized by a protracted crisis, with volatile contexts in the Central African Republic, Libya, Nigeria and South Sudan.

Chad is ranked 184 out of 186 on the 2012 Human Development Index. Some 62 per cent of people earn less than $1.25 per day in purchasing power parity (United Nations Development Programme Human Development Report 2011). Poor governance, poverty and insufficient funding of basic social services remain barriers to improving children's and women's future.

References

Banque Mondiale (2005). 'Rapport d'Etat du Système Educatif National tchadien pour une politique éducative nouvelle'. MEN/Pole de Dakar.
Chang, G. C. and Radi, M. (2002). 'Chad Education and Training: Thematic Study Collection'. Constitution de la République du Tchad. Version révisée du 31 Mars 1996.
Economic Intelligence Unit (EIU) (2008). Country Profile. Chad. London, England.

Executive Committee of the High Commissioner's Programme Standing Committee, 53rd Meeting, 13–15 March 2012.

General Population and Housing Census (2009). N'Djaména, Chad.

Kagbe, R. (2012). 'The 2012 High School Exam Results in Burkina Faso, Cameroon and Chad'. Democratic Wealth, N'Djaména, Chad.

Loi N° 16/PR/2006 du 13 Mars 2006 portant Orientation du système éducatif tchadien. Présidence de la République, Mars 2006. N'Djaména, Tchad.

Ministère de l'Education (2012). 'Stratégie intérimaire pour l'Education et l'alphabétisation, 2013–2015'. N'Djaména, Tchad.

Ministry of the Economy, Planning, and International Cooperation (2013). 'National Development Plan 2013–2015'.

Ministère du Plan du Développement et de la Coopération (2003). 'Document de Strategie de Réduction de la Pauvreté'. N'Djaména, Tchad.

Ministère de l'Education Nationale (2010). 'Année Scolaire 2010/11. Données statistiques'. N'Djaména, Tchad.

Ministère du Plan, de l'Economie et de la Coopération Internationale (2009). 'Recensement Général de la Population et de l'Habitat (RGPH2)'. N'Djaména, Tchad.

Nomaye, M. (1998). *L'Education de base au Tchad: situation, enjeux et perspectives.* L'Harmattan, Paris, France.

Third survey on Consumption and the Informal Sector in Chad (ECOSIT III) completed in 2011 UIS (2014b). *Data Centre.* Available from http://stats.uis.unesco.org/unesco/TableViewer/document.aspx?ReportId=143&IF_Language=eng (accessed on 29 January 2014). Montreal: UIS.

United Nations Development Programme (2011). 'Human Development Report 2011'.

UNDP (2013). *Human Development Report 2013. Explanatory note on 2013 HDR composite indices: Mauritania.* New York: UNDP.

UNESCO (2011). 'Financing Education in Sub-Saharan Africa. Meeting the Challenges of Expansion, Equity and Quality'.

UNESCO-BREDA (2012). 'Household Education Spending. An Analytical and Comparative Perspective for 15 African Countries'. Pôle de Dakar. Dakar, Senegal.

UNICEF CHAD (2012). 'Peace building, education and advocacy in conflict-affected contexts programme. Annual Report'. N'Djaména, Chad.

8

The Gambia: An Overview, Trends and Futures

Makaireh A. Njie

General education developments

Introduction

This chapter provides an overview of education in The Gambia, examines the evolution of education policies from the pre-independence era to date, the trends and their implications for the future.

The author divides the chapter into two parts. Part 1 offers information on the country's education policies over the years, and discusses policy making and implementation processes. The discussion includes the participation of stakeholders in the government's public expenditure review process, education policy dialogues, as well as policy implementation, under which he defines the current structure of The Gambia's education system. The author also makes reference to the decentralization process, to Madrassas, and to early childhood development.

In Part 2, the author devotes the discussion to technical and vocational education and training policy in The Gambia.

Overview

The Gambia's high population growth rate over the years (prior to 1993) has been one of the dominant factors that has adversely impacted on its environmental, and social and economic development. This factor has put added pressures on our health and education systems in the past and at present. The planning and development of education policies have therefore taken into consideration the issue of access, in the earlier years, and later started addressing issues of quality and relevance in education.

The Ministry of Basic and Secondary Education has articulated strategies and plans to ensure the improvement of learning outcomes in terms of teacher training in the areas of pedagogy, knowledge content, curriculum review, instructional design, access, assessment and examination procedures, computing, early childhood development and open and distance learning.

A recent study entitled 'Technical assistance for improving relevance and efficiency in TVET and Higher Education in The Gambia' (2005), by the Ministry of Higher Education Research Science and Technology (MoHERST) has identified the key challenges in TVET and Higher Education such as relevance, quality, and efficiency including cost effectiveness.

TVET has become a key priority area in The Gambia and is now playing an increasingly significant role with regard to the country's education system and The Gambia Government considers it as an important tool that contributes to economic prosperity. In addition, the government's Programme for Accelerated Growth and Employment (PAGE) (2011–15) buttresses the implementation Strategies to improve access, equity, quality and equality by financing education which The Gambia Government intends to achieve by linking capacity building initiatives (including TVET programmes) to job market requirements, and ensuring access to quality basic education as well as tertiary and higher education. In order to achieve these objectives there is the need for interventions to improve access, establish relevance, quality and sector management, and to have an effective funding system.

The National Training Authority (NTA) in collaboration with the Ministry of Higher Education, Research, Science and Technology are now embarking on a number of innovative projects to address the needs of TVET and ensure its relevance to labour market needs. All existing education and Training Policies are now expected to conform and be re-aligned to the Programme for Accelerated Growth and Employment Policy objectives. The Government of The Gambia now attaches great importance to relating education and training policies and strategies to the needs of the job market. PAGE aims to enhance employment opportunities, income *per capita*, social services, gender equity and the country's economic competitiveness.

Problem statement

The main aim of this chapter is to address the issue of education developments in The Gambia and to find out how general education, technical and vocational education and training (TVET) and higher education have evolved.

Methodology

The author used the method of descriptive research and used various sources to extract relevant information for the research. Thus, relevant documents from the Ministry of Basic and Secondary Education (MoBSE), and the Ministry of Higher Education, Research Science and Technology, were reviewed and further data were obtained from relevant Parliamentary Acts, Policy documents, seminar and conference papers, and journal articles.

The report analyses the evolution of education in The Gambia from the pre-independence era to date with a particular focus on general education, TVET, Madrassas, and early childhood development, and on processes, namely, policy making processes, and the decentralization process.

Evolution of education policies

The Gambia inherited basically the British system of education, that is to say, predominantly an education system aimed at the acquisition of basic skills in reading, writing and numeracy, at primary level, with progression to secondary level determined by an examination called the Common Entrance Examination, which tended to categorize people as those capable of white-collar jobs and those destined for manual work. This system has had a negative impact on human resource utilization and development in The Gambia and in the region (N'Jie 1979).

Pre-independence era

During this era, the education system in The Gambia was in most cases offered by Christian missionaries in the country, and provided three years of pre-school education and seven years of elementary/primary school education. Successful students at the Standard Seven School Leaving Certificate Examination proceeded to secondary/high schools to undertake a three-year programme leading to the Cambridge School Certificate. The education policy of the last colonial government in The Gambia (that is, the policy for 1961–5) brought in reforms that witnessed the introduction of a Six-year Primary School Education programme and an entry age of six but, with the discretion for the education of children left to their parents. Secondary school education was then provided at Junior Secondary Schools and Senior Secondary Schools or High schools. At the time, The Gambia had only four Senior Secondary Schools with only one, the Gambia High School, offering a Sixth Form Education for the

16–19 year olds. At the post-Secondary School level, there was a Vocational Training Centre in Banjul and a Teacher Training College initially located in Georgetown, but later transferred to Yundum. They were the only tertiary institutions in the country.

The 1965–76 era

As a priority, the Gambia Government saw the need to transform the education system, from the controlled provision of an elitist education for the few, to an education for all, with the inevitable consequence of an upsurge in school enrolment. The 1961–5 Education Policy introduced a six-year-primary education programme aimed at making education available to all children in The Gambia and with special attention to girls' education. The period after independence (that is, after 1965) witnessed major reforms in education. The Sleight Report – 'The Development programme in Education for The Gambia 1965–1975' formed the policy framework and aimed both at radical increases in school enrolments and at attaining universal primary education in The Gambia by 1970.

The 1976–86 policy

The reforms introduced in this policy included the raising of the entry age to school from six to eight, the inclusion of literacy in the local languages (Mandika, Fula and Wollof), and Environmental Studies into the primary school curriculum. This curriculum was also re-developed to become more oriented towards Agriculture and Vocational training. There was also the shift of the burden for private expenditure in education to government with a view to having a system of free but non-compulsory primary education by September 1977. There was also the aim of introducing free compulsory primary education, as soon as sufficient accommodation and staffing were available. Class size was increased from 29.3 to 40; religious and moral instruction was introduced in schools. The Government took full responsibility for teachers of Arabic/Islamic studies in all schools.

During this period, public post secondary school education was provided at:

- The Yundum College for Teacher-Training (which was renamed The Gambia College). Its provision of courses expanded to include Public Health, Midwifery, and Nursing and Agriculture.
- The Gambia Technical Training Institute (GTTI);
- The Management Development Institute (MDI);

- The Hotel School; and
- The Gambia Telecommunication and Media Institute (GTMI).

The GTTI, MDI and GTMI institutions offered courses which led to local and external qualifications, while The Gambia College and the Hotel School offered only local qualifications.

Regarding the financing of education, the policy specified that this must remain the responsibility of the government. Fees paid by non-government-sponsored students were received and paid to central government. High schools were financed through a grant-in-aid subvention which enabled institutions to cater for the salaries of the teaching staff. The revenue generated went towards the procurement of supplies. At the Gambia College, GTTI, MDI and the Hotel School, Government provided for the salaries of the teaching staff, for capital expenditure, and for training materials, although the provisions for training and education were not adequate; as the allocations of funds were not based on Programme Budgeting. However in addition, Government provided generous scholarships to students.

The 1988–2003 policy

The fundamental objectives of the 1988–2003 policy were to increase access to education and to improve its quality and relevance. The school entry age was lowered from 8 to 7 and the grading of classes was changed in order to meet the objectives of 9 years of uninterrupted Basic Education, while Secondary Technical Schools and High schools were re-named Middle and Senior Secondary Schools, respectively. Thus, the general structure of education became one of 6–3–3–2 (that is, six years of Primary School education, three years of Lower Secondary/Middle School, three years of Upper Secondary/Senior Secondary School, and two years of Sixth Form education). During the first half of the Policy, the Teacher Training programme at The Gambia College was reduced from three years to two years to meet the requirements for the number of qualified teachers in the newly expanded and restructured system. However, in the second half, the duration of the programme returned to three years and was restructured in such a way that those in the Higher Teachers' Certificate (HTC) programme received two years of face-to-face College-based training and one year field-based studies by Distance Learning mode while the Primary Teachers' Certificate (PTC) received one year College-based training and two years of field-based training.

The transition rate from Primary Schools to Middle schools was to increase from 30 per cent in 1987 to 60 per cent in 2003, with a Primary School Gross Enrolment Ratio (GER) target of 75 per cent by the end of the policy period. The transition was, however, still determined by a selection process at Grade 6 (based on the Primary School Leaving Certificate Examination). The policy also targeted the training of all unqualified teachers to be completed by 2003 and the expenditure on teaching-learning materials to be significantly increased in order to improve the quality of education in the country. The school curriculum was to be revised and the teaching of local languages further strengthened.

Unlike some of its neighbours, The Gambia continued to be lacking in the provision of education at the Tertiary level. However, university education was a long-term objective, and the policy stated that government would, in the later stages of the policy period 1988–2003 and beyond, seriously examine and pursue the possibility of establishing the nucleus of a university at the Gambia College. This education policy did acknowledge the significance of vocational education and training in terms of Human Resource Development (HRD), but no specific reforms were made in this regard, though the need for expansion and training opportunities was expressed in the policy document.

The 2004–15 policy

The focus of the Education reforms after the 1988–2003 policy was for the 2004–15 policy to provide a policy framework that seeks to establish a national agenda for education in The Gambia.

The 2004–15 Policy aims and objectives outlined for education in the country, are clearly synchronized with the Education-related Millennium Development Goals (MDGs), the EFA imperative, the New Partnerships for African Development (NEPAD) and The Gambia's Poverty Reduction Strategy Paper (PRSP). It was anticipated that the policy priorities identified at the time would allow for the growth of educational opportunities, and would see an improvement in the effectiveness of education at all levels, from Early Childhood Development (ECD) to tertiary and higher education. The policy priorities and objectives included but were not limited to the following:

- To increase the basic education GER to 100 per cent by 2015, taking into account enrolment in Madrassas.
- Increasing completion rates in basic education to 100 per cent by 2015.
- Increasing the supply of trained teachers to enhance a 45:1 teacher ratio.
- Increasing the enrolment ratio of Early Childhood by 50 per cent especially in the rural areas.

- To provide marketable skills to enable individuals to deal effectively with the demands and challenges of everyday life.
- To establish a sound financial basis for the long-term development and sustainability of TVET.
- Institutionalize access programmes for Higher Education especially for girls, particularly in Mathematics and Technology (DOSE 2004: 17).

The formulation of the present Education Policy 2004–15 gave serious consideration to the blue print of the Gambian Government's Strategic Plan for socio-economic development, incorporated in its 'Vision 2020' document (GoG 1996). The Vision gives emphasis to 'Education and Vocational and skill-based training' and to the encouragement of entrepreneurship ('as a corner-stone for Human Resource Development'), coupled with high quality academic and professional training.

The policy-making process in education

During the appraisal and development of the 1988–2003 policy, due consideration was given to the scope, limitations and failures of the Education Policy (1976–86) and the findings raised important issues that had to be considered to improve and make relevant the policy. It was realized that the process at the first stage of policy formulation, needed to take into consideration, the National Guidelines, the policies and Development Plans of Government, such as the First and Second Five-year Development Plans (1975/80 and 1981/1985, respectively), the 'Vision 2020' blueprint, and the country's PRSP. The 1988–2003 Policy had also envisaged a built-in mechanism which was that there would be a continuous process of regular policy reviews, in order to meet the need to update and adapt policy objectives to the realities and the changing needs on the ground. And indeed, this principle of continuous needs assessment at the Ministry of Education did enhance the measures taken for the 'unparalleled expansion of the education system at all levels, from early childhood education to tertiary and higher Education' and resulted in 'gender parity, having been almost achieved at the Lower Basic (Primary) level and enrolment, retention and performance in the local regions substantially improved' (DOSE 2004: 26).

This process of assessing and reviewing earlier education policies included the following:

Participation in the Public Expenditure Review

Given the benefits derived from the first public expenditure review (PER) in 1997, another one was carried out in 2001, as part of an on-going process of monitoring the education system. The PER (2001) pointed out the shortfalls in the areas of expenditure in education, access, enrolment, private costs and benefits of education, efficiency, as well as quality and relevance of education.

Education policy dialogues

The formulation of the 2004–15 Education Policy involved the contributions of all stakeholders in the country, through a participatory process. The process included the participation of children, adults, illiterate and literate members of society, government departments, private sector representatives, and civil society in general in both urban and rural areas. Formal and informal meetings were organized to discuss and examine the strengths and weaknesses of the 1988–2003 Policy, in order to guide the development of the 2004–15 Policy. The dialogues between various interest groups took place through regional conferences supported by radio and television programmes. The consultations provided the then Department of State for Education with critical issues for debate during the Education Conference for the development of the 2004–15 policy framework. Critical issues were raised and discussed which included improving access to quality education for all, Madrassas, non-formal, early childhood and special needs education, expansion of secondary education, skills development, TVET, local government decentralization reforms and capacity and professional development. A national conference was held at The Gambia College in 2003 and came up with recommendations and resolutions for addressing the above issues.

Policy implementation

The present structure of the education system

The Ministry of Education is headed by a Minister of State appointed by the President of the Republic and he/she is supported by a Senior Management Team (SMT) and they advise the Minister on policy matters. The Ministry of Education in The Gambia has brought in a number of innovations in order to enhance the effective implementation of the policy objectives. Among the pertinent innovations is the setting up of Directorates:

(a) The Directorate of Non- Formal Education has been merged with the Basic Education Directorate which deals with Grades 1 to 9, the Ministry having in mind the expanded vision of Basic Education internationally, with the emphasis on quality education for adult learners and Out of School Youth through non-formal approaches.
(b) The Directorate of Science and Technology.
(c) The Directorate of Services merged with Project Co-ordination Unit (PCU).

Decentralization

The Gambia's Local Government Act of 2002 required and directed that the provision of educational opportunities be decentralized in order to enhance better project implementation strategies and policies. In a bid to achieve this objective, the Ministry of Education effected the decentralization of education services into six Regional Education Offices that support the Ministry's activities at headquarters. The offices were later upgraded to Regional Directorates (and headed by Directors). This strategic action has enhanced the participation of Local Government Authorities in the management of Education at the community level, with a view to achieving the crucial objective of providing nine years of uninterrupted EFA.

Madrassas

The Ministry of Basic and Secondary Education now accepts the fact that it will be extremely difficult to achieve the goals of EFA without the inclusion and development of Non-Formal Education and the Madrassas. It therefore recognizes the contribution that Islamic Schooling Centres can make to educational development as they are institutions within the Non-Formal Sector of Education. The fact is that in most African countries, it has been the inability of public institutions to fulfil the demand for education, which leads them to commit to Non-Formal Education (Boly 2005). The Islamic Schools system has traditionally been to offer a Conventional Islamic School curriculum, that is, one which combines a study of the Quran with studies in various fields of secular knowledge. However, the reform of Islamic Schools in The Gambia is making steady and significant progress. The Education Policy 2004–15 recognizes the role of Madrassas in the attainment of policy targets. The policy states that: 'The Madrassas will be supported and strengthened to cater for children whose parents opt for instruction in these institutions. Such support will include the provision of teachers of English, instructional materials, and the upgrading and training of Madrassa teachers for quality assurance' (DOSE 2004: 20)

In line with and to support this provision, the MoBSE is now supporting the development of syllabuses and text books for Madrassas. It has also allocated subventions in the annual budgets which are disbursed to the General Secretariat for Islamic Studies for the payment of salaries to English language teachers in Madrassas.

The Early Childhood Development (ECD) sector

In the past, ECD was not given due consideration: it came mainly under the ambit of the private sector. Recent developments in education have however seen action taken by the Ministry of Education to develop the sector. The Ministry now sees ECD as an important element of quality basic education. As a consequence, the Lower Basic/Primary Schools in The Gambia, particularly those in the rural areas now have an ECD component annexed to them within the framework of the delivery of the national school curriculum. The Government considers ECD so important that an Operational Policy for Early Childhood Development was developed, the components of which have been incorporated into the Revised Education Policy 2004–15.

Technical and vocational education and training: The evolution of TVET policy in The Gambia

TVET policy during the post-independence era

As earlier indicated, during the pre-independence era, TVET was under the preview of the then Ministry of Education, with the exception of the non-formal type of apprentice training in the Informal and non-formal sectors of the economy. The only provider of formal technical training and education was offered at the Banjul Technical Training School under the Ministry of Education. The technical training programmes did not lead to any external qualifications. The main areas of training offered were in Carpentry and Joinery, and Construction, but eventually Sheet Metal work, Welding Crafts, Blacksmithing, Mechanical Engineering and Telecommunication Engineering were added to the curriculum. However, the training programmes offered were not tied to the national occupational manpower needs of the country and The Gambia Government found it necessary to address the problem of manpower needs. In 1975, it launched its First Development Plan, 'The five-year plan for Economic and Social Development' (1975/1976–80). It was the first document to make an attempt to formulate a 'National Development Plan' that covered most sectors of the economy. The Plan made a serious effort to take steps towards meaningful re-construction and development at the national level. The planning process then involved, in particular, the specific definitions of national objectives, priorities and possible targets. The plan established a framework for maximizing integration, co-ordination and the executing capacity of the public sector. It was seen and judged not as a programming exercise, but primarily as a national statement of firm intent.

The preparation and launching of this Development Plan coincided with the release of a report by the Ministry of Economic Planning and Industrial Development in 1974, which dealt with the manpower requirements of the country; and relevant to this paper was the fact that the report concluded that the main areas of labour shortages were skilled craftsmen, technicians and trained stenographers. 'The shortage of these workers is felt widely through the private and public sectors where, and in the case of skilled craftsmen and technicians it was reported that in several cases this shortage had adversely affected production' (Wood 1974: 2).

The 1970s were a period of national development in most developing countries, and most manpower reports at the time pointed to a serious shortage in the supply of middle level technical manpower. The warning was that if developing countries were ever to bridge the gap that separates them from the economically advanced nations, there was the urgent need for them (at a time of rapid scientific and technological advancement), to have in place, a trained manpower at all levels. Mass education and the maximum possible provision of facilities for vocational and technical training which would deliver a source of skilled labour was an essential prerequisite for economic growth.

The Education Policy 1976–86 had made mention of TVET aims and of its direction, but only in general terms. The first Five-Year Plan had stated that the primary aim of education was to create in the shortest possible time, and with the available resources, a stock of trained manpower that was going to be capable of servicing the socio-economic needs of the country. It was then that, by a directive of government, steps were taken to re-orientate the school curriculum (to include Commercial, Secretarial, Scientific and Technical subjects into the Junior and Secondary Schools as they were then called), and that by a further directive, the names of all Junior Secondary Schools were changed to Technical Secondary Schools. However, consideration was not given to the planning, management, and resourcing of TVET and later studies of TVET confirmed this as a reason for the failure of the Technical Secondary Schools.

Additionally, within the Administrative/Management structure of the Ministry of Education, there was no Directorate or Division (headed by an Education officer), to oversee and advise on the planning, implementation and development of technical and vocational education and training in the country.

Further developments of the TVET policy

In a very serious effort of the Government to give priority to this sector, in 1976 the World Bank was approached for assistance with the review and development of plans to rectify and redirect developments in TVET, and to include the construction of the first Government Technical Training Institute in The Gambia. It was located in the Kanifing Industrial Area. This was the first World Bank Education Project to be launched in The Gambia and it included, as a pilot programme, the construction and equipping of technical workshops in selected Secondary Schools, in particular, Metal and Carpentry workshops. The schools followed the school curriculum agreed upon between the Ministry of Education and the well-established Examinations body in the region, namely, the West African Examination Council (WAEC). The new Technical Training Institute was built in 1977 at the Kanifing Industrial Estate, with the condition that a New Directorate of Technical and Vocational Education and Training was to be established under the office of the country's President.

TVET within the 1976/86 education policy (and the 1975/80 and 1981/86 development plans)

The 1976/1986 education policy had merely referred to TVET in a statement that gave indications as to the sort of programmes it would offer. The strategies and policies for identifying needs, for resourcing, and for capacity development policies were not adequately dealt with. This situation was similar to what transpired in most countries in the region, that is, priority for investment and planning in education was given to general academic education to the detriment of TVET development and investment.

The fact is that, in the developing world, employment opportunities for even well-trained technical manpower are very limited within Government, and, at the time, Governments in the region were by far the largest employers, and in a situation with high numbers of unemployed graduates, this could create frustration and might cause political and/or social instability. With this situation in mind and in the context of planning for the TVET, the Government took certain decisions to ensure that it intended to get the TVET system right and to have structures in place for the continuing monitoring and development of the system. A critical issue which the Government noted at the time (in addition to other systemic problems) was the lack of co-operation between training providers and employers in both the public and private sectors, including the non-formal sector. This necessary link was absent or non-functional in a formal sense, and the mismatch between the demand side for skills in the labour market and the supply side (that is, the training that institutions were providing), resulted in the problem of youth unemployment. The report of the Colombo Plan, on training facilities at the technician level had described the lack of co-operation between Government, educational institutions and industry as one of the biggest obstacles to progress in technical education and training (ILO 1962: 14). This statement was not confined to The Gambia; other developing countries experienced the same.

In order to re-direct and reform the TVET system, in 1979 the government established, the National Vocational Training Board (NVTB).

Developments in TVET and future trends

The Gambia Government, through its PRSP I and II intended to eradicate poverty in The Gambia as soon as it was feasible. To achieve this objective, the Government will need to maintain a sustainable growth, create more opportunities for employment and develop a framework for strategies, as regards the creation of more jobs.

As indicated earlier in this paper, the Government of The Gambia has long recognized the need for a trained workforce, particularly one that possesses technological and vocational skills. In its endeavour to address the problem of youth unemployment, it has initiated over the years many strategies and policies to address the situation of early school leavers, and an untrained and unskilled labour force; for example, both the 1975–80 and the 1981–5 Development Plans stated the following as priority objectives:

- To increase the skill and efficiency of individual workers;
- To increase the collective efficiency of the workforce through organization and management;
- To reduce the risk of unemployment among the educated youth, through moderate expansion of education at the secondary level.

The present Gambia Government's Strategic Plan for socio-economic development, as incorporated in its Vision 2020 (GoG 1996), has given serious consideration to and emphasis on vocational and skills-based training and the encouragement of entrepreneurship (as a cornerstone for human resource development) coupled with high quality academic and professional training.

In spite of all the above initiatives by Government and by various institutions, and of the economic growth recorded over the years, poverty is not being alleviated. The National Training Act of 2002 on TVET indicated that poverty was partly due to the lack of skills, and the Government concluded that TVET and skills development were not strategically structured; lacked direction; and failed to meet the need to stimulate the country's growth and production.

A more recent study by Adjivon (2007) reveals that employers are not happy with the output from the training system.

Current state of affairs for TVET

Following the recent developments, a new Ministry of Higher Education, Research, Science and Technology has been established. The TVET sector is now under the purview of that Ministry and the latter has delegated the overall management and supervision of the TVET sub-sectors (such as the Informal Sector, Apprenticeships and In-plant Training), to the National Training Authority (NTA) for co-ordination and supervision. The NTA Act (2002) mandates the Authority to:

- Regulate National Vocational Qualifications;
- Co-ordinate the quality of delivery of technical and vocational education and training;
- Make technical and vocational education and training relevant to all occupations (skilled artisans, and semi-skilled workers), and to the occupations classified as unskilled;
- Encourage and promote life-long learning to all Gambians.

The NTA has become the regulatory body responsible for the award of National Vocational Qualifications (NVQs) in association with both education and training establishments, and with employers in The Gambia. It has now developed The Gambia Skills Qualification Framework (GSQF) to guide and regulate skills qualifications and their levels in the country. In addition, the NTA is in the process of establishing a Labour Market Information System (LMIS). Also established now, is a system that continuously analyses and monitors occupational needs. The NTA is now established as a semi-autonomous organization partnering the private sector with government. The key and urgent issues for the policy to address include: consultations with stakeholders; installing an effective LMIS; and having in place a sustainable financial system.

Conclusion

This chapter has provided an overview of education in The Gambia, and has examined the evolution of education policies (from the pre-independence era to date) and their implications for the future. The chapter is in two parts. Part 1 discusses the policy-making and implementation processes for the education system in The Gambia. These have included the system's participation in the government's public expenditure review process, the education policy dialogues, the decentralization process, the development of Madrassas, and early childhood development.

In Part 2, the chapter discusses technical and vocational education and training policy in The Gambia. The chapter addresses the challenges that face the government of The Gambia in terms of unemployment and underemployment, and describes the employment policies and strategies that the government has formulated and adopted in order to address this situation (whilst encouraging the idea of a green economy and the growth of the national economy, and promoting access to credit for productive investment.) The chapter underscores the steps which the government of The Gambia has taken in order to respond to the increasing rate of unemployment and of poverty, (particularly, among women and young people). These steps include facilitating credit facilities for women and youth, and supporting skills training and green jobs initiatives (with a view to promoting entrepreneurship in the formal and informal sectors of the economy).

The various policy and strategic initiatives that the Government has initiated and implemented are commendable, in particular, the present PAGE policy initiative which has laid down constructive strategies to deal with the problem of poverty, and the development of its human resource capital, in order to ensure the achievement of the policy objectives. However, critical challenges remain, such as inefficient national co-ordinating and monitoring mechanisms, insufficient funding for job creation, and inadequate advocacy strategies.

References

Adjivon, A. (2007). *A Study of the Co-ordination of Skill Development with Employment Needs in The Gambia*. Bakau, The Gambia: ERNWACA Office.

Boly, A. (2005). What Language of Instruction in Non-formal Education? *ADEA Newsletter*, 17 (2): 9.

Gambia Government (GoG) (1975). *Five Year Plan for Economic and Social Development 1975/76 -79/80*. Banjul: Government Printer.

—(1979). *An Act of Parliament to Establish a National Training Board*. Banjul: Government Printer.

—(1980). *Second Five Year Plan for Economic and Social Development 1980–85*. Banjul: Government Printer.

—(1988). *Education Policy (1988–2003)*. Banjul: Department of State for Education.

—(1996). *The Gambia Incorporated. Vision 2020*. Banjul. Government of The Gambia.

—(2004). *The Education Policy 2004–2015*. Banjul: Department of State for Education.

—(2011). *Programme for Accelerated Growth and Employment* (PAGE). Banjul: Ministry of Finance.

International Labour Organization (ILO) (1962). *Vocational Training and Management Development (Fifth Asia Regional Conference)*. Geneva.

Lewis, G. (1977). *Report of the ILO consulting on proposals for a New Technical Institute in The Gambia*. Banjul.

MoHERST (2005). *Technical assistance for improving relevance and efficiency in TVET and Higher Education in The Gambia (Ministry of Higher Education, Research, Science and Technology.*

Ministry of Local Government and Lands (2002). *The Local Government Act for Decentralization (2002)*. Banjul: Ministry of Local Government (MoLG).

National Training Authority (2002). *Technical Education and Vocational Training Act. (TVET) National Training Authority (NTA)*. The Gambia.

N'Jie, M. A. (1979). *Technical and Vocational Education in The Gambia. The Road Ahead*. Master's Degree Thesis, University of Sheffield, England.

Wood, D. (1974). *Manpower Report on the Requirements of Technical Personnel in The Gambia*. The Gambia: Ministry of Economic Planning and Industrial Development.

Ghana: An Overview

Ruby Selenu Avotri

Introduction

This chapter gives a historical perspective of education from indigenous traditional informal education through to the introduction and development of a 'Western' type of education from the pre-independence to post-independence era. The chapter also describes different types of education reforms that were initiated since independence to make education relevant to the socio-economic needs and aspirations of Ghana. Some challenges of education, specifically on the structure of education, curriculum, educational financing and provision of infrastructure and educational materials and some measures adopted to resolve these are highlighted.

It is reiterated that despite several interventions and injection of considerable resources, with substantial support from development partners, Ghana is yet to overcome the perennial challenges facing the education system.

The chapter is based on a reflective analysis of the author's personal observations as an educationist and researcher with a 21-year work experience at the Curriculum Research and Development Division (CRDD) of the Ghana Education Service. In addition to several educational reports, documents were analysed to support assertions in the chapter.

The chapter begins with historical perspectives of education from indigenous education to the introduction of formal education in the pre-colonial era. It further elaborates on various forms education reforms after independence, highlights challenges and achievements of some of the reforms. It concludes with suggestions to make education relevant to the needs of Ghana.

Historical perspective

Indigenous Ghanaian education

Indigenous Ghanaian education was in practice in the then Gold Coast before formal education was introduced. This was non-formal, non-certificated but very pragmatic and was based on past experiences as well as present way of life (Fiah 1979). Memorization, strict imitation and reproduction of adult behaviour were very essential ingredients of this form of education. The objectives of the indigenous informal education were to preserve and perpetuate traditions and cultural practices inherited from past generations as well as maintaining social solidarity.

Pre-colonial era

Formal education in Ghana was introduced by the European merchants and the early Basel, Wesleyans, the Bremen Missionaries and the Roman Catholic Church. While the missionaries needed educated local assistants to propagate Christianity, the European merchants set up the early schools to educate their mulatto children by native women. The curriculum comprised reading, writing, the language of the governing country and later some arithmetic and religious knowledge (McWilliam 1967) in addition to practical skills in carpentry, masonry, blacksmithing, shoemaking and sewing for girls, agriculture and medical and health education.

Colonia era

A wide variety of education systems were in practice at the time the British Government assumed full control of the Gold Coast in 1874. The first Plan for Development of Education was therefore drawn up in 1882 to harmonize education in the Gold Coast leading to the inception of the 'Westminster' type of education in Ghana.

The education system introduced in Ghana was similar to traditional education for the working class with very little involvement of locals in education. The lecture method and chorus chanting of statements partially understood by pupils, asserted by McWilliam (1967), were used. The curriculum focused on teaching of English, arithmetic and writing and 'Payment by Results', was introduced with more grants being paid for passes in 'core' subjects of

English, arithmetic and reading and less was allocated to other subjects which were perceived to be less important, such as technical and vocational education. Consequently, the 'elite' Ghanaians were not attracted to these areas because they were perceived to be for those who were not 'academically' endowed (McWilliam 1967).

This system reinforced rote learning and the teaching and mastery of specific subjects. (McWilliam 1967). The British bookish type of education thus permeated the entire social fabric of Ghanaians through to post-independence era. Education was geared towards the skills required in clerical and administration jobs in the civil service. In Ghana's desire to industrialize, the Accelerated Development Plan for Education, which made primary education free and compulsory for all Ghanaian children was accordingly drawn up because education was perceived to be the backbone of national development (ibid.).

Inception of educational reforms

The rapid structural expansion in education in the Accelerated Development Plan for Education did not have corresponding changes in the content of the curriculum to match the aspirations of the new Government of creating fast-changing modern society. Instead, the British curriculum was maintained. As a result, a pool of unemployed, and in some cases, 'unemployable' school leavers were turned out leading to a rural–urban drift of young school leavers who paraded the corridors of various ministries looking for non-existent clerical and administrative jobs (Avotri 1995).

The Amissah Committee

In the late 1960s, the Amissah Committee which was set up to assess the situation and advise the Government on curriculum reforms recommended a practical and vocational type of education that would develop necessary skilled manpower and technicians for modernization and industrialization (Ghana Education Service, CRDD 1988). Based on this, the Eight-Year Primary School Programme and Two-Year Continuation Schools Scheme were introduced in the 1970s in addition to the conventional subjects like English, mathematics, science and music. The Continuation School structure was to expose children to a wide range of indigenous vocations such as masonry, pottery, blacksmithing, dressmaking and fishing. Poor planning, inadequate resources and implementation challenges were largely responsible for the failure of the scheme.

The education system of 1974

As a result of public agitation to find a more relevant system of education for the country, an Educational Review Committee, chaired by Professor Dzobo, was therefore set up in 1973 to review the existing education system and advise the Government (Ministry of Education 1974). The Dzobo Committee recommended the establishment of a three-year Junior Secondary School (JSS) and a three-year Senior Secondary Schools (SSS) to replace the existing four-year middle schools and seven-year secondary schools respectively. One hundred and eighteen experimental Junior Secondary Schools (JSS) were established across the country in 1976 (Ministry of Education 1990).

Education reform of 1987 (EVANS-ANFOM)

An Education Commission chaired by Evans-Anfom, which was later set up to examine concerns of the public identified similar challenges as the Dzobo Committee. Based on its report, a new education reform was introduced in 1987 nationwide and the old system gradually phased out (Avotri 1995).

The 1987 Education Reform was the first major post-independence education reform in the country. Apart from reducing the length of pre-tertiary education from 19 to 12 years, the traditional curriculum was also replaced with an integrated curriculum that emphasized a child-centred inquiry approach to teaching and learning. In addition, more emphasis was placed on the acquisition of basic vocational, agricultural and technical skills (Ministry of Education 1990).

The structure of the old pre-tertiary educational system comprised ten years basic education called Elementary Schooling comprising a six-year primary and a four-year middle school education, a five-year secondary/technical education based on a selection examination, the Common Entrance Examination; and probably a further two years sixth form secondary education. Students who could not enter the secondary/technical school could enter any post-elementary institutions such as Teacher Training, commercial institutions or nurses training colleges.

The new education structure was made of 18–24 months of Kindergarten (KG) for four- to six-year-olds, nine years basic education (six years primary and three years JSS) and three years' secondary education and three to four years' post-secondary and tertiary education in institutions such as the polytechnics, teacher training and nurses' training colleges and universities. This was the first time KG education was formally included into the education system. The curriculum was reviewed with emphasis on practical, vocational, technical and agricultural courses to expose junior high school (JHS) students to pre-technical and pre-vocational skills. Apart from changing the structure and content of the education system, the reform also aimed to increase access to basic education by abolishing selection examination into JHS. This was to meet a 1992 Constitutional requirement of giving every child the opportunity to access basic education.

Despite the advantages of the 1987 Education Reform, the Ministry of Education was confronted with implementation challenges which eroded some of the anticipated benefits. The reform was designed such that pupils began school in the old traditional education, continued in the new system at the JHS level after which students were expected to complete in the old system. Implementation of this design was problematic and could best be described as 'a quick fix' measure, which had proved to have limited impact (Wallace and Louden 1992).

Community involvement was an integral part of the education reform and substantial community contribution was required in the provision of classrooms and workshops for vocational and technical education. However, many communities were unable to supplement government initiatives in terms of infrastructure, resources and skilled personnel, especially for indigenous vocational subjects largely due to poverty and poor infrastructure that characterized many rural communities. The situation was worsened by the perennial rural–urban drift of the youth who were expected to support the elderly to manage the schools (Avotri 1995).

The reform also introduced a new curriculum that was different from the traditional curriculum that teachers were trained in and had also been teaching. Teachers, who were supposed to implement the curriculum, had very little involvement in its development and the brief orientation given some of them was inadequate in equipping them with the requisite skills to effectively teach it. School performance did not improve as was anticipated in the 1987 education reform.

The free compulsory universal basic education

In 1994, the Education Reform Review Committee (ERRC) was set up to review the 1987 Education Reforms, assess its efficacy, identify its challenges and make recommendations for its improvement (Ministry of Education 1997). Some of the weaknesses identified in the ERRC report were overloading of the curriculum, continued decline in quality of education, general lack of educational facilities and materials and resource mismanagement. The Basic Education Sector Improvement Programme (BESIP) therefore was set to prioritize the problems identified by the ERRC and propose appropriate strategies to address them (Ministry of Education 1999a).

Based on this, the Government introduced the Free Compulsory Universal Basic Education (FCUBE) in September, 1995, as a 1992 Constitutional requirement under Article 38(2) which made provision for free compulsory and universal basic education by the year 2005 and this was to be progressively extended to secondary education and beyond, depending on resource availability. The FCUBE aimed to achieve three main goals in two-five-year phases:

- Enhance quality of teaching and learning outcomes;
- Improve access and participation to basic education with special focus on girls and the poor;
- Efficient allocation, management and utilization of fiscal, material and human resources in the education sector (Ministry of Education 1997).

As a result, the pre-service and in-service teacher training programmes were redesigned to produce well-qualified teachers to improve quality of education in addition to a review of the curriculum and development of adequate appropriate instructional materials. Rehabilitation and construction of school infrastructure and measures to increase participation of girls and the disadvantaged were to be pursued. Decentralization and district-level capacity building and effective monitoring and supervision, among others, were proposed to ensure efficient school management.

Cost of the first phase of FCUBE (1996–2000), was estimated at $1.35 billion and was largely funded by the Government of Ghana with support from development partners such as United States Agency for International Development (USAID), Department for International Development (DFID), European Union (EU) Deutsche Gesellschaft fur Technische Zusammenarbeit (GTZ), Canadian International Development Agency (CIDA) and Japan International Cooperation Agency (JICA) (Ministry of Education 1996).

Notable achievements of the FCUBE were a major review of the pre-tertiary curriculum, development of a textbook policy and provision of educational materials and textbooks to schools. Access to basic education for children of school-going age was improved. More JSS were built throughout the country to absorb the increasing primary enrolment. Between 1994 and 1997, for example, enrolment increased by 5.5 per cent and 5.4 per cent in primary and JSS levels respectively with no significant increase of enrolment of girls over boys (Ministry of Education 1999b; Avotri et al. 1999).

However, the issue of quality continued to be a challenge in basic education as a result of inadequate infrastructure, teaching-learning materials, poor calibre of teachers, rate of teacher lateness and absenteeism, among others. Problems with access, retention and performance persisted as well as regional gender inequalities.

Review of Education Reforms 2002

In January, 2002, the government inaugurated a Presidential Committee on Review of Education Reforms in Ghana under the chairmanship of Professor Jophus Anamuah-Mensah, to again review the entire educational system in the country, identify the inadequacies and shortcomings in the previous reforms and make recommendations for a more effective education. This led to the inception of the 2007 Education Reforms.

A two-year KG became an integral part of basic education 2007 education reforms. Although the Committee maintained the three-year senior secondary education, the government increased it to four 'to improve academic output of students at the end of the secondary level of education' due to the large number of students who failed the West Africa Senior Secondary Certificate Examination (WASSCE). Junior and Senior Secondary schools were renamed Junior High and Senior High Schools respectively. Apprenticeship training was formalized into the education system (Ministry of Education, Youth and Sports, 2004).

A major review of the structure and content of the pre-tertiary school curriculum began based on the provisions of the Education Reforms. ICT was integrated across the broad spectrum of the curriculum as well as made a core subject at the JHS and senior high school (SHS) levels of education. The reform also required extensive infrastructural development. A continuous teacher development was proposed resulting in the establishment of the National Teaching Council and upgrading of all Teacher Training Colleges into diploma-awarding institutions with affiliation to education-oriented universities. The National Council for Technical and Vocational Education (NCTVET) was also established to transform technical, agricultural and vocational education at the pre-tertiary education.

The implementation of the 2007 Education Reform which began in September 2007/8 academic year was received with much apprehension from a cross-section of the public. Critics questioned the timing when adequate preparations had not been made for the takeoff of the reform. The new curriculum for the reform and subsequent training of teachers in its use, for example, were yet to be completed. Supply of syllabuses and accompanying textbooks to schools was delayed. FCUBE was still plagued with myriads of perennial challenges, including inadequate infrastructure that were yet to be solved to address the poor academic standards across all levels of education.

The rationale and relevance of the extension of the SHS education by one year was another contentious issue considering the inadequacy of the existing educational facilities, especially infrastructure. The extension of the duration of SHS invariably increased the problems facing the entire education system. Although the Government introduced some interventions such as the School Feeding Programme and capitation grant at the primary and basic levels of education respectively to increase access to primary schools, these measures rather compounded the problems of inadequate infrastructure and professional personnel.

While the controversy about the introduction of the 2007 reform was still going on, there was a policy shift in which the duration of the SHS was reversed from four to three years at the change of governance in 2009. The SHS curriculum was accordingly revised to bring it in line with the proposed three-year programme. However, the two programmes ran parallel to each other for the next four years until the last batch of students in the four-year programme graduated in 2012/13 academic year together with the first batch of the reversed three-year programme. During this period, the inadequacy of school infrastructure became very critical leading to many schools being accommodated in makeshift structures. Several ad hoc measures were put in place while government quickly mobilized resources to provide accommodation and classroom facilities for schools. Some of these structures, which were earlier started, were yet to be completed.

Overview of Ghana's education reforms

One major characteristic of all the education reforms introduced since independence was inadequate preparations for the take-off of the programmes. In all cases extensive plans were made but the implementation was always faulted because adequate preparations were not made to address identified challenges of the existing education system and structures put in place before the introduction of the new one. This always resulted in perpetuation of the challenges of the previous system. Lack of capacity in terms of infrastructure and personnel was a key challenge in the enforcement of the compulsory component of the FCUBE and to date no solution has been found to this problem as an incredible number of schools are conducted under trees. It also implies that if all the out-of-school children were to go back to school, the government would be confronted with the dilemma of providing enough classrooms to accommodate all of them. Demand for trained and qualified teachers still outstrips supply by all the teacher training institutions, especially at the basic level of education.

Information Communication and Technology (ICT) in the school curriculum

The importance of ICT in accelerating development and a knowledge- and information-based economy cannot be overemphasized. It is on this premise that, the Ghana Government developed a policy framework document, 'Ghana ICT for Accelerated Development' (ICT4AD) to accelerate socio-economic development of the nation in the early 2000s (Republic of Ghana 2003) and also collaborated with the Government of India to establish the Kofi Annan Centre of Excellence in Information Technology (IT) to promote IT education and usage in the country.

The importance of education as a cross-cutting issue within the national ICT frame was unequivocally stated. One of the objectives in the policy is to 'promote an improved educational system within which ICTs are widely deployed to facilitate the delivery of educational service at all levels of the education system' (Ministry of Education 2008). The accompanying strategy in the policy explicitly stated that Ghana's education system will be modernized using ICTs to improve and expand access to education, training and research as well as improve quality of education to make education responsive to the needs of society. Furthermore, the first two pillars of the policy targeted accelerated human resource development and promoting ICT in education. Finally, the first ICT4AD rolling Plan (2003–6) identified promoting ICT in education as a priority focus area. If education is perceived as the engine of growth, the onus lies on the education sector to facilitate ICT skills acquisition in the country.

This was explicitly stated in the ICT4AD and goes to buttress the importance government attached to ICTs in education.

As a result of a policy directive in the 2007 education reform to integrate ICT into the curriculum to promote teaching and e-learning at pre-tertiary levels of education, the government rolled out a plan to introduce computers into all primary, secondary, vocational and technical schools to support the initiative. The 'One-to-one Laptop per Child (OLPC)' initiative by government has so far made available several laptop computers to basic schools throughout the country. In addition, all educational institutions were to be progressively equipped with computer laboratories and ICT tools. Tertiary institutions were to be resourced to train skilled personnel for the ICT centres. Ghana was among 16 countries that implemented the first phase of the demonstration project of the NEPAD e-Schools Initiative at the pre-tertiary level to promote access, quality and equity within ten years (Ministry of Education 2008). Assessment of the ICT initiatives in 2005 noted among others, an increased number of both students and teachers acquiring ICT skills and developing a strong interest in ICT and science. As a result, most schools were motivated to source funding through their PTAs and other initiatives to expand the project and acquire more ICT equipment (Education Research Network of Central and West Africa 2006).

The implementation of the Initiative was thwarted by a number of challenges, notably among them was a lack of policy direction at all levels for integrating ICT in education, heavy dependence on external funding, 'dumping' of obsolete and inappropriate equipment in support of the initiative and the lack of trained ICT personnel for the centres.

To increase the supply of skilled teachers to the schools, computers and internet connectivity were provided to all 38 teacher training colleges and 37 Technical Institutes. Many JHS and SHS also received internet connectivity. Teachers were also trained in basic computer skills, and C21st skills in pedagogy. The MoE in partnership with other agencies and private organizations promoted the sale of computers to teachers on hire purchase terms. However, the issue of skilled teachers willing to teach ICT is a major challenge that confronts the government because of comparatively higher demand with better service conditions in other sectors of the economy.

Access, gender and education

Education initiatives since post-independence Ghana, aimed at increasing school enrolment, made reasonable progress in expansion of access to education. However, there is still a yawning gap yet to be filled, especially for disadvantaged communities and children with special educational needs. Moreover, there has been a progressive decrease in total enrolment with increase in level of education over the years (Table 9.1). In 1997–8, for example, the gross enrolment rates (GER) were 77.5 and 59.9 per cent for primary and secondary schools respectively. GER for tertiary education for the same period was 24 per cent of the primary cohort (MoE 1998; quoted in Avotri et al. 1999). The GER for 2009/10 were 94.9 and 79.5 per cent for primary and JHS respectively. This dropped to 37.1 per cent at the secondary level (Ministry of Education, EMIS 2011).

Furthermore, fewer girls than boys were enroled at all levels of education with gender disparity increasing with level of education (Table 9.1). The retention rate for girls is also lower than for boys.

Several interventions have been put in place since the 1987 education reforms to reduce gender disparity at all levels of education. The curriculum and textbooks were reviewed and made more gender-sensitive (Ministry of Education 2002a). The Girls' Education Unit (GEU) was established in 1997 to support girls' education across the country. District Assemblies introduced scholarship schemes for girls to promote girls' education at JSS and SSS levels. Several donors such as the United Nations Children's Fund (UNICEF), USAID, and non-governmental organizations (NGOs) such as Forum for African Women Educationalists (FAWE) and Catholic Relief Services, supported interventions that specifically targeted girls. Some of the interventions targeted specific issues

Table 9.1 GER: Pre-tertiary education (2007–12)

Year	KG Total	KG Boys	KG Girls	Primary Total	Primary Boys	Primary Girls	JHS Total	JHS Boys	JHS Girls	SHS Total	SHS Boys	SHS Girls
2007/08	89.7	90.4	88.9	95.0	97.1	92.8	78.8	82.2	75.2	42.8	72.9	27.9
2008/09	92.9	93.5	92.2	94.9	97.0	92.8	80.6	83.9	77.0	33.9	36.7	30.8
2009/10	97.3	98.1	96.5	94.9	96.7	93.0	79.5	82.5	76.3	36.1	38.9	33.2
2010/11	98.4	99.2	97.5	96.4	98.0	94.7	79.6	82.6	76.4	36.5	38.9	33.9
2011/12	99.4	100.4	98.4	96.5	97.9	95.0	80.6	83.0	78.1	37.1	Na	Na

Source: Compiled from Ministry of Education, EMIS Reports of 2008 to 2012

such as access to education, improving quality, awareness creation and parental responsibility, health and HIV/AIDS and food security and nutrition. The GEU developed the National Vision for Girls' Education to promote gender equity at the basic level of education. Provisions in the 2007 education reform also targeted enhancing gender equity at all levels and programmes (Ministry of Youth and Sports 2004).

At the tertiary level, affirmative action in favour of female students was introduced to increase female enrolment as well as reduce gender discrimination. Special access courses were organized in mathematics and science for female students who had the potential and interest to enter the teacher training colleges. The 2009/10 gender profile of the 38 teachers' training colleges in the country shows one only male, six only female and 31 co-educational institutions (Ministry of Education, EMIS 2010). This was a deliberate effort to increase the number of female teacher-trainees. However, the proportion of qualified female teachers reduced by 0.9 per cent while that of males reduced by 0.3 per cent when compared with the 2008/9 figures. The enrolment of teacher-trainees in 2009/10 in Colleges was 26,629, an increase of 6.1 per cent over the previous year. However enrolment of males increased by 10.4 per cent while that of females increased by 0.3 per cent within the same period (Ministry of Education, EMIS 2010).

In-school interventions, such as girls' clubs, girls' vacation programmes to build self-esteem and leadership skills, to encourage girls to mobilize their peers and to embark on sensitization issues, were introduced at various times. These interventions had achieved considerable results but much needs to be done to sustain the gains and completely bridge the gender gap.

Quality of education

Quality of education has been a major challenge in Ghana for several years, especially at the pre-tertiary level of education and interventions to improve quality over the years have yielded limited results. The criterion-referenced tests which were used to assess level of proficiency at the basic level of education in the 1987 reform were replaced with the National Education Assessment (NEA) tests in 2005. The results in all cases revealed low proficiency in mathematics and English, far below the acceptable level.

Among the factors that influence quality of education are: pupil-teacher ratio, time on task, the availability of teaching and learning materials, including textbooks and poor or inadequate school infrastructure and teacher quality.

Government made significant strides to train quality teachers for all levels of education. The University of Cape Coast and later the University of Education, Winneba, were specifically established to train teachers, particularly, for basic and secondary education. The subsequent increase in the number of teacher training colleges to 38 and upgrading to diploma-awarding institutions buttresses government's commitment to teacher education. These initiatives, notwithstanding, the supply of quality teachers remains a contentious issue. In 2009/10 for example, less than 60 per cent of teachers were qualified, with the number of qualified female teachers significantly higher than that of males (Ministry of Education 2012).

The high demand for teachers necessitated the recruitment of pupil teachers from the National Service Scheme and the National Youth Employment Programme (NYEP) to temporarily fill vacancies in schools, especially at the basic level. This has had a considerable effect on the quality of education because of the low calibre of the NYEP personnel, now Ghana Youth Employment and Entrepreneurial Agency.

Financing education

The Government of Ghana is the main source of funding to education in Ghana. Apart from internally generated funds, the Government also gets external assistance from development partners such as USAID, DFID, UNICEF, the World Bank, CIDA, JICA and the French government. Total government expenditure of 35–40 per cent for the Ministry of Education is inadequate. Thus the establishment of the Ghana Education Trust Fund (GETFUND) by Act 581 on 25 August 2000 to provide funds to supplement the provision of education at all levels. The main source of funding for GETFUND is a two and a half percentage charge on the value added tax and any other allocation by Parliament. The GETFUND funding brought about a remarkable improvement in the provision of educational infrastructure, particularly at the tertiary level.

In addition, philanthropist and corporate funding at times augment government initiatives. Old student associations and Parent-teacher Associations (PTAs) have played very active roles in supplementing government efforts in relation to infrastructure for pre-tertiary education.

Financing education continues to be a major problem in Ghana. There is the need for government to broaden the scope of mobilizing funding for education to ensure that quality education is provided at all levels of education in Ghana.

Religious organizations, for example, must commit more funds to support educational initiatives, and special education levies should be imposed on mining companies.

Challenges of education

Education in Ghana has undergone several reforms. However, the same problems recur with each education reform. Education in Ghana has challenges with structure, access, quality, performance, teacher quality, availability of infrastructure and educational materials.

The decentralization policy, whereby district assemblies are required to provide infrastructure for schools is not effective because most district assemblies are not able to raise sufficient resources to fund infrastructure projects. District assemblies must widen their tax networks to increase revenue for education.

The demand for qualified teachers far outstrips turnout of trained teachers by the various teacher training institutions. The proposed 20 new teacher training colleges, it is anticipated, would eventually increase qualified teacher supply to lay a sound foundation for future education and eventually improve the quality of education.

Conclusion

It is obvious from the above that education in Ghana is not meeting the needs of a fast-changing society despite enormous investments, both human and financial, made into it over the years. Education is still plagued with both human and economic challenges. As a result, issues of education need not and should not be the responsibility of the central government alone. All stakeholders, parents, communities, individuals as well as private organizations and enterprises must pool resources together to support government and collaborate to improve access, quality and outcome of education to make it relevant to the socio-economic needs of Ghana. It is only then that education can drive the engine of development in the country.

References

Avotri, R. S. (1995). *The Efficacy of the 1987 Educational Reform in Ghana: The Case of Social Studies*. A Ph.D. Thesis, Murdoch University, Perth, Western Australia.

Avotri, R., Owusu-Darko, L., Eghan and H. Ocansey, S. (1999). *Partnership for Strategic Resource Planning for Girls' Education in Africa: Gender and Primary Schooling in Ghana*. Forum for African Women Educationalists (FAWE), Institute of Development Studies (IDS), University of Sussex.

Education Research Network of Central and West Africa (ERNWACA) (2006). *Integration of ICT into Education in West and Central Africa*. A multinational research on integration of ICT.

Fiah, F. (1979). *Ghana's Universal Public Educational Schools. A Review*. Dissertation for Master of Science, University of Edinburgh.

Ghana Education Service (2009). *Needs Assessment for KG Education*. Curriculum Research and Development Division, September, 2009.

Ghana Education Service, C.R.D.D. (1988). *Social Studies for Junior High Secondary Schools. Pupils' Book 2*. Accra and London: Unimax Publishers and Macmillan Publishers Ltd.

McWilliam, H. O. (1967). *The Development of Education in Ghana: An Outline*. London: Longmans Green and Co. Ltd.

Ministry of Education (1974). *The New Structure and Content of Education for Ghana*. Accra: Ministry of Education.

—(1990). *An Evaluation Report of Junior Secondary Schools Established in Ghana between 1976 and 1987 (A Report)*. Accra: Curriculum Research and Development Division.

—(1996). *Achievements under the Fourth Republic (1992–1996)*.

—(1997). *FCUBE Programme: Report on status of FCUBE programme implementation*. February–July 1997.

—(1999a). *BESIP Implementation Programme Report*.

—(1999b). *Basic Education Sub-sector Improvement Programme: Implementation Progress Report (1996–98)*. For achieving Free Compulsory and Universal Basic Education (FCUBE) by the year 2005.

—(2002a). *Report of the President's Committee on Review of Education Reforms in Ghana (Anamuah-Mensah Report)*, Ministry of Education, Accra, 2002, pp. 1–3.

—(2002b). *Situational Analysis of Gender Issues in Education: from Literate Girls to Educated Women*. Report prepared by L. Casely-Hayford for the Ministry of Education as part of the Education Sector Review (ESR) with assistance from the ESR Gender Task Team. 17 June 2002.

—(2008). *ICT in Education Policy*. November 2008.

—(2008/9) *Report on Basic Statistics and Planning Parameters for Basic Education in Ghana 2008/2009*. EMIS. March 2009.

—(2010). *Report on Basic Statistics and Planning Parameters for Colleges of Education in Ghana 2009/2010*. EMIS. September 2010.

—(2011). *Report on Basic Statistics and Planning Parameters for Basic Education in Ghana 2010/2011*. EMIS. April 2011.
—(2012). *Appraisal of Ghana's Education Sector Plan 2010–2020*. March 2012.
Ministry of Education, Youth and Sports (2004). *White Paper on the Report of the Education Reform Review Committee*, October 2004.
Republic of Ghana (2003). *The Ghana ICT for Accelerated Development (ICT4AD) Policy*. A Policy Statement for the Realization of the Vision to Transform Ghana into an Information-Rich Knowledge-based Society and Economy through the Development, Deployment and Exploitation of ICTs within the Economy and Society (2003). Available from www.ict.gov.gh (accessed 2003).
Wallace, J. and Louden, W. (1992). 'Science teaching and teachers: prospects for reform of elementary classrooms. *Science Education*, 76 (5): 507–12.

10

Ghana: Trends and Futures

Daniel Justice Eshun

Introduction

This chapter focuses on current trends within pre-tertiary and tertiary education in Ghana and an exploration of future developments. This chapter is a reflection on the present writer's participant experiences and observations and analytical engagement with various genres of literature on Ghanaian education systems. The writer was educated in Ghana at both pre-tertiary and tertiary levels. Also, the writer has taught at primary, secondary and tertiary schools in both rural and urban parts of Ghana. Furthermore, from 1997 to the present, the writer has visited Ghana every two years to teach at a tertiary institution, converse with teachers, opinion leaders and parents who are all worried about trends within education, the lack of vocational training, the discrepancies between universities' visions and graduate employability and scarce resources – both human and material – to support the education system. Also, the chapter critically draws on various academic researches, reports, parliamentary acts, public pronouncements of opinion leaders and newspapers' reporting on ongoing changes and policies in Ghanaian education.

The contention of this chapter is that whereas Ghana's education system has undergone many reforms in recent times, it is shrouded in ambivalence, paradoxes, ironies and inequalities. But education would have a bright future if there were clarity about the nation's free compulsory education policy, and if links were established between education and Ghana's economic and labour needs and teachers were taken seriously. To pursue these arguments, first, we examine current educational trends: pre-tertiary and tertiary, focusing on various ironies, inequalities, ambivalence and paradoxes. Second, we shall explore various issues that need attention in future if Ghanaian education is to be perceived as fit for purpose.

Trends: Pre-tertiary and tertiary

Until very recently there seemed to be a consensus within the literature that the problems of Ghanaian education were: 1) that there were not enough schools; 2) that retention of children, particularly, girls in schools was a problem; 3) that the government did not spend enough money on education; 4) that the content of the educational curriculum was irrelevant to local needs and employability; and 5) that teachers were badly paid (Hurd and Johnson 1967; Robertson 1984; Oduro 2000). The continuous identification of these problems listed as the roots of Ghana's educational problems have led to many reforms.

As part of the reforms within the sector, the Ghanaian educational system is now structured on the 6–3–3–4 system:

- Pre-School – 2 years (ages 4–6)
- Primary School – 6 years (ages 6–11)
- Junior Secondary/High School – 3 years (ages 12–14)
- Senior High Secondary School – 3 years (ages 15–17)
- University Bachelor's degree – 4 years (ages 18–22)

Of course one could start school at any age as a mature student learning alongside younger people, and there have been cases where many adults have gone to school to learn to read and write. Strictly speaking, age is not a barrier to educational opportunities in Ghana. Besides, Ghanaians love titles, and qualifications and certificates are perceived as demonstrations of achievements and status within the social stratum. Many students spend years pursuing higher degrees, provided they have the ability and the financial resources. In the past, the Ghanaian government used to fund gifted students and potential future academic leaders to study abroad in reputable universities in Europe and America and then to serve the mother country but this has become more infrequent in recent years.

The official language of instruction throughout the Ghanaian educational system is English. However, during pre-school and the first three years of primary school, pupils may be taught in their mother tongue – Ewe, Twi, Fanti, Hausa, Dagomba and other indigenous languages, after which English becomes the sole medium. Students who desire could continue to study a Ghanaian language as well as French as classroom subjects through to the end of senior secondary school and even sit exams for them. But all the textbooks and materials are otherwise in English. Here lies an ambivalence and inequality: it is established that children who receive schooling in their mother-tongue language in the early years of education have better learning outcomes overall and, in particular, significantly better literacy levels and the second language is learned best when the child's first indigenous language has been learned well (Mackenzie et al. 2012; Ouane and Glanz 2010). As Mackenzie et al. have argued: 'mother tongue learning should be the initial key language of instruction in education, with a second language introduced later in carefully managed stages' (Mackenzie et al. 2012: 2). Yet, the Ghanaian education system does not sufficiently invest in Ghanaian indigenous languages. One struggles within the system to find a culturally contextualized curriculum with appropriate and adequate material written in a language that is relevant to children. Besides, many of the teachers are not equipped to teach indigenous language. When the present writer was an undergraduate in the 1990s in Ghana, students who were reading for a degree in Ghanaian indigenous languages were often not taken seriously, they were often laughed at; their subjects were not considered to be worth a degree programme. Teachers are, therefore, ill-equipped to teach in Ghanaian indigenous languages. Besides, there is misplacement of teachers who could teach in a particular indigenous language. It is not uncommon for an Akan speaker who cannot express him/herself in the Ga language to teach pre-school children in Accra. Also, teaching in indigenous languages in pre-school reveals inequalities within the educational system. In southern Ghana the dominant indigenous language within urban centres is Akan – a combination of Fanti and Twi. Pre-school children who speak Ewe, Hausa and Dogomba as their mother tongue are often taught in Fanti and Twi. So the policy of using indigenous languages during the pre-school and part of the early primary education places some children from minority groups within urban centres at a disadvantage right from the beginning of their education.

According to the Ghana Education Act of 2008, the educational system is intended to produce well-balanced individuals with the requisite knowledge skills, aptitudes and attitudes to become functional and productive citizens for the total development and the democratic advancement of the nation, and related matters (Ghana Education Act 2008). Furthermore, the Education Act of 2008 explicitly stated that 'Education at the basic level is free and compulsory'. Parents who refuse to send a child who has attained school-going age to schools are breaking the law (Ghana Education Act 2008: 4).

Since Ghanaians encountered European missionaries and colonialism they have always valued education, certificates and qualifications. Part of the explanation of mass conversion to Christianity in the nineteenth and early twentieth centuries was to have access to missionaries' schools (Bartels 1965; Graham 1971). Culturally, education came to be associated with the acquisition of useful and employable knowledge that led to wealth creation and access to political power and social influence. Ghanaian social mobility is very tight, economic opportunities are scarce and power is in the hands of a few. The perception was that education held the key to many possibilities and this made parents desire a good education for their children (ibid.).

This Ghanaian perception of education completely contradicts Blackmore's claim that the main reason Ghanaian parents resist formal education is 'their perception that uneducated sons are more "sociable" and that they will stay near to home to ensure the continuity of the family and of traditional, religious, or practical skills' (Blackmore 1975: 238). Since Christian missionaries and colonials introduced formal education, it has been seen as a source of power – economic, social and political. This perception continues to shape current trends in parents' desire to send their children to school. Yes, some pupils do drop out and do not complete their basic education but the reasons are far more complicated than Blackmore's observation. Even in the most rural parts of Ghana, parents and guardians, often with meagre economic means, have high educational ambitions and aspirations for their children. Parents wish to see their sons and daughters become doctors, lawyers, accountants, and other professionals in secure employment.

The irony is that current statistics indicate that graduate unemployment is becoming a major feature in Ghana. It is reported that as many as 50 per cent of graduates who leave Ghanaian universities and polytechnics will not find jobs for two years after their national service, and 20 per cent of them will not find jobs for three years (Aryeetey 2013). This statistic is high compared to the global unemployment rate of 6.1 per cent, and even that of South Africa where a third of the active labour force is unemployed (Owusu-Ansah 2014). This high graduate unemployment rate appears to lend support to recent research findings that reveal that the capabilities being developed in Ghanaian graduates are not matching the national manpower needs (Afenyadu et al. 2001; Afenyadu 1998). This demonstrates the mirage and reality in the trends within Ghanaian education.

Ghana has experienced a population explosion in the past 20 years. The rapid growth of the population has resulted in two in every five people in the country being less than 15 years old (Population Census Report of Ghana 2000). The current projections seem to suggest that by 2015, one person in four (26.5 per cent) in Ghana will be a child of less than 10 years (Population Census Report of Ghana 2010). This young population and the government's insistence on compulsory education for every child has led to rapid expansion in the education sector. Currently, the Ghanaian government allocates 23.20 per cent of its budget to education while the World Bank benchmark recommends 20 per cent. This implies the government is spending more than it should on education (Ghana Education Finance Brief 2012). This overspending is a demonstration of the government's commitment to the achievement of Universal Primary Education for all children by 2015. Bearing in mind the burgeoning young population this comes across as a lofty ambition. But the government has introduced several measures to accelerate their vision of universal education for all by 2015.

Current measures include grants to all public pre-schools (4- to 5-years old) to provide a compulsory education that gives every child a good start in the education system. It is often mentioned that many poor parents do not send their children to school because the children are hungry. To address this problem the government has introduced a free school feeding programme for all children in primary schools. Also, there has been a special campaign in the media to bridge the gender gap in education and targeted programmes to improve access to education in rural areas. All these efforts have resulted in good progress in the education sector, especially in the past seven years (Ghana Ministry of Education 2009).

For example, the government's decision to remove school fees has positively impacted enrolment figures. In the 2005/6 school year: Primary school gross enrolment rose by nearly 10 per cent, bringing total primary enrolment to 92.4 per cent nationwide. Primary school net enrolment increased from 62 per cent to 69 per cent. Every region in Ghana experienced a rise in enrolment; Northern Region (where enrolment rates have always been at their lowest) experienced the largest increase from 58 per cent to 76 per cent. Overall enrolment in basic school increased by 16.7 per cent in the 2005/6 school year compared to 2004/5. Furthermore, the enrolment of girls increased slightly more than that of boys, 18.1 and 15.3 per cent for both sexes respectively (UNICEF 2006).

The increase in enrolment of girls is a real achievement in recent Ghanaian educational development. For in some parts of Ghana economic and socio-cultural factors contribute to low enrolment and attendance rates of girls. Often, girls play a key role in the survival of poor families who are struggling to make a living either by working to contribute to family income or taking care of household chores like looking after younger siblings. In these situations, girls are less likely to be sent to school (UNICEF 2007; Ampiah Adu-Yaboah 2011). In many of the rural communities where the present writer has taught, the assumption is that the girl child will be married and provided for by her husband so traditionally there is less understanding of her need for education in comparison with the boy child.

In recent study there is an indication that in real expenditure providing compulsory free education leads to the government spending 50.5 per cent of the total budget on pre-school, primary and junior secondary sectors (Ghana Education Finance Brief 2012). But despite this big slice of the budget Ghana's public education system is saddled with discrepancies, inequalities, underperformance and mismanagement.

The Ghanaian get-ahead culture has taught the emerging middle-class parents that to send your child or ward to the public school for basic education is disadvantaging and limits the child's chances to go to a better senior secondary and excellent public university. In contrast, before independence in 1957 and until the 1980s, many middle-class children went to public school (Evans-Anfom Report 1986). The current trend among the emerging middle classes is to pay for their children to go to private schools for their basic education. The middle classes have come to appreciate the forces of globalization and the attending tough competition in the job market and they want to give their children the best possible advantage.

The current trends are that the public basic education system is inadequate to equip young pupils with the basic reading, writing and numeracy skills required for further studies at the secondary level and to international standards. Besides, subjects taught at the public primary and junior secondary school (JSS) levels were too poorly taught owing to shortages of qualified teachers and relevant learning materials (Government White Paper 2010). In effect, pupils of average ability are not able to acquire sufficient foundation in the basic literacy, numeracy and social studies to enable them to move on either to senior secondary school or enter into the job market' (Government White Paper 2010).

This indictment on the public education sector is supported by the current pupil-teacher ratio in 2006/7 of 35.7:1 at the national level, while at the regional levels the ratio is even higher. For example, in the Upper East Region it was 58:1 in 2003/4, 57.4:1 in 2004/5 and 53.9:1 in 20006/7 (UNICEF 2007). It could be argued that there has been progressive improvement in the pupil-teacher ratio. For in 2012/13 the pupil-teacher ratio at the public primary school was 33:1 but the private ratio is lower (27:1). This lower pupil-teacher ratio in the private sector means teachers are able to give more attention to each child than in the public schools.

The recent increased enrolment of children into public primary schools has led to a massive overcrowding of classrooms. It is estimated that for Ghana to meet the target of Universal Primary Education by 2015 there will be a deficit of 1,048 classrooms to be built every year for the next four years in the public basic schools in the country. There has also been a corresponding shortage of furniture and sanitation facilities. Also, there is going to be a shortage of qualified teachers, deepening the inability of the country to provide quality primary education for the growing numbers of the primary school-aged children (6–11 years) in the public sector, especially in rural and deprived areas. It is estimated if the population rates continues to grow unabated a teacher will be expected to handle as many as 100 or more pupils. Once again, the deprived districts have been the worst off (UNICEF 2007). This scenario is going to increase the desire for private education at the basic level.

Private education has a long history in Ghana; it could be argued that private education was interwoven with the history of education in the country as many of the missionaries provided education for their converts during colonial periods (Bartels 1965; Graham 1971). However, the current desire for private education is being influenced by unspoken class consciousness. Ghanaians generally do not feel comfortable talking about class consciousness and aspiration; it is rather expressed through symbolism (Akyeampong 1996). It is known and accepted in the current educational trend that many aspirational parents have realized that when their children interact with schoolmates from similar parental backgrounds there is high academic motivations within the school. Also, the pushy parental backgrounds of the pupils influence the quality of teaching and the calibre of teachers employed, particularly in private schools (*Ghana Daily Mirror* 2013). Furthermore, from present writer observations, the private schools desired by the middle classes consciously transmit global cultural capital and inculcate study habits. These private schools force pupils to take books home to read, give them access to the internet and computer facilities within the school that give them global perspectives. Many middle-class parents have become conscious that their children are going to compete in the global market and the earlier they are imbued with global perspectives on things the better. But this leaves children from the less affluent and privileged backgrounds behind in the educational attainment (*Ghana Daily Graphic* 21 July 2013).

Nevertheless, many of the private schools are clustered within the regional capitals – Accra, Cape Coast, Sekondi-Takoradi, Kumasi, Ho, Brong-Ahafo, and Tamale. It is understandable that current private schools are set up within the cities where many of the emerging middle classes live. However, increasingly, private schools are equally being set up in the rural areas. A case in point is the Omega Schools founded by Ken and Lisa Donkoh, and James Tooley in 2008, backed by Pearson's Affordable Learning Fund with a sole mission to deliver quality education at the lowest cost on a grand scale in rural areas and town centres in Ghana. Whatever controversy that surrounds Omega Schools innovation of the 'Pay-As-You- Learn' privatization policy (Omega Schools 2014), there are still inequalities in the educational system.

There are inequalities and discrepancies between the cities and the rural schools. These inequalities apply to both private and public schools. Comparatively, the public basic education in the city is better than those within the rural areas as lack of basic amenities in the rural areas demotivates qualified and better teachers to take positions in these areas (Salifu et al. 2013; *Ghana Daily Graphic* 16 August 2013). For example, the government has 'embarked on a policy of one-child one laptop'. But children in the rural areas do not have access to electricity to power their laptops. Presently, in the urban areas, one in ten children lives in a household with either a laptop or desktop while in rural areas it is one in a hundred (Ghana National Population Statistics 2010). Inequitable distribution of social amenities have concentrated good public and private schools in the urban centres and determines the future prospects of many innocent children.

Private education is as old as the introduction of education in Ghana. What is new is that to get a good basic education means attending a private school. The discrepancies between urban and rural education, be it in the private or public sectors, have become too obvious to many in the rural areas and some have started setting up their own private schools to provide similar quality basic education in rural communities. A case in point is the private school of Paulina set up for poor children in a rural community near Accra where each pupil pays $500 per term. The school caters for 450 children and the aim is to provide education similar to that enjoyed by middle-class children. The fee is meagre in comparison to many other private schools in the urban centres where parents pay up to $3000 per term. In fact, Omega Schools providing private education on the Pay-As-You-Learn model charge as low as 'all-inclusive daily fees of about 65 US cents' (Omega School 2014). On face value the Omega Schools' private fees are a bargain! However, in a country where the majority of people live on nearly less than a dollar a day is private education the solution to the provision of Ghana's basic education?

Supporters of private schools argue that their creation is partly responsible for Ghana's progress toward achieving universal primary education for all. Opponents point out that the money families spend on private-school fees could be better spent on health, food, water and shelter, if they took advantage of the free government schools. For the poorest Ghanaian families, it has been observed that even enroling a child in a low-fee private school would amount to about a third of their household income (Lewin 2013). But a recent survey of poor families who send their wards to private school found that poor parents view the government schools as poorly managed. There is little teacher accountability, and the schools are 'insensitive' to parents' concerns (ibid.). This ongoing debate demonstrates the ambivalence that surrounds Ghanaian education. By the Act of Parliament basic education ought to be free and compulsory (Ghana Education Act 2008). But how 'free' is the compulsory basic education in Ghana if private schools are replacing the public?

It appears there is support within government circles for a shift from state-funded public basic schools to private schools. The assumption is that the private sector provides opportunities for 'decentralization', and there is more efficiency, proper school governance, management and accountability; particularly as private schools are directly accountable to fee-paying parents. (Presently, it is estimated that 25 per cent of Ghanaian pupils are enroled in private schools.) It seems various political parties trumpeting the vision of compulsory free quality basic education that comprises: 'kindergarten, primary and junior high for between the ages of 4–14years' (GES Basic Education Brief 2014) are coming to the realization that the nation cannot afford compulsory free education for all.

'Free compulsory basic education' has become so unsustainable that head teachers of public schools wishing to give good basic education to their pupils so that they can compete with their peers in the private sectors are charging fees. But this is constitutionally illegal. Recently, the Minister for Ghana Education Service, Professor Jane Opoku-Agyemang warned heads of schools against the charging of illegal fees. The Minister pointed out: 'while the government is working very hard to bring down the cost of basic education it is important that heads of schools do not use other unapproved means to raise the cost of education' (*Adom News* 21 May 2013). It is true that, officially, head teachers of public schools providing basic education are not supposed to charge fees. But the reality is that for many parents who cannot afford sophisticated and expensive private basic education for children to get ahead in life, their children's future is inextricably linked with paying an 'unofficial' contribution towards their children's education in the public sector, despite the constitutional arrangement of 'free compulsory education' which in all reality is unaffordable.

The President of Ghana, John Mahama has been very open about the unaffordability of the free compulsory basic education for all children. The President is of the view that part of the reason for a near-collapse of Ghana's basic education is the 'compulsory free education' that the nation is attempting to provide all children (*Ghana Daily Graphic* 2014). Dr Paa Kwesi Nduom, the leader of the Progressive People Party, has re-echoed the President's positions. Dr Nduom argues that President Mahama's view by-passes the constitutional requirement of 'free compulsory basic education'. But the reality and factual evidence on the ground indicate that the nation cannot afford compulsory free education. As Dr Ndoum puts it: 'Give me new facts and I will change my mind. Only a fool does not change his mind on evidence of new facts' (*Ghana Daily Graphic* 3 March 2014). The debate whether there should be free compulsory education is ongoing but it demonstrates the inconsistency between policy and practice that characterizes Ghanaian education.

The inconsistency is even more visible in the area of Inclusive Education and Special Educational Needs. The official education policy suggests that the delivery of education to young people with disabilities and special educational needs is informed by three guiding principles: 1) the right to education; 2) the right to equality of educational opportunities; 3) the right and obligation to be included in and participate fully in the affairs of society (Ghana Ministry of Education 2010). But public awareness on disability issues and special educational needs is very poor. The disabled population in Ghana is estimated at 10 per cent of the total population, which equates approximately 2.2 million people. Yet, people with disabilities face many forms of exclusion in society as well as in education. As Slikker observes: 'although disability policies exist on paper, the implementation is very limited and awareness of the Disability Act is low amongst society and people with disabilities themselves' (Slikker 2009: 10). Disability is often equated with educational inability. This thinking about disability results in several barriers for people with disabilities and forms of exclusion and discrimination, which have in turn influenced the self-confidence of many people with disabilities. Out of 400 people who were interviewed in the Eastern, Volta and Central Regions of Ghana in 2009 who were all above primary and secondary school age (11–18) 45.5 per cent have never had the opportunity to access primary or secondary education (ibid.).

Senior secondary schools: Three years (ages 15-18)

Part of the paradox of Ghana's education system is that whereas publicly funded basic schools are treated with scorn, perceived to be poor in their performance, the desire of every parent is to send his/her child to the traditional publicly funded elitist senior secondary schools. There are 670 senior secondary schools in Ghana, 493 public and 177 private. 156,743 and 17,949 students have enroled in public and private senior secondary schools respectively (Ministry of Education, Senior High School Report 2013).

Despite the huge number of senior secondary schools, there are few selective schools that parents wish their children and wards to attend. These schools include Mfanstipim, Adisadel, Achimota, St Augustine's, Wesley Girls, Prempeh Senior Secondary, St Johns College, Ghana Secondary Technical, Holy Child Girls', Presbyterian Boys Secondary, and a few others in the regional capitals and towns. The observation of the present writer is that the competition to get into these schools is very high; parents who wish to send their children to these elitist secondary schools must make sure that their children possess impeccable exams results, and they are connected to 'a big man' or 'big woman' in the country who belongs to the old boy or old girl association of the school selected. Old boys and girls contribute substantial sums to their alma mater and are often given preferential treatment when it comes to admission (Ghana *Daily Graphic* 27 September 2013). So accessibility to an elitist public school demands, on the one hand, a huge capital and social investments on the part of the parent, and on the other, hard work on the part of the child in private schools paid for by the parents. Parents sending their children to private schools for their initial basic education are more likely to have access to the best public senior secondary schools.

Tertiary education: Four years (ages 18-22)

Perhaps the biggest question facing Ghanaian tertiary education is: what is it for? The assumption that underpins present senior secondary education is that it must lead the students to a university degree or Higher National Diploma, hence, the content of the senior secondary curriculum does not make allowance for those who do not have the academic abilities to proceed to university. Yet, presently, only half of the Senior Secondary graduates proceed to University, Teacher Training or Polytechnic (Ghana Ministry of Education 2010). Whatever happens to the other 50 per cent is not clear. Current secondary and tertiary education does give serious attention to vocational and technical training. Vocational and technical education have always been perceived as inferior to general academic education. As Aryeetey et al. observe, there is a widely held perception 'that only people who are academically weak undertake technical and vocational education' (Aryeetey et al. 2011: 2). The focus within tertiary education appears to be to produce graduates who will take up 'white collar' jobs (Forster 2002) which are increasingly becoming difficult to find in Ghana.

Future of Ghana's education system

Ghana's education system is presently characterized by paradoxes, ironies and inconsistencies between policies and practice, the future of the education system, therefore depends on how the nation clarifies and addresses the various issues raised. Education policy makers need to address some key questions.

First, can the state provide free compulsory basic education for all children? Ghana cannot continue to depend on donor agencies for the provision of basic education for her citizens. Central government needs to collect taxes to finance public services including the provision of 'free compulsory education'. However, a majority of the graduates who should be in employment and paying taxes are unemployed. Where will the needed funds come from?"

Second, what is the link between tertiary education and the economic needs of Ghanaians? Policy makers and educators need to address this with all alacrity. It has been observed that there is a mismatch between tertiary education and the needs of industries (Aryeetey et el. 2013). There are skills, including those needed by competent teachers, administrators, accountants, medical doctors, researchers, responsible, visionary and accountable leaders, engineers, mechanics and strategists that are highly needed in the private and public sectors to drive the nation's developmental and economic vision forward. But the tertiary education sector continues to produce graduates who often lack abilities to analyse data/situations and propose solutions. Tertiary education is not producing students with creativity, imagination, innovation, and technical skills or graduates who are able to take responsibility for their own actions and inactions.

Finally, the future of Ghanaian education hugely depends on how the government and nation as a whole perceives the teachers. Teachers are often excluded from the decision-making process during educational reforms and national developmental strategies and they are badly remunerated. Despite their important contribution to society, teachers are peripheral in most national educational reform initiatives (Osei 2008). But as Owusu-Mensa observes 'teachers must be made to feel recognised and motivated, so that the country's educational system could play its role of being the key to the door of our development' (*Ghana Daily Graphic* 2013).

It is not uncommon for a Ghanaian parent to discourage a bright child from becoming a teacher. It is as if the whole nation has forgotten that lawyers, researchers, professors, medical doctors, engineers, politicians and all those glittering careers that are viewed to be the channel of social, political, and economic power owe their beginnings to teachers teaching young people how to read and count. Education for education's sake, learning just for the pleasure of learning new things and, pursuing a career with the view to contributing to the common good of the nation rather than having access to wealth and influence ought to be inculcated into the whole citizenry for the future of Ghanaian education – basic, secondary and tertiary levels to be effective.

Conclusion

Ghana's education system is shrouded in ambivalence, paradoxes, ironies and inequalities. To address these enigmas, the government needs to be clear about the nation's policy of 'free compulsory basis education'; the nation needs to address the link between education and the labour market needs and to take teachers seriously.

References

Afenyadu, D., King, K., McGrath, S., Oketch, H., Rogerson, C. and Visser, K. (2011). *Learning to Compete: Education, Training and Enterprise in Ghana, Kenya and South Africa*. Edinburgh: Centre for African Studies, University of Edinburgh.

Akyeampong, E. (1996). 'What's in a drink? Class struggle, popular culture and the politics of Akpeteshie (local gin) in Ghana, 1930–67'. *The Journal of African History*, 37 (2): 215–36.

Ampiah, J. G. and Adu-Yaboah, C. (2011). *Understanding the Social and Economic Lives of Never-enroled Children: A Case Study of Communities in Northern and Southern Ghana*, Accra: Ghana Education.

Aryeetey, E. (2013). 'Jobs are our greatest worry', *Business and Financial Times*. Ghana.

Asante, F. (2011). 'State of the Ghanaian Economy 2010', *Business and Financial Times*, Ghana, September.

Bartels, F. L. (1965). *The Roots of Ghana Methodism*. Accra: Ghana Methodist Press.

Bawakyillenuo, S., Akoto, I.O., Ahiadeke, C., Bortei-Doku Aryeetey, E. Agbe, E.K. (2013). Tertiary Education and Industrial Development in Ghana, Accra: University of Ghana.

Blackmore, K. P. (1975). 'Resistance to formal education in Ghana: Its implications for the status of school leavers'. *Comparative Education Review* 19 (2): 237-51.

Busia, K. A. (1969). *Purposeful Education for Africa*. The Hague: Mouton.

Evans-Anfom, E. (1986). *Report of the Education Commission on Basic Education 1986*. Accra, Ghana Ministry of Education.

Foster, P. J. (2002). 'The vocational school fallacy revisited: education, aspiration and work in Ghana 1959-2000'. *International Journal of Educational Development*, 22 (1): 27-8.

Ghana Ministry of Education (1974). *Report of the Education Advisory Committee on the Proposed New Structure and Content of Education for Ghana*. Accra, Ghana Ministry of Education.

—(1986). *Educational Strategic Plan*. Accra, Ghana Ministry of Education.

—(2009). *One-Year Implementation of Education Reform*. Accra, Ghana Ministry of Education.

—(2010). *Educational Strategic Plan*. Accra, Ghana Ministry of Education.

—(2013). *Senior High School Report*. Accra, Ghana Ministry of Education.

Ghana Daily Graphic. 21 July 2013.

Ghana Daily Graphic. 16 August 2013.

Ghana Daily Graphic. 30 October 2013.

Ghana Daily Graphic. 27 September 2013.

Ghana Daily Graphic. 25 February 2014.

Ghana Daily Graphic. 3 March 2014.

Ghana Daily Mirror. 16 August 2013.

Ghana Education Act 2008, Accra, Parliament of Ghana.

Ghana Education Finance Brief, 2012, Accra, Ghana Ministry of Education.

Ghana Education Service Basic Education Brief, 2014.

Ghana Government White Paper, 2010.

Ghana National Population Statistics, 2010. *Ghana National Population Statistics 2010*. Accra: Ghana Statistical Service.

Graham, C. K. (1971). *The History of Education in Ghana From Earliest Times to the Declaration on Independence*. Abingdon: Frank Cass and Company Ltd.

Hurd, G. E and T. J. Johnson. (1967). Education and Social Mobility in Ghana, *Sociology of Education*, 40, (1): 55-79.

Jeffries, R. (1975). 'The Labour Aristocracy? Ghana Case Study', *Review of African Political Economy*, (3): 59-70.

Lewin, K. (2013). *Consortium for Research on Educational Access, Transitions and Equity*. Accra: CREATE.

Mackenzie, P. J. and Walker. J. (2013). *Global Campaign for Education Brief, Mother-tongue Education: Policy Lessons for Equality and Inclusion*. Johannesburg: Rosebank.

Oduro, A. D. (2000). *Basic Education in the Post-Reform Period, Accra Centre for Policy Analysis*. Accra: Ghana Ministry of Education.

Omega Schools Franchise Ltd (2014) Available from http://www.omega-schools.com

Opoku-Agyemang, J. (2013). *Adom News*. 21 May 2013.

Ouane, A. and Glanz, C. (2010). *Why and How Africa Should Invest in African Languages and Multilingual Education*. Hamburg: UNESCO Institute for Lifelong Learning.

Owusu-Ansah, W. (2012), 'Entrepreneurship education, a panacea to graduate unemployment in Ghana?' *International Journal of Humanities and Social Science* 2 (2): 361–9.

Osei, G. M. (2008). 'Career ladder policy for teachers: the case of Ghana'. *International Review of Education* 54, (1): 5–31.

Population Census Report of Ghana, 2000. Accra, Ghana Statistical Service.

Population Census Report of Ghana, 2010. Accra, Ghana Statistical Service.

Robertson, C. (1984). 'Formal or nonformal education? Entrepreneurial women in Ghana'. *Comparative Education Review*, 28, (4): 639–58.

Slikker, J. (2009). *Attitudes towards Persons with Disability in Ghana*. Accra: Voluntary Service.

UNICEF (2007). *Achieving Universal Primary Education in Ghana by 2015: A Reality or Dream*. New York: UNICEF.

UNICEF Ghana (2006). 'Abolition of school fees', *Issue Briefing Note* (9), July 2006.

11

Ghana: Education Financing

Ato Essuman

Introduction

The quality of education has been a major agenda for discussion at both national and international fora. The debate has not only heightened in recent times but assumed considerable attention by the developing world, particularly, when it is considered that the percentage developing countries spend on education is about two times as that spent by OECD countries on education, yet the quality of education and achievement are consistently on the decline in many developing countries (Mourshed et al. 2010). This raises questions that require critical analysis, which includes the need for increased financing for education, but more importantly, how these funds are allocated and utilized. In this chapter, I examine the path that education financing in Ghana has taken in the last five decades. I begin by looking at issues of education financing from different perspectives, the history and development of education financing in Ghana and sources and trends of education financing. A section of the chapter is focused on development partner contributions to education and aid effectiveness. Issues about sustainability and resource allocation are also highlighted and discussed. I conclude the chapter with some feasible financing choices as Ghana strives to make education a major contributor to its development aspirations. Although the chapter focuses on Ghana, there are obviously some implications and messages for countries in sub-Saharan Africa since many of them have shared similar aspirations as Ghana.

Methodology

The aim of this paper is to establish a documentary review of education financing and its effectiveness in Ghana. It is a reflective analysis rooted in both historical and contemporary expressions of the evolution of education financing in Ghana over five decades by means of participant observation and documentary analysis. As a past 'insider' of education policy formulation and management, in the capacity as the Chief Director of the Ministry of Education, I located and reviewed extensively documents from the Ministry of Education, the Ministry of Finance and other governmental reports, including government White Papers on various Commissions on education. It also involved the review of journal articles on education financing in general and as they related to Ghana in particular. Studies commissioned by the government of Ghana and development partners were also examined. In a number of cases discussions were held with some stakeholders to gain further insights on issues and their various perspectives.

Education financing: Issues and perspectives

Issues about education financing have been dominant in the human development literature across the world with the State being the biggest financier of education. In OECD countries for example, on the average, 83 per cent of all funds in the education sector comes from public sources (OECD 2011), while in sub-Saharan Africa the state funds 70.8 per cent at primary level, 53.5 per cent at secondary level and 78 per cent at tertiary level of education expenditure (Mourshed et al. 2010). The reason for the increasing role of the state in the financing of education has been attributed to the positive social impact derived from education as well as ideologies and priorities of governments, even though in some cases development partners have influenced such decisions.

The levels of commitment shown by African governments in financing education reflect the level of expenditure as a percentage of GDP, which has generally been on the increase. Akyeampong (2010) acknowledges the massive injection of financial capital into education by governments in Africa, but is quick to point out that despite these injections, there still exist a large number of disadvanted people who are still excluded from accessing education. He calls for a more direct chanelling of funds to institutions and individuals who need them most, as an effective way of overcoming the cost barrier in education and argues that funding should not only be about how much is given out, but how such monies are utilized. Yamda (2005), citing the examples of Kenya, Tanzania and Ethiopia, reports however, that teachers' salaries took up the largest chunk of recurrent education expenditure.

Lewin (2006) contends that there is a lack of attention to secondary education. He highlights the disparities in terms of sector financing in education in sub-Saharan Africa, pointing out that many countries in the region often put more resources into funding primary and tertiary education than education at the secondary level and advise that correcting this imbalance would have a more positive impact on the needed growth that will aid access to education by all.

The funding capacity of most African governments has led to the increasing growth of non-governmental/private schools in Africa (Lewin and Sayed 2005) thus making the case for external funding – private and donor support. Wise (2012) and Casely-Hayford et al. (2007), however highlight the effect of the erratic and unreliable nature of donor support for education in Africa that often adds to the funding gap in education, thus, affecting aid effectiveness.

The principle guiding the spending of public resources on education has been that education is a public good, i.e. its benefits are for all in society. This principle is premised on the evidence of the human capital theory that states that, human capital is crucial for the growth of an economy. Thus, by inference, investment in education is seen as an investment that will benefit the futures of societies and nations (UNESCO 2002).

Global studies by the World Bank have also shown that the unit cost of higher education is about 60 times higher than that of primary education (World Bank 1988). Similarly in Ghana, in 2010, the cost of educating a student at the tertiary level as against educating a student at the primary level was nine times higher– GHS1,932: GHS213 (MOE 2012). Higher education has thus become a target for cuts in economies, aiming at implementing greater austerity measures. Therefore, there has always been an urge from donors and international community to countries in the developing world, particularly, in sub-Saharan Africa to reduce government spending at the higher level and focus more resources on primary education, which has higher returns. The World Bank views this as a more justified way of efficiently and equitably allocating resources (Youssef 2005). On the back of such evidence, the World Bank has argued that many countries have misallocated resources to sub sectors of education by increasing spending on secondary and tertiary education (Azcona et al. 2008).

The changing position of the World Bank is reflected in its study titled – 'Higher Education in Developing Countries: Peril and Promise', (World Bank

2000a) which questions the use of traditional economic models that have very limited understanding of the importance of higher education in determining the allocation of resources in education. They argue that using a model that only sees the contribution of people by the taxes they pay and their higher wages are not a true reflection of what pertains in the real world. The contributions of higher education are far-reaching and lie at the heart of every economic development. In reality, regardless of the higher unit cost in higher education, it is instructive to note that for sub-Saharan Africa to develop, there is a need for the indigenous capacity of its people to be developed. The full potential of education will only be felt on the socio-economic development of countries if greater attention is given to higher education.

Over the past few decades, decentralization has become one of the most debated policy issues throughout both the developing and the developed worlds (Faguet and Sanchez 2006). It is seen as central to national development efforts and is placed squarely in the foreground of policy discourse in many countries (Essuman and Akyeampong 2011). This debate has been extended to whether to centralize or decentralize issues about funding of education. Proponents of decentralized funding and management of education have argued that decentralization brings together beneficiaries and policy makers which results in a more efficient management of resources, improves quality and creates spaces for local people's participation (World Bank 2000b; Essuman and Bosumtwi-Sam 2010). Critics of decentralized education funding argue that it often leads to the widening of inequalities.

Historical development of education financing in Ghana

As the first independent country in sub-Saharan Africa, Ghana, propelled by ideology, self-determination and a new national identity, pursued a rapid primary education expansion under the 'Universal Compulsory Education' programme, which started in 1952. This was followed by the expansion of secondary, technical and tertiary education expansion through the opening of several schools and two new universities (Kwame Nkrumah University of Science and Technology and the University of Cape Coast). Riding on the euphoric wave of freedom and self-determination, the newly independent Ghana tried to conceptualize education as a vehicle for crystallizing new national goals and visions (McWilliam and Kwamena-Poh 1975).

The Education Act of 1961 sought to make primary and middle school education compulsory, universal and free. Section 21(1) of the 1961 Education Act, stipulates that, 'No fee, other than the payment for the provision of essential books or stationery or materials required by pupils for use in practical work, shall be charged in respect of tuition at a public primary, middle or special school' (GoG 1961). There was however no mention of the fees to be charged at the higher levels of education. The Act further defined the roles of the central and local government and the various aspects of the education expenditure each was to take care of. The central government was to foot the wages of teachers whereas the local assemblies were responsible for the building and maintenance of classrooms and other education infrastructure.

The military regime that took over from Nkrumah's government in 1966 maintained existing funding policies (Pola 2008). However, in 1969 the Busia Government's attempt to introduce a loan scheme at the University level to students who hitherto were enjoying free education was very unpopular. This was the first attempt to introduce private financing into funding tertiary education in the country (Adu-Boahen 2010). Military dictatorship took over the reins of governance at various times between 1971 and 1992 and government spending on education during this period kept falling as a result of the high petroleum prices and low investment in the country due to lack of confidence in the military dictatorship by the international community (Thompson and Casely-Hayford 2008). Government expenditure on education fell from over 6.5 per cent of GDP in 1976 to 1.5 per cent in 1983 (World Bank 2004).

From the mid 1980s, Ghana's policy on education financing began to be influenced by market-oriented thinking, which was part of the IMF/World Bank demands calling for reduced public spending and cost recovery in education. These led to, for example, the institution of cost recovery measures across the sector and the setting up of the University Rationalization Committee to restructure university education in terms of content and funding. During this reform period, education came under strong international influence and education financing focused almost exclusively on primary (basic) education (Akyeampong 2010).

The issue of cost sharing was given real meaning when the student loan scheme was introduced in 1988 in public tertiary institutions. The scheme was improvised to become the Student Loan Trust in 2007 and was viewed as deferred cost sharing (Attuahene 2007). Cost sharing and fee paying in public universities triggered the participation of the private sector. Between 2004 and 2010, the number of private and public tertiary institutions shot up to 120, an increase of about 13-fold (World Bank 2011).

The 1992 Constitution also made provision for the establishment of the District Assembly Common Fund (DACF). This fund was to receive 5 per cent of the central government's revenue. In 2007 this was increased to 7.5 per cent. Furthermore, the laws governing the administration of the fund mandates that up to 20 per cent of the allocation be spent on education (Thompson and Casley-Hayford 2008).

With the introduction of the Ghana Education Trust Fund (GETFund) in August 2000, Ghana has managed a relatively successful diversification of funding for tertiary education. A percentage of Value Added Tax (2.5 per cent) is deducted and paid to the Fund for educational infrastructure, scholarships, loans to students, training and research.

Donor financing of education in Ghana

The World Bank and other donor community participation in education came within the broader context of economic reforms when Ghana adopted the Bank's Economic Recovery Program that called for major reforms within the Ghanaian economy in the early 1980's (Tuffuor 2005). This reform initiative had its own implications on education. Donor financing of education in Ghana comes in four main forms – direct allocation, technical support, consultancy services and budgetary support. About 10 per cent of governmental spending on education is allocated to investments, while close to 90 per cent is spent on services and other administrative areas.

Efforts towards a sector-wide approach and programmatic support for the sector at various times have not had any positive outcome and aid is still skewed towards a donor's own traditions and preferences. However, the stable political environment, the implementation of the Ghana Poverty Reduction Strategy 1 and the implementation of an education strategic plan in 2002, earned donor confidence and resulted in an appreciable level of donor support.

These notwithstanding, donor positions on some issues were uncompromising and sometimes created tensions and doubts as to who was really in charge and what interest donors pursue. The conflicting agenda of the Ministry per its Strategic Plan objectives and government agenda reflected by its White Paper on the recommendation on the 2007 Educational Reforms, triggered different stances that left no doubt regarding the weakness and the capacity of the Ministry in negotiating what it considered best in addressing its key objectives. For example, whereas the government White Paper clearly showed a bias on shifting attention to post basic education and skill training, the donor interest focused on the achievement of the MDGs, which had its focus on achieving universal primary education.

The extension of focus beyond primary education was also viewed as a contravention of Fast Track Initiative (FTI) guidelines that called for at least 50 per cent of budgetary allocation to be given to primary education. With budgetary allocation to primary education falling from 40 per cent in 2003 and 28 per cent in 2006, donors put a lot of pressure on the government of Ghana to reverse the trend (Palmer 2005). It is instructive to mention however, that regardless of the opposition raised, the government of Ghana stuck to its grounds and admonished the donors to respect its decision.

There were however, genuine concerns by the donor community. Deficits in capacity in executing the Ministry's own agenda as well as that of donor programmes was a key issue. In such circumstances, ownership became problematic as officials saw such projects/programmes as donor activities rather than the Ministry's. The frequency of attrition of political leadership did not give comfort to the donor community and this brought along the issue of trust. For example, within a period of ten years there were as many as seven ministers of education appointed. Again, decisions and approaches to educational issues were usually politically 'coloured'. Key officers at the bureaucracy are transferred or removed when new ministers are appointed or where there is a change in political leadership. Such practices do not only affect the preservation and reliability of institutional memory, but hamper the strengthening of institutions to carry on its mandate effectively from period to period and raises sustainability concerns. In such contexts, donors may not be entirely blamed for taking some of the positions they adopt to push some agenda already agreed with the Ministry.

Sources/trends of education financing in Ghana

Education in Ghana has been funded from mainly five sources. These include Government of Ghana's discretionary budget (GoG), Donor Funds, Internally Generated Funds (IGF) from educational institutions, Highly Indebted Poor Countries (HIPC/MDRI) Funds and the Ghana Education Trust Fund (GETFund).

Table 11.1 shows that the government of Ghana still remains the highest contributor, contributing at least 70 per cent of the education expenditure.

Table 11.1 Trends in education resource envelope and expenditure as a share of GDP and total public spending

Source	2008	2009	2010	2011
GoG	70.0%	74.96%	71.20%	71.90%
	1,219,028,427	1,461,721,144	1,825,819,889	2,563,391,576
Donor	5.77%	4.88%	2.52%	3.6%
	100,652,087	95,067,893	64,742,440	127,255,813
IGF	9.41%	10.80%	11.77%	9.9%
	164,097,989	210,524,567	302,013,754	354,288,649
GETfund	12.19%	7.72%	12.21%	14.5%
	212,541,633	150,636,100	313,283,250	518,486,027
HIPC/MDRI	2.71%	1.63%	2.30%	0.1%
	47,251,582	31,818,711	58,504,024	2,288,506
Total Education Expenditure	1,743,571,718	1,949,768,414	2,564,363,357	3,565,710,570
GDP[1]	30,179,000,000	36,598,000,000	46,232,000,000	57,013,000,000
Total Government Expenditure	9,538,244,209	8,756,146,694	11,532,209,320	13,837,325,330
Education Exp. as a % of GDP	5.8%	5.3%	5.5%	6.3%
Education Exp. as a % of GoG Exp.	18.3%	22.3%	22.2%	25.8%

Source: Ministry of Education

However, as indicated in Table 11.2 below 68.7 per cent was spent on personal emoluments/salaries in 2011. This resonates with Yamda's (2005) assertion that even though many African states appear to be spending more on education, a sizable portion of this is used to pay salaries. Clearly, this has implications on quality. Despite the high donor participation in the education sector, Table 11.1 shows that donor contribution to the entire education budget may appear insignificant. Donor support for the sector also appears erratic. The highest contribution by donors to the sector between 2008 and 2011 was less than 7 per cent in relative terms – 5.8 per cent in 2008. Since then, donor input into the education expenditure has gone as low as 2.5 per cent in 2010 and increasing to 3.6 per cent in 2011.

However, this is only one side of the story. Table 11.2 indicates the allocation of the GoG discretionary budget by expenditure item. Three out of the four expenditure items – personnel emoluments, administration and investments, represent about 85.2 per cent. Service, which represents expenditure on the core activities of education, has an allocation of only 14.8 per cent. Donor contribution to Service on the other hand, for 2011 was GHS97,469,383 representing

18.5 per cent of total expenditure on services. Even though there are other sources of funding applied towards Service, it is instructive to relate what GoG allocates to Service as against donor contribution, which is over 76.6 per cent of total donor contribution. Thus, even though donor support may seem relatively low in relation to the total education expenditure, its impact on quality teaching and learning (Service) cannot be overemphasized.

Table 11.2 Education resource envelope and item expenditure 2011

Sources	PE	Administration	Service	Investment	Total	%
GoG	2,450,824,393	41,114,714	17,469,398	53,983,071	2,563,391,576	71.9%
Donor			97,469,383	29,786,430	127,255,813	3.6%
IGF	–	45,855,049	307,437,490	996,110	354,288,649	9.9%
GETfund			99,645,410	418,840,617	518,486,027	14.5%
HIPC			2,288,506	–	2,288,506	0.1%
Total	2,450,824,393	86,969,763	524,310,187	503,606,228	3,565,710,570	1.00
%	68.7%	2.4%	14.7%	14.1%		

Source: Ministry of Education

Table 11.3 Trends in expenditure by level of education

Sources	2008		2009		2010		2011	
	Amt. (GH¢)	%	Amt. (GH¢)	%	Amt. (GH¢)	%	Amt. (GH¢)	%
Pre-school	65,901,027	3.8	60,272,779	3.1	72,036,051	2.8	103,391,337	2.9
Primary	613,661,054	35	594,950,694	30.5	715,160,506	27.9	1,234,146,460	34.6
JHS	292,419,320	16.8	297,665,072	15.3	370,235,825	14.4	411,648,553	11.5
SHS	171,058,251	9.8	337,369,027	17.3	400,030,646	15.6	526,809,606	14.8
TVET	18,311,207	1.1	35,038,819	1.8	38,436,313	1.5	126,982,366	3.6
SPED	10,662,566	0.6	7,493,238	0.4	17,214,633	0.7	19,149,996	0.5
NFED	6,327,284	0.4	3,715,031	0.2	13,357,023	0.5	15,154,167	0.4
Teacher Education	55,274,368	3.2	50,377,753	2.6	62,056,093	2.4	–	–
Tertiary	378,615,134	21.7	401,191,936	20.6	511,806,744	20	639,230,889	17.9
Mgt. & Subvtd	130,011,299	7.5	160,837,566	8.2	362,459,208	14.1	487,809,862	13.7
HIV-AIDS	1,330,209	0.1	856,499	0	1,570,316	0.1	1,387,335	0.04
Total	1,743,571,719	100	1,949,768,414	100	2,564,363,357	100	3,565,710,570	100

Source: Ministry of Education

This then opens up the debate on resource allocation, which is discussed at the next section. Other significant contributors to the education budget have been the GETFUND and Internally Generated Funds. The two sources contribute on the average more than 22 per cent of the education expenditure between 2008 and 2011.

Table 11.3 indicates that basic education receives the highest in the education expenditure (35 per cent), followed by tertiary (18 per cent) and secondary education (15 per cent). Commitment to technical and vocational education has been mere rhetoric by successive governments. This is reflected in resources allocated to the division over the years. With the exception of the year 2011, when it received an allocation of 3.6 per cent of total education expenditure, in prior years, allocation had been less than 2 per cent falling to its lowest in 2008, i.e. 1.1 per cent of total spending in education.

Feasible financing choices

In this section, I conclude by highlighting key financial options and suggest some feasible financial choices as Ghana strives to make education a major contributor to its development aspirations. In 2001, the Government of Ghana introduced subsidies at the Senior High School level with the view of reducing the burden on parents and guardians of wards in such schools. Recently (2012), there has been intensive debate on fee-free senior high school education in Ghana. While some see this as preposterous and unimaginable, others consider it as a poverty alleviation option and a panacea to providing the required cadre of youths with skills needed for the economic development of Ghana. Without getting into the debate of its feasibility or otherwise, what is clear is that it has enormous financial outlay implications, which give the signals about the need to rethink about feasible as well as sustainable choices of education resource allocation and more importantly, how such funds are utilized. In the discussions that follow, I will tease out specific areas of opportunity, discuss and offer choices that could impact on the sustainability of educational funding in Ghana.

Teacher issues and funding

Since the early 1980s equilibrium for the demand and supply of teachers has never been achieved even though many interventions have been made to address the numbers of professional teachers in schools. These include increase in the annual cohort of teacher trainee admissions, training for pupil teachers, sandwich and distance learning programmes. The World Bank Report on Education In Ghana (2011) presents the dwindling numbers of teachers in the last three years 2008–10) despite the scale of interventions and resources put into teacher training to shore up the numbers.

Again study leave has been available to Ghanaian teachers since 1997. At any one time, up to 15,000 teachers are enroled in universities full-time to study for degrees (World Bank 2011). The expectation is that teachers will return to teaching following the award of degrees. This largely, does not happen. The scheme is very expensive as teachers continue to be paid their full salaries for the duration and Government pays all fees and accommodation allowances. Additionally, 9,000 teacher trainees are admitted into the colleges of education annually and the full expenses borne by Government.

The funding of study leave for teachers and the payment of allowances to students in teacher training colleges are both anachronistic and non-productive since the majority of teachers so supported never return to teaching and merely see it as a stepping stone to greener pastures. For over a decade, the debate on study leave with pay has been raging on, but government after government appear not to have marshalled the political will to rationalize the scheme, while providing credible alternatives for continued professional educational development and Life Long Learning for teachers. Indeed the 2007 National Education Reform Implementation Committee (NERIC) teacher training sub-committee, specifically recommended abolition of study leave with pay.

The reality of the matter, however, is that unless the teaching profession becomes competitive, compared to many of the professional bodies, attrition will continue in greater numbers than we have ever witnessed. Though this may be a challenge it provides an opportunity. Within Ghana's own constitutional demands of providing education for all and the MDGs, the use of conventional access to teacher training may not produce the number of teachers needed to clear the over 25,000 professional teacher deficits. The scale of the challenge is huge and the educational system requires large numbers of teachers and a pedagogy that is different from the predominant chalk and talk, teacher-dominated approach that has bedevilled teaching for a long time (Anamuah-Mensah 2011).

Alignment of resource allocation to national priority goals

A key challenge Ghana faces is the alignment of the allocation of resources to national priority goals. Political considerations of successive governments seem to have driven allocation of resources for short-term political advantage than long-term development considerations. The question is, where should Ghana prioritize funding of education to maximize impact on economic development? Financial projections for the future clearly indicate that Ghana will still need the support of development partners to meet its education growth targets (MOESS 2007). For tertiary education, the challenge is to ensure that funding is targeted to coincide with government priority areas.

Currently, there is a mismatch between government priority and practice on the ground. Most of tertiary funding (universities and polytechnics) goes to support students pursuing liberal arts, humanities and business programmes. In state universities, the ratio of enrolment in humanities to science and technology-based programmes is about 65:35 falling short of the official government policy of 60:40 science to humanities (MOESS 2007).

What Ghana can celebrate is the contribution that the private sector is currently making to tertiary education, and the growing number of distance education and sandwich programmes on offer in universities. As private access expands, this will reduce pressure on state funds so that more of it can be channelled to support other education sectors. In addition, government perception about private entrepreneurs' participation in education should change from a position of suspicion of profit motivation only, to a position that would recognize them as partners/collaborators in education delivery. This would create fruitful engagement and enhance effective use of resources.

Improving the management of funds (GETFund and IGF)

It was indicated earlier that the GETFund and IGF together contribute over 22 per cent of the total resource envelope for education. In order to increase good returns on investments, it is important that the administration of the fund is insulated from political influences and dictation and rather aligns its utilization to reflect the educational development needs of the country.

Over 50 per cent of the internally generated funds are used on extra allowances to lecturers, procuring expensive vehicles, and other expenditure items that may not necessarily add value to effective education delivery. If a new policy framework is introduced and accountability improved, this could be an important resource to educational funding.

Conclusion

As I reflect on the issues raised, a central issue that resonates among all issues about education financing is funding adequacy and how funding requirement can be sustained in the midst of domestic challenges and dwindling donor support. Funding will never be enough and this calls for prudent use of resources, alignment of funding resources to national/education developmental goals and the pursuit of a policy of revenue diversification as a strategy for financing education. The challenge of limited funds availability in a developing world context should reorient policy makers to think more of pro-poor funding options, since policies that focus on equal opportunity for all may not necessarily be equitable in countries where wide gaps of income already exist.

References

Adu-Boahen, A. (2010). *Meeting the Financial Needs of Tertiary Students: the Role of Students Loan Trust Fund (SLTF)*. Kumasi: KNUST.

Akyeampong (2010). *Educational Expansion and Access in Ghana: A Review of 50 Years of Challenge and Progress.* Centre for International Education. University of Sussex, UK.

Anamuah-Mensah, J. (2011). *Creating Teachers for Tomorrow: Making Professional Development Work.* Available from WISE: http://www.wise-qatar.org/content/teacher-education-sub-saharan-africa-tessa-0 (accessed 12 October 2012).

Atuahene, F. (2007). *The Challenge of Financing Higher Education and the Role of Student Loans Scheme: An Analysis of the Student Loan Trust Fund (SLTF) in Ghana. Higher Education.* Kumasi: KNUST.

Azcona, G., Chute, R., Dip, F., Dookhony, L., Loyacano-Perl, D., Randazzo, D. (2008). *Harvesting the Future: The Case for Tertiary Education in Sub-Saharan Africa.* The Maxwell School of Syracuse University.

Casely-Hayford, L., Palmer, R., Thompson, M. N. and Ayamdoo, C. (2007). *Aid and Donor Partnerships in the Ghana Education Sector: A Critical Review of the Literature and Progress.* Accra: ResearchConsortium on Education Outcomes and Poverty (RECOUP).

Essuman, A. and Akyeampong, K. (2011). 'Decentralisation policy and practice in

Ghana: the promise and reality of community participation in education in rural communities'. *Journal of Education Policy* 26 (4) 513–27.

Essuman, A. and Bosomtwi-Sam, C. (2010). 'Decentralisation and the management of basic schools: a critical analysis of the management of the capitation grant scheme in Ghana'. *Ghana Journal of Education and Teaching* (GHAJET), 11, 33–48.

Faguet, J. P. and Sanchez, F. (2006). 'Decentralisation's Effects on Educational Outcomes in Bolivia and Colombia'. Available from http://sticerd.lse.ac.uk/dedps/47 (accessed 23 November 2008)

Government of Ghana Document (GoG) (1961). Ghana Education Act 1961. Accra.

Lewin, K. (2006). *Financing Secondary Education in Commonwealth Countries: New Challenges for Policy and Practicewea.* CREATE.

Lewin, K. and Sayed, Y. (2005). *Non-government Secondary Schooling in Sub-Saharan Africa. Exploring the Evidence in South Africa and Malawi.* London: DFID.

McWilliam, H. and Kwamena-Poh, M. (1975). *The Development of Education in Ghana.* London: Longman.

MOE (2012). *National Education Sector Annual Review (NESAR) Report.* Accra: Ministry of Education Science and Sports.

MOESS (2007). *Preliminary Education Sector Performance Report.* Accra: Ministry of Education Science and Sports.

Mourshed, M., Chijioke, C., and Barber, M. (2010, November). 'How the world's most improved school systems keep getting better.' Available from McKinsey and Company: http://www.mckinsey.com/client_service/social_sector/latest_thinking/worlds_most_improved_schools (accessed 11 November 2012).

OECD (2011). Education at a Glance 2011: OECD Indicators, OECD Publishing. http://dx.doi.org/10.1787/eag-2011-en (accessed February 2014).

Palmer, R. (2005). *Beyond the Basics: Post-basic Education and Training and Poverty Reduction in Ghana.* Edinburgh: Centre of African Studies, University of Edinburgh.

Pola, I. (2008). 'Great Pola Foundation'. Available from History of Education in Ghana: http://politicalpola.wetpaint.com/page/HISTORY+OF+EDUCATION+IN+GHANA (accessed 4 October 2012).

Thompson, N. M. and Casely-Hayford, L. (2008). *The Financing and Outcome of Education in Ghana.* Oxford: Research Consortium on Educational Outcomes and Poverty.

Tuffour, J. A. (2005). *Multi-Donor Direct Budget Support in Ghana: the Implication for Aid Delivery and Aid Effectiveness.* Accra: Center for Economic Policy Analysis (CEPA).

UNESCO (2002). *Financing Education – Investments and Returns.* Montreal: UNESCO.

Wise (2012). 'Funding education: new models for our times'. Available from http://www.wise-qatar.org/content/funding-education-new-models-our-times (accessed 9 September 2010).

World Bank (1988). *Education in Sub-Saharan Africa: Policies for Adjustment, Revitalization and Expansion*. Washington, DC: World Bank.

—(2000a). *Higher Education and Developing Countries: Peril and Promise*. Washington, DC: World Bank.

—(2000b). *Decentralisation: Rethinking Government*. New York: Oxford University Press.

—(2004). *Books, Buildings, and Learning Outcomes: An Impact Evaluation of World Bank Support to Ghana*. Washington, DC: World Bank.

—(2011). 14 November, available from 'University education should be a ladder out of poverty, World Bank vice president says'. Available from http://web.worldbank.org/WBSITE/EXTERNAL/COUNTRIES/AFRICAEXT/0,,contentMDK:23047662~menuPK:258659~pagePK:2865106~piPK:2865128~theSitePK:258644,00.html (accessed 11 November 2012).

Yamda, S. (2005). *Educational Finance and Poverty Reduction:The Cases of Kenya, Tanzania, and Ethiopia*. Tokyo: GRIPS Development Forum.

Youssef C. (2005). World Bank Priorities in Education Lending. A Graduate Journal of International Affairs. Volume 6, 1–29.

Guinea: An Overview of Higher Education

A. Tidjane Diallo, M. Kodiougou Diallo and Sékou Konate

Introduction

The competitiveness and the prosperity of a country depend to a large extent on the quality of its educational system in general, of its Higher Education, scientific research and ability to innovate.

Like anywhere in the world, the missions of the Higher Education in Guinea are the education, research and community service.

This chapter is based on reports written by the Higher Education Institutions and the Ministry of Higher Education and of Scientific Research as well as visits to universities and Institutes carried out between 2009 and 2012.

In what follows, we are going to address the site inventory of the Higher Education in Guinea and the vision of its development before defining some strategic objectives for the period 2013–20.

The following points will be developed:

- Context
- The great reforms from 1989 to 2012
- State of the Higher Education
- Vision and strategic objectives

Context

Salient points of physical, demographic, economic, political and educational contexts are emphasized in this section.

Physical, demographic and economic contexts:

The Republic of Guinea, a coastal country, is situated in West Africa with an area of 245 857 km². Its demography is characterized by a rapid growth of the population with great regional disparities. In fact, the total population went from 9.7 million inhabitants in 2007 to approximately 11.3 million in 2012 with an average annual growth rate of 3.1 per cent (equivalent to a doubling every 25 years) and constituted of 52 per cent of females and (44 per cent) of youth with an age group of either lower or equal to 15.

Despite important mining and agricultural potentialities and abundant rainfalls, Guinea is classified within the least advanced countries of the planet. In 2012, 58 per cent of the population lived under the poverty line against 53 per cent in 2007.

After a serious decrease between 2006 and 2010, the macroeconomic situation redresses from 2011.

The results of deployed efforts by Guinea have placed the economy on a direction of growth. In fact, the growth rate of the real GDP rose from 1.9 per cent in 2010 to 3.9 per cent in 2011 and 4.8 per cent in 2012.

In other respects, the strategy document of alleviating poverty recognizes a strategic role to education in general, and to the Higher Education in particular in the attainment of the Millennium Development Goals (MDG) and the improvement of living conditions of the population. It emphasizes an integrated approach of different public policies and it constitutes the reference frame of the governmental action and the partners' support to the development in Guinea.

Political context

Since independence in 1958 till 2010 the Republic of Guinea experienced different political regimes successively. Rebel attacks in 2000 at the country borders as well as social and political claims between 2006 and 2009 provoked violence detrimental to the economic and social development of the country. From democratic presidential elections held in 2010, Professor Alpha Conde was elected President of the country. At his inauguration on 21 December 2010, the President reiterated his willingness to transform Guinea by improving the governance and the quality of basic social services.

Education context:

Following the example of other sub-Saharan countries, the Republic of Guinea with the support of its partners is committed to the development and realization of universal primary education before 2015. The gross enrolment rate of schooling in primary education in 2012 was 81 per cent against 79 per cent in 2007/8. This rate was 45 per cent in the junior high school (33 per cent for girls) and 17 per cent in the senior high school (12 per cent for girls) in 2011–12.

Student enrolments in technical education and vocational training are insignificant compared to the demand. This form of education and training records only 19,000 registered students while senior secondary schools (lycées) record 181,000 students from 2011 to 2012. It is worth pointing out that lycées offer only three fields of study: mathematical sciences, experimental sciences and social sciences.

Common public expenditures devoted to the education sector oscillate around 2 per cent of the GDP. In 2011, those expenditures represented 18.2 per cent of the state budget while they were 30 per cent in some neighbouring countries like Senegal.

Concerning the distribution of the budget among different education orders, a decrease from 9 per cent in 2002 to 4 per cent in 2011 was noted for technical education and vocational training, and during the same period the budget of the higher education increased from 23 per cent to 37 per cent because of bursaries and social transfers in university grants.

Main reforms from 1989 to 2012

The evolution of higher education and scientific research in Guinea during the last 25 years is characterized by three fundamental reforms: the transformation of higher education institutions into administrative public establishments, the extension and the diversification of the network of higher education institutions, and the progressive change to the BMD system, i.e. Bachelor-Master-Doctorate.

The setting-up of higher education institutions into public establishments

Between 1989 and 1990, the existing two universities and the three higher institutes were transformed into public establishments with some autonomy of administrative, pedagogic and financial management. Although this autonomy was limited, it was perceived as a considerable progress compared to the previous situation of 1989, characterized by an excessive centralization of the process of decision making at the level of the Ministry of Higher Education and Scientific Research.

The extension and the diversification of the network

The increase in enrolments of those who passed the Baccalaureate, a consequence of the massive schooling in primary education and the explosion of numbers in secondary education has not been accompanied by an increase in the training capability in the higher education. Until 2003, only one-third of candidates who took the placement test, accessed higher education. To adjust this situation, the government took the following measures: to bring higher education institutions closer to beneficiaries by creating regional university centres, to promote the development of private higher education, to encourage distance training and to create professional programmes. The consequence of these arrangements has been an increase in public higher education institutions from 5 to 17 and private higher education institutions from 0 to about 40.

The Bachelor-Master-Doctorate reform

Considering the weak school-to-work transition of school leavers of the higher education institutions in the job market, it was decided in 2002 to undertake a huge curricular reform aiming at improving a graduate's employability. This reform of study programmes was carried out between 2005 and 2007 with the financial support of the World Bank and technical support of the University of Quebec in Montreal. According to international trends, this reform has been registered as soon as the start of the BMD system.

Thus, at the beginning of the academic year 2007/8, about 50 Bachelors programmes were offered to first-year students. The change to other grades was progressively conducted. The three reforms determined the size of the network of higher education as they are known today.

State of higher education and scientific research

The mission of the Ministry of Higher Education and of Scientific Research is: the conception, elaboration and implementation of government policy in the fields of higher education, scientific and technical research as well as technological innovation and ensuring evaluation and monitoring. To ensure its mission, the Ministry of Higher Education and Scientific Research has at its disposal:

- 17 institutions of public higher education among which 10 are situated outside Conakry. They cover the whole eight administrative regions of the country. This network includes three universities, three university centres and eleven higher institutes including one distance training institution.
- 39 operating private higher education institutions in 2012–13, i.e. an increase of four compared to the previous academic year. Thirty-five of them are located in Conakry;
- 30 institutions of research and documentation scattered throughout the country.

In this section, we examine issues regarding governance of the system and of institutions of higher education and scientific research, access to tertiary education, training, research, human resources, infrastructures, equipment and laboratories, IT and financial resources.

Governance

According to Decree N°93/PRG/SSG/2011 of 18 March 2011, the Ministry of Higher Education and Scientific Research includes four national departments: public higher education, private higher education, scientific research and technological innovation, university and scientific infrastructures.

The institutions of Higher Education and some research centres have slowly evolved and attained a certain form of autonomy. In this context, Decree N°175/PRG/SSG/ of 27 September 1989 relating to the status of Conakry and Kankan universities has served as a model for all other public institutions.

After several years of operation of bodies planned in this decree, shortcomings remain in the composition of the board of trustees that give priority to ministerial department representatives to the detriment of those of the socio-economic world.

On the operational plan, the exercise of essential allocations and responsibilities of the Ministry is shared out between several departments and technical services.

At the core level, bodies like the conference of rectors and general directors of public higher education institutions (CRDG), the Board of Directors of research institutions and the Chamber of the Higher Education of the Promoters Office of the Private Education are regularly consulted in order to solve problems like the admission of new successful students at the baccalaureate in the institutions and to share information and get their opinions on burning questions.

It turns out that the managerial training of the main institution leaders is not enough for responsibilities to be assumed in complex organizations. So, management based on results, several times stated by official speeches, is still delayed. Likewise, the vocational training of the staff of administrative and technical support includes numerous knowledge gaps. This requires academic executives at all levels to carry out secretariat assignments.

In other respects, the problem of reliable and available data on time is a handicap in the management of institutions and the steering of the Ministry. The statistic yearbooks of the Higher Education are sporadically published.

Access to undergraduate studies

Until 2005, the requirement to access graduate studies was passing a test opened to successful students at the baccalaureate of the three last sessions. The rate of admission to higher education has never gone beyond 45 per cent of candidates. In 2006, the Government took two major decisions, the first one, the suppression of this test and the second, to offer an education grant to young successful students at the baccalaureate who should be placed in private higher education institutions. The evolution of enrolments in the first year of IES

Table 12.1 Admission of successful students at the baccalaureate in higher education

Year	2004	2005	2006	2007	2008	2009	2010	2011	2012
Candidates number	26,269	26,84	32,586	9,029	23,955	22,822	19,998	13,062	27,021
Successful numbers	9,571	12,060	22,129	7,582	17,082	22,294	19,504	12,792	26,672
%	36.4%	44.7%	67.9%	84%	71.3%	97.7%	97.5%	97.9%	98.7%

Source: Conférence des Recteurs et Directeurs Généraux (CRDG), 2012

(higher education institution) is a tribute to the thoroughness with which the baccalaureate sessions are organized by the Ministry of Pre-University and Civic Education. Let us point out that from 2006, the majority of successful students at the baccalaureate were enroled in higher education. Attempts made in 2008 and 2010 to regulate this flow of students failed.

This table shows that due to the suppression of the access test to higher education which took place in 2006, the admission rate has increased to exceed 97 per cent since 2009.

Moreover, proportions of successful students at the baccalaureate in the social sciences have considerably increased from 2007. In fact, the table below shows that the proportion of students in the social sciences placed in the first year varied to a quarter of candidates in 2005 and to three-quarters in 2011. This situation complicates their placement in higher education and later their school-to-work transition.

Table 12.2 Numbers of successful students of social sciences, placed in the 1st year in the IES

Year	2004	2005	2006	2007	2008	2009	2010	2011	2012
Numbers	9,571	12,060	22,129	7,582	17,082	22,294	19,504	12,792	26,672
Social Sc. number	3,147	3,299	6,146	5,005	9,484	14,093	9,407	9,730	17,418
Social Sc. %	32.9%	27.4%	27.8%	66%	55.5%	63.2%	48.2%	76.4%	65.3%

Source: Conférence des Recteurs et Directeurs Généraux (CRDG), 2012

In other respects, the table below shows that Conakry regrouped almost half of the candidates to higher education in 2012:

Table 12.3 Statistics of candidates by selection centre in 2012

Center	Boké	Conakry	Faranah	Kankan	Kindia	Labé	Mamou	N'Zerekore	Total
Number	1,762	13,274	1,331	2,001	3,658	1,467	1,031	2,557	27,081
%	6.51%	49.02%	4.91%	7.39%	13.51%	5.42%	3.81%	9.44%	100%

Source: Conférence des Recteurs et Directeurs Généraux (CRDG), 2012

Note that 2011 and 2012 sessions of the baccalaureate recorded respectively rates of success of 21.27 per cent and 33.33 per cent.

Training

Curricula

The majority of the curricula in force in the IES have been elaborated in the context of the BMD system after consulting representatives of professional sectors of reference. seventy-five programmes of Bachelor, about 20 for the Master's Degree and seven of specialty in medicine, pharmacy and odonto-stomatology are offered in public higher education institutions. The same programmes of Bachelor Degree are adopted in private higher education institutions. However, most of the private higher education institutions offer only programmes of Law, Political Sciences, Economic Sciences, Business Administration, Marketing, Sociology, Computing and English putting aside Sciences and Engineering.

Doctorate theses defences are scanty. Only two defences of theses took place in 2011, one in Mathematics and the other in Biology. In 2012, no defence of doctorate thesis took place. Five doctorate-awarding schools have just been created. To exactly develop, they necessitate a consistent follow-up spread through several years. The proportion of students reading for the Master's Degree and Doctorate is low. To illustrate, Sonfonia University with 18,874 students counts only 287 students of post-graduate studies, that is to say 1.52 per cent of its number.

For some years, some professional Bachelors were offered at the Polytechnic Institute of the University of Conakry, the Higher School of Tourism and Hotel Industry, the Institute of Geology and Mines of Boké and the Technology Higher Institute of Mamou.

The lack of study spaces and the numerical inadequacy of teaching personnel reduce considerably the duration Bachelor students have to be present on campus. Most public institutions offer only three days (15 to 20 hours of course) per week of contact with teachers, and private institutions four days/week.

In the curricula that include training periods, students are confronted with enormous difficulties of placement because of huge sizes which largely go beyond the control capabilities of most small and medium-size enterprises. The relationships between universities and enterprises are very weak.

An evaluation of the Bachelor curricula implementation of the LMD system has just been carried out by Guinean experts with the financial support of UNESCO. If the curricula have been elaborated with the required expertise, their implementation met a lot of difficulties (large groups of students, lack of alignment between objectives, teaching and learning strategies and assessment of students).

Students

During the academic year 2010–11, 77,049 students were registered in the 17 public IES of which 17,858 were girls, 26,143 students of which 9,998 were girls and 95 were foreigners registered in the private higher education. In total, there were 103,192 students among whom 26,656 were girls (26.8 per cent) and 1,352 were foreigners (1.3 per cent). The latter are mainly concentrated in graduate studies and departments of Medicine and Pharmacy. In 2005–6, the IES counted only 42,711 students among whom 9,119 girls, i.e 21.3 per cent of the number. Thus, from 2006 to 2011, i.e in five years, numbers multiplied by 2.4!

As the majority of successful students at the baccalaureate were from the Social Sciences field of study, it was not surprising to notice that 22.9 per cent and 13.6 per cent registered respectively in the Faculties of Arts and Human Sciences and Political and Law Sciences. Moreover, economic sciences and management programmes attract more students than technical sciences (21.30 per cent against 13.3 per cent).

In other respects, the level of successful students at the baccalaureate is weak especially in French the language of instruction. As far as students are concerned, they complain about the little use of drawing software and information technologies and of communication in their training.

The school- to-work transition of young graduates runs into numerous obstacles some of which are the weakness of the private sector and the inadequate skills of school leavers according to prospective employers. An obvious inconsistency to be noted is between the training offered in higher education and the needs of the job market. Following a study cited by the AGUIPE in 2000, the urban unemployment rate of youth from 25 to 29 years old was 61.5 per cent for higher education graduates.

To conclude this sub-section, it should be noted that about 2,500 students continue their studies abroad through co-operation agreements with partner countries. Those students experience severe delays in the payment of their bursaries putting them in difficult situations. In addition to this government support, a lot of students are supported abroad by their parents. For example, in France, their number was estimated at 3,000 in 2010.

Scientific research

Scientific research is carried out in public higher education institutions, centres and research institutes. The size of the latter is very varied. There is a proliferation of small institutions without any real link with universities and with the socio-economic environment.

The IES grant part devoted to research is insignificant. This prevents the implementation of long-term research programmes that are impactful. Most of the research is individually conducted for the promotion to a higher academic grade or the obtaining of a degree (DES, Master's etc.). Some refereed journals are regularly published at Gamal Abdel Nasser University (UGANC), General Lansana Conte University (UGLC), Agricultural Higher Institute of Faranah (ISAF), Pasteur Institute of Guinea (IPG) and at the Scientific Research Center of Conakry-Rogbane (CERESCOR). However, most of them are not listed in the abstracts. Research institutions receive subsidies inadequate to undertake significant research projects. However, some of them succeed in obtaining published articles in the national and foreign journals. The valorization of research findings and innovation encounters a major difficulty, which is that numerous obtained patents during the last ten years have not been exploited.

Some institutions manage to get consultancy contracts with enterprises or development partners. But, there are very few institutions that secure these contracts at the institutional level since academics and researchers prefer to negotiate individual contracts and not through their institution.

Human resources

The teaching staff, estimated at 2,384 in the public sector in 2010–11 is inadequate. While female teachers (139) represent 5.8 per cent, doctorate holders represent less than 19.6 per cent of the total number. The teaching assistants who constitute three-quarters of the personnel have either a Master's degree or the Higher Studies Diploma. Moreover, the most qualified personnel proportion of this total number is aging. The average age of doctorate holders is 58. These lecturers teach not only in the public but also in the private institutions. It should be noted that the pupil-teacher ratio is estimated at 32:1.

Between 2006 and 2011, the composition of the faculty deteriorated in the public sector. Doctorate holders represented 27.9 per cent of this faculty in 2006 against 19.6 per cent in 2011 and professors and associate professors 16.4 per cent against 9.9 per cent. Students in private higher education institutions were trained in 2011 by 1,490 teachers, most of them permanent employees of public institutions.

The recruitment and promotion of research lecturers and Guinean researchers are organized autonomously by the National Committee of Recruitment and of

Promotion (CNRP) on the basis of defined criteria and procedures mandated in Decree N°176/PRG/SSG of 27 September 1989 regarding positions in Higher Education and Scientific Research and the particular status of their holders.

Available jobs in public IES are not filled by call of nomination, but internal co-optation then validated by the CNRP. This is contrary to international practices.

The teacher-researcher role is far from being attractive because the career plan is not stimulating, and it explains the exodus of the most talented young teachers to the private sector.

Numerous teachers in higher education are obliged to take jobs in the private IES in order to supplement their earnings. This complicates management issues within their institution of origin. This prospect discourages young people from a teaching career. Consequently, there is an urgent need to renew the faculty to deal with massive retirement, the expansion of the system and requirements of the BMD system.

Public IES employ 681 civil servants in the administration and 936 maintainers. As far as private IES are concerned, they utilize 461 people in the administration and 338 maintainers.

It is worth pointing out that enrolments of the technical, pedagogical and administrative support staff are insufficient so that the most qualified teacher researchers are obliged to carry out subordinate assignments.

Infrastructures, equipment, laboratories and TIC

Infrastructures are insufficient compared to needs.

The age and lack of laboratory equipment and consumables constitute serious challenges in most institutions. Internet connection and facilities are not well spread in public higher education and research institutions. Private IES have more computers compared to public ones. Most attempts of internet connection with V-SAT antennas ran into high costs. Thus, the deployment of fibre optics first in Conakry, then in the up country is seen with great hope.

Recurrent shortage of electricity and water hinders the activities of institutions of higher education and research.

Documentary resources

Documentary resources are insufficient. There is less than one book per student in the libraries. To enhance the documentation level, some institutions have bought books from their own funds, and most have recourse to gifts from NGOs, Embassies, private people and foreign institutions.

Finances

Education expenses are in general very weak compared to those of the sub-region. In Guinea, they decreased from 3.6 per cent of the GDP in 2009 to 2.3 per cent of the GDP in 2011. During the last ten years, the budget of higher education in the education budget increased from 23 per cent in 2002 to 37 per cent in 2011. This evolution was due to the weight of social aids granted to both students of the public and the private higher education institutions. The amount of bursaries represents 38 per cent in average of the budget of the public higher education institutions according to the 2012 initial budget act.

To avoid compromising the quality of training, it would be convenient to find acceptable strategies of drastic abatement of this proportion. Social assistances to students represent less than 20 per cent of university grants in most African English-speaking countries.

The amount of public grants awarded to public IES depend fundamentally on the number of their students. The type of curriculum is not taken into consideration. This situation creates difficulties for scientific, technical and medical channels.

Financial management procedures are embodied in a manual. Frequent audits have been organized in 2011 by competent authorities to ensure conformity to regulations and the reliability of the reported requirement concerning the number of students.

The table below shows the evolution of the IES and IRS budget from 2005 to 2012.

Table 12.4 Evolution of the IES and CR budget from 2005 to 2012 (in thousands of Guinean francs)

Year	IES and IRS Budget	State budget	IES and IRS budget part in the GDP
2005	32,563,000	1,680,454,050	0.32%
2006	51,619,980	3,109,992,534	0.34%
2007	106,539,135	3,440,392,462	0.54%
2008	120,733,845	3,998,309,691	0.51%
2009	157,960,645	4,614,247,940	0.66%
2010	282,039 945	4,979,049,055	1.18%
2011	286,658,605	7,830,388,359	0.86%
2012	406,548,316	10,734,365,324	1.02%

Source: Ministère Délégué au Budget (MDB)/Direction Nationale du Budget(DNB), 2012

The unit cost of the Guinean student in public institutions is weak compared to that of the sub-region as the table below shows.

Table 12.5 Unit costs in CFA Francs in public institutions of Guinea, Mali, Senegal and Togo

Country	Medicine	Engineering	Fundamental sciences	Arts and Human sciences	Economic sciences
Guinea	362,090	362,090	362,090	362,090	362,090
Mali	–	1,350,000	–	810,000	950,000
Senegal	4,600,000	2,200,000	–	1,200,000	1,700,000
Togo	2,160,189	1,635,690	1,400,000	1,331,523	–

Source: MESRS: General report of consensus-building on the higher education of 24 and 25 August 2012

Thus, an engineering Malian student costs four times more than a Guinean student of the same field.

In the context of their autonomy, the public institutions of higher education and great research institutions have the possibility to generate income by their own activities. It is the reason their budget forewords include components inflows and expenditures. The inflows include student registration and fees, delivery services offered by different units (initial or paying trainings for example), research contracts, consultation and expertise, notarization of schooling documents. However, the proportion of revenues is very meagre, about 1.5 per cent for certain establishments. Students registration fees of public IES remained constant during the last five years (15,000 GNF per year).

Strong points of the higher education system and of scientific research

Each of the eight administrative regions of the country houses at least one public higher education facility whose mission sometimes matches the main activities of the region in question. To illustrate, the mines in Boké and the veterinary medicine of Dalaba are examples.

The network of higher education and scientific research is diversified and includes a varied range of specialities. It encompasses universities, higher education institutes specialized in agriculture, veterinary medicine, mines, education sciences, technology, tourism and hotel industry and arts. An institute fully dedicated to distance training is prepared to back up other IES in the delivery of courses at a distance in addition to its traditional missions.

Among the 30 institutions of research and documentation, there are a great variety of specialities: medical biology, oceanography, environment, biodiversity, medical plants, historical heritage etc.

Private higher education is significantly on the rise. Until 1999, there was only one private higher education facility, today private IES amount to 39.

Guinean higher education played the role of pioneer in Francophone West Africa in the introduction of the BMD system in 2007.

Opportunities, threats and challenges

Among opportunities offered to higher education and of scientific research, here are some of them:

- The government commitment to building a higher education system and scientific research capable of efficiently contributing to poverty alleviation, improvement of living conditions of populations and the transformation of Guinea into an emerging economy;
- The dynamics of the mining sector which results in the momentum of other sectors like agriculture, tourism and hotel industry, civil engineering, industrial production, energy banks and insurances, lux craft, information technologies and communication, all entrepreneurs among whom some will be job executives and senior technicians;
- The emergence of a knowledge economy societies worldwide obliges the country to innovate to improve their competitiveness;
- The increased interest of development partners to support the development of higher education of quality in low-income countries.

Some threats to higher education and the scientific research system:

- The pressure of interest groups likely to block essential reforms of higher education and of scientific research;
- The recurring social and political crises which can prevent political decision-makers from concentrating on development issues;
- The world economic crisis favouring a wait-and-see policy among potential investors.

The main challenges that higher education and scientific research should overcome:

- Improving governance and system management of higher education institutions and scientific research;

- Improving access and fairness;
- Improving the relevance and quality of teaching and learning;
- Improving the employability of the graduates;
- Reinforcing IES and IRS partnership with the socio-economic world;
- Reactivating research and technological innovation;
- Improving the living environment and work conditions of students, teachers and researchers;
- Increasing funding devoted to training, research and technological innovation.

Vision and strategic objectives for 2013–20

The vision is to build a performing and diversified system of higher education and scientific research, responding to the country's needs, likely to speed up the economic and social emergence of Guinea and capable of training competent citizens, determined to live together in a democratic society.

Goal

The purpose is to promote in a globalized world, a higher education and scientific research system of high quality and relevance in order to effectively deal with the economic, social, cultural and environmental demands.

Strategic objectives for the 2013–20 period:

It is to take action to reshape higher education and to revitalize research in view of:

- Improving the governance and the management of the system of higher education institutions and of scientific research;
- Accelerating the training of young teacher-researchers and researchers for the expansion of the higher education system and scientific research;
- Improving access to tertiary education;
- Promoting short programmes of higher professional training;
- Improving the quality of teaching and learning;
- Developing private higher education, public/private partnership, co-operation and the participation of Guineans from abroad;
- Developing research and innovation;
- Promoting IT use in higher education and scientific research;
- Improving the funding of higher education and scientific research.

Conclusion

Overall, higher education and scientific research have been described. While student enrolments have increased significantly since 2006, unfortunately, infrastructures, equipment, number and quality of teachers have not followed the momentum. Moreover, several urgent problems persist for numerous years without any appropriate responses and solutions.

Fortunately, signs of change are perceptible: a clearer vision of the role of higher education and scientific research in the country which desires economic and social emergence and stronger commitment of actors and partners to improve the relevance and quality of this sector.

References

Corporate (2013). 'Strategy document of poverty alleviation (2013–2015)'. Conakry: Ministry of Economy and Finance (MESRS)

Diallo, M. C., Camara, A. I. and Barry, A. (2011). 'Evaluation report of Bachelor programs of the BMD system'. Conakry: MESRS.

Statistic Service and Planning (2011). 'Trend chart of the higher education'. Conakry: MESRS.

Acronyms

BMD	Bachelor-Master-Doctorate
CNRP	National Commission of Recruitment and Promotion
CRDG	Rectors and General Directors Conference of Public Higher Education Institutions
DNB	National Department of the Budget
HEI	Higher Education Institution
IPC	Polytechnic Institute of Conakry
IRS	Scientific Research Institution
IRST	Scientific and Technologic Research Institution
ISMG	Higher Institute of Mines and Geology
ISSMV	Higher Institute of Veterinary Medicine Sciences
IST	Higher Institute of Technology
IT	Information Technology
MDB	Delegated Ministry to the Budget

MDG	Millennium Development Goals
MEETFP	Ministry of Employment, Technical Education and of Vocational Training
MESRS	Ministry of Higher Education and Scientific Research
PRG	Presidency of the Republic of Guinea
R-D	Research-Development
SGG	Government General Secretariat
UGANC	University Gamal Abdel Nasser of Conakry
UGLC-S	University Generaal Lansana Conte of Sonfonia
UJNK	University Julius Nyerere of Kankan

13

Guinea-Bissau: An Overview, Trends and Futures

Akemi Yonemura[1]

Introduction

Guinea-Bissau is a fragile post-conflict country, with an unstable political situation, and weak infrastructures. The coup d'état that took place in April 2012 not only paralyzed the political life but the entire social field, leaving the country in a state of lawlessness. Before the coup, the education system in the country had expanded tremendously at almost all levels. However, the situation is still far from ideal and it has worsened after the coup.

This chapter is a reflective analysis of both the post-colonial and contemporary evolution of education in Guinea-Bissau. Based on data collected mainly from documentation of the government as well as international organizations, the chapter aims to provide an overview, the trends and futures of education in Guinea-Bissau. It provides key information on the historical, political, sociolinguistic, demographic and economic context of the country, followed by an overview of the education system in the country and the trends by exploring major issues and policies. The chapter concludes with an emphasis on political stability as an essential condition for the progress of the education sector in the country and for the future prospects of educational development.

An overview

Guinea-Bissau is a Lusophone (Portuguese-speaking) country[2] located on the West African coast, bordered by Senegal to the north and Guinea to the south. It is listed as one of the Least Developed Countries (LDCs), which are characterized as having 'weak human and institutional capacities, low and unequally distributed income and scarcity of domestic financial resources ... often suffer from governance crisis, political instability and, in some cases, internal and external conflicts'. Guinea-Bissau is also listed as a member of the Small Island Developing States (SIDS), which is recognized as a distinct group that shares common geographic characteristics and similar constraints in their sustainable development efforts. The LDCs' largely agrarian economy is affected by low productivity and low investment, and their reliance on the export of a few primary commodities as a major source of income is extremely vulnerable to external trade shocks. These constraints limit the capacity in domestic resource mobilization, leading to chronic external deficits and heavy dependence on external financing that have kept them in a poverty trap (UN-OHRLLS 2013).

Guinea-Bissau is one of the poorest countries in the world with Gross National Income (GNI) per capita US$550 in 2012, much lower than the average of sub-Saharan Africa (SSA), US$1,345. More than two-thirds of the population lives under the poverty line (69.3 per cent in 2010) (World Bank 2013a, 2013b). The Human Development Index for Guinea-Bissau ranked 176 out of 187 countries in 2012 (UNDP 2013).

Guinea-Bissau's population represents only 1.6 million in 2012, but with the annual growth rate of more than 2 per cent and a large proportion of young people (the population between the ages of 0 and 14 comprises 42 per cent of the total population), the population is expected to reach more than 2 million in 2020 (United Nations Population Division 2012). As is the case for many small countries, brain drain is an issue in Guinea-Bissau. The overall emigration rate of Guinea-Bissau was 6.8 per cent in 2010, with one quarter of them being tertiary-educated. The country lost more than 70 per cent of the physicians and 25 per cent of the nurses born in the country (World Bank 2011). Around half of the population follows indigenous beliefs, 45 per cent Muslim, and 5 per cent Christianity (EIU 2008). The population of Guinea-Bissau is composed of a number of ethnic groups, including Balanta (the largest group representing approximately 20 per cent of the population), Fula, Manjaca, Mandinga, Papel, and other small ethnic groups as well as European and mulatto, and they speak their ethnic languages. The official language is Portuguese, but it is spoken by only 11 per cent of the population, while 80 per cent of the population can speak Portuguese Creole. Portuguese is the only language of instruction, and most textbooks come from Portugal. From colonial times, all children had to learn French as a second language in high school (Leclerc 2013).

Guinea-Bissau was colonized by Portugal in the sixteenth century, but colonial control was weak and limited to the coast and rivers. An independence movement was started in 1956 by the Partido Africano para a Independência da Guiné e Cabo Verde (PAIGC) and independence was achieved in 1974. Since then, political instability has continued and a series of coups d'état were attempted especially during the 1980s, which were mostly caused by party infighting and discontent among the Balanta (EIU 2008). The conflict that took place in 1998–9 was particularly serious, and caused the destruction of nearly 80 per cent of the infrastructures. The election in 2009 marked the return to a more normal and peaceful political environment. However, following the 2010 military unrest, concerns over security, lack of subordination of the military to the civilian power and drug trafficking, prompted the suspension of major development assistance in the country (RoGB 2010; World Bank 2013b). In March 2012, the first round of the presidential elections took place, but the second round was interrupted by a military coup on 12 April 2012 (EIU 2013), and political uncertainty continues.

Due to these geographic and demographic characteristics and economic and political limitations, the country faces challenges in the education sector. This chapter presents the overview of the education system in Guinea-Bissau, by reviewing the overall context of the country that led to the current state of the education system, its trends in the past several decades, and the future prospects of the education system in Guinea-Bissau.

Education system, status, and sector strategy

Guinea-Bissau's education sector strategy is developed in line with the Poverty Reduction Strategy Paper (PRSP), which evolves around key areas critical to the national development, including to: 1) strengthen governance, upgrade public administration and ensure macroeconomic strategy; 2) promote economic growth and job creation; 3) increase access to social services and basic infrastructures; and 4) improve the living standards of vulnerable groups (IMF 2007). It is unlikely that Guinea-Bissau will achieve the education goals of MDGs and EFA targets by 2015. Therefore, the government developed an education sector programme for the period of 2009–2020 and set more realistic targets to be achieved by 2020, taking into account the country's needs and capacities (see Table 13.1). To realize these targets, the government will be required to increase the education share of the national budget to 17 per cent by the end of the

Table 13.1 Government's 2020 targets and strategies by level of education

Level of education	Target by 2020	Strategy
Pre-school	GER = 10.6% (4.7% in 2005)	1. Community participation 2. Increase in capacity of the system 3. Promotion of private education
Primary education (PE) cycles 1 and 2 (6 years)	Universal completion (100% completion)	1. Policy development for teacher training and recruitment to improve standards
Primary education cycle 3 (3 years)	Increase enrolment as much as possible. About 110,000 pupils (41,000 in 2006)	2. Improvement of ongoing teacher training 3. Measures to reduce grade repetition
Secondary education (3 years)	Increase enrolment according to higher education targets. About 21,000 students (13,000 in 2006)	4. Enhancement of retention and equality, particularly vulnerable groups 5. Increase of the private schools 6. Improvement of teaching standards by teaching aids and increased teaching hours 7. Expansion of infrastructure 8. National examination at the end of the education cycle (primary and secondary)
Technical and Vocational Education and Training (TVET)	Enrol about 800 (250 in 2006), short training courses to provide vocational qualifications / apprenticeships; 15% to graduate in the 6th year and 15% to graduate in the 9th year (6,800 apprentices)	1. Establishment, strengthening and restructure of short-term training courses with professional organizations and non-governmental organizations (NGOs)
Higher education	Enrol approximately 6,200 students (compared to 3,700 in 2006)	1. Streamlining of departments 2. Development of private education 3. Merit-base scholarships for disadvantaged students 4. Development of distance learning schemes 5. Increase in research funding

Source: RoGB, 2010

period, in addition to rigorous implementation of the programs and external technical and financial support (RoGB 2010).

In 2013, Pôle de Dakar of UNESCO published the status of the education sector in Guinea-Bissau, analysing the situation of the past 20 years between 1991 and 2010. Major findings were the following:

Access

- **Demography:** The population of primary education age, i.e. ages 7–12, comprises nearly one-fifth of the total population and this share is expected to continue in the coming years.
- **Macroeconomic challenge:** Poor performance of the country's economic growth keeps it heavily dependent on foreign aid.
- **Education expansion:** The education system has good performance in quantitative terms with a marked improvement in school coverage (between 1999/2000 and 2009/10, the annual increase was 5 per cent for pre-school and primary school, and 9 per cent for secondary school). However, universal primary education is still far from being achieved.

Quality and learning

- **Low internal efficiency:** Between 1998/9 and 2009/10, 24 per cent and 14 per cent, respectively, were repeaters at the primary and secondary levels.
- **Low literacy rate:** The education system produces too little lasting literacy after six years of schooling.
- **School shifts and learning:** A school organization in basic education with multiple shifts may have a negative impact on the learning curve.

Finance of education

- **Low government spending:** The share of education spending in total current government spending is the lowest in SSA (11 per cent in 2010). All other countries in SSA, such as Central African Republic (CAR), the Gambia, Malawi, allocate 14 per cent or higher share of public expenditure in education.
- **Resource allocation:** In terms of intra-sector distribution, the current expenditure on education is in favour of primary and secondary education.

It is overwhelmingly spent on staff costs at the expense of teaching and administrative expenses.
- **Private contribution:** Due to the insufficient government investment in education, contribution of households to educate their children is critical.

Equality

- **Key disparity areas:** Very marked disparities exist in enrolment by the level of family income, location of residence, and gender.
- **Unequal resource allocation:** Unequal distribution of resources for education is less pronounced than in other countries with similar levels of wealthy population. Countries comparable with Guinea-Bissau in terms of GDP/capita, allocate between 47 per cent (Tanzania) and 64 per cent (Rwanda) of their resources for the most educated 10 per cent of the population while in Guinea-Bissau only 28 per cent of the resources are allocated for the most educated 10 per cent of the population. However, still, strong social disparities exist in ownership of these resources.
- **Unequal teacher salaries:** The allocation of teacher salaries in the basic education schools needs to be improved and made more equitable across regions. (Teacher salaries in Guinea-Bissau are below the average of 10 countries[3] with a similar level of wealth, i.e. 2.3 GDP/capita against the average of the 10 countries, 4.4 GDP/capita, and also below the average remuneration indicated by the context of the Fast Track Initiative (3.5 GDP/capita) (UNESCO Pôle de Dakar 2013).

The next section describes the educational development of Guinea-Bissau in the historical and international contexts to identify further what makes it unique and what kind of country-specific efforts have been made.

Historical and emerging trends in educational development in Guinea-Bissau

Access and participation[4]

One problem of post-conflict countries is that comprehensive data are often not available. In Guinea-Bissau, regularly collected internationally comparable data for pre-primary and tertiary education is almost non-existent. However, available data from the UNESCO Institute for Statistics (UIS) demonstrates that during the past four decades, the overall participation of education at all levels has significantly increased. Particularly large strides for primary education are observed twice during the same period.

The first large stride was the increase of the gross enrolment ratio (GER) of primary education from 47 per cent in 1973 to 98 per cent in 1976. The second large increase occurred from the mid-nineties to 2000s – during which time the primary education GER increased from 56 per cent in 1995 to 78 per cent in 1999, to 93 per cent in 2001 and to more than 100 per cent by 2004. Between these two big positive strides, there was a stagnant period in the 1980s and early 1990s. Having once achieved 98 per cent in 1978, the GER started declining from that peak year, and throughout the eighties up to around 1995, it remained low between 73 per cent and 56 per cent. Gender disparity has been quite large throughout this period except for two times, when the gap was closed somewhat in 1973 and significantly in 2010. The GER for boys in 1971 was 47 per cent and only 20 per cent for girls, and in 1978, 133 per cent for boys and 64 per cent for girls. Only in 2010, was the gender gap diminished (127 per cent GER for boys and 119 per cent GER for girls) (see Figure 13.1) (UIS 2013).

During the stagnant period of the eighties, the country experienced political instability and a number of coups d'état. The first stride took place around the time of the independence of 1974. The second increase in 2000 can be explained

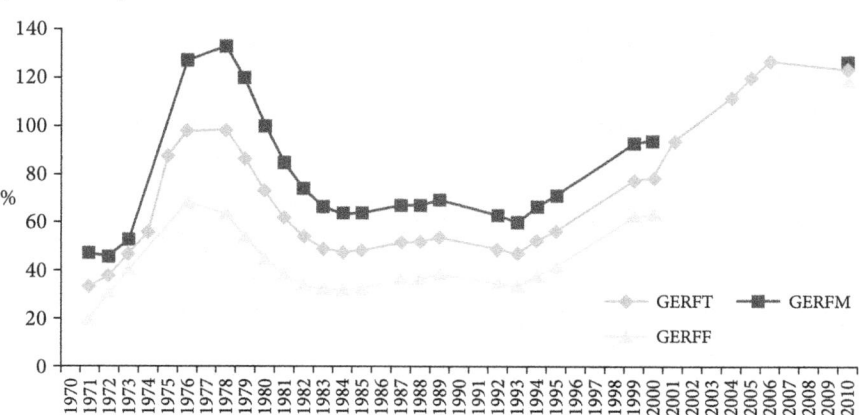

Figure 13.1 Trends in gross enrolment ratios at the primary level in Guinea-Bissau (1971–2010)

Source : UIS database, May 2013
GERFT: Gross Enrolment Ratio for both sexes
GERFM: Gross Enrolment Ratio for males
GERFF: Gross Enrolment Ratio for females

by the international campaigns, such as the Millennium Development Goals (MDGs) and EFA that set specific goals to achieve Universal Primary Education (UPE) and gender parity by 2015. Another aim of these campaigns was to promote donors' behaviour to use these targets as the principal reference to set the government's priorities. Although these MDG targets for education gained much attention, other EFA goals, related to pre-primary, literacy, life-long learning, and quality education, were not considered as high on the policy agenda among the competing priorities.

By approximately 2000, relatively comprehensive data across all levels became available, probably in relation to the global campaign for EFA that

Table 13.2 Enrolment by levels of education in Guinea-Bissau (1999 and most recent data) and the SSA regional average (2011)

			1999	Most recently available data (year)	Regional Average 2011
Gross Enrolment Ratio (GER) %	Pre-primary	MF	4	7 (2010)	18
		M	4	7 (2010)	18
		F	4	7 (2010)	18
	Primary (ISCED 1)	MF	78	123 (2010)	101
		M	93	127 (2010)	105
		F	63	119 (2010)	98
	Secondary (ISCED 2 and 3)	MF	...	36 (2006)	41
		M	...	...	45
		F	...	...	37
	Tertiary (ISCED 5 and 6)[1]	MF	...	3 (2006)	8
		M	...	...	10
		F	...	...	6
Net Enrolment Ratio (NER) %	Pre-primary	MF	...	5 (2010)	8
		M	...	5 (2010)	10
		F	...	5 (2010)	6
	Primary	MF	50	74 (2010)	77
		M	59	75 (2010)	79
		F	42	72 (2010)	75
	Secondary	MF	...	9 (2000)	...
		M	...	11 (2000)	...
		F	...	6 (2000)	...

Source: UIS, 2011a and 2013

1 According to the International Standard Classification of Education (ISCED), primary level (ISCED 1) refers to first and second cycles of primary education only; secondary level (ISCED 2 and 3) refers to third cycle of primary and secondary education; ISCED 5 refers to first stage of tertiary education and ISCED 6 refers to second stage of tertiary education (UNESCO 1997).

sought for internationally comparable data to monitor the progress of EFA. According to these statistics, the progress since the baseline year (before the EFA commitment was set in 2000) to 2010, almost all levels of education participation increased significantly. The greatest achievement was at the primary level reaching almost 74 per cent of net enrolment ratio (NER) with very little gender disparity (75 per cent for boys and 72 per cent for girls) in 2010, which is almost the same level of the SSA regional average of 77 per cent. But still the country falls short of the goal of UPE with a quarter of the primary-age students out-of-school. At the other levels of education, pre-primary education GER in 2010 was only 7 per cent, which was much lower than the regional average of 18 per cent. Secondary education participation was typically low in SSA, and GER in Guinea-Bissau was only 36 per cent in 2006, almost the same level of the 2011 SSA average of 41 per cent. Only 3 per cent of the college-age people attended tertiary education in 2006, whereas the 2011 regional average was 8 per cent (see Table 13.2).

Early childhood education development and pre-primary education

There is little information available on enrolment for pre-primary education in Guinea-Bissau. One available study shows that attendance at pre-primary education programmes in Guinea-Bissau varies from less than 5 per cent in the poorest 20 per cent of households to 25 per cent in the wealthiest 20 per cent of households (Nonoyama-Tarumi and Ota 2010 cited in EFA Global Monitoring Report 2011). For early childhood education development and pre-primary education, not only enrolment in pre-primary education, but two other criteria on health and nutrition, which are critical for child development, were used (UNESCO 2012).[5] Guinea-Bissau was ranked by the Early Childhood Care and Education (ECCE) index at 62nd among 68 countries in 2010 with a health indicator of 82 per cent, nutrition indicator of 72 per cent, and education indicator of 22 per cent (UNESCO 2012).

Literacy

Most countries in SSA are likely to miss the EFA adult literacy target to achieve a 50 per cent improvement by 2015.[6] The majority of the illiterate adults are, in fact, concentrated in a small group of countries. In SSA, eleven countries have an adult literacy rate below 50 per cent, of which eight are in West Africa (UNESCO 2012). Guinea-Bissau's adult literacy rate (age 15+) in 2011 was 55.3

per cent (68.9 per cent for men and 42.1 per cent for women), slightly lower than the regional average of 59.1 per cent (68.1 per cent for men and 50.6 per cent for women). The youth literacy rate (ages 15–24) was 73.2 per cent (79.3 per cent for men and 67.1 per cent for women), slightly higher than the regional average of 69.5 per cent (75.6 per cent for men and 63.7 per cent for women) (UIS 2011a).

Armed conflict and education

Many poor countries spend more on arms than on primary education. The EFA Global Monitoring Report (GMR) 2011 identified countries where military spending outstripped spending on primary education. The Report surveyed 39 countries and identified 21 countries that spent more on their military budget than on primary education. If all these 21 countries cut military spending by 10 per cent, they could put 9.5 million additional children in school, which represents around 40 per cent of their out-of-school children. In Guinea-Bissau, the military spending was equivalent to 3.8 per cent of its GDP and if it was to be cut by 10 per cent and used for education, an extra 34,000 children could be enroled in primary school. The military budget in Guinea-Bissau was four times higher than the primary education budget (UNESCO 2011).

Quality

All aspects of the quality of education are not easily recognized and quantifiable, but one of the major methods is to assess learning outcomes, especially in literacy, numeracy and essential life skills, which can be measured by exams or school survival rates. Limited data from the EFA GMR show that Guinea-Bissau's education quality was below the SSA average: the pupil/teacher ratio in primary education was 44 in 1999 and 52 in 2010, whereas the SSA average in 2010 was 43. The increase between 1999 and 2010 was probably due to the pressure to achieve UPE and the supply of teacher has not caught up with the increase of students. The share of female teachers in primary education is used as an indicator on the assumption that female teachers encourage female students' participation. Guinea-Bissau is not making much progress in this area, which was 20 per cent in 1999 and 22 per cent in 2010, far below the SSA average of 43 per cent. Trained primary school teachers represented only 35 per cent of total teachers in 1999 and 39 per cent in 2010, whereas the SSA average in 2010 was 80 per cent (UNESCO 2012).

Student mobility

One of the small states' problems is that they do not have a large higher education system in the country and a high rate of tertiary students goes abroad. According to the UIS, 45 per cent of the tertiary students of Guinea-Bissau studied abroad in 2005 (UIS 2013). This indicates that Guinea-Bissau's higher education needs to be expanded significantly and its quality should be enhanced to retain good students in the country in the long run. As a shorter-term response, many countries are trying to facilitate mobility by harmonizing the higher education system.

The role of regional organization

Other than the global international bodies, African continental and regional organizations are playing an important role in the political, economic and social affairs in Africa. One of the key organizations for Guinea-Bissau is the Economic Community of West Africa States (ECOWAS). Among the 15 members of the ECOWAS, the majority of the countries are Francophone (Benin, Burkina Faso, Côte d'Ivoire, Guinea, Mali, Niger, Senegal, and Togo); there are five Anglophone countries (the Gambia, Ghana, Liberia, Nigeria, and Sierra Leone) and the remaining two are Lusophone countries (Cape Verde and Guinea-Bissau). Guinea-Bissau is also a member of an interstate organization called Países Africanos de Língua Oficial Portuguesa (PALOP), which has a number of official agreements with Portugal and development partners in the fields of culture, education and Portuguese language development and preservation. In 1996, together with Portugal and Brazil, the PALOP countries established the Comunidade dos Países de Língua Portuguesa (CPLP) (European Commission 2013).

While major international organizations are focusing on basic education, these regional organizations are working on post-secondary and professional education, based on the common regional interests and/or common language ties. One example is harmonization of the tertiary education system. This effort has been on the education policy agenda for several decades, as can be seen in the Regional Convention on the Recognition of Studies, Certificates, Diplomas, Degrees and other Academic Qualifications in Higher Education in the African States, commonly known as 'Arusha Convention', which was ratified by 22 African countries in 1981. The African Union (AU) is promoting harmonization of the tertiary education system across Africa through collaboration and systematic quality assurance, using common and agreed benchmarks of excellence, which also facilitates mobility of graduates and academics across the continent (Butcher et al. 2009). Although Guinea-Bissau has not yet ratified this convention, there is a specific area of initiative to harmonize the system by regional economic or official language blocks. For example, the curriculum harmonization for undergraduate medical training in the ECOWAS region is an effort initiated by the West African Health Organization (WAHO), a specialized institution of ECOWAS, to harmonize training curricula of general medical practice in English-, French- and Portuguese-speaking countries within ECOWAS. The benefits of such an initiative include: a unified accreditation process for the ECOWAS region, acquisition of equivalent skills to facilitate free movement of health professionals, and a possibility of pooling health workers in favour of national systems within ECOWAS in order to reduce brain drain (ECOWAS 2013).

Education finance and external support

Guinea-Bissau allocated 11.9 per cent of government spending to education in 1999, which was 5.2 per cent of GDP. Its aid dependency was relatively high among SSA countries, and Guinea-Bissau's net official development assistance (ODA) as a percentage of GDP in 2009 was 18 per cent, whereas the average of SSA countries was 10 per cent (UNESCO 2012). The ODA for education per population aged 5–24 in 2008 was US$18 (UIS 2011b). At the global level, fiscal adjustments resulting from the financial crisis, have damaged prospects for getting all of the world's children into schooling by 2015 and Guinea-Bissau cut more than 15 per cent of its education spending in 2009 (UNESCO 2011). This situation indicates that Guinea-Bissau is likely to depend heavily on external financial support.

Although consolidated data are not available in the Organization for Economic Co-operation and Development (OECD)'s database on aid, emerging influence of non-traditional donors is increasing (OECD 2013). Since the military coup in 2012, the relationship with traditional development partners has been changing. While European donors and the International Monetary Fund (IMF) have suspended their programmes, Angola, which had become an important donor for Guinea-Bissau, also withdrew its support following the ousting of its ally. Part of the resource gap is likely to be financed by other sources, particularly the ECOWAS and Nigeria. China, which has been expanding its influence in Africa, and had provided financial support prior to the coup, might also sustain its support. The United States of America's major concern in the country is primarily related to the drug-trafficking networks, which may affect the US financial support (EIU 2013).

As an international effort in reducing poverty through skills development, Brazil, an emerging donor, has a great potential to provide assistance to Lusophone African countries. Brazil's government-industry body that oversees vocational training, Serviço Nacional de Aprendizagem Industrial (SENAI), has provided technical assistance to several Portuguese-speaking African countries, including Guinea-Bissau. Skills development is high on Brazil's development assistance agenda although the amounts spent are still small. Brazil's support is based on its own country's experience in lifting many youth out of poverty through skills development by apprentices in the informal sector and smallholders, which can be replicated further (UNESCO 2012).

Conclusions and future prospects

Political stability is the essential condition

This chapter provided an overview of the education system of Guinea-Bissau, by exploring: the sector strategy and policy framework; and the status and structure of the education system. It then outlined the trends by exploring issues regarding access and participation at all levels of the education system; early childhood education development and pre-primary education; literacy; armed conflict and education quality; student mobility; the role of regional organizations; education finance and external support. Analysis of these sections reveals that in Guinea-Bissau, political stability is the essential condition for educational development.

Since its independence, Guinea-Bissau has been known as one of the most politically unstable countries in Africa, where an elected president has yet to successfully complete a term in office (Wilson Center 2013). The political disruptions following the coup in April 2012 undermined policy implementation in most of the public and private sectors. The international community considers that political stability will depend on credible elections and a legitimate civilian administration, which are included in international organizations' programming principles. Most of the international donors support will be dependent on re-establishing constitutional order. A new programme of the IMF to boost economic growth and improve public financial management will be negotiated after the elections and is likely to trigger other support from donors. The failure to hold the elections will delay aid disbursements and make the planned activities stagnant. Once constitutional order is re-established, donors will urge the government to resume structural reforms, including pro-poor spending (EIU 2013).

Disadvantageous characteristics of LDCs and SIDS are further articulated by Collier (2008) as the poverty traps, of which, 'the conflict trap' and 'bad governance in a small country' are the characteristics of Guinea-Bissau. He explains that conflicts that are distinctive to those in the poverty trap are characterized as being stuck in a pattern of internal challenges against government. In Africa, societies with one big ethnic group are also risk factor, which is the case for Guinea-Bissau. The theory of the coup trap is that once a country has had a coup, it is more likely to have further coups. To break these conflict traps, Collier proposes aid, military intervention, laws and charters, and trade policy for reversing marginalization. To break the bad governance trap, he maintains that it requires reform from within and it takes courage. As seen in the historical trends in the educational development in Guinea-Bissau, in addition to the global campaign for education, political stability is an essential condition to develop and maintain a strong education system.

Future prospects

There are many historical and political explanations for the instability, which are beyond the scope of this chapter. However, one explanation from the educational policy point of view can be related to ethnic groups and language issues, especially when Portuguese, which is spoken only by 11 per cent of the population, is the only language of instruction. How can all the ethnic groups, which do not speak Portuguese, participate in the Western-style democratic process by having a free and fair election and having the rule of law described in the official language of Portuguese? Language diversity seems to present a challenge in representing the majority of the public opinion. Education helps empower people and allow them to participate in the political process and access to the information; therefore, civic education in different languages needs more attention, in addition to the traditional curriculum that emphasizes the language skills of Portuguese.

In order to improve conditions in the educational sector of Guinea-Bissau, future efforts should consider not merely achieving the UPE, but also the content of education that is supported by the beneficiary population. The level should go beyond the primary and secondary, and pre-primary and post-secondary education should gain more attention. The impact of globalization and advancement of technology will increase the opportunity for distance learning that should increase the tertiary enrolment. This may be linked to regional harmonization efforts to promote common quality standards that are already taking place in some of the professional training. In relation to curriculum harmonization, standardized exams to assess the learning outcomes may be developed as a regular monitoring instrument in collaboration with regional organizations. Development of inclusive life-long learning opportunities, considering language and social diversity, is crucial for long-lasting development.

Notes

1. Disclaimer: The ideas and opinions expressed in this chapter are those of the author, and do not necessarily represent the views of UNESCO and do not commit the Organization.
2. The Lusophone countries in Africa include: Angola, Cape Verde, Guinea-Bissau, Mozambique, and Sao Tome and Principe, and in 2011, Equatorial Guinea adopted Portuguese as an official language, in addition to French and Spanish.
3. These countries are: Burkina Faso (2006), Mali (2008), Central African Republic (2008), the Gambia (2009), Tanzania (2009), Niger (2008), Rwanda (2008), Madagascar (2006), Ghana (2007) and Togo (2007).
4. The terminology and the classification of the education system used by the Government and other sources, are not consistent with the internationally agreed standardized terminology and the classification used by UNESCO, but for this chapter, the original data were used without adjusting them and the sources are provided.
5. Child health indicator is measured by the percentage of children who survive beyond their fifth birthday. Nutrition indicator is measured by the percentage of children under five who do not suffer from moderate or severe stunting. Education indicator is measured by the percentage of children aged 3 to 7 who are enroled either in pre-primary or in primary school (UNESCO 2012).
6. This formulation cannot be operationalized when adult literacy rate is higher than 67 per cent. For monitoring purpose, a 50 per cent reduction in adult illiteracy rate is used.

References

Butcher, N., Hoosen, S. and Njenga, B. K. (2009). 'Harmonization of higher education programmes: a strategy for the African Union'. *African Integration Review* 3 (1): 1–36.

Collier, P. (2008). *The Bottom Billion*. New York: Oxford University Press.
ECOWAS (2013). *Harmonised Curriculum for Undergraduate Medical Training in the ECOWAS Region*.
EIU (Economist Intelligence Unit) (2008). *Country Profile Guinea-Bissau*. London: EIU.
—(2013). *Country Report 3rd Quarter 2013: Guinea-Bissau*. London: EIU.
European Commission (2013). EUROSTAT. PALOP. Available from http://epp.eurostat.ec.europa.eu/portal/page/portal/international_statistical_cooperation/africa_caribbean_pacific/africa_sub_saharan/palop (accessed 6 October 2013).
IMF (International Monetary Fund) (2007). *Guinea-Bissau: Poverty Reduction Strategy Paper*. Washington, DC: IMF and IDA.
Leclerc, J. (2013). 'L'aménagement linguistique dans le monde. Guinée-Bissau'. http://www.axl.cefan.ulaval.ca/afrique/Guinee-Bissau.htm (accessed 7 October 2013).
Nonoyama-Tarumi, Y. and Ota, Y. (2010). 'Early childhood development in developing countries: pre-primary education, parenting, and health care'. Background paper for *EFA Global Monitoring Report 2011*. UNESCO: Paris.
OECD (2013). 'Aid Statistics'. Available from http://www.oecd.org/dac/stats/ (accessed 24 September 2013).
RoGB (Republic of Guinea-Bissau) (2010). *Three-year Plan for the Development of Education: 2011–2013*. Bissau: RoGB, Ministry of National Education, Culture, Science, Youth and Sports.
UIS (UNESCO Institute for Statistics) (2011a). *Education (all levels) Profile – Guinea-Bissau*. Montreal: UIS.
—(2011b). *Financing Education in Sub-Saharan Africa*. Montreal: UIS.
—(2013). Data Center. Montreal: UIS http://www.uis.unesco.org/datacentre/pages/default.aspx (accessed 27 September 2013).
UN-OHRLLS (United Nations Office of the High Representative for Least Developed Countries, Landlocked Developing Countries and Small Island Developing States) (2013) 'Least Developed Countries'. http://www.unohrlls.org/en/ldc/25/. Small Island Developing Countries. http://www.unohrlls.org/en/sids/44/ (accessed 2013).
UNDP (2013). *Human Development Report 2013. Explanatory Note on 2013 HDR Composite Indices: Guinea-Bissau*. New York: UNDP.
UNESCO (1997). *International Standard Classification of Education ISCED 1997*. Paris: UNESCO.
—(2011). *Education for All Global Monitoring Report 2011*. Paris: UNESCO.
—(2012). *Education for All Global Monitoring Report 2012*. Paris: UNESCO.
UNESCO Pôle de Dakar (2013). *Guinée-Bissau: Rapport d'état du system éducatif*. Dakar: UNESCO Pôle de Dakar.
United Nations Population Division (2012). *World Population Prospects: The 2012 Revision*. New York: United Nations Population Division of the Department of Economic and Social Affairs. Available from http://esa.un.org/unpd/wpp/index.htm (accessed 22 September 2013).

Wilson Center (2013). *In Brief – Elections in Guinea-Bissau*. Washington, DC: Wilson Center. Available from http://www.scribd.com/doc/170646564/In-Brief-Elections-in-Guinea-Bissau (accessed 11 October 2013).

World Bank (2011). *The Migration and Remittance Factbook 2011*. Washington, DC: World Bank.

—(2013a). Data: Guinea-Bissau. Washington, DC: World Bank. Available from http://data.worldbank.org/country/guinea-bissau (accessed 12 October 2013).

—(2013b). *Country Overview: Guinea-Bissau*. Washington, DC: World Bank. Available fromhttp://www.worldbank.org/en/country/guineabissau/overview (accessed 12 October 2013).

14

Ivory Coast: An Overview, Trends and Futures

François-Joseph Azoh

Introduction

The chapter examines the status of education in the Ivory Coast according to the objectives of EFA. The government has assuredly made some efforts but it is still unable to cope with the schooling of children. To answer the demands of education, initiatives are taken by communities to make up for the deficit of the government's provision. Moreover, the education sector was strongly affected by the military-political crisis but it has managed to continue its operation. The chapter outlines the strategies developed to promote education and protect children. If education in the Ivory Coast has made significant progress, crucial issues exist with the quality, inclusion and the pedagogical integration of Information and Communications Technology (ICT). This chapter is based on documentary analysis of official documents as well as research.

Context

The Ivory Coast occupies an area of 322,462 square kilometres and is bordered by Burkina Faso and Mali in the North, Liberia and Guinea in the West, Ghana in the East, and the Atlantic Ocean in the South. The country has witnessed rapid population growth with a size of 6.6 million inhabitants in 1975 which increased threefold to 18.5 million in 2005; 20.8 million in 2008. It is estimated to reach 22.3 million of inhabitants in 2015 (UNDP 2008). The national density is 47.90 square kilometres per inhabitant.

In 1960 the Ivory Coast gained independence and since this date, education has always been the responsibility of the state which ensures its financing.

The proportion of the budget allocated to the education sector had always been higher than that billed to other ministerial departments or sectors, but it declined with the economic recession since 1980. In 1992, funding allocated to education was 40 per cent of government budget for recurrent and investment costs but this declined to 19.37 per cent in 1999 and 17.8 per cent in 2000.

From 2002 till 2006, the percentage of the budget assigned to education remained constant and was around 22 per cent (Ministère d'Etat, Ministère du Plan et du Développement, DSRP 2009: 52). In spite of this reduction, the percentage of Gross Domestic Product (GDP) for the public running costs for education is 4.1 per cent in the Ivory Coast against a regional average of 3.3 per cent.

The period from 1985 till 1995 was characterized by a growing increase in poverty levels. Indeed, the rate of poverty increased from 10 per cent in 1985 to 36.8 per cent in 1995, with an average increase of 2.7 percentage points a year. It then climbed to 48.9 per cent in 2008. The number of poor people estimated at 974 000 in 1985 (on a population of 10 million) grew to 10,174,000 in 2008 (on a population of 20.8 million). From 2002 till 2008, which was within six years, there had been a 10 per cent rise in the level of poverty in the Ivory Coast, which strongly affected the education sector. The distribution of the spending categories among households for the whole population indicates a low allocation of 3.7 per cent. This expense item is classified among three last ones with the acquisition of durable goods and real property.

Education is a public responsibility of the state. However, historic and structural reasons have enabled the state to entrust part of its duty regarding education to churches and the private sector. Indeed, since independence in 1960, the state has been granting subsidies to schools managed by churches/religious entities and the private sector. This measure was aimed at complementing the efforts of the state in education. Consequently, the state subsidies oblige denominational schools to welcome pupils irrespective of religious background (Lanoue 2002). With the administrative decentralization policy in 2001, the central power had transferred a part of its missions to districts (for primary schools) and to the regions (for secondary schools) for the building of infrastructure, equipment and payment of locally recruited staff. The central power is the body that defines its prerogatives in defining programmes, conducting evaluations, recruitment and training of teachers and defining teachers' salary scale. Current developments in the education sector have led to the emergence of alternative educational forms, which are integrated into the formal system, for instance, functional elimination of illiteracy, community schools, and Islamic schools.

The educational system: Organization and function

The first public school was established in 1887 under the pre-colonial era in the south of the country, which became colonized in 1896. As for the Catholic denominational schools, they appeared from 1950 and were annexed to the public education system (Lanoue 2004a, 2004b). The educational system consists of four cycles, which include preschool, primary, secondary and higher education. The preschool welcomes children from 3 to 5 years old and lasts three years. Its main objective is to socialize children and develop their skills regarding perception and recognition of objects. However, preschools tend to benefit urban areas more than rural areas largely because they are located in the former. They also serve children of the wealthy and the elite more than those of the poor.

The primary cycle comprises 6 years and enrols children for a period of 6 to 11 years. Pupils graduate from this cycle through a competitive examination, which awards them a diploma to enable them to enrol in the secondary cycle. While the private sector manages only 9 per cent of this level of education, public schools dominate with 91 per cent in planning and infrastructural development. To an extent, this helps to address the disparities that exist between urban and rural areas with regards to enrolment rates, girls' access to education and staffing.

The secondary cycle is made up of general education and technical education. The general secondary education is subdivided into two levels with the first level welcoming pupils aged between 12 and 15 years and lasting 4 years signified by a diploma earned through a competitive examination, which enables pupils to access the second level. The second level extends over 3 years and receives pupils from 16 to 18 years old. This cycle also ends with a diploma, which guarantees pupils an entry into the next cycle of education.

Technical education and vocational training aims at developing the skills for jobs in the domains of small crafts and industry. The private sector also participates in this level of education which comprises three hierarchically ordered levels in a decreasing manner:

- 1st level with duration of three years allows entry into employment or higher education;
- 2nd level which lasts two years results in employment or allows one to have access to the previous level;
- 3rd level which lasts two years leads to employment or the previous level.

This type of education is considered less attractive by the pupils and parents because it is perceived as the last resort for the pupils who failed in the general secondary school.

The fourth cycle is the upper level of education, which consists of university and high school with durations of study ranging between 2 and 7 years ending in a Doctorate. It includes general studies and specialized training ensured by the public and private sector. The system Bachelor-Master-Doctorate will be adopted for the next school year (2012–13).

The educational supply and demand

In the Ivory Coast, statistical data for education are rarely available and those obtainable give a very general picture and are not disaggregated. However, the observations on the ground and disaggregation of the statistical data suggest that demand is higher than supply. The statistics indicate that percentages of children in full-time education are still far from the goals of the EFA which will not be reached in 2015 (Azoh et al. 2010).

It is estimated that in the population of 15 to 45 years old, 63 per cent are illiterate. The problem of demand exceeding supply is a cause that excludes some groups from school. Indicators show that through efforts progress was made, and gross enrolment rates (GER) between 1998–9 and 2000–1 rose from 71.7 per cent to 76 per cent, which indicates a 4.3 per cent increase in three school years, compared to an annual rate of 1.5 per cent growth.

None the less, the military-political crisis of 2002 led to a significant reduction in the enrolment rates which declined to 47.3 per cent in 2002–3, that is a fall of 28.7 per cent. However from 2006 to 2007, enrolment rates soared to 74.3 per cent. Then again, this growth rate still fell below that of 2001 (before the crisis 76 per cent). Available data indicate that the Ivory Coast counts approximately 3.6 million children of less than six years and this population is estimated to be 4.2 million in 2020. It is estimated that approximately 42 per cent of the young people old enough to be in primary school are not there. In 2007, this population included 1.2 million 7 to 12 years old. Most of these young people are from poor and rural families, and are largely girls. There are many reasons for this situation but four are outlined below.

First, the numerous inefficiencies that characterize the administrative system prevent the recording of births, which in turn undermines school registration/enrolment.

Second, the family and socio-cultural factors, which privileges boys over girls offer more opportunities to the former while constraining the latter (Dedy et al. 1997).

Additionally, the long distances that children in the rural areas compared to those in the urban areas have to walk result in lower access to schools in rural settings. The study of the RESEN (World Bank 2011) indicates that the global distance is of the order of 17 points (66 per cent in rural areas against 83 per cent in urban zones). Consequently, the chances of access to school decrease in a rather significant way to 59 per cent when the child must walk between 30 and 60 minutes to reach the primary school, and fall below 50 per cent if the school is more than a one-hour walk farther away from the child's home.

Furthermore, education cost is higher for households, particularly, when accessed from the private sector.

Preschool

Preschool still remains the privilege of a low number of children as the gross enrolment rate did not exceed 3.3 per cent in 2005–6. Indeed, preschool education recovered during years of dominance by the private sector. Despite the State's increase in resources and access to large numbers of children, the rural environment still stays under-equipped with 198 preschools in rural areas (18.5 per cent) against 871 in urban zones (81.5 per cent). Out of a total number of 64,136 pupils, 54,081 are in the urban areas and only 10,055 in a rural environment (16 per cent). It is worthy to note that 49 per cent of the 64,136 children are girls.

The education policy implemented from 1992 to 1993 required that preschool and primary levels had to be given equal importance in public education.

Available data suggest that in 2008–9, out of a total of 1,069 preschools, 689 (that is to say 64 per cent) were public while 380 (that is to say 36 per cent) were private. Preschool represents a total size of 640 out of which 582 (91 per cent) are public and 58 (9 per cent) are private.

- The integrated preschools in primary schools represent a total size of 429 out of which 107 (that is to say 25 per cent) are public and 322 (that is to say 75 per cent) are private.

Primary school

The focus of the state on this level of education has been significant hence the increase in enrolment rate to 76 per cent in 2001–2. However, it experienced a decline during the military-political crisis dropping to 47 per cent since 2002–3 but rose again to 74 per cent in 2006–7. From 2007 to 2008, it had risen to 78 per cent. In 2008–9, the total number of pupils in primary schools were 2 383 359 out of which 45 per cent, that is 1,065,371 were girls, then again, enrolment and gender parity figures remain inadequate. Thus, demand exceeding supply remains the problem of access to children in the age bracket of 7–12 years. Table 14.1 below compares the data for 2006 and 2009.

Table 14.1 Situation of children of schooling age

Year	2006	2009
Age bracket	7–12 years	7–12 years
Number of children to be schooled	2,777,414	3,062,944
Number of children schooled	1,606,319	1,824,944
Number of children not schooled	1,171,095	1,238,000

Source: *Ministère de l'Education Nationale*, 2009

From 2006 to 2009, there was a rise in the number of children enroled in school. The number of children in school shows a slight increase from 1,606,319 to 1,824,944 between 2006 and 2009, that is, an increase of 218,625. Numerous efforts remain to be made for the schooling of 1,238,000 children who remain out of school, and whose number increased by 66,905 children from 2006.

The data of 2006 allow a differentiation of two groups of children:

- Those who have never been to school were estimated at 833,224 individuals,
- Those who have been registered once but dropped out before reaching the first year of secondary school were estimated at 337,870 young people

The high pupil-teacher ratio of 1:44 is also another challenge in the provision of quality primary education.

General and technical secondary school

In the general secondary cycle, the gross enrolment rate is rising even if it is still low and does not exceed 32 per cent at Level 1 and 16 per cent at Level 2. The general secondary education enroled a total of 929,606 pupils of which 353,953 are girls, which signifies a 38 per cent rate. The public sector receives a total number of 602,212 pupils of which 218,608 are girls, which represent 36 per cent. As for the private sector, it records a total number of 327,394 pupils of which 135,345 are girls, which represent 41 per cent.

Altogether, the average pupils/class ratio is 63:1 with a ratio higher in the public sector than in the private sector, that is 89:1 against 41:1.

For what affects technical education and vocational training, the data in Table 14.2 indicate increasing staff with an increase of the structures of the private which exceed those of the public sector from 2005–6.

Table 14.2 Staff of pupils in technical education

Year	2003–4	2004–5	2005–6	2006–7
Public	25,345	25,730	22,457	24,018
Private	7,775	16,597	25,209	26,481
Total	33,120	42,327	47,666	50,499

Source: RESEN, World Bank, 2011

Staff for all the public and private sectors numbered 28,793 during the period 1996 to 1997 and rose to 50,499 in 2006–7, that is an annual average increase of 5.8 per cent. If staff were more important in the public sector, we noticed that in 2006 to 2007, 52.4 per cent of the pupils were schooled in the private sector. Staff remains globally constant: for 100,000 inhabitants, as we count 258 learners from 1998 to 1999 and 257 learners from 2006 to 2007. The peak was reached from 1999 to 2000 with 275 learners for 100,000 inhabitants.

Academic

For two decades, public education provision progressed and the private sector came on board in 1995.

Over a period of 10 years (1996–7 to 2006–7), there has been an increase in staff rates by 80 per cent in public education. The increase from 87,873 students to 156,772 students is a rate of annual average increase estimated at about 6 per cent. All in all, the public universities welcome 48 per cent of the students.

In the private sector, staff evolved quickly over the same period, passing from 20,492 to 56,907 students, that is an annual average increase of about 11 per cent.

The number of students for 100,000 inhabitants increased to 666 in the period from 1998 to 1999 and 798 between the years 2006 and 2007.

The performance of the educational system

In spite of the progress that the educational system of the Ivory Coast has made, when evaluated, its performance remains not encouraging. Performance remains low in terms of access. While 70 per cent of children of school-going age have access to primary school, 30 per cent are not schooled. Also, only 33 per cent have access to general secondary school. Data indicate that repetition and dropout rates remain high.

At primary level, the rate of repetition is 19 per cent and completion is 46 per cent. In the secondary cycle, repetition rate is higher in Level 2 than in Level 1 and it is observed that this phenomenon occurs more in the private sector than in the public sector. At Level 1, the rate of repetition is 13 per cent with 10 per cent in the public sector and 19 per cent in the private sector.

In the Ivory Coast, for the school year 2006–7 we noticed that performance in primary education (74 per cent) falls below the African average (93 per cent) with a distance of 19 percentage points. In general secondary education (33 per cent) it falls within the African average (36 per cent) but drops significantly below the performance of other countries. While technical education and vocational training performs (257 learners for 100,000 inhabitants) below the African average (309 learners), the university system (798 students for 100,000 inhabitants) has a coverage rate which is above the continental average (299 learners for 100,000 inhabitants) (World Bank 2011: 26).

Education during the politico-military conflict

The crisis which started in 2002 had a considerable impact on education for several reasons. There was the departure of the solar administration and teachers from the zones of conflict. Out of the 11,234 teachers at post in the primary schools in these zones, only 1,771 (that is approximately 16 per cent) stayed (Azoh et al. 2004). More than half of the children of school-going age, that is, more than 700,000 overall, were forced to give up their studies (Coen 2005). The armed conflict led to the destruction of infrastructure and plundering of educational resources.

During the conflict education had to continue to protect the children and teenagers from being recruited to join armed groups and against all forms of violence (Azoh et al. 2009a). Thus, various initiatives were developed to ensure the continuity of education in both conflict zones of the country (Azoh et al. 2009b). One was the introduction of the shift system where the class was divided into two pedagogical groups and organized alternately, a group for the morning and another for the afternoon. Another was the bridges classes, which involved a system of transition allowing the children to integrate into the education system. The lessons taught are reduced taking into account the fundamental disciplines. Also, there were the multi-grade classes, a system allowing the same teacher to teach pupils from different academic classes and of different abilities. Simultaneously, the training of voluntary teachers with the help of communities, national and international non-governmental organizations (NGOs) was another initiative. Community participation then became more crucial, and so another initiative to involve the community in the school life through administration, material support and financial management came into being. This initiative led to the creation of community schools, which provided such a credible alternative that today they are to be integrated into the official system.

All these initiatives led to the observation that in the:

- 'governmental area', the system of running a double shift catered for all displaced pupils avoiding the plethoric ones. This system took care of 133,826 pupils among whom 74,470 were from primary schools.
- 'non-governmental area', qualified teachers were retained and supported by voluntary teachers (60 per cent) to ensure the education of 166,796 pupils.

Perspectives

The development of education in the Ivory Coast indicates a series of short-term perspectives seen mainly from two levels: education access and adapting the provision of education.

Increasing education access

Because supply cannot meet demand in the educational system targets have been set to address the issue. First, there have been steps to raise the enrolment rates of girls in education because it was observed that while the gender parity index (GPI) at preschool level was 0.99, this was not the same for the other cycles of education. While the primary level indicated a GPI score of 0.88, at the general secondary level a score of 0.58 was recorded.

Moreover, because repetition and dropout rates in the system mostly affect girls, measures had to be put in place to correct this unfavourable situation for girls.

Also initiated was inclusive education which aimed to integrate all children with specific needs into the system and it enabled access to basic education. Thus, children gained access to formal education irrespective of their socio-economic or cultural status.

Adapting the offer of education

Adapting the provision of education to global and cyber best practices may enrich the education system by including the new effective knowledges and improve teacher training (PANAF 2007).

Due to the politico-military crisis that occurred for many years (2002–11), in the particular context of the Ivory Coast, there is increasing need for new approaches and two are presented here. The first approach concerns a guarantee, a way of improving education giving its potential to reach a great proportion of the population to be educated. The second approach involved peace education and citizenship, which underlined questions of sustainable development and management of natural resources such as water which are the sources of conflict. The integration of this approach into the education system will lead to improved living conditions among communities through intra- and inter-communal relations

Conclusion

Education in the Ivory Coast has progressed but many goals still remain to be achieved in order to reach education for all. These goals include improving the rate of enrolment and the gender parity index as well as boosting finances considering that education costs are still high. Authorities need to ensure that education caters for the vulnerable population, particularly, girls and women. The provision of education must take cognizance of and develop the emerging young adult generation, able to ensure the scientific development and economic progress in an environment without violence (Ministère d'Etat, Ministère du Plan et du Développement, 2012, Plan National de Développement 2012–2015). The education system must also enable the training of future citizens willing to participate in dialogues between cultures and contribute to the development of the global village. These are the educational challenges of the twenty-first century facing the Ivory Coast and other numerous countries in Africa.

References

Azoh, F-J., Koné, R., Kouadio, K. O., Okon, G. M. and N'Guessan, M. V. (2004). 'Evaluation de l'impact du conflit armé sur le système scolaire dans les zones sous contrôle de la rébellion (2004)'. Ministère de l'Education Nationale de Côte d'Ivoire, Banque Mondiale et ROCARE.

Azoh, F-J., Lanoue, E. and Tchombé, T. (2009a). *Education, Violence, Conflits et Perspectives de paix en Afrique Subsaharienne*. Paris: Karthala.

Azoh, F-J., Koutou, N. C. and Chelpi-den Hamer, M. (2009b). 'Impact du conflit armé sur l'éducation primaire: Quel Financement pour les Ecoles? Quels Freins à la Scolarisation? Quelles Réponses Locales?' Save The Children-Pays Bas, Université d'Amsterdam et ROCARE.

Azoh, F-Joseph, Ettien, A. A-M. and Goin, B. Z. T I (2010). 'Ecoles communautaires: alternative crédible ou offre crédible intégrée au système d'éducation primaire en Côte d'Ivoire?. Ministère de l'Education Nationale, UNICEF, ROCARE.

Coen, B., (2005). 'Après trois ans de conflit, les enfants de Côte d'Ivoire retournent à l'école'. UNICEF. Available from http://www.unicef.org/french/infobycountry/cotedivoire_30572.html (consulté le 29 septembre 2012).

Dedy, S., Bih, E. and Koné, R. (1997). 'Étude des déterminants familiaux de la scolarisation des filles et des enfants en zone de sous-scolarisation de Côte d'Ivoire'. Ministère de l'Education Nationale/ROCARE

Lanoue, E. (2002). 'Les politiques de l'école catholique en Afrique de l'Ouest. Le cas de la Côte d'Ivoire'. Thèse de doctorat, EHESS, Paris.

—(2004a). 'Les écoles catholiques et la construction des identités scolaires en Côte d'Ivoire'. *Cahiers de la recherche sur l'éducation et les savoirs, n°3, 2004*, pp. 79–95.

—(2004b). 'École catholique et décolonisation ecclésiale socio-histoire d'une controverse sous la 1ère république de Côte d'Ivoire'. *Archives de Sciences sociales des Religions*, 2004, 128, pp. 5–24.

Ministère de l'Education Nationale (2009). *Annuaire statistique de la DPES*, Abidjan.

Ministère d'Etat, Ministère du Plan et du Développement (2009). Document de Stratégie de Réduction de la Pauvreté (DSRP) 2009–2013, Abidjan.

—(2012). 'Plan National de Développement 2012–2015'. Abidjan. Ministère du Plan et du Développement.

PANAF (2007). 'Agenda Panafricain de Recherche sur l'Intégration Pédagogique des Techniques de l'Information et de la Communication'. Centre de Recherches et de Développement International (CRDI)/Université de Montréal (Canada) et Réseau Ouest et Centre Africain de Recherche en Education (ROCARE). Available from www.observatoiretic.org (consulté le 29 septembre 2012).

UNDP (2008). Rapport Mondial sur le Développement Humain 2007/2008. La lutte contre le changement climatique : un impératif de solidarité dans un monde divisé. New York, UNDP.

World Bank (2011). 'Le système éducatif de la Côte d'Ivoire. Comprendre les forces et les faiblesses du système pour identifier les bases d'une politique nouvelle et ambitieuse'. Rapport d'Etat sur le Système Educatif National (RESEN). Washington. Banque Mondiale.

15

Ivory Coast: Evolving Gender Representation in Higher Education from Peace to the Era of Political Instability and Post-Conflict Reconstruction

N'Dri Thérèse Assié-Lumumba

Introduction

This paper is a reflective essay grounded on both a conceptual and historical articulation (with some empirical illustrations) of the evolution of formal education in Côte d'Ivoire inherited from the colonial experience, with a focus on gender. The arguments are presented within the methodological framework of historical-structuralism. It is defined by the fundamental principles and assumptions that social phenomena, and the structure of society at large with its institutions and policies, reflect the socio-historical contingencies within which institutions evolve. The analysis of the interface of gender, higher education, and development in Africa in general, can be well articulated within this framework. The historical factors define colonial contexts and post-colonial processes of the Ivorian higher education institutions as well as the location of women and articulation of gender.

Since the inception of colonial rule in Africa, there have been debates and struggles surrounding the fundamental issues that still pertain to contemporary African education such as whether this colonially designed formal education as conceptualized and organized from a European perspective can lead to socio-economic development in post-colonial Africa. Issues of how to make an initially alien system grow new roots to be Africanized enough to reflect African ethos and social fabric have been critically addressed. Of these issues, the gender question remains the quintessential challenge in the quest for social progress.

In the past decade or so, African countries, including Côte d'Ivoire have been defining strategic planning for their future development in the twenty-first century. Education constitutes a central factor for human resource development targeted for the acquisition of the skills to create and sustain the envisioned competitive economies amidst increasing globalization. The centrality of the education and gender nexus in economic planning is an additional factor in discussing future development. One of the enduring characteristics of formal education in Côte d'Ivoire, like in many other African countries, has been the persistent gender imbalance in the representation at all levels of the system. Whether education is defined as a basic human right and/or as an investment, the gender parity question remains critical.

Côte d'Ivoire, as a contemporary nation-state, was carved out of its socio-geographic context in the nineteenth century with marks on the state of the social institutions that have endured through to the twenty-first century including those related to education. Following the partitioning of the entire African continent at the Berlin Conference in 1884/5, Côte d'Ivoire was established as a formal French colony in 1893 and subsequently became part of French West Africa.[1]

The French colonial administration, like the other colonial powers, designed and implemented its policy of education to suit colonial imperatives. European colonization in Africa was an arrogant expression of patriarchy. Even when colonial powers were represented by non-traditional groups like women, these female leaders acted as 'honorary males' in advancing patriarchal agendas. Colonial policies were guided primarily by the interests of the colonizers. Thus, formal education, with its societal reproductive and transformative capacity, was an instrument to not only shape the African societies for that time, but to also shape the future of colonized societies.

This paper addresses key aspects of the fundamental gender factor in the inherited French formal education system in Côte d'Ivoire. With the historical and colonial legacy, what have been the trajectory and patterns in the decades following the immediate post-independence decade in the mid-twentieth century up to the beginning of this second decade of the twenty-first century?

The paper is structured under three main headings. The first section deals with the perverted effect and unintended consequences of the convergence of colonial policies and indigenous resistance to European education as the root of contemporary gender-based unequal educational opportunities, especially at the higher education level. The second section examines the post-colonial reality in the Ivorian education system from the 1960s to the Dawn of the New Millennium. The third section discusses gender in education in meeting the challenges of post-conflict reconstruction and development. The conclusion reflects on the search for renewal looking forward.

The roots of contemporary gender imbalance in education: Unintended convergence of colonial policies and indigenous resistance to Europeanization

Colonial policies of education in Africa reflected the broader ideology and administrative models of different European powers at that time and their adaptation to regional and local realities in the colonies to achieve their respective goals. The British colonial education policy, designed from the broader philosophy of indirect rule, was characterized by almost full control of the different Christian denominations, based upon the authority of the British Crown. In turn, these denominations were in charge of the education of the colonized with very few exceptions of direct state involvement such as in Northern Nigeria for strategic purposes. In the case of Belgium, an agreement between King Leopold II and the Vatican granted full control of the policy and administration of the education for the Congolese to the Catholic Church to serve the colonial administration and its corporations.

In contrast, the French colonial administration was directly and fully in charge of the design and implementation of education policy for the colonized Africans. Administrators operated within a highly centralized system whereby decisions were adopted in the Ministry of the Colonies in Paris and then trickled down to the Dakar office for French West Africa and Brazzaville for French Equatorial Africa.

The single most famous (or notorious) feature of the French colonial policy of education was assimilation. Philosophically, assimilation aimed at using formal education to produce colonized Africans who would think and behave like the French without the same freedom and equality. How could it work then? In the broader European thinking of the time that rejected the idea and reality of African history and civilization, assimilation was presented as the gateway to culture and civilization. However, this philosophy of assimilation that was predicated on equal education in type and content for the metropolitan French and the colonized Africans was in direct conflict with the exigencies of colonization that were grounded on systematic inequality between the colonizers and the colonized. The legal status of the 'natives' invented by the colonial administration provided the justification for unequal rights and treatment. Thus, assimilation suffered from fundamental contradictions.

However, despite these contradictions, the French colonial education policy affected the existence of the indigenous systems. Education in French colonies was profoundly structured with uniquely enduring effects. Yet many of the attributes of the inherited system have been deemed hindering factors in postcolonial development agenda. Therefore, for a better understanding of the gender factor in the Ivorian contemporary education with a focus on higher education, it is necessary to recall the roots of some of these factors that continue to affect education with direct consequences for socio-economic development and social progress.

It is worth mentioning a few ideas about gender in the nineteenth century during which time the colonial policies took shape. For instance, according to Napoleon 1, the founder of the élite and higher education-driven secondary school of lycée,

> The weakness of women's brain, the mobility of their ideas, their future position in the social order, the 'necessity of a constant and perpetual submissiveness and of a certain indulgent and easy charity', all this can be obtained only through religion, a charitable and smooth religion ... (Prost 1968: 268).

At the time of the design of the French policies towards its colonies, the prevalent views on education for females in France were also captured in this statement by a religious authority, Mgr. Dupanloup's statement (Prost 1968: 268):

> Girls are raised for private life in private life; I request that they be not sent to courses, examinations, diplomas, qualifications which prepare men to public life. ... I request that women for the future be not educated to become free thinkers.

The idea of the division of the social space into a public sphere controlled by men with its corresponding formal education versus a private sphere that ought to offer at best only rudiments of formal education, was the mainstream throughout Europe, certainly in France's bourgeoisie/aristocracy. Women from the Third Estate who were working outside the home did not receive even the parochial vocational education that their male counterpart received. Although there were some progressive opposing positions that articulated the importance of providing some or even equal education to the female population, these views did not inform colonial policy.

Like elsewhere in Africa, the Africans in the French colonies and specifically in Côte d'Ivoire, resisted colonial domination and its policies of dismantling or disorganizing indigenous social institutions including education (Assié-Lumumba 1998, 2006). Ivorian resistance to French colonial rule was reflected in the rejection of two types of French education: school for chiefs' sons to train future leaders expected to support and serve as agents of colonial rule and school to train workers for the colonial economy. The two types of schools targeted the boys only. In the context of resistance the youth that attended these schools were drafted as if they were in the military and were enroled by force. Initially, the schools provided only a few years of elementary education. Nevertheless, the main aspects of the assimilation policy were implemented. They included the use of French as the sole language of instruction in all schools, the selective/elitist nature of the education even if it was reduced to a few elementary school years, and the unequivocal gendered and unequal treatment of girls.

In their struggle to safeguard their civilization, Ivorian families and societies more generally vowed to protect the girls from the corrosive impact of the French assimilation-based education, as women were recognized as the foundation of culture and civilization. Thus, for Ivorian families, a defining battleground was how to prevent the enrolment of their daughters in any type of French schools, when the colonial administration and also a few scattered Catholic missionaries attempted to do so. In addition to the ideological rejection, the fact that education for girls was conceived and designed mostly around home economics contributed to explain the resistance at a later stage, when families realized that their daughters would enter de facto a process of domestication as women. Even if the vocational schools for the males provided only basic skills for low-ranking positions as auxiliaries in teaching, agricultural extension, medical assistance, and so forth, French education was shaping a gendered occupational structure.

This rejection of French education did not last throughout the entire colonial era. Colonial education was limiting, as a key concern in the mind of the colonial authorities was how to control the 'natives'. In spite of the nature of colonial education those who attended the schools even by force acquired new skills that positioned them relatively better in the irreversibly Europeanizing society (Ki-Zerbo 1972). They were the males who could qualify for the new positions, including the political leadership positions following the struggle for independence in which women, even without the benefit of any European formal education including the ability to read and write, were equally engaged at the forefront.

The ironic convergence of two contradictory policies – the French search for control of the African and reproduction of French historical views on the worthlessness of female education on the one hand and on the other hand the Africans' struggle for freedom through their rejection of European education, especially for the females – constituted the seeds of deep-seated gender inequality planted in the Ivorian/African soil. Though unintended, the consequences of the nexus of colonial policies and indigenous resistance to Europeanization by way of the more unequivocal rejection of education for the female population created the initial gender gap. While the value of that education had evolved and increased by the time of independence, the initial differential access based on gender is still impacting the Ivorian education process, especially at the tertiary level.

Post-colonial policies and practices from the 1960s to the dawn of the New Millennium

Since Côte d'Ivoire acquired its independence in 1960, the government has signed and even ratified numerous agreements and conventions adopted by African and International organizations that aim to eradicate gender-based inequality and ensure the protection of the rights of the girl child and the woman.[2] On 17 July 1980, it signed the Convention on the Elimination of All Forms of Discrimination Against Women (CEDAW), which includes specific articles on the elimination or prevention of all forms of inequality in education regarding access to all types and levels, retention, completion, output, the content and values promoted in the curriculum the process, and the outcome relating to the occupational structure.

Côte d'Ivoire was among the first African countries to create a Ministry of Women's Affairs in the beginning of the United Nations Women's decade.[3] It was headed by Mrs. Jeanne Gervais from 1976 to 1983. The country was also strongly represented by women in the September 1995 Beijing Conference after which, on 18 December 1995, it ratified CEDAW. In spite of these noteworthy achievements, it is important to ask what have been the broader and specific domestic policies and practices toward effective elimination of the gender gap in education, especially at the tertiary level.

From independence in 1960 to the military coup d'etat of 24 December 1999, Côte d'Ivoire was considered an emerging country ready for economic 'take-off' (Roques 1966). Even if there were critical and sceptical positions (Amin 1967), it registered spectacular economic growth rates, second only to Japan during the first two post-colonial decades. On the political front Côte d'Ivoire was considered a land of peace and stability under the leadership of its first President, Félix Houphouët-Boigny.

The government was represented at the Addis Ababa Conference of 1961, where African leaders defined their education needs and agreed to achieve by 1980:

- Universal free and compulsory primary schooling,
- Secondary education for 30 per cent of all children finishing primary school
- University places for 20 per cent of secondary school completers.

In Côte d'Ivoire, the actual or perceived centrality of education led to the official declaration of education as 'the priority of all priorities'. As such, formal education often tied up several ministries with their respective portfolios, including the Ministry of Primary Education (and Television Education in the 1970s–1980s), the Ministries of Education of Higher Education, Scientific Research, Technical Education and Vocational Training. Other ministries such as those for Youth and Sports and Cultural Affairs were also involved in formal education.

Thus, the Ivorian government devoted considerable proportions of its increasing resources and public expenditures to education. For instance, in 1965, public monetary resources allocated to education represented up to 5.4 per cent of the GNP and 20 per cent of the total public expenditure. The corresponding figures for 1973 are 7.4 per cent and 31.7 per cent respectively. In 1973, Côte d'Ivoire was arguably the country that allocated the largest proportion of its recurrent budget to education (Tuinder 1978: 281–2).

The increase in general enrolment rates at all the levels of the education system reflected to a certain extent the official declaration and aforementioned budgetary commitment. The increase in enrolment was even more spectacular at higher education levels, especially considering the negligible number of students enroled at independence. Thus, the total enrolment grew from just 48 students from 1959–60 to 5,366 in 1978–9 (Assié 1982: 155). At the primary level, the proportions of female students grew from 24.6 per cent to 38.8 per cent in the same period. The corresponding figures for the secondary level are 14.3 per cent to 26.4 per cent (ibid. 165).

When broken down by gender, however, the distribution at the higher education level reflected the historical legacy of female under-representation, a pattern that is widespread throughout the African continent with only a few exceptions mostly in Southern Africa and a few other emerging cases such as Tunisia or Southeastern Nigeria with a parity of male under-representation.

The two converging historical factors mentioned in the first section have been compounded by the nexus of persistent internal cultural, economic, and policy-related factors and exogenous dynamics in the context of neo-liberal policies amidst globalization, especially since the structural adjustment programmes (SAPs) of the international financial institutions that started in the 1980s (Assié-Lumumba and Lumumba-Kasongo 1996; Assié-Lumumba 2000).

From the 1950s to the 1960s/1970s, the idea that education was an investment toward individual upward mobility and national development as articulated in human capital theory was popular in Africa and across the globe (Schultz 1961; Harbison and Myers 1964). Convinced by the arguments of human capital theorists, researchers and policy analysts and based on observation in the early post-independence years, and also given the hierarchical conception of the structure of the education system, actual and potential students and their families, policymakers and society at large viewed higher education as the most desirable avenue to achieve and maximize private and social returns to education. Considering the original gender imbalance, a critical question is how the Ivorian decision-makers proceeded to ensure equality.

The Ivorian government adopted several policies to achieve a declared goal of eliminating gender inequality, first at the lower levels of the education system, namely the primary and lower secondary levels. The logic for the lower level was that by achieving universal enrolment it would de facto resolve the problem. However, many of the reforms that deal in part with access were not implemented (Assié-Lumumba and Lumumba-Kasongo 1991). Specific policies included the adoption of technology, with a highly publicized television programme to achieve quickly universal primary enrolment, the most efficient means to eliminate any form of inequality in basic access. At the secondary school level, policies concerned, for instance, the adoption of an affirmative measure that consisted in admitting female students to secondary schools in general at a lower level than the level for male secondary school candidates[4] and the creation of all-girls secondary schools.[5]

However, structurally, in addition to persistently lower initial enrolment in primary schools, girls continued to encounter numerous obstacles that resulted in lower enrolment rates and higher repetition, dropout and forced-out rates than among the males. Girls from low socio-economic statuses, who reach puberty and start to have their menstrual periods, generally in upper primary classes, tend to miss class at least once a month for sanitary reasons. As a result, they fall behind. The cumulative effects lead to failing grades, repetition or even dismissal.

Early/unwanted pregnancy usually resulted in dismissal from school and/or difficulties in managing the life of young and unprepared mothers with no specific family, social and institutional support. In fact, even when their partners were fellow students or teachers, for that matter, they were considered as the sole person responsible for their situation. Hence dismissal was a punishment. In low socio-economic status families, especially in rural communities (Assie-Lumumba 1994) but also in growing urban peripheries in Abidjan and other large urban centres, direct and opportunity cost remained higher for female than for male youth. Thus the female students' use of time for housework instead of homework contributes to lower achievements. The cumulative effect of these factors explains the higher female repetition and dropout rates.

As a result of lower enrolment rates and higher attrition rates among females in primary school, there has been a persistent gender literacy gap as illustrated in the data published in the Guide to the Analysis and Use of Household Survey and Census Education Data (UIS 2004) based on the MICS (Multiple indicator cluster survey.[6] They indicate that among people aged 15–24 years, 69.6 per cent of the males compared to 51.5 per cent of the females are literate. The corresponding figures for 25–34 years, 35–44 years, 45–54 years, 55–64, and finally 65 years and above are 67.6 per cent and 41.2 per cent, 60.7 per cent and 32.3 per cent, 52.0 per cent and 17.9 per cent, 26.6 per cent and 5.2 per cent and 17.1 per cent and 3.6 per cent, respectively.

The relatively smaller gap among the youngest population group suggests that the gap is diminishing. The smaller gap in the oldest age group, which would have reached elementary school age during the last decade of the colonial period, reflects the restrictive French colonial administration policy that did not promote popular basic education. Thus, while the proportion of female students was negligible at that time, enrolment of male youth was not high either. In addition to high attrition in a selective system, the application of legal dismissals based on academic performance led to many students leaving the system too soon to acquire and consolidate literacy. African youth that were enroled experienced an elitist system even at the primary level.[7]

Generally, in earlier post-independence decades and the current context, another continuous consequence of unequal access and high attrition rates among schoolgirls at the lower levels of the system is the considerably wider gap between males and females at the tertiary level.

Table 15.1 Tertiary education gross enrolment ratio as percentage of total eligible population by gender (years with missing data or non-gender disaggregated data are not included)

	School enrolment, tertiary (% gross)	School enrolment, tertiary, female (% gross)	School enrolment, tertiary, male (% gross)	Gender Gap	Selectivity Index
1971	1.02	0.30	1.66	1.36	5.53
1972	1.03	0.32	1.68	1.36	5.25
1973	1.21	0.39	1.97	1.58	5.05
1974	1.25	0.42	2.02	1.60	4.80
1976	1.32	0.47	2.12	1.65	4.51
1977	1.53	0.56	2.43	1.87	4.33
1979	1.98	0.72	3.16	2.44	4.38
1980	2.19	0.80	3.47	2.67	4.33
1984	2.37	0.86	3.78	2.92	4.39
1987	2.61	0.97	4.15	3.18	4.27
1994	4.12	1.94	6.21	4.27	3.20
1995	3.99	1.99	5.93	3.94	2.97
1999	6.37	3.38	9.30	5.92	2.75
2000	6.63	3.69	9.52	5.83	2.57
2006	8.56	5.61	11.51	5.90	2.05
2007	8.87	5.91	11.82	5.91	2.00

Source: World Bank, World Development Indicators (Adjusted with additions of Gender Gap and Gender Selectivity Index Calculated by author, accessed on June 12, 2013)

At the higher education level in general, especially at the university, there is an even smaller proportion of female students registered in fields such as sciences in comparison to the humanities and social sciences. Typically, in addition to the general and persistent under-representation of women in higher education, there is the severe problem of the reproduction of classical disciplinary clusters by gender whereby female students enrol disproportionately in larger numbers in disciplines that are less competitive according to the hierarchy and the values attributed to them on the labour market and in society at large and yield less return. The enrolment ratios and gender gaps and selectivity index show a persistent gender inequality over the decades. As recently as 2007, a female university-age youth has half the chance of a male counterpart to enrol.

In her study of 'Ivorian Women: Education and Integration in the Economic Development of Côte d'Ivoire' based on data from the 1980s to the early 1990s, Rose Eholié (2007), now a retired professor of Inorganic Chemistry, lamented the entrenched inequality in quantitative representation of Ivorian women in higher education in general and even more blatantly in the scientific fields and subfields. The unequal representation in the fields of study is reproduced in educational outcome and translates into a gendered and unequal occupational structure. Thus, there is a vicious cycle and reproduction of gender inequality ironically produced through education, an institution that has been called the great equalizer. Eholié authoritatively articulated the negative consequences of the gender gap hindering women's rights and advancement and their roles in the national development process.

In another study titled 'Women and Scientific Education: The Case of Higher Education in Côte d'Ivoire' Denise Houphouët-Boigny and Frederica Koblavi Mansilla (2007) critically examine the distribution of female students in the fields of science in the Ivorian higher education, including universities as well as *Grandes* Écoles, which are very selective elite professional schools in the fields of science. In a way this study is a follow up to the aforementioned study by Eholié. Based on their assessment and comparisons of some of the data from Eholié's study and new data of their own, they concluded, while acknowledging the higher proportion of female students that the patterns of female underrepresentation and negative disciplinary clusters persist. Thus, the system still remains essentially characterized by gender inequality.

An earlier study (Assié 1982: 215) based on 'selectivity indices' found 'that a son with a university educated father has 3.5 more chances than one whose father has no formal education to attend an academic secondary school'. The corresponding figure for female offspring is 35.2. This gives more weight to the argument that female enrolment is much more determined by ascriptive factors. While few female students come from 'uneducated homes, virtually all daughters with at least one university educated parent, usually the father, are enroled in secondary schools' (ibid.).

More generally, it is well established that disadvantaged social circumstances, and especially poverty, are good predictors of initial low enrolment of girls, their higher attrition rates, limited completion rates in the lower levels of education, leading to their under-representation at the higher education level. As will be shown in the next section, due to the combined effects of many factors, especially the decade-long political crisis, Côte d'Ivoire that was hailed for its economic success is now challenged by increased poverty. What then are the trends of gender issues in the educational system, higher education and society at large?

Political instability, the search for peace and implications for gender equity and education

Côte d'Ivoire marred its entrance into the new Century/Millennium, with the 24 December 1999 military coup, exactly a week before the New Year. Subsequently, the entire first decade of the new Millennium was marked by rebellions and armed conflicts that were transformed into full-fledged civil war. After a full five-year term (2005–10) with no elections of the president and representatives of the National Assembly, the 2010 elections were expected to normalize the political process and bring back peace. However, following the highly contested results of the November 2010 second round, the presidential election led to further violence until April 2011. Given the essentially patriarchal nature of the colonial standing army and its legacy in the post-colonial society, this military coup was in itself a setback in the efforts to close the gender gap in education.

In the 1980s, the spectacular economic and educational achievements of earlier decades started to slow down and almost stagnated with the economic crisis. The subsequent austerity measures of the SAPs of the World Bank and the IMF that were supposed to help resolve the problems in fact exacerbated the situation in the 1980s and 1990s. The 1999 military coup and the subsequent violence and instability precipitated further stagnation and decline. As shown in Figure 15.1, the proportion of people living under the poverty line increased significantly in the 1990s. However, the country was on the path

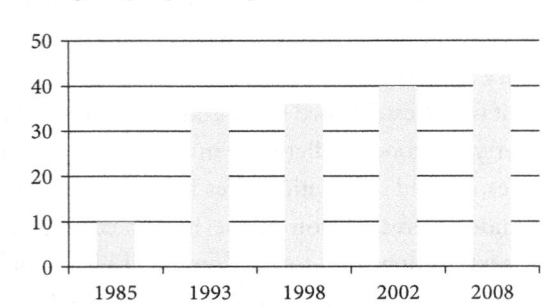

Figure 15.1 Percentage of people living below national poverty line

Source: Data from World development Indicators, World Bank April 2011 (accessed on 10 May 2013)

of recovery that was put to a sudden halt by the military coup d'état and the destructive violence that endured throughout the first decade of the twenty-first century.

The international comparisons based on economic, social and a wider range of indicators show that Côte d'Ivoire has experienced considerable setbacks during the period. The Human Development Index (HDI – with four categories (very high: 1–47, high: 48–94, medium: 95–141, and low: 142–186) of the United Nations Development Programmes (UNDP) shows that by the time the military coup occurred, Côte d'Ivoire's rank had already declined to 154. However, the situation worsened resulting in a ranking of 170 in 2011 and 168 over the past two years. While measurements of the HDI are not precise and have consistently provoked controversy, they give an indication of the general and comparative socio-economic trends of different countries.

As a result of the general decline, the most vulnerable groups have been feeling the setback even more. Ironically, while the proportion of impoverished people who need a caring state to meet basic needs including the cost of education, healthcare, etc., was increasing, the state's investment in education was in decline. Thus, despite highly publicized programmes of distribution of school supplies to needy students, in reality data from the UNESCO Institute of Statistics (UIS) show the steady decline of the public expenditure on education as a proportion of the GNI. *Africa for Women's Rights: Côte d'Ivoire,* for instance,[8] made a scathing general assessment of the gendered dimensions of continued 'obstacles to access to education', stating that:

> The general level of schooling in Côte d'Ivoire is very low, especially for girls: in the northern areas of the country, under the influence of tradition, the population remains reluctant to educate girls, who are often responsible for domestic tasks. In 2009, only 49% of girls were educated at primary school level as opposed to 61% of boys, and over 75% of girls received no secondary school education. The literacy rate for young women aged between 15 and 25 was only 40%.

Nearly all the African countries have recently articulated their respective strategic long-term visions and also medium-term plans to lead their countries to the status of middle-income and emerging economies that can withstand increasing global competitiveness. Ironically, while at least in terms of growth Côte d'Ivoire reached decades earlier some of the newly targeted, in rebuilding the torn post-conflict country, the leaders of the country have also presented their planning arguments.

Given the dismal state of gender in the country, what are the measures that the authorities are envisioning for gender parity in the future? In the medium-term document (*Plan National de Développement 2012-2015*, Tome III 2012: 73-6) for instance, there are references to plan the promotion of 'gender equality' 'economic security and human rights' and the 'reduction of gender-based violence'. Concerning education, the document refers to 'encouraging girls' access to education' and 'improving access of the female population to ICTs'.

However, there is no bold higher education policy statement or engagements to empower women through equal access to the highest level of education and production of knowledge and equal capacity to participate in decision-making processes. This is particularly true as it relates to training in the fields of science and technology, which the state considers to be the foundation for the future competitive economy. In order to fundamentally transform the Ivorian social fabric to create a gender-balanced and egalitarian society, the policies must be daring.

Conclusion

Amartya Sen (1999) articulated that women throughout the world and especially in the Third World are not allowed to fulfill their human capabilities as they have limited opportunities in education and subsequently in the workplace. Yet this unused potential negatively affects the lives of all people (Sen 1999: 191). I have also (Assie-Lumumba 2007) made a case for the need to rethink the 'Gender Factor in Human Capabilities' meaning that we start with the premise that any form of unequal opportunity is both a violation of the basic human rights of the individual and a loss for society in terms of the potential contribution toward social progress. It does not matter whether it is the female population that is under-represented or the males. Any imbalance in access, progression in the educational system from the basic to the higher education levels and in the different fields, successful academic achievement and socio-economic attainment create loss that may or may not be easily observable.

Côte d'Ivoire ought to envision a bold policy of leapfrogging toward gender as a sine qua non for social progress. Unleashing the neglected or suppressed human capabilities of the female population is both a human rights issue and investment in the future. New forward-looking policies must also consider the synergy and co-ordination within the regional economic communities (RECs) such as the ECOWAS and also the perspectives of the continent and diaspora to achieve economies of scale and mutual reinforcement.

Notes

1. Beside Senegal where the capital of Dakar of French West Africa (Afrique Occidentale Française-AOF) was located and Côte d'Ivoire, the other colonies were Benin, Burkina Faso, Guinea, Mali, Mauritania, and Niger.
2. For instance the African Charter on Human and People's Rights of the Organization of African Unity (OAU) and subsequent measures by the African Union (AU), Universal Declaration of Human Right, International Covenant on Civil and Political Rights, and Optional Protocol to International Covenant on Civil and Political Rights; Convention against Discrimination in Education, to cite a few.
3. The Women's started with the1976 inaugural conference in Mexico City, followed by the mid-way Copenhagen Conference of 1980 and was concluded with the 1985 Nairobi Conference.
4. This author criticized this measure as being insufficient as female students admitted under such policies would not perform well in secondary school without support.
5. The first and most prominently innovative of such institutions was Collège Sainte Marie which became later Lycée, a public institution completely run by French nuns of the Saint François-Xavier Congregation that had created two high-achieving élite secondary schools.
6. www.uis.unesco.org/Library/Documents/hhsguide04-en.pdf (last accessed on 13 July 2013).
7. The French invented the strange system of 'higher primary education' (école primaire supérieure) for the natives.
8. http://www.wikigender.org/index.php/Africa_for_Women%27s_Rights:_Cote_D%27Ivoire#Obstacles_to_access_to_education (accessed on 28 April 2013).

References

Africa for Women's Rights: Côte d'Ivoire. Available from http://www.wikigender.org/index.php/Africa_for_Women%27s_Rights:_Cote_D%27Ivoire#Obstacles_to_access_to_education (accessed on 28 April 2013).

Amin, S. (1967). *Le Développement du Capitalisme en Côte d'Ivoire*. Paris: les Éditions de Minuit.

Assié, N. T. (1982). 'Educational Selection and Social Inequality in Africa: The Case of the Ivory Coast', unpublished Ph.D. Thesis, University of Chicago, Chicago, Illinois.

Assié-Lumumba, N. T. (1994). 'Rural students in urban settings in Africa: the experiences of female students in secondary schools'. In N. Stromquist (ed.), *Education in the Urban Areas: Cross-National Dimensions*. Westport, CT: Praeger, pp. 199–218.

—(1998). 'Women in West Africa'. In N. Stromquist (ed.), *Women in the Third World: an Encyclopedia of Contemporary Issues*. New York: Garland Publishing, Inc., pp. 533–42.

—(2000). 'Educational and economic reforms, gender equity, and access to schooling in Africa'. *International Journal of Comparative Sociology*, Vol. XLI: 1.

—(2006). 'Structural Change and Continuity in the African Family: The Case of Côte d'Ivoire. In Y. Oheneba-Sakyi and B. K. Takyi (eds), *African Families at the Turn of the 21st Century*. Westport, CT: Greenwood Publishing Group.

—(2007). 'Human Capital, Human Capabilities, and Gender Equality: Harnessing the Development of Human Potential as a Human Right and the Foundation for Social Progress'. In N. Assie-Lumumba (ed.), *Women and Higher Education in Africa: Reconceptualizing Gender-Based Human Capabilities and Upgrading Human Rights to Knowledge*. Abidjan: CEPARRED, pp. 15–37.

Assié-Lumumba, N. T. and Lumumba-Kasongo, T. (1991). 'Economic Crisis, State and Educational Reforms in Africa: The Case of Côte d'Ivoire'. In M. B. Ginsburg (ed.), *Educational Reform in International Context: Ideology, Economy and the State*. New York: Garland Publishing Inc.

—(1996). 'The impact of structural adjustment programs on higher education in Africa'. One of the studies of the network 'An African perspective on structural adjustment programs' of CODESRIA.

Eholié, R. (2007). 'Ivorian Women: Education and Integration in the Economic Development of Côte d'Ivoire'. In N. Assie-Lumumba (ed.), *Women and Higher Education in Africa: Reconceptualizing Gender-Based Human Capabilities and Upgrading Human Rights to Knowledge*. Abidjan: CEPARRED, pp. 233–75.

Harbison, F. H. and Myers, C. A. (1964). *Education, Manpower, and Economic Growth; Strategies of Human Resource Development*. New York: McGraw-Hill.

Houphouët-Boigny, D. and Koblavi Mansilla, F. (2007). 'Women and Scientific Education: The Case of Higher Education in Côte d'Ivoire'. In N. Assie-Lumumba (ed.), *Women and Higher Education in Africa: Reconceptualizing Gender-Based Human Capabilities and Upgrading Human Rights to Knowledge*. Abidjan. CEPARRED, pp. 307–51.

Ki-Zerbo, J. (1972). *Histoire de l'Afrique Noire, d'Hier à Demain*. Paris: Hatier.

Prost, A. (1968). *Histoire de l'Enseignement en France: 1800–1967*. Paris: Armand Colin.

République de Côte d'Ivoire (2012). *Plan National de Développement 2012–2015*. Abidjan: République de Côte d'Ivoire.

Roques, P. (1966). 'La Côte d'Ivoire vers le "take-off" économique'. *Penant*, 76, 711, 137–48. avr.-mai-juin.

Schultz, T. W. (1961). 'Investment in human capital'. *American Economic Review* 51: 1–17.

Sen, A. (1999). *Development as Freedom*. New York: Alfred A. Knopf, Inc.

Tuinder, B. A. (1978). *Ivory Coast, The Challenge of Success: Report of a Mission Sent to the Ivory Coast by the World Bank*. Baltimore: Johns Hopkins University Press.

UNESCO Institute of Statistics (UIS) (2004). Guide to The Analysis and Use of Household Survey and Census Education Data, based on the MICS (Multiple indicator cluster survey). Available from www.uis.unesco.org/Library/Documents/hhsguide04-en.pdf (last accessed 13 July 2013).

World Bank (2011). *World Development Indicators*, April 2011.

16

Liberia: Conflicts and Post-Conflict Trends

Barbara G. Reynolds[1]

Introduction

When I speak with colleagues about Liberia, including Liberian colleagues, there is a sense that the 1989–2003 conflict was a truly defining moment in Liberia's modern history. As with every war, these colleagues and their communities lost the things ordinary people hold most dear – family and friends, home and health, limb and livelihood. The people I met in four short months when I worked in Liberia in 1997, whether in the office, at church, at the hairdresser's, in the market were warm and kind. Some were tired, others frustrated, some bitter and cynical. But everyone kept going, kept trying, kept focusing on the future and I admire the indomitable determination and courage that kept them moving. They shared their lunch and their laughter, their hymn books and their life-stories. From these interactions, I realised that for the foreseeable future, Liberia's narrative would be defined by the conflict.

To gain an accurate picture of the current education system in Liberia, it is important to understand Liberia's recent educational history. Sadly, very little data exists about Liberian education since the civil war, and due to this lack of data, very little has been written (Tsimpo and Wodon 2012). In researching this chapter, therefore, I thought it would be instructive to use the conflict to compare and contrast the education situation in Liberia, looking beyond the current snapshot of data and facts to set out the historical factors that most shaped the current situation of education in Liberia, and to begin to look at perspectives for the future. The chapter relies heavily on data and information from government, UN and similar reliable sources, supplemented by brief interviews with Liberians.

Country Profile

Liberia has a population of 3,441,790. Approximately 50 per cent of the population are under 18 years old, with a relatively low life expectancy of 58 years and a high level of poverty (IDLO 2010). Since the war, fertility rates have steadily declined, from 6.6 children per woman from 1981–5 to 5.2 children in 2007, although fertility rates differ greatly between urban and rural areas, with 6.2 children per woman in rural areas, and 3.8 in urban regions (LISGIS et al. 2008). Tuberculosis, malaria, HIV/AIDS and yellow fever present serious health threats in Liberia, and contribute to the relative high levels of mortality and morbidity (UNDP 2010).

Originally founded by freed black American slaves in 1847, Liberia has endured a long history of conflict and dispute. Despite the fact that the American-Liberian population constituted only around 5 per cent of the population (Adebajo 2002), these settlers created an exclusive rich elite within Liberia, which was primarily based in Monrovia. The indigenous peoples of the hinterland were largely excluded, over time causing friction between the two main parts of Liberian society and, ultimately, was the cause of the civil war from 1989 to 2003 (Ellis 1995).

The 14 years of civil war have decimated Liberia's infrastructure and left it in economic turmoil (IDLO 2010). The nation's social fabric, including churches, schools and hospitals, were left in tatters. Over the course of the conflict, 800,000 Liberians were displaced, and around 270,000 were killed (UNDAF 2007). Great atrocities have been committed, including sexual abuse, cannibalism, and the training and use of child soldiers. Ellis (1995) comments 'even professional soldiers ... who may be assumed to be hardened to acts of violence, recoil before the savagery of the Liberian conflict in which cannibalism, random violence and tortures of every sort imaginable have become commonplace'. (p. 165).

The negative effects of war on civilian populations are well documented. Figure 16.1 shows that the majority of deaths during war occur outside of active fighting, due to decreased health care provision and worsening social and economic situations. Thus, the number of deaths in Liberia may well be higher than the 270,000 quoted by UNDAF, compounded by the fact that the decreased healthcare and poor social provision is likely to continue well after any war has finished. Thus, while the war is now a memory of the past, the effects linger and may well take decades to address.

Figure 16.1 Indirect mortality as a percentage of conflict related deaths

Country (Years)	% of total conflict-related deaths
Iraq (2003–2007)	63
Sudan (Darfur 2003–2005)	69
Iraq (1991)	77
Burundi (1993–2003)	78
Timor-Leste (1974–99)	82
Congo (2003)	83
Uganda (2005)	85
Liberia (1989–1996)	86
Angola (1975–2002)	89
Sudan (South 1999–2005)	90
Sierra Leone (1991–2002)	94
D. R. Congo (1998–2007)	96

Source: UNESCO (2011) Global Monitoring Report

When the Comprehensive Peace Agreement was signed in 2003, a transitional government was formed, and by 2004 more than 100,000 ex-combatants, 12 per cent of whom were children, were disarmed. By 2007 more than 700,000 internally displaced persons had returned to their home towns and cities (UNDAF 2007). In 2013, a staggering 80 per cent of Liberia's population lived below the poverty line (IDLO 2010), with 48 per cent of the population living in 'extreme poverty' (USAID 2009). The agricultural industry, including mining and timber, employs around 70 per cent of the workforce, and Liberian land contains around 40 per cent of the rain forests in West Africa, playing a large role in the economy of the country (LISGIS et al. 2008). Nonetheless, only 3 per cent of Liberia's youth express an interest in farming (USAID 2009), and rural retention is low, which could pose a problem for further economic development. Control over land as well as resources needs to be carefully monitored, however, as high-value resources, such as diamonds, have been looted in the past by rebel forces to finance the war (UNESCO 2011).

Figure 16.2 shows Liberia's performance on the Human Development Index from 1980 to 2013. The dip in development between 2001 and 2005 can be attributed to the war and post-conflict challenges. While it lags behind the rest of sub-Saharan Africa, the country's development rate is on the rise, and at a rate that appears to be higher than its sub-Saharan counterparts.

Liberia is generally considered a 'fragile state' in international development discourse, a term used to describe a state when its structures 'lack political will and/or capacity to provide the basic functions needed for poverty reduction, development and to safeguard the security and human rights of its populations' (OECD 2009: 18). While Liberia under Ms Johnson Sirleaf has manifested the political will to pursue a robust development agenda, the civil war severely diminished Liberia's infrastructure and human capital.

Furthermore, there are recent concerns that Liberia, now at peace for 10 years, might be at risk of additional conflict due to high levels of poverty and economic instability. At a UN meeting in 2009, the Secretary General's Special Representative in Liberia, Ellen Margrethe Loj noted that 'Massive youth unemployment and current job layoffs constitute a real security concern ... Without regular and stable jobs, more Liberians, especially the younger generation, could be tempted by the easy money associated with illegal economic activities or potentially by those wanting to recruit for subversive activities once again' (All Africa.com 19 March 2009).

In 2005, Ellen Johnson Sirleaf was elected president, the first female Head of State in sub-Saharan Africa. With the help of the international community, Liberia has since made steady progress on the recovery process (UNDAF

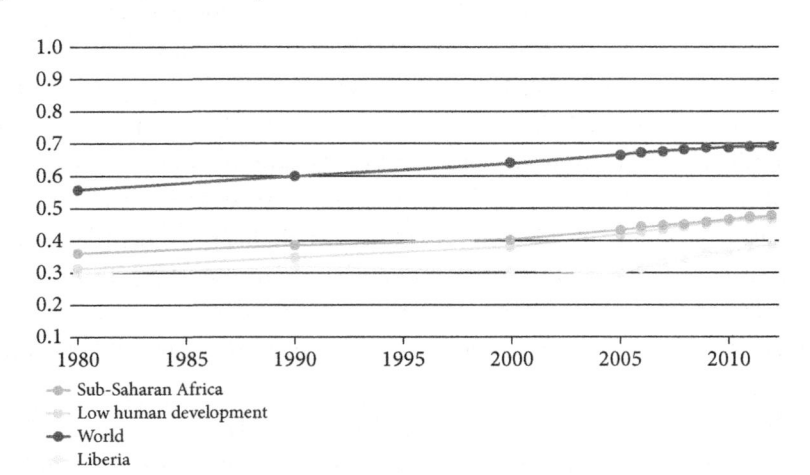

Figure 16.2 Human development index trends

- Sub-Saharan Africa
- Low human development
- World
- Liberia

Source: 2013 Human Development Report

2007; IDLO 2010), with a significant shift in attitudes across Liberia, particularly, towards girls and women. However, although huge successes have been celebrated, many challenges remain, including repairing destroyed infrastructure, rebuilding and rethinking school systems, and a journey towards economic recovery and opportunities for citizens to regain livelihood.

Education in Liberia

Issues of access

Education, if delivered effectively and universally, has the capacity to decrease poverty and even to mitigate fragility in Liberia. Unfortunately, however, in the case of Liberia, education is still not universal, and as there are insufficient job opportunities after education, there is growing concern and frustration among young people. These frustrations can lead to unrest and conflict which, in its fragile state, is perhaps too close for comfort for most Liberians. In their 2009 report, the International Crisis Group discusses the serious risks that unemployment presents to Liberia's stability.

Almost an entire generation of Liberians that have grown up during the war has had no education whatsoever, with the exception of those who have gone to refugee and internally displaced persons camps (USAID 2009). This left an enormous gap in knowledge in an entire generation of children. According to the International Rescue Committee (2002),

> The Liberian education system has been devastated by the war: schools have been destroyed, trained staff lost and governmental infrastructure disconnected. Of an estimated population of 2.5 million of which 55 per cent are of school-going age, 45 per cent have no access to education. This is especially true in the rural areas for younger children and for girls (p. 12).

Only a very small proportion of Liberians has had the opportunity to attend school, with only 44 per cent of females and 61 per cent of males having attended any form (LISGIS et al. 2008). Figures worsen when it comes to secondary schooling, as only 5 per cent of females and 13 per cent of males have completed secondary or tertiary education. These figures of course come from a time which was only four years after the end of the war, and since that time there has been some improvement.

As a result of the huge proportion of the population which had not attended school, and taking into account other consequences of the war, the Government of

Liberia has defined 'youth' as being between the ages of 15 and 35 (USAID 2009). Children aged 14 and under constitute around 47 per cent of the population (GoL 2008), and a further 28 per cent of the population are defined as 'youth' (USAID 2009). Since 75 per cent of the population are below the age of 35, this presents an incredible challenge for the Government of Liberia, which now has a high number of over-age students to educate as well as the current children of school-going age. Understandably, this places an immeasurable strain on Liberia's already depleted resources. Approximately 12.1 per cent of government spending goes to education, which accounts for 1.9 per cent of the GDP (UNESCO 2011).

There are significant disparities in access between the poorest households and wealthy ones. The Net Attendance Rate (NAR) is 23 per cent for the poorest quintile and 66 per cent for the wealthiest at primary school level (Tsimpo and Wodon 2012). Further disparities exist between regions within the country, with NAR being at 60.6 per cent in the Monrovia area, and nearly half that figure in most other regions of the country at around 29–32 per cent for the North West, South Central, South Eastern and South Central regions (LISGIS et al. 2008).

The gaps between rich and poor and between urban and rural groups mirror long-standing divisions in Liberia. Tensions in Liberia have traditionally been due to disparities between groups in Monrovia and its surrounding areas and the hinterland. In his paper (1995), Ellis notes 'The construction of ethnic patronage systems by rival soldiers ... was probably the single most important cause of Liberia's subsequent collapse' (p. 178), and indeed this needs to be remembered. Further partitioning of peoples within the country due to region or wealth quintile is likely to stir further conflict.

Regional differences are even more apparent at secondary school level, with NAR at 34 per cent in Monrovia and as low as 8 per cent in the North Central region (LISGIS et al. 2008). Furthermore, the urban/rural disparity is greater at secondary level, with three times more urban children attending school than rural. The lowest quintile of the population is extremely unlikely to attend secondary school, with NAR figures at only 4.5; and the highest quintile at 38.2 (LISGIS et al. 2008).

Universal Free Primary Education has been implemented in Liberia since 2002, complemented by the Accelerated Learning Programme (ALP) to address the education needs of the thousands of over-age children whose education was interrupted by the civil war. This has been a considerable achievement as the number of children going to school since then has increased dramatically (IDLO 2010). However, a very large proportion of children withdraw from school after the state-funded primary phase, and the next challenge for the

Table 16.1 Liberia – net attendance ratios

	Primary	Secondary
Residence		
Urban	57.5	30.4
Rural	28.9	9.7
Region		
Monrovia	60.6	34.2
North Western	32.0	19.1
South Central	31.2	17.5
South Eastern A	30.6	8.9
South Eastern B	44.3	10.9
North Central	29.1	8.1
Wealth Quintile		
Lowest	22.6	4.5
Second	26.4	7.3
Middle	37.1	12.0
Fourth	41.8	20.5
Highest	66.4	38.2
Total	40.0	19.6

Source: Liberia DHS 2007

Government of Liberia will be to increase retention rates of children after the primary level.

Because of the instability during the war and the extreme strain on government resources, private schools account for a large proportion of overall schools in Liberia, with approximately 40 per cent of enrolment being at non-government schools at primary level and over half at secondary level (Tsimpo and Wodon 2012). More interestingly perhaps, looking at Table 16.2, is the distribution of children from urban and rural areas to government and private schools. As can be seen, children from rural areas are more likely to attend government schools, while children from urban areas are more likely to attend private schools. There are more children overall, however, attending government schools at primary level, and more children attending private schools at secondary level. These statistics illustrate the current education system in Liberia.

Tsimpo and Wodon (2012) identify three main factors that explain why attendance rates are not as high as perhaps they could be – cost, distance and age. Cost was the main factor which caused children's diminished attendance even when schooling was tuition-free. These costs were related to uniforms, lunches and school materials, and were perceived as being too expensive. In

Table 16.2 School attendance by type (2007)

	Primary		Secondary	
	Urban	Rural	Urban	Rural
Government	25.8	71.1	28.3	65.0
Private	63.0	18.0	65.0	28.4
Other	11.2	10.9	6.7	6.6

Source: Tsimpo and Wodon (2012)

addition, the opportunity cost of losing a child's help in the home or at work was a significant factor in school attendance.

Second, distance from schools, which has increased for most children as a result of schools being destroyed during the war, was another inhibiting factor. Primary schools are around 30 minutes from the average home in urban areas, and 45 minutes from the average home rurally; whereas secondary schools, which seem to be much less frequently attended, are on average over three hours away (Tsimpo and Wodon 2012).

At the tertiary level, Liberia offers university education, but it is available only in Monrovia. This is a contentious issue as a lot of the civil unrest has come as a result of differences between the descendants of 'American-Liberians', who are mostly based in Monrovia, and 'African-Liberians' from the hinterland. Offering tertiary education only in Monrovia immediately alienates a large proportion of the population located too far away to attend, risking continued tensions and conflict.

While vocational training is more widespread than tertiary education, as many as 84 per cent of vocational trainers are unqualified (USAID 2009). To exacerbate matters, large numbers of training institutions have been destroyed in the war, and there is little or no equipment that can be used in training. Large proportions of students equally complain that vocational training does not lead to gainful employment afterwards, because skills are not directly linked with the job market (USAID 2009).

'The higher education system has remained paralyzed and the technical and vocational education and training system is still in disarray due to the looting of the training equipment during the war'. – From the Interim Poverty Reduction Strategy, as quoted in UNDAF (2007: 11).

Issues of quality

The contribution of quality education, or the lack thereof, to unemployment and poverty is now a well-established fact. 'When large numbers of young people are denied access to decent quality basic education, the resulting poverty, unemployment and sense of hopelessness can act as forceful recruiting agents for armed militia' (UNESCO 2011: p. 16). Given Liberia's recent history, the quality of education is an important area of focus.

The 14-year civil war has presented Liberia's education system with a number of challenges regarding access and quality. Huge numbers of qualified teachers left the country in search of safety and work. Roads have been destroyed making children's journeys more arduous, and schools have been damaged or destroyed increasing the distance children must cover to attend school. These issues are slowly being addressed by the Government of Liberia as infrastructure is rebuilt. However, significant challenges still remain.

A number of inhibiting factors exist in terms of quality. Around 70 per cent of schools in Liberia were destroyed during the war (IDLS 2010), leaving children to travel great distances with attendant challenges around security and fatigue. Furthermore, schools which have not been completely destroyed often lack adequate facilities such as toilets, much less enrichment facilities such as libraries and laboratories. The high number of ex-combatants wishing to take part in the Accelerated Learning Programme is a further demand on the limited education resources.

The number of trained and qualified teachers has dropped dramatically since the war, with a huge proportion of them fleeing the country to seek work and safety elsewhere. Great numbers of teacher training centres have been destroyed as well, meaning there is a serious lack of qualified teaching staff across the country, with over 60 per cent of teachers lacking adequate qualifications for teaching (Tsimpo and Wodon 2012). Many facilitators of learning have received no teacher training whatsoever, and many have had only secondary level education themselves.

Further inhibitors of quality have to do with the resources available. Books and other learning resources have been hard to recover and finance since the end of the war, and many children and teachers have few or no textbooks or materials. Pupil to textbook ratios are low, at one book for every 27 children at primary level, and one book for every nine children at secondary level (MoE 2007).

Parent satisfaction, although not necessarily the most unbiased indicator, is still an interesting factor to consider when discussing quality of education. With the lack of resources, schools at great distances, and untrained teachers, it is perhaps unsurprising that parents are concerned about the quality of education. Approximately half of parents whose children attend government schooling are satisfied with the school; and 60 per cent of parents whose children attend private schools are satisfied (Tsimpo and Wodon 2012). Among the concerns parents most frequently cited were the lack of books and supplies, insufficient teachers, facilities in bad conditions, poor teaching, and long distances to school. Certainly it will be an uphill battle to attempt to address all of these, as more money, resources and time are needed to build schools, resource them appropriately and train teachers.

While retention and pass rates are a crude measure of education quality, they are still useful. As might be expected, retention rates are relatively low in Liberia, and a majority of children do not move on to secondary schools. Unfortunately, data are not available regarding pass rates, which in itself is somewhat concerning.

The quality of schooling is of paramount importance in this critical stage of Liberia's post-conflict recovery. Quality education improves perceptions of the importance of schooling, and thereby increases attendance and retention rates. It is incredibly vital that children successfully complete their schooling without having to repeat, to reduce the private and public costs of education. Enhancing the quality of education in Liberia, therefore, will remain a priority in the foreseeable future.

Peace, conflict and security: Post- conflict initiatives and the ALP

One of the most egregious violations of the rights of Liberian children was the wide-scale recruitment of child-soldiers. Many of these children were abducted, others forced to enter the war or face the most excruciating personal trauma resulting from loss of limb or family member. Child-soldiers received no formal education. Rather, much of what they learned in the military will have to be un-learned and addressed not only through catch-up education but through psychological and social support to reintegrate into civilian life.

In response to this situation, the Government of Liberia established the 'Accelerated Learning Programme' (ALP), which attempts to consolidate six years of primary school into just three. The aim of the programme is to provide over-aged school-goers with the basic tools they will need to move on towards a secondary education, if they so desire. Once the programme has been completed, the student is eligible to sit the National Primary School Certificate Examination (NPSCE), which determines whether he or she is able to progress to Grade 7.

Because a majority of students attending the ALP are former child-soldiers or have been affected by the war in some way, the Ministry of Education has

Table 16.3 Liberia – ALP enrolment figures

Year	Total enrolment	% Girls
Pilot	771	n/a
1999–2000	3,402	46%
2000–1	5,146	42%
2001–2	4,370	46%
2002–3	4,969	47%
2003–5	Not available	
2005–6	**53, 697**	46%

Source: Baxter and Bethke (2009)

recommended additional learning modules to accompany the ALP. These include peace, human rights and HIV/AIDS education. Other additional modules include agriculture, an attempt on the part of the Government to increase interest in the most lucrative part of Liberia's economy, and physical education. These subjects are not mandatory, however, and many of the NGOs responsible for implementing ALP have not included these modules (Nicholson 2007).

The programme itself was developed by a number of parties, including specialists from the Liberian Ministry of Education, Save the Children UK, UNESCO, UNICEF, the University of Liberia, the West African Examination Council (WAEC) and the Church-Related Education Development Organization (CREDO) (Baxter and Bethke 2009). In constructing the curriculum, the aim was to contract the existing Liberian curriculum, without losing any substantive value.

Table 16.3 shows the ALP enrolment figures from the pilot. By 2006, the programme had expanded considerably to around 500 schools in 11 counties.

Although the ALP is a formidable attempt from the government to try to ensure that children involved in the conflict secure primary education, there are several shortcomings in the programme. According to Nicholson (2007), a majority of the teachers had only received secondary level education themselves, whereas the materials developed for ALP were designed for teacher facilitators with higher levels of education. Further, only ten days of training was provided to ALP teachers which, particularly for teachers without formal training, would be grossly insufficient. As the training for ALP teachers was conducted mostly in lecture-style lessons with few demonstrations, the utility of the training was very constrained.

Theoretically, the need for the ALP should have been for a few years: just long enough for over-aged school-goers to have the chance to complete their primary education. The programme, however, has continued to be implemented, possibly due to the high number of ex-combatants who are in need of a primary education, possibly because regular primary education has not been able to keep pace with regular demand. According to the 2011 Global Monitoring Report, some 75,000 students were enroled in the ALP by the end of the decade.

Originally meant to target children aged 8 to 16, some providers have enroled youth aged 10 to 17, others adults aged 19 to 35, as children who were younger than 10 were found to be less able to deal with the accelerated nature of the programme and unable to handle the study without systematic review and time to process information. Ironically, because of demand, younger school-aged children who could have attended primary school ended up enroling in ALP and effectively taking the places of their older counterparts.

In addition to the ALP, some 'Education for Peace' programmes have been implemented (EFA 2011). These programmes were promoted by UNESCO and UNICEF in an effort to ensure that schools are an integral part of peace-making in post-conflict countries like Liberia. Curriculum development and training of teachers for these programmes have begun to gain more importance with the MoE, however, little is known about the effectiveness of them, as very little data exists on their evaluation (UNESCO 2011).

Gender

Since the election of Ellen Johnson Sirleaf in 2005, gender parity has become a priority. A significant shift in attitude towards women and girls is perhaps the most substantial change, and the president has vowed to increase access to education for girls, as well as the level of protection for women nationwide (IDLO 2010).

As Table 16.4 shows, the greatest gender divides seem to appear in the lowest wealth quintile, with NAR for boys being at 25.2 and 19.8 for girls. In all areas, boys attend school more than girls do; however the gap is not as large as one might have anticipated in a post-conflict situation and it is clear that Johnson Sirleaf's presidency and the work the Government of Liberia has done has helped to increase gender parity.

Beyond school attendance, literacy rates show a staggering difference between genders, with 60.8 per cent of adult males being literate and only 27 per cent of females in 2007 (UNESCO 2013). Since the gender gap in current school attendance is much smaller, it is expected that over time literacy rates will also be more balanced.

Table 16.4 Net attendance ratios by gender (2007)

NAR	Male	Female
Residence		
Urban	60.8	54.6
Rural	30.5	27.1
Region		
Monrovia	65.3	56.5
North Western	33.5	30.6
South Central	32.5	30.0
South Eastern A	31.9	28.9
South Eastern B	46.8	41.7
North Central	29.9	28.2
Wealth Quintile		
Lowest	25.2	19.8
Second	27.6	24.9
Middle	36.4	38.0
Fourth	47.4	36.8
Highest	69.1	64.1
Total	41.4	38.6

Source: Liberia DHS 2007 (LISGIS et al. 2008)

There are a number of factors which might inhibit girls from attending secondary school in Liberia. Understanding these factors and attempting to address them will, over time, increase attendance rates for girls, and hopefully gender parity. First, strong societal beliefs are still embedded within the population that girls are somehow less worthy of an education than boys are. The patriarchal society has preconceptions about the life path of males and females, and traditionally it is thought that females need only basic education as they will become wives and mothers later in life. Linked with this, pregnancy often prevents female students from attending school, and once they have given birth, child-care becomes the primary concern.

Sexual abuse and sexual harassment within schools of girls is still an issue, with few cultural and legal inhibitors of these negative behaviours. Elevated levels of rape and sexual harassment are still being reported in Liberia, even years after the end of the conflict (UNESCO 2011).

Because of the fact that primary education is not only free, but compulsory in Liberia, it's clear that it's had an impact on female attendance at school. Unfortunately, this does mean that a large number of children withdraw from education once they have completed their cost-free portion of their education. Furthermore, the fact that the gender gap widens at this time shows that the perception of value of education for female children is lower than that of male children. Equally, it demonstrates that issues of cost of education are still largely inhibiting factors, which are keeping children out of school at a secondary level, particularly females.

Liberia has seen significant progress in prioritizing gender parity within education. Girls, however, continue to experience difficulties in pursuing their education, and the government must address issues of high dropout rates for girls, increase female safety in and out of school and out, and encourage more underprivileged girls to attend school (IDLO 2010).

Governance and finance

Poor governance is the main factor which has contributed to Liberia's fragility and conflict (Study Synthesis Report 2009), and many would argue that the roots of the war were derived from inequitable allocation of government resources. Huge disparities have existed between the American-Liberians, mainly based in and around Monrovia, and the indigenous people, based in the hinterlands, ever since the freed black American slaves returned in 1847. Despite the fact that the American-Liberians constituted a mere 5 per cent of the population (Adebajo 2002), they managed to create a rich elite which would largely exclude and alienate the rest of the population, thus creating civil unrest. According to the UN, 'Poor leadership and the misuse of power: The failure of previous national leaders to create broad-based, transparent and accountable systems of governance, and their reliance on a system of patronage, undermined social cohesion and sustained a mistrust and fear, particularly among ethnic communities' (UNDAF 2007: 3). Thus, governance, accountability and social cohesion are at the forefront of Liberia's development plan.

Very much aware of its history, the Government of Liberia has placed education very high on its reconstruction and development agenda. Education is seen as one of the pillars and principal instruments in the hands of government and people to ensure personal and societal progress. Within this context, 12.1 per cent of government spending goes towards education (Tsimpo and Wodon 2012). In spite of this high percentage of government spending on education, there is considerable non-government investment in education. According to Tsimpo and Wodon, funding from NGOs is still supporting teachers' salaries, as well as the provision of books and other school supplies. The government does not accurately track these additional finances from NGOs, however, so it is unclear how much is being spent overall.

Teacher salaries are a major issue in terms of funding, as at the moment they are extremely low, at only $200–$300 per year, meaning that teachers are being forced to find other sources of income. Admittedly budget allocation is already under strain due to the need for such extensive rebuilding across the nation, but teachers who have fled will not have adequate incentives to return should salaries remain so staggeringly low, and with high numbers of children in the classroom.

While Liberia receives a certain amount of international aid, as the EFA Global Monitoring Report (UNESCO 2011) demonstrates, a large number of poor conflict-affected countries are not receiving the similar proportions of aid. Figure 16.3 shows that the distribution of aid is not necessarily equal, and some countries receive far more than others.

In terms of private spending, the average urban household spends 30.8 per cent of education expenditure on school uniforms, by far the biggest expenditure, followed by 20.5 per cent on primary school fees and 15.1 per cent on secondary school fees. Rural households spend most of their education expenditure on primary and secondary school fees at 25.6 per cent and 25.5 per cent respectively, and just 12.3 per cent on uniforms (Tsimpo and Wodon 2012).

Figure 16.3 Aid received in low and mid-low income countries

Country	Value
Iraq	9.8
Afghanistan	4.1
Ethiopia	2.9
Sudan	2.1
Pakistan	1.8
O. Palestinian T.	1.8
Uganda	1.7
D. R. Congo	1.6
Philippines	1.1
Liberia	1.0
Sri Lanka	0.9
Rwanda	0.8
Sierra Leone	0.7
Nepal	0.7
Georgia	0.6
Somalia	0.6
Côte d'Ivoire	0.6
Burundi	0.5
Chad	0.4

Source: UNESCO 2011 Global Monitoring Report

Considering that cost was one of the main factors addressed above in terms of inhibiting factors preventing children from attending school, it is instructive to note quite how much of the family educational budget must be spent on uniforms, perhaps something schools could do away with in these mitigating circumstances.

A Governance assistance programme entitled GEMAP – Governance and Economic Management Assistance Program has been implemented with aid from Liberia's development partners, and infrastructure, basic services and the social sector is beginning to show improvements. Moreover, the UN Security Council has now lifted sanctions on the country's diamonds and timber (UNDAF 2007). The overall outlook is positive, but for families who are struggling to meet basic needs, financing their children's education will remain a challenge for the foreseeable future.

Conclusion

I asked a former colleague of mine to sum up the education situation in Liberia. Having served in the sector all his life, in the classroom, in the Ministry of Education and now in the philanthropic sector, this is what he had to say:

- Education in Liberia was a decentralized management process, beginning with a community- service focus. The spread of Islam added the Quranic Madrasat curriculum to most of the North-Western parts of Liberia.
- Public/Western education, inter-spiced with philanthropic ventures introduced the decentralizing management of education.
- The present challenge in education today is more like attempting to reclaim an education system that we lost – going back to where it all started.
  Our most recent education reform policy is toward decentralization of facilities and management. The challenges continue to be 'the devolution of authority', engaging factors of 'access', 'fiscal support', policy implementation and management of 'input factors'.
- Key players in education today are the President, House Standing Committee, Senate and legislators, the Minister of Education, some NGOs and mining concessions.
- Parents continue to make the necessary sacrifices to keep their children in school. There are now six (6) degree-granting universities including a Seventh Day Adventist University for West Africa. There are Associate-degree granting colleges in almost every county headquarters.

- The future of education in Liberia continues to be promising but this depends largely on if the government abides by its current education laws. It is urgent that the government hasten the decentralization process; e.g. establish county school systems – for effective policy implementation and quality control, etc.

I could not have penned a more balanced and reflective summary. The insights of my former colleague are instructive. His optimism is tempered with a practicality that is typical of many of his countrymen and women I know. His comments underline the significant role that key individuals play in Liberia, as has come out clearly in the literature which repeatedly refers to President Johnson Sirleaf's influence on the rehabilitation of the sector. What struck me is that nowhere in the literature had I seen the role of mining concessions analysed, reflecting the need, as always to balance the objective with the subjective views.

As an interested bystander, I echo my former colleague's optimism. I have seen the grit and determination in his countrymen and women, and hope that ten years from now, a different kind of narrative will be penned of education in Liberia.

Note

1 Many thanks to Ms Vicky Wiley, Intern at Save the Children UK, who assisted me with some basic research

References

Adebajo, A. (2002). *Building Peace in West Africa: Liberia, Sierra Leone and Guinea-Bissau*. Colorado/London: International Peace Academy; Colorado/London: Lynne Rienner Publishers, Inc.

Baxter, P. and Bethke, L. (2009). *Alternative Education: Filling the gap in emergency and post-conflict situations*. Paris and Reading: IIEP-UNESCO and CfBT.

Ellis, S. (1995). 'Liberia 1989–1994: a study of ethnic and spiritual violence'. *African Affairs*, 94 (375) (April: 165–97).

Government of Liberia. Monrovia (GoL) (2008). '2008 National Population and Housing Census: Preliminary Results'. Government of Liberia p. 6. Liberia.

International Crisis Group (2009). 'Liberia: uneven progress in security sector reform'. (London: Report No. 148, 13 January 2009)

International Development Law Organisation (IDLO) (2010). 'Liberia country report. Strengthening the legal protection framework for girls in India, Bangladesh, Kenya and Liberia'. Women's NGO Secretariat of Liberia (WONGOSOL).

International Monetary Fund (2012). 'Liberia poverty reduction strategy paper – annual progress report'. IMF Country Report No. 12/45. Available from http://www.lr.undp.org/Documents/PDF/reduction_strategy.pdf (accessed March 2014)

International Rescue Committee (2002). 'Leveraging learning: Revitalizing education in post-conflict Liberia'. USA: International Rescue Committee.

Liberia Institute of Statistics and Geo-Information Services (LISGIS) [Liberia], Ministry of Health and Social Welfare [Liberia], National AIDS Control Program [Liberia], and Macro International Inc. (2008). *Liberia Demographic and Health Survey (2007)*. Liberia: Monrovia.

Ministry of Education (2007). 'Liberian primary education recovery program'. Monrovia, Ministry of Education. (Report prepared for Fast Track Initiative.)

Nicholson, S. (2007). *Assessment of the National Accelerated Learning Programme in Liberia*. Report prepared for the Ministry of Education of the Republic of Liberia and UNICEF. Unpublished manuscript.

OECD (2009). 'Concepts and dilemmas of state building in fragile states: From fragility to resilience'. *OECD Journal on Development*, 9/3: 1–91.

Tsimpo, C. and Wodon, Q. (2012). *Education in Liberia: Basic Diagnostic Using the 2007 CWIQ Survey*. In: *Poverty and the Policy Response to the Economic Crisis in Liberia* (edited by Quentin Wodon). Washington, DC: World Bank (April 2012): pp. 35–59.

UNDP (2010). 'UNDP's partnership with The Global Fund in Liberia: supporting implementation, developing capacity'. Liberia: UNDP Liberia Country Office.

—(2013). 'Human development report. The rise of the South: human progress in a diverse world'. New York: UNDP.

UNESCO (2011). 'Global monitoring report. The hidden crisis: armed conflict and education'. Paris: UNESCO Publishing.

United Nations (UNDAF) (2007). 'UN Development Assistance Framework for Liberia 2008–2012: Consolidating Peace and National Recovery for Sustainable Development'. Monrovia: United Nations in Liberia.

USAID (2009). 'Advancing youth project: labor market assessment – Liberia'. Liberia: USAID.

17

Liberia: Citizenship Education in the Post-Conflict Era

Laura Quaynor

Introduction

The ways that young people enact citizenship has always had importance for their communities, nations and world. This fact has never been more relevant than at the present moment, a point raised by Gordon Brown when he noted that 'The new year has begun – just as 2012 ended – with young people on the march' (Brown 2013). The formation of youth to be such participatory citizens continues to be central to the educational enterprise (Banks 2008; Dewey 1916). The need for education to provide youth with tools to engage in their societies is even more pronounced in emerging democracies and post-conflict environments, many of which are on the African continent (Resnick and Casale 2011).

This chapter considers education for citizenship in Liberia, a unique nation in West Africa. I illustrate the effects of colonization and conflict on citizenship education, as well as describe the ways youth currently learn about citizenship in this context. The chapter is organized into four main parts: the context of belonging in Liberia; the ways the Liberian Civil Wars disrupted ideas of citizenship and belonging; current research on political socialization and citizenship education in Liberia; and considerations for the future.

The context of belonging

Like most countries in Africa, Liberia is home to a multitude of ethnic and linguistic groups. Anthropologists have documented differing indigenous

Liberian forms of youth socialization in the northern and southern regions of Liberia. In the central and northern regions, groups such as the Kpelle, Gio, and Krahn have historically socialized young people into adulthood via initiation societies known as Poro for men and Sande for women. Commonly referred to as 'bush schools', these societies served as places where adolescents learned values and skills needed for full participation in the community. Before engaging in communal decision making, an individual needed to be an initiated member of these societies (Lancy 1996).

Southern groups such as the Krahn and the Grebo do not have these types of secret societies. Rather, scholars document collective decision making with a communally chosen chief and checks and balances on his power (Moran 2006; Sawyer 2005). Councils of elders, warriors or women could convene for a variety of reasons. In one instance, Moran recounts a situation where a group of women gathered to petition the chief regarding communal concerns and refused to work unless their concerns were addressed. In both northern and southern groups, youth were taught decision making as part of community rather than a system of individual votes.

In addition to the influences of indigenous ethnic groups, the history of the nation of Liberia contributes to ideas about citizenship, belonging, and citizenship education today. As a nation founded by African Americans in 1847, Liberia is unique in West Africa as it was not colonized by European powers. Rather, it was settled by free blacks from the Americas who considered themselves 'the means of introducing civilization and religion among the barbarous nations of this country' (Liebenow 1987: 153). This worldview was expressed in the founding constitution of Liberia, which excluded tribal persons from citizenship, but required them to pay taxes to the national government (Cassell 1970; Liebenow 1987; Shick 1980).

Although Americo-Liberians made up a small percentage of the population of the nation, this group controlled the government from 1847 to 1980 (Liebenow 1987). Constitutional restrictions did not include time limits for the presidency: President William Tolbert was elected to seven consecutive terms from 1944 to 1971, when he died in office (Cassell 1970). His term marked a slow increase in opportunities and rights for indigenous Liberians, including the rights to vote and attend public universities (Liebenow 1987).

Despite the eventual incorporation of indigenous Liberians into politics, the centralization of the government, slow rate of change, and presidential sovereignty all helped to lead to the recent civil wars (Sawyer 2005). In 1980, Samuel Doe, an indigenous Liberian, overthrew the government and established an authoritarian regime, which dissolved into conflict when Charles Taylor led a group of rebels to invade Nimba County in the north of the country. This was followed by 14 years of conflict when hundreds of thousands were killed and millions were displaced (BBC 2013). This conflict officially ended with a peace agreement in 2003. Ellen Johnson Sirleaf, a World Bank economist of mixed indigenous and Americo-Liberian descent, was then elected president in 2005 (BBC 2013). Although President Johnson was a co-recipient of the Nobel Peace Prize in 2012, allegations of corruption and nepotism mar her administration (BBC 2012).

Education and citizenship during the Liberian civil wars

Citizenship education was both a catalyst and result of the instability in Liberia. While students' and young people's ideas about civic duties and rights contributed to conflict, this conflict changed young people's conceptions of citizenship. In the second half of the twentieth century in Liberia, student civic activism was tied to popular uprisings and political transitions.

When the war disrupted schooling for the majority of Liberian students, young people's ideas about belonging and citizenship were moulded by the conflict. The conflict resulted in an increased awareness of civic rights, human rights, and individualism among youth (Bohrer 1999; Utas 2003). Both students and undereducated, unemployed youth became key political actors during the war (Diouf 2003).

Recent Afrobarometer surveys indicate that these young people are part of a populace that supports democracy. Liberian respondents indicated a preference for democracy over other types of government, but are somewhat critical of democracy in Liberia. Fifty-one per cent of respondents reported satisfaction with the way democracy worked in Liberia, and less than 50 per cent expressed trust in governmental institutions, local government officials, the police and political parties (Tokpa et al. 2008).

Schooling and citizenship education

In Liberia, Western-style schools were imported by Americo-Liberians, initially only to educate their own children. In the late nineteenth and early twentieth century, school attendance defined one's status as *civilized*, or kwii (David

1992). The knowledge that one acquired in school, *kwii meni*, was defined in opposition to local knowledge or *zo meni* (Utas 2003). As part of the nation-state, schools inherently prepared nation-focused citizens.

Currently, formal civic education takes place in social studies classrooms, specifically during the 8th and 12th grades when students study civics and government. Students also learn about citizenship in classes focused on history and geography, and through practices such as electing class representatives. Recent programmes supporting school-based civic education include an initiative to promote critical thinking in teacher education from the Open Society Institute and the United States Association for International Development (USAID). In addition, a new citizenship education curriculum was produced by the Ministry of Education in partnership with UNESCO.

However, schools are not the only place that students learn about citizenship. Like young people all over the world, students in Liberia learn about citizenship through their home, religious institutions, peers and the media. Informal civic education commonly takes place through radio programmes, neighbourhood youth associations, sports teams, and groups titled Intellectual Development Forums that meet at atai (tea) shops.

Although large-scale studies document civic education and measure youth civic understandings in countries around the world, no countries from Africa have been included in such studies (Schulz et al. 2010) and there is sparse empirical information on civic education in Liberia. In two recent studies, I researched the intended, implemented, and internalized civic education curriculum in four schools in Greater Monrovia, the urban centre of Liberia (Quaynor 2012; Quaynor 2014). These studies are described below.

Methods

To address the notable gap in scholarship on citizenship education in Liberia, I conducted two case studies: one single case study of the intended and implemented citizenship education curriculum in an NGO school, completed in May 2009; and one multi-site study of the intended and internalized citizenship education curriculum in four schools across the greater Monrovia area in October 2011. The 2009 single case study involved a textual analysis of the official civics text; three interviews with the civics teacher; and participant observation in an 8th grade civics classroom over the course of one month. The 2011 multi-site study was sponsored by the Open Society Institute and included individual interviews with teachers and administrators; focus group interviews with students; and a quantitative survey distributed to students. In the second study, I conducted interviews with six social studies teachers and four administrators, speaking with one to two teachers and one administrator at each school; completed focus group interviews with a total of 53 students, speaking with two groups of six to seven students at each school for interviews lasting 30–45 minutes each; and collected an 82-item survey from 286 8th grade students from four schools. These schools were identified by purposeful convenience sampling, to include one school run by a non-governmental organization, one run by a church, and two government schools. All schools were located in Greater Monrovia, and served low to middle income students. A report with the full details from this study was filed with the Open Society Institute (Quaynor 2012).

Findings

Below, I share what the findings from these two case studies illuminate about intended, implemented, and internalized citizenship education curricula in Liberia. First, I present findings from the textbook, which outlined a conception of citizenship that stressed a national conception of citizenship, focusing on citizens' rights over citizens' responsibilities, and encouraged students to question established holidays and governmental norms. Then, I report the varying ways that the teachers responsible for implementing the curriculum discussed citizenship, although all recognized the importance citizenship education has for peace.

Following this discussion of the intended curriculum, I share findings from the 2009 single case study to show how citizenship education was implemented by one teacher who also participated in the multi-site study. This teacher gave notes from the book in a call and response fashion, although he often paused to address student questions and comments on the material, giving examples relevant to their lives. Finally, I present the ways that students internalized the citizenship curriculum, drawing on the survey and focus groups completed by 8th grade students in the multi-site study. Students overwhelmingly associated citizenship with the responsibility to engage in development. However, there were also significant differences between male and female student responses, and between the responses of students at different schools. To some extent, student responses showed influences of their teachers, their school, and their neighbourhood on their conceptions of citizenship.

Intended citizenship curriculum

When investigating the nature of systems of education, international organizations divide the study of the intended, implemented, and internalized curriculum: although these are often related, they are rarely the same. Research on intended curricula focuses on official policy documents, including curriculum guides, white papers, and textbooks (Anderson-Levitt 2007). Here I report on the intended curriculum at the school level, including themes from the textbook and teachers' understandings of citizenship education.

Citizenship in the textbook: a critical, national focus.

Findings from a textbook analysis indicated a focus on national conceptions of citizenship, rights and responsibilities of both citizens and the government, and a critical perspective on problems in Liberian democracy (Avery and Simmons 2000). This critical focus is notable for a post-conflict society (Quaynor 2012). Below, I present excerpts from the textbook to illustrate these themes.

National belonging. Although the textbook referenced all levels of citizenship, it emphasized national unity and belonging. Ethnic identity and participation in global and regional networks was discussed in relation to national citizenship: an individual's identity as Liberian should come before affiliation with local or global groups. For example, the textbook stated 'There is nothing wrong with being a member of a tribe' (Guannu 2004: 80), but that that problems arise 'when members of one tribe … give their allegiance and loyalty to their tribe and not the Liberian state' (ibid.).

Rights and responsibilities. The textbook spent multiple chapters detailing the political and economic rights, as well as responsibilities, of citizens. The most frequently mentioned responsibilities of citizens, voting and being informed, were also framed as rights; these were also the most active methods of civic participation discussed. In addition, civil and political rights (e.g. the right to vote), were more frequently cited than social and economic rights (e.g. the right to earn a living) were also mentioned. According to the textbook, citizens only had responsibilities to their government when the government fulfilled its responsibilities to its citizens. These responsibilities included providing education and protecting citizens' rights.

Critique of democratic failings. Notably for a textbook in post-conflict societies (Quaynor 2012), the textbook was frank about past and current failures of Liberian democracy. At one point the textbook listed some of these past injustices:

Between 1904 and 1980, some Liberians could not get the jobs for which they were qualified because their behavior was not Western. Other citizens could not get a speedy and fair trial because they were poor. Further still, the economy during the last half of the 20th century benefited only a small group of Liberians and their foreign friends. (Guannu 2004: 7)

This willingness to criticize shortcomings of democracy was extended to current issues, such as corruption, an over-powerful executive branch, and the celebration of the Thanksgiving holiday. Thanksgiving is a controversial holiday in Liberia, as it originated from Americo-Liberians giving thanks that they survived attacks by indigenous Liberians. The tone of the critiques in the textbook can be observed in this description of corruption:

> Because the number of public servants in the past embezzled public funds and abused public office with impunity, these two negative behaviors have become widely accepted in Liberia as a way of life in public service. This is wrong and is also a beginning of revolution. (p. 56)

Teachers' intentions and civic understandings: variation as the rule. Although each school in the multi-site case study used the same textbook, each teacher elevated slightly different aspects of citizens' rights and responsibilities in their interviews. Teachers who worked in the same school agreed on the role of controversial issues in citizenship education. Like most teachers in Liberia (Stromquist et al. 2013), the teachers in this study were all male. For the sake of space and clarity, these findings are presented in Table 17.1 overleaf.

As seen in the table, public school teachers focused on personal responsibility and the links between citizenship and family; private school teachers tended to describe ways that student actions were related to a democracy, whether through voting as at Lisa Bayer or through accepting different opinions at the Neighborhood Baptist School. All of the teachers I spoke with underlined the importance of citizenship education in helping students be informed, learn about rights, and learn respect. In three out of four schools, teachers specifically discussed the fear that a lack of either knowledge or patriotism could be responsible for conflict (Quaynor 2012).

Implemented citizenship curriculum

This section reports on findings related to the implemented curriculum (Anderson-Levitt 2007) gathered during one month of civic classroom observations in Pastor John's class at the Lisa Bayer School in 2009 (Quaynor 2015). Just as the textbook in this study did not shy away from controversial issues,

Table 17.1 Teachers' conceptions of citizenship

Teacher	School	School Type	Subject	Themes	Representative Quotes
Pastor John[1]	Lisa Bayer	Local NGO	History, Civics (6th–12th)	Citizenship means informed decision making	'The students must know the judiciary … and why the legislators are there because they are the future leaders tomorrow they will be electing their presidents and their senators and representatives. If they don't know the right, they will not be able to choose a right leader'. 'Even if the person [politician] is lying to them … they will read between the lines to know who that person is because the person lives with them in the community'. (10/17/11).
Mr. Ballah	Neighbourhood Church Baptist School		Civics (7th–9th)	Citizenship means patriotism and respect	'In the past – problems came from not having a love of your country'. 'If you know that controversial issues exist, you will respect the views of others – that will make controversial issues to work'. (10/20/11)
Mr. Janneh	Neighbourhood Church Baptist School		History (7th–9th)	Citizenship education promotes peace	'If students were educated about their functions in society and upheld the laws of the community, there would be peace'. (10/20/11). 'When students ask me my opinion, I take the question back to them' (10/20/11).
Mr. Johnson	Elizabeth School	Public	Civics (7th–9th)	Informed citizens will be unified	'Students that are misinformed can be a threat. When they look at issues in the newspaper or on the radio, if they don't understand it, they'll repeat in the wrong way'. (10/24/11)
Mr. Williams	Elizabeth School	Public	Civics (7th–9th)	Citizenship means transnational unity	'Liberians should accept nationals from other countries who come to Liberia'. 'When we discuss controversial issues we move from disagreeing to agreeing'. (10/24/11)
Mr. Moore	Tolbert School	Public	Civics and History (8th)	Citizenship means morality and responsibility	'Citizens differ from "aliens" because they have specific rights, and they must learn about them' 'We [Liberians] should be church-going people and should be responsible'.

1 All names reported are pseudonyms

classroom discourse allowed students to engage with the subject material. A typical class would involve a call and response pattern (Noment 2005) for half of the period, interspersed with student questions and discussion for the other half.

Lessons always included personal connections to the material by the teacher and the students. For example, while teaching about the legislative process, Pastor John talked about the current budget before the legislative body, which proposed to raise the salary of civil servants in the government to $100 a month from $70. He then worked students through a breakdown of the costs associated with working and running a household, illustrating the actual value of this salary change.

Students engaged in critiques of power. Both the teacher and students noted the differences between the ideals of democracy in the textbook and their everyday experiences. Although the teacher emphasized national citizenship, state allegiance, and constitutionalism (Bahmueller 1991), students most often commented about faults in the ways democracy worked in Liberia. Students critiqued corruption, the lack of good governance, and a lack of equal and fair representation. Typically, after the teacher gave notes on the structure and function of the government, students noted ways that it did not operate as described (Quaynor 2015).

Having the means to speak. Students repeatedly commented on the ways poverty limited their political rights. When students brought up the problem of corruption, Pastor John told students that they should use their freedom of speech to help solve this problem. One male student, Peter, responded, 'I can't challenge them [politicians]. My ma is broke and my pa is broke'. A female student, Fatima, added,

> Yes – for me because I do not have the means to speak if I speak against someone with money their money will send me to Salt Beach [a prison] for my lifetime. Not just for half time but for my lifetime.

In this example, Fatima and Peter saw parallels between economic and political power. Without sufficient economic power, they stated that they could not access basic civil rights. For them, freedom of speech required the means to speak (Quaynor 2015).

Students as active citizens. Both the teacher and students repeatedly expressed the ways they not only expected to act as citizens in the future but acted as citizens in the current moment. This theme aligns with student activism in historical and contemporary Liberia. In recent years, Liberian secondary students have demonstrated to protest against school conditions and teacher absenteeism (Abalo 2011; Hanson 2012; Weedee and Johnson 2011). The teacher underlined his expectation that students be active citizens the day that he lectured about the legislative branch of the government. When students brought up the complaint that legislators were not fulfilling their constitutional duties, Pastor John reminded them that 'Without you there will be no what? [hypothetical question] Government'. When a female student said she would not vote in the next election because 'they [those in power] already know who they want', another student challenged her, saying 'the government is the society ... if you don't [vote] you will never get access' (Quaynor 2015).

Internalized civics curriculum

In the 2012 study, I used both focus group interviews and surveys to determine how 8th grade students in four schools understood citizenship and described their civic trajectories (Quaynor 2012). Below, I discuss themes from the focus groups and general descriptive findings from the survey at each school. I then discuss the differences in responses between female and male students.

Focus Group Findings. When students were asked how people put citizenship into action, students at all schools gave responses focused on the national aspect of citizenship and specifically developing their nation. However, different aspects of citizenship and civic trajectories were highlighted at each school. Students at Tolbert School emphasized respect for diversity as critical for citizenship. At Elizabeth school, which was located in a neighbourhood in the city centre, some students emphasized the role of citizens in promoting peace, as the war had robbed them of years of schooling; at the same time, other students stated that citizens should fight for their rights even if this precipitated conflict. Student participants at Neighborhood Baptist School were the most likely to indicate that good citizens protest, and students at Lisa Bayer School were the most likely to value participation in community development projects, obeying rules, voting and defending their country (ibid.).

Because of increased interest in the effects of globalization on youth socialization, I also asked students about global citizenship. Overall, students discussed global citizenship in ways that mirrored the textbook, focusing on representing Liberia at international events or bringing resources from other places to develop Liberia. One interesting way that many students adopted transnational affiliations was through identification with a particular European premier league: for example, many students stated they were 'gunners' or fans of the Arsenal Football

Club in England. Although Liberians have been celebrated on the international stage for achievements from football to peace (BBC 2013), students never discussed Liberians as contributors to the world around them, but as consumers of information and resources from elsewhere (Quaynor 2012).

To analyse results from the quantitative survey, I combined items into scales and compared the outcomes of these scales between public and private schools. As some schools had small classes, there were not enough respondents from each school to compare the mean survey score from each school. All items included in the survey showed sufficient distribution across response categories. Mean responses on the four-point scale ranged from 2.22 to 3.44 with a standard error range from .054 to .076 (Quaynor 2012).

Survey Results. Internal consistency as measured by Cronbach's coefficient α for the entire 82-item survey was found to be high at .957, suggesting that the items provide a reliable measure of the construct under investigation. The scores from the 82 items were summed and unweighted to create an overall score. Based on theories of citizenship, 13 subscales were identified ranging from 3 to 19 items. Cronbach's coefficient α was identified for the subscales with values that ranged from .598 (Media Use) to .867 (Community Participation). Average item-to-total correlations ranged from .402 to .557. Inter-subscale correlations ranged from .248 to .895. Higher scores correspond to stronger senses of citizenship. Means and standard deviations for each subscale were calculated by gender and school type; then, mean comparisons were performed for scale scores and each item on the survey to identify statistically significant mean differences for gender and school type (Quaynor 2012).

There were notable differences on this survey by both gender and school type as assessed through t-tests. Males (M=12.42, SD =3.28) had a statistically higher scale score than females (M=11.66, SD=3.10) on the Ethnic Identity Scale, t(275)=-1.97, p=.049. On Item 13, or the belief that good citizens teach others in their community, females had more favourable responses than males, t(275)=2.48, p=.016, meaning that females held the belief that good citizens teach others at a significantly higher level than males reported holding the same belief. Males had more favourable responses than females on Item 62 (t(275) =-2.651, p=.008), 'I believe in the values of my religious group' and Item 63 (t(275)=-2.83, p=.005), 'being part of my religious group is important to me' (Quaynor 2012).

It was clear from both the focus groups and the survey that students have a variety of understandings of citizenship, although they focus on nation-centred, development-based ideas. Different civic understandings were evident at each school, highlighting the potential importance of variation in teachers' conceptions of citizenship on student understandings. Students are also aware of the tension between peace and justice in a post-conflict society, and many believed that protests were an acceptable nonviolent way to fight for their rights. Finally, it is notable that male students expressed higher affinities with their ethnic and religious groups than female students: girls' understandings of citizenship may be more flexible.

Considerations for the future

Citizenship education in Liberia has rich potential to be a powerful force, providing students with the skills needed to create a just, peaceful society. Citizenship education is built on a rich tradition of student activism in Liberia, as well as local political socialization in ethnic groups and national political socialization in schools. The studies discussed in this chapter suggest that the civics classroom in post-conflict Liberia can be a place for young people to learn about democracy as a concept. When young people realize the disjuncture between this and their daily experiences, it may spur them to greater civic engagement. In addition, the multi-site study highlights that messages conveyed in schools about citizenship can vary widely, although teachers are nominally using the same curriculum. Teacher education for teaching citizenship may be imperative, as the ways teachers help to shape student understandings may influence whether students see themselves as patrons of a client state or participatory citizens in a democracy (Coe 2005). Future efforts could focus on action research, helping teachers to assess how changes in their practice affect students' ideas about citizenship.

Despite a worldwide focus on global citizenship education (Banks 2008), students and teachers in these studies reported few global ties and overwhelmingly associated citizenship with the nation-state. Nonetheless, most students had transnational affiliations with football teams and consider the world outside of their nation as a source of knowledge. In the future, research on citizenship education in Liberia might examine the development of global citizenship in Liberia and other West African nations.

References

Abalo, E. (2011) 'Student protests disrupt classes in Monrovia', *The Inquirer*, 23 March 2011. Available from http://africatv1.com/Dawala/2011/03/ (accessed 9 August 2013).

Anderson-Levitt, K. M. (2003). *Local Meanings, Global Schooling: Anthropology & World Culture Today*. New York: Palgrave MacMillan.

Avery, P. G. and Simmons, A. M. (2000). 'Civic life as conveyed in United States civics and history textbooks'. *International Journal of Social Education*, 15: 105–30.

Bahmueller, C. F. (1991). *CIVITAS: A Framework for Civic Education*. Calabasas, CA: Center for Civic Education.

Banks, J. A. (2008). 'Diversity, group identity, and citizenship education in a global age'. *Educational Researcher*, 37: 129–39.

Bohrer, K. (1999). *'It's Hard to Be a Refugee': Cultural Citizenship and the Experience of Modernity among Urban Liberians in Exile*. The University of Wisconsin-Madison Ph.D. dissertation. OCLC No. 45392277.

British Broadcasting Corporation (BBC 2012). 'Liberia laureate Gbowee chides Sirleaf on corruption', 8 October 2012. Available from http://www.bbc.co.uk/news/world-africa-19876111 (accessed 1 October 2013).

—(2013). 'Liberia profile'. Available from http://www.bbc.co.uk/news/world-africa-13729504 (accessed 1 October 2013).

Brown, G. (2013, January 14). 'Youth in revolt'. *Newsweek*. Available from http://www.newsweek.com/gordon-brown-youth-protests-india-and-pakistan-63193 (accessed 15 September 2013).

Cassell, C. A. (1970). *Liberia: History of the First African Republic*. New York: Fountainhead Publishers.

Coe, C. (2005). *Dilemmas of Culture in African Schools*. Chicago: University of Chicago Press.

David, S. M. (1992). '"To be kwii is good": a personal account of research in a Kpelle village'. *Liberian Studies Journal*, xvii (2): 203–15.

Dewey, J. (1916). *Democracy and Education: An Introduction to the Philosophy of Education*. New York: Free Press.

Diouf, M. (2003). 'Engaging postcolonial cultures: African youth and public space'. *African Studies Review*, 46 (2): 1–12.

Guannu, J. S. (2004). *Liberian Civics*. Monrovia, Liberia: Cuttington University.

Hanson, V. C., 'As teachers continue strike action – mcss students demonstrate', *The Inquirer*, 23 October 2012. Available from http://allafrica.com/stories/201210231266.html (accessed 22 September 2013).

Lancy, D. (1996). *Playing on the Mother Ground: Cultural Routines for Children's Development*. New York: The Guilford Press.

Liebenow, G. (1987). *Liberia: The Quest for Democracy*. Bloomington, IN: Indiana University Press.

Moran, M. (2006). *Liberia: The Violence of Democracy*. Philadelphia: University of Pennsylvania Press.

Noment, N. (2005). *Readings in African American Language: Aspects, Features, and Perspectives*. Vol. 2. New York: Peter Lang.

Quaynor, L. (2012). *The Implications of Privatization for Citizenship Education: Views from Four Liberian Schools*. Budapest, Hungary: The Open Society Institute. Available from http://www.periglobal.org/role-state/document/document-implications-privatization-citizenship-education-views-four-liberian-sc (accessed 1 October 2013).

—(2015). '"The means to speak": Educating youth for citizenship in post-conflict Liberia'. *Journal of Peace Education*, 15(1), 15–36. doi:10.1080/17400201.2014.931277.

Resnick, D. and Casale, D. (2011). 'The political participation of Africa's youth: turnout, partisanship, and protest'. Working Paper 2011/56. Helsinki, Finland: United Nation University.

Sawyer, A. (2005). *Beyond Plunder: Toward Democratic Governance in Liberia*. Boulder, CO: Lynne Reinner Publishers.

Schulz W., Ainley J., Fraillon J., Kerr D. and Losito B. (2010). *ICCS 2009 International Report: Civic Knowledge Attitudes, and Engagement among Lower Secondary School Students in 28 Countries*. Amsterdam, Netherlands: International Association for the Evaluation of Educational Achievement (IEA).

Shick, T. W. (1980). *Behold the Promised Land: A History of Afro-American Settler Society in Nineteenth-Century Liberia*. Baltimore, MD: Johns Hopkins University Press.

Stromquist, N. P., Lin J., Corneilse C., Klees S. J., Choti T. and Haugen C. S. (2013). 'Women teachers in Liberia: social and institutional forces accounting for their underrepresentation'. *International Journal of Educational Development*, 33 (5): 521–30.

Tokpa, A., Zeze S., Saryee D., Greene L., Thompson J. A., Gyimah-Boadi E., Loga C., Bratton M. and Mattes R. (2008). *Afrobarometer Round 4: The Quality of Democracy and Governance in Liberia*. Ann Arbor, MI: Inter-university Consortium for Political and Social Research.

Utas, M. (2003). *Sweet Battlefields: Youth and the Liberian Civil War*. Uppsala, Sweden: Uppsala University.

Weedee, E. and Johnson O. (2011). 'Bloody Monday', *The Heritage*, 9 November.

18

Mali: An Overview, Trends and Futures

Mohamed Chérif Diarra

Introduction

The aim of this chapter is to present an overview, the trends and future prospects of Mali's educational system. The chapter provides a brief description of the historical background geography, demographics, and political evolution of Mali during the post-colonial period. It further describes and analyses its educational system in the independence era with a specific focus on reforms undertaken, on its structural organization, its governance and administration, its funding and the legal and institutional context governing the system. The chapter further analyses the current education trends such as access/participation, quality, equity and relevance, decentralization and devolution and their bearings on the system. Finally, the system is faced with numerous challenges such as enrolment explosion, shortage of quality human resources and weak institutional capacity that affect its ability to deliver quality educational services.

Overview

Introduction

The Republic of Mali is a landlocked country in the semiarid interior of West Africa. It covers a surface area of 478,767 square miles (1,240,190 square kilometres) about five times the size of Great Britain. Mali shares common borders with seven former French colonies: Guinea and Côte d'Ivoire to the south and south-west, Burkina Faso and Niger to the east, Senegal and Mauritania to the west, and Algeria to the north. During the colonial period (1885–1960), the name of the colony changed four times. These name changes included Soudan

Français (French Sudan 1890–99), Senegambie et Niger (Senegambia and Niger 1902–4), Haut Sénégal et Niger (Upper Senegal and Niger 1904–20), and again Soudan Français (French Sudan 1920–60) (Imerato 1989).

Mali's population was estimated to be 16 million and its annual growth rate 3.01 per cent in 2013. At this current rate, Mali's population would reach 21 million in 2023, and 27 million in 2033. This population is extremely young: 47.7 per cent is 14 years or less, 19 per cent is between 15–24 years of age meaning that nearly two-thirds of the Malian population is 25 years old or less. It is predominantly rural (75 per cent) and Muslim (95 per cent). Bamako the capital city has a population estimated to be 2 million in 2013. The principal ethnic groups are the Mandingo (50 per cent), the Fulanis (10 per cent), the Dogons (7 per cent), the Songhai (6 per cent) and the Tuaregs (3.5 per cent). French is the official language (Diarra 1997).

Mali has been the seat of three great empires – Ghana, Mali, and Songhai – and many Kingdoms. After achieving independence in 1960, Mali and Senegal formed the short-lived Federation of Mali (April–August 1960). After the collapse of the Federation in August 1960, Mali proclaimed its independence on 22 September 1960, under the leadership of Modibo Keita, whose regime – l'Union Soudanaise du Rassemblement Démocratique Africain – (U.S.R.D.A), a radical left-wing government (1960-8), encouraged the creation of a state-run economy. The socialist regime was overthrown in 1968 in a military coup orchestrated by Lt. Moussa Traoré. The military regime ruled the country until 1979, when a one-party system was installed. This period from 1979 through 1991 was characterized by the return to civilian rule under a military-sponsored political party. The rise of pro-democracy movements led to a second coup in March 1991 under the leadership of Lt. Colonel Amadou Toumani Touré. A transitional government ruled the country from March 1991 through May 1992, when multi-party democracy was realized. In February 1992, a new constitution was approved, and free and fair elections (municipal, legislative and presidential) were conducted. Alpha Oumar Konaré was elected the President of the Third Republic of Mali in April 1992. After Konaré, Geneal Touré was elected for two terms. He was overthrown in March 2012, by Captain Amadou Haya Sanogo. Concurrently, a rebellion of the Tuareg ethnic group known as the Movement for the National Liberation of Azawad (MNLA) in northern Mali backed by armed Jihadists resulted in the occupation of the three northern regions (Timbuktu, Gao and Kidal) Under the pressure of the international community led by the African Union (AU) and the Economic Community of West African States (ECOWAS), Captain Sanogo stepped down as Head of State in April 2012 and a transition government headed by Professor Dioncounda Traoré as President took over. In January 2013, on the demand of President Traore, France's military intervention freed Mali from the yoke of the Jihadists. Presidential elections were held in July 2013. Ibrahim Boubacar Keita was elected President.

Mali is divided into eight administrative regions (Kayes, Koulikoro, Sikasso, Segou, Mopti, Timbuktu, Gao and Kidal) and the District of Bamako. The regions comprise 50 'cercles' (administrative circumscriptions) whereas the District of Bamako is divided into six communes. Mali has 703 communes (the smallest administrative unit (Diarra 1997).

The methodology used in the chapter is basically qualitative. It consists of a desktop review of all the available sources of data, mainly secondary but also primary and others. Websites also provided useful information.

The public educational system

Background and setting

Mali's educational system is a legacy of French colonization. However after the country gained independence it went through profound structural as well as major content reforms. These reforms were dictated by the new political orientation of the country (Socialism) whose key objective was to construct a new educational system rooted in the Malian values, culture, society and traditions. One may make a strong case that Mali's educational system, from 1960 to 1990, went through three major phases of evolution that basically correspond to the following post-independence period: a phase of stability (1960–70); of growth (1970–80) and of crisis (1980 onwards Diarra 1997).

Educational reforms

After Mali became independent, its government faced the formidable challenge of designing an educational system responsive to the needs of an independent African state. This task resulted in the design and implementation of the 1962 Educational Reform that constitutes the major cornerstone of the current educational system of Mali on the one hand, and marks the beginning of a dramatic change from the French colonial system of education on the other hand. Haidara (1977) posits that, in essence, the reform focused on the following five major objectives: 1) The provision of a quality education accessible to the masses; 2) the design of a public educational system that meets the manpower requirements of the country and educates the majority of children within a limited time span and at a minimum cost possible; 3) the identification and implementation of educational standards that guarantee recognition by other countries of the Malian educational credentials; 4) the promotion of a new curriculum that integrates universal values but that is first and foremost afro-centred; and 5) the implementation of the concept of education for liberation and emancipation, that is, an education that decolonizes the minds of the people. Other important forums were held to reinforce the 1962 educational reform. They are: the National Consultation (1978), the Etats Généraux (1989) the National Debate (1992) and the National Forum (2008)

This restructuring movement and organizational change provided a new framework and impetus aimed at encouraging the equality of educational opportunities and expanding dramatically the educational system. Haidara (1977) points out that to ensure a total educational decolonization, the reform also included an adult literacy programme known as the Functional Literacy Project (FLP) whose major objective was to teach adults who did not attend formal schooling, reading, writing and arithmetic in their native languages.

Structure of the educational system

Structurally, the education system of Mali looked like a pyramid with kindergarten or preschool as the base and graduate education as the top. Preprimary education has been run for a long time by private institutions outside the control of the Ministry of Education. Prior to the 2012 basic education reform, fundamental education comprised of two cycles, the first cycle covered 1st grade to 6th grade whereas the second cycle went from 7th grade to 9th grade. With the new primary education reform initiated in 2011 by the authorities, the two cycles were merged into an uninterrupted 9–10 year cycle known as basic education. In the past, Cycle 1 consisted of Grades 1 through 6. Pupils took an entrance exam into Grade 7 known as the Certificat de Fin d'Etudes du Premier Cycle (C.E.P). As for Cycle II, it consisted of Grade 7 through Grade 9, leading to the Diplôme d'Etudes Fondamentales (D.E.F) which gives students access to secondary education.

Second, secondary education includes technical, vocational, normal, and academic general track, i.e. the Lycée (high school). After completion of fundamental education, students may attend vocational or high schools. Vocational schools offer a two-year or a four-year programme that confer on their graduates low and medium level technical degrees. As for the Lycée, a three-year track institution from Grades 10 through 12, seniors (in Grade 12) take an entrance examination into higher education called the 'Baccalaureat'.

Third, the Baccalaureat is the passport to higher and tertiary education. This level of education, unlike primary and secondary, is the replication of the French dual type of higher education composed of the 'grandes écoles' (three, and five-year institutions) and the university. (Diarra 1997).

Governance and administration

First of all, unlike many other African countries, Mali did not experience a rampant proliferation of Ministries of Education at any given time of the historical development of its educational system. From the 1991 transition period to the first government of the post 2012 coup, education has been governed by one or two ministries. For example, in the aftermath of the launch of the Ten-Year Educational Development Plan – (PRODEC), in September 2001, the institutional architecture of the Ministry of Education was changed and the system was piloted by only one National Ministry. The National Ministry of Education was subsequently split into two ministries (Basic Education, Literacy and National Languages and Higher Education and Scientific Research) in 2004. Currently, Mali has two ministries (National Education and Higher Education, Universities, and Scientific Research) that are responsible for running the country's educational system.

The governance structure of Mali's educational system comprises three layers: national, regional and local. Its organogram shows at the national level the Minister's Office even Central Directorates in charge of various domains report to the Minister. Devolved entities, the Académies d'Enseignement –AE- (Regional Education Offices) at the regional level, and the CAP – (Centres for Pedagogical Activities) at the local level are in charge of the implementation of educational policies formulated at the central level . School governance is also a key policy implementer at the local level.

A central structure of Ministry of Higher Education, Universities, and Scientific Research is the National Directorate of Higher Education (DNES). Mali has five public universities each headed by a Rector.

Funding

The financing of education is the constitutional responsibility of the government. Further, the 1992 constitution stipulates that public education (primary and secondary) is free and compulsory. As for higher education, limited tuition and fees (about US$12 are paid annually by students enroled in various universities and grandes écoles (Diarra 1997). However confronted with severe financial constraints coupled with the ever-increasing cost of education, households, communities and development partners were urged to contribute. Thus the diversification of the funding sources of the education machinery at all levels was introduced. However, the bulk of the cost of education is borne by the government. The share of the national budget allocated to the education sector has gradually increased over the past two decades. For example, It rose from 25.5 per cent in 2006 to 31.5 per cent in 2010 (PISE II), a 6 per cent increase over a five-year- period and an average annual increase rate of 1.2 percentage point. Households and communities' contribution has been also significant. It was estimated to be 16 per cent in 2008 (RESEN 2010). Development partners through bilateral and multilateral co-operation contribute significantly to the funding of education . Further the Global Partnership for Education (GPE) is also contributing and approved a US$41.7 million grant to the government of Mali in 2013 for infusion into the education sector.

Private and community schools

The rising demand for education coupled with the inability of the government to provide enough educational services led to the liberalization of the education sector through the provision of all kinds of private schools. In fact, confessional schools owned and operated by religious institutions such as the church have been in existence since colonial days. The proliferation of private schools started in the early 1980s and accentuated with the ever-increasing social demand for schooling at all levels. Concentrated in the capital city for the majority of them in the 1960s and 1970s, private schools gradually spread over the whole country constituting an alternative to public schools whose quality was deteriorating due to the shortage of qualified teachers resulting in overcrowded classrooms especially in primary schools and urban areas such as Bamako and the lack of infrastructure and instructional materials. Although private schools are fee-paying institutions, the demand for them never decreased because of their relatively good quality.

A 1994 law defines community schools, a subcategory of private schools, as any not-for-profit education centre created and managed by a community or association, as opposed to an individual or corporation (De Stefano et al. 2006). In fact, community schools were spontaneously opened by communities across three regions of Mali (Koulikoro, Sikasso and Ségou) and supported by the USAID through three American Private Voluntary Organizations (PVOs) World Education, Africare and Save the Children and local NGOs. According to PISE 2 (2006), the weight of public primary schools in the education sector as a whole declined from 80 per cent in 1996-7, to 63 per cent in 2004-5, whereas the number of private and community schools along with CED (Education Centers for Development) significantly increased from 20 per cent in 1996/7 to 37 per cent in 2004-5 with community schools accounting for 17 per cent of the total. The community schools in Mali are in the process of becoming communal schools. Ministry of National Education: Bureau of Statistics and Planning (2014) reveals that, in the 2013/14 school year, there were 2. 1 million pupils enroled in 10794 primary public schools and 744,166 in 5,546 private schools. For secondary schools, there were 90,113 pupils enroled in 110 schools and 228,905 pupils enroled in 1,132 schools.

Legal and policy framework

To ensure a coherent development of its educational system, Mali moved from the project to the sector-wide approach, a systemic and management reform that views education as an inclusive, integrated and holistic body. Therefore, Mali National Parliament adopted on 29 December 1999, Education Act N°99-046 AN RM (Loi d'Orientation de l'Education), an important piece of legislation, the first of its kind, that regulates and organizes the system. A year prior to the adoption of the Act, the Ten-Year Educational Development Plan – (PRODEC) covering the 1998-2008 period was designed and launched in September 2001. The plan targeted all the components of the system from Early Childhood Care Education (ECCE) to Higher Education. The operational plan of PRODEC, the Education Sector Investment Program – (PISE) an initially two phase rollout plan comprising PISE I (2000-4) was extended till 2005, PISE II (2006-8). PISE III that was eventually added covered the 2010-12 period. PRODEC's three strategic objectives were to:

i) Improve the quality of education through a training policy and curriculum development
ii) Improve and increase the gross enrolment ratio (GER) and
iii) devolve and decentralize the educational system.

Trends

Numerous trends will continue to dominate Mali's educational system for some time. They are multifaceted and percolate through all the levels and types of education. As they are intrinsically linked, they negatively affect the system in terms of internal and external efficiency.

Access and participation

Access to and participation in education especially primary education expanded significantly in the 1990s and 2000s as a consequence of Mali's commitment to the implementation of numerous initiatives such as the World Declaration on Education for All, Jomtien (World Education Conference 1990), the Dakar Framework for Action (World Education Forum 2000) and PRODEC. According to UIS (2014b) as may be observed in Figure 18.1, primary education gross enrolment ratio (GER) more than doubled in just 20 years. For example, it increased from only 32 per cent (39 for boys and 24 for girls) in 1992 to 88 per cent in 2012 (94 for boys and 83 for girls) a 275 per cent increase. Data for secondary education are not available, however, it is common knowledge that its GER also increased significantly as a direct consequence of the dramatic expansion of primary education. Higher education experienced an explosion in enrolments from the early 1990s to 2014. Total enrolments increased from 6000 students in 1991/2 to about 100,000 students in 2013/14 (DNES 2014) (of which 6000 are enroled in private institutions), a sixteen fold increase in 24 years. This has caused enormous challenges for the government. The shortage of faculty members is dramatic as they totalled only 991 (all categories and ranks combined) in 2013/14 (DNES 2014).

Quality

The quality of teaching and learning has always been a central issue for education in Mali, perhaps with the exception of the first decade of the independence era (1960–70). Recent data on quality assessment are not available but it is generally

Figure 18.1 Primary gross enrolment ratio (GER) for boys and girls (%) world, sub-Saharan Africa (1971–2011)

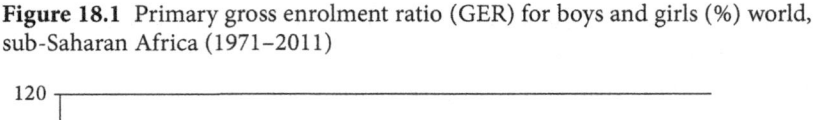

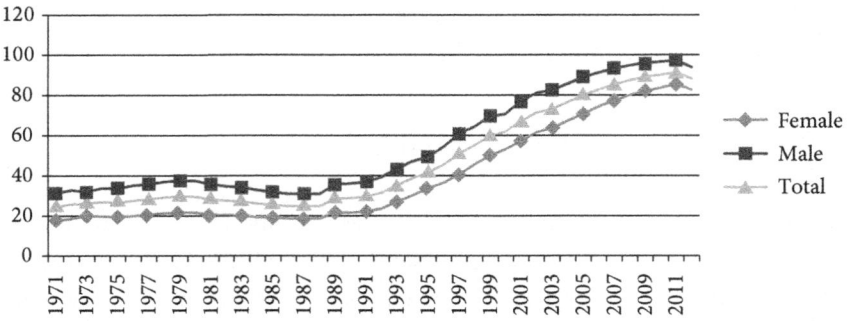

Source: UIS 2014 Data Center

recognized that education is of poor quality. As access continues to expand, educational quality at all levels continues to deteriorate. To illustrate the quality imperative, two major indicators, the Net Enrolment Ratio (NER) and the Grade Repetition Rates (GRR) were examined in the 2006 PISE II evaluation report. The results of the evaluation provide enough evidence to demonstrate that the performance of the system (quality wise) over a long period of time has been falling. Although the primary school NER has made progress during the period under review it still remains remarkably low in absolute terms. For example, it increased from 25.1 per cent in 1996/7 to 43.2 per cent in 2004/5 and hovered around 58.2 per cent in 2012. As for GRR, they have been very high all along. In 1996/7, they were 19.5 and 23.5 per cent respectively for Cycle I and Cycle II of primary education. They have almost remained unchanged at 18.7 and 24 per cent respectively for Cycles I and II in 2004/5. The pupil/teacher ratio (PTR) another key indicator of educational quality has not improved at all. During PISE II it was 63 in 2004/5, a situation that negatively impacts quality. The time on task another quality indicator is very low. It was estimated to be 821 hours/year compared to 950 in developed countries (MoE/Ministere de l'Education 2006).

Equity and relevance

Two other significant trends that will continue to plague the educational system are equity and relevance. The system is characterized by huge inequities at all levels and for all types of education. Disparities such as poor/rich, urban/rural and boy/girl are rampant and persistent. Regarding the poor/rich cleavage, the great majority of children from rich families attends school and stays in school while the opposite has been observed in poor families. For example, 14.8 per cent of primary school children belong to the poorest 20 per centile of the population whereas, 22.4 per cent of them are from the richest 20 per centile of the population PISE II (2006). Gender disparity is examined through the GER. For example, the primary education GER was 88 per cent in 2012 (94 for boys and 83 for girls), an 11 per cent differential percentage point. As for the urban/rural disparity, the primary school Grade 1 admission rate was 89.5 for urban children compared to 61.1 per cent for rural children. The NER was 64.2 and 35.6 per cent respectively for urban and rural children.

The relevance of education, given the high level of youth unemployment in Mali, has been a hotly debated issue. The youth unemployment rate at the national level hovers around 30 per cent as young graduates are unable to find jobs on the market commensurate with their degrees and qualifications. This situation is further characterized by the mismatch between the degrees conferred by the educational and training institutions and the job market.

Decentralization and devolution

The 1992 Mali constitution institutionalized administrative decentralization as a balanced economic and social development strategy for the country (Diarra 2003). With the adoption and enactment of Public Law N° 95–034 governing Local Government, a new redistricting was initiated and new local government entities were established in 1996. But a year earlier, the 1991 National Conference (NC) paved the way for this fundamental constitutional reform to take place. (Hyden 1983) argues that decentralization of responsibilities in African countries rose out of the rapid expansion of government activities. It was further argued that excessive central control stifles operations of government and reduces public accountability. Decentralization is the delegation of authority to lower levels of government, for example, states/departments, provinces or districts or as well as the creation of parastatal bodies to carry out public responsibilities for which government departments are ill equipped. At the regional level, the government established the Regional Council, at the Circumscription level, the Circumscription Council and at the commune level the Communal Council Pre and Primary education are under the Circumscription control whereas secondary education is under the responsibility of the Circumscription Council.

As for devolution, it refers to an inter-organizational transfer of power to geographic units of the local government that lay outside the command structure of the central government. At the Regional and local levels, devolved authorities of the Ministry of Education are the AEs and CAPs established in 1999. The Centre d'Appui à la Décentralization et à la Déconcentration (CADDE) was also established to facilitate the co-ordination within and between various devolved entities of the Ministry of Education. Although decentralization and devolution have been in existence in Mali for 20 years, their impact is still limited because the transfer of financial resources from the central government to the devolved entities is slow and the new structures are faced with the daunting challenge of the shortage of financial and human resources.

Human capacity

Human capacity is instrumental for development. The quality and quantity of human capital is an issue of paramount importance in Africa nowadays (Diarra 2007). A key impediment to the implementation of PRODEC since its inception has been the acute shortage of human capacity especially in the pedagogical staff (teachers) and non-pedagogical staff (planners, statisticians, evaluators, etc.). First of all, 3,000 teachers were needed annually to ensure the attainment of the Education for All objectives especially objective 2, universal primary education. In this respect, the various pre and in-service teacher training programmes were undertaken by the Teachers Training Institutes – IFM) and the Alternative Strategy for the Recruitment of Teachers – (SARPE). They did not produce enough graduates to meet the demand. The 17 existing IFMs are able to graduate around 2,200 teachers annually. Second, among the non-pedagogical staff, planners were trained and deployed in all the REOS to closely monitor the implementation of PISE. However, the other categories of non-pedagogical personnel (statisticians, evaluators and policy analysts) are still in short supply. School administrators whose overwhelming majority is classroom teachers promoted to their positions are not adequately trained to be instructional leaders, educational managers and administrators. Therefore, capacity building of the human resources should be conducted nationwide and for all categories of school personnel.

Literacy

One of the major objectives of 1962 was to promote adult literacy. Thus an extensive literacy campaign was launched and functional literacy centers were established in the country in the early 1960s. The notion of basic literacy used in Mali is for the initial learning of reading and writing which adults who have never been to school need to go through. As for functional literacy, it refers to the level of reading and writing which adults are thought to need to perform some specific jobs in a complex modern society. The use of the terms underlines the idea that although people may have basic levels of literacy, they need a different level to operate in their day-to-day lives (Barton 2006). Functional literacy centres were established in 1960 to train adults who could read and write. Furthermore, the CEDs and Centers for Women's Education (CAFés) were established. Despite significant efforts undertaken in the 1960s, Mali has one of the highest adult illiteracy rates in the world with 52.2 per cent of males and 66.8 per cent of females being illiterate (Mali MDP 2010). Furthermore, according to the 2009 Mali Population Census results, the literacy rate in the urban setting was 51.5 per cent whereas in the rural setting it was 19.5 per cent. Thus illiteracy in Mali is predominantly rural- and gender-based. Despite the allocation of 3 per cent of the Ministry of Education's budget to literacy, in 2008, illiteracy is still rampant and much needs to be done to significantly reverse the current trend.

Integration of ICT

Mali is a pioneer in the area of ICT. As early as 1987, the first national forum on the Information and Communication Technologies (ICT) was held. This led in 2005, at the national level, to the adoption of ICT Act N°05–002 of 10 January 2005. The same year the Agency for the Information and Communication Technologies (AGETIC) was established. AGETIC aims at promoting ICT, training a critical mass of specialists and undertaking research in the area, given the remarkable progress the country has recorded in the domain since the mid-1980s. Interestingly, at the education sector level, a national ICT strategy was developed and adopted in 2011. Prior to this, numerous initiatives were launched by the Technical and Financial Partners (TFP), Non-Governmental Organizations (NGOs) and individual school principals around the country (Kersanti et al. 2011). The ICT infrastructure was gradually put in place to address the connectivity bottleneck. The national strategic plan has a capacity-building component articulated around the following objectives; 1) integrate ICT in formal and non-formal education curriculum, school administration and scientific research; 2) design and implement an initial training programme in ICT aimed at introducing it in the syllabus of all the Higher Education Institutions (HEIs); and 3) open a computer room in all the public high schools and other secondary institutions.

Regional integration

Mali is a member of several sub-regional organizations: the WAEMU that comprises seven other West African countries of which six are former French colonies (Benin, Burkina Faso, Côte d'Ivoire, Niger, Senegal and Togo) and one Portuguese (Guinea Bissau). The Union whose objectives focus primarily on economic integration is in the process of integrating its Member States' secondary educational systems. In this respect, the harmonization initiative of their secondary education curriculum was launched in 2011 with the view of offering one high school diploma for all the Union's member states. WAEMU is also involved in the revitalization of the higher education system of its member states through its assistance to its (PAES) Assistance Program to Higher Education – implemented in all its member states.

At the sub-regional level, Mali is also a member of the Regional Economic Community (REC) of West Africa known as the Economic Community of West African States (ECOWAS), which comprises 15 Member States (the eight WAEMU Member States) plus Cape Verde, Guinea and the five Anglophone countries of West Africa: The Gambia, Ghana, Liberia, Nigeria and Sierra Leone. As part of its Education and Training Protocol, ECOWAS launched in 2010 an initiative whose major objective is to harmonize the higher education systems of its member states through the mutual recognition of degrees, diplomas and qualifications conferred by their HEIs. The long-term objective of the initiative is to facilitate the mobility of faculty members, students and labour within the REC.

Conclusion and future prospects

Mali's educational system is a legacy of French colonialism but was also shaped by internal forces, traditions and values. In the search for a new model adapted to local realities, it underwent several structural reforms, under various political regimes. It is currently facing several challenges that threaten its very existence and its future development. First of all, a financial resources shortage may accentuate and affect its ability to provide quality services. If peace and political stability are not quickly consolidated, economic growth may be compromised depriving the government of useful resources for development. A better allocation and management of these resources is also a challenge. Second, the continuous explosion in enrolments at all levels and for all types of education is another key challenge. Third, as enrolments continue to increase at all levels and types of education, the provision of qualified teachers and their insufficient supply will be a major bottleneck. As a consequence of this shortage, the quality of teaching and learning will continue to deteriorate jeopardizing the country's effort to promote its economic development. Fourth, new innovations such as ICT, need to be scaled up. Fifth and finally, local communities' control of the communal schools should be encouraged. They should be operated by the communlties in the name of the subsidiarity principle and empowering them to run these schools for better performance.

References

Barton, D. (2010). *Literacy: An Introduction to the Ecology of Written Language*, 2nd edn. Wiley Blackwell.

De Stefano, J., Schush Moore, A., Balwanz, D., and Hartwell, A. (2006). Equip2 Working Paper: Meeting EFA: Reaching the Underserved Through Complementary Models of Effective Schooling, Washington, DC: USAID. http://www.equip123.net/docs/e2-MeetingEFASynth WP (accessed March 2014).

Diarra, M. C. (1992). 'Educational funding in Mali: past trends and contemporary issues'. Unpublished Master's Thesis. Baton Rouge: Louisiana State University.

—(1997). 'Educational costs and cost recovery in developing countries: the case of Mali'. Unpublished Dissertation. Baton Rouge: Louisiana State University.

—(2003). 'Financial management of education in a decentralized and devolved setting: the cases of Mali, Nigeria and Uganda'. Paris: Association for the Development of Education in Africa.

—(2007). *Education and Human Capital Development in Africa in Shaping a New Africa*. Amsterdam: Kit Publishers, pp. 95–127.

Haidara, B. A. (1977). 'An example of a higher education training college: Bamako'. *Prospects*, 3: 383–90.

Hyden, G. (1983). *No Shortcut to Progress: African Development Management In Perspective*. Berkeley and Los Angeles: University of California Press.

Imperato, P. J. (1989). *Mali: A Search for Direction*. Boulder: West View Press.

Kersenti, T., Collin, S. and Harper-Merrett, T. (2011). *Pedagogical Integration of ICT: Successes and Challenges of 87 African Schools*. Ottawa: ON, IDRC.

Mali MDP (2010). http://sites.google.com/a/tcd.ie/mali-mdp/education (accessed March 2014).

Ministère de l'Education, Nationale, Secrétariat Général (2006). 'Proposition de Plan d'Action pour la Mise en Œuvre Accélérée du PISE 2 pour la Scolarisation Primaire Universelle'. Bamako, Mali.

Ministry of Higher Education and Scientific Research, National Directorate of Higher Education (DNES) (2014). Mali: Bamako.

Ministry of National Education: Bureau of Statistics and Planning (2014). 'Public and Private Schools in Mali'. Mali: Bamako.

Rapport d'état sur le Système Educatif National (2010). 'Analyse Sectorielle pour une amélioration de la qualité et de l'efficacité du système'. Banque Mondiale, Pôle de Dakar, Washington, DC: UNESCO.

UIS (UNESCO Institute for Statistics) (2014). Data Center. *Country Profiles: Mali*. Montréal: UIS. http://stats.uis.unesco.org/unesco/TableViewer/document.aspx?ReportId=143&IF_Language=eng (accessed March 2014).

World Education Conference, Jomtien, Thailand (1990). UNESCO, Paris: France.

World Education Forum, Dakar Framework for Action (2000) Dakar, Senegal: UNESCO, Paris, France.

19

Mauritania: An Overview, Trends and Futures

Akemi Yonemura[1] and Mohamed Chérif Diarra

Introduction

This chapter is a reflective analysis of both a post-colonial and contemporary evolution of education in Mauritania. Based on data collected mainly from documentation of the government as well as international organizations, this chapter aims to provide an overview, the trends and futures of education in Mauritania.

It first offers background information on the historical, political, socio-linguistic, demographic and economic contexts of the country, followed by an overview of the education system of Mauritania and the trends on the major issues and policies. Finally, the chapter discusses the future prospects in terms of achieving universal primary education, quality of training, literacy, the relevance of education in the face of high unemployment rates, commitment to developing the country's human resource base, and provision of peace education to stem social and political instability.

Overview

Mauritania covers a land area of 1,030,700 square km (4.25 times the size of Great Britain), of which about 80 per cent is desert. It is located in the Maghreb region of western North Africa, bordered by the Atlantic Ocean in the west, Western Sahara in the north, Algeria in the north-east, Mali in the east and south-east, and Senegal in the south-west. Mauritania has four ecological zones, including the Saharan, the Sahelian, the Senegal River Valley, and the Coastal Zones. The climate has changed dramatically since the prolonged drought in the 1960s. This change was partly due to a recurrent pattern of wet and dry cycles common to

Sahelian Africa, but experts also agree that some are man-made, such as overgrazing, deforestation, poor farming methods, and over-population. During the 1980s, the desert was advanced southward and by the late 1980s, desertification had changed agro-pastoral and human settlement patterns, driving its inhabitants southward in search for food and water. Simultaneously, the advancement of dunes threatened some villages (Handloff 1988).

Mauritania became independent in 1960 after six decades of French rule. In 1978, a bloodless coup marked the start of military rule that lasted nearly three decades (Economist Intelligence Unit [EIU] 2008). After another military coup in 2005, followed by democratic elections in 2006–7, the new government engaged in dialogue with development partners with an agenda focusing on economic governance. However, in 2008, the civilian president was removed from office by another military coup. The political crisis resulted in most of international support being placed on hold. In 2009, the successful presidential elections led to the establishment of a national unity government and the lifting of international sanctions. Nevertheless, the country remains vulnerable to political instability with issues, such as domestic social tensions and the rebellion in northern Mali (World Bank 2013).

In 2013, Mauritania's population was estimated to be about 3.8 million inhabitants doubled in less than 40 years and is predominantly young. According to the National Statistics Office (ONS) (2012), 42 per cent of the country's population is less than 15 years of age. Further, Mauritania is a lower-middle-income country with a Gross National Income (GNI) per capita of about US$1,110 in 2012. Forty-two per cent of the population lived under the national poverty line in 2008 (World Bank 2014). Nomads made up the majority of the population at the time of independence, but today 90 per cent of the population has settled. Desertification and economic opportunities in cities have accelerated urbanization and settlement. Moors, of mixed Arab and Berber descent, are culturally close to the Haratine, their former slaves, and Moors and Haratines together account for around 80 per cent of the population. The black population comprising Wolof, Toucouluer, Soninké, and Peul ethnic groups, is concentrated in the south. The official language is Arabic, but French and local languages, such as Pular, Soninké and Wolof, are also spoken (EIU 2008).

Mauritania's recent discoveries of minerals have supported the economic growth and raised incomes. Mauritania exports iron ore, gold, and copper, and also has become a modest offshore oil producer. Mauritania's waters have abundant fish stocks and the country's livestock is important. It has a strong potential for irrigated agriculture along the Senegal River. The country's economic and social development depends on its ability to manage these resources and their revenues in an inclusive manner (World Bank 2013). Despite these potentials, poverty affects a majority of Mauritanians, particularly, in rural areas mainly due to the weakness of the rural economy, which depends on capital-intensive sectors, such as mining and fishing, unfair distribution of resources, and vulnerability to both environmental and economic shocks. In rural areas, where 78 per cent of the poor live, the poverty rate remained 59 per cent between 2004 and 2008, while in urban areas, poverty declined from 28.9 per cent to 20.8 per cent. Inequality level in the country is average for sub-Saharan Africa (SSA) and similar to that of Senegal. The Gini coefficient was at 0.38 in 2008, which means the top 20 per cent of the population has seven times as much as the bottom 20 per cent (ibid.). Its human development index (HDI) in 2012 was 0.467, lower than the sub-Saharan African average of 0.475, ranking 155 out of 187 countries. Between 1980 and 2012, the mean years of schooling increased from 1.8 years to 3.7 years, and expected years of schooling increased from 3.8 years to 8.1 years (United Nations Development Program [UNDP] 2013). MDGs regarding universal primary education (UPE) and gender equity appear achievable, but the most deficiencies in achieving the MDGs are related to health, environment, and employment (World Bank 2013).

The public education system

This section presents the major reforms undertaken all along the post-independence era as well as the sector strategy and policy framework. It also covers the structure of the system as well as its institutional piloting in terms of governance and administration. Its funding and the private sector development are finally highlighted.

The educational system of Mauritania is a legacy of French colonization, but has thrived to adapt to the socio-cultural environment of which it is also a product.

Educational reforms and sector strategy

Like most African Francophone countries, Mauritania initiated several educational reforms during the national period whose purpose was, on the one hand, to promote the national culture, and on the other, downgrade the French influence in the country. First, the 1967 reform centred around the language issue with the replacement of French with Arabic as the official language of Mauritania. This reform also has educational ramifications. The 1973 reform articulated the Arabic language promotion policy called 'Arabization' in French whereby the use of Arabic was promoted in all the spheres of the country (administration, medium of instruction, etc.). In the 1978 reform, the hegemony of Arabic was decreased as French's status changed again with its revalorization. Since 1999 Mauritania has embarked on a structural reform of its educational system that is characterized by the transition from a double medium of instruction to a unified one, articulated around the Arabic-French bilingualism tandem. The reform resulted in the design of a National Program for the Development of the Education Sector (Programme National pour le Développement du Secteur de l'Education – PNDSE in French) whose first phase covered the 2002–10 period. The second phase was launched in 2012 and covers the 2012–20 period. Thus, Mauritania moved away from the educational project approach to the sector-wide approach that is systemic, comprehensive and integrated (Ministry of Education of the Islamic Republic of Mauritania [MOE] 2011).

Governance and administration

The institutional pilot of the system is the State Ministry of National and Higher Education and Scientific Research which has under its responsibility three Deputy Ministries in charge of Basic Education, Secondary Education and Employment, Vocational Training and New Technologies of Information and Communication. Two other Ministries – Islamic Affairs and Traditional Education (mahadras) and Social Affairs, Childhood, Family and Pre-Primary – are also in charge of education (MoE 2011).

Structure and organization

The organizational structure of the system is articulated around five key components: pre-primary, basic, secondary general, technical and vocational training and higher education. The official age bracket for schooling is 3 to 5 for pre-primary, 6 to 11 for primary education, 12 to 18 for secondary education, and 19–20 for tertiary education. Education is compulsory from 6 to 15 years old. For primary to post-secondary education, the academic year begins in October and ends in June (UNESCO Institute for Statistics [UIS] 2014a). Basic education was made compulsory for all children in 2001, and consequently the enrolment in primary education increased. Although the secondary education enrolment is still low, the official statistics does not include private and Quranic schools (EIU 2008).

Funding and external support

The funding of education is the constitutional responsibility of the government that is, therefore, its main funder but donors and communities also contribute significantly. According to PNDSE II, the country's revenues more than doubled in a period of eight years. They rose from Monetary Units (MU)[2] 104 billion, in 2002, to MU 257.1 billion in 2010. As for the external revenues comprised by grants and donations provided by development agencies, they rose from MU 8.9 billion, in 2002, to MU 22.4 billion in 2010. In 2010, the contribution of the communities represented about 12 per cent of the total investment in education. Mauritania allocated 4.5 per cent of its Gross Domestic Product (GDP) to education, which is a bit higher than that allocated by its neighbouring West African countries. The average annual economic growth rate that is higher than the average annual population growth rate has been an asset for the education sector in that it has enabled the increase in its budgetary allocations over the past ten years. Primary education has been the major beneficiary of this increased allocation (MoE 2011).

The Global Partnership for Education (GPE) is an important source of external financing for basic education for low- and lower-middle-income countries, and its influence seems to be increasing over time. Between 2004 and 2011, donors spent US$32 billion in aid to basic education, including US$ 2 billion to the GPE. In 2011, one third of the aid to basic education in Mauritania came from the GPE (UNESCO 2014).

Development and education

Three major development challenges in Mauritania are identified as lack of inclusive growth, lack of competitiveness and poor governance (World Bank 2013). The Poverty Reduction Strategy Paper (PRSP) is the medium-term framework of reference for the government's economic and social development policies with the goals of poverty reduction and improved standards of living for the population of the country, which is used as the main benchmark for technical and financial partners. Development of human resources and improving access to basic services are one of the key strategic pillars of the

Table 19.1 PRSP III action plan for education 2011–post-2015

Level / Type of Education	Specific Objectives	Some priority actions
Primary	(i) Increasing retention rate to 79% in 2015; (ii) eliminating gender disparities; (iii) improving quality; (iv) enhancing leadership by results-based management	Educating girls and supporting family life education, providing schools for disadvantaged groups, producing textbooks and teaching aids, restructuring teacher training, upgrading the teacher qualifications
Post primary	(i) Improving enrolment capacity; (ii) Raising the quality and relevance of education to jobs; (iii) Improving co-ordination with tertiary education	Purchasing school furniture and laboratory equipment, developing scientific research, training and retaining teachers in science discipline, equipping all schools with canteens and accessibility to the underprivileged
Tertiary	Restructuring and improving the provision and quality	Building a modern campus for selected universities, developing professionalism in industry by offering distance education, on-the-job continuing education, and implementing scholarship management policy, developing the legal and institutional framework and introducing private sector development incentives
Technical and vocational	(i) Establishing a structure for training instructors and management personnel, (ii) updating programmes continuously by using a competency-based approach, (iii) pursuing a quality-based approach in training institutions	Increasing relevance and effectiveness, diversifying the provision of technical vocational training, including public works, information and communications technologies, tourism industry, agriculture and rural economic trades
Traditional teaching	(i) Including traditional education in the provision of the basic education, at the pre-school and primary levels and in adult literacy, (ii) allowing traditionally educated students to transfer into different levels of the formal education system	Establishing a structure for the training of imams (Islamic leadership position), building and outfitting mosques, strengthening the decentralization of traditional education
Literacy	(i) Strengthening leadership and management of literacy programmes, (ii) developing and diversifying literacy programmes	Streamlining the management and co-ordination of the literacy program

Source: IMF and IDA, 2011

PRSP in Mauritania. The PRSP is prepared within other international development frameworks and/or in alignment with them, such as the MDGs. Mauritania prepared PRSP for the period of 2001–15, which has been implemented by 5-year action plans. The third PRSP (PRSP III 2011–15) consolidates the achievements made under the PRSP II, continues to focus on health and education as the key areas necessary for sustainable development and attempts to close the educational disparities based on gender, socio-economic background and regions. Particularly, it emphasizes improving equality at all levels of education. Skills development is critical as about 350,000 children did not complete secondary education and 65,000 unskilled school dropouts enter the labour market annually. The PRSP III also recommends that specific measures to renew education and professional training programmes to better target skills and knowledge to meet the needs of the private sector. Priority objectives set for 2011–15 for education are universal access to quality primary education of a minimum period of 9 years and the reduction of the adult illiteracy rate to 15 per cent. The achievements made over the first 10 years of the PRSP at the primary level should be extended to other levels. Although many weaknesses have been observed, including failure to align to the various programming tools, lack of co-ordination, low levels of participation by beneficiary populations, etc., the potential of sustained development spurred by an abundant reserve of natural resources, in the areas of agriculture and mining exists. Yet, Mauritania still has various obstacles, including: weak governance, heavy external dependence and vulnerability to external shocks, and insufficient capacity to absorb foreign aid. The specific objectives and some priority actions of the PRSP III are summarized in Table 19.1 above (International Monetary Fund [IMF] and International Development Association [IDA] 2011).

Trends

In the past decade, overall education indicators in Mauritania have improved significantly. In relation to the EFA progress, expressed by EFA Development Index (EDI), which is a composite index of the mean of four components (universal primary education, adult literacy, gender parity and quality of education measured by the survival rate to grade 5), Mauritania was ranked as a low EDI country (less than 0.80), but between 1999 and 2011, the EDI increased more than 20 per cent, mainly as a result of improvement in the probability of children reaching the fifth grade (from 55 per cent in 2001 to 82 per cent in 2008) (UNESCO 2014). The following trends may continue to be observed in the country's educational landscape for many years to come.

Access and participation

Access has dramatically expanded especially over the past two decades. Internationally comparable data are not available on a regular basis for all levels, but the availability of statistics has improved particularly from around 2000. The data on pre-primary education is not collected regularly, but according to the UNESCO Institute of Statistics (UIS 2014b), its gross enrolment rate (GER) was only 2 per cent. In 1971, the gross enrolment ratio (GER) for primary education in Mauritania was only 14 per cent (8 per cent for girls), whereas it was 90 per cent globally, and 52 per cent for sub-Saharan Africa (SSA) on average. The GER steadily increased during the seventies and eighties, and took great strides in the nineties passing from around 50 per cent to close to 100 per cent in 2011 as may be observed on Graph 19.1.

The gender disparity was closed at the primary level and from 2004, girls' participation surpassed boys'. This is probably due to the global campaign to achieve universal primary education and girls' education through MDGs and EFA. However the post-primary participation still lags behind. The GER for secondary education in 2012 was only 27 per cent (25 per cent for female) and 5 per cent for tertiary level (3 per cent for female) (see Table 19.2).

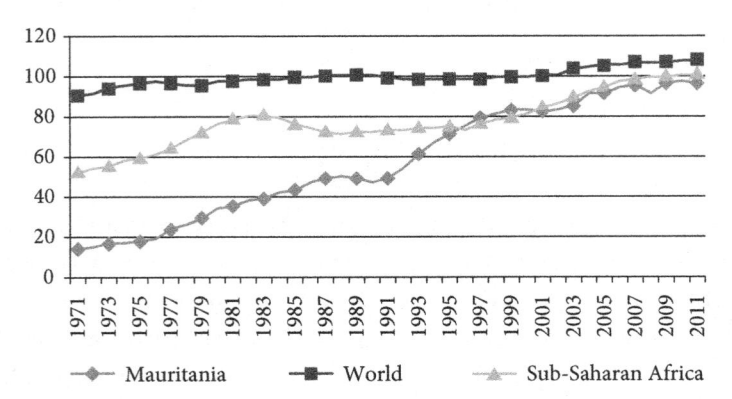

Figure 19.1 Gross enrolment ratio, primary, both sexes (%), World, sub-Saharan Africa, and Mauritania (1971–2011)

Table 19.2 Participation in education by level and gender (2003–2012)

			2003	2004	2005	2006	2007	2008	2009	2010	2011	2012
Pre-primary	GER	total	2	2	..	..	..	..	..	..	..	..
		female	..	..	..	..	..	..	..	..	..	..
Primary	GER	total	85	91	91	94	95	91	96	97	96	97
		female	85	92	93	95	97	93	98	99	99	99
	NER	total	65	72	71	73	74	71	70	71	71	70
		female	65	73	72	74	75	72	71	72	73	72
Secondary	GER	total	21	22	22	23	23	19	20	20	22	27
		female	19	20	21	21	22	18	18	19	21	25
Tertiary	GER	Total	3	3	3	3	4	4	4	4	5	5
		female	1	2	1	2	..	2	2	3	3	3

GER = Gross Enrolment Rate
NER = Net Enrolment Rate
Source: UIS. 2014b. Data Center

Quality and relevance

International campaigns and national efforts in increasing access have met with remarkable success especially at the primary level, but quality of education and learning level, measured by the basic skills in reading and mathematics, have not accompanied the level of participation. Students' scholastic achievements are determined by their ability and efforts, but in reality, circumstances at birth, such as poverty, gender, ethnicity, disability or location are more influential determinants of whether children go to school and learn. According to UNESCO (2014), using information on entry into school and progression and an international common scale of learning achievement, in Mauritania, about 80 per cent of children reached grade 4, but did not learn the basics, and less than 10 per cent of children reached grade 4 and learned the basics. Wealth affects basic learning significantly in Africa. In Mauritania, more than 30 per cent of children from rich families completed primary school and achieved minimum learning standards in mathematics while only less than 10 per cent of children from poor families have done so (2004–8 PASEC – Programme d'Analyse des Systèmes Educatifs de la CONFEMEN – Conférence des ministres de l'Éducation des États et gouvernements de la Francophonie) (UNESCO 2014).

Equality and equity

In Mauritania, among the major indices of inequality in education, location and family wealth are the greatest determinants of disparity in out-of-school children (aged 7–14). Children from the worst-performing provinces are 3.6 times as likely to be out-of-school as those from the best performing provinces; and children from the poorest families are 3.3 times as likely to be out-of-school as those from the richest families. The out-of-school rate in rural areas is 1.9 times higher than that in urban areas. Unlike many other African countries, gender disparity in Mauritania is in favour of girls; fewer girls (37 per cent) are out-of-school than boys (40 per cent) (FHI 360, n.d.).[3]

Literacy

Literacy data is not collected regularly, but the available data show that in 2000, the adult literacy rate (15+) was 51.2 per cent (43.4 per cent for females), slightly lower than the average of SSA, 57.2 per cent (48 per cent for females), and much lower than the world average of 81.9 per cent (77 per cent for females). Overall youth literacy rate (age 15–24), in 2000, was 61.3 per cent and 55.5 per cent for females (UIS 2014b).

Gender

Efforts to bridge the gender gap have somehow not been extended beyond primary education. On the Gender Inequality Index (GII) calculated by the United Nations Development Program (UNDP) based on three dimensions (reproductive health, empowerment, and economic activity), Mauritania was ranked 139 out of 148 countries in 2012. Only 8 per cent of adult women have reached secondary or higher education, compared to 20.8 per cent of their male counterparts. This is much lower than the SSA's average, which was 23.7 per cent for females and 35.1 per cent for males. Gender disparity in labour force participation is more evident, which was 28.7 per cent for females and 79.2 per cent for males (UNDP 2013).

Internal efficiency

From 2002 to 2010, the internal efficiency of education in Mauritania steadily improved. According to the RESEN (Rapport d'état sur le Système Educatif) Interim Report on the Education System, the retention rates for primary education improved and the repetition rates declined. For example, the retention rates increased from 45.1 per cent in 2002 to 72.1 per cent in 2010, a significant increase of 27 per cent in just a period of eight years. As for repetition rates, they decreased from 14.7 per cent in 2002 to only 3.9 per cent in 2010 (Pole de Dakar 2010).

However, for secondary education, the repetition rates were quite high, i.e. 12.9 per cent for both the first and second cycles in 2008. Further, the secondary education Global Efficiency Index (GEI – first and second cycles combined) was 70.9 per cent in 2008. As a matter of fact, the internal efficiency issue of education in Mauritania is being gradually resolved (MoE 2011).

Conflict and security

Mauritania experienced a prolonged political instability marked by successive coups that negatively impacted peace and security in the country. It is clear that education can play a key role in mitigating conflicts, in building peace and enhancing security in the country and the region as a whole. Finally, education may be a powerful tool and vehicle for policy dialogue among various conflicting parties in the country. Therefore, there is need to utilize education as a key instrument for mitigating conflict and building security in the country. This may be undertaken by curriculum revision and integrating into it concepts, such as conflict prevention, resolution and the like. Education can also promote peace.

Skills development

Despite its integration into a more and more globalized world economy exemplified by increasing foreign direct investments (FDI) totalling US$1.2 billion in 2013 and a rather robust average annual economic growth rate of 5.65 per cent over the past three years (Jeune Afrique 2014), the supply of jobs is still limited. To better understand the mismatch between employment and training, the ONS conducted a national survey in 2008 EPCV (Enquête Permanente de Conditions de Vie [Permanent Survey of Living Conditions]) of young school leavers aged 25–35. The main objective of EPCV was to compare the structure of the flux of school leavers with that of new entry workers (MoE 2011). The EPCV study reached the following conclusions: 1) the unemployment rate among primary school leavers (with no skills) was 58 per cent; 2) 12 out of 14 per cent of secondary education cycle 1 school leavers were to take up jobs in the informal sector of the economy; and 3) young school leavers have serious difficulties in finding jobs commensurate with their qualifications because the unemployment rates among secondary and tertiary education graduates were 29 and 42 per cent, respectively. These difficulties are further explained by the fact that a relatively high proportion of post-secondary graduates are employed in the informal sector, i.e. tertiary education (11 per cent), vocational training (21 per cent), and the second cycle of secondary education (19 per cent).

Student mobility

Brain drain in Mauritania like in most African countries basically characterized by the mobility of faculty members and students is an issue of paramount importance. Although statistics are not available to accurately measure the magnitude of brain drain, the phenomenon deprives Mauritania of highly skilled manpower which is vital for its economic development. Thus, the quantity and quality of human capital in Mauritania must be looked into, the perspective of the increased rise in labour productivity.

Regarding student mobility measured by the outbound mobility ratio, (the proportion of Mauritanian students leaving the country to go and study abroad), it was estimated to be 22 per cent in 2012, the highest percentage in the Maghreb region (UIS 2014b). Mauritania's outbound high mobility rate could be attributed to the low quality of its higher education institutions or the willingness of Mauritanian students from high socio-economic status to study abroad, in such countries as France (1,408 in 2011), Morocco (1,326 in 2010), Saudi Arabia (457 in 2012), Germany (93 in 2011) the United States of America (59 in 2011), Qatar (57 in 2012) and Malaysia (55 in 2011) (UIS 2014b), having in mind that a degree from a reputable institution could maximize their chance of getting highly paid jobs in their country or elsewhere.

Technology and education

Mauritania has embraced since 1995 the Information and Communication Technologies (ICT) as a tool for integration, development and pedagogy among others. This resulted in the design of a national plan for the development of information and communication infrastructure (1999–2002) with the support of the United Nations Economic Commission for Africa (UNECA) to boost the use of ICT in various sectors. Further, the government of Mauritania with the support of the UNDP started an e-government initiative in 1999, whose major objective was to enhance communication and the exchange of information among the various ministries of the country. The ICT strategy, articulated around eight strategic objectives, was extended for the 2002–6 period and the policy is still currently being implemented with the e-government, being one of its major components. With specific reference to education, initiatives such as the opening of multimedia centres in selected public and private high schools around the country are being implemented (MoE 2011).

Language policies

Mauritania was colonized by France for six decades (1901–60). Thus, the French language became the official language as well as the language of instruction of the country for this period and a significant portion of that of the post-independence era. Nevertheless, 75 per cent of its population are Moors whose native language is Arabic, and the remaining 25 per cent of the population speak three different African languages. In such a multilingual context, the language issue becomes a major challenge from a political, cultural as well as an education perspective. Since 1999, the Mauritanian authorities have attempted to introduce bold reforms about the use of the languages in the school system that unfortunately produced mixed results. Several educational reforms were undertaken by different governments [see section on educational reforms (1967, 1973, 1978 and 1999)], which also have had implications for the language policy that constantly impacts French and has affected its status as the official language of the country as well as the medium of instruction. In a multilingual situation, where the speakers of the three African languages have a limited proficiency in Arabic, the functional bilingualism alluded to in the reforms section of the chapter seems to be the best possible option to address the language issue (MoE 2011).

Regional integration

Mauritania, a buffer zone between the Maghreb and West Africa, is part of the Arab Maghreb Union (AMU), comprising four other countries (Algeria, Libya, Morocco, and Tunisia). It should be noted that the AMU has been dormant for the past two decades or so because of internal political divisions among its Member States. The educational systems of the AMU Member States in general, and especially the systems of higher education are fully harmonized, resulting in a high level of mobility of faculty members and students within the AMU region. Although the AMU has a highly harmonized system of higher education, political integration is still a big challenge and attempts were made in 2013 by the authorities of Tunisia to revitalize the Arab Regional Economic Community (REC).

Summary and future prospects

The chapter provided an overview of the education system of Mauritania, which included major reforms after independence; the sector strategy and policy framework; the structure of the education system; its institutional piloting with regards to governance and administration; and its funding and the private sector development. It then outlined the trends by exploring issues regarding access and participation at all levels of the education system; quality and relevance; equality and equity; literacy; gender; internal efficiency of education; conflict and security; skills development; student mobility and brain drain; technology and education-integration of ICT; language policies; and regional integration. From the discussions on the overview and trends of Mauritania's educational system, it may be concluded as the following future prospects:

First, demography will continue to impact education posing a challenge for the provision of adequate and quality educational services because the population will continue to increase rapidly. According to the United Nations (UN), with average annual rate of population change of 2.8 per cent during the period of 2005–10, the country's population will reach 5 million in the 2020s (UN 2012). This increase will, most certainly, affect the majority of education indicators from pre-primary to higher education and expansion of the education system at all levels is expected.

Second, with the current trend, although universal primary education may not be achieved in the near future, primary and secondary education will expand significantly in the next decade. According to the projections by FHI 360, the transition rate from primary to lower secondary education will increase steadily, reaching 90 per cent for males and 80 per cent for females in 2025. Nearly 90 per cent of both boys and girls are expected to complete primary education and 64 per cent of boys and 54 per cent of girls are expected to complete lower secondary education in 2025 (FHI 360 2013).

Third, high unemployment among school graduates of all levels from primary to tertiary and higher education will question the relevance of education in its current form and raise issues, such as the value of a degree as well as the mismatch between training and employment that is the interface between training institutions and the job market.

Fourth, this situation raises the importance of developing the country's human resources base in order to have a critical mass of scientists, engineers and doctors to fulfill the country's human resources' needs. This should interrogate Mauritania's current development model and underscore the role the educational and training system (including the private sector) can play and the responses they can provide.

Fifth, this situation will dramatically affect the funding of education in the country. Resources generation and management as well as inter and intra sectoral resource allocation at all levels will be key to quantity and quality human capital development. Despite the significant economic growth observed over the past decade, education in Mauritania is still not adequately funded and a huge infusion of financial resources should promote critical skills and competencies and raise the productivity that, in its turn, boosts inclusive economic growth and is a powerful wealth creation tool.

Finally, Mauritania is prone to social and political instability. Thus, it is important to use education as a mitigating factor for effective peace building, conflict prevention and resolution and enhancing security in the country, creating an environment that is conducive for a sustainable socio-economic growth and an orderly and planned development of Mauritania's education system.

Notes

1. Disclaimer: The ideas and opinions expressed in this chapter are those of the author or the co-author, and do not necessarily represent the views of UNESCO and do not commit the Organization.
2. The Monetary Unit (MU) or Mauritania Ouguiya (MRO) is the currency of the country, whose today's exchange rate to the US dollar is 290.5. http://www.xe.com/currencyconverter/convert/?Amount=1&From=USD&To=MRO (accessed 3 April 2014).
3. Source of the data is Multiple Indicator Cluster Survey (MICS) 2007.

References

EIU (Economist Intelligence Unit) (2008). *Country Profile Mauritania*. London: EIU.

FHI 360 (2013). 'Education Policy and Data Center (EPDC) Education Trends and Projections 2000–2025: Mauritania'. Washington, DC: FHI 360 Global Learning Group.

—(n.d.) *Mauritania: Out of School Children of the Population Ages 7–14*. Washington, DC: FHI 360 Global Learning Group.

Handloff, R. E, (ed.) (1988). *Mauritania: A Country Study*. Washington, DC: GPO for the Library of Congress. http://countrystudies.us/mauritania/ (accessed 26 January 2014).

IMF (International Monetary Fund) and IDA (International Development Association) (2011). *The Islamic Republic of Mauritania Poverty Reduction Strategy Paper and Joint Staff Advisory Note*. Washington, DC: IMF and IDA.

Jeune Afrique (2014). 'Le Classement Exclusif des 54 Pays Africains'. Hors-Série N°35. L'Afrique en 2014. Paris: Jeune Afrique.

MoE (Ministry of Education, Islamic Republic of Mauritania) (2011). *Programme National de Développement du Secteur Educatif (PNDSE-II) 2012–2014*. Nouakchott: MOE.

Pole de Dakar (2010). RESEN (Rapport d'état sur le Sysème Educatif) – Interim Report on the Education System, Dakar: Pole de Dakar.

UNDP (2013). 'Human Development Report 2013. Explanatory note on 2013 HDR composite indices: Mauritania'. New York: UNDP.

UNESCO (2014). 'Education for All Global Monitoring Report'. Paris: UNESCO.

UIS (UNESCO Institute for Statistics) (2014a). *Country Profiles: Mauritania*. Montreal: UIS.

—(2014b). *Data Centre*. Available from http://stats.uis.unesco.org/unesco/TableViewer/document.aspx?ReportId=143&IF_Language=eng (accessed on 29 January 2014). Montreal: UIS.

United Nations (UN) (2012). *World Population Prospects: The 2012 Revision Volume II: Demographic Profiles: Mauritania*. New York: United Nations Department of Economic and Social Affairs Population Divisions.

World Bank (2013). *Mauritania Overview*. http://www.worldbank.org/en/country/mauritania/overview (accessed 25 January 2014). Washington, DC: World Bank.

—(2014). *Data: Mauritania*. http://data.worldbank.org/country/mauritania (accessed on 9, February 2014). Washington, DC: World Bank.

Niger: An Overview

Nana Aicha Goza and Ibro Chekaraou

Introduction

A thorough account of the historical development of education in Niger calls for an overview of the general context within which it evolved. Education in Niger, being an offshoot of that of the French colonial system in West Africa, has had limited expansion due to the resistance of the local populations, the scarcity of financial resources and the lack of adequate means of access to the country due to its being landlocked.

This chapter focuses on the educational system in Niger and its evolution from the pre-colonial period to today. To enable a better understanding of the system, we first present the geographical, linguistic, cultural and administrative context of the country and how this context has influenced the spread of education in the country. Further, we borrow the concept of 'school civilization' from Dupont (1990) to serve as our conceptual framework for analysing the state of school from the colonial to the current period. We conclude the chapter by arguing that, in spite of the very many challenges that school in Niger still faces, the educational system has evolved especially from independence in 1960 to today.

To carry out the study resulting in the writing of this chapter, we used descriptive methodology which consisted of a document analysis of contemporary authors' and educators' work on education. Most of the data used were drawn from Sandi's (1993: 5–58) doctoral thesis.

The geographical, linguistic, cultural and administrative aspects and their impact on the educational system

Niger is a vast dry and landlocked country in West Central Africa. It is bordered by Nigeria and Benin to the South, Algeria and Libya to the North, Burkina Faso and Mali to the West, and Chad to the East, with an area of 1,267,000 square kilometres, over twice as large as France. The country's closest sea port is in Cotonou, Benin, at 1,035 kilometres (kms) from the capital city, Niamey. Two-thirds of the country consists of the Sahara Desert in the north and center. The country is one of the hottest areas of the world with three main seasons including:

- The rainy season from May/June to September/October;
- The dry and cold season, also known as the Harmattan, from October/November to February/March;
- The dry and hot season, from March to May.

The main economic activities in Niger include agriculture, animal husbandry, art work and fishing, which are highly dependent on the climate change. The country also produces coal, uranium and gold, and, since 2011, it has joined the restricted number of oil-producing countries around the world. However, all these natural resources are exploited by foreign companies such as AREVA for uranium and the Chinese SORAZ for oil.

The geography in Niger contributed to a large extent to the scarcity of education access. Waeyenberghe (1964), for example, mentioned a few of these factors which had blocked the development of education including: the fact that country was landlocked, thus its remoteness, the scattering of the inhabitants in a territory more than twice as vast as France, the lack of rapid means of communication and transportation, the nomadic or semi-nomadic life of the population and the fact that 95% of the national economy was based on subsistence agriculture and animal husbandry.

At independence in 1960, the rate of school-attending children in Niger was 3.6 per cent, the lowest in French colonial Africa. The geography in Niger contributed to a large extent to the scarcity of education access.

Until today, these geographical aspects continue to impact the evolution of the educational system in Niger, which ranked 174th according to the last human development report (PNUD 2013). The scattering of the habitat still constitutes a major obstacle to the expansion of schools in Niger, a country that is composed of 14,000 towns while the road structure is yet to fully develop. The harshness of the climate, exacerbated by a long dry and hot season, has led to a special adaptation of the school system and its calendars in a scarcity of resources. For example, the school year has always ended as soon as the rainy season starts to accommodate and encourage the nomads, animal breeders and farmers.

It seems antithetical that, in spite of the free basic education policy enacted by the government, the recurrent food crises in the country and the persistent poverty among the population (61 per cent are below the poverty line in the country) make the average citizen still bear the indirect school costs. Yet, with a population of 15,203,822 inhabitants, the demand in schooling continues to increase given the high yearly population growth rate of 3.3 per cent according to M/F/INS (2011).

Impact of the linguistic and cultural aspect on the educational system

Serving as a bridge between North and sub-Saharan Africa, Niger was for a long time inhabited by people of different races including whites and blacks. Today, Niger counts ten national languages and a variety of corresponding cultural practices. This multiplicity of languages and cultures has posed numerous challenges to the educational system, making the western French education face difficulties of implantation in the country. In particular, the general public has resisted the exclusive use of the French language, which was only spoken by a bare 10 per cent who have had a chance to attend school, as the only medium of instruction from the primary to the tertiary/university level. Moumouni (1998) blamed the failure of the education system in Niger on this 'refusal' to adapt it to the local socio-cultural realities.

Yet, since the country gained independence in 1960, the inclusion of the national languages in education has been one of the government's preoccupations, and, as early as 1978, the use of five national languages as media of instruction (French is taught as a subject) has been tried out in specific schools known as écoles *expérimentales* [experimental schools]. This long experimentation has discouraged the majority of the proponents of the inclusion of local languages and cultures in education. As a result, although to a lesser degree, the tension still remains, especially when the general public knows that the 1998 education reform law (commonly known as LOSEN, i.e. *Loi d'Orientation du System Educatif Nigerien* [Niger Education System Reform Law]) (MEBA, 1998), in its articles 10 and 19, mandates the use of national languages as media of instruction in the education system throughout primary school.

To show its commitment to address the concern, the government created a special office in charge of the promotion of national languages in the Ministry of Education and, in 2011, the ministry was even renamed as the Ministry of Education, Literacy and the Promotion of National Languages (in French, *le Ministère de l'Education National, de l'Alphabétisation et de la Promotion des Langues Nationales – MEN/A/PLN*).

The administrative aspect and its influence on education

The Niger colony was created in 1922 under the French protectorate after long resistance movements from the locals. A colonial decree by the French signed into law on 17 July 1964 divided the country into 'départements' [prefectures], 'arrondissements' [districts] and 'communes' [cities], which were respectively headed by governors, district administrative officers and mayors. This colonial administration was seconded by the traditional power structure which consisted of sultans, kings and village chiefs, who earned more trust among the local populace than the new 'modern' authorities. These two types of administrations have worked jointly to manage and maintain the education system. While the colonial administration was the only organizing force with the challenge of ensuring access to and quality of the colonial education system (49 per cent of the population was under 15 years of age), it relied heavily on the traditional authorities for school propagation (sensitizing the general public about the new school system and urging them to attend it).

This brief overview of the geographical, linguistic and administrative characteristics of the country shows the influence of these factors on the evolution of the educational system. The new 1998 education reform law (LOSEN), strategically took into consideration these impacting aspects by acknowledging a shared responsibility of all education stakeholders (teachers, school administrators, parents and the whole community) and urging them to join efforts for the development of a successful education system. We believe that this synopsis is relevant to a study of the evolution of the colonial and postcolonial education system in Niger.

Conceptualizing the study

We borrow the expression 'school civilization' from Dupont (1990) to serve as our conceptual framework because it perfectly illustrates the study of the educational system in Niger that we propose to make in this chapter. Thus, in his book entitled *The School Civilization*, Dupont (1990) showed that what he called the 'school civilization' consisted of a broad enterprise, which is in charge of education. He added that 'it may be astonishing that, in the same book, one speaks of "the past school" and "the future school"! At first sight, one may think that one should preclude the other. Yet this view remains erroneous! Supporting it is synonymous to overlooking, unfortunately, the dynamic and irreversible character of an evolution …. The "school of yesterday" (i.e. "the past school"), with its dynamism, needs to be understood whole before [one could pretend] comprehending any possible future [school] [the translation is ours]'. Following this notion of 'school civilization', which to us is a type of paradigm, we will analyse the educational system in Niger from its past colonial heritage to its current postcolonial state.

The Niger education system yesterday and today

In this section, we use the concept of 'school civilization' to analyse the state of the Niger school from the colonial to the current period.

The Niger 'school of yesterday': The colonial period

During the colonial era, Niger was a member of the federation of French West African Colonies. Thus, the history of education in Niger is intimately linked to that of the French colonial West African Federation (known in French as AOF, Afrique de l'Ouest Française [French West Africa]), which came into being in 1895 and included Senegal, Middle Niger, The Upper Senegal, Cote d'Ivoire, The Dahomey (now Benin) joined later by Mauritania, Niger and Upper Volta (now Burkina Faso). Capelle (1990) acknowledged the vastness of the empire which had a population of 18 million inhabitants spread unevenly over a massive land mass of 4,675,000 square kilometres.

Several studies (Desalmand 1983 cited in Sandi 1993; Inné 1988) indicated that until the turn of the twentieth century, the task of organizing education in the Federation of West African Colonies was assigned to the Lieutenant Governor of Senegal, Cancille, who presented a report on the subject. The foundation of education in the federation was laid down after the ratification by General Governor Roume of three drafts on 24 November 1903. The ratified drafts were to remain in force until the Brazzaville conference in 1944.

Three levels of education were acknowledged by the 24 November 1903 drafts including an elementary primary education, a higher primary level and the federal schools. In Niger, the first school was created in 1903 in Filingué after several unsuccessful attempts in Doulsou in 1898, in Dosso in 1889, in Sorbon Hawsa in 1900 and in Niamey in 1902.

At the beginning, education, according to Inné (1988: 202), was fraught with much unprofessionalism and hesitation and 'the first education institutions were not real schools'. However, it was not until 1922 when the colony of Niger was created that attention was paid to the problems of the new schools. The colony took advantage of its administrative and financial autonomy to organize its education system according to its professional needs and goals consisting of promoting handicraft and farming activities. Salifou (1977) noted that education efforts continued and the number of schools increased from 16 in 1922 to 22 in 1930, 18 of which were located in rural areas. Within this period, the number of students tripled accordingly.

Nonetheless, speaking of the evolution of schools until Niger became independent in 1960, Inné (1988: 206) pointed out that '21,054 pupils, representing barely 3.6 per cent of school age children, were registered in primary schools while only 1,040 students were registered at the secondary and higher education levels'.

Several reasons might account for the unsatisfactory results in the sector including uprisings and resistance of the population against colonial expansion, parents' aversion toward the 'white man's school' and the failure of school itself to attract the youth by not being able to produce graduates who could serve as role models. Furthermore, with the education system's limited efforts to arouse people's enthusiasm and the discouraging first results, rural populations became particularly reluctant towards school especially when their partially-schooled children would refuse to return to farm work when they left.

However, to improve school quality, 'the first teacher training institution was created in 1945 in Kollo, an area located 50 kms from Niamey. After completing their primary school education, pupils underwent three-year training in this teacher-training school after which they were sent to teach in rural schools. A similar school followed in the same Niamey area in 1947. Niger had its own office in charge of pedagogical supervision in 1950. Efforts to provide adequate training to teachers continued with the creation of two more colleges of education, respectively in Zinder in 1957, and in Tillabery (one specifically hosting female pre-service teachers) in 1959' (Inné 1988: 205).

The education system in the crossroads (first republic and the military regime)

Despite various factors that contributed to hampering the development of Niger's education system after its independence from the French in 1960, in March 1961 in the Addis Ababa Francophone African Ministers of Education Conference, the country committed itself to the 'education for all by 1980' convention alongside other French speaking African countries. The conference formulated the following long-term recommendations:

- Compulsory and free primary education;
- Secondary education for 30 per cent of the students having completed their primary education;
- Higher education for 20 per cent of the students having completed their secondary studies; and
- Improvement of the quality of education in schools and universities.

Meunier (2000: 112) added that 'the government of the first Republic ensures harmony and suitability between western schools and the socio-cultural and economic specificities of the country'. He further reported that the first democratically elected president of independent Niger, Diori Hamani, supported that, as opposed to the pre-independence school elite, the post-independence citizens would receive an education that valued local cultures while, at the same time, providing the nation with future trained farmers and animal breeders who were open to cultural and economic progress.

This vision contributed to the extension of the school organization chart to include preschool especially under the supervision of the missionaries, which experienced a very low expansion and the primary schools sector which was made up of three different types of schools mainly:

- Schools known as 'traditional schools' based on the model inherited from colonization where the sole medium of instruction is French. It took six years to complete for children 7 to 13 years old;
- Madrasas, the first of which was created in 1957 in Say in which French and Arabic were used; and
- Experimental schools whose medium of instruction was the mother tongue of the children. In these schools, the use of five local languages (Fulfulde, Hausa, Kanuri, Zarma-sonray and Tamashek) as medium of instruction has been experimented since 1978.

The next sector included the secondary schools level which was subdivided into the first cycle with four years of general education ending with a national certificate known as the Brevet d'Etudes du Premier Cycle (BEPC) [First Secondary Cycle Certificate] and the second cycle which consisted of three years of education graduating with a baccalaureate diploma in one of the three majors that students chose to pursue, i.e. natural science/biology, math/physical science/chemistry and the art/social science majors.

The chart also included professional/vocational education sector to satisfy the increasing demand for state officials in the young nation's administration. As a result, professional training centres were progressively created under the supervision of the relevant ministries. Virtually all of them came under the same system (three years of duration of study ending with BEPC as shown in Table 20.1.

The professional education process was completed with the creation of Centre for Technology Studies (CET – *Centre d'Enseignement Technique* in French) in 1977. The creation of a technical high school (LET – *Lycée d'Enseignement Technique* in French) in 1955 in the form of a training centre is also noteworthy. The centre was transformed into a junior secondary technical school in 1963 to become a technical high school later.

However, the colonial legacy in secondary education was as insignificant as it was in the primary sector. Inné (1988: 214) noted that 'until 1969, there were only two high schools, one of which was exclusively attended by female students. Both were located in Niamey. There were also 17 middle schools, three private schools, three centers for education and training and a college of education'.

Table 20.1 Evolution of professional schools from 1963 to 1977

Institutes	Date of creation
National School of Administration	1963
National School of Health	1965
Electricity and Water Management Training Centre	1965
Post and Telecommunication Training Centre	1969
School of Animal Sciences	1971
Air School of Mining Studies	1975
Training Centre for Literacy Agents	1977
National Institute for Youth, Sports and Culture	1979

Source: Meunier, 2000: 151–2

At the beginning of the 1970s, barely a decade after independence, Inné (1988: 216) continued, 'secondary schools were struck by students' uprisings and repetitive strikes. A tremendous agitation destabilized the education system in Niger. The idea of reforming the education system emerged from this gloomy context. With the approval of public authorities, a presidential decree dated 19 May 1972 set up a National Commission for Educational Reforms and Planning. The commission produced a document entitled 'Educational reforms and new directions' after a meeting from 23 to 27 of February 1974. This document highlighted the major achievements and weaknesses of the education system in Niger and recommended that reforms were necessary'.

The education system faced huge challenges while the social and economic situation of the country also worsened. The context favoured a military coup on 15 April 1974. One of the major concerns of the new military leaders was a fair administration that guaranteed the right to education to all (Amadou 2000). Meunier (2000: 134) pointed out that 'the military leaders' commitment was revealed through the organization of a national seminar on the reform of education from September 4th, to September 12th, 1975'. Subsequently, numerous debates and actions were conducted to bail out the educational system through exploration of new directions to improve its efficacy including:

- 1976: Experimentation of the national language education in Tillabery
- 1979: General education symposium and the extension of teaching languages to three other languages (Fulfulde, Tamashek, Kanuri) than Hausa and Zarma
- 1982: National Debate on Education in Niger
- 1991: National conference's education Report
- 1992: General state of education forum
- 1998: LOSEN
- 1999: Meeting of the veterans of Education
- 2003: Ten-year Program for Educational Development (PDDE 2003-2013) (MEBA, 2003).

In addition, as early as 1974, the then military Head of State Colonel Seyni Kountché in his inaugural speech expressed the determination to create an educational system that was in harmony with the socio-cultural values of the communities and capable of producing educated citizens who will take care of the development of the country (Bergmann et al. 1999 quoted in Chekaraou 2009: 30). During that period, research indicated that significant results were achieved as shown in Table 2 (Inné 1988).

Table 20.2 Schools and number of their students in 1986

Schools	Public	Private	Number of Classrooms	Number of Students
Pre-school	30	10	-N/A	5,430
Primary	1,837	N/A	6,615	272,622
Middle schools	68	16	1,120	45,255
High schools	10	N/A	171	6,768
Technical high schools	2	0	33	673

Source: Inné 1988: 229–30

In addition to the primary, secondary and professional schools, four teacher training schools, known as écoles *normales*, were created for pre-service teacher training while another was turned into an in-service teacher training school, with a total of 75 classes. Moreover, the University of Niamey was added with six faculties (Faculty of Arts and Social Sciences, Faculty of Sciences, Faculty of Health Sciences, Faculty of Law and Economics, Faculty of Pedagogy and the Faculty of Agriculture) and two Institutes (Institut de Recherche en Sciences Humaines [Institute for Research in Human Sciences] (IRSH) and Institut de Recherche en Mathématiques [Research Institute for Mathematical Studies] (IREM)). A student population of 2,787 Niger students was registered at the University.

The education system improved during the 1980s and the 1990s as a result of considerable funding that the sector received from the government (a quarter of the national budget was devoted to education) due to the uranium boom of the eighties. To continue ensuring the government's commitment to the promotion of education, the LOSEN, which aimed at reforming the education system, was voted into law in June 1998. As the first officially written education policy document in the history of the country, this reform law specifies the vision, goals, content and type of teaching methodology orientation of the national education agenda. It also invites all stakeholders (parents, students, community, government, civil society and donors) to join efforts towards the promotion of education in the country by clearly defining the roles to play by every one of them (see LOSEN Articles 60, 65–9, 70 and 73).

However, these achievements were undermined by the combination of several factors such as students' riots (from 1990 to 1998), the emergence of economic hardship once again during these decades, the structural adjustment programme (IMF) in the 1980s, the devaluation of CFA Franc, the local currency, on 12 January 1994 and the fall of the uranium price, which contributed heavily to destabilizing the country's economic fabric. Various actions were taken among which a new salary grid to satisfy the international donors' demands to adjust, suspension of workers' allowances payment in 1997, and the application of an exceptionally made law, which anticipated workers' retirement after serving 30 years.

In addition, a crucial decrease of the budget allocated to education from 19.9 per cent in 1992 to only 8.6 per cent in 2003, contributed to tamper with the efforts made. Once again, to meet national and international commitments of the government regarding education, the educational system in Niger still has a long way to go. It remains to be seen whether the implementation of the PDDE (Ten-year Program for Educational Development), which was enacted in 2003, will remedy the difficult situation in which the education sector in Niger finds itself.

The Niger school today

The State-of-the-Nation speech by the Prime Minister in 2000 before the National Assembly highlighted that 'the educational system is, from now on, at the center of the national concerns among Niger citizens. One needs to deeply look at the institutional fabric that supports the educational system to accommodate it with the actual capacities of the government. The primary education sector, in particular, needs to adapt to the context of territorial decentralization [...] more attention needs to also be paid to functional literacy and the revitalization of experimental bilingual schools for effective inclusion of our national languages in the education system' (Amadou 2000).

Following this, Niger adopted the poverty reduction strategy (SRP in French, i.e. *Stratégie de Réduction de Pauvreté*), which placed education at the centre of the government's policies as an indispensable asset that allowed every citizen to move towards ideals of liberty and social justice as well as aspire to welfare and fight against poverty. The SRP pays special attention to the improvement of quality in education and training as well as the quantity of schools in a successful educational system, which will contribute better to reducing poverty. The second report on the implementation of the SRP even emphasized the objectives of basic primary education and literacy policies, putting a specific accent on the improvement of quality and making the teaching relevant.

In addition, the educational policy plan for the 2002–12 decade recommends 'the acceleration of universal education and literacy, the improvement of quality and relevance of the education system including the non-professional and the professional/technical training sector, and the improvement of quality in education by reforming the curriculum and decentralizing the management of education". Based on these recommendations, the government of Niger elaborated, in 2003, the Ten-year Program for Education Development known as the PDDE. The PDDE not only specified the country's education policy orientations but also prepared the government to implement the various national and international conventions on education to which they subscribed including the Education for All by 2015 convention and the MDGs, to mention a few.

A few years after its conception, it seemed that the PDDE implementation started paying off. Doubtless, the gross schooling rate was one of the lowest in the sub-region (3.6 per cent) at independence in 1960. By 2011, however, it grew to 76.1 per cent in primary school, 19.8 per cent and 4.1 per cent in the first and second cycle schools respectively while there were 135 university students for every 100,000 inhabitants. It still is low especially at the secondary and tertiary levels but considering its being 3.6 per cent at independence, there have been tremendous improvements. Evaluations of the PDDE implementation have hinted that it has contributed to the development of access at the expense of quality and that it has failed to confront the gender and rural/urban disparities in school (thus the lack of equity) (Daouda 2013). It remains to be seen whether even these access-related improvements can be sustained and the challenges of quality and equity be addressed with efficacy.

Conclusion

This chapter examined the evolution of the educational system in Niger from the colonial to the post-colonial periods. Prior to this, however, the chapter exposes the geographical, cultural, linguistic and administrative organization of the country and how it impacted the expansion of education. This analysis points to an educational system which has developed significantly throughout the two periods in spite of the many challenges it faces, mainly, due to the lack of training for teachers, the socio-cultural traditions and the scarcity of resources exacerbated by corruption, and, at times, the harshness of the climate.

In the years 2000s, the PDDE implementation has contributed to the improvement of the system especially regarding access to schooling but gender and rural/urban disparities remain (Daouda 2013). However, looking at the statistics, the success of the education system in Niger gives a rather pyramidal picture of its evolution and improvement, i.e. the higher up the sector, the gloomier the picture regarding its trends. A study of the trends in the system as we propose to do in our second chapter in this volume, will probably give a better picture.

Bibliography

Amadou, H. (2000). *Déclaration de politique générale (DPG) 2000*. Niamey: Cabinet du Premier Ministre.

Capelle, J. (1990). *L'éducation en Afrique noire à la veille des indépendances (1946-1958)*. Paris: Ed. Karthala.

Chekaraou, I. (2009). *Teachers' appropriation of an educational reform policy in Africa: A socio-cultural study of two bilingual Hausa-French schools in Niger*. Saarbrücken, Germany: Lambert Academic Publishing.

Daouda, H. (2013). 'Souci de redorer le blason de notre système éducatif'. *Le Sahel Quotidien*, 8535, (May 29): 5.

Dupont, P. (1990). *La civilisation de l'école*. Bruxelles: Labor.

Inné, M. (1988). 'La politique d'éducation au Niger'. In Anon. (eds), *Pédagogie Pratique pour l'Afrique vol 1*, pp. 199-232. Paris: Imprimerie Aubenas d'Ardèche.

M/F/INS (2011). '*Annuaire Statistique 2009/2010*'. Niamey: M/F/INS.

MEBA (1998). *Loi d'Orientation du Système Educatif Nigérien* [LOSEN]. Version Intégrale. Niamey: MEBA.

—(2003). 'Programme décennal pour le développement de l'éducation (PDDE).' Niamey, Niger: Ministère de l'Education de Base et de l'Alphabétisation (MEBA).

Meunier, O. (2000). *Bilan d'un siècle de politiques éducatives au Niger*. Paris: L'Harmattan.

Moumouni, A. (1998). *L'éducation en Afrique*. Paris: Présence Africaine.

Programme des Nations Unies pour le développement (PNUD) (2013). 'Rapport sur l'indice du développement humain'. Paris: PNUD.

Salifou, A. (1977). *L'histoire du Niger*. Thèse de Doctorat (Paris VII) (France).

Sandi, N. A. (1993). *Analyse théorique et expérimentale de quelques déterminants du décrochage scolaire dans l'enseignement secondaire au Niger*. Thèse de Doctorat Université Mons Hainaut (Belgique).

Waeyenberghe, R. van. (1964). Planification de l'enseignement: République du Niger – (mission) 1961-1962 [Mission Report]. Paris : UNESCO.

21

Niger: Trends and Futures

Ibro Chekaraou and Nana Aicha Goza

Introduction

The Niger formal education system is a 6–4–3-year system (six years in the primary or Basic Education I, four years in the first cycle of secondary or Basic Education II and three in the second cycle of secondary school or simply secondary school). It also includes pre-school and higher education. It constitutes a legacy from the French colonial system as proven by its exclusive use of the French language as the medium of instruction from pre-school to university. This has resulted in a mismatch between the curricular content and the school socio-cultural context.

Many educators perceive the 'language problem' to be the principal issue that hinders the efficacy of Niger's education system since independence in 1960. According to Moumouni (1998), the colonial education and the traditional African education were worlds apart, the former attaching no value to the latter and treating it with contempt. Colonial education sought to force itself onto the African population without considering the valuable resources of the traditional mode of education. Yet, apart from a few isolated experimental schools where five national languages have been tested as media of instruction since 1973, the government has not been able to solve this language-in-education issue. This situation persists in spite of the overt mandate of the 1998 *Loi d'Orientation du Système Educatif Nigérien* [Niger Education System Reform Law] (LOSEN) to include the children's primary languages as media of instruction in primary schools and subjects in Basic Education II (Articles 10 and 19).

The Niger education system started with a few junior officers trying to teach in their camps as early as 1889 in Dosso 1898 in Doulsou 1900 in Sorbon Hausa and 1902 in Niamey. These 'schools' were short-lived, giving very limited results. The creation of the first real school followed in 1903 in Filingué (176 kilometres north-east of the capital city, Niamey). Nevertheless, pre-independence education yielded limited results with the literacy rate as low as 3.6 per cent, the worst in French West African colonies.

In spite of these various challenges and low performance, the education system in Niger has experienced significant trends that are worth exploring. In this chapter, we used descriptive methodology which consisted of a document analysis of education-related national laws and official discourse (for example, education policy documents, state-of-the-nation speeches by former officials known as DPGs, etc.), contemporary authors' and educators' work on education, to expose the general tendencies of education in Niger and, later, reflect on its future perspectives. However, first, a synopsis of its structure might contribute to a better understanding of the trends and perspectives that we propose to explore.

The structure of the Niger education system

In Title III, Chapter I, Article 16 of LOSEN, the formal education system is defined as 'a means of acquiring an education and professional training in a school context' [translation is ours]. It consists of basic education, secondary education and higher education.

Articles 17 through 22 highlight what basic education entails. It is composed of two sub-sectors: Preschool and basic education (first cycle and second cycle). In official documents, the two cycles of basic education are often referred to as Basic Education I or primary school education and Basic Education II or secondary school first cycle education respectively. Preschool accepts three- to five-year-old children for a one- to three-year-long cycle of study while Basic Education I recruits six- and seven-year-olds for a six-year study period which ends with a diploma called the CFEPD (*Certificat de Fin d'Etudes du Premier Degré* [End of First Cycle Studies Certificate]. Basic Education II accepts children aged 11 to 13, who hold their CFEPD certificate, for a four-year-long study period, which ends with another certificate referred to in LOSEN, Article 21, as the '*Diplôme de Fin d'Etudes de Base* (DFEB) [End of Basic Education Studies Dilopma]' but currently known to the public and many education officials by its former name, the BEPC (*Brevet de Fin d'Etudes Premier Cycle*) [End of First Cycle Studies Certificate].

Articles 23 to 26 specify what secondary education involves. It recruits children who hold the DFEB, roughly at an age between 15 and 17 (LOSEN is not specific about the age) for a study period of three years. This sector includes the general education on the one hand and the professional and technical education on the other. The general public and even official documents refer to this sector as the *lycée*, a name inherited from the French colonial education system. LOSEN falls short of clarifying the exact name of the diploma that students receive after the three-year long study period in the *lycée*. However, the general public and official documents refer to this diploma as the BAC, short for baccalaureate, which has many denominations to reflect the general, the technical and professional majors that compose this sub-sector. For example, for general education studies, we have BAC A for arts and social science majors, the BAC D for natural sciences and biology majors and BAC C for the math, physics and chemistry majors. In the technical field, we have BAC G or BAC F depending on the majors students pursue. The BAC allows students to enter higher education institutions.

Articles 27 through 35 identify what higher education includes. Structurally, Articles 30-2 mention three main cycles: the first (first year through the BA or BS degrees), the second (master's programme through receipt of the degree) and the third (the doctoral programme through the actual degree receipt). As opposed to the former system where the BA or BS degrees were followed by a one-year-study period at the end of which a student would obtain a *Maitrise* diploma, the former French master's degree, today, higher education institutions in Niger with the universities leading, have adopted the LMD (*Licence-Master-Doctorate* [BA/BS, Master's and Doctorate]) system that allows Niger to be in harmony with the sub-regional West African higher education structure that reflects the French higher education reform which, itself echoes the Anglophone, specifically the North American, university system.

Article 33 stipulates that four main types of institutions provide higher education training in Niger: the Universities, the Higher Education Institutes, which are similar to community colleges in the US, the *Grandes Ecoles* [higher education schools] such as the National School of Administration and Law (ENAM), which trains potential and returning government employees in finance, law, administration, social security, labour studies to mention a few and the Mining and Geology School (EMIG), which provides Niger and other West African countries with engineers in studies in fields such as electricity, energy mining, etc. The fourth category of institutions that provide higher education consists of what LOSEN refers to as the *Centres Spécialisés* [Specialized Higher Education Centres].

To sum up, the structure of the formal education system in Niger is not so different from that of the majority of countries around the world including such affluent nations as France, the US and Canada. The question that remains now is whether this neat structure reflects positive outcomes. The next section responds to this question by focusing on the system's general trends from independence in 1960 to date.

Earlier trends of the education system from independence

At independence in 1960, the new leaders of Niger inherited an almost non-existent education system with disparate schools that were mostly concerned with providing the colonial system with *subalternes*, i.e. low degree blue collar employees, to serve the colonial master. Kelly (1992) argued that schooling 'was to diffuse spoken French among those who were, by birth, destined to become an [*sic*] elite'. The elites in question, on the other hand, only 'needed to know [...] how to communicate with the Frenchmen' for eventually becoming their interpreters (p. 15).'

To explain the scarcity of schools that existed at independence in Niger, Inné (1988) reported that only 21,054 pupils, representing barely 3.6 per cent of school age children, were registered in primary schools while only 1,040 students were registered at the secondary and higher education levels in 1960. Until 1969, he continued, there were only two high schools, one of which was exclusively attended by female students and both were located in Niamey. There were also 17 middle schools [i.e. Basic Education II schools], three private schools, three centers for education and training and a normal school. With the efforts that the government made, in 1986, i.e. 26 years after independence, Inné (1988) added, the system contained 6,615 primary schools with 272,622 pupils, 1,120 middle schools with 45,255 students and 171 high schools [i.e. *lycées*] with 6,768 attendees. The technical high schools had 673 trainees.

From the figures above, we realize that the educational system improved significantly from independence to 1986, a period that corresponds to the first republic and the military regimes. Next, we turn to the trends in the last decade, a period through which the country has experimented with democracy.

Trends of the Niger educational system during the 2003–13 decade

At the advent of the elaboration of the PDDE, all diagnostic studies of the educational system in Niger showed that the situation in primary schools especially, remained critical in particular regarding access, quality development and equity. However, after ten years of PDDE, positive trends were registered especially concerning access to school throughout the country in all education sectors.

Trends in the pre-school basic education sector

To determine access and effective coverage in the pre-school sector, we use the attendance and gross enrolment rates as indicators as illustrated in Table 21.1.

Table 21.1 shows significant progress in the number of pre-school attendees. The gross enrolment rate rose up to 5.7 per cent in 2011, slightly above the rate projected in the PDDE. It is also noticeable that community and private schools played a significant role in pre-school education with 38 per cent attendees, 24 per cent in community kindergartens and 14 per cent in private preschools. However, preschool remained the domain of urban areas with 61 per cent of the attendees in 2011 being in urban centre schools. One important point to make is the lack of gender disparity in preschools (5.6 per cent for boys and 5.7 per cent for girls).

Table 21.1 Evolution of number of preschool attendees and gross enrolment rate of Niger preschools

	Schools	Attendees	2008–9	2009–10	2010–11	Gain in %
Number of attendees	All	Boys	25,275	34,027	47,580	37.2
		Girls	22,844	33,651	48,442	45.6
		Total	48,119	67,678	96,022	41.3
	Rural schools	Boys	5,707	10,333	18,027	77.8
		Girls	5,677	10,008	18,381	80,0
		Total	11,384	20,341	36,408	78.8
	Community Schools	Boys	3,177	5,733	10,991	86.1
		Girls	3,101	5,688	11,710	94.6
		Total	**6,278**	**11,421**	**22,701**	**90.3**
	Private schools	Boys	7,791	5,944	6,955	-3.3
		Girls	5,357	6,036	7,012	14.4
		Total	13,148	11,980	13,967	3.9
Gross enrolment rate (in %)		Boys	2.7	4.7	5.6	2.9
Girls			2.4	4.6	5.7	3.3
Total			**2.5**	**4.6**	**5.7**	**3.2**

Source: MEN/A/PLN, 2010–11

In addition, positive trends were found in the number of teachers, which passed from 1,995 in 2009-10 to 2,961 in 2010-11, an increase of 48.4 per cent and also in the number of schools which grew from 826 in 2009-10 to 1,283 in 2010-11, a rise of 43.7 per cent. However, these positive results should not hide the necessity of reducing the number of students per classroom, which increased from 42 in 2009-10 to 54 in 2010-11 while the norm is 25. Also, problems related to, for instance, the lack of or the out-datedness of the equipment used in the classrooms, the latrines and electricity should also be tackled to ensure effectiveness of preschool education.

Trends in the primary education (Basic Education I) sector

Still according to the Ministry of Education statistics of 2010-11, indicators used to determine trends in the primary basic education sector included the evolution of numbers of registered students in the first year, the total numbers of attendees, the rate of enrolment in the first year, and the overall rate of schooling in the sector. The following table highlights these indicators.

Table 21.2 shows an increase of 11.1 per cent among the first year registered primary school pupils while Table 21.3 reveals exposes an overall rate of

Table 21.2 Evolution of students registered in first year of primary education

	2007-8	2008-9	2009-10	2010-11	Yearly gain %
Total of Attendees	342 360	410 975	463 160	469 917	11.1 %
Boys	187 303	226 453	249 941	254 235	10.7 %
Girls	155 057	184 522	213 219	215 682	11.6 %

Source: MEN/A/PLN 2011

Table 21.3 Evolution of enrolment rate in the first year of primary education

	2007-8	2008-9	2009-10	2010-11	Gain in %
Rate of admission	77.8	90.4	98.6	99.8	22
For boys	84.1	98.4	105.2	106.6	22.5
For girls	71.4	82.2	92	92.7	21.5
In Urban areas	118	116	117.1	111.3	-5.5
In rural areas	69.9	84.9	94.3	96.7	26,8

Source: MEN/A/PLN 2011

Table 21.4 Evolution of numbers of primary school attendees by gender

	2007–8	2008–9	2009–10	2010–11	Gain (%)
Total Attendees	1 389 194	1 554 270	1 726 452	1 910 166	11.2
Boys	796 395	883 710	970 276	1 066 576	10.2
Girls	592 799	670 560	756 176	843 590	12.5

Source: MEN/A/PLN, 2011

Table 21.5 Evolution primary basic schooling rate per area and by gender

	2007–8	2008–9	2009–10	2010–11	Gain (%)
Total Attendees	62.1	67.8	72.9	76.1	14
Boys	71.2	77	81.9	84.9	13.7
Girls	53.1	58.6	63.9	67.3	14.2
Urban areas	73.2	78	80.8	99.1	25.9
Rural areas	58.4	64.4	70.3	70	11.6
Girl/Boy Parity Rate	0.75	0.76	0.78	0.79	0.04
Urban/ Rural Parity Rate	1.25	1.21	1.15	1.42	0.17

Source: MEN/A/PLN 2011

access to the first year of primary basic education of 22 per cent between the academic years of 2007–8 and 2010–11. However, according to these Ministry of Education statistics of 2010–11, regional disparities concerning access to the first year of primary school still existed and the difference of 17.8 per cent between Agadez, the region with the highest rate (107.7 per cent) and Zinder, the province with the lowest (89.9 per cent) needs to be addressed.

In spite of efforts made by the government since independence, the expansion of schools in Niger is still hindered by socio-cultural factors especially in certain areas where, for example, girls are still marginalized in terms of access to education, as hinted in Table 21.4.

Positive trends were registered from 2007 to 2011 as shown in Tables 21.4 and 21.5. These resulted from numerous efforts by the government as a response to the commitment made to the nation through, for example, the LOSEN which stipulates that every citizen has a right to education and, benefit from the EFA goals of the international community. The gross schooling rate gained 14 per cent points (62.1 per cent to 76.1 per cent between 2007–8 and 2010–11. On the contrary, the growth of the girl/ boy parity rate was slow from 0.75 per cent in 2007–8 to 0.79 in 2010–11 while the urban/ rural area disparity worsened between the same periods. The education access challenge thus, remains the gender and urban/rural area disparity. The situation is more challenging when we know that in many rural areas, up till today, '[p]arents are willing to go to great lengths to avoid sending a child [especially a girl child] to school [...]' (Wynd 2000: 105).

Regarding quality in primary basic education, we use three indicators to evaluate performance: the completion rate, the rate of success in the-end-of-cycle exam (CFEPD) and the retention rate.

Significant gains were registered regarding the completion rate as indicated in Table 21.8. It passed from 45.8 per cent in 2007-8 to 51.2 per cent in 2010-11. However, many pupils failed to complete the cycle of six years. A minimum of one out of every two children failed to complete the cycle he/she had started, with heavy disparities between urban and rural areas and boys and girls.

Table 21.6 Primary education completion rate by gender and area

	2007-8	2008-9	2009-10	2010-11	Gain (%)
Total Rate	45.8	48.2	49.3	51.2	54
Boys	56	58	57.1	59.7	37
Girls	35.8	38.6	41.5	41.6	6.8
Urban	54	62.5	64.9	74.5	15.1
Rural	40	43.5	44.2	45	4.9

Source: MEN/A/PLN 2011

Table 21.7 Evolution of the success rate in the CFEPD by gender and area

	2007-8	2008-9	2009-10	2010-11	Gain (%)
Total Rate	44	53.3	58.7	63.5	14.7
Boys	45.3	55.3	50.2	64.9	14.9
Girls	41.9	50.3	56.6	61.6	14.7
Urban	49.6	50.3	63	67.1	13.4
Rural	41.1	59.4	56.5	61.8	15.4

Source: MEN/A/PLN 2011

Table 21.8 Retention rate by gender in the academic year 2010-11

Indicators	Girls	Boys	Total
Retention rate CM2 (sixth and last grade in primary school)	66.7	71.3	69.2
Efficacy Coefficient in %	48.2	51.7	50.3
Graduates with certificate	402	448	429
Graduates with certificates who did not repeat the year	290	330	311

Source: MEN/A/PLN 2011

Likewise, although the rate of success in CFEPD (Table 21.7) improved from 53.3 per cent in 2009 to 63.5 per cent in 2011, one out of every three school-attending children failed his/her exam at the end of the cycle. This lack of efficacy in the education system is confirmed to a great extent by the low retention rates in Table 21.8. Only one hundred children in primary schools (69.2 per cent) succeeded in pursuing their education through the final year, including those who repeated the years. The efficacy coefficient of 50.3 per cent in 2010–11 implied that, to produce one successful graduate, two children needed to be registered in the first year of the cycle. Moreover, in 2010–11, out of 1000 pupils, 429 received their CFEPD of whom 311 without repeating the year even once until they reached the sixth grade. Once again the retention rate is lower for girls (66.7 per cent) than for boys (71.3 per cent). Lastly, the completion rate increased from 45.8 per cent in 2008 to 51.2 per cent in 2011.

Significant funding had been allocated to the education sector (from 59.3 billion CFA francs, more than 115 million US dollars in 2006 to 103.2 billion CFA, about 206 million US dollars in 2011). This huge investment contributed to substantial improvement of education indicators such as the gross enrolment rate (5.7 per cent in preschool and 76.1 per cent in Basic Education I in 2011). However, with great gender and regional disparities, a retention rate of 69.2 per cent and an efficacy coefficient of 50.3 per cent in 2011, Niger is unlikely to honour the 'Education for All by 2015' commitment.

Trends in the first secondary school cycle (Basic Education II)

In Niger, this sector is known as the first secondary school cycle or the Basic Education II sector. We, thus, use these terms interchangeably. Referring to the Ministry of Education statistics, we use the first year enrolment rate, the total numbers of students registered and the gross schooling rate to analyse the trends in this sector. Similarly to the primary education sector, this sector benefited from great efforts by the government especially in terms of access (76.1 per cent in 2010–11). This means that there should be a massive influx of secondary school students in the first year.

The analysis of this table shows that all pupils from primary school were accommodated in Basic Education II. The gross enrolment rate of 29.6 per cent (24.4 per cent for girls) meant that only one out of every three students was able to access this level of study after primary school. Many factors contribute to this situation up until today including early marriage for girls and the uneven distribution of the national school map. Thus, in spite of the government's various efforts to create secondary schools in rural areas, many students' schooling has

Table 21.9 Gross enrolment rate per region and nationally

	Number of 13-year olds			Newly registered pupils in first year (6ème)			Gross Enrolment to 6ème Rate		
	Boys	Girls	Total	Boys	Girls	Total	Boys	Girls	Total
AGADEZ	7,319	7,035	14,354	2,192	2,112	4,304	29.9%	30%	30%
DIFFA	6,810	6,571	13,381	1,401	1,182	2,583	20.6%	18%	19.3%
DOSSO	32,459	29,969	62,428	8,989	5,390	14,379	27.7%	18%	23.%
MARADI	35,287	32,394	67,681	17,286	9,159	26,445	49.0%	28.3%	39.1%
NIAMEY	18,320	19,563	37,883	8,826	8,874	17,700	48.2%	45.4%	46.7%
TAHOUA	35,325	29,656	64,981	12,690	5,662	18,352	35.9%	19.1%	28.2%
TILLABERY	42,139	41,357	83,496	7,672	6,088	13,760	18.2%	14.7%	16.5%
ZINDER	32,470	31,441	63,911	13,252	9,919	23,171	40.8%	31.5%	36.3%
NIGER	210,129	197,986	408,115	72,308	48,386	120,694	34.4%	24.4%	29.6%

Source: MEN/A/PLN 2011

Table 21.10 Gross schooling rate according to gender

	Number of 13–16 year olds			Number of first secondary school attendees			Gross schooling rate		
	Boys	Girls	Total	Boys	Girls	Total	Boys	Girls	Total
Total	769,518	735,892	**1,505,410**	180,018	118,198	**298,216**	23.4%	16.1%	**19.8%**

Source: MEN/A/PLN 2011

been hindered by the distances between their homes and the schools. Parents become reluctant to send their teenagers to secondary schools that remain far from their home towns due to fear of incidents resulting from possible insecurity.

As we can see from this table, only 298,216 teenagers aged between 13 and 16 attended secondary school out of a total of 1,505,410, representing 19.8 per cent with only 16.1 per cent for girls. This implies that only one teenager out of five has access to the first cycle of secondary school. This rate is only less than one out of five for girls.

Table 21.11 Retention rate in the first cycle of secondary school by gender

	Completion rate			Gross Admission Rate			Retention Rate		
	Boys	Girls	Total	Boys	Girls	Total	Boys	Girls	Total
Total	11.9%	8.4%	10.2%	34.4%	24.4%	29.6%	34.6%	34.2%	34.4%

Source: MEN/A/PLN 2011

From Table 21.11 we learn that only 10.2 per cent of children completed the first secondary school cycle. A comparison with the gross enrolment rate of 29.6 per cent allows us to see the degree of difficulty of the system to enable students to finish their secondary school studies (almost only one child out of every three finished his/her schooling). The retention rate being of 34.4 per cent, it also helps us understand that barely one child out of three was maintained in school, the rest being expelled or dropping out on the way. According to a report by the then Ministry of Higher and Secondary Education (MESS/R 2010), the highest drop-out rate among students in the first cycle of secondary school (43.3 per cent) took place in the first year while the highest repeater rate was found among fourth-year students (29.5 per cent). These negative trends were due to many reasons mainly:

- The lack of shelter for teenagers leaving their homes to attend school in other more hostile towns or cities;
- The scarcity of trained tenured teachers as opposed to a heavy influx of the teaching staff on the National Youth Service teaching duties and contractual teachers, both of whom lack adequate pedagogical training if any;
- Early marriage for girls. Students in this cycle being teenagers, parents do not hesitate to withdraw their female children and marry them out, which, as one may expect, results in skyrocketing disparities between boys and girls in school.

Trends in the second secondary school cycle

Generally speaking, the Niger education system presents a situation where the numbers of school attendees diminish tremendously as we climb up the cycles. This statement is fully illustrated when we look at the statistics of trends in the second cycle of secondary school compared to the first cycle and the primary school data. Let us look at Table 21.12.

Table 21.12 shows that the gross schooling rate in the second cycle of secondary school is 4.1 per cent with 5.6 per cent for boys and 2.6 per cent for

Table 21.12 Gross schooling rate in the second cycle of secondary school

	Number of 17–19 year olds			2nd Cycle Attendees			Gross Schooling Rate		
	Boys	Girls	Total	Boys	Girls	Total	Boys	Girls	Total
Total	457,084	455,532	912,616	25,735	11,827	37,562	5.6%	2.6%	4.1%

Source: MEN 2011

girls. This implies that for every two girls in school there are six boys. Negative trends are also shown through the regional disparities where the region with the highest attendees, Niamey, has a rate of 20.8 per cent, seconded by Agadez (10.6 per cent) while the region with the lowest rate is Tillabery with 1.3 per cent seconded by Tahoua with 2 per cent.

This is due to the scarcity of funds in the secondary school sector compared to the primary sector, where most efforts, especially for developing girls' education, are put. The girl/ boy disparities are also due to early marriage of girls and their heavy influx in professional or vocational schools which happen to be more accommodating in case they get married. In addition, statistics regarding secondary school revealed a high rate of failure in exams. Less than 50 per cent received their exam in the first cycle while a bare 30 per cent earned theirs in the second cycle in 2011. The lack of training for teachers who are mostly Youth Service employees and on contract, as well as the scarcity of teaching materials and laboratory equipment, also account for these disparities.

Trends in the professional and technical schools

The professional and technical secondary education sector is a three-year cycle which ends with various diplomas as follows:

- A technical baccalaureate at the end of a three-year study period;
- The *Brevet d'Aptitude Professionnelle* (BAP) [professional competence certificate] after two years of study; and
- The *Diplôme d'Aptitude Professionnelle* (DAP) [professional competence diploma] after three years of study.

Due to the new BA/BS – MA/MS – Ph.D. reform that was adopted for higher education in Niger, students have now the option of obtaining professional Bachelor's and Master's degrees. The professional schools are managed by the Ministry of Higher Education but also by the Ministry of Professional and Technical Training and that of health. The professional schools play a very important role in the socio-economic development of the country but they need to be better organized and provided with more adequate resources both by the government for public schools and founders of private institutions.

Trends in Higher Education

Higher education institutions in Niger include universities, institutes, other public higher education schools such as the Higher School of Mining and

Geology (EMIG), the School of Administration and Law (ENAM) and the Public Health School (ISP). They also encompass private higher education schools focusing on such fields as education, health, engineering, accounting, management and business. To access higher education, one needs to obtain the end-of-second-cycle-of-secondary-school diploma, the baccalaureate.

In the public sector of higher education

Until 2010, Niger only had one public university in Niamey, the capital city, one sub-regional Islamic University in Say (50 kms south of Niamey) and three Technological University Institutes (known as the *Instituts Universitaires de Technologie, IUT*, in French). Today, three more universities exist in three regions (Maradi, Tahoua and Zinder). In addition, many public institutions had either upgraded their offer capacities to include higher education (for example, ENAM) or been created (ISP, for example). In 2010, Niamey alone housed ten of these schools, according to MESS/R (2010).

In private higher education schools

The growing demand in higher education born of a significant increase in baccalaureate diploma owners (11.3 per cent in 2006 to 28.1 per cent in 2010) and such candidates as civil servants who return to university to upgrade their skills, resulted in a plethora of private higher education institutions including one University in Niamey (The Canadian University), another in Maradi and about 30 other higher education schools.

Access to higher education

In Niger, the higher education ratio compared to the general population is 135 students per every 100,000 inhabitants. As indicated in the following table, the female to male ratio in higher education is 29.3 in public institutions and 88.6 in private schools, the total being 40.7.

Table 21.13 Number of higher education students by gender and type of school

Types of Institution	Female	Male	N/A	Total	Female to male ration
Public Universities	2,660	9,694	7	12,361	27.4
Private Universities	12	8	173	193	N/A
Total	2,672	9,702	180	12,554	27.5
Public Higher Education Schools	440	875	1,006	2,321	N/A
Private Higher Education Schools	2,203	2,486	220	4,909	88.6
Total	2,643	3,361	1,226	7,230	78.6
Grand Total	5,315	13,063	1,406	19,784	40.7

Source: PAES/UEMOA 2010

In relation to male students, the number of female students is greater in public and private higher education schools (2,643 females to 3,361 males) than in universities (2,672 females to 9,702 males). This translates into a female/male ratio (proportion of females for every 100 male students) of 27.5 in universities and that of 78.6 in higher education schools. This ratio is of 40.7 for the total student population. Female students choose to attend public or private higher education schools, not the university, because their programme of study takes fewer years, accommodates a possible marital status (many get married as students) and is replete with various professional diploma options.

Future perspectives

Four recently made innovations in the Niger education system serve as a springboard for our reflection on future perspectives:

- The 1998 reform law (LOSEN) and the corresponding PDDE, which include a call for the use of the national languages as media of instruction in Basic Education I;
- The 2005 curricular innovations such as the math and French initiatives;
- The LMD reform in higher education; and
- The gender promotion initiatives.

LOSEN and the PDDE

For a long time the educational system has been criticized for its lack of adaptability to the local realities (Moumouni 1998; Chekaraou 2009). To reflect this criticism, the government initiated a reform law known as LOSEN, which supports the use of local languages in school as a solution to this problem of inadaptability. A few experimental schools were created to implement the policy stipulation. However, in spite of promising results due to educating children in their own language (Alidou 1997; Bergmann et al. 1999; Chekaraou 2009; Chekaraou and Goza 2013a, 2013b), these native language schools are still at their experimental level while LOSEN supports making primary school in the entire country bilingual where the child's native language is used as the medium of instruction while French is taught as a subject.

The system will be of tremendous benefit both in terms of acquisition of and access to knowledge (Chekaraou 2009) if all primary schools use the national languages as media of instruction as is being done in experimental schools. In addition, the implementation of the PDDE had already shown significant positive trends in the Niger education system especially regarding access (over 79.2 per cent in primary school, according to Daouda (2013)). If these trends continue, by the year 2015, the gross enrolment rate in the primary school will approximate 100 per cent. In addition, with the guarantee of equity and quality in education on which both international donors and the government have agreed to focus while still pursuing efforts of ensuring access (Daouda 2013), there is likelihood for higher rates of pupil retention in schools in the near future.

On another ground, drawing from a report by Diagne (1999) that a Niger pupil would spend up to 11.2 years before graduating from primary school where only six were required, and another by MEN (2008a, 2008b) that merely 6.4 per cent of the primary school students had the required competence in French language arts in 2005 (only 2 per cent in 2007) while only 5 per cent performed as required in mathematics in the same year compared to only 1.9 per cent in 2007, the Ministry of Education designed a few initiatives in order to improve the educational system, particularly, in the primary school.

The first of these initiatives was the language, arts and mathematics reform law, which aimed at contributing 'to the improvement of the internal efficacy of teaching in basic education through mastery of basic competence in language and mathematics' (MEN 2008a: 4; 2008b: 4). Based on three phases (see Chekaraou 2011) including a diagnostic/entrance test to determine a child's level in the two subjects, an intervention or remediation period and an evaluation/exit test phase, this initiative has been implemented in the school districts of Niamey, the capital city. Although results are not available to date, in terms of perspective, if fully implemented, it could significantly improve the quality of the education system, especially when it was accompanied with two other initiatives, i.e. the teacher education and training reforms.

Based on the realization that the quality of students' learning could not be improved separately from that of teacher training, an institutional and curricular reform was introduced in teacher training schools in 2007 (MEN 2008c; n.d.). This initiative involves five points mainly; a) doubling the pre-service training period from one to two years; b) adopting the competence-based methodology to give teachers 'power to act, to succeed and progress that allows for the efficient realization of the tasks and activities at one's work place and that is based on an organized set of acquisitions (knowledge skills in various domains, perceptions, attitudes, etc.' (MEN 2008c: 5); c) the need for intelligible teacher practice; d) the mastery of all subjects taught for an interdisciplinary approach to teaching; and e) development of skills of evaluation techniques on the part of the pre-service teacher (see Chekaraou 2011 for more details). It could also echo the language, arts and mathematics initiative to improve quality if effectively implemented.

Alongside the above mentioned initiatives came the commitment to continuously train unskilled contractual teachers which has been guaranteed since 2007 by such donors as the UNICEF in Tahoua, Maradi, Agadez, Zinder and Diffa regions and by Cooperation Suisse in the remainder of the regions (Tillabery, Niamey and Dosso) as of 2010. The pre-service and in-service teacher training supported in these initiatives was to happen in such a way that teachers should be made to link their classroom activities with the local socio-cultural realities of the country (Chekaraou 2011) to respond to the constant criticism that the education system did not reflect the cultural context of the students (Inné 1988; Moumouni 1998).

Furthermore, the Niger educational system having revealed acute rural/urban and gender disparities as shown in our earlier discussion on trends, a few gender-promotion-in-school actions were undertaken by the government as a way of taking care of equity, the other components highlighted in the PDDE. According to Hissiaka (2013), initiatives such as the increase of the national education budget to 25 per cent of the GDP coupled with the obligation for all children to attend school until the age of 16, the promotion of schooling for girls and young women to be reinforced by the newly created Office of Promotion of Girls' Schooling (*Direction de la Scolarisation des Filles* in French), the creation of second-chance schools to especially promote older girls' and school dropouts' schooling and the signing into law of a national gender promotion policy (Ministère en Charge de L'Education et la Formation, i.e. MEN/A/PLN 2011) will likely help efface the gender differential in education.

Moreover, to promote girls' schooling, the national gender policy is to be implemented through six phases including: promoting a gender-supporting school environment, providing enough gender-competent men and women including role models for developing girls' education and training, developing a federating mechanism of actions towards and actors in support of girls' schooling, enhancing a sufficient resource mobilization plan which adapts to the promotion of girls' schooling, adopting affirmative action measures that support girls' access to and retention in schools and reducing socio-cultural obstacles to girls' education and training.

This policy further recommends the creation of a High Commission for Girls' Education and Training (*Haut Commissariat à l'Education et à la Formation des*

Filles (HCPEF) which will function as a ministry in itself since affiliated offices related to the office were to open in every one of the eight regions of the country.

A combination of these initiatives and the PDDE provisions implementation on the one hand, and the inclusion of national languages in educating children (Articles 10 and 19 of LOSEN) as proven to yield positive trends in learning, especially for girls (Chekaraou and Goza 2013b) on the other hand, are likely to foster significant change in the rural/urban and gender differential that exists in Niger formal education.

Conclusion

In this paper we first presented a brief overview of the Niger education system structure and its general trends since independence, especially in the last decade 2002–13. Next, we highlighted a few perspectives for future change of trends. These perspectives, we argue, are fundamentally based on initiatives and policies (the French and mathematics initiatives, the curricular reform innovations in teacher training schools and the gender promotion policy) which are mostly related to improving the three components of the Ten-year Education Plan (PDDE), itself an offshoot of the new 1998 national education policy (LOSEN) mainly quality, access and equity.

It is our contention that should all the initiatives and policies that we discussed be effectively implemented, education in Niger will greatly improve by the year 2020. This means that Niger would have failed the Education for All by 2015 agenda but with the scarcity of resources that the country endures, being only five years off the 2015 goals is much better than not reaching them at all.

References

Alidou, H. (1997). 'Education language policy and bilingual education: The impact of French language policy in primary education in Niger'. (Ph.D. dissertation. The University of Illinois at Urbana-Champaign 1997). UMI, 9737030.

Bergmann, H., Buttner, T., Hovens, M., Kamayé, H. O., Mallam, G. M. and Saley, J. (1999). *Evaluation de l'école expérimentale: Esquisse d'un bilan de 25 ans d'expérimentation de l'enseignement bilingue au Niger (Rapport final, Juin 1999).* Niamey: Ministère de l'Education Nationale (Coopération Technique Allemande – GTZ – and Projet Education de Base: Promotion de l'enseignement Bilingue).

Chekaraou, I. (2009). *Teachers' Appropriation of an Educational Reform Policy in Africa: A Socio-cultural Study of Two Bilingual Hausa-French Schools in Niger*. Saarbrücken, Germany: Lambert Academic Publishing.

—(2011). 'Improving quality in basic education in Niger: Initiatives, implementation and challenges'. *CICE Series 4*: 73–85.

Chekaraou, I. and Goza, N. A. (2013a). 'Gender and education in Niger: Access, retention of women in higher education institutions'. *CICE Series 5*: 65–77.

—(2013b). 'Teachers implementing an educational policy and implications for pupils' (especially girls') access, performance and retention'. *Journal of International Cooperation in Education (CICE)* 15 (3): 169–85.

Daouda, H. (2013). 'Souci de redorer le blason de notre système éducatif'. *Le Sahel Quotidien*, 8535, (May 29): 5.

Diagne, A. W. (1999). *Amélioration de l'accès, de la qualité et de la gestion de l'éducation de base au Niger par le développement des écoles de base: Version définitive*. Ministère de l'Education Nationale: Niamey.

Hissiaka, H. (2013). 'Genre, education et interventions sociales: Quelques expériences au Niger'. *Cuadernos de Género 3:* Género, educación e intervención social: Experiencias compartidas entre Espana y Niger, 7–15.

Inné, M. (1988). 'La politique d'éducation au Niger'. In Anon. (eds), *Pédagogie Pratique pour l'Afrique*, pp. 199–232. Paris: Imprimerie Aubenas d'Ardèche.

Kelly, G. P. (1992). 'Colonialism, indigenous society, and school practices: French West Africa and Indochina 1918–1938'. In P. Altbach and G. P. Kelly (eds), *Education and the Colonial Experience*, 2nd edn. Brunswick, pp. 9–32.

M/F/INS (2011). *Annuaire Statistique 2009–2010*. Niamey: M/F/INS.

MEBA (1998). *Loi No. 98–12 du 1er Juin 1998 portant orientation du système éducatif Nigérien (version intégrale)* [Law No. 98 of 1 June 1998 on reforming the Niger education system (complete version). Niamey: Editions Alpha.

—(2003). *Programme décennal pour le développement de l'éducation (PDDE)*. Niamey, Niger: Ministère de l'Education de Base et de l'Alphabétisation (MEBA).

MEN (2008a). *Initiative: Relever le défi de la qualité: Maitrise de la langue – Guide unique du maitre*. Nouvelle Imprimerie du Niger: Niamey, Niger.

—(2008b). *Initiative: Relever le défi de la qualité: Mathématiques – Guide d'accompagnement des tests*. Nouvelle Imprimerie du Niger: Niamey, Niger.

—(2008c). *Programme d'études des Ecoles Normales d'Instituteurs (Version Provisoire)*. Ministère de l'Education Nationale: Niamey, Niger.

—(n.d.). 'Contexte d'élaboration des nouveaux programmes des ENI'. Ministère de l'Education Nationale (Rapport).

MEN/A/PLN (2010–11). *Statistiques de l'Education de Base, Annuaire 2010–2011*. Niamey: MEN/A/PLN.

MESS/R (2010). *Annuaires statistiques de l'enseignement supérieur*. Niamey. MESS/R.

Ministère en Charge de L'Education et la Formation (MEN/A/PLN) (2011). *Politique*

Nationale de l'Education et de la Formation des filles au Niger 2012-2020. Niamey: Ministère en Charge de L'Education et la Formation.

Moumouni, A. (1998). *L'éducation en Afrique Noire*. Paris: Présence Africaine.

PAES/UEMOA (2010). *Enquête auprès des établissements d'enseignement supérieur 2010*. Niamey: PAES/ UEMOA.

Wynd, S. (1999). 'Education, Schooling and Fertility in Niger'. In C. Heward and S. Bunwaree (eds), *Gender, Education & Development: Beyond Access to Empowerment*. London and New York: Zed Books, pp. 101-16.

Nigeria: An Overview

Naomi A. Moland

Introduction

The diversity of educational experiences in Nigeria mirrors the diversity of the 177 million people living in this giant of a country. In addition to being diverse, Nigeria is deeply divided along ethnic and religious boundaries – boundaries that become the fault lines for ongoing conflicts. Gross inequalities between regions serve to further demarcate these divisions, making national unity seem unlikely. Educational inequalities between regions are rooted in colonial practices, but have been perpetuated by decades of poor governance by the Nigerian state. Failures in the Nigerian education system have implications for issues of access and quality, as well as literacy, girls' education, higher education, and conflict resolution. If Nigeria is to meet its enormous potential, it must prioritize the improvement of its education system – a strategy which could help to increase faith in the state, as well as help develop Nigeria's human capital. As the giant in West Africa, and as an 'old' oil country, Nigeria has the opportunity to set an example for countries such as Ghana, Cote D'Ivoire, and Sierra Leone that have recently discovered oil. To date, regrettably, Nigeria has provided a harrowing example of how oil wealth can contribute to corruption, weak governance, inequality, and conflict (Falola and Heaton 2008). By prioritizing the provision of quality education for its citizenry, the Nigerian state could model how resource wealth can help to support education, promote equality, and reduce conflict.

This chapter is based on a growing secondary literature about Nigerian history and politics, as well as my own research in Nigeria investigating education, ethnic relations, and nation-building. I spent nine months between 2011–12 in Nigeria, interviewing over 60 educators and Ministry of Education officials, and observing in over 25 schools in six cities throughout Nigeria:

Kano; Ibadan; Lagos; Abuja; Abakaliki; and Calabar. While this chapter draws primarily on secondary sources, my analysis is informed by my fieldwork in Nigerian schools. My goal is to analyse how inequality permeates through the layers of the Nigerian education system, and how reforms to education may help to alleviate divisions and build a more peaceful nation.

Historical and political context

Several historical and demographic factors have led to deep inequalities between groups in Nigeria. As in many colonies, Nigeria's boundaries were drawn for colonists' purposes with little regard for previous regional groups, and colonial policies exacerbated ethnic rivalries (Bach 2006; Falola and Heaton 2008: 209). The British ruled northern Nigeria more indirectly than southern Nigeria, and prohibited Christian missionaries – and their schools – in order to maintain peace in the Islamic Sokoto Caliphate in the north. As a result, at independence in 1960, the south was significantly more 'developed' and had much higher levels of education than the north (Mustapha 2004: 274).

In the immediate post-colonial period, Nigerian leaders allocated significant resources to education, believing that schools were key to forging national unity (Falola and Heaton 2008). However, the optimism of that period soon faded with the onset of the Biafran War (1967–70) and subsequent decades of economic volatility.

Many educational inequalities persist today – for example, 2010 literacy rates are 79 per cent in the South-West region and 17 per cent in the North-East region.[1] When divisions between religious and ethnic groups correspond to massive gaps in economic and educational levels, differences are manipulated by leaders (Campbell 2013). The continual fear of domination by one ethnic, religious, or regional group over another has fuelled innumerable conflicts.

Since the restoration of democracy in Nigeria in 1999, ethnic and religious divisions have deepened (Falola and Heaton 2008). The economy has worsened since the implementation of a World Bank-recommended Structural Adjustment Plan in 1985, and socio-economic gaps have widened (Geo-Jaja and Mangum 2003; Mustapha 2004). Moreover, the failure of the state to improve ordinary citizens' lives has undermined faith in the government by most Nigerian citizens. The Nigerian government has little incentive to be accountable to its population, since its power and 80 per cent of its revenues come from foreign oil companies (Paden 2008: 12). This context of high revenues and low accountability has led to rampant corruption. While Nigeria is the seventh largest oil producer, 70 per cent of Nigerians live on less than 1 USD per day; Nigeria has one of the most unequal income distributions in the world (Campbell 2013: 12; Paden 2008: 13)

Herbst and Mills (2006) classify Nigeria as a 'dysfunctional state' because it fails to provide welfare and opportunity to its citizens, and has experienced continuous unrest and decline (2006: 1). Scholars debate how serious Nigeria's problems are; while some deny that Nigeria is a 'failed' state (Hagher 2011), others contend that it should at least be classified as 'fragile' (Francois and Sud 2006). Francois and Sud (2006) describe a continuum of state failure that ranges from weak, to fragile, failing, failed and collapsed (2006: 143). Many sub-Saharan African countries (including the Democratic Republic of Congo, Angola, Sudan, Somalia, and Ethiopia, among others) also fall along this continuum, and also struggle with educational provision. While Nigeria's GDP per capita (and its percentage of government expenditures dedicated to education) are higher than some fragile states',[2] its literacy rate and Human Development Index are average or low compared to other fragile states (Herbst and Mills 2006; Omolewa 2008). The fact that one of the wealthiest countries in Africa still scores poorly in literacy and human development leads to questions about economic priorities and distribution.

Scholars emphasize that educational provision is often the most visible social service that governments provide, and therefore crucial for establishing governmental legitimacy (Barakat et al. 2008; Rose and Greeley 2006). Conversely, lack of quality education, or unequal educational services, can undermine citizens' faith in the government. When the government does not meet people's demands for education, or for security or a sense of belonging, some turn to ethnicity or religion as 'an alternative to citizenship' (Falola and Heaton 2008: 205). In a mean vicious cycle, strengthened ethnic and religious identities coupled with a dysfunctional state leads to ethno-religious conflict, which further undermines national unity. At least 13,500 people have been killed in religious and ethnic conflicts in Nigeria since 1999 (Campbell 2013: xvii). Religious conflicts in Jos have killed hundreds since 2000, and attacks by the extremist Islamic group Boko Haram, whose name means 'Western Education is Sinful', have left over 5,600 people dead.[3] These increases in violence have led to renewed calls for secession by some groups (Ross 2012).

Demographic factors also contribute to the divided nature of the Nigerian nation. Nigeria does not have one majority ethnic group – the three largest constitute 29 per cent (Hausa-Fulani), 21 per cent (Yoruba), and 18 per cent

(Igbo) of the population.[4] The rest of the population is divided into over 250 ethnic groups. None of Nigeria's ethnic groups are securely dominant by numbers or by other means; the fear that another group has 'hegemonic tendencies' has caused conflicts throughout Nigerian history (Bach 2006; Mustapha 2004).

The absence of a dominant majority in Nigeria also plays out along the religious axis of difference. Nigeria is the largest country in the world that has a near equal divide between its Christian and Muslim populations (Paden 2008: 3). When the country returned to democratic rule in 1999, 12 northern states adopted Sharia Law, leading to fear amongst Christians that Muslims were attempting to turn Nigeria into an Islamic state (Campbell 2013). Muslims have similar fears about potential Christian domination (Falola and Heaton 2008).

While there is no dominant ethnic or religious majority in Nigeria as a whole, there are definite majorities in certain regions. Herbst and Mills (2006) explain that such geographic segregation poses particular problems for nations because spatially distinct groups can be mobilized around ethnic loyalties that compete with the state (2006: 10). Ethnic, religious, regional, and political boundaries coincide in Nigeria, making divisions deep and durable.

To say the least, the 'national question' – the debate about what Nigeria is, and who Nigerians are – has plagued the country since independence (Falola and Heaton 2008: 158). One of my interviewees captured this thought well when he painted this picture:

> As of now, every Nigerian person is a person, is an individual. It is not a community. When a man builds a house, and builds a fence so high, and puts barbed wire on the fence, and employs a mean-looking security person, and has lots of kids, and you call it Nigeria? Of course he's a state on his own. He's got his own army. He's got his own reservoir so he provides his own electricity, that's a generator. He provides his own water; he could as well provide his own education for his children. And then he becomes the Federal Republic of [his last name], that's my own country. And then I'm all good ... There is no part of us that says that we're one.[5]

This comment captures how Nigeria's problems of a dysfunctional state, weak national identity and vast inequalities are deeply intertwined. This interviewee explains that when individuals do not receive any services from their government, they feel no connection to the Nigerian nation. Such a scenario also illustrates how a weak state exacerbates educational inequalities; education becomes a privilege for those who can afford to pay for private schools, rather than a civil right that is distributed to all citizens equally. If the Nigerian state were to prioritize providing quality education for all of its citizens, this could help to balance regional inequalities, which is a necessary prerequisite for decreasing conflict.

Current challenges

Most current challenges in the Nigerian education system are related to the inequalities and government fragility described above. These have resulted in an unequal system that fails to provide basic education to many Nigerian citizens.

Finance

The volatility of the oil market and the failed Structural Adjustment Programmes of the 1980s have caused great fluctuations in Nigerian government spending on education. While government resources have been limited, the resources that are available have been mismanaged. Jenkins (2006) estimates that since independence, Nigerian regimes have misappropriated more than 200 billion USD, 'potentially enough to have raised the country's standard of living to European levels' (2006: 142). Despite Nigeria's wealth, it has consistently given fewer resources to education than many other African nations; for example, in 2000, Nigeria dedicated 9.0 per cent of total government expenditures to education, while Ghana spent 22.3 per cent, Cameroon spent 14.6 per cent, and Ethiopia spent 13.8 per cent (Geo-Jaja 2006). In recent years, the Nigerian state has progressively decentralized education funding, leading to greater educational inequalities as poorer local governments cannot afford the costs of education and are increasingly charging school fees (Geo-Jaja 2006; Sunal et al. 2003). Increased enrolments coupled with limited funding have led to a dysfunctional system where school buildings are collapsing, teachers are poorly trained, textbooks are outdated, and classes are enormous (Paden 2008; Sunal et al. 2003).

Access and enrolment

The Nigerian government has advocated for universal primary education since 1976 and has signed on to numerous international agreements such as Education for All (in Dakar, Senegal 2000). The most recent National Policy on Education (2004) establishes that education should be compulsory and free for six years of primary and three years of secondary (National Policy on Education 2004). Despite these efforts, statistics show that significant progress is necessary to meet the goal of universal primary enrolment by 2015. The fact that Nigeria has 8 million children out of school – the highest number in sub-Saharan Africa – reflects Nigeria's massive population and relatively low enrolment rates (Kazeem et al. 2010: 295). Nigeria's 2012 Net Enrolment Ratio (NER) is 0.58.[6] Enrolment varies widely by region, with 49 per cent of children in the northern regions and 80 per cent of children in the southern regions attending school (see Table 22.1).[7] Urban-rural gaps also exist; enrolment rates are 75 per cent and 55 per cent, respectively.[8] At the secondary school level, the NER decreases to 44 per cent and the gap widens, with 27 per cent of children in the northern regions and 61 per cent of children in the southern regions attending secondary school.[9]

Most barriers to school enrolment are economic. As the federal government reduces and decentralizes education funding, and as the school-aged population booms, local governments are increasingly charging school fees – causing a decline in the NER (Geo-Jaja 2006: 145). In tough economic times, school fees result in double losses for parents who lose the child's labour contributions and need to pay fees (Kazeem et al. 2010; Sunal et al. 2003). When families see many unemployed school graduates, they may doubt whether the investment will bear returns. Kazeem et al. (2010) explain that parents do not send their children to school for economic, cultural and religious reasons; they recommend media campaigns to encourage parents to send their children to school (2010: 315). Other scholars believe that barriers to educational access are more economic than cultural, making the benefits of such campaigns seem dubious (Geo-Jaja 2006). If the Nigerian state is truly dedicated to education for all, enforcing and supporting the elimination of school fees is a crucial first step.

Table 22.1 Educational inequalities between North and South Nigeria (Source: National Population Commission and RTI 2011)[10]

	Southern Regions	Northern Regions	Nationwide
Net Enrolment Ratio- Primary	80%	49%	58%
Net Enrolment Ratio- Secondary	61%	27%	44%
Literacy among children aged 5–16	72%	29%	47%

Quality

As in many African countries, rapidly increasing enrolments in the decades following independence, coupled with unchanging or decreasing budgets, led to ballooning class sizes, teacher shortages, and a subsequent decrease in educational quality. Nigerians I spoke with in 2012 referred to the 'glory days' of education in the 1960s and 1970s when books were new, laboratories were stocked, and students competed for the highest test scores in West Africa. This was a time when a much smaller percentage of the population was attending school, and when the 1970s oil boom allowed the government to expand spending on public services. While quality is more difficult to measure than the quantity of children enroled, researchers rely on data such as student-teacher ratios, teachers' certification levels, and literacy rates. 2002 data lists the national average student-teacher ratio as 45:1 (Geo-Jaja 2006: 142); many classes that I observed had more than 70 students. Teacher quality is of concern; Sunal et al. (2003) explain that many teachers have not passed the prerequisite certifying exams. When they are poorly remunerated, teachers often take on additional jobs to make a living, leading to teacher absenteeism (Ndiyo 2007), which has obvious negative implications for achievement.

Literacy

As achievement data is difficult to obtain in Nigeria, scholars often draw on literacy figures to gauge educational efficacy. While the overall literacy rate for children aged 5-16 is 47 per cent, this rate again varies significantly by region, with approximately 29 per cent of children in northern regions and 72 per cent of children in southern regions who are literate. Not surprisingly, significant urban-rural gaps exist; 70 per cent of urban children and 36 per cent of rural children are literate.[11] In regards to adult literacy, Nigeria's 67 per cent lags behind several African countries, such as Tanzania (70 per cent), Botswana (79 per cent), and Lesotho (81 per cent) – a fact that some find surprising in light of Nigeria's significant resources (Omolewa 2008: 699).

In order to support literacy, the government has encouraged instruction in Nigerian languages. Researchers consistently claim that children are more likely to achieve academically in any language when they start education in their mother tongue (Brock-Utne 2007), but significant barriers prevent this from happening in the Nigerian case. While the most recent National Policy on Education (2004) states that the 'language of the environment' should be taught in the first three years of primary school (p. 16), studies show that practice varies substantially. In rural areas, local languages are often used throughout primary and secondary school, while in most urban areas, English is the only medium of instruction (Akinnaso 1993). With over 400 languages, Nigeria is the most linguistically diverse country in Africa. Significant resources would be necessary to develop the teacher competencies and curricular resources to increase instruction in local languages (ibid.). Providing quality education in all 400 Nigerian languages is not feasible, but unless more resources are dedicated to teaching in mother tongues, language will continue to be a significant barrier to academic achievement for many Nigerian children.

Gender issues

In many developing countries, significant educational reforms within the last decades have focused on girls' education. In Nigeria, girls' enrolment rates have improved, although they still lag behind their male counterparts at 58 per cent versus 64 per cent.[12] Girls' literacy rates in 2010 were 45 per cent nationwide, while boys' literacy reached 48 per cent.[13] Gender parity varies by region; southeastern Nigeria presents an unusual case where enrolment is equal and literacy levels are higher among girls – possibly due to Igbo parents withdrawing their sons early from school to learn a trade.[14] In northern Nigeria, girls' enrolment is lower, a phenomenon that some link to Muslim religious beliefs, to beliefs that formal schools are fundamentally Christian institutions, and to parental concerns about girls' safety (Kazeem et al. 2010: 302). Other studies argue that most parents want to send their daughters to school, but when they are forced to make difficult economic choices, they assume that educating their sons is more likely to result in financial benefits (Geo-Jaja 2006; Sunal et al. 2003).

Higher education

Since independence, tertiary institutions have been seen as critical for developing Nigeria's human capital and forging national unity (Anyanwu 2011). The government invested substantially in higher education, and Nigerian universities were considered beacons of learning, attracting students from across West Africa and beyond (Eribo 1996). This early prioritization of higher education, coupled with Nigeria's size, has produced what Mazrui (2006) calls the 'largest Black intelligentsia anywhere in the world' (2006: x). Since independence, however, scholars recognized how the university system was perpetuating patterns of uneven development between southern and northern regions of the country (Ajayi 1975). During the first decade of the first federal university in Ibadan, 865 southern and 74 northern students were educated (Anyanwu 2011: 7). While this gap has decreased in subsequent decades, inequalities persist. Quota systems and scholarships, designed to draw more northern students into federal universities, have been largely ineffective (Anyanwu 2011).

In the decades following independence, higher education became a 'shadow of the past lively and productive academic community' as repeated military regimes, characterized by anti-intellectualism, led to the emigration of numerous Nigerian professors (Eribo 1996: 65). Brain drain has affected all sectors; Falola and Heaton (2008) estimate that by 2000, a staggering 50 per cent of Nigerians with university degrees lived outside of the country (2008: 223). Today, higher education faces many of the same financial challenges that primary and secondary education face: large class sizes; deteriorating facilities; and rising tuition costs (Anyanwu 2011). These problems are exacerbated by intense political dynamics which lead to frequent strikes and shutdowns that inhibit scholarship and student progress (Ndiyo 2007). The demand for higher education is much higher than the available supply; less than 15 per cent of annual applicants are accepted for enrolment (Anyanwu 2011: 222). This has led to a proliferation of private universities, some of which have questionable credentials. More private universities are opening in the south, which may further the north-south tertiary education gap (Anyanwu 2011).

Privatization

While some have heralded the propagation of private schools and universities as a potential corrective to the deterioration of public education, others predict that the privatization of education in Nigeria will lead to further inequalities. Geo-Jaja (2006) explains how the privatization of education can allow the government to avoid their responsibility to provide social goods (2006: 127). The proliferation of (sometimes for-profit) private schools in Nigeria – with fees ranging from 24 USD/ year for tuition that rivals elite American private schools[15] – means that only the very poor attend public schools. Some private schools that I visited in Nigeria had better-trained staff, more materials, and more sophisticated technological resources than many American schools, while nearby public schools had roofs that were caving in. When a government fails to provide quality public education (as is the case in some Western countries, to a lesser degree), those who can will take their children to private schools, and education becomes more of a tool for reproducing social class than for equalizing citizens.

Attacks on education

A more explicitly dangerous threat to education is developing in north-eastern Nigeria in the form of attacks on schools by the extremist Islamic organization Boko Haram. Since 2012, at least 70 teachers and 100 students have been killed, 50 schools have been damaged and 60 other schools have been forced to close (Amnesty International 2013: 4). In April 2014, Boko Haram gained international infamy after kidnapping over 250 schoolgirls. These attacks have devastating implications for students in north-eastern Nigeria and other regions. In addition to the tragic loss of life and halted education in schools that have been attacked, this violence leads other families to fear sending children to school and the government to close more schools. In a vicious cycle, inadequate education becomes both a cause and a consequence of violence. Militant groups such as Boko Haram destroy educational institutions, leading to more uneducated youth. These disaffected youth, in turn, become Boko Haram's target recruits, and often are the perpetrators of violence (Campbell 2013). Unfortunately, the Nigerian government's 2013 crackdown on Boko Haram has been critiqued as violating human rights, as the Nigerian military allegedly indiscriminately killed Muslims in north-eastern Nigeria – further alienating many northerners.[16]

If the Nigerian government is to reduce the likelihood of continued insurrections, it must increase educational levels in northern Nigeria in order to gain the trust of northern citizens and reduce the number of uneducated youth who can be recruited to violence. Currently, Christian children are five times as likely to go to school in Nigeria as Muslim children (Kazeem et al. 2010: 312). Politicians recognize this disparity; one promising programme begun by the Jonathan administration in 2013 seeks to improve educational provision to 'almajiris', children sent to study with Islamic teachers who often end up begging and homeless.[17]

Conflict resolution through education

In Nigeria, inequalities between groups – which the education system has exacerbated – have contributed to ongoing conflicts. The government has taken some measures to equalize access to education, which could help to build national unity. For example, the government created Federal Unity

Colleges (secondary schools which integrate students from all over Nigeria) and a quota system in federal universities to increase student enrolment from northern states (Anyanwu 2011). While the controversial quota system has been ineffective and needs revising, the government should not abandon efforts to equalize enrolment and achievement at all levels of education.

In addition to structural reforms to equalize access, the Nigerian government has used the curriculum to help promote intergroup tolerance among schoolchildren. Textbooks contain chapters about Nigeria's diverse groups and the benefits of national unity (see, for example, Gambo et al. 2007). Additionally, a new television program called *Sesame Square* (funded by USAID and aired on the Nigerian government station) aims to teach ethno-religious tolerance to Nigeria's youngest citizens (Moland 2015). While scholars caution that a multicultural curriculum can reinforce stereotypes (King 2005; Moland 2015), such efforts – when approached cautiously – may help to educate children about their co-citizens.

Conclusion

The Nigerian government faces many challenges – from violent attacks in the north-east to continuing ethnic conflict in Jos – not to mention a disaffected population that is increasingly impoverished. Because of Nigeria's size and influence in West Africa, this increasing insecurity has the potential to destabilize other states in the region (Campbell 2013). Other West African countries, particularly those that have recently discovered oil, can learn from Nigeria's past mistakes. For example, heightened accountability is vital to ensure that oil revenues are used to enhance the living and education standards for the whole population. Nigeria has invested enormously in the oil sector at the expense of other sectors; the volatility of the oil market means that the country's entire budget – including its education budget – has been on a boom and bust cycle that social services cannot afford to be tied to. Maintaining a stable financial commitment to education is paramount.

While improving education is not a panacea for all of these dangers, it is one thing the government could do that may help to alleviate the social inequalities and grievances that are leading to conflict. Improved education could help millions of disaffected youth to acquire the knowledge and skills they need to contribute to the Nigerian economy. Perhaps more importantly, improved provision of education will increase Nigerians' faith in their state and their identity as Nigerians, which may help to alleviate intergroup conflicts. Persistent and widening economic and educational gaps will only exacerbate intergroup tensions. Providing quality education to all citizens is one way that Nigeria can move away from being a 'dysfunctional state' that is 'ostensibly democratic' (Campbell 2013; Herbst and Mills 2006). Scholars often use these terms to describe Nigeria, but many also use the term 'potential' to describe Nigeria's enormous promise to be a leader in the region and the continent. Particularly in a country where 43 per cent of the population is under 15 years old,[18] improving educational provision is key to building this latent potential.

Notes

1. National Population Commission and RTI International 2011, p. 47.
2. In 2000, Nigeria spent less of total government expenditures on education than Ghana, Ethiopia, Cameroon, and Botswana (Geo-Jaja 2006). However, Nigeria's education expenditures are somewhat higher than some other 'fragile states' (as classified by Francois and Sud 2006). See CIA World Factbook, https://www.cia.gov/library/publications/the-world-factbook/
3. The Associated Press. 'Explosion Rocks Mall in Nigerian Capital'. *The New York Times*. 25 June 2014.
4. CIA World Factbook. Available from https://www.cia.gov/library/publications/the-world-factbook/geos/ni.html (accessed 12 August 2014).
5. Personal Communication, 23 April 2012.
6. The NER represents the percentage of primary-age-children in the population enroled in school. Education For All Development Index, http://www.unesco.org/new/en/education/themes/leading-the-international-agenda/efareport/statistics/efa-development-index/ (accessed 12 August 2014).
7. National Population Commission and RTI 2011, p. 55.
8. Ibid., p. 55.
9. Ibid., p. 59.
10. Ibid., pp. 44–55.
11. Ibid., p. 47.
12. Ibid., p. 55.
13. Ibid., pp. 45–6.
14. Ibid., pp. 45–6.
15. Personal communication with Nigerian educators, February–April 2012.
16. See Gordon, Michael R. 'Kerry, in Africa, Presses Nigeria on Human Rights'. *The New York Times*, 25 May 2013.

17   Shehu, Garba (2013). 'Nigeria's Glittering Almajiri Education Plan'. *Premium Times*, 8 August 2013. Available from http://allafrica.com/stories/201308080779.html (accessed 12 August 2014).
18   CIA World Factbook. Available from https://www.cia.gov/library/publications/the-world-factbook/geos/ni.html (accessed 12 August 2014).

References

Ajayi, J. F. A. (1975). 'Higher education in Nigeria'. *African Affairs*, 74: 420–6.

Akinnaso, F. N. (1993). 'Policy and experiment in mother tongue literacy in Nigeria'. *International Review of Education*, 39: 255–85.

Amnesty International (2013). *'Keep Away from Schools or We'll Kill You': Right to Education Under Attack in Nigeria*. London: Amnesty International Ltd.

Anyanwu, O. E. (2011). *The Politics of Access: University Education and Nation-Building in Nigeria, 1948–2000*. Calgary: University of Calgary Press.

Bach, D. C. (2006). 'Inching Towards a Country without a State: Prebendalism, Violence, and State Betrayal in Nigeria'. In Clapham, C., Herbst, J. and Mills, G. (eds) *Big African States*. Johannesburg: Wits University Press.

Barakat, B., Karpinska, Z. and Paulson, J. (2008). *Desk Study: Education and Fragility*. New York: Inter-Agency Network for Education in Emergencies (INEE) Working Group on Education and Fragility.

Brock-Utne, B. (2007). 'Language of instruction and student performance: New insights from research in Tanzania and South Africa'. *International Review of Education*, 53: 509–30.

Campbell, J. (2013). *Nigeria: Dancing on the Brink*. New York: Rowman and Littlefield Publishers, Inc.

Eribo, F. (1996). 'Higher education in Nigeria: decades of development and decline'. *Issue: A Journal of Opinion*, 24: 64–7.

Falola, T. and Heaton, M. M. (2008). *A History of Nigeria*. Cambridge: Cambridge University Press.

Francois, M. and Sud, I. (2006). 'Promoting stability and development in fragile and failed states'. *Development Policy Review*, 24: 141–60.

Gambo, A., Danladi, E. N. and Halilu, L. (2007). *Amana Social Studies for Junior Secondary Schools (Universal Basic Education Edition)*. Zaria, Nigeria: Amana Publishers Ltd.

Geo-Jaja, M. A. (2006). 'Educational decentralization, public spending, and social justice in Nigeria'. *International Review of Education*, 52: 125–48.

Geo-Jaja, M. A. and Mangum, G. (2003). 'Economic adjustment, education and human resource development in Africa: The case of Nigeria'. *International Review of Education*, 49: 293–318.

Hagher, I. (2011). *Nigeria: After the Nightmare*. Lanham, MD: University Press of America, Inc.

Herbst, J. and Mills, G. (2006). 'Africa's Big Dysfunctional States: An Introductory Overview'. In Clapham, C., Herbst, J. and Mills, G. (eds) *Big African States*. Johannesburg: Wits University Press.

Jenkins, P. (2006). *The New Faces of Christianity: Believing the Bible in the Global South*. Oxford and New York: Oxford University Press.

Kazeem, A., Jensen, L. and Stokes, C. S. (2010). 'School attendance in Nigeria: Understanding the impact and intersection of gender, urban-rural residence, and socioeconomic status'. *Comparative Education Review*, 54: 295–319.

King, E. (2005). 'Educating for conflict or peace: Challenges and dilemmas in post-conflict Rwanda'. *International Journal*, 60: 904–18.

Mazrui, A. A. (2006). *A Tale of Two Africas: Nigeria and South Africa as Contrasting Visions*. London: Adonis and Abbey Publishers Ltd.

Moland, N. (2015). 'Can multiculturalism be exported? Dilemmas of diversity on Nigeria's Sesame Square'. *Comparative Education Review*, 59: 1–23.

Mustapha, R. A. (2004). 'Ethnicity and the politics of democratization in Nigeria'. In Berman, B., Eyoh, D. and Kymlicka, W. (eds) *Ethnicity and Democracy in Africa*. Oxford: James Currey.

National Policy on Education (2004). *National Policy on Education- 4th Edition*. Lagos, Nigeria: Nigeria Educational Research and Development Council (NERDC).

National Population Commission (Nigeria) and RTI International (2011). *Nigeria demographic and health survey 2010 (DHS) EdData profile 1990, 2003, 2008, and 2010: Education data for decision making*. Washington, DC: National Population Commission and RTI International.

Ndiyo, N. A. (2007). 'A dynamic analysis of education and economic growth in Nigeria'. *The Journal of Developing Areas*, 41: 1–16.

Omolewa, M. (2008). 'Adult literacy in Africa: The push and pull factors'. *International Review of Education*, 54: 697–711.

Paden, J. N. (2008). *Faith and Politics in Nigeria: Nigeria as a Pivotal State in the Muslim World*. Washington, DC: United States Institute of Peace Press.

Rose, P. and Greeley, M. (2006). *Education in Fragile States: Capturing Lessons and Identifying Good Practice*. Prepared for the DAC Fragile States Group.

Ross, W. (2012). The Biafrans Who Still Dream of Leaving Nigeria. *BBC News*.

Sunal, C. S., Sunal, D. W., Rufai, R., Inuwa, A. and Haas, M. E. (2003). 'Perceptions of unequal access to primary and secondary education: Findings from Nigeria'. *African Studies Review*, 46: 93–116.

23

Nigeria: Technical, Vocational Education and Training

Benjamin Ogwo

Introduction

Education in Nigeria, like in many other countries of the world, is charged with passing on worthwhile knowledge and skills to the citizenry for: work, leading the good life and responsible citizenship. Within the workforce, education is used to train and retrain workers on the relevant knowledge and skills that are needed to secure, retain and progress in any given occupation. If such education is conducted at sub-degree level, it is referred to as vocational education but if it is offered at the degree and postgraduate levels, it is referred to as professional education. However, there is a prevailing misconception and misunderstanding of the meaning and scope of vocational education among policy makers, educational administrators, general education teachers, students and the general public. Thus this chapter aims at providing useful conceptual, historical and functional background information on TVET. It then offers an overview of the scope, trends in the various TVET policies from 1981 to 2013. Additionally, it outlines the major TVET institutions in the country and lists the past and current technical and vocational qualifications in Nigeria. Finally, the chapter highlights the central issues that will undermine or promote TVET nationally. In order to attain the aims of the chapter, the write-up adopted the contemplative analysis approach that is rooted in both a historical and contemporary study of conceptual expressions of the evolution of TVET in Nigeria, by means of participant observation and documentary analysis.

According to the Federal Government of Nigeria (FGN) (2013) Technical and Vocational Education and Training (TVET) is used as a comprehensive term referring to those aspects of the educational process involving, in addition to general education, the study of technologies and related sciences and the acquisition of practical skills, attitudes, understanding and knowledge relating to occupations in various sectors of economic and social life. It covers the following areas: Technical Colleges, Vocational Enterprise Institutions (VEIs) and National Vocational Qualifications Framework (NVQF). Furthermore, TVET is understood to be:

a) an integral part of general education;
b) a means of preparing for occupational fields and for effective participation in the world of work;
c) an aspect of lifelong learning and a preparation for responsible citizenship;
d) and instrument for promoting environmentally sound sustainable development;
e) a method of facilitating poverty alleviation (UNESCO and ILO 2002: 7).

The goals of Technical and Vocational Education and Training (TVET) in Nigeria, according to the national policy on education, are to: provide trained manpower in the applied sciences, technology and business, particularly, at craft, advance craft and technical levels; provide the technical knowledge and vocational skills necessary for agricultural, commercial and economic development; and give training and impart the necessary skills to the individual for self-reliance economically.

In this era of proliferations of TVET programmes and conceptual misinformation, it is pertinent to clarify the terms technical education and vocational education because in some write-ups they are used interchangeably. Technical education is that aspect of education that leads to the acquisition of practical and applied skills as well as basic scientific knowledge (FGN 1981) while vocational education provides the skills, knowledge and attitudes necessary for effective employment in specific occupation at sub-professional cadre (Okoro 1993). It should be noted that all vocational education programmes are technical but not all technical educational programmes are vocational. Technical education in itself is not directed towards employment in any specific occupation but could be found usable in multiple occupations. Hence a couple of trade secrets, attitudes and practices needed to succeed in a given occupation are not found in the technical education curriculum. Thus, technical education could be viewed as a complementary aspect of or a sub-set of the vocational education programme. However, vocational training is the term referring to skill training wherein there is no written curriculum and the basic scientific knowledge and theoretical principles inherent in the skills are not emphasized. Examples include trainings that are offered in the informal apprenticeship programmes like roadside mechanics and carpentry (Ogwo and Oranu 2006a).

There are various ways of typifying TVET, namely formal (conducted under public supervision and under contract with a state board or local education agency (Osuala 2004), non-formal (undertaken outside the school system) and informal (done in the form of vocational training and without a written curriculum). Informal TVET is the type of vocational programmes provided by parents, guardians, relatives, significant others, craftsmen/women of different trades within the informal sector of the economy. It also includes learning resulting from everyday activities relating to work, family or relaxation/entertainment. This type of education predated the precolonial history of Nigeria and it is the indigenous educational system. Informal TVET programmes include agricultural training (farming, fishing and animal rearing, etc.), trades/crafts (weaving, smithing, carving, carpentry, dancing, wine-tapping, catering, etc.) and the professions (herbalist, witch doctors, etc.) (Fafunwa 1974). The informal TVET is fundamentally conducted under the apprenticeship programme wherein the craftsmen/women train the apprentices on their specific trades. On the other hand, the non-formal TVET is conducted outside the school system. This type of TVET programme, conducted at the workplace, is structured, and often, its certificates are not transferable, and it is, usually, of a short duration. Osuala (2004) indicated that the earliest history of non-formal TVET in Nigeria was traced to the multinational companies such as John Holt (in the 1930s), United Africa Company (UAC) (in 1954), and Shell-BP (in 1956). Between 1908 and 1935, the Nigerian Railway, Marine and Public Works Department, etc. established in-service TVET programmes (Fafunwa 1974). These non-formal TVET programmes were related to business, agriculture and trades relating to the operations of the multinational companies. Today, non-formal TVET programmes are still conducted by private/public sector organizations in the areas of computer appreciation, in-plant retraining, small and medium enterprises' skills, agricultural practices, technical trades, etc. The non-formal TVET has been used to offer the youth, underprivileged, women, men, and physically challenged saleable skills and knowledge of basic or advanced levels across a wide range of occupations as well as in workplace situations and in multifaceted socio-economic frameworks.

The formal TVET is offered within the school system. It is offered in the primary school, junior secondary school, senior secondary school and at the tertiary education level. At the primary and junior secondary school levels,

TVET is offered as pre-vocational subjects such as basic technology, information technology, agriculture, and home economics. The TVET subjects offered at the primary and junior secondary school levels are referred to as pre-vocational since they are designed to offer exploratory discourse of occupation and not aimed at providing employment preparations. At the senior secondary school level, the TVET subjects include agriculture, computer studies, applied electricity, electronics, building construction, General Metal Work, Technical Drawing, Auto Mechanics, Woodwork, Home Management, Food and Nutrition, Stores Management, Accounting, Commerce, Office Practice and Insurance. At the tertiary level, the polytechnics, monotechnics, technical colleges and vocational schools offer TVET programmes at advanced levels. The TVET programmes offered at the colleges of education and education faculties of universities are professional education programmes designed to train professional TVET teachers for the various levels of the education system. These are not, strictly speaking, vocational education programmes because vocational education is offered at sub-professional (below bachelor's degree or higher national diploma) levels.

Historically, formal TVET had a humble beginning in the Nigerian education system. According to Fafunwa (1974), some of the mission schools in the last century included bricklaying, farming and carpentry as part of their curriculum, but these skills were not seriously regarded by pupils and parents as an integral part of western education because it led to blue collar jobs and not the white collar types. Okoro (1993) stated that by 1909 the Hope Waddell Training Institute and Nassarawa Government School offered courses in tailoring, carpentry some commercial subjects and, metal work, carpentry, weaving and leatherwork respectively. However, the programme established by different public services departments (Public Works Department, Nigerian Railway, Post and Telegraph Department, etc.) can also be classified as formal TVET because the students took the London City and Guilds Examinations at the end of their programmes (ibid.). The first tertiary level TVET institution was the Yaba Higher College that introduced engineering courses in 1932 (Fafunwa 1974). Today there are many TVET institutions in Nigeria as reported by the National Board for Technical Education (NBTE 2013) in Table 23.1 overleaf.

From the foregone, it can be deduced that the scope of TVET is very broad and has been used in Nigeria for ensuring equity, justice, work skills, gender equality, citizenship education, social responsibility by different government programmes such as EFA, MDGs, poverty alleviation, and borstal or reformatory institutions

Table 23.1 Summary of number, type and ownership of polytechnics, monotechnics and technical colleges in Nigeria

Institution Type	Ownership			Total
	Federal govt.	State govt.	Private	
Polytechnics	21	38	15	74
Monotechnics	23	2	2	27
Colleges of Agriculture	17	19	–	36
Colleges of health Technology	9	40	1	50
Other Specialized Institutions	13	–	3	16
Innovation Enterprise Institutions (IEIs) and Vocational Enterprise Institutions (VEIs)	–	–	71	71
Technical Colleges	19	110	3	132

Source: compiled from data provided by the National Board for Technical Education (NBTE, 2013): http://www.nbte.gov.ng/index.html

(prisons), international development agencies and Subsidy Reinvestment and Empowerment Programme (SURE-P). With increasing youth and general unemployment, various governments are resorting to TVET programmes for job and wealth creation. The United Nations Educational, Scientific and Cultural Organization (UNESCO) (2009) asserted that TVET is complex and has several facets some of which are:

1 It may come under the attributes of several ministries thus making it multi-sectoral in nature
2 Theoretical and practical learning may constitute important TVET building blocks. TVET makes specialized knowledge and skills acquisition possible in schools, specialized training centres, and in the workplace;
3 TVET may be available at secondary, post-secondary and higher education levels;
4 TVET may include basic training for beginners as well as training throughout the professional life of productive workers. It can also open doors to post-secondary and higher education;
5 TVET may be a part of the formal education system, but may also be offered in an informal manner at work or through non formal methods.

The potentials of TVET for the individual, community and national development (Okorie 2000) are hardly controvertible. According to Olaitan (1996), TVET like other forms of education is a potent means for positive change and development. At the individual level, TVET enables the individual to enhance his/her economic and social worth by improved prospects for productive work, either on self-employment or paid employment and earned respect for service rendered (Ogwo and Oranu 2006b) and it could also increase the individual's level of productivity and earning capacity (Uwadiae 1992). At the community and national levels, TVET provides the human capital needed to sustain technological development, increase national productivity index, improve the quality of life, create wealth/alleviate poverty, tackle unemployment and promote national pride through food security, achieve technological identity/feats and attain favourable balance of trade with other countries. These gains of TVET cannot be attained by wishful thinking, sheer chance, and disparaging investment on recklessly/unevaluated capacity-building programmes but by thoughtfully designed and dedicated implementation of TVET programmes.

Trends in TVET policy provisions in Nigeria in the past three decades

Public policy remains the instrument of state for implementing government programmes. Thus, the wordings of the policy, its spirit and scope will determine how a particular development challenge will be tackled by government. TVET as well as the education system in Nigeria got the major post-independence policy thrust by the 1969 national conference which helped usher in the 1977 national policy of education. The 1977 policy and other associated government documents (FME 1977) stated government's condemnation of the negative public attitude towards technical occupations and consequently offered free technical education programme in response. Unfortunately, like most other grandiose but poorly articulated policies, the free technical education programme did not last longer than two years owing to the enormous financial involvement, which the programme's architects did not properly think through (Ogwo and Oranu 2006b). There have been other hit and miss issues arising from TVET policy formulation and implementation in the past three decades which can best be appreciated by a closer look at the policy provisions of the national policies on education. The most striking one is inconsistent usage of concepts like technical education, vocational education and technical and vocational education. It is pertinent to mention that Nigeria is yet to formulate and develop its first distinct TVET policy; as all the references to TVET have been delimited to the few pages ascribed to TVET in the overall national policies on education.

Overview of the 1981 TVET provisions in the national policy on education

The 1981 national policy on education was a well-thought-out document that provided generously for technical education. It defined technical education as that aspect of education which leads to the acquisition of practical and applied skills as well as basic scientific knowledge (FGN 1981). The policy made very remarkable provisions for technical education but did not mention any thing about vocational education and training even when some of its provisions were apparently for vocational training. It mandated the National Board for Technical Education (NBTE) to accredit training offered by roadside mechanics and directed the Industrial Training Fund (ITF) to organize appropriate apprenticeship training schemes for Nigeria. It is obvious that the policy makers regarded technical and vocational education to mean the same thing. The policy remarkably placed holders of the Higher National Diploma in Engineering and allied fields on grade level 08 similar to Bachelor's degree holders. This move did a lot of good for the image of technical education as being equivalent to general education. There are other ambitious provisions of the policy regarding adequate funding for technical education especially against the background of the 6-3-3-4 system of education. More so, it was at a time that preceded the era of a buoyant Nigerian economy owing to the earnings from the oil boom.

Overview of the 1998 TVET provisions in the national policy on education

The 1998 national policy on education provided for vocational education and eliminated the use of the concept: technical education. It defined vocational education as that form of education which is obtainable at the technical colleges and being equivalent to the senior secondary education but designed to prepare individuals to acquire practical skills, basic and scientific knowledge and attitude required as craftsmen and technicians at the sub-professional level (FGN 1998). This policy did not use the concept of technical education, rather it discussed polytechnic and monotechnic education in apparent reference to technical education offered in such institutions. Another important image-boosting provision in terms of parity with general education is the admission of students who graduated from the artisan training centre into the technical colleges. The policy also stated that more efforts shall be made to encourage women to embrace technical education.

Overview of the 2004 and the 2008 TVET provisions in the national policy on education

Section 7 of the 2004 national policy on education provided for Science, Technical and Vocational Education in which it adopted the UNESCO and International Labour Organization (ILO) (2002: 7) definition of TVET. It also described the concept of pre-technical and vocational education. The policy stated that the goals of technical and vocational education shall be to:

a) provide trained manpower in the applied sciences, technology and business, particularly, at craft, advanced craft and technical levels;
b) provide the technical knowledge and vocational skills necessary for agricultural, commercial and economic development;
c) give training and impart the necessary skills to individuals who shall be self-reliant economically (FGN 2004: 30–1).

In terms of funding, the policy stated that a greater proportion of education expenditure shall continue to be devoted to vocational education at federal and state levels. The 2004 policy restated other issues like gender, artisan training and apprenticeship training.

The 2008 national policy on education did not define TVET, rather it incorporated technology education subjects into basic, post-basic education and tertiary education. It also mentioned the establishment of Vocational Enterprise Institutions (VEIs) for the transformation of students' knowledge through technological processes into wealth and a broader economic base (FGN 2008).

Overview of the current TVET provisions in the 2013 national policy on education

The 2013 national education policy reflected the full nomenclature of TVET and also adopted the UNESCO and ILO (2002) definition of TVET. This is a good sign that the policy makers have learnt the inherent conceptual differences in technical education, vocational education and technology education. The goals of TVET are also the same as the 2004 and 2008 national policies on education in terms of including TVET under the chapters on post-basic and career development. However, the Vocational Enterprise Institutions (VEIs) and National Vocational Qualifications Framework (NVQF) were introduced into the policy document in order to accommodate private sector provision of non-formal TVET and recognition of prior learning as well as transferability of

TVET credentials. The VEIs and NVQF are the very significant inclusions in the 2013 national policy. The section on tertiary education described the details of technology education at the polytechnics, monotechnics and colleges of education (technical). This clearly indicates that the policy is able to distinguish between TVET and technology education.

These policies reviewed above and the Federal Ministry of Education's (FME 2000) national MasterPlan for technical and vocational education (TVE) development in Nigeria in the twenty-first century with The Blue-Print for Decade 2001–2010 as well as the 4-year strategic plan for the development of the educational sector: 2011–15 have been the guiding documents for policy makers and implementers in the recent past. These documents have prescribed the roles of the major TVET institutions in Nigeria and how they will contribute towards meeting the policy objectives.

Major TVET institutions in Nigeria

The attainment of the TVET policies objectives is dependent on the capacity and commitment of the major TVET institutions to fulfil their various mandates. The major TVET institutions include but not exclusively: the Federal and State Ministries of Education, the National Board for Technical Education (NBTE), technical colleges, the Innovative Enterprise Institutes (IEIs) and VEIs, the National Commission for Colleges of Education (NCCE), the National Business and Technical Examination Board (NABTEB), International Centre for Technical and Vocational Education and Training (UNESCO-UNEVOC) centres in Nigeria, Industrial Training Fund (ITF) and National Directorate for Employment (NDE).

The Federal and State Ministries of Education are the government departments that formulate, regulate and enforce TVET polices, most times through the various government parastatals. The Federal Ministry of Education is in charge of the TVET policies at the national level while the states' ministries of education are responsible in the 36 states of the federation. At the Federal Capital Territory (FCT), Abuja, the Territory's department of education is in charge of its TVET policies. The NBTE is the major government parastatals of the Federal Ministry of Education established in 1977 to regulate TVET programmes at the technical colleges, vocational schools, and more recently the IEIs and VEIs. It is also in charge of technology education at the polytechnics and monotechnics. The Board discharges its functions through the accreditation process, establishment of the national minimum standards and liaising with government for overseeing the funding of the federally owned institutions. The technical colleges are equivalent to senior secondary level of education. They offer practical and theoretical contents in mechanics, building, wood, electrical, textile, printing, beauty culture and business trades as well as hospitality and computer craft practice. The curriculum for each trade consists of four components: General education, Theory and related courses, Workshop practice, Industrial training/production work and Entrepreneurial training (FGN 2013).

The VEIs and IEIs are recent introductions in TVET. They are also regulated and overseen by the NBTE. Unlike the technical colleges, the VEIs and IEIs are privately owned and offer courses on some indigenous skill areas by adopting the apprenticeship structure for some trades. The National Commission for Colleges of Education (NCCE) is charged with teacher education and as such, regulates and accredits the courses offered at the colleges of education (technical). These colleges train the technical teachers that teach at the technical colleges and other related institutions. The National Business and Technical Examinations Board (NABTEB) was established in 1992 to conduct the following examinations: National Technical Certificate (NTC), Advance National Technical Certificate (ANTC), National Business Certificate (NBC), Advance National Business Certificate (ANBC), Royal Society of Arts (RSA) and City and Guild (C&G) and entrance examinations into Federal Technical Colleges.

There are three UNESCO-UNEVOC centres in Nigeria. They are located at the Yaba College of Technology, Lagos, the Centre for Technical Vocational Education, Training and Research (CETVETAR), University of Nigeria, Nsukka and the NBTE Centre of Excellence at Kaduna. These UNEVOC (International Centre for Technical and Vocational Education and Training) centres engage in activities relating to knowledge sharing and management among TVET practitioners in Nigeria. They also relate with other UNEVOC centres in the world to conduct TVET researches and disseminate research findings to policy makers. The Industrial Training Fund (ITF) is a parastatal in the Federal Ministry of Industry, Trade and Investment which was established in 1971 by an act which was amended in 2011. ITF has lots of programmes relating to TVET development in Nigeria, for example, its Vocational and Apprentice Training, Research and in-plant retraining programmes for industries. The National Directorate of Employment (NDE) is a parastatal in the Federal Ministry of Labour and Productivity. It was established in 1986 for designing and implementing programmes to combat mass unemployment. Among others, the NDE runs the following TVET-related programmes: Basic National Open

Apprenticeship Scheme (B-NOAS), Advanced National Open Apprenticeship Scheme (A-NOAS), School-on-Wheel Scheme (SOW) and Resettlement Loan Scheme. In recent times, the NDE has established training centres across the country.

Technical and vocational qualifications in Nigeria: Past and current

The TVET educational institutions in Nigeria offer different types of certifications. The trade tests (I, II and III) are offered, by the Ministry of Labour and Productivity, to candidates that completed TVET training outside the formal institutions. The NABTEB offer examinations leading to the award of the National Technical Certificate (NTC), National Business Certificate (NBC) and National Vocational Certificate (NVC). Some training institutions still prepare candidates for the City and Guilds of London trade tests (intermediate and advanced levels). According to the national policy on education (FGN 2013), The National Vocational Qualification Framework NVQF shall consist of six levels:

- NVQ Level 1: Entry Level or unskilled employees
- NVQ Level 2: Foundation or basic skilled employees
- NVQ Level 3: Operators or semiskilled employees
- NVQ Level 4: Technicians, skilled and supervisory employees
- NVQ Level 5: Technical and junior management positions
- NVQ Level 6: Professional engineers and senior management positions

The other qualifications such as national diploma (ND) and higher national diploma (HND) and Bachelor of Technology degree are considered as certificates issued under technology education as well as professional level education and as such may not be regarded as TVET qualifications.

Trending issues in technical vocatioal education and training (TVET) in Nigeria

The most pressing issue in Nigeria relating to TVET is the overbearing weight of youth unemployment especially in relation to half-hearted implementation of TVET programmes. In order to address this debilitating development challenge various governments in Nigeria appear to be throwing money at the problem without building needed synergy among the TVET institutions. Owing to the amount of money provided by different government ministries and international development agencies, everybody is now in the business of capacity building on TVET. Sometimes, these capacity-building programmes are undertaken by agencies that are least able to handle them but have enough connections at the resource allocation venues. There is urgent need to have a commission/council/committee in charge of galvanizing the TVET training efforts in Nigeria such that it will be easy to ascertain the impact of any programme, state of knowledge in any trade, reconcile the mandates of all TVET agencies so as not to have them run at cross purposes with each other. The army of unskilled, ill-trained and under-employed youths are all but a time bomb almost about to explode. There is need to have a national TVET policy that will address issues such as public–private partnership in quality assurance, access and wealth creation.

In all the TVET policies reviewed in this chapter, the issue of gender, women's empowerment and the reputation of TVET graduates had been recurring. Good image and reputation of any occupation are not conferred by acts of parliament or policy provisions. Wherever they are found, they were earned and not compelled. If the graduates of TVET programmes continue to improve on the level of skills shown at work; this will in turn translate to an equal rise in reputation and regard. Look around the construction sites in Nigeria, finished furniture in homes, vehicles on Nigerian roads; one will see overwhelming evidence of the poor quality of craftsmanship of TVET graduates. This type of low skills cannot enhance the image and reputation of the graduates, rather, it will sustain the perception of ineptitude in which they are held. Women's empowerment and access on the other hand can be improved by carefully articulated programmes relative to particular trades. The EFA as well as the MDGs programmes have improved access to TVET programmes, hence the outstanding issue now is for the programmes to pursue the goal of learning for all. This will ensure gender equity as well as improve the reputation of the TVET graduates.

Poverty alleviation, entrepreneurship and the success of TVET programmes in Nigeria have remained a mixed bag. Most times the graduates of TVET lack the soft skills (affective competencies) needed to wait on a business to mature. Many of the TVET graduates lack the perseverance, dedication and patience needed to acquire/hone technical skills, and as such, cannot establish and run their new outfits. They prefer to ride commercial motor bike/tricycles ('okada/keke' NAPEP – National Poverty Eradication Programme). instead of working on the trade for which they trained. The commercial motor-riding enterprise tends to yield immediate cash returns to these graduates at a faster rate than practising their respective trades.

These formal, non-formal and informal TVET graduates lack the prerequisite technical and soft skills to work on their respective trades hence they keep moving from one job to another thus sustaining the cycle of poverty as they transit from one trade to another. Admission to TVET programmes should be based on aptitude and not on ease of access. The return on investment for training in TVET programmes will be extremely low when admission criteria are based on any factor other than aptitude and interest of the student.

Globalization and information communication technology (ICT) are issues that are constantly captured in many government policies on TVET. The potentials of ICT in promoting TVET in Nigeria are limitless. Cheaper training cost, increased access and high-quality delivery are some of the benefits of introducing more ICT-based delivery systems and management of TVET programmes. In the area of ICT utilization, there are an array of vicious cycles, such as low capacity of teachers, mis-procurement of equipment, administrators' debilitating ignorance and corrupt practices. These challenges, notwithstanding, the pressures by the international development agencies as well as globalization will continue to require pursuit of transparency and skilful use of ICT. Globalization has also brought to the fore the inadequate skills issue of TVET graduates since many of the multinational organizations are insisting on outsourcing for positions that should ordinarily be filled by Nigerian TVET graduates. However on a bright note, TVET graduates can still acquire internationally recognized certificates such as offered by Microsoft, Cisco and SAP, while residing in Nigeria.

TVET has lots of potentials for human capital and technological development, and for the socio-economic and political prosperity of Nigeria. Like all other facets of Nigeria polity, other forms of vices (tribalism, nepotism, corruption, etc.) are impeding the sustainable development of the country. These vices are not peculiar to Nigeria but have continued to be at the root of underdevelopment of the low-income/developing countries. It will entail joint efforts of all governments of the world to mitigate the proliferation of these vices since the government officials/investors from the developed countries induce those from the less-developed countries; who succumb because of the prevailing poverty of material/mind. Love of country, patriotism and pride of craftsmanship should be part of TVET curriculum in all forms of education. Irrespective of the volume of its inclusion on various government policies/

documents, TVET will only contribute to the development of Nigeria to the extent to which these policies are sincerely implemented. All over the informal sector of the economy, the ingenious, creative and industrious nature of Nigerians are manifest and will only entail sincere leadership at all levels of governance to translate these into a national asset.

Conclusion

TVET has been acknowledged internationally as being a veritable means for skills acquisition within the informal, non-formal and formal education system. By building strong institutions and less of powerful/lawless leaders, Nigerian TVET systems will be used to curb youth unemployment, reduce poverty, improve social justice, and promote skills empowerment for all. The chapter has attempted to clarify the meaning and scope of TVET for ready reference for policy makers, administrators and students so as to enable all major stakeholders to maximally explore its potentials. The historical accounts indicate the trail TVET followed and the trend projects the trajectory for its future. The country can learn from its past, construct the present and envision its future of TVET by strategic positioning and committed policy implementation. Nigeria does not have any other alternative to an efficient TVET system for its development hence TVET is the Hobson's choice in her bid for sustainable growth and development.

References

Fafunwa, A. B. (1974). *History of Education in Nigeria.* London: George Allen and Unwin Ltd.
Federal Government of Nigeria (FGN) (1981). *National Policy on Education*, 2nd edn. Lagos: Federal Ministry of Information Printing Division.
—(1998). *National Policy on Education*, 3rd edn. Lagos: Federal Ministry of Information Printing Division.
—(2004). *National Policy on Education*, 4th edn. Lagos: NERDC Press.
—(2008). *National Policy on Education*, 5th edn. Lagos: NERDC Press.
—(2013). *National Policy on Education*, 6th edn. Lagos: NERDC Press.
Federal Ministry Education (FME) (1977). Free Technical Education. *F.M.E. Information Curricular No. SME 363/5.1/93* Lagos: F.M.E.
—(2000). *The National Master – Plan for Technical and Vocational Education (TVE)*

Development in Nigeria in the 21st Century with the Blue-Print for Decade 2001–2010. Abuja: Author.
National Board for Technical Education (NBTE) (2013). 'Brief History of National Board for Technical Education (NBTE)'. Available from http://www.nbte.gov.ng/history.html (accessed 6 October 2013).
Ogwo, B. A. and Oranu, R. N. (2006a). *Methodology in Formal and Non-Formal Technical/Vocational Education*. Nsukka: University of Nigeria Press
—(2006b). *Poor Image of Technical/Vocational Education Programmes in Nigeria: Causes, Problems and Interventions*. [Funded Technical Report by Education Trust Fund (ETF), Abuja]
Okorie, J. U. (2000). *Developing Nigeria's Workforce*. Calabar, Nigeria: Page Environs Publishers.
Okoro, O. M. (1993). *Principles & Methods in Vocational & Technical Education*. Enugu, Nigeria: University Trust Publishers.
Olaitan, S. O. (1996). *Vocational and Technical Education in Nigeria: Issues and Analysis*. Onitsha, Nigeria: Noble Graphic Press.
Osuala, E. C. (2004). *Foundations of Vocational Education*, 5th edn. Enugu: Cheston Agency Ltd.
UNESCO (2009). 'Regional Contribution to statistical Information Systems Development for Technical and Vocational Education and Training: Diagnosis and Comparative Analysis for identifying Quality Improvement Strategies'. Available from http://unesdoc.unesco.org/images/0021/002115/211512e.pdf (accessed 6 October 2013).
UNESCO and ILO (2002). *Technical and Vocational Education and Training for the Twenty-first Century*. Paris and Geneva: Authors.
Uwadiae, S. A. (1992). 'Coping with the challenges of technology on the pursuit of excellence in vocational-technical education' (Paper presented at the Alvana International Conference on Educational Studies, AICOE, Owerri).

Nigeria: Financing Education

Mary Ogechi Esere

Introduction

Nigeria, like every other developing country, is presently striving towards nation building and national development. The key to achieving this aim lies in effective mass mobilization whose facilitative instrument is functional and well-funded education in all its ramifications. Education contributes to nation building in two major ways. On the one hand, it is expected to maintain and sustain the well-engrained and well-established normative social and cultural practices of the society and community. On the other hand, education is expected to extend the frontiers of knowledge thereby, extending the capabilities of the nation. In terms of nation building, from the economic perspective, education is expected to provide the nation with a reservoir of able and capable human resources (Esere 2004). It is expected to equip the people with relevant knowledge and skills. In other words, education is expected to play a duality of roles namely, that of preservation and that of advancement.

Education, at various stages, translated into their respective curricular, aims at giving the nation a sense of history, a sense of national pride and identity, a sense of belonging, a sense of ownership, a sense of unity in cultural diversity, and a sense of direction for national cohesiveness. Just as it enhances all these, including a sense of social justice and patriotism, education must, at the same time, attempt to eradicate a sense of selfishness, prejudice and chauvinism which all threaten to break a nation (Idowu 2001). Access to education is an indication of a country's preparedness to meet its manpower needs. The products of a well-funded educational system are capital investment, which will over time lead to the development of the nation in all its ramifications. Access to education in industrialized nations and developing nations is, perhaps, the engine that drives the boat of their development.

As a nation, Nigeria cannot reach her maximum potential without education. To be able to live and survive, both body and mind must be nurtured from birth to death. Education is food for the mind. Nigeria cannot afford to postpone the supply of this food to some future time. Postponement of the supply of education may just mean that our minds will either be undernourished or malnourished. The process of nation building presupposes the prevalence of progressive transformational values. Out of education comes the human capital that has the capacity and responsibility for conducting research to assist us to find solutions to pressing national problems (Esere 2004). As long as Nigerians do not prioritize the improvement of the knowledge base and skills, they will continue to be exploited by other nations that have woken up to the importance of developing human capital through well funded and quality education.

Quality education has been described as the greatest legacy that any nation can bequeath to its citizenry (Idowu 2001). Its greatness still lies in the fact that it is a means of achieving national growth and development. Education has always been highly rated in developed countries as the main and basic step towards self-enhancement, survival and usefulness to the society (Mallinson 1998). Functional and well-funded education is very basic and crucial for social, economic and technological development of any nation. It is a means of improving both the individual and the society. It is maybe due to this awareness that the Nigerian National Policy on Education (1981) is emphatic on government's decision to uphold education as 'an instrument par excellence for effecting national development' (p. 5). Furthermore, the 1999 Constitution provides in Section 18 that:

i) Government shall direct its policy towards ensuring that there are equal and adequate educational opportunities at all levels.
ii) Government shall promote science and technology.
iii) Government shall strive to eradicate illiteracy, and to this end, Government shall as and when practicable provide:
iv) (a) free, compulsory and universal primary education;
   (b) Free secondary education;
   (c) Free university education;
   (d) Free adult literacy programme (Constitution of the Federal Republic of Nigeria 1999).

These fine policy statements notwithstanding, there is no denying the fact that education is very poorly funded in Nigeria. Toward this end, this paper examines financing education in Nigeria. In so doing, the paper x-rays the journey so far, by considering some vital statistics, consequences of poor funding of the education sector, the debate surrounding who funds education in Nigeria and the way forward.

Funding education in Nigeria: The journey so far

During the colonial era in Nigeria, the funding of education was left to the missionary organizations until around 1882 when the colonial government enacted an Educational Ordinance to end the exclusive control of education by the missionaries. A new Educational Ordinance was enacted in 1887 when the two colonies of Nigeria and Ghana (formerly known as Gold Coast) were separated. This ordinance provided for a Board of Education with powers to give grants to schools for teachers' salaries, buildings, etc. At that time, government primary schools were established and maintained in part from public funds. An arrangement was usually made whereby local chiefs or native court presidents accepted responsibilities for erecting and maintaining school buildings and teachers' houses and paying an annual subscription varying from 40 pounds to 100 pounds. There were also assisted schools which were given government grants and were to meet the deficit of their requirement by fees and church contribution (Fafunwa 1974; Durosaro 2012).

In Nigeria, the period from the 1960s to the 1970s witnessed the most rapid expansion of education because the government invested heavily in education (World Bank 1988). During this period the education system in Nigeria could be said to be in a state of boom. As a matter of fact, facilities that existed in Nigerian educational institutions were on a par with what existed in other parts of the world (Eisemon 1980; Babaloa et al. 1996). However, the economic crises of the 1980s led to the introduction of Structural Adjustment Programmes (SAP) with their attendant prescription from the International Monetary Fund (IMF) and the World Bank for reduction in public investment in education (Igbuzor 2006). The policy prescription of these world bodies were succinctly captured by Bonat (2003) who pointed out that:

> The Bank did not suggest that public spending on education should be boosted at the expense of servicing external debts. The World Bank prescribed adjustment, revitalisation and selective expansion policies in order to address the education problems ... the purpose of adjustment was to 'alleviate the burden of education and training on public budgets'. Because the Bank expected continuing structural adjustment to further erode public spending on education, it recommended adjustment to diversify sources of educational finance 'through

increased cost sharing in public education', and the 'encouragement of nongovernmental supplies of educational services'. The Bank recommended 'increased user charges' in public education, especially for tertiary education. The Bank also recommended 'containment of unit costs' 'especially in utilisation of teachers' (low pay policy for teachers), lowering construction standards for educational infrastructure, and benefitting from 'the tendency of students to repeat grades of drop out of school'.

These policies actually led to a decrease in public expenditure on education, increased participation of the private sector, commercialization of education and stagnation of teachers' salaries in the face of inflation leading to a decline in the quality of education (Igbuzor 2006). One other way that has led to the declining quality of education is the neglect of tertiary institutions in Nigeria especially as from the mid-1980s. According to Fasina (2003),

> The World Bank has, since the mid-1980s, canvassed the position that Nigeria and African countries do not need higher education but only training of its youth in basic education and technical education. The UBE is predicated on the same assumption. Pay less attention to university education and fund UBE. Leave universities to private hands; re-introduce the 1986 Structural Adjustment Programme (SAP) formula of cost recovery, rationalisation, and commercialisation and public universities will die a natural death. But UBE will survive because the World Bank will fund it. This is the illusion of the decade.

Education capital expenditure has therefore declined sharply since the 1980s, and by 1988, the real value of capital expenditure was less than 17 per cent of the average value of the 1980s (CISCOPE 2005). This trend has continued unabated and the budgetary allocations to education in Nigeria have been less than 10 per cent of the total federal budget since 1995 to date. This is in sharp contrast to UNESCO's recommendation of 26 per cent. Some current statistics on education funding in Nigeria is further elucidated in the next section of this paper.

Some vital statistics

There is no denying the fact that education is very poorly funded in Nigeria, which is yet to comply with the UNESCO recommendation that 26 per cent of annual budget be spent on education. Nigeria spends less than 10 per cent of her annual budget on education. Botswana spends 19.0 per cent; Swaziland,

Table 24.1 Share of education on the national budget, 2005–12

Years	Total National Budget	Allowance to Education	% Share of Education
2005	1,846,000,000,000	92,000,000,000	4.98
2006	1,900,000,000,000	92,000,000,000	4.84
2007	2,300,000,000,000	186,000,000,000	8.09
2008	2,870,000,000,000	33,600,000,000	9.64
2009	3,101,813,750,626	216,639,437,111	6.98
2010	4,608,616,278,213	249,080,000,000	5.40
2011	4,226,191,559,255	339,481,528,685	8.03
2012	4,749,100,821,171	400,148,037,983	8.43

Source: Budget Office, Federal Ministry of Finance, Approved budget, 2005–12

24.6 per cent; Lesotho, 17.0 per cent; South Africa, 25.8 per cent; Cote d'Ivoire, 30 per cent; Burkina Faso, 16.8 per cent; Ghana, 31 per cent; Kenya, 23 per cent; Uganda, 27.0 per cent; Tunisia, 17 per cent; and, Morocco, 17.7 per cent (Abayomi 2012).

A cursory look at Table 24.1 shows the trend in the allocation of fund to the education sector in Nigeria covering the period 2005 to 2012. The table indicates that the percentage allocation to education from the federal government annual budget ranged between 4.84 per cent and 9.64 per cent. This allocation appears too low (Durosaro 2012) when compared with what other nations in Africa spend on education (see Table 24.2).

In Nigeria today, concerned education stakeholders have continued to call for the upward revision of the budget to meet the 26 per cent recommended by UNESCO, as the amount voted for education fails to adequately address the funding of this vital sector. According to a breakdown of the 2012 budget, the sum

Table 24.2 Expenditure on education as percentage of gross national production in some African nations

Country	% GNP on Education
Angola	4.9
Cote d' Ivoire	5.0
Ghana	4.4
Kenya	6.5
South Africa	7.9
Malawi	5.4
Mozambique	4.1
Nigeria	0.76
Tanzania	3.4
Uganda	2.6

Source: Lawal, M. B. (2011)

of N400.15 billion, representing 8.43 per cent of the budget has been allocated to education. Out of this, N345.091bn (82 per cent) was allotted to recurrent expenditure while a meagre N55.056bn (18 per cent) is for capital expenditure. N317.896bn was proposed for personnel cost and N27.192bn was for overheads. Also, the main ministry had a budget proposal of N5.491bn; MDGs N2.173bn; parastatals N5.196bn; universities, N14.411bn; colleges of education, N4.555bn and unity colleges N7.663bn. The ministry got a total capital allocation of N5.49bn in 2011, out of which N3.688bn was released; total commitment was N3.497bn and actual draw down was N2.699bn (Abayomi 2012).

Disturbed by the huge gap between amount for capital and recurrent expenditure, the Senate Committee on Education has queried the large percentage of the ministry's budget voted for recurrent expenditure to the detriment of capital expenditure for infrastructure in the sector. According to Senator Uche Chukwumerije, Chairman of the committee, the distribution of funds between recurrent and capital poses challenges of slow pace in infrastructural development in the agencies and institutions. A further breakdown showed that while personnel allocation increased by N38.584bn, overheads got N1.836bn and capital N3.231bn respectively, which Chukwumerije argued 'are not remarkable enough to offer great changes from last year's achievements'.

In Nigeria, education is put on the concurrent legislative list. By implication, states are given the power to fund and control education in their domains along with the federal government (Durosaro 2012). Table 24.3 presents the level of priority accorded education by some states in Nigeria.

Table 24.3 shows that during the 2010 and 2011 fiscal year, Delta State devoted between 5.45 per cent and 14.15 per cent of her annual expenditure to

Table 24.3 Share of education on state budgets in Nigeria, 2010 and 2011

State Total Expenditure	Delta		Enugu		Kogi		Lagos	
	2010	2011	2010	2011	2010	2011	2010	2011
	N	N	N	N	N	N	N	N
	215.98 7.094.971	144.84 0.000.000	57.770 000.000	66.442 293.596	78.669 082.681	78.455 332.453	389.57 0.766.372	445.18 0.000.000
Expenditure on Education	11.768 477.966	20.500 .000.000	3.600 .000.000	3.700 .000.000	9.762 819.696	7.969	52.588 .137.958	61.713 .000.000
% on Education	5.47	14.15	4.48	4.5	12.41	10.16	13.50	13.87

Source: Durosaro, D. O. (2012)

education. For Enugu State, 4.48 per cent and 4.5 per cent of her expenditure during the period under review was devoted to education. Kogi State allocated between 10-16 per cent and 12.41 per cent of her annual expenditure to education while Lagos State devoted between 13.50 per cent and 13.87 per cent of her annual expenditure to education. According to Durosaro (2012: 22), if this expenditure on education in these States is shared per head of the school age population in each of the States, the amount would be mere stipend and grossly inadequate.

Consequences of poor funding

The scenario painted above shows that Nigeria's educational system is still bedevilled by a myriad of problems, which keeps worsening by the day, all as a result of poor funding. These include: shortage of quality staff; dearth of infrastructure; inadequate classrooms and offices; inadequate laboratories for teaching and research; shortage of books and journals; indiscipline; inconsistent and ill-conceived policies; corruption at high and low places; cultism; irregular payments of salaries; examination malpractices; embezzlement of funds; low staff-student ratios; poor record keeping; fraud and self-deception with regard to accreditation; failure to send staff regularly on short courses to improve and enhance their competences; and, the fact that government often reneges on the mutual agreements between it and the unions of educational institutions (Abayomi 2012).

In the Universal Basic Education (UBE) guidelines, every primary or junior secondary school in Nigeria is expected to have one general science laboratory for elementary science and domestic science; one ventilated improved toilet for a maximum of 40 pupils or students per toilet; and, one teacher to handle only 40 pupils or students in a class. But these criteria are yet to be met due to scarcity of funds.

In some primary schools, pupils sit on the bare floor in a classroom. Most secondary schools lack classrooms, libraries, laboratories and equipment. In the universities, the scarcity of funds manifests itself everywhere on campus as there are no current books or journals, no laboratory equipment, limited number of lecture rooms, acute shortage of water, no basic chemicals, no specialized chemicals, 'no nothing' as Abayomi (2012) puts it. Furthermore, teachers in the primary and secondary schools are poorly paid, lecturers in Nigerian tertiary institutions are also poorly remunerated. The basic annual salary of a professor is N753, 549, whereas a professor in Singapore receives ten times the salary of his Nigerian counterpart. This abysmal scenario has led to the question of who really should fund education.

The debate on who funds education

According to Igbuzor (2006), one major question about financing education is who should finance education? The argument has always been whether the cost of education should be borne by government or by the individuals receiving education. Three schools of thought are recognizable in this debate.

i) The first group are those who believe and argue strongly that the cost of education should be borne essentially by parents with government providing the enabling environment. They are of the view that education should be subjected to free market discipline (Igbuzor 2006). This group are of the opinion that families and individuals ought to pay fees in order to access nominally available public services, otherwise these services would not be available or their quality would become unacceptably low (Tomasevski 2003). Going by the position of this group, the poor, as a matter of fact would not be able to access education. Education is a human right that should be accorded to all human beings solely by reason of their being human. A number of international human rights instruments provide for education as a fundamental human right. These include the Universal Declaration of Human Rights (1948), the International Covenant on Economic, Social and Cultural Rights (1966), the African Charter on Human and Peoples' Rights (1981) and the Child's Right Act. It is maybe on this basis that the second school of thought derives their argument.

ii) The second group argues that education is a right and as such must be funded by government. To them, there are enough resources in the world to fund at least basic education for all children. According to this school of thought, the problem of education is not the problem of lack of funds but that of mismanagement of funds, corruption, misplaced priority, and poor policy choices (Igbuzor 2006). They argue that education should not only be free but also compulsory. They posit that government should bear all the cost of education because even if the direct costs are borne by government, the indirect costs (such as uniform, transport and school meals) may be beyond the capacity of the family while the opportunity cost may be impossible to bear (Tomasevski 2003). They also argue that no right could exist without corresponding government obligation and that government is obliged to make education available, accessible, acceptable and adaptable.

iii) The third school of thought in this debate, while coming from the rights-based stance like the second group maintain that education is a right and as such government must not only endeavour to remove all the barriers to education but must also take steps to utilize to the maximum its available resources to achieve progressively the full realisation of the right to education and other social and economic rights. This group argues that there are layers of obligations in matters of social and economic rights. These are obligations to respect, protect and fulfil. The obligation to respect requires states to refrain from interfering with social and economic rights e.g. refrain from forced eviction. The obligation to protect requires states to prevent violations by third parties, for example, ensuring that private employers comply with labour standards. The obligation to fulfil requires states to take appropriate legislative, administrative, budgetary, judicial and other measures towards the full realisation of such rights (Igbuzor 2006).

From the foregoing, it is obvious that scholars are not in agreement on a cost-sharing arrangement for education. What then exactly is the practice as regards education funding in Nigeria?

Sources of funding of education in Nigeria

Education funding comes from different sources. The major one for all levels of government is public revenue from taxation. Education funds are reported to be distributed among primary, secondary and tertiary education levels in the proportion of 30 per cent, 30 per cent and 40 per cent respectively (Balami 2003). The public funding includes direct government expenditure (for teachers' salaries and instructional materials) as well as indirect expenditure in the form of subsidies to households such as tax reductions, scholarships, loans and grants.

Given the rising cost of education, the federal government took steps to improve her financial base by promulgating Decree 7 of 1993 on Education Tax which stipulates that 2 per cent of the profit of companies registered in Nigeria should be collected by the Federal Board of Internal Revenue and be paid into a Fund called Education Tax Fund, (now called Education Trust Fund), which would be disbursed to Federal, State and Local Government Authority educational institutions in Nigeria to improve educational funding (Durosaro 2012). This decree has since its promulgation been in operation bringing relief to various tiers of government on education funding, though still grossly inadequate.

Another group of stakeholders in the Nigerian educational system are the international development partners such as the United Nations Children's Fund (UNICEF), the British Council, the United Nations Educational, Scientific and Cultural Organisation (UNESCO) and the World Bank. These international development partners have also been committing much of their own resources to educational development in Nigeria. For instance, UNICEF had been funding Basic Education and Gender programmes and Strategic Education Sector Planning in many states across the federation. The British Council has also been investing much in capacity building for education sector workers in Nigeria while the World Bank had been assisting Nigeria with loans to fund the Universal Basic Education programme (Durosaro 2012).

The way forward/recommendations

The state of education in Nigeria is still precarious (Common Wealth Education Fund 2005). As reported by Atueyi (2012), how to provide alternative funding opportunities for Nigerian undergraduates formed the basis of the discourse, at the first international student finance conference, held recently in Lagos. Participants challenged the government to channel the bulk of the nation's stolen wealth into educating its citizenry. Participants also deliberated on the need to provide multiple funding options for prospective Nigerian undergraduates by providing students' loans, bursaries, scholarships and grants. This is because, when there is assured funding quality, output will improve for any country with large natural resources and endowment, without the right human capital is heading towards its Waterloo.

Other participants who spoke at the event argued that the older generations enjoyed scholarship, bursaries and other grants and now they are not able to give the same opportunity to the present generation. They urged government to desist from bad policies and concentrate on programmes that would impact on the poor masses. They also requested that all recovered funds from the nation's corrupt officers should be channelled towards assisting indigent but brilliant undergraduates. The salaries of educators must be raised considerably as Nigeria has the wherewithal to do so, education being the key to the development of any society. It is obvious that government's decision to spend 8.43 per cent of the budget on education is insufficient to guarantee this right in Nigeria. There is, therefore, the need to close this variance with the 26 per cent to fast track education-related MDGs.

One of the most brilliant initiatives, undertaken during the tenure of Mrs. Obiageli Ezekwesili as Education minister, as reported by Oyekanmi (2012) was the Community Accountability and Transparency Initiative (CATI) launched in March 2007. The idea behind CATI, which the FME designed in conjunction with the Universal Basic Education Commission (UBEC) and the Civil Society Action Coalition on Education for All (CSACEFA), was to let Nigerians know how much money the Federal Government was spending on education in their respective communities. The CATI was expected to inform the citizens about their entitlements and encourage town associations, community development associations, civil society groups and individuals to play more active roles in monitoring how the money budgeted for education is spent. More importantly, it was also intended to encourage various stakeholders to hold government officials, State Universal Basic Education Boards (SUBEBs), contractors, school administrators and managers accountable for both the efficient utilization of public funds and the expected returns in investment in education. To that effect, the FME and UBEC published information on the disbursement to all states between July 2005 and July 2006 on the FME website. Information on various disbursements was to be publicized twice a year.

The CATI office was located at UBEC, where reports of mismanagement are to be channelled, for onward transmission to the Education Minister's office. The minister would then report to the President and send the findings to appropriate bodies for further action. The CATI desk at UBEC was to be manned by an independent officer to be nominated by CSACEFA, who would then work closely with the CATI Desk Officers at the FME and liaise with Parent Teacher Associations (PTAs), Civil Society Groups, town unions, international development partners, faith-based organizations, community development groups to ensure integrity. The beautiful side of the initiative, Oyekanmi (2012) posited was that, it was also to serve as an instrument to evaluate schools, which would have efficiently utilized public funds and grade them on accountability and transparency. Those adjudged to be the best were to receive additional allocation from the five per cent Good Performance Fund of the two per cent Consolidated Revenue Fund being administered by UBEC.

However, this initiative was strangled to death immediately Ezekwesili left office. Since then, no Education minister has bothered to re-examine them, yet, so much noise was made, variously, on the problems associated with corruption and examination malpractice, which were direct consequences of their failure to act appropriately. This writer on this note joins other well-meaning Nigerians to request that CATI be resuscitated for optimal management of Nigerian scarce finances in education. There is a great need for better budgeting process with participation of stakeholders and tracking of the use of resources for education. Civil Society Organizations and Schools Management Committee have a big role to play in this regard.

Conclusion

This paper has been an attempt at x-raying issues on financing education in Nigeria. As highlighted in the Roadmap on Education document (FMOE 2009), basically the challenges facing the Nigerian educational system can be classified into four key areas – Access and Equity, Standards and Quality Assurance, Technical and Vocational Education and Funding. In the area of funding, Nigeria needs to improve on actual financial provision for education, fund management and accountability (Durosaro 2012).

References

Abayomi, A. (2012). 'Education budget'. Available from http://www.vanguardngr.com/2012/04/2012-education-budget-and-its-implications-analysis/ (accessed 20 May 2012).
Atueyi, U .(2012). 'Conference considers alternative funding'. Available from http://www.ngrguardiannews.com/index.php?option=com_content&view=article&id=91257:conference-considers-alternative-funding-for-undergraduates-&catid=80:education&Itemid=610 (accessed 20 May 2012).
Babalola, C.J.; Okunola, J.; Adeyemi, M.L. & Ibekwe, C.O. (1996). Education in Nigeria. Ibadan: Falktec Press.
Balami, D. (2003). 'Finance of education in Nigeria'. Paper presented at the Forum on Cost and Finance of Education in Nigeria, Abuja.
Civil Society Coalition for Poverty Eradication (CISCOPE) (2005). *Liberalisation, Deregulation and Privatisation of Education Services in Nigeria.* Abuja: CISCOPE.

Commonwealth Education Fund (2005). Study on the Nigeria Federal Education Budget Performance 2003–2005.

CSCOPE (2005). Retrieved from http://en.wikipedia.org/wiki/CSCOPE_%28education%29 (accessed 13 September 2012).

Durosaro, D. O. (2012). 'Where the shoe pinches: The cost of education'. Being text of 103rd inaugural lecture of University of Ilorin 29 March.

Eisemon, T. O. (1980). 'Scientists in Africa'. *The Bulletin*: 17–22.

Esere, M. O. (2004). 'Globalisation and the challenges of human development in Nigeria: The counsellor's factor'. *The Nigerian Journal of Guidance and Counselling*, 9 (1): 71–84.

Fafunwa, B. (1974). *History of Education in Nigeria*. London: George Allen and Urwin.

Fasina, D. (2003). 'Building the Future on Sound Education: The Problems and Prospects of Universal Basic Education Programme'. In F. Abayomi, D. Atilade and M. Matswamgbe (eds), *State of Education in Nigeria: What Hope for the Future?* Lagos: Ajasin Foundation.

Federal Ministry of Education (1981). *National Policy on Education*. Lagos: Government Press.

—(2009). *Roadmap for the Nigerian Education Sector*. Abuja: Ministry of Education.

Federal Republic of Nigeria (1999). *Constitution of the Federal Republic of Nigeria*. Lagos: Government Press.

Idowu, A. I. (2001). *Education for National Reconstruction, Reformation and Development*. Being text of a lead paper presented at the first national conference of the school of education, college of Education, Oro, Kwara State, between 1–4 May, 2001.

Igbuzor, O. (2006). *Financing Quality Basic Education in Nigeria*. Being text of a keynote address delivered at a roundtable organised by the Commonwealth Education at Rockview Hotel, Abuja, 5 September, 2006.

Lawal, M. B. (2011). 'Funding Tertiary Education in a Depressed Economy: Public-Private Partnership to the Rescue'. In K. Adeyemi and B. Awe (eds), *Rebranding Nigerian Educational System*. Lagos: National Open University of Nigeria.

Mallinson, V. (1998). *An Introduction to the Study of Comparative Education*. London: Heinemann.

Oyekanmi, M.J. (2012). *Universal Basic Education: Challlenges and the Way Forward*. Ilorin: TIM-Sal Publishers.

Tomasevski, K. (2003). *Education Denied: Costs and Remedies*. London: Zed Books, p. 72.

World Bank Report (1988). Retrived from https://openknowledge.worldbank.org/handle/10986/5971 (accessed 10 April 2012).

Senegal: An Overview

Léa Salmon and Latif Dramani

Introduction

Education is essential for development. The economic boom observed in Asian countries such as Japan and Taiwan, illustrates the important role played by human capital through education in growth (Becker 1993). These nations managed to achieve high growth rates based on education and training, despite a highly competitive international environment. Furthermore, Dramani (2012) highlights an intergenerational mechanism of transmission of human capital between parents and their children. Indeed, the children of educated parents had a much higher probability of being educated compared to other children. Moreover, according to Riddell (2004) and Woodhall (2001), the theory of education economics is based on two principles. First, it is primarily interested in the relationship between the investment in education/training, and the productivity/income distribution. The application of this theory in Senegal highlights significant distortions in the development of education infrastructure on the one hand, and the mechanisms of income distribution on the other. Indeed, a large part of the labour force in Senegal works in the informal sector which is very low in human capital.

The results of a recent study in Senegal show (Dramani 2011) that education is the main factor for escaping chronic poverty, as it also helps to develop mechanisms for resilience to economic shocks and to better support these (Dramani 2013). Despite all the research that indicates the link between education and growth, the education system in Senegal remains challenging.

This chapter provides an overview of the education system in Senegal. The study is based on a quantitative analysis of available survey data at all levels of education, from pre-primary to higher grade at national level. It also assesses the effectiveness and efficiency of the education system.

Context

Senegal in West Africa is considered as a politically stable country, certainly in comparison with its neighbouring countries. It is often seen as a success story in terms of economic growth and poverty reduction, at least prior to the economic crisis (Salmon 2012). Most of the indicators below show progress over the first decade of the new millennium. (Table 25.1)

The GNI per capita increased from $1.380 to $2.000 in almost 10 years, the GDP has almost tripled, but there is a drop in the growth rate of GDP, from 6.7 per cent in 2003 to 2.6 per cent in 2013. Social indicators are also encouraging with an increase in life expectancy from 56.7 to 59 years.

The major challenge facing Senegal is the constant growth of its population, which has increased dramatically in the last few years to almost 13 million inhabitants, living in an area of 196,712 km². The education system has had great difficulty integrating this young population (51 per cent of the population). This severely compromises the quality of learning. Despite the efforts of the Senegalese government to reach the second MDG, which is to achieve primary education for all by 2015, the results remain mixed. Several studies, however, have shown that the development of education is progressing to meet the MDG. Indeed, the redirecting of investments provided by the country's partners in the education sector has had a direct impact on children's access to formal education after the high dropout rates of the 1980s and 1990s which were linked to severe cutbacks.

In Senegal, the gross enrolment rate (GER) has reached 94.1 per cent[1] at primary school level. In contrast, the net enrolment rate (NER) remains relatively low; with 59.1 per cent children not having been enroled in primary schooling in 2010.[2] To this we must add those children who have never been

Table 25.1 Key Senegal indicators

Senegal Indicator	2002	2003	2010	2011
GNI per capita, PPP (current international in USD)	1,380.0	1,470.0	1,910.0	1,940.0
Population, total (in millions)	10.0	10.3	12.4	12.8
GDP (current USD) (in millions)	5,333.9	6,857.9	12,855.3	14,291.5
GDP growth (Annual %)	0.7	6.7	4.1	2.6
Life expectancy at birth; Total (years)	56.4	56.7	59.0	59.3

Source: World databank, 2013

to school or who receive schooling in the informal system and therefore do not appear in official statistics.

Moreover, the NER decreases according to the level of the educational cycle. The NER is lower in secondary and higher education, due to constant strikes in the educational sector in Senegal. Taking stock of these dismal results, it is necessary to understand the challenges of the education system in Senegal and the low performance that hinders its development.

The objective of this chapter is to draw an overall picture of the education system, with a particular emphasis on access and the quality of learning at national level, the main causes of this low quality of education performance, as well as the lessons to be learned to attain the MDGs.

Following this introduction, the chapter is organized into four sections. The first section is devoted to the socio-economic causes of the education crisis in Senegal. The second section presents the quality of the education system through the performance indicators at all levels from pre-primary to the higher education level. The third section addresses the management of the education system. The final section offers conclusions and recommendations.

Education: A difficult challenge

Education is crucial in the development of an individual and of a nation. This led to the need to create a 'right to education' as stated in the Universal Declaration of Human Rights (UDHR) and the African Charter (AC). Similarly, education is the second MDG, after the reduction of poverty and hunger.

Educational systems in Senegal however, have paid a heavy price due to previous economic crises. As a response to the crises, the structural adjustment programmes in the 1980s and 1990s are notable examples (UNESCO 1995: 6). As a result, these two decades witnessed a widespread deterioration of educational standards. The school dropout process is a good illustration of this situation. This process had the peculiarity of penalizing the most vulnerable groups, among which girls were the first victims. Senegal suffered from that crisis as a 'double penalty' because the problem of dropping out came on top of the issue of unequal access to education, which the country was already experiencing before the economic collapse of the 1980s. Today the education system has improved a lot compared to the 1990s, even if the quality of education is still hampered by economic and social barriers.

According to some studies, religion is one of the main factors impacting the choice of the family whether to send their children to school or not. As an example, the child of a Mourid follower (the most prominent Islamic Sufi order in Senegal) is less likely to attend school than the child of a Christian (Dramani 2012). Indeed, cultural and religious communities have a strong influence on Senegalese families. Religion plays a key role in the family and community's strategies and the decisions to send their children to school; especially when they have the perception that the state has failed. Given the limitations of the state budget which fails to offer a good education; some families choose to send their children to a non-formal or semi-formal education. As a result, the number of Islamic schools and centres has increased dramatically and there are now between 10,000 and 15,000 *Daraas* according to sources.[3] The distinctiveness of the *Daraas* is that the Quran is taught but not necessarily the basics of learning such as reading, numeracy, and general knowledge. Once students finish schooling, they are unprepared for the modern world or to be independent in life. Hybrid systems such as the *French Arabic schools* have also sprung up, and they now account for 374 primary schools and 22 middle and high schools in the public sector. The private sector respectively records 324 primary schools and 150 middle and high schools.[4]

There is also a correlation between living conditions and education. The parents' own education has a significant influence on the probability of their child going to school. If a parent has no education, the chances of his/her child going to school fall by 69 per cent compared to a child whose parent attended middle school. Moreover, poverty does not favour the access of children to schooling. The child of an individual who is chronically poor has almost 60 per cent less chance of going to school (Dramani 2011).

These families have little resources to cover the school expenses in public schools despite the low fees. Furthermore, they often have a lot of children to take care of, which further increases the burden of education costs. Parents and their communities therefore have a huge bearing on children's education.

Access to education

In Senegal, the education system is composed of formal, non-formal and informal education. The formal education sector is structured around early childhood (0–6 years), elementary education (7–12 years), middle school

(13-15 years), general and technical secondary (16-18 years) and higher education (18 and over).

The non-formal education could be defined as any organized educational activity outside the formal education system (Diouf et al. 2001). Finally, the informal education refers to any educational practices and training not structured.

In this analysis, we have been focusing on the formal education system and we mostly referred to the Ministry of Education, which designs the country's strategy for education within the next 10 years (2013-25), namely the programme to improve the quality, the equity and the transparency (PAQUET). We also used data from the national statistical agency (ANSD 2011). The access to education is measured by the Gross Enrolment Rate, the parity indices and the share of private education in the school system. In kindergarten, as elsewhere in the world, enrolment is not compulsory in Senegal. This explains the low enrolment rates of children in school at an early age. Indeed, the enrolment rate was 2.3 per cent in 2000 and increased to 10.7 per cent in 2011, slightly below the target value defined in 2007. In 2011, the gender ratio showed that 11.4 per cent of girls were enroled, compared to 10 per cent of boys. Private kindergartens played an important role in the education of young children.

The situation is different in elementary school, where progress has been remarkable regarding the access to education. For example, the gross intake rate in Grade 1 exceeded by 2.7 points, the target value of 2011, and rose from 85.1 per cent in 2000 to 113 per cent in 11 years; and the GER in primary school also increased in 11 years, from 67.2 per cent to 93.9 per cent, slightly below the target value. Some efforts have also been undertaken in the field of parity, with an index that rose from 96.4 per cent to 110.9 per cent. The percentage of students in private education also grew by 4 per cent in a decade (from 10.6 per cent to 14.4 per cent).

In middle school, GER has grown significantly in ten years, with 19.6 per cent in 2000 to 53.2 per cent in 2011, with more state places available. The general secondary school also showed progress in ten years with a GER which barely reached 10 per cent doubling in 2011. The available data showed a huge improvement on girls' access to education whose enrolment tripled from 2000 (6.7 per cent in 2000 and 18.9 per cent in 2011). There is also an increase in the share of the private school of 5 per cent in eight years.

Concerning the gender distribution in high secondary schools, it can be observed that, as in middle secondary schools, the enrolment of boys (24.3 per cent) is greater than girls (18.9 per cent).

In higher education, the number of graduates has more than tripled in ten years, from 8,178 in 2001 to 30,017. The overall number of students has also increased from 30,000 in 2001 to 91,359 in 2010. The data of the Ministry of Education (PAQUET) also shows an increase in the share of private universities of 5 per cent in eight years. In 2011, higher education institutions (colleges and universities) collated the number of 111,749 students of which 42,322 were girls, representing 37.9 per cent. The private higher education numbers account for 18.9 per cent of this total, 21,162 students being enroled in private institutions.

The quality of education

For all school cycles, the quality of education is measured in terms of school completion rate, success rate, dropout rate, and grade repetition rate. Early childhood is the period when children learn the five preliminary steps in reading and writing, which represents a crucial step in determining the performance of children at the higher grade. Children who have followed this stage of cognitive development will have the facility to learn more than other children (Gove and Cvelich 2010: 2). At an early age, there are no data available to show if children have learnt the basic skills, because in most developing countries like Senegal, they are not evaluated according to standardized models. At the primary level, World Bank data show that the primary completion rate remains low (59 per cent), compared to other African countries such as Cameroon (78.7 per cent), Cape Verde (98.9 per cent) and Togo (73.67 per cent) (refer to http://data.worldbank.org/).

Moreover, in Senegal, data show that a 1st grader has only a 62 per cent chance of reaching Grade 6. In 2011, this rate was 63 per cent which was below the target value of 70 per cent. The repetition rate dropped fourfold in ten years, from 12.4 per cent to 3.5 per cent. This is mainly due to a Senegalese policy which advocates zero grade repetition in 1st and 2nd grade, and less than 5 per cent in other grades in elementary school. The dropout rate also decreased from 10.3 per cent in 2004 to 8.6 per cent in 2011. The number of children who reached Grade 6 increased from 49.1 per cent in 2004 to 88.4 per cent in 2011.

In middle school, the success rate of the final exam slightly increased over ten years reaching 50 per cent. At this level of schooling, grade repetition is allowed and it is constantly increasing, from 13 per cent in 2004 to 18 per cent in 2011, while the dropout rate remains stable with 8 per cent compared to 7.5 per cent in 2000.

In high school, progress has been made regarding the number of students going to university. The national transition rate is 55.1 per cent, an increase of five percentage points from 2010 when the rate was 50.1 per cent. The transition rate is higher for boys than girls (57.3 per cent against 52.5 per cent). An analysis of the situation at the regional academies reveals a high rate of transition for St. Louis (71.8 per cent) against a low transition rate of 33.5 per cent in Kédougou. The repetition rate is the indicator used to measure internal efficiency in the high secondary schools. The success rate of colleges and universities in 2010 stood at 42.2 per cent and is slightly higher for men (42.6 per cent) than women (41.6 per cent) (ANSD 2011: 84, 89).

In order to achieve education for all as stated by the MDGs in 2000, several studies have been conducted to evaluate the performance of children around the world. Thus, several definitions have been proposed.[5] A variety of indicators of the quality of education exist (Latour 2006).[6] The main indicators used in Africa are the *Programme d'Analyse des Systèmes Educatifs* (PASEC), *des Pays de la Conférences des Ministres de l'Education des Pays Francophone* (CONFEMEN)) and the Southern and Eastern Africa Consortium for Monitoring Education Quality (SACMEQ).[7] The quality of learning is a measure of school results – i.e. schooling achievements, social, political and moral values transmitted by the school.[8] In Senegal, several measures have been used to assess pupils' performance (USAID 2012). According to the National Assessment for learning outcomes (SNERS) data, 20 per cent of 6th graders achieved the required results in French, and 10 per cent achieved the results in Mathematics. In 2007, PASEC data showed that the average score (out of 100) in French for 5th graders was 40.6, and the average score (out of 100) in Maths for 5th graders was 42.1. In 2009, most students had not acquired basic reading skills by the end of 3rd grade and 26 per cent of students assessed could not read a single 1- or 2-syllable word. Students read on average five words per minute in Grade 1, 20 words per minute in Grade 2, 35 words per minute in Grade 3, which is below the level of fluency for reading comprehension. In 2012, Jangandoo data (2012)[9] showed that 64 per cent of children tested failed the reading test for the 3rd Grade and 81.4 per cent failed the numerical test for the 3rd Grade.

Education management

In Senegal, the implementation of the Structural Adjustment Programmes (SAP) in the 1980s and 1990s resulted in cuts to the government budget for the health and education sectors. Rurimwishiga (1992) noted that the decrease in the budget resulted in the closure of more than three hundred classes in rural areas due to lack of teachers; a stagnation of school enrolment in primary school; an introduction of doubled-shift and multigrade classes to cope with the increase of the school-going population; an increase in the dropout rate and abandonment particularly at the end-of-cycle classes (5th and 9th grades).

In such circumstances, it was very difficult for teachers to cover the programme, so the quality of education suffered greatly. From 2000 onwards, there was a significant improvement in terms of the share of education expenditures as part of the total government expenditure. In fact, the ratio increased from 30.9 per cent in 2000 to 40.3 per cent in 2007 showing the importance of the sector as a development factor for Senegal, which is greater than the UNESCO requirement of 20 per cent.

The budget allocated varies from one cycle to another. In early grade, the share of the state budget allocated to early education is extremely low, less than 1 per cent in 2011, compared to elementary school (15.9 per cent), middle school (24.01 per cent), high school (24.01 per cent) and university (19 per cent). While the allocated budget increased in middle and high school, it declined at university level. The modest budget allocated to elementary school has an impact on the education system as a whole and on teaching and learning in particular. Indeed, such a budget which pays teachers inadequately and fails to motivate them cannot even provide classes with teaching books and materials. Depending on the source, children may only have 2.5 books at their disposal; one book can be shared by five children. Added to this, is the issue of overcrowded classrooms, often with more than 60 students per class. In rural areas, there is often a shortage of canteens at school and children cannot eat on site.

Moreover, Table 25.2 below reveals that only 16 per cent of schools have running water, electricity and sanitation facilities. Yet, access to toilet facilities is essential and their absence and lack of hygiene is a key issue, especially for girls.

Here is a profile of a good teacher as drawn up within the profession:[10] In terms of skills, teachers must: 1) have the appropriate job knowledge; 2) have a mastery of their field but also have the desire to share; 3) be good listeners; 4) be ready to provide support and use positive language; 5) disseminate information in an accessible way; 6) have a sense of humour and have good ethics. In terms of character, the teacher must be motivated, imaginative, competent, a role model, a good communicator, responsive, attentive, open-minded, dynamic, punctual, friendly, etc. This is far from the case in Senegal. Approximately, 29 per cent of teachers had a basic minimal competency in the official language

(French) and 75 per cent of them had minimal knowledge in Mathematics. Moreover, teachers are poorly motivated with an 18 per cent absenteeism rate. The total daily classroom hours, which is 4 hours 36 minutes, is not completed because in practice, children only receive 3 hours 15 minutes of classroom teaching daily. Therefore, children lose 1 hour 21 minutes of teaching per day. In addition, there are many strikes which disturb normal teaching and the learning process at school.

In Senegal, the percentage of total public expenditure of the government on education has varied greatly over the past decade. An analysis of the distribution of the budget allocated to education in 2009 shows a significant absorption of resources by the primary education sub-sector (42 per cent) of the total. This concentration of resources could be justified by the fact that primary education for all was the most important education goal that the country was trying to achieve.

In addition, only 9.1 per cent of resources were allocated to technical education and vocational training. This could be justified by the low numbers of vocational and technical training vis-à-vis other sub-sectors of education. In terms of resource allocation, it is still behind the college and universities (19.9 per cent), high level education (12.6 per cent) and secondary education (11.3 per cent).

Even if the State is the main contributor for funding the education sector, local communities through skills transfer and decentralized management also contribute in providing resources. Households also participate in the educational provision for their children, especially concerning the costs of

Table 25.2 Education indicators

Components of Indicators for education	Indicators
School	
Facilities (water, electricity and sanitation)	16%
Number of students per class	34
Number of students per teacher	29
Number of books per student	2.5
Teacher	
Teacher's absence rate per scheduled class	18%
Classroom learning time per day	3h15
Percentage of teachers with basic language competency	29%
Percentage of teachers with basic Math competency	75%
Resources	
Cost for primary schools per student in cfa	77000
Percentage of teachers cumulating two months of pay delay	0%

Source: A. Diagne (2012: 207)

supplies and registration fees. It should also be noted that the technical and financial partners (TFP) contribute to funding in various forms. In 2010, the distribution of contributions from key players is as follows: State (70 per cent), local authorities (17 per cent), donors (12 per cent) and households (1 per cent).

Conclusion

Education performance indicators in Senegal indicate that significant work remains to ensure the smooth transmission of human capital (education of children, youth and adults). Many efforts have been made by the Government of Senegal in the last decade in regard to PDEF results. However, it is important to note that in terms of quality the results remain disappointing. Dropout rates, exclusion and repetition are still high and the standards required to implement quality education are sorely lacking. The main challenge in Senegal, like in many other African countries, is to improve the completion rate of primary school and the quality of learning. This should be a priority in the MDGs and post 2015.

Faced with this challenge the Laboratory of Research on Economic and Social Transformation (LARTES) has suggested recommendations aimed at improving cognitive learning and the input at national and international level (LARTES 2012a, 2012b). These recommendations are in line with the priorities described in Center for Universal Education (2011). They aim at supporting early childhood development and equity in learning opportunities for boys and girls and building up basic reading and numeracy competencies at primary school. They also emphasize transitional programmes in order to complete the high school cycle and provide training to students who did not complete primary school in order to give them the opportunity to have access to the labour market.

In terms of cognitive learning, children should master basic skills such as reading, writing, mathematics and general knowledge which are necessary to progress in the school system. The cognitive contents should be adapted to the level of the child. Kindergarten schooling should be promoted. Learners should acquire knowledge that would allow them to take part in the economic, political and cultural life of their society and in a global economy. Children should be assessed on a regular basis by using simple and inexpensive methods. Quality of learning indicators should be improved by using skills-based tests.

In terms of inputs, the availability of books/manuals at learning places should be improved. Teachers should be trained in the cognitive teaching and learning method. They should also be trained in new methods which are likely to guarantee a positive attitude or aptitude with regard to mathematics as it develops analysis, logic, numeracy reasoning and problem-solving skills. Notions of citizenship, democracy, individual rights, and the question of equity between boys and girls should be introduced into the curriculum.

Notes

1   Ministère de l'Education Nationale du Sénégal (2012), 'Note Introductive au Conseil Interministériel d'évaluation de l'année scolaire 2011–2012 et de suivi de la rentrée scolaire 2012–2013', Dakar, Sénégal.
2   DSRP II (2010), 'Formulation du document de politique économique et sociale 2011–2015: Bilan diagnostic', République du Sénégal.
3   Department of Arabic Learning, Ministry of Education and local NGOs.
4   Ministère de l'Education Nationale du Sénégal (2013), 'Programme d'Amélioration de la Qualité, de l'Equité et de la Transparence (PAQUET: Secteur Education Formation 2013–2025'), Dakar, Sénégal.
5   Education and learning are sometimes misused. The first refers to general development of an individual, at different levels, religious, moral, social, technique, scientific, medical, etc. The second notion is more specific in that it refers to the transmission of knowledge through signs.
6   M. Latour (2006), 'L'évaluation au service de la qualité en éducation: Pratiques et enjeux'. Available from http://www.ciep.fr (accessed 6 June 2006). The author makes a very detailed bibliography review of the educational systems and background evaluation.
7   Center for Universal Education at Brookings Africa Learning Barometer, 'Technical Appendix'. Available from http://www.brookings.edu/research/interactives/africa-learning-barometer (accessed 17 September 2012).
8   Jangandoo is a research programme, managed by LARTES (Laboratory of Research on Economic and Social Transformations) and funded by the Hewlett Packard Foundation. Its objective is to evaluate the level of education in the household in Senegal following other countries' experiences like India, Pakistan, Kenya, Tanzania, Uganda and Mali. These results come from the pilot survey assessing 1,600 children in four regions in Senegal.
9   H. Boudreault, 'Un profil d'enseignant par des enseignants' University of Quebec Montreal, (UQAM), available from http://didapro.wordpress.com/lalbum/un-profil-denseignant-par-des-enseignants

References

Anda, M. Adams. (2012). 'The education Link. Why learning is central to the post 2015 global development agenda'. *Center for Universal Education, Working paper,* #8.

ANSD (2011). 'Situation Economique et Sociale: Education', Edition 2011, Dakar, Sénégal.

Becker, G. S. (1993). *Human Capital: A Theoretical and Empirical Analysis with Special Reference to Education,* 3rd edn. University of Chicago Press.

Center for Universal Education (2011). 'A global compact on learning: taking action on education in developing countries', *Brookings Institute,* Washington, DC.

Diagne, A. (2012). *Le Sénégal Face aux Défis de l'Education: Enjeux et Perspectives pour le 21e siècle.* Paris: Karthala Edition.

Diouf, A., Mbaye, M. and Nachtman, Y. (2001). 'L'éducation non formelle au Sénégal: description, évaluation et perspectives'. Dakar, Sénégal: UNESCO.

Dramani, L. (2011). 'Escaping chronic poverty in Senegal: Intergenerational determinants'. *Conference Paper 8, Eighth Meeting of the Working Group on Macroeconomic Aspects of Intergenerational Transfers,* Brazil, December 2011.

—(2012). 'Intergenerational transmission of human capital in Senegal'. *International Journal of Educational Research and Technology,* IJERT 3 (3): 37, 52.

—(2013). 'Educational and resilience to economic shocks in Senegal'. *International Journal of development and Sustainability,* 2 (2).

DSRP II (2010). 'Formulation du document de politique économique et sociale 2011–2015: Bilan diagnostic', République du Sénégal.

European Commission (2002). 'European Report on Quality Indicators of Lifelong Learning', Brussels.

Gove, A. and Cvelich, P. (2010). 'Early Reading: Igniting Education for All', A report by Early Grade Learning Community of Practice. Research Triangle Park, NC: Research Triangle Institute.

LARTES (2012a). 'Baromètre de la qualité des apprentissages des enfants au Sénégal'. Dakar, Sénégal.

—(2012b). 'Dynamiques de la pauvreté et conséquences sur l'éducation au Sénégal: Un agenda pour l'action'. Dakar, Sénégal.

Latour, M. (2006). 'L'évaluation au service de la qualité en éducation: Pratiques et enjeux'. http://www.ciep.fr (accessed 6 June 2006).

Ministère de l'Education Nationale du Sénégal (2012). 'Note Introductive au Conseil Interministériel d'évaluation de l'année scolaire 2011–2012 et de suivi de la rentrée scolaire 2012–2013'. Dakar, Sénégal.

—(2013). 'Programme d'Amélioration de la Qualité, de l'Equité et de la Transparence (PAQUET: Secteur Education Formation 2013–2025'. Dakar, Sénégal.

Riddell, W. Craig. (2004). 'Education, Skills and Labour Market Outcomes: Exploring the Linkages in Canada'. In Gaskell, Jane and Rubenson, Kjell, *Educational Outcomes for the Canadian Workplace.* Toronto: University of Toronto Press.

Robert, F. (2005). 'Une approche conceptuelle de la qualité en éducation', *Dossiers des sciences de l'éducation,* #13, Revue Internationale des sciences de l'éducation, Toulouse, France.

Rurimwishiga, E. (1992). 'L'ajustement structurel'. African Institute for Economic Development and Planning, IDEP. Dakar, Sénégal, pp. 16–34.

Salmon, L. (2012). 'Perceptions of the economic crisis and poverty in Senegal: A quantitative and qualitative analysis'. In *Living Through Crisis.* World Bank Publications. Washington DC, USA.

UNESCO (1995). 'Rapport sur l'état de l'Education en Afrique', BREDA, Sénégal.

—(2005). 'Education for All: the quality imperative', *Global Monitoring Report on EFA.* Paris, France.

USAID (2009). 'La qualité de l'éducation de base au Sénégal : une revue' Center for Collaboration and the future of schooling, rapport final, 14 Avril, Sénégal.

Woodhal, M. (2001). 'Human Capital: educational aspects'. Neil J. Smelser and Paul B. Baltes (eds). *International Encyclopedia of Social & Behavioral Sciences.* USA.

World Bank (2013). World databank, World Development Indicators, Washington DC, USA.

26

Senegal: Trends and Futures

Caroline Manion

Like most countries around the world, education has been expected to play a central role in social, economic and cultural development in Senegal, an ethnically and linguistically diverse West African country. At independence in 1960, Senegal, as a former French colony, inherited a national education system inadequately equipped to meet the imperatives of equitable, quality and relevant education for all in the service of national development aspirations. Successive education reforms and programmes that have guided processes of educational development in the country have produced mixed results over the last half-century. On the one hand, over the past decade educational access and completion rates have improved at the basic education level. On the other hand, the overall quality of basic education has remained low, with related concerns about access, quality and relevance persisting at the post-basic and higher education levels.

Using primary and secondary data obtained through analysis of government, donor and civil society documents and databases, as well as reviewing the scholarly literature, the goal of this chapter is to provide a succinct snapshot of current education trends in Senegal, at basic and higher education levels, and suggest future issues that the country faces as it strives to achieve its ambitious sector development goals.

Education policy landscape: Priorities and targets

While a range of targeted policies exist that direct action with respect to inclusive education (see Aslett-Rydbjerg 2003), the integration of ICT into Senegalese schools and educational administration (see Fall 2007) etc., the Programme de développement de l'éducation et de la formation/Development

Plan for Education and Training (PDEF)[1] is the key overarching policy framework that has been guiding educational development in Senegal since 1998. Created in collaboration with key stakeholders, including civil society and donors, PDEF sets out key sector targets, plans of action to achieve them and the resources needed (Ndiaye 2006; World Bank 2009). The third implementation phase of PDEF (2008–11) has recently completed, focusing in particular on enhancing the management capacity of the sector (DeStefano et al. 2009; World Bank 2009).

A key theme across successive phases of the PDEF, as well as Senegal's 2013–25 Education for All Sector Plan, is the expansion in the system across all levels and sub-sectors, particularly as a means to address geographic, gender and other disparities in education participation (DeStefano et al. 2009; Global Partnership for Education 2014). Through the Global Partnership for Education, Senegal received an $81.5 million grant in 2009 in support of improved access to primary education, focusing on the construction of schools and improving school facilities (e.g. provide running water) (Global Partnership for Education 2014). Between 2009 and 2013 over 3,000 primary schools have been constructed (ibid.).

Other key education policy goals include improving the quality and relevance of learning, and the promotion of a 'coherent, modern, decentralized efficient and effective education system as a whole' (République du Sénégal 2003: 7; 2013). Thus, the PDEF and the current education sector plan basically share the same goals as those emerging from the 1981 General Meeting on Education and Training (EGEF) – a 'turning point' in educational development in Senegal, and the subsequent National Commission on the Reform of Education and Training (CNREF) (Ndiaye 2006: 224; Ndoye 1997, République du Sénégal 2013). Additionally, as per the foundations laid by EGEF and CNREF for the development of democratic schooling in the country, PDEF continues to extend the partnership model, '[ensuring] that communities participate fully in the development of education', including the design, implementation and evaluation of education policies and programmes (Ndiaye 2006: 226).

Further policy priorities identified in the current EFA sector plan include the development of technical and vocational training, in partnership with the private sector, to strengthen schooling-work-economic growth linkages; improved management capacity; reduce drop-out and repetition rates to improve the system's efficiency; improve educational staff productivity and; promote and enhance the use of national languages in the formal education system (Global Partnership for Education 2014; République du Sénégal 2013)

With respect to the challenges associated with achieving the goals and targets identified in the PDEF, the Planning and Education Reform Department (DPRE) has suggested several, including,

> ... coordinating across three ministries of education; the need to recruit, train, support and maintain teachers at a rate never before achieved; meeting the rising salary costs associated with expansion; the construction of increasing numbers of classrooms, also at a rate never before achieved in Senegal; the purchasing and distribution of millions of books and other pedagogical materials including those required by the introduction of a new school curriculum. The government will be attempting to manage these demanding implementation-intensive strategies and activities at the same time, during a period where expansion alone will continue to eat up many of the additional resources flowing to the sector (p. iv)

Trends in formal education: Expansion and quality at the basic and secondary levels

Since 2000, and in line with its EFA commitments, Senegal has registered significant gains in terms of increasing access to education, largely as a product of infrastructure and physical expansion projects implemented throughout the country. With expansion in the public and private sectors, early childhood care and education (ECCE) the Gross Enrolment Ratio (GER) in pre-primary schools increased from 3 per cent in 1999 to 13 per cent in 2010, with girls enroling at higher rates than boys (UNESCO 2012). Education is compulsory for those aged seven to twelve. Whereas enrolment in private institutions as a percentage of total enrolment was 50 per cent in 2005 at the pre-primary level, enrolment in private institutions at the primary level in Senegal was 14 per cent – the key point here is to suggest the scope of the public system of education in the country (ibid.). Table 26.1 highlights the remarkable gains made in terms of education expansion.

Table 26.1 Progress in expanding access to education

Level/Sub-Sector	Enrolment Rates		
	2000/01	2007/08	Growth
Pre-School	2%	9%	350%
Elementary	72%	90%	25%
Middle	20%	39%	95%
Secondary	9%	16%	78%

Source: Ministère de l'Education, 2008 cited in DeStefano et al., 2009: 6

Since 2000 the gender gap in elementary education has been reversed, with more girls than boys now enroling at this level (DeStefano et al. 2009; UNESCO 2012). For example, in 2010 the Net Enrolment Rate (NER) for girls at the primary level was 78 per cent; whereas for boys, the NER was 73 per cent (UNESCO 2012). Given the negative shifts in boys' enrolment rates, it is expected that boys' education could emerge as a key equity concern going forward, much as is the case in many parts of the world.

Private providers of education services are increasing in number and are attracting relatively large numbers of students willing to pay tuition fees (plus other direct and indirect costs of schooling) in exchange for what is often perceived to be a higher quality of education (and thus, higher status). In particular, the historical bottleneck at the transition from elementary to middle/secondary school has drawn a large influx of private providers, eager to fill the gaps in state service in communities, especially those in urban areas. For example, in 1999 enrolment in private institutions as a percentage of total enrolment at the primary level was 12 per cent, and by 2010 was 14 per cent (UNESCO 2012). At the middle school/secondary level, 21 per cent of all students enroled attended private institutions (ibid.).

Despite the impressive gains in terms of educational expansion, there has been much concern expressed about the low quality of education generally available to the citizens of Senegal (Republic of Senegal 2013). Relatively low literacy rates for adults and youth reflect the low quality of education available in the system: In 2010 less than half of the adult population (those 15 years of age and over), and only 65 per cent of the youth population (those aged 15–24) were considered literate (UNESCO 2012). Results of the Poverty Monitoring Survey in Senegal (2011) suggest that 72.4 per cent of household heads polled had no formal education (Republic of Senegal 2013: 32). A 2009 USAID report offers a very pointed discussion about the quality of education in Senegal, highlighting poor pupil performance, low survival/high dropout rates, and low transition rates from elementary to middle/secondary school (DeStefano 2009: iii). Given the low quality of education, the system cannot be said to be efficient. In 2010 the total drop-out rate from basic education was just over 40 per cent, with slightly more boys than girls leaving school (UNESCO 2012). In 2009 the survival rate to grade five was 75 per cent, and the survival rate to the last grade was only 60 per cent, with slightly more boys surviving longer than girls (ibid.)

One of the key challenges and sources of contentious debate internally and externally, concerns French as the dominant language of instruction and a compulsory subject in Senegalese schools from kindergarten to university (Clemons and Yerende 2009; Diallo 2011; Ngom 2002; Sane 2010). For many (especially rural Senegalese citizens), French is simply not the language that they use on a daily basis: it is not relevant to their lives or livelihoods. As Naumann and Wolf (2001) argue, '… using French as the only teaching language constitutes a major handicap for most students, and especially in primary education' (p. 374). Yet, while Naumann and Wolf go on to suggest that public debate on the incorporation of (African) mother-tongue languages in primary education is 'practically taboo' (p. 374), research in 2002 revealed that 87 per cent of the Senegalese supported the introduction of national languages[2] into the formal education system, with 37 per cent believing that education should be delivered using national languages (Diallo 2011: 208). Reasons for these responses included 'pedagogical benefits, effective communication, and language and cultural maintenance' (ibid.).

Another key challenge in terms of improving the quality of education concerns the inadequate conditions of schools themselves, with regional disparities in school conditions a defining feature of the system (Boubacar and Francois 2007). Many schools, especially in rural and remote areas lack running water, electricity and working latrines. Inadequate amounts of teaching and learning resources also negatively impact the quality of education. Overcrowding in some schools has also been highlighted as a problem affecting educational quality (DeStefano et al. 2009). Frequent disruptions due to teachers and students striking, festivals, teacher absenteeism etc. reduce the time available for learning and disturb the pedagogical flow of the classroom, ultimately affecting quality.

Teacher quality, inextricably connected to the quality of pre-service and in-service training, as well as availability of teaching resources and working conditions, is another key challenge for the Senegalese education system. As the education system has expanded over the past 15 years (i.e. through the construction of new facilities), the need for teachers has increased tremendously, leading to the practice, begun in the mid-1990s of hiring 'volunteer' teachers, who lack formal teaching qualifications. Such teachers would receive a basic six-month pre-service training before entering the classroom, and would receive lower salaries than certified teachers (Marphatia et al. 2010b). A controversial reform in the late 1990s, also intended to speed up the entry of teachers into the system, was the reduction in the formal teacher training programme from four years to three months(!), although this has been subsequently changed to the current requirement of a six-month pre-service training programme that all teachers must complete (ibid.).

Ultimately, DeStefano et al. (2009) outline six paths by which to improve the quality of education:

- Meeting training needs of teachers who were hastily hired and who are serving as 'voluntaries' or 'vacataires', in particular the large backlog of teachers waiting to get the equivalent of their basic pre-service training.
- Provide training that works more closely and systematically with teachers on how they manage their classrooms and deliver instruction.
- Provide training for school directors and principals that enable them to act as on-site pedagogical supports to teachers in their schools.
- Improve middle school curriculum and eventually to make it aligned with the new elementary curriculum which is competency-based.
- Improve local governance and better define roles for parents and community members in managing school improvements that move beyond concerns for the physical plant.
- Improve the management of academic time, including increasing the total number of hours in the school year, limiting the number of disruptions and closures, monitoring teacher attendance and maximizing teaching time in each school day (p. 10)

Non-formal education

Since gaining political sovereignty from France in 1960, non-formal education (NFE) has come to play an important role in adult literacy and basic education training in Senegal, particularly for women and marginalized youth. Government, donors and a range of transnational, national and local non-governmental organizations (NGOs) have been involved with the funding, design and delivery of non-formal educational programmes and activities in the country, with the latter playing an arguably stronger and more coherent role, particularly since the early 1990s when a policy of government–civil society partnership[3] was adopted that emphasized the service provision roles of NGOs (Diagne 2008; Nordveit 2008).

A ten-year literacy policy was adopted in 1993 that aimed to reduce the illiteracy rate by 5 per cent per year (Nordveit 2008; Shiohata 2010). Key government–civil society literacy projects initiated in Senegal have included: the CIDA supported *Projet d'appui au plan d'action*/Project to Support the Action Plan for NFE, or PAPA; the World Bank supported *Project alphabétization priorité femmes*/Project for Promoting Literacy among Women, or PAPF; the GTZ supported *Projet d'alphabétisation des élus et notables locaux*/Project for Promoting Literacy for Village Leaders and Local Dignitaries, or PADEN and *Alpha Femme* and; the Government of Senegal supported *Programme d'alphabétisation intensive du Sénégal*/Programme for Intensive Literacy Training in Senegal, or PAIS (Care and Cherry 2006). By 2000, over one million individuals had completed some form of literacy class (Ministry of Education 2000: 27, cited in Shiohata 2010: 247); however, evaluations have cast doubt on the effectiveness of literacy programmes, with some arguing that the central problem is one of language and specifically the differences between the language(s) used at home and that in formal schools (French) and that in NFE programmes (indigenous or national languages) (Shiohata 2010).

Emerging in the national context of the first wave of educational decentralization policies in the 1990s and the global context of the Education for All movement, basic community schools (ecoles communautaires de bases) or 'ECBs' in common parlance, remain a key feature of the non-formal education landscape in Senegal (Clemons and Yerende 2009; Clemons and Vogt 2004). Recognizing the need for lower-cost, relevant alternatives to the formal education system, ECBs are the products of public–private partnerships first established in the 1990s by three key NGOs: Association Pour Le Développement De L'éducation de la Formation en Afrique (ADEF) (1993); Action Aid (1994), and Plan International (1996) (Miller-Grandvaux and Yoder 2002). Since then a range of local and transnational NGOs have entered into partnership with the government to run hundreds of ECBs across the country, (Clemons and Yerende 2009: 419). Of all the basic education schools available to Senegalese youth, ECBs account for approximately two per cent (Diarra et al. 2000; Miller-Grandvaux and Yoder 2002, cited in Clemons and Yerende 2009: 419). ECBs are financed either by the NGOs running them or through the CIDA-funded Projet d'appui au Plan d'Action (PAPA). The Ministry of Culture is responsible for the governance of ECBs (and other forms of NFE and adult education), including 'orientation, motivation, data collection, planning, co-ordination, monitoring and evaluation, and technical assistance' (ibid.).

The ECB movement has several key aims: 1) to develop an educational alternative; 2) to counteract the quantitative and qualitative limitations of the formal sector; 3) to promote community development; 4) to institutionalize the use of national languages; 5) to disengage the state from local educational efforts; and 6) to motivate untapped support for development activities in the field (Republique du Senegal 1997, cited in Clemons and Yerende 2009: 419).

ECBs offer a four-year cycle of basic education, with a curriculum that focuses on building practical skills and promoting community development (Miller-Grandvaux and Yoder 2002: A-10). The dominant use of local languages in ECBs is a further distinguishing feature of these schools relative to formal schools. In theory, students completing the ECB cycle are able to pass into the formal public school system (ibid.). As locally-rooted and run schools, ECBs tend to be smaller than regular public schools, and are managed by committees of parents and village elders who are responsible for the construction, maintenance and management of the schools, as well as paying teacher salaries with money from local income generating activities (Clemons and Yerende 2009: 419).

The non-governmental organization, Tostan has been an important actor in the non-formal education sector in Senegal since 1991, providing problem, literacy and human rights-based educational programmes for adult learners, particularly rural women (Gillespie and Melching 2010). Tostan's Community Empowerment Project is based on a holistic approach to social change, targeting village-level governance, education, health, environment and economic sectors and 'addresses the cross-cutting issues of child protection, early childhood development, female genital cutting, child/forced marriage and the empowerment of women and girls' (UNESCO 2013).

Post-secondary education

There are a variety of public and private tertiary education institutions in Senegal, including four public and three private universities.[4] There are approximately 90 private tertiary institutions operating in Senegal, offering programmes in accounting, business, tourism, communication and ICT programmes, and enroling 27 per cent of higher education students (World Bank 2011: 2). Enrolments in university have increased from 59,400 in 2005 to 98,000 in 2010, representing a 15 per cent annual growth rate (ibid.). In terms of equity in access, women constitute 33 per cent of the total university enrolment (ibid.).

There are a number of challenges facing the higher education sub-sector in Senegal, including those related to supply, quality, relevance and equity. First, the system lacks an adequate supply capacity to meet demand for places in universities and other post-secondary training facilities (World Bank 2011). A second issue is the low internal efficiency in the higher education system, particularly given high repetition and low survival rates, often linked with quality and relevance concerns (Boccanfuso et al. 2012; World Bank 2011). Efficiency problems and higher professor salaries in the sub-sector are compounded by the growth in student subsidies, which has affected the ability of government to adequately fund the core functions of the universities, ultimately affecting the quality of education or the ability of the government to channel resources to improving quality (World Bank 2011: 3). A further challenge concerns equity, and specifically persistent inequalities in resource allocation: 'Studies in 2004 and 2005 showed that students in the top 50 per cent of income groups received 4.3 times more education subsidies than students in the bottom 50 per cent' (World Bank 2011: 4). And finally, concerns have been raised about mismatch between the types of programmes students are enroling in, labour market trends and the needs of the economy (World Bank 2011). For example enrolments in science, applied science, technology and medicine decreased 10 per cent between 1991 and 2008, with available spaces in such programmes not able to meet student demand. Meanwhile enrolments in arts and social sciences have boomed (ibid. 2).

While PDEF has focused primarily on increasing access and improving the quality of basic education, it also details reforms intended to improve access to and quality higher education, with the latter dominantly defined in relation to the labour market outcomes of graduates. Between 2000 and 2005 government spending on higher education rose at a steady pace concomitant with increases in public funding for basic education (Boccanfuso et al. 2012).

Higher education reforms under PDEF have included the construction of regional university centres to help meet demand and reduce the pressure on the country's two main universities: Cheikh Anta Diop in Dakar and Gaston Berger in Saint Louis; however, the first of these regional university centres did not open until 2007 and overcrowding remains a problem (Boccanfuso et al. 2012: 7; Ritter 2011). A second set of reforms targeting quality improvements in higher education included a range of actions: improving the use of technology in classrooms; enhancements to libraries and information systems; additional research funding support and; a realignment of fields of specialization (technical and non-technical) to better match the needs of the labour market (République du Sénégal, cited in Boccanfuso et al. 2012: 7).

Most recently and modeled after the European Union's Bologna Process, Senegal has been working with its counterparts in the WAEMU to integrate and harmonize higher education across the countries. The reforms LDM have been funded by the WAEMU (US$5.8 million), are co-ordinated by the UNESCO regional office in Dakar, and include the following actions:

'to establish a system made up of three levels "bachelor-master-doctorate", an organization of teaching in semesters and teaching units, and the implementation of credit and the delivery of an appendix describing the degree' (UNESCO 2014). While the LMD has been widely lauded by multilateral institutions, including UNESCO, particularly as part of the internationalization of higher education agenda, the changes have met with some resistance on the part of students who feel that they have not been adequately informed of the changes and feel unsupported as they attempt to navigate the new system (Ritter 2011).

Concluding remarks

It is clear that the Senegalese Government, working with donors and the non-governmental sector has made progress in terms of improving the capacity and management of the formal and non-formal education systems; however, equally clear are the significant challenges that lie ahead in terms of achieving continued expansion (as per policy objectives) alongside improvements to quality, especially in the primary and middle/secondary sub-sectors. Moreover, the bottleneck that is seen at the post-secondary level, caused by insufficient supply relative to demand, is a growing concern for the Government of Senegal. At the time of writing, the Senegalese government, relevant ministries, civil society and donors recognize that the biggest obstacle to successful reform towards quality education for all is not the quantity of resources; rather, it is the capacity of the system to use existing resources efficiently and effectively.

Notes

1 Programme Décennal de l'Éducation et de la Formation.
2 A Constitutional amendment in 1971 reaffirmed French as the official language of Senegal, but formally established six 'national languages': Diola, Malinke, Pulaar, Serrere, Soninke and Wolof. In 2001, a further change was made that would allow any indigenous language to become an 'officially recognized language', if it was codified (Diallo 2011). By 2007, the number of recognized national languages jumped to 17, although these languages remain peripheral to official spaces, including the formal education system in Senegal (Diallo 2010).
3 As Nordveit describes, 'In Senegal, the approach was called partnership

(le partenariat) or, more commonly, faire-faire, literally "to make do," indicating that the state "made" the civil society associations "do" something' (2008: 183).
4 Public universities include, Cheikh Anta Diop (Dakar); Gaston Berger (Saint-Louis); Ziguinchor (Ziguinchor); and, Alioune Diop (Thies). Private universities include, Suffolk University Dakar Campus (Dakar); Dakar Bourguiba (Dakar); and, Universite du Sahel (Dakar).

References

Aslett-Rydbjerg, C. (2003). *Inclusive Education – Early Lessons Learned from Senegal L'Étude de Faisabilité – Éducation Spéciale et Intégratrice.* NDF, No 306. Washington, DC

Boccanfuso, D., Larouche, A. and Trandafir, M. (2012). *Quality of Higher Education and the Labor Market in Developing Countries: Evidence from an Education Reform in Senegal. Working Paper 11–17.* Sherbrooke, Quebec: Groupe de Recherche en Économie et Développement International.

Boubacar, N. and Francois, R. (2007). *Country Profile Prepared for the Education for All* Global Monitoring Report 2007: Strong Foundations: Early Childhood.

Care and Cherry, S. (2006). *Civil Society Participation and the Governance of Educational Systems in the Context of Sector-Wide Approaches to Basic Education: Senegal.* Toronto: Ontario Institute for Studies in Education, University of Toronto.

Clemons, A. and Vogt, C. (2004). 'Theorizing, restructuring and rethinking nonformal education in East and West African communities'. *Current Issues in Comparative Education,* 6 (2): 88–99.

Clemons, A. and Yerende, E. (2009). 'Interrelationships of non-formal mother tongue education and citizenship in Guinea and Senegal'. *International Journal of Bilingual Education and Bilingualism,* 12 (4): 415–27.

DeStefano, J., Lynd, M. R. and Thornton, B. (2009). *The Quality of Basic Education in Senegal: A Review: Final report,* pp. 1–105. Washington, DC: USAID/Center for Collaboration and the Future of Schooling.

Diagne, A. W. (2008). *Case Study: The Costs and Financing for Reducing Illiteracy in Senegal.* Paris: UNESCO.

Diallo, I. (2010). *The Politics of National Languages in Postcolonial Senegal.* New York: Cambria Press.

—(2011). 'To understand lessons, think through your own languages'. An analysis of narratives in support of the introduction of indigenous languages in the education system in Senegal. *Language Matters,* 42 (2): 207–30.

Diarra, D., Fall, M., Gueye, P., Mara, M. and Marchand, J. (2000). *Les Ecoles Communautaires de Base au Sénégal.* Paris: Institut International de planification de l'éducation (IIEP)/UNESCO.

Fall, B. (2007). *ICT in Education in Senegal*. Washington, DC: InfoDev.

Gillespie, D. and Melching, M. (2010). 'The transformative power of democracy and human rights education in nonformal education: The case of Tostan'. *Adult Education Quarterly*, 60 (5): 477–98.

Global Partnership for Education (2014). *Senegal: Overview*. Available from http://www.globalpartnership.org/country/senegal (accessed 18 March 2014).

Government of Canada (2012). *International Education: A Key Driver of Canada's Future Prosperity*. Available from Foreign Affairs and International Trade Canada http://www.international.gc.ca/education/assets/pdfs/ies_report_rapport_sei-eng.pdf (accessed 2 October 2012).

Marphatia, A. A., Legault, E., Edge, K. and Archer, D. (2010). *The Role of Teachers in Learning in Burundi, Malawi, Senegal and Uganda: Great Expectations, Little Support*. London: Action Aid/Institute of Education, University of London.

Mbow, P. (2009). *Secularism, Religious Education and Human Rights in Senegal: Working paper 09–007*. Working paper series. Evanstan, IL: Institute for the Study of Islamic Thought in Africa (ISITA), The Roberta Buffet Center for International and Comparative Studies, Northwestern University.

Miller-Grandvaux, Y. and Yoder, K. (2002). *A Literature Review of Community Schools in Africa*. Support for Analysis and Research in Africa (SARA) Project. United States Agency for International Development (USAID). Washington, DC.

Naumann, J. and Wolf, P. (2001). 'The performance of African primary education systems: Critique and new analysis of PASEC data for Senegal'. *Prospects*, 31 (3): 373–91.

Ndiaye, M. (2006). 'Partnerships in the education system of Senegal'. *Prospects*, 36 (2): 223–49.

Ndoye, M. (1997). 'Senegal: Defining and implementing priorities in the education sector'. *Prospects*, 27 (4): 609–17.

Ngom, F. (2002). 'Linguistic resistance in the Murid speech community in Senegal'. *Journal of Multilingual and Multicultural Development*, 23 (3): 214–26.

Nordtveit, B. H. (2008). 'Producing literacy and civil society: The case of Senegal'. *Comparative Education Review*, 52 (2): 175–98.

Republic of Senegal (2013). *National Strategy for Economic and Social Development (2013–2017)*. Senegal: Poverty Reduction Strategy Paper. Washington, DC: International Monetary Fund.

République du Sénégal (2003). *Programme de developpement de l'education et de la formation (Education Pour Tous) [P.D.E.F/E.P.T]*. Dakar, Senegal: Ministère de L'Education.

—(2006). *Senegal: Poverty Reduction Strategy Paper*. Available from http://siteresources.worldbank.org/INTPRS1/Resources/Senegal-PRSP(Sept2007).pdf (accessed 20 August 2012).

—(2013). *Programme d'Amélioration de la Qualité, de l'Equité et de la Transparence (PAQUET): Secteur Education Formation 2013–2025*. Dakar, Senegal: République du Sénégal.

République du Sénégal MEN and PAPA (1997). *Les Problèmes Lies à la Qualité de L'enseignement dans le Non-formel*. Dakar, Senegal: Projet d'Appui au Plan d'Action.

République du Sénégal/Ministere de l'education de l'enseignement technique et de la professionalle (2008). *Programme decennal de l'èducation et de la formation: Rapport national sur la situation de l'education 2007*. Dakar, Senegal: Direction de la Planification et de la reforme de l'education (DPRE).

Ritter, J. (2011). 'Senegal: Radical Reforms for Higher Education'. *World University News*. Available from http://www.universityworldnews.com/article.php?story=20110917101401318 (accessed 8 February 2014).

Sane, S. (2010). 'Decolonization and questions of language: The case of Senegal'. *Hagar*, 9 (2): 181–7.

Shiohata, M. (2010). 'Exploring the literacy environment: A case study from urban Senegal'. *Comparative Education Review*, 54 (2): 243–69.

—(2012). *Global Monitoring Report: Youth and Skills: Putting Education to Work*. Paris: UNESCO.

—(2013). *The Tostan Community Empowerment Program*. Available from http://www.unesco.org/uil/litbase/?menu=4&programme=86 (accessed 15 February 2014).

—(2014). *Project to Support the 'Bachelor – Master – Doctorate' Reform by Building Capacities of Universities through IT platforms*. Available from http://www.unesco.org/new/en/dakar/education/higher-education/project-to-support-bachelor-master-and-doctorate-reform-through-it/ (accessed 8 February 2014).

World Bank (2007). *International Development Association and International Finance Cooperation Country Assistance Strategy for the Republic of Senegal for the Period FY07-FY10*. Washington, DC: World Bank.

—(2009). *Project Appraisal Document of the Education for All – Fast Track Initiative in the Amount of US$81 Million to the Government of the Republic of Senegal for a Proposed Catalytic Fund Grant*. Washington, DC: World Bank.

—(2011). *Project Appraisal Document on a Proposed Credit of SDR 63.9 Million to the Republic of Senegal for the Tertiary Education Governance and Financing for Results Project*. Washington, DC: World Bank.

Sierra Leone: An Overview

Kingsley Banya

Introduction

Once referred to as the 'Athens of West Africa', Sierra Leone boasted the first school for boys (CMS Grammar School) founded in 1845; the first school for girls (Annie Walsh Memorial School founded in 1849; and the first tertiary education institution [Fourah Bay College] founded in 1827). Today Sierra Leone's educational system is in desperate need of reform; for example in 2008, students' performance in the Basic Education Certificate Examination (BECE) and the West Africa Senior School Certificate Examination (WASSCE) were the worst in the history of public examinations in the country and in West Africa. At the University of Sierra Leone, Fourah Bay College, final examinations had to be cancelled due to the lack of paper to write the examinations. This provided the backdrop in which the current chapter is written. The paper is divided into three major areas: viz: background of the country; the various structures of the educational system, and their drawbacks; and future trends. This empirical research paper also draws on the Constitution of Sierra Leone and other supporting legislative and policy documents including: The Education Act (2004b), The Government White Paper on Education (2010a), The Local Government Act (2004c), The Education Sector Plan 2007–15, The National Policy for Technical and Vocational Education and Training (TVET) (2010b), and the National Policy for Teacher Training and Development (2010c).

Context

Sierra Leone is a small West African nation bordered to the west by the Atlantic Ocean, to the north and north-east by Guinea, and to the south and south-east by Liberia. Sierra Leone is richly endowed with natural resources and fertile lands. Its mineral wealth includes deposits of diamonds, bauxite, rutile (titanium dioxide), iron ore and chromite. The latest population of the country is estimated to be 5.3 million with around 38 per cent of the population living in urban areas. There are a considerable number of diverse ethno-linguistic groups. The dominant ethnic groups include the Temne (35 per cent), Mende (31 per cent), Limba (8 per cent), and Kono (5 per cent). In addition, 2 per cent of the population is Kriole (or 'Krio'), an ethnic group comprised of descendants of freed slaves from the Americas who were settled in the capital of Freetown in the late eighteenth and early nineteenth centuries. Life expectancy in Sierra Leone is approximately 55 years, and the infant mortality rate is 80 deaths per 1,000 births. Literacy rate among the total population is 31 per cent, with the average Sierra Leonean completing 7 years of schooling.[1]

Despite rich natural resources, Sierra Leone is an extremely poor nation with tremendous income inequality. There is also a high level of official corruption that is impeding the country's development (more on this later). Nearly half of the working-age population engages in small-scale agriculture. Manufacturing consists of the processing of raw materials and light manufacturing for the domestic market. Alluvial diamond mining remains the major source of hard currency earnings, accounting for nearly half of Sierra Leone's exports. The 2010 GDP totalled USD 4.8 billion (ranked 161 in the world), with a GDP per capita of USD 900. Agriculture comprises 49 per cent of the GDP, industry 31 per cent, and services 21 per cent (2005 est.). The population below the poverty line is 70.5 per cent. The majority of people are living in abject poverty. Per capita gross national income (GNI) of US$320 in 2008 is much lower than the average of US$1082 for sub-Saharan African countries or $564 for low-income countries. About two-thirds of the working-age population engages in subsistence agriculture.[2]

Sierra Leone's history partially accounts for its troubles. In 1787, the British founded Freetown as a base to stop the Atlantic slave trade. Later in the nineteenth century, British forces conquered the inland tribes and organized a state comprised of different peoples, speaking 23 languages and dialects. As part of the trend towards formal independence of former colonial countries, Sierra Leone was granted independence in 1961. Reaction against corrupt ruling elites was a contributing factor in the country's 11-year civil war.[3] From 1992 to early 2001, civil war plagued the country, and many citizens fled or sought refuge in the capital, Freetown, the so-called internally displaced persons. For much of the war, anarchy prevailed and massive human rights abuses were committed. Much of the conflict spawned from an unequal distribution of natural resources, money and power, but it was also fuelled to a great extent by the illicit trade in 'blood diamonds'.[4]

In recent years, the country has slowly begun to recover from the conflict that decimated infrastructure, halted agricultural production, almost destroyed the educational system, and most important of all, crippled the confidence and welfare of the population. Large numbers of school structures were destroyed resulting in thousands of children with no schools to attend for a period of almost ten years. At least 31 per cent, Sierra Leone's adult literacy rate is one of the lowest in the world. The provision of basic education and increasing access, especially in the rural areas, are key challenges for the government. In many rural communities there is a serious absence of basic essentials of life and with high unemployment there is little incentive for parents to send their children to school. Also, in rural communities with a functioning primary school, it is estimated that over 50 per cent of the teachers are unqualified and untrained. In many of these schools, there is serious overcrowding resulting in high pupil/teacher ratios of 69 to 1. In 2004 the country ranked last – 177 of 177 nations in the United Nations Development Program (UNDP) Human Development Index (due to low literacy rates, high maternal and infant mortality rates and low life expectancy). By 2010, it has risen to 158 to 169 countries on the Index.[5]

The youths (defined by the National Youth Policy (2007) as people between the ages of 15–35) constitute about 34 per cent of the population and are mostly illiterate (about 40 per cent),[6] unemployed and unemployable (about 70 per cent) because of a lack of employable skills and little working experience (conditions compounded by the long civil war).[7] The provision of well-designed, accessible, credible and labour-market and employment-focused TVET constitutes one of the most strategic programmes for social and economic development in Sierra Leone. The issue of youth unemployment ought to be taken seriously. For in the past two decades, civil wars in three African countries (Sierra Leone, Liberia, and Ivory Coast) were partially fuelled by chronic youth unemployment or underemployment. The youth population provided the 'folder' for various unscrupulous politicians to further their agendas. All over the continent, the challenges facing young people and how to engage them into productive lives are tasking governments, as seen in the Maghreb, North Africa.

Educational structure

A brief description of each sector follows with some salient points:

Primary level

After the war in 2002, significant progress has been made in increasing access to education. Primary school enrolments have increased from about 400,000 in the late 1980s to about 660,000 at the end of the war in 2001/2. This is part of an effort by government to meet the Constitutions Declaration that 'all children in Sierra Leone have a right to free compulsory basic education at primary and junior secondary school levels'. Since then, primary enrolments have more than doubled reaching 1.3 million in 2006/7.[8]

The White Paper of 2010 mandated a new structure of education; the main changes to the existing system were the inclusion of compulsory pre-school for children aged 3–5 and the extension by one year of secondary level education. Previously, compulsory education had been 9 years in length – 6 years primary and 3 years of junior secondary. The current system of education envisions 12 years of compulsory schooling – 3 years preschool, 6 years primary and 3 years of junior secondary. Primary education is 6 years in duration and for children aged 6–11 years old. It is free and compulsory; although hidden costs make schooling expensive. This level of education emphasizes the acquisition of literacy, numeracy, communication, and critical thinking skills. There are no entry requirements and it is open to all children of appropriate age. It forms the first part of basic education. It is mainly provided in formal primary schools, but there are non-formal providers of primary education for older children and youth. Pre-school education is for children aged 3–5 years old. It is supposed to be free and compulsory. According to the Government White Paper (2010a), every primary school shall have a pre-school wing attached. Pre-school education will support the all-round development of the child and lay the foundation for future learning success.

Secondary education

Similar to the primary school, the secondary enrolment has doubled since 2002. Since 2010 structural changes have been introduced to secondary education as follows:

Junior secondary education follows primary education and lasts for 3 years. It is compulsory, and shall be made progressively free. It is open to all students who have acquired basic literacy and numeracy skills determined by passing the National Primary School Examination (NPSE). The junior secondary school level provides basic general education and preparation for general or technical and vocational upper secondary school education. At the end of junior secondary school all students will sit for the Basic Education Certificate Examination (BECE). Junior secondary education marks the end of compulsory education.

Senior secondary school education follows the junior secondary school level. There are two types of senior secondary education – one that offers general education (SSS) and another offers technical and vocational education and training (SSTV). Senior secondary education is open to students who meet the government-stipulated requirements in the BECE. They can choose subject areas that allow them to specialize and prepare for tertiary level courses. Students at the end of the senior secondary level sit either for the West African Senior Secondary Certificate Examinations (WASSCE) or the National Vocational Qualifications Examination (NVE). Despite this, many school-aged children are still out of school; according to the DHS 2008, 26 per cent of children aged 10–14 have had no formal education, and there are disparities with respect to gender, rural-urban residence, region and wealth.[9]

Post-secondary, non-tertiary education programmes straddle the boundary between senior secondary and tertiary education. The entry requirement is that students have at least a BECE certificate. Some may have attempted WASSCE, but did not have the minimum criteria necessary to enter tertiary level programmes. These programmes are typically more specialized than what is offered at the senior secondary level. Such programmes are typically offered at Technical Vocational Institutes, Agricultural Institutes, Junior College of Technology, and Polytechnics and lead towards the award of a certificate.

Tertiary education

Tertiary education follows the senior secondary level. Tertiary Education is provided by different types of institutions, colleges, polytechnics, and universities. Until recently, private providers were not actively encouraged to establish tertiary institutions. Tertiary education is offered by polytechnics, professional colleges, and universities. Minimum requirement for entry into tertiary education is set by institutions, but a prerequisite is WASSCE. Tertiary education programmes lead to the award of diplomas, certificates, and degrees. Teacher education occurs at the tertiary level and is offered by polytechnics and universities. In addition to teaching, universities are also involved in research.

Teacher education

One of the major problems with education in the country is the preponderance of unqualified teachers, i.e. teachers teaching at a level higher than appropriate for their academic qualification and teachers with no formal pedagogical training. Since teachers are crucial for providing students with the necessary skills and knowledge to function appropriately in society, it follows that the literacy rate is so low. In the school year 2004/5 there were around 19,300 teachers in primary school and 9,500 teachers in secondary schools. Female teachers make up around 30 per cent of the primary and 20 per cent of the Junior secondary school teaching force.[10] The training of teachers has traditionally taken place in teacher colleges. Before the enactment of the Polytechnics Act of 2001, there were five teacher colleges for the training of teachers. There has been a low turnout of high quality primary and secondary school teachers. Currently, it is estimated that 65 per cent of teachers are untrained and unqualified (Government of Sierra Leone 2007).

A gap exists in the teaching expertise in the key subjects and skills that are needed to be taught in the 6–3–3–4 system; that is six years of primary school, three years of junior secondary school, three years of senior secondary school, and four years of tertiary school. The Act specified that all of these colleges (with the exception of Bo Teachers College) will be eventually transformed into polytechnics by merging with TVET institutions. The Bo Teachers College has been incorporated into the School of Education of Njala University under the 2004 Universities Act. The number of graduates from these institutions was relatively low up until 2000. This was mainly due to the weak absorptive capacity of the institutions and low interest in the teaching profession resulting from poor conditions of service. The major incentive for entry into the profession has been the granting of scholarships. The two universities, three polytechnics and two teacher colleges that train teachers in Sierra Leone are all government owned. The recent Universities Act provides for private universities, so private institutions for training teachers in the future will be possible. Until very recently only one teacher college offered a Secondary Higher Teachers Certificates (HTC-S) programme, but today all teacher colleges and polytechnics can offer the programme. The certification of pre-service teachers is the responsibility of the National Council for Technical, Vocational and other Academic Awards (NCTVA).[11]

Many graduates of teacher training institutions do not end up in schools and a significant number of those who do end up in the classroom stay in the teaching profession for less than four years. Due to the poor conditions of service and working conditions in schools for teachers, young qualified and trained teachers are always leaving the profession. Many who exit the teaching profession head to the police force to train as officers or for non-governmental organizations (NGOs) which they believe offer better conditions of service. Additionally, many teachers who graduate from institutions in the capital and district headquarters town do not return to their home areas to take up employment. The consequence of this migration is that rural areas are deprived of trained and qualified teachers. In addition, teacher management issues such as recruitment, deployment, transfer, replacement, promotion, and supervision are carried out in an ad hoc manner, and there is no central department responsible for these tasks. There is also the issue of non-formal management training for institutional heads leading to weaknesses in management, structure and inefficient delivery. Better deployment and placement procedures are also needed to alleviate the acute shortages of qualified teachers in the rural district areas. Because teachers can apply directly to their schools of choice, and the incentives to work in rural areas are few, the better-qualified teachers tend to work in larger towns. A disproportionate number of community teachers work in rural schools. Problems with late payment of salaries, poor housing conditions and low salaries compared to the private sector have all contributed to a lack of motivation among teachers, possibly leading to high rates of absenteeism and lateness.

In a 2010 policy document, National Policy on Teacher Training and Development, the government indicated the main objective of teacher education, viz: 'to produce professional teachers who have the subject knowledge and understanding, practical skills and competencies, and professional ethics to teach' (Government of Sierra Leone 2010c: 9). In order to accomplish this objective, the government promised to do the following:

- Strengthen the monitoring, supervision, and control mechanisms of teacher training and development and the roles of partners;
- ensure that teacher education institutions are well-resourced;
- develop guidelines for in-service teacher training and distance education;
- support the implementation of the *Code of Conduct for Teachers and other Educational Personnel* with appropriate sanctions against those that violate the code;

- establish and adequately support the Teaching Service Commission which will be responsible for all aspects related to teacher management; and,
- create partnerships with local communities, national and international agencies in support of teacher education and development (ibid.).[12]

These are lofty goals, but there is real doubt whether they can be implemented with the high level of corruption in the country and the lack of critical human resources. As part of globalization and marketization, the Universities Act 2005 permitted private tertiary institutions to establish universities. At the same time the government undertook to provide grants in aid to eligible students at public tertiary institutions, with priority given to groups of students in the following categories:

- Unqualified teachers in rural schools enroled in a distance education teacher certificate programme;
- female students in the sciences and engineering;
- students enroled in needs areas, Language Arts, Early Childhood Education; and,
- students with special needs.

There is a general belief that these are platitudes that cannot be implemented for several reasons, including resolve to carry them through.

Technical and Vocational Education and Training (TVET)

As part of tertiary education, the 2004 New Education policy targeted TVET as a critical component of the system of education and placed some emphasis on acquisition of relevant and self-reliant skills. The end of the civil conflict created greater needs for an impetus to technical and vocational skills training for the large number of young people who could not be educated or were unable to continue their education in the formal mode due to demographic, social, economic and related reasons. The post-war contraction of the labour market employment coupled with the transformation of economic systems has resulted in a demand for skilled personnel with technical and vocational qualifications.

Thus, it is becoming increasingly apparent that issues such as peace, national security, poverty reduction, and overall national development depend on the quality of acquired skills and the dynamics of the labour and productive environment in which the skills can be applied. TVET, particularly for thousands of the unemployed and unemployable youth in the country form the hub around which all of these issues revolve. Unfortunately, quality, standards, and usability of the skills obtained in most of the existing vocational and technical training institutions and centres both for employment and for the realist entrepreneurship cannot be assured. There are several factors responsible for this state of affairs:

- Poor staffing (for example, out of the 2,057 training and administrative staff in 191 institutions only 28 per cent were professionally qualified, while 50 per cent of the staff were holders of trade certificates).
- Low to zero entry qualifications for the students enroled in the institutes and centres (only 20.4 per cent of the institutions had a formal entry requirement).

The Accreditation and Certification of graduates of formal post-basic TVET institutions is undertaken by the National Council for Technical Vocational

Table 27.1 A summary of the formal education structure

Level	Name of the education programme	Minimum entrance requirements	Main diplomas, qualifications or certificates awarded at end	Official entrance age	Duration in years	Part of Compulsory Education
Early Childhood Education	Pre-Primary	3 years old	n.a.	3	1–3	Y
Basic Education	Primary	6 years old	n.a.	6	6	Y
	Lower Secondary	Pass NPSE	BECE	12	3	Y
Upper Secondary	Upper Secondary	BECE	WASSCE	15	3	N
Post-Secondary, Non-tertiary	Primary teachers' certificate	BECE	Teacher Certificate (TC)	15+	1	N
	Technical Vocational Institute	WASSCE or NVQ	Ordinary National diploma (OND)	18	2	N
Tertiary	University	WASSCE	Bachelor's degree	18	4	N
	Secondary teachers' certificate	WASSCE	Higher teacher certificate (HTC)	18	3	N
	Polytechnic	WASSCE	Higher National diploma (HND)	18	2	N

Source: Government of Sierra Leone – National Education Policy 2010

and other Academic Awards (NCTVA). But it is not clear if and how the NCTVA provides services to the numerous sub-tertiary and private technical and vocational skills training institutions, and there is no indication of how the training obtained in such centers is validated (MEYS 2008). To remedy the situation, the government of Sierra Leone has entered into partnership agreements with several UN agencies, national and international NGOs, including United Nations Educational Scientific Cultural Organization (UNESCO); Department of Foreign International Development, United Kingdom (DFID-UK); United Nations Development Program (UNDP); African Development Bank, (AfDB); United Nations Industrial Development Organization (UNIDO); International Labor Organization (ILO); Food and Agricultural Organization, (FAO); United States of America International Development (USAID), and World Health Organization (WHO).

Gender education

In 2000, all 192 United Nations member states adopted the UN Millennium Declaration, a new global partnership to reduce extreme poverty in all of its forms by half by 2015. By 2001, agreement was reached on eight goals supported by 21 quantifiable targets and 60 indicators through which progress could be measured. For the purposes of this paper, Goal 2: universal primary education key target: ensure that by 2015, children everywhere (boys and girls alike) will be able to complete a full course of primary school) and Goal 3: promote gender equality and empower women (eliminate gender disparity in primary and secondary education, preferably by 2005, and at all levels of education no later than 2015) are pertinent. To accomplish these lofty goals, the country had identified the goal of providing six years of quality education to all children of primary school-age (6–11 years) and the over-aged who have missed out, including those with special needs.

Non-formal education

Non-formal education (NFE) includes all organized educational and training activities and processes outside the formal education system that are designed to meet the learning needs of out-of-school children, youth and adults. These include adult and continuing education, NFE for children, skills training and apprenticeships for youths, community education, and adult literacy programmes. About 300,000 primary school-aged children are reported to be out of school due to various factors including poverty, and many of these children may not be able to enter formal schools. At 45 per cent for men and 24 per cent for women, the adult literacy rate in Sierra Leone is one of the lowest in the world. The literacy rates are much lower for rural residents.[13]

The objective of apprenticeship training and skills training is to enable learners or trainees to acquire specific occupational skills as artisans, craftsmen, technicians and technologists by working alongside skilled and experienced trainers. Out-of-school youth (between the ages of 15 and 35) are the primary targets for apprenticeship and skills training. The framework for the development of apprenticeships and skills training is set out in the 2010 National Policy on Technical and Vocational Education and Training (TVET).

The management and control of education

In addition to the Ministry of Education, Youth and Sports, various councils, commissions and boards help to manage and supervise the education system. Below is a snapshot of some of the agencies and what they are charged to do:

- *The National Commission for Basic Education* was established by Decree No. 4 of 1994 to advise, co-ordinate, monitor, evaluate, and conduct research on a basic education programme in the country.
- *The National Board of Education* – reconstituted and reactivated in March 2007; to assist the Ministry of Education in addressing challenges to education in Sierra Leone.
- *The Tertiary Education Commission* – established by the Tertiary Education Act of 2001; to advise government on all matters relating to tertiary education; fund-raising for tertiary education; vetting the budgets of tertiary education, ensuring relevance of programmes offered, ensuring equity in admission, recommending modifications in conditions of service, and ensuring parity in appointment and promotion of staff. The TEC will be responsible for the accreditation of tertiary institutions.
- *The Teaching Service Commission* shall be responsible for all matters related to teacher management and professional development.
- *The National Institute for Education Training and Research* shall be responsible for curriculum development, teacher development, and educational research. NIETAR shall incorporate the National Curriculum Research and Development Centre, and the National Council for Technical, Vocational and other Academic Awards.
- *The Non-Formal Education Council* was established by an act of Parliament

in 2004. It is responsible for advising on all matters related to literacy and non-formal education programmes in Sierra Leone.
- *The National Council for Science and Technology* was established by a decision of Cabinet in 2001 as an organ providing policy guidelines relating to the development, dissemination, and application of science and technology countrywide.

It should be noted that all the above agencies report to the over-extended Ministry of Education, Youth and Sports.[13]

Ethnicity and corruption

No article on the education system of Sierra Leone is complete without reference to ethnicity and the high level of corruption in the country. One of the key legacies of imperial rule in sub-Saharan Africa (SSA) is the ethnic linguistic diversity of the states. With perhaps the exception of the Maghreb, all parts of the SSA are riddled with ethnic divisions that formally and informally affect every aspect of society. An assortment of political economy models suggests that polarized societies will be prone to competitive rent-seeking by the different groups and will have difficulty agreeing on public good like infrastructure, education, and good policies (Alesina and Drazen 1991; Alesina and Rodrik 1994; Alesina and Spoalare 1995; Alesina and Tabellini 1989; Shliefer and Vishny 1993; Throup 1985). Alesina and Drazen (1991) argue that 'society's polarization and decree of social conflict' (p. 7) are key factors underlying policy decisions. Ethnic diversity may increase polarization and thereby impede agreement about the provision of public goods. This creates positive incentives for growth-reducing policies, such as financial repression and overvalued exchange rates, which create rents for the groups in power at the expense of society at large (Easterly and Levine 1997).

The Berlin Conference of 1885 that determined the borders of modern African nations through a tragicomic sense of negotiation between European powers split up ethnic groups and exacerbated pre-existing ethno-linguistic divisions (Pakenman 1991). Ethnic diversity influences economic performance and most of this effect works indirectly through public policies, political stability, and other economic factors. Ethnic conflicts affect the economy in more subtle ways than stimulating interethnic violence. Political instability, rent-creating economic policies, and poor public good may reflect a more fundamental country characteristic. African state borders were determined by where each

European state happened to wander instead of existing ethnic borders. This resulted in the division of ethnic groups among neighbouring communities; for example, the Kissi ethnic group is found in the eastern part of three West African countries: Sierra Leone, Guinea, and Liberia. The high levels of ethnic diversity have encamped growth-impeding policies. As observed by Ake (1996),

> conflict among nationalities, ethnic groups, and communal and interest groups broke out after the independence of African nations. The resulting struggle for power was so absorbing that everything else, including government, was marginalized (p. 10).

Other scholars have pointed out that African economic decline was due to the destruction caused by 'rival kinship networks, whether of "ethnic" clientelism or its camouflage in no less clientelist "multiparty systems"' (Davidson 1992: 21). Ethnically diverse societies often give rise to policy situations formally analogous to Shleifer and Vishny's unco-ordinated bribe-takers, beyond straight bribe collection. It is common in weak multiethnic coalitions for each ethnic interest group to be allocated a ministry or area of control. These unco-ordinated ministries may each pursue a rent-seeking strategy without taking into account the effect of their actions on other groups' rents. For example, one group may impose an overvalued exchange rate and strict exchange controls on the black market. Another group may impose very low interest rates (e.g. negative in real terms) on savers for the purpose of generating rents in the form of low-interest loans for their ethnic supporters. In general, separation of powers between distinct groups can lead to 'common pool' problems (Perrson et al. 1997). Each group seizes its share of the 'pool' of rents until the pool is exhausted. The common pool problem is alleviated only if checks and balances exist that gives each group a veto over the other groups. The 'common pool' story could help explain the otherwise inexplicable phenomenon of 'killing the goose that lays the golden egg'. (p. 15) It is not uncommon to observe some activity nearly taxed out of existence in Africa, that is, taxed far beyond its profitable margin to operate (Davidson 1992).

Unfortunately, Sierra Leone is one of the most corrupt countries in the world. According to Transparency International, the country is at the bottom of the global corruption perception index with an appalling 2.5. Since 2007, the level of corruption has increased dramatically with ethnic policies. For example, 70.8 per cent of ministerial appointments in the current government come from the northern part of the country, from where the President hails. The Minister of Education and his deputy come from the same area as the President. As recently as 2014, in the midst of a severe Ebola outbreak, that has killed more than a thousand people and infected countless others with the disease, the Ernest Bai Koroma University was created by the current President in his home town despite the lack of need for another white elephant.

Conclusion

The ten-plus years of war resulted in a major setback for education in the country. Hundreds of schools were destroyed and thousands of students lost a decade of schooling. Despite the terrible upheaval, immediately after the war the government embarked on an ambitious programme to rehabilitate the educational system. The government solicited external resources and expatriate services for the education sector. For example, in 2002, the government allocated US $9 million to be expended on various programmes and activities by the Ministry of Education, Science and Technology. The amount is 25 per cent of the total Highly Indebted Poor Countries (HIPC) funds available to Sierra Leone. This funding was used to rehabilitate/reconstruct 83 institutions from primary, secondary, and technical-vocational, two teachers' colleges, and five district inspectorate offices. A total of 5,500 sets of school furniture and beds were supplied to schools (The Sababu Education Project). The Ministry, in collaboration with UNICEF, Plan Sierra Leone, the Norwegian Refugee Council, and a host of other organizations undertakes various programmes in the development of education in Sierra Leone. For example, the African Development Bank assisted in procuring science equipment, materials and chemicals and technical/vocation subject equipment for schools and in rehabilitating school laboratories. UNICEF is implementing the three-year Non-Formal Primary Education Programme (NFPEP) and the Complementary Rapid Education Programme Schemes (CREPS). UNESCO supported the development of a national science and technology policy in Sierra Leone, while the United Kingdom-based NGO project known as Knowledge Aid Sierra Leone has introduced internet service to schools and colleges in the country (Ministry of Education/Government of Sierra Leone 2005).

While the government should be commended for its ambitious programmes in all educational sectors the realities are that implementation may not be possible in the current economic situation and an atmosphere of massive corruption. Heavy dependence on donor agencies will not be enough to sustain the long-term development of the country. There is a general awareness in the country that innovation and change in the educational system has a direct effect on social, economic, cultural, technological and political development, yet the level of corruption and ethnic politics may hold the country back for many years to come.

Notes

1. CIA World Factbook, http://www.cia.gov/library/publications/theworld-factbook/goes/sl.htm (accessed 2010).
2. CIA World Factbook, http://www.cia.gov/library/publications/theworld-factbook/goes/sl.htm (accessed 2010).
3. CIA World Factbook, http://www.cia.gov/library/publications/theworld-factbook/goes/sl.htm (accessed 2011).
4. See, for example: Lansana Gberie (2005), *Adinty War in West Africa – the RUF and the Destruction of Sierra Leone*, Bloomington, Indiana University Press. John L. Hirsh (2001), *Sierra Leone: Diamonds and the Struggle for Democracy*, Boulder, CO: Lynne Rienner Publishing.
5. United Nations Development Program (UNDP) 'International Human Development Indicators, Sierra Leone', http://hdr.undp.org/eu//statistics (accessed 2007).
6. Ministry of Education Youths and Sports, (2008) *National Youth Policy* (draft).
7. Government of Sierra Leone (2003), *Sierra Leone Integrated Household Survey*, SLIHS, Freetown.
8. Government of Sierra Leone (2005), S*tatistics Sierra Leone (1963–2005)*.
9. Ministry of Education and Sports (2008), *Household Survey, Freetown, Sierra Leone*.
10. Ministry of Education, Youth and Sports (2005), *Teacher Education in Sierra Leone: Freetown, Sierra Leone*.
11. GTZ (2005) *Technical and Vocational Training Centers in Sierra Leone (below TECs) Freetown* (unpublished).
12. Ministry Of Education Youth and Sports (2010), *National Policy on Teacher Training and Development, Freetown Sierra Leone*.
13. Ministry of Education, Youth and Sports (2009), *Non-formal Education in Sierra Leone. Freetown Sierra Leone*.

References

Ake, C. (1996). *Democracy and Development in Africa*. Washington, DC: The Brookings Institution.
Alesina, A. and Drazen, A. (1991). 'Why are stabilizations delayed?'. *American Economic Review*, 81 (5): 1170–88.

Alesina, A. and Rodrik, D. (1994). 'Distributive politics and economic growth'. *Quarterly Journal of Economics*, 109 (2): 465–90. Available from http://www.jstor.org/stable/2118470 (accessed 2010).

Alesina, A. and Spoalare, E. (1995). 'On the number and size of nations'. *American Economic Review*, 96 (31): 1312–20.

Alesina, A. and Tabellini, G. (1989). 'External debt, capital flight and political risk', *Journal of International Economics*, XXVII: 199–220.

Best, J. W., & Kahn, J. V. (2006). *Research in Education*. Boston, MA: Pearson.

Davidson, B. (1992). *'The Black Man's Burden: Africa and the Curse of the Nation State'*. New York: Times Books.

Easterly, W. and Levine, R. (1997). *'Africa's Growth Tragedy: Policies and Ethnic Divisions'*, Washington, DC: World Bank.

Government of Sierra Leone (2004a). *The Educational Act 2004*. Freetown: Government Printer.

—(2004b). *The Education Act 2004*. Ministry of Education, Sports. Freetown: Government Printer.

—(2004c). *The Local Education Act (2004)*. Freetown: Government Printer.

—(2007). *The Education Sector Plan 2007–2015*. Freetown: Government Printer.

—(2008a). *Ministry of Education, Youth and Sports Vocational Schools in Sierra Leone*. Freetown: Government Printer.

—(2008b). *National Youth Policy*. Freetown: Government Printer.

—(2010a). *White Paper on Education*. Freetown: Government Printer.

—(2010b). *The National Policy for Technical and Vocational Education and Training (TVET)*. Freetown: Government Printer.

—(2010c). *The National Policy for Teacher Training and Development*. Freetown: Government Printer.

Government of Sierra Leone/Ministry of Education (2005). Annual Science and Technology Report. Freetown: Government Printer.

Government of Sierra Leone/Ministry of Education, Youths and Sports (2006). *The Education Sector Plan. (2007–2015)*. Freetown: Government Printer.

Ministry of Education Youths and Sports (2008) *National Youth Policy* (draft). Sierra Leone: MEYS.

Pakenman, T. (1991). *The Scramble for Africa*. New York: Random House.

Perrson, T., Gerald, R. and Tabellini, G. (1997). 'Separation of powers and political accountability'. *Quarterly Journal of Economics*, 112 (4): 1163–202.

Shleifer, A. and Vishny, R. W. (1993). 'Corruption'. *Quarterly Journal of Economics*, 108 (3): 599–617.

Throup, D. (1985). 'The origins of Mau Mau'. *African Affairs*, 84 (336): 399–433. Published by Oxford University Press on behalf of The Royal African Society. Available from http://www.jstor.org/stable/723073 (accessed 2011).

UNDP (2004). *Human Development Index*. New York and Washington, DC: UNDP.

—(2010). *Human Development Index*. New York and Washington DC: UNDP.

Sierra Leone: Educational Trends and Futures

Kwabena Dei Ofori-Attah

Introduction

Until the arrival of missionaries in Sierra Leone in the early fifteenth century, the education of children was essentially organized by tribal leaders and groups (Kup 1961). Boys received education in the bush schools through the Poro society, while girls had theirs through the Sande society (Bledsoe 2000). Although the development of education in Sierra Leone is beset with numerous problems, the government has introduced a number of policies and partnerships that appear to revive interest in learning in Sierra Leone. The aim of this chapter is to explore the development and problems of providing quality education in Sierra Leone. In the next sections of this chapter, the organization, conceptual framework, methodology, trends and the future directions of education in the country will be examined.

The chapter begins with a brief discussion of the conceptual framework, methodology and historical development of education in Sierra Leone and ends with a discussion on the futures of the education system in the country.

Substantial research on education and development finds that education is key to the development of any country (Atteh 1996; Ofori-Attah 2006). In view of this argument, any nation that wants to develop its human and natural resources pays attention to the development of education (Haddad et al. 1990). This study is rooted in World culture theory which accounts for the spread of education throughout the world (Meyer et al. 1977; Carney et al. 2012).

Content analysis was used to collect data for this chapter. The research methodology therefore focused on analysing and interpreting recorded materials such as books, journal articles and websites (Ary et al. 2014). This approach was used because it is a method of inquiry that provided access to data relevant to the current chapter (Best and Kahn 2006).

Historical trends in educational development

The colonial education system in Sierra Leone consisted of seven years of primary education, five years of secondary education and an additional two years of education to prepare for university education (7-5-2) (Anderson and Baker 1969; Wise 1956). Elementary education was provided by both the missionaries and the government and later by the Muslims. Most of these schools were located in the urban areas along the coastal areas. By the close of the 1921/2 academic year, missionaries had established 54 elementary schools in the Colony (Freetown) mainly in the urban areas and 44 in the Protectorate, mainly in the inland and rural areas (Fyle 1981; Sumner 1963; Seddall 1874). Total enrolments in the mission schools in the Colony stood at 4,347 while the total enrolments in the mission schools in the Protectorate stood at 1,585 (Anderson and Baker 1969). By the close of the 1921/2 academic year, the Colonial government established elementary schools in the Colony with a total enrolment of 662 children and 6 primary schools in the Protectorate with a total enrolment of 352 children (Anderson and Baker 1969; Corby 1990; Kandeh 1992). The bulk of these students were children, both boys and girls, of freed African slaves (Seddall 1874).

Muslim schools or the Madrassas have a long history in Sierra Leone (Conteh 2009; Kandeh 1992). Muslims entered Freetown in large numbers from

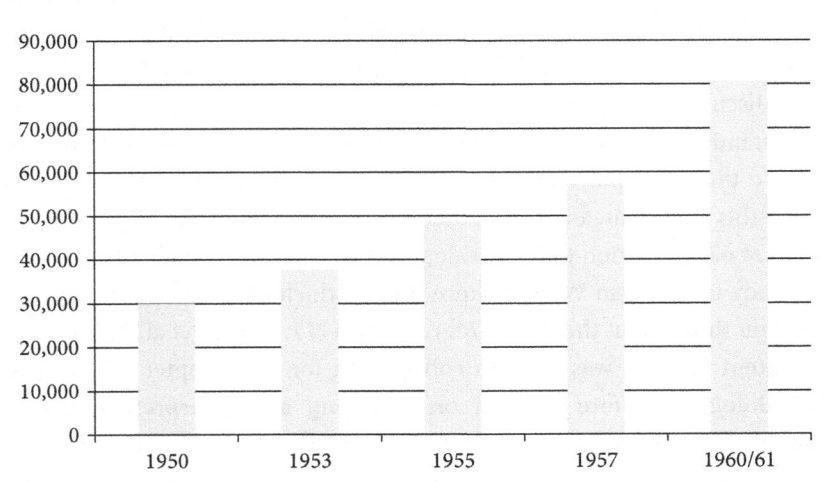

Figure 28.1 Primary school enrolment trends in Sierra Leone for selected years, 1950 to 1960/1

Source: Adopted from Anderson and Baker 1969: 118

Guinea, Senegal and Mali, and Nigeria, long before Britain claimed the area as a Protectorate in 1808 (Skinner 1976; Fyle 1981). Because of the large number of Muslims in the Colony, in 1902, the colonial government introduced an Ordinance that provided Western education for the Muslims (Sumner 1963).

As the years wore on, parents showed keen interest in enroling their children in school because literacy skills became a hallmark of civilization and offered freedom from hard labour (Bledsoe 2000; Fyle 1981). Between 1950 and 1961, enrolment in the primary schools continued to soar (see Figure 28.1).

The curriculum of the elementary schools

The curriculum of the elementary schools in Sierra Leone was based upon the British system (Brown 1964; Mouser 2009). The language of instruction was English because the missionary teachers could not speak any of the local languages (Obanya 1995; Bai-Sheka 2002; Kamanda 2002; Porter 1953). This approach implied covertly that a Western type of education with Christian education as the foundation would be adapted to all schools in Sierra Leone (Hair 1997). In view of this, the curriculum consisted of what is now commonly referred to as the three R's, namely, reading, writing, and arithmetic, with singing and sewing for girls (Hilliard 1957; D'Souza 1975; Ofori-Attah 2006).

Christian religion was infused in the curriculum because the missionaries controlled what was taught and what was not (Hair 1997; Ofori-Attah 2006). Thus, ideas that were considered anathema to the Christian faith and practice, like witchcraft, tribal gods, or animism were not entertained in the curriculum. Children were taught not to believe in the religious rites and practices of their parents (Kandeh 1992). Such teachings alienated many parents and so they often confronted school administrators about the negative impact schooling was having on their cultural practices. In some cases, prominent local chiefs refused to send their children to school when invited to do so. Instead, some of the chiefs sent off their domestic servants to school as their own biological children (Anderson and Baker 1969; Mouser 2009; Hargreaves 1953). The curriculum for schools such as the Government School in Bo which had Muslim children included Arabic, practical training in farming, carpentry, bridge building, road making and land surveying (Hilliard 1957; Corby 1990).

Secondary education

The establishment of secondary schools became important because there was a strong need to find room in the educational system for children who had completed their elementary education in the country. The Church Missionary Society (CMS) took the lead in this direction and by 1845 had established two secondary schools in Freetown, one for boys and the other for girls (Hilliard 1957). The Catholic Church in 1912 opened the St Joseph's Catholic Secondary School for girls in Freetown. The Wesleyan Methodist Mission also opened a secondary school for boys in Freetown in 1874 (Baker 1963). The Bo Ahmadiyya secondary school for boys was set up in 1960 by the Ahmadiyya Muslims in the interior of the country (Skinner 1976). Because of a lack of trained teachers, Muslim students were often taught by the Christian Missionaries (Sumner 1963).

One interesting feature of the colonial secondary system was the addition of boarding facilities to the schools. Boarding facilities were essential because the school authorities wanted to provide complete supervision over the academic, cultural and moral behaviour of the students. In the boarding schools, the students lived in dormitories governed by their own student leaders (Corby 1981). Each dormitory had a unique identity and name. In the Bo Government Secondary School, the students lived in four main dormitories. These were named Manchester, Liverpool, London, and Paris. These names demonstrate the closer ties that the institution enjoyed with its European counterparts.

The early secondary schools established in the country were based upon the English grammar school model (Sumner 1963). The Christian mission schools put emphasis on the teaching of English Grammar and Composition, Arithmetic, Algebra, Geometry, Modern World History, Latin, French, Greek, Religious Knowledge Hygiene, and General Science. A local language, Mende, appeared on the curriculum of a few secondary schools in the early twentieth century. These were the Collegiate School (1914) and the Albert Academy (1920) (Anderson and Baker 1969).

Enrolment in secondary school education soared between 1945 and 1960/1 academic years. With a total student enrolment of 2,064 in 1945, the figure jumped to 7,512 by the close of the 1960/1 academic year. At the same time, the number of recognized secondary institutions rose from 11 in 1945 to 37 by the end of the 1960/1 school year (Anderson and Baker 1969: 136). Although local interest in secondary education peaked, secondary education was not meeting the needs of the majority of the students who graduated with poor test scores.

In order to arrest this sad situation, the government introduced technical and agricultural education after a long public debate and a change in government policy concerning the administration and organization of secondary education in the country (Hilliard 1957; Ketkar 1977).

Technical and agricultural education

In 1889, the Church Missionary Society (CMS) opened a technical school in Freetown. The curriculum of the school included courses in building, plumbing, carpentry, needlework (for girls), sewing, ironing, washing, and starching (Anderson and Baker 1969: 42). The colonial government showed interest in technical education and in 1953 opened the Freetown Technical Institute. The school offered full- and part-time classes so that workers could enrol to take part-time courses to improve their technical skills. The school also offered evening classes in commercial and business courses for working adults who prepared for the Royal Society of Arts Examination.

Agricultural education lagged far behind the other forms of secondary education. The reasons are obvious; many Sierra Leoneans did not want to enter a programme that would tie them to the land. Moreover, training in agriculture was not the way out to avoid manual labour. Finally, training in agriculture had little to do with social elevation. The early institutions that provided courses in agriculture between 1927 and 1928 were the Njala School and the Mabang Academy (Anderson and Baker 1969: 105). Njala University College has its origins in the government-established agricultural station built in 1912 at Njala in the Southern Region of the country. The colonial government established Njala Agricultural College to promote the interests of students in agricultural education.

Teacher education

One problem that schools faced in Sierra Leone during the early years of the development of formal schooling was the unavailability of qualified teachers. All the initial teachers were foreigners (Corby 1990). Most of them were missionaries from England and the United States and many of them were not trained or qualified to teach in the schools. In 1893, only 41 teachers were recognized by the colonial government as being certified or qualified to teach in the public school system.

During this period, teachers were classified as pupil teachers, assistant teachers, provisionally certified teachers, and certified teachers. Pupil teachers had the lowest academic training. Completion of Standard IV or VII and a successful completion of an examination conducted by the government (Anderson and Baker 1969) were all the necessary qualifications the teachers possessed. Assistant teachers were those who had completed the pupil-teacher programme with an additional pass at the teacher examination also conducted by the government. Provisionally Certified Teachers were pupil-teachers who had passed the Government Scholarship Examination with distinction. The final group consisted of Certified Teachers. These were teacher candidates who had successfully passed the final-year examination at a recognized teacher training institution.

Admission into teacher training institution was three years of teaching experience as a pupil teacher. Teacher training lasted a minimum of two years. The curriculum for teacher training included content as well as pedagogical principles. The early institutions that prepared candidates for the teaching profession were Fourah Bay College, the United Christian Council's teacher training college at Bunumbu and the Catholic Teacher Training College at Bo.

Higher education

Until 1948, Sierra Leone served as the centre of learning for British colonies in West Africa. Fourah Bay College, which was founded in 1827 by the Christian Mission Church (CMS) became the seat of learning in colonial West Africa, earning Sierra Leone the moniker the 'Athens of West Africa' (UNESCO 2014; Ajayi et al. 1996). The university offered higher educational credentials to students from Ghana, Nigeria, the Gambia and other countries in Africa (Keith 1946; D'Souza 1975; Corby 1990; Baker 1963). Because Fourah Bay College (now the University of Sierra Leone) was affiliated with Durham University in England, its curriculum followed the English tradition. The college awarded Bachelor degrees and License in Theology (Redwood-Sawyerr 2011).

The civil war and education

After independence in 1961, the government introduced a number of policies that changed the organization and administration of education in the country. However, the 1991 to 2002 Civil War hampered education in the country. During the war, over 1,270 schools were destroyed; qualified teachers fled the conflict zones or even the country and 67 per cent of all school-age children were forced out of school (UNESCO 2007). Njala University was almost burned to the ground; Makeni Teachers' College and Magburaka Technical Institute were badly vandalized and parts were set ablaze; Freetown Teachers' College and the former Bunumbu Teachers College were looted and vandalized (World Bank 2007: 90). Some parents who had the means had to send their children to neighbouring countries such as Liberia, Guinea or Ghana to attend school. Enrolments in schools at all levels declined considerably. For instance, enrolment in primary schools declined from 370,564 in 1989/90 to 315,146 in 1991/2 when the war intensified (World Bank 2007; UNESCO 2006).

During the war era, the government introduced a number of policies to help improve the quality and delivery of instruction in the country. The establishment of the National Commission for Basic Education in 1993, the 1995 Education Policy, and the Education Master Plan in 1997 all had the ultimate aim of creating education that responded to the needs of students. For instance, the 1995 Education Policy created a new education system, the 6-3-3-4 model, which included six years of primary education (from 6 to 12 years of age, three years of secondary education, three years of senior secondary schooling, or technical/vocational education and four years of higher or tertiary education (Williams 2014). This replaced the old system of seven years of primary education, five years of secondary education and an additional two years of education to prepare for university education (7-5-2) (Anderson and Baker 1969).

In 2001, the government introduced a series of educational policies that determined the course of education in the country. The 2001 Educational Acts included the National Council for Technical, Vocational, and other Academic Awards (NCTVA) Act, The Polytechnics Act, Tertiary Education Commission Act (World Bank 2007: 136). The Tertiary Education Act 2001 regulated university admissions, and dealt with the relevance of course offerings. These numerous policies led to increases in enrolment in schools at all levels. For instance, enrolment in primary schools rose from 315,146 in 1990/1 to 659,503 by the close of the 2001/2 school year, enrolment in tertiary institutions rose from 6,429 in 1989/90 to 12,895 at the end of the 2001/2 academic year (World Bank 2007).

Education after the civil war

The civil war had a devastating effect on the education system in the country. In order to correct this sad situation, the government had to introduce a new policy to revive interest in schooling at all levels. This resulted in the introduction of the 2004 Education Act (Berghs 2012). The 2004 Education Act included standards for the improvement in the quality and delivery of instruction in pre-primary, primary, secondary and tertiary institutions. This Act made it mandatory for all parents to send their children to school or face legal action (Williams 2014).

The 2004 Education Act had a significant impact on organization and administration of education in the country. A total of 1,633 new primary and 816 new secondary schools were established during this period (Williams 2014: 27). According to the 2010 school census report, of 7,671 pre-primary, primary, junior and senior secondary schools in Sierra Leone, the government of Sierra owned and operated about 1,152 (15 per cent), the missions, (Christians and Muslims) 4,790 (62 per cent), private sector, 745 (10 per cent), community groups, 926 (12 per cent), other agencies, 58 (1 per cent). Between the 2004/5 and 2006/7 academic years, enrolment in schools increased at nearly all levels. The enrolment in pre-primary jumped from 20,632 to 24,807; enrolment in primary schools rose from 1 280 853 to 1,322,238; enrolment in junior secondary schools increased from 155,052 to 177,917; senior secondary schools, 44,924 to 60,329; tertiary, 16,625 to 18,831 (ibid: 28). The large increases in the school enrolments resulted in part from the free and compulsory primary education policy of the government through the 2004 Education Act and partly as a result of the determination of parents to get education for the children following the disruption of education in the country during the civil war.

In 2010, the government introduced a new education policy to help students improve upon their learning outcome. The policy is known as the 2010 Education Act, and modified the existing 6–3–3–3 system to a 6–3–4–4 system. This policy added one more year to the duration of senior secondary school education. The new system is commonly referred to as the 6–3–4–4 system, that is six years of primary education, three years of junior secondary education, four years of senior secondary education and four years of tertiary education. The increase in the number of three years to four years is designed to help students perform better on the secondary school graduation examination conducted for all candidates in West Africa (World Bank 2007).

Teacher shortage has hit Sierra Leone since the beginning of formal schooling. Although the government has since independence established several teacher training institutions, the problem persists. To solve this problem the government has trained a number of teachers through distance education and through the normal face-to-face medium of instruction (Alghali et al. 2005). By the close of the 2004/5 academic year, Sierra Leone had over 25,839 qualified teachers in the education sector. At the end of the 2005/7 school year, the number had jumped to over 40,263 (Williams 2014).

Futures: Performance, persistence, and promising initiatives

The education system in Sierra Leone has achieved an extraordinary recovery, reflected in the doubling of student enrolments in nearly all levels, from primary to tertiary. Fresh air is blowing through the corridors of the education sector. The government of Sierra Leone is investing large sums of public funds in education. According to the Ministry of Education Science and Technology (2007):

> Approximately 20% of current government spending, the largest of any of the sectors, is allocated to education. An estimated 48% to 50% is allocated to primary education, and about 25% of the rest to secondary education with junior secondary having around 19%. In GDP terms, around 4.9% of government expenditure is presently on education. (p. 27)

Students from poor homes, especially those in the rural areas, are being provided with assistance to remain in school. Sometimes the assistance is in the form of the provision of solar lamps to be used at home in the evening to do school work while away from school. Other times, the assistance is in the form of financial assistance. In a country where about 70 per cent of the population lives below the poverty line, the school feeding programme takes a lot of the heat off family expenditure. Funds for the school feeding programme are used to purchase, deliver and distribute nutritious food, primarily, to school children, particularly, girls, as a means of increasing enrolment and attendance rates, decreasing drop-out rates, as well as improving children's concentration, learning and academic performance (Government of Canada 2014).

Since 2003, two large programmes to support basic education have been in effect: 1) The Rehabilitation of Basic Education Project/SABABU Education Project, funded by the Government of Sierra Leone, the World Bank and African Development Bank, provides support to basic education in the areas of school construction and rehabilitation, provision of teaching and learning materials and teacher education; 2) The Girls' Education Support Programme, an affirmative action programme that provides all girl pupils in the North and East regions with free junior secondary education, including payment of their school fees, provision of books, uniforms and other educational materials for their use in school (Government of Sierra Leone 2011; Republic of Sierra Leone 2006).

Despite considerable progress in the education sector, the status of many young children in Sierra Leone remains disturbing (UNESCO 2006). Early childhood education has therefore attracted the attention of the government of Sierra Leone (Williams 2014). In Sierra Leone, however, only 14 per cent of children between ages 3 and 5 receive any form of early childhood education. Although the Government's policies aimed at increasing pre-primary education are yet to be translated into successful early childhood education programmes and interventions, the participation of the private sector in early childhood education is gradually improving the situation. In 2010, about 5 per cent of first graders had attended preschool the prior year (Focus 1000 2014).

The ten-year civil war left thousands of children in hopeless states. Many children today in Sierra Leone are either orphans, or many have no homes; several hundreds of children have been disabled for life. In response to the new Disability Act of 2011, higher educational institutions have introduced special education programmes where they train and prepare teachers to teach special needs children (UNHR 2011). The University of Makeni is a leader in this field. The University offers Certificate, Diploma and Bachelors in Special Education for Specialist Teachers, as well as an Introduction to Special Needs Education certificate for mainstream teachers (University of Makeni 2012).

Many children during the ten-year civil war lost the opportunity to receive education. These children have now grown to be adults with little or no literacy skills. Adult education is now the way out for these people. By the end of the civil war in 2002, it was estimated that over 300,000 people were out of the normal traditional education system (Government of Sierra Leone 2011). The educational needs of most of these students have been addressed by several policies including the reduction of primary school teaching time from 6 to 3 years in a programme called Complementary Rapid Education (CREPS), vocational and skills training of the young adults between 15 and 30 years. (UNESCO 2004). In 2002, there were over 8,000 adults enroled in adult learning classes all over the country (Alghali et al. 2005).

Since 2002, Sierra Leone has received numerous educational aids from several countries and organizations. The countries include Australia, Britain, Canada, China, France, Germany, Israel, Russia, and the United States (IBS 2014). New elementary and secondary schools are being built in several parts of the country. These schools are equipped with modern technology to help facilitate teaching and learning in a modern way. Ayoub International School (A.I.S.) was founded in 2004 as an American-based co-educational independent school to serve bright and highly motivated students (Ayoub International School 2014). The American International School in Freetown has modern facilities including 19 full-time classrooms in three buildings, a dedicated science lab, technology lab/media centre with computers. The entire school is WiFi accessible with access points throughout for students, staff and visitors alike. The Lebanese School in Freetown, Sierra Leone has kindergarten, elementary and high schools sections (American International School of Freetown 2014; Lebanese International School 2014).

Conclusion

The determination and commitment of the government to return the country to the old status of 'the Athens of West Africa' is paying positive dividends and has attracted the attention of several stakeholders in the development and improvement of education in the country. Although the education sector is still riddled with problems of corruption, inefficiency, mismanagement and ill-equipped schools, with the government's strong commitment to education and favourable resource allocation to the sector, the education system has great potential for sustainable development (World Bank 2007: 14).

References

Ajayi, J. F. A., Goma, L. K. H. and Johnson, G. A. (1996). *The African Experience with Higher Education*. Accra, Ghana: Association of African Universities (AAU).
Alghali, A. M., Turay, E. D. A., Thompson, E. J. D. and Kandeh, J. B. A. (2005). 'Environmental Scan on Education in Sierra Leone with Particular Reference to Open

and Distance Learning and Information and Communication Technologies'. Available from http://www.col.org/sitecollectiondocuments/05sierraleone_enviroscan.pdf (accessed 16 April 2014).

American International School of Freetown (2014). 'Facilities'. Available from http://ais-freetown.org/at-a-glance/ (accessed 18 April 2014).

Anderson, E. C. and Baker, E. D. (1969). *Educational Development in Sierra Leone*. Ann Arbor, MI: Malloy Lithoprinting.

Ary, D., Jacobs, L. C., Sorensen, C. K. and Walker, D. A. (2014). *Introduction to Research in Education*. Belmont, CA: Cengage Learning.

Atteh, S. O. (1996). 'The crisis in higher education in Africa'. *Issue: A Journal of Opinion*, 24 (1): 36–421.

Ayoub International School (2014). 'Welcome to our School'. Available from http://www.ayoub-international-school.org/ (accessed 20 April 2014).

Bai-Sheka, A. (2002). 'Mother Tongue Education in Sierra Leone'. Available from http://www.thepatrioticvanguard.com/spip.php?article1280 (accessed 8 April 2014).

Baker, E. D. (1963). *The Development of Secondary Education in Sierra Leone*. Ann Arbor: MI: University of Michigan Press.

Banya, K. (1993). 'Illiteracy, colonial legacy and education: the case of modern Sierra Leone'. *Comparative Education*, 29 (2): 159–70.

Berghs M. (2012). *War and Embodied Memory*. Burlington, VT: Ashgate Publishing Company.

Bledsoe, C. (2000). 'The Cultural Transformation of Western Education in Sierra Leone'. In B. A. U Levinson (ed), *Schooling the Symbolic Animal*. Lanham, MD: Littlefield Publishers, pp. 137–57.

Brown, G. N. (1964). 'British educational policy in West and Central Africa'. *The Journal of Modern African Studies*, 2 (3): 365–77.

Carney, S. Rappleye and Silova, I. (2012). 'Between faith and science: world culture theory and comparative education'. *Comparative Education Review*, 56: 366–93.

Conteh, P. S. (2009). *Traditionalists, Muslims, and Christians in Africa: Inter religious Encounters and Dialogue*. Amherst, NY: Cambia Press

Corby, R. A. (1981). 'Bo School and its graduates in colonial Sierra Leone', *Canadian Journal of African Studies*, 15 (2): 323–33.

—(1990). 'Educating Africans for inferiority under British rule: Bo School in Sierra Leone'. *Comparative Education Review*, 34 (3): 314–49.

D'Souza, H. (1975). 'External influences on the development of educational policy in British Tropical Africa from 1923 to 1939'. *African Studies Review*, 18 (2): 35–43.

Focus 1000 (2014). 'Early Childhood Education'. Available from http://focus1000.org/index.php/background-information/early-childhood-education (accessed 6 May 2014).

Fyle, C. M. (1981). *The History of Sierra Leone: A Concise Introduction*. London: Evans.

Government of Canada (2014). 'Project profile: School Feeding Program in Sierra

Leone – WFP 2010-2012'. Available from http://www.acdi-cida.gc.ca/ (accessed 6 May 2014).

Government of Sierra Leone (2011). 'Sierra Leone Education Sector Capacity Development Strategy 2012-2016'. Available from http://planipolis.iiep.unesco.org/

Haddad, W. D., Carnoy, R. R., Rinaldi, R. and Regel, O. (1990). *Education and Development: Evidence for New Priorities*. Washington, DC: The World Bank.

Hair, P. E. (1997). 'Christian influences in Sierra Leone before 1787'. *Journal of Religion in Africa*, 27: 3–14.

Hargreaves, J. D. (1953). 'Political prospects in Sierra Leone'. *The World Today*, 9 (5): 208–17.

Hilliard, F. H. (1957). *A History of Education in British West Africa*. London: Thomas Nelson and Sons.

IBS, Education for Development (2014). *Education for Change Programme 2009 – 2014*. Available from http://ibissierraleone.org/ (accessed 5 May 2014).

Kamanda, M. C. (2002). 'Mother tongue education and transitional literacy in Sierra Leone: Prospects and challenges in the 21st Century'. *Language and Education*, 16 (3): 195–211, DOI: 10.1080/09500780208666828

Kandeh, J. D. (1992). 'Politicization of ethnic identities in Sierra Leone'. *African Studies Review*, 35 (1): 81–99.

Keith, J. L. (1946). 'African students in Great Britain'. *African Affairs*, 45 (179): 65–72.

Ketkar, S. L. (1977). 'The economics of education in Sierra Leone'. *The Journal of Modern African Studies*, 15 (2): 301–9.

Kup, A. P. (1961). *A History of Sierra Leone: 1400-1787*. Cambridge: Cambridge University Press.

Lebanese International School (2014). 'Curriculum'. Available http://lebanese internationalschool.com/site/ (accessed 10 April 2014).

Meyer, J. W., Ramirez, F. O., Rubinson, R. and Boli-Bennett, J. (1977). 'The world educational revolution, 1950-1970'. *Sociology of Education*, 50: 242–58.

Ministry of Education, Science and Technology, Sierra Leone (2007). 'Sierra Leone education sector plan: A road map to a better future'. Available from http://planipolis.iiep.unesco.org/upload/Sierra%20Leone/Sierra_Leone_ESP.pdf (accessed 10 April 2014).

Mouser, B. L. (2009). 'Origins of church missionary society accommodation to imperial policy: the Sierra Leone quagmire and the closing of the Susu Mission, 1804-17'. *Journal of Religion in Africa*, 39: 375–402.

Obanya, P. (1995). 'Case studies of curriculum innovations in Western Africa'. *International Review of Education / Internationale Zeitschrift für Erziehungswissenschaft / Revue Internationale de l'Education*, 41 (5): 315–36.

Ofori-Attah, K. D. (2006). 'The British and curriculum development in West Africa: a historical discourse'. *Review of Education* 52: 409–23.

Porter, T. (1953). 'Religious Affiliation in Freetown, Sierra Leone'. *Journal of the International African Institute*, 23 (1): 3–14.

Redwood-Sawyerr, J. A. S. (2011). 'Rebuilding the Athens of West Africa'. Available from http://www.cedol.org/wp-content/uploads/2012/02/Professor-Jonas-Redwood-Sawyerr-article.pdf (accessed 1 May 2014).

Republic of Sierra Leone (2006). 'New Njala University Inaugurated'. Available from http://www.statehouse-sl.org/mest-news-page.html (accessed 1 May 2014).

Seddall, H. (1874). *The Missionary Mission of Sierra Leone*. London: Picadilly.

Skinner, D. E. (1976). 'Islam and education in the Colony and hinterland of Sierra Leone (1750–1914)'. *Canadian Journal of African Studies / Revue Canadienne des Études Africaines*, 10 (3): 499–520.

—(1978). 'Mande Settlement and the development of Islamic institutions in Sierra Leone'. *The International Journal of African Historical Studies*, 11 (1): 32–62.

Sumner, D. L. (1963). *Education in Sierra Leone*. Freetown: Government Printer.

UNESCO (2004). 'National Report on the Development of Education in Sierra Leone, West Africa for the Year 2003'. Available from http://www.ibe.unesco.org/National_Reports/ICE_2004 (accessed 5 May 2014).

—(2006). *Strong Foundations: Early Childhood Care and Education*. Paris: UNESCO.

—(2007). 'Support to Strengthen the Capacity of the Community Education Centres for Literacy and Vocational Skills for Women and Girls'. Available from http://www.unesco.org/ (accessed 5 May 2014).

—(2014). 'Old Fourah Bay College Building'. Available from http://whc.unesco.org/en/tentativelists/5744/ (accessed 28 April 2014).

UNESCO, IBE (2005). 'Quality Education for all Young People: Reflections and Contributions Emerging from the 47th International Conference on Education of UNESCO Geneva, 8-11- September'. Available from http://www.ibe.unesco.org/publications/free_publications/educ_qualite_angl.pdf (accessed 28 April 2014).

United Nations Human Rights (UNHR) (2011). 'Report on the Rights of Persons with Disabilities in Sierra Leone'. Available from http://unipsil.unmissions.org/ (accessed 28 April 2014).

University of Makeni (2012). 'Promoting Special Needs Education in Sierra Leone'. Available from http://universityofmakeni.com/wordpress/?p=754 (accessed 26 April 2014).

Williams, C. B. (2014). 'Sierra Leone: Effective Delivery of Public Education Services'. Johannesburg, South Africa, Open Society Foundation. Available from http://www.afrimap.org/ (accessed 25 April 2014).

Wise, C. (1956). *A History of Education in British West Africa*. London: Longmans, Green and Company.

World Bank (2007). 'Education in Sierra Leone: Present Challenges, Future Opportunities'. Available from https://openknowledge.worldbank.org/handle/10986/6653 (accessed 6 May 2014).

Togo: An Overview

Philippe Amevigbe

Education does not consist of an acquisition of disconnected knowledges, or a series of practical recipes, exercises and assignments with graduated difficulties. It seems rather embodied and active in someone who has the curiosity for learning. Informal education facilitated the link between manual and intellectual work. It was the only form of education in practice on the eve of the colonial conquest which disrupted that education in Togo. Three successive colonial power administrations with their different ideologies followed till the independence of Togo in 1960. In what measure do these colonial administrations train the Togolese? The answer would be found in the following pages.

The German government did not want the autochthon young to be massively educated. According to the German missionaries, the school is an instrument for evangelizing the populations through which it would realize its mission to train interpreters and executers for administration and commercial activities. The British and French Governments had almost the same mission with their ideologies.

After the independence of Togo, education was based on French policy education. Then from 1975 to date, many education initiatives had begun to reflect the Togolese realities with appropriate manuals with selective education being replaced by mass education. The result has been an unfair mismatch between training and the labour market. The chapter gives an overview of education in Togo by exploring the following: informal education in Togo, colonial administration education, education from independence 1960 to 1974, and then, the 1975 education reform to date.

Informal education in Togo

Generally in Togo, the aim of informal education is to lay the foundations of good moral behaviour of the individual in society as well as impart knowledge and training received from communities. This education, which is orally transmitted through the word and gestures, connects manual and intellectual work. Schooling tends to be a daily and timeless event and through exchanges between adults, the young learn by listening and observing.

In practice, they learnt by imitation. And so, skills and professional training were integrated into the culture. Learners memorized and adopted ways, values, concepts, style of communication and proverbs and respect for one's elders was paramount. Society maintained the balance of different communities through major occupations that protected and preserved the traditional status quo preventing all kinds of innovation. Education was central not only to the secular but also the sacred which permeated all lives. Parents held the important place in their children's education. Fathers and mothers taught their sons and daughters respectively. Old age was perceived as a positive value and played an important role in the pedagogic plan. The models and system of education were supported by communities using their own languages.

Consequently, the society was harmonized and everybody was socially integrated and there were no unemployed persons. This traditional education was the only form of education existing during the pre-colonial times. In 1842, however, the Christian missions opened the first European school in Togo at Petit Popo. Then, the three successive colonial power administrations came with their different ideologies, which influenced the Togolese education system.

Colonial administration educations

This section will now examine five points which are: tentative education of the indigenous in Togo, the German system of education in Togo from 1884 to 1914, the education system under the administration of British and French from 1914 to 1920, the setting up of the French education system from 1921 to 1932, and the education system after the second World War from 1945 to 1960.

Tentative schooling by the autochthon in Togo

In the nineteenth century, European education expanded to the Gold Coast. This led to the establishment of the first European school in Togo at Petit Popo in 1842 for the indigenous people. The aim was to train intermediaries to facilitate trade between Africans and Europeans. During the same period, missionaries were teaching their Christian religion using English in confessional schools without a public programme.

German education system in Togo from 1884 to 1914

When the German empire established in 1884 on the coast of Togo, it had to integrate the existent cultural system by recruiting interpreters among the past pupils from the school of the coast. The Western schools established in the south of Togo disrupted the old educational system. The North stayed excluded from this instruction unlike the German tentative till 1912.

The German government did not want the young from the indigenous population to be highly educated. So since 1887 to 1912, the Colonial Administration built only three public primary schools, one agricultural school for three years training to become young agriculture mentors. There was also one professional school which trained final year pupils from primary school and illiterate youth to become workers. Also, there was one improvement school which recruited pupils who had completed primary school. Pupils of the improvement school, authorized by the administration to be trained for two years were able to access good jobs in administration and factories. The fact was that the government refused to promote the German language because it did not want to train the German Black. Being driven by nationalist and financial considerations, the administration established moved to set up German missions in Togo where Pidgin English and Ewe, the popular local language of the south of Togo were used. The Catholic Mission Society founded first of all private schools along the coast with the study programme centred on religion. As they were private schools, the administration could not directly influence the content but allocated grants for the courses where the media of instruction were Ewe and Pidgin English. Finally, the German government wanted to teach a very small minority of interpreters and avoided massive teaching.

According to the German missionaries, the school was an instrument for evangelizing the populations. In consequence, the different missions: Bremen mission, Catholic mission, and Methodist created two improvement courses, one professional school and 344 primary schools with 13,852 pupils. The German Administration created one improvement school, one professional school and three primary schools as noted above. At the end of the German colonial period, only one Togolese child for 1,500 children attended public schools while one for 35 attended mission schools. While seminars trained the teachers and catechists, Catholic professional school founded in 1905 in Lome played an important role in the training of the specialized workers.

Education system under the administration of the British and French from 1914 to 1920

Teaching in Togo under the administration of the British and French from 1914 to 1920 was imprecise and the system of education was disorganized. Ewe, a local language and the medium of instruction was suppressed and English only taught in the area occupied by the British. The English school spread throughout the country. The pupils and their parents had a preference for English studying. The aim to have French priority did not succeed in these regions, and in others, the programme was half French, half English.

Setting up of the French teaching from 1921 to 1932

In 1920, the French administration began to organize the schooling system where there were already 5,305 pupils in the French schools in Togo with six public schools and 63 confessional schools. It was on this basis that the Administration began to create a lot of schools with a formal organization of schooling system in 1922.

The aim of the French Administration was to adopt the principles of gratuity, obligation and secularity of primary teaching for all, and to prevent the indigenes developing individualist and liberal ideas and from using the French schools as a vehicle for revolt and nationalism. Thus for these countries, the best strategy was to confine the indigene instruction to a professional training geared towards manual activities.

The German administration later insisted on the teaching of the German language, and its educational system showed a sure sign of a social evolution in Togo. Nevertheless, the social and economic influence of the British colony of the Gold Coast continued to fascinate literate Togolese, most of whom would send their children to further their secondary school education in the Gold Coast. All these particularities complicated the implementation of the teaching system in Togo.

In 1921, at the time of the German administration, the schools of the French period were divided into confessional and public schools: six public schools with 1,242 pupils and then 63 confessional schools with 4,043 pupils. According to the educational system of the Territories of the French Western Africa, the schooling system had three levels: Elementary primary teaching, superior primary teaching, and professional primary teaching. In the French public schools, the elementary primary teaching subdivided into two levels aimed to familiarize the indigenes with the French language and to prepare them to become efficient workers in their own country.

The village school formed the basis of the teaching received by pupils from the ages of 7 to 14. The teaching brought pupils into contact with the French culture and language. After four years of schooling, the best pupils were selected to follow the more elaborate teaching of the regional school.

The regional school, the second level of the primary school had 3 years of schooling. The teaching comprised French, natural science, agriculture, arithmetic, drawing, moral education, practical activities in agriculture for boys and housework for girls. The elementary primary study certificate was a diploma which recognized the successful conclusion of the regional school.

The improvement courses in the superior primary teaching in Lome was opened in 1922 for pupils who obtained the elementary primary study certificate after a competitive examination prepared in six months. The studies lasted three years during which the pupils received a training which prepared them for a career in teaching, health, general administration or trade. This school prepared talented pupils for competitive examination and entry to federal schools of general Government of French Western Africa.

The first professional school created in 1922 recruited young men physically fit to work in workshops. They received a 4-year general teaching in French, Arithmetic and Drawing, completed by practical training in Carpentry, Brickwork, Weaving, Foundry and Forge.

One agriculture school trained agricultural mentors in botany, vegetal biology, practical topography, appendages, agriculture parasitology, preparation of main agricultural products for export and expertise in these products. Also, included among these professional schools are the schools to train railway workers and the professional section of the regional school of Lome which recruited a limited number of ten candidates from the regional schools of southern towns of Togo in 1926. These pupils received 45 francs, health care and two-year training to become carpenters, forgers, and builders.

The French Administration decided to control the influence and the development of the private confessional teaching but failed because its own schools had inadequate number of places for pupils in 1930. The missions had the infrastructure but nevertheless lacked the grants that the German missions would have to send them. So, the financial problem became a handicap for them. Moreover, parents of pupils had to pay fees and the teacher salaries were modest unlike the public schools which were free and its teachers well paid. In consequence, the mission schools decreased from 7,500 to 5,000 pupils till the war. As a result, the missions had to negotiate an agreement with the French Administration to obtain grants to pay teachers' salaries according to the results from the final primary examination and from the inspection carried out of all their confessional schools under the supervision of the public schools inspector.

The economic crisis in 1930 obliged the colonial authorities to change the teaching politics in Togo. They stopped opening new village schools. The first classes were annexed to existent regional schools. The only improvement school was then transferred to the superior primary school at Victor Ballot in Dahomey (present Republic of Benin). Thus, the teaching system comprised:

- A popular rural teaching given in all towns with the intention to instruct the child in his own area spoken French, new methods of agricultural activities, farming and hygiene aimed at providing the child with skills for work and behaviour;
- An elementary primary teaching comprising rural and urban schools where pupils followed the programme of first and second class, completed by manual and agricultural activities with the intention to diffuse the usage of French in the mass and inculcate in adults the necessary notions of economic life in the country;
- And then the superior primary school, which prepared pupils in a year for the entry competitive examination to the improvement school where studies lasted three years, that is, two years for general teaching and one year for the specialization in one of these proposed sections 'teaching, administration and trade'. At the end, the qualified pupils could prepare for the entry competitive examination to the general government schools of French Western Africa.

To limit the number of qualified pupils who would be unemployed, the administration imposed the system of limited age which got rid of a great number of young pupils with the intention to encourage pupils to return to agriculture, an unpopular measure, which failed. In consequence, several qualified pupils left for neighbouring countries like Ivory Coast, the Gold Coast, Nigeria and

Central Africa. In any case, the school pupil population rose from 7,000 in 1932 to 17,000 in 1945.

The teaching after the second World War from 1945 to 1960

Under political pressure after the war, the colonial authorities adopted the teaching system in France. So, primary school lasted six years: two years in first class, two years in second and two years in third. At the end of these six years study, pupils obtained Elementary Primary Study Certificate. During this period, the size of primary schools grew from 17,230 pupils in 1946 to 81,062 in 1959 with 33 per cent of girls and 34 per cent of schooling rate.

In the secondary school, the improvement school of the capital became superior primary school in 1942, which was transformed into classic and modern college in 1947, and then into secondary school (Lycée Governor Bonnecarrere) in 1953. At the same time, a modern college was opened at Sokode situated in the centre of the country. From 1954, Togo counted five secondary schools: two public with boarding school and three confessionals (Evangelical College and Catholic College for Boys and Catholic College for Girls), all in Lome. The size of the secondary schools grew from 500 pupils in 1948 to 2,000 in 1960.

The colleges prepared the candidates for O Level Diploma, during which subjects were selected and the examination results announced by the academic authorities of the University of Paris. Secondary school (Lycée) also prepared candidates for O Level Diploma, and then for Baccalaureates I and II whose subjects and jury came from the University of Bordeaux in France. A hundred scholarships (56 for superior education in France) were distributed in 1950.

The professional school of Sokode was transformed into a practical school of trade and industry. Reorganized in 1956, the apprentice centre situated in the South West area prepared candidates in three years for the Agricultural Professional Aptitude Certificate.

In 1958, the teaching personnel counted 1,584 comprising 99 metropolitans, 1,454 for the primary school and 100 for the secondary school and then 30 for the technical. In the same academic year, 1958–9, 300 Togolese students in France were identified of whom 137 were grants holders, 139 non-grants holders and 24 trainees.

There were two centres which trained teachers: a training college at Atakpame for teachers with a low grade, which became Primary Teachers Training College in 1951 and a Catholic Teachers Training College at Togoville. These training colleges formed teachers for five years. During the same period, the Evangelical Improvement School too comprised a pedagogic section for the training of teachers for the evangelical mission.

At the end of the French period, Togo was the country that had the best rate of schooling (24 per cent) in French West Africa in 1951. The north of Togo which was for a long time marginalized began to make up for lost time.

Education from independence: 1960 to 1974

In 1960, the population of Togo had begun to grow rapidly. In 1960, there were fewer than 100,000 pupils but by 1975, the number of pupils had increased to 362,895 in a country with a population of 3,500,000 inhabitants. The Togolese educational system was structured as follows: Basic education, secondary school first level, secondary school second level, university and higher education. There were four teaching orders: public education, confessional education, private schools, and Islamic schools which existed locally but had no formal records in the national yearbook of school statistics of direction of educational planning and evaluation.

Thus, the educational system was based on the colonial system till the reform of 1975. According to the spirit of the reform of 1975, the school had to play a capital role in the promotion of economic growth. The improvements introduced in the educational system aimed at linking schools closely with the needs of the labour market. The income generated by phosphate allowed Togo to adopt an industrialization politics particularly during the period from 1975 to 1980 enabling an expansion of the educational system where teaching reform was decreed. The reform aimed to develop all levels of teaching, particularly, the primary school where all children from the ages of three to 15 years will be in school. The competitive exam to attend the first and fifth class of the secondary school was suppressed, and so, was the obligation to possess Primary School Certificate and O Level Diploma to give access to Secondary 1 and Secondary 2. These different measures authorized a spectacular expansion of schooling size at all levels between 1960 and 1980. The development of teacher training which had been stopped resumed with the building of two training colleges. The National Pedagogic Institute was transformed and strengthened to play an education advisory role; conduct action and pedagogic research with new missions, permanent adaptation of methods and programmes, and personal development, distance education, and then generate and disseminate information.

The reform of education (1975) to date

The government authorities, aware of the sad educational situation, set up an ambitious reform where education was based on Togolese realities with appropriate manuals, and where selective education had been replaced by mass education. As the objectives of the reforms had not been attained, and in addition, the teachers had not been well-prepared to use the new methodology, the education has aimed to develop the process of knowledge production without evaluation to raise the challenges of educational reform, the innovations and the general development. The period has been appropriate thanks to the price of phosphate.

Unfortunately, this period was followed by an economic recession in 1979 due to the collapse of the price of phosphate. The government froze recruitment in the public sector in 1979 and salaries in 1982. So, the Togolese education system became very selective again and reduced the rate of success. Two important sources of wastage of public resources in education are the dropouts and repeating the year. In the primary school, the percentage of those who repeated the year reduced from 29.6 per cent in 1998 to 23.9 per cent in 2007, while in Secondary 1 it reduced from 24.6 per cent to 24 per cent, and in Secondary 2 it rose from 27.4 per cent to 30.4 per cent.

The education crisis obliged the government to replace the initial teacher training unqualified teachers' improvement programme for three months. This was followed by the school directors' training. It prevented the establishment of new schools. In the same perspective, the Direction of permanent education, action and pedagogic research and the National Institute of Sciences of Education ensured the initial training of school inspectors and mentors. The former intervened in matters of didactic material adapted to national realities for primary schools and the latter trained school inspectors for Secondary 1. The school inspectors for Secondary 2 were trained at St Cloud in Paris, although before this period, all kinds of school inspectors were trained at St Cloud in Paris.

The education budget was reduced and parents had to bear a significant part of the cost. The sensible growth of the number of teachers was possible thanks to the massive recruitment of contractual teachers and village teachers in the public, and in the confessional private. The country hit by the economic crisis was unable to fund important expansion of the educational system. It had to appeal to local resources. The community schools and private schools responded to the appeal of the government. A growing number of individuals or associations obtained the authorizations from the State to create and manage private schools with school fees paid by the parents of pupils. The communities which did not have public schools or confessional schools in their areas organized themselves and built schools, as well as recruited and paid teachers.

From 1998 to 2007, the average annual growth rate of preschool education was 13.7 per cent. From 2010 to 2011, the number of children attending preschool had increased in almost all regions of the country.

At the primary school level there was an average annual growth of 3.5 per cent due to the development of private schools and community schools. However, there was no general access to primary school. Less than one child over two aged 6 years old attends primary school with disparities between regions. Consequently, there was late enrolment of children in school. Pupil retention in the educational system was weak. Out of the 100 children who were enroled in the first class of primary in 2008, only 68 reached the primary superior class, 40 in the terminal class of Secondary 1, and 12 in the terminal class of Secondary 2. Gender parity is not attained in secondary education, and number of girls in school decreases as the level of education rises.

From 2008 to 2009, the school suppressed fees at primary and this led to an annual average growth of 14 per cent of pupils in primary school. This indicated improved access to primary school. By 2011, the increase was more remarkable in public schools with 50.53 per cent. The number of girls had increased to 50.72 per cent in three years against 50.36 per cent for boys. While enrolment rates had improved in primary school completion rates had been low and thus primary universal education has not been accomplished. Seventy per cent of children at 6 years old enroled in primary school but only a few complete primary schools.

In Secondary 1, the average annual growth is 10 per cent with 6.6 per cent in public school and 26.5 per cent in private schools. Secondary 2 also expanded from 1998 to 2007 with a population of 32,862 to 91,904, an average annual growth of 12 per cent. This growth was higher in private schools (19.6 per cent) than in public (10.3 per cent).

Equity has not yet been attained especially at the secondary school level. New classrooms have to be built to increase access. Pupil numbers decrease as the level of education rises. High repetition rates undermine the attainment of a diploma. Secondary education deserves improved quality for the best results.

Higher education expanded from 1998 to 2007 and shows very high quantitative growth during the years after. More than 38,059 students in public schools in 2007–8 were recorded while there were only 15,000 in 2004. In 2011, the total number of the students of both the University of Lome and University of Kara increased from 38,059 students (8,234 girls and 29,825 boys) in 2008 to 54,819 students (13,163 girls and 41,656 boys) in 2011. The two universities in three years experienced rapid growth in numbers of 16,760 students (11,831 boys and 4,929 girls). The number of lecturers according to gender for both universities increased from 556 teachers (490 males and 66 females) in 2008 to 579 teachers (517 males and 62 females) in 2011 with only 23 lecturers and a decline in female teachers. Inadequate numbers of actual lecturers was the result.

There was the problem of unemployed university graduates because of a mismatch between education/training and the demand of the labour market in Togo. This situation obliged the authorities of universities to launch the LMD reform to make higher education more relevant.

Technical and professional education from 1998 to 2007 had equally experienced quantitative progression. The number of learners grew from less than 11,000 in 1998 to about 31,846 in 2007, a 12.8 per cent of average annual growth.

The inefficiency of general education justifies the creation by the tertiary sector, of a lot of high technical and professional schools for preparing students to Superior Technician Diploma.

These strategies not appropriate to the slow development of the industrial and commercial sectors in the country produce a lot of dropouts who do not find jobs in the labour market.

Conclusion

The traditional education was the only form of education existing during the pre-colonial time. People learned by imitation. So the society was harmonized and everybody was socially integrated and there were no unemployed persons. It was the only form of education on the eve of the colonial conquest which disrupted that education in Togo.

Three successive colonial power administrations with their different ideologies followed till the independence of Togo in 1960.

In 1842, however, the Christian missions opened the first European school in Togo at Petit Popo. The aim was to train intermediaries to facilitate trade between Africans and Europeans.

When the German empire established in 1884 on the coast of Togo, it had to integrate the existent cultural system by recruiting interpreters among the past pupils from the school of the coast.

The German government did not want the young from the indigenous population to be highly educated. The fact was that the government refused to promote the German language because it did not want to train the German Black. Finally, the German government wanted to teach a very small minority of interpreters and avoided massive teaching. At the end of the German colonial period, only one Togolese child for 1,500 children attended public schools while one for 35 attended mission schools.

Teaching in Togo under the administration of the British and French from 1914 to 1920 was imprecise and the system of education was disorganized.

The aim of the French Administration was to adopt the principles of gratuity, obligation and secularity of primary teaching for all, and to prevent the indigenes developing individualist and liberal ideas and from using the French schools as a vehicle for revolt and nationalism.

To limit the number of qualified pupils but who would be unemployed, the administration imposed the system of limited age which got rid of a great number of young pupils with the intention to encourage pupils to return to agriculture, an unpopular measure, which failed.

Under political pressure after the war, the colonial authorities adopted the teaching system in France. In 1958, the teaching personnel counted 1,584 comprising 99 metropolitans, 1,454 for the primary school and 100 for the secondary school and then 30 for the technical. Three Primary Teachers Training College were opened comprising two confessional and one public.

At the end of the French period, Togo was the country that had the best rate of schooling (24 per cent) in French West Africa in 1951.

The educational system was based on the colonial system till the reform of 1975. The government authorities, aware of the sad educational situation, set up an ambitious reform where education was based on Togolese realities with appropriate manuals, and where selective education had been replaced by mass education. As the teachers had not been well-prepared to use the new methodology, the objectives of the reforms had not been attained.

The education budget was reduced and parents had to bear a significant part of the cost. The sensible growth of the number of teachers was possible thanks to the massive recruitment of contractual teachers and village teachers in the public, and in the confessional private. The country hit by the economic crisis was unable to fund important expansion of the educational system. It had to appeal to local resources. The community schools and private schools responded to the appeal of the government.

At the primary school level there was an average annual growth of 3.5

per cent due to the development of private schools and community schools. However, there was no general access to primary school.

Higher education expanded from 1998 to 2007 and shows very high quantitative growth during the years after. There was the problem of unemployed university graduates because of a mismatch between education/training and the demand of the labour market in Togo. This situation obliged the authorities of universities to launch the LMD reform to make higher education more relevant.

Technical and professional education from 1998 to 2007 had equally experienced quantitative progression. The inefficiency of general education justifies the creation by the tertiary sector, of a lot of high technical and professional schools for preparing students to Superior Technician Diploma.

These strategies not appropriate to the slow development of the industrial and commercial sectors in the country produce a lot of dropouts who do not find jobs in the labour market.

References

Books

Direction de la Planification de l'éducation et de l'Evaluation (1996, 1999, 2009, 2011). *Annuaire national des statistiques scolaires*. Togo: Direction générale de la planification de l'éducation.

Gayibor, N. L. (2005). '*Histoire des Togolais Tome II de 1884 à 1960*'. Presse de l'UL.

Hornby, S. (2000). *Oxford Advanced Learner's Dictionary*, 6th edn. Oxford University Press.

Reports

Diambomba, M. (1990). ' Les causes de la non-fréquentation et de l'abandon scolaires dans l'enseignement au Togo'.

Colloque (2002). 'Le système éducatif togolais. Eléments d'analyse pour une revitalisation'.

—(2009). 'Plan sectoriel de l'éducation'.

Togo: Trends and Futures

Kossi Souley Gbeto and Koffi Nutéfe Tsigbé

Introduction

To assess the trends of the education system in Togo as well as its prospects amounts to reviewing the orientations and the vision defined by the state authorities for this sector from the colonial period to this day. Before colonization the inhabitants of the territory that was to be known later as Togo, benefited from a traditional education system within the family circle, peer education or in religious convents. This system was either general or practical, in which the mastery of a language or a trade was taught (Assima-Kpatcha 2005: 101–57).

With the advent of colonization, this education system was substituted by the Western system that pursued two distinct objectives. The Western school, on the one hand, aimed at helping the Christian missions, which opened the first schools in Togo, to achieve their evangelization objectives. It also helped the colonizers to meet their needs through the training of assistants for administration and trading centres. (Lassey 2011: 111–32). It is this very colonial school that trained the elites in Togo who later fought for its independence proclaimed on 27 April 1960.

After, conferences and reforms were organized and sector policies for education were defined. From these initiatives it is possible to identify the trends and prospects of the education system in Togo.

The aim of this chapter is to review the various orientations that have been given to the education system and study the prospects for the future. The work is based on documentary analysis. It is a thorough analysis of administrative documents such as reports, conference documents, education sector policy documents as well as any other official documents related to the education system in Togo. It also aims at reviewing existing research related to the subject being examined.

This chapter is subdivided into four main parts. The first reviews the education system from independence up to the reform of education in 1975, and the second part analyses the content of the reform and its subsequent trends up to 1992. The third part deals with the trends in the education system from the national conference on education up to date. Lastly, the fourth delves into the prospects of the education sector in Togo. This analysis will cover the various cycles of education in order to point out the peculiar aspect of each one.

The education system in Togo just after the colonial period: What kind of orientation for what kind of results? (1960–75)

From 1884 to 1960, Togo was under the domination of three colonial rulers, namely Germany (1884–1914) France and Great Britain (a joint rule 1914–19) and France (1919–60). Under these various periods, the education system in place aimed at maintaining the domination of the colonial administration over the population. It was out of the question to train medium-level civil servants who might later question colonial rule and start struggling for the emancipation of their territories. It was better to give them rudimentary education that would help them understand and obey the orders of the colonizer. It was meant to provide them with technical and vocational training to prevent the development of bureaucracy (Gayibor 1997: 78–9). This is the reason why the various colonial administrations had to open in the first place primary schools, and later on some secondary schools. Under these circumstances those who wished to pursue higher education were obliged to go to regional schools in Bamako or in Dakar, or even go to France.

Just after the second World War the complementarities between the missions' schools and the colonial administration yielded positive results. At the primary school level the number of pupils ranged from 17,400 in 1946 to 57,000 in 1954 (with 21 per cent of girls) and reached 87,400 (with 26 per cent of girls) in 1960, which represents a five-fold increase in 15 years. At the secondary level the number of students varied from 500 in 1948 to 1,000 in 1952, 1,600 in 1957 and to 2,000 in 1960, which was an increase of 300 per cent in 12 years (Assima-Kpatcha et al. 2005: 142–3). Missionary schools showed a tendency towards an increase especially at the primary school level. It was with this drive towards education that Togo got its independence.

Therefore, the education system was meant to meet the socio-economic, political and cultural needs of the Africans as stipulated in the Universal Declaration of Human Rights. For this, the new education system had to be progressively cut off from the colonial ideology under which learners were to be mentally and ideologically moulded by the French colonial ideology. To reach this objective the Togolese authorities decided to align their educational system with the general orientation that was defined by the African communities through a series of conferences such as those of Addis Ababa, Abidjan and Nairobi.

The Addis Ababa conference was the first of its kind in post-colonial Africa. The conference that took place from 15 to 21 May 1961, made important recommendations to African states pertaining to education. The conference invited them to organize their educational systems in such a way that the enrolment rate reaches 100 per cent in the primary school, 30 per cent in the secondary school and 5 per cent in higher education by the end of 1980. For this reason, particular emphasis was laid on the funding for education. It was agreed that authorities should raise the budget allocated to education from 3 per cent to 6 per cent by the end of 1980. Concerning the planning of education, the conference recommended to the ministers of education to set up planning offices with adequate qualified personnel whose role would be to collect statistical data, determine the planning of the education system, make recommendations for the revision of curricula, plan the recruitment and the training of teachers, do research on new pedagogical methods, as well as future prospects for the long term (UNESCO 1961: 20–1).

Thus, great emphasis was laid on the improvement of access to education at all the levels. The number of students then increased significantly to the detriment of the quality of teaching. In addition, the necessity to adapt the contents of the curricula to African cultural realities was not met. A mid-term assessment of the degree of implementation of these recommendations was carried out during the second conference of African countries ministers of education of (MINDAF) in Abidjan from 17 to 24 March 1964.

This conference, about funding of education in African countries gave them the opportunity to evaluate the level of implementation of the Addis Ababa recommendations. During this conference, UNESCO (Organisation des Nations Unies pour l'Education la Science et la Culture) was discharged from its duty to carry out the follow up of the Addis Ababa action plan in favour of the Commission of the Organisation of the African Unity (OAU) (UNESCO-Afrique, Breda 1991: 7).

Finally, between 1960 and 1975 a third conference (MINDAF III) was held in Nairobi in Kenya from 16 to 27 July 1968. Jointly organized by the OAU and UNESCO, this conference aimed at evaluating the strengths and weakness of the educational sector since 1961. It was recorded that, the illiteracy rate in Africa varied from 71 per cent to 69 per cent between 1960 and 1968. At the primary school level the failures and the dropouts were higher than the successes which varied respectively from 54 per cent for the failures to 46 per cent for the successes. It was emphasized that everywhere an attempt was made to adapt the teaching to rural realities, but met with hostility from both parents and students. The disparity between the students' population and the available seats in classrooms led to overcrowding and the inadequacy of equipment in schools. The gap between the curriculum and the employment opportunities exacerbated the problems of unemployment (Ameganwovo 2010: 51).

Togo took an active part in all these conferences before deciding to make their recommendations part of its curricula. The office for the planning of education was set up. The problem of overcrowding in schools resulted in inadequate equipment and number of qualified teachers. Under these conditions, the quality of education deteriorated. But from 1970, precise orientations were defined for education by the High Council for Education set up by decree No. 70–141 of 13 July 1970 (Ministry of National Education and Scientific Research 1989: 4). It is this council that worked on the projections on the vision of the Togolese educational system at all the levels of education.

At the primary school level, it was agreed to build more classrooms in order to improve access to education. This included the creation of vocational and professional training centres for primary school pupils who could not further their education at the secondary school level. Another reason was to improve the quality of teaching through the recruitment of highly qualified teachers (Batchoduom 2006: 71).

As far as secondary education was concerned, it was noticed that there was a multiplication of six forms. The authorities therefore decided to put an end to this system by creating the second cycles at the end of the primary schools which were later transformed into secondary schools. It was also recommended to introduce the teaching of technology in the secondary schools. Finally, it was decided to orient some students who have completed the secondary school towards the technical and professional training centres (Batchoduom 2006: 71).

A complete reform of the technical education system was initiated in order to adapt its curricula to the development needs of the national economy for it to meet the requirements of the employment market (Batchoduom 2006: 71).

A teacher training college was opened at Atakpame with the aim of training high-quality teachers in order to improve the quality of education (Occanssey 1972: 120).

At the same period, the pressure of necessity justified the opening of a national university with a regional dimension. Its objective was to train high-level civil servants, who would work for the development of the country. The university was then set up by decree N°70-156 of 14 September 1970 under the name Université du Benin, which is now known since the year 2002 as University of Lomé (UL-DAAS 2002: 5).

To reach these objectives required a long-term planning process. In fact, as Togo was engaged in a two-decade programme since 1966, the authorities targeted 1985 as the year by which the country was to achieve its socio-economic development. This period was subdivided into four five-year terms (1966–70, 1971–5, 1976–80, 1981–5) generally known as five year-plans for the socio-economic development. The above mentioned objectives were to be achieved within the second five-year term (1971–5). Unfortunately, on the eve of 1975 it was noticed that these objectives were not easily attainable.

From the reform of the education system to the National Conference on Education: What kind of trends? (1975–92)

The idea behind the reform of the education system of 1975 was expressed in the following way in the manifesto of Rally of the Togolese People (RPT: single political party in Togo from 1969 to 1991) 'If one does not want the education system to be a great waste, a hurdle to the social and economic development, and if one does not wish to see the school become a producer of unemployed graduates, it is important to operate a fundamental reform' (Assima-Kpatcha 2007: 85). This quote shows clearly that the Togolese authorities wanted to reform the education system in such a way that the school does not become a place where unemployed graduates are produced, but rather a place where the social and economic development of the country are fostered. The authors of the reform baptized it as 'the new school' that will occur once the said reform is adopted. The aim of this reform was to train a new type of citizens who are 'balanced in their behaviour, open minded, capable of adapting themselves easily to every new situation, full of initiatives and capable of transforming their milieu' (Ministry of National Education 1975: 9).

In addition, the reform pursued three main objectives, namely the democratization of the education system, its profitability, and its capacity to adapt itself to the realities of the milieu for development. The first objective aimed at giving equal opportunities to all in terms of education, to girls and boys and to orient the students according to their skills (Gbikpi-Benissan 2012: 166). The second objective was based on the professional qualification of the teaching and administrative staff trained in sufficient numbers and the construction of adequate infrastructure. The last objective was based on the need to adapt the teaching to the realities of a developing country like Togo. This implied the rehabilitation of the local languages as well as the Togolese cultural values that will facilitate social and economic development. In addition, all the philosophical values would benefit from the freedom of speech at school, without neglecting all the African and Togolese forms of expression, such as oral expression, artistic expression, musical expression, and technology etc. To achieve this, the reform recommended the creation of an African Linguistic Institute which would focus on the study of Togolese languages. The institute was also to be in charge of outlining the necessary tools for the teaching of these languages. It also was to introduce, by 1975, an advanced study of the languages to give the opportunity to every citizen to learn at least two Togolese languages, and to train teachers for this new situation (Ministry of National Education 1975: 8-9).

The 'new school' was subdivided into four levels of teaching: the first level, (kindergarten and primary school), the second level, (junior secondary school) the third level (senior secondary school and the technical secondary school) and the fourth level (university and other institutes of higher education). How then was the reform implemented?

It must be underlined that the reform took effect on the date it received presidential assent, which was on 6 May 1975. Paradoxically, Jean Adama Nyame and Yao Nuakey (2000: 72) in their assessment of the curricula of the reform concluded that 'the new programmes and official instructions pertaining to the orientations of the reform were written and published by a national commission, only five years later, that is, in April 1980'. This constituted a great delay. Pushing further their analysis, the two experts observed that these programmes were developed through a strategy that followed the disciplinary approach, and this was not efficient.

In 1989, the National Institute of Education (INSE 1989: 9) organized a mid-term assessment of the reform and obtained mitigated results. Efforts were made by the state authorities to reach the objectives by opening new schools, as well as teacher training institutions reinforced by administrative structures, and the modification of teaching programmes. The assessment then concluded that despite the 'objective of democratisation of access to education, the goals were not achieved'.

At all the levels of education, student population varied from 432,000 in 1975 to 730,000 in 1990, which represents an average annual increase of 3.55 per cent (Assisma-Kpatcha 2007: 85).This general tendency towards an increase must not however hide the realities of the 1980s.

In fact, with the recession in the Togolese economy at the beginning of the 1980s which led to the imposition of the structural adjustment programmes by the World Bank, authorities were obliged to reduce investments in the education sector. The system then yielded a great number of school dropouts. School enrolment that was 72 per cent in 1980 dropped to 68.4 per cent in 1981, and reached 52.2 per cent in 1985. It is from 1990 that a growth rate of 62.9 per cent was registered. This tendency toward an increase hides many disparities in the educational regions that are as follows: 73.6 per cent for the Maritime Region, 69.7 per cent for the Plateaux Region, 61.5 per cent for Central Region, 53 per cent for the Kara Region and 29 per cent for the Savanna Region (ibid.). It is evident that the regions in the southern part of the country have higher rates of enrolment than those in the north, despite the efforts made by the authorities to reduce regional disparities in the rates of enrolment.

Concerning the fight against illiteracy which is another aspect of the reform, a relative success was chalked, as far as the literacy programmes for women are concerned. As a result, in 1989 662 literacy co-education programmes were organized all over the country, with 337 centres for women and another 113 additional centres that were able to enrol respectively, 9,634; 7,985 and 2,186 learners (INRS 1991: 48–9).

The number of teachers unfortunately did not correspond with the increase in the number of pupils. From 1975 to 1980, at the kindergarten and primary school level, the number of teachers registered a growth rate of 7.91 per cent with 5,627 teachers in 1975. Between 1980 and 1985, this rate decreased and reached 2.7 per cent. Between 1985 and 1990 this growth rate became negative that is 0.18 per cent. This negative tendency, to some exceptions, was almost the same at the junior secondary school level for the same period. At the senior secondary school level by the end of 1980s only 764 relatively qualified teachers were recorded and most of them were part-time teachers and most importantly the majority did not reach the level of the General Certificate of Education,

Advanced Level. In addition, there was a lack of qualified teachers in science subjects, music, and home economics. As far as higher education was concerned in 1989 a total of 276 teachers with 211 Togolese were recorded. Out of this total, lecturers and senior lecturers were predominant, compared to associate professors and full professors who were scarcely found in the faculties. There was a total absence of full professors in charge of chairs (INRS 1991: 48–54; Assima-Kpatcha 2007: 86–7).

The period corresponding to the economic crisis of 1980s, did not favour the increase in the number of teachers. As a result, the quality of teaching declined, there was the lack of teaching and learning resources and adequate training for teachers (Assima-Kpatcha 2007: 87).

However, it was during the national sovereign conference (July to August 1991) that the limitations of the reform were clearly established and a recommendation to hold the National Conference on Education was adopted, and it eventually took place in 1992. It must be recalled that, Togo took part in the Jomtien conference on education for all in 1990. The recommendations of the National Conference on Education at this conference coupled with those of the national conferences of 1991 worked in favour of the National Conference on Education.

In fact, known under the name 'National Conference on Education, of Training and Scientific Research' this meeting was held in Lomé from 4 to 13 May 1992. The mission assigned to the meeting was 'to examine, analyse, and assess the education system in its functioning', its results, and its relation with the world at large'. The conclusion was that the reform was a complete failure in terms of the quality of the teaching. But for Assima-Kpatcha (2007: 87), instead of concluding that it was a total failure, it would rather be relevant to say that the reform was not implemented, due to the economic difficulties facing the country. All the assessments of the reform today reveal that the internal and external efficacy of the Togolese system of education suffered many setbacks at every level. Furthermore, the development of technical education and vocational training was regarded a complete failure, despite the creation in 1984 of a ministry in charge of this sector. Also, failure to develop the informal education system in the country was an issue (Gbikpi-Benissan 2012: 167).

These recommendations of the National Conference on Education could not be implemented as was expected. The reason being that in the 1990s, Togo went through a social and political crisis which was characterized by a severe lack of financial resources following the suspension of co-operation with its partners in development. As a result, the state authorities opted for measures, developed in the next section of this chapter, to solve the immediate problems.

The Togolese education sector from 1993 to date: What are the realities?

This section focuses on three programmes. The first is the Declaration of Sector Policy for Education (1993), the second is the Project for the Support to the Management of Education (PAGED) 1995–2001, and the third is the National Action Plan for Education for All 2005–15. All these programmes are the major orientations given to the Togolese education system for the periods concerned.

The declaration of sector policy for education (1993)

According to Jean Adama Nyame and Yao Nuakey (2000: 74), this declaration falls within the framework of the spirit of Jomtien (Education for All) and it illustrates Togo's commitment to pursuing a great social justice. For the two experts, the sector policy maintains the three priority objectives defined by the reform of 1975. To reach these three objectives, they concluded, the government undertook emergency and well-focused actions upon which a request was submitted to the World Bank funding in the form of the Project for the Support to the Management of Education (PAGED).

The project for the support to the management of education (PAGED) 1995–2001

At the beginning, it was presented in the shape of a technical assistance from the World Bank in 1990 for the rehabilitation of the education sector. In 1992 the project was reoriented in order to cover the entire problems confronting the sector following the political crisis through which the country went. The project covered two aspects, namely, the improvement of the quality of education and the management of the education system.

The aspect concerning the 'in service training of teachers and the quality of education' constitutes the innovation of the project. This aspect was meant to provide a logistical support to all the primary schools in the country (Nyame and Nuakey 2000: 74).

In fact, in September 1996, the government defined the educational programmes related to the improvement of the school environment, the reinforcement of school management capacities, the improvement of educational programmes and the setting of a permanent policy for professional training (ibid.). Through this programme the government wanted to lay an emphasis on primary school education in order to reach a net enrolment rate of 80 per cent in 2010 by the latest. The government reaffirmed its support to this programme in 1998 because it wanted to do everything possible to reach the goals of the Jomtien Conference. At the same time, it was noticed that the objectives of the Education for All could be reached by the year 2000. It is in this vein that the action plan of Dakar came into being.

The World Forum on Education held in Dakar from 26 to 28 April 2000, had to reschedule the deadline for the achievement of the Jomtien objectives until 2015. It also defined a framework of action to help these countries in the elaboration of their policy as well as the national strategies for the education for all (Gbikpi-Benissan 2012: 169). It is in this context, that Togo elaborated its national action plan for education for all.

The national action plan for the education for all 2005-15

After having underlined the great shortcomings in the Togolese education sector, the action plan defined by six priorities are summarized by François Gbikpi-Benissan (2012) as follows:

> 1-improve upon access, equity and keeping children in school at different levels of education, and particularly at the primary school level, and especially girls, children with special difficulties, the physically impaired, the vulnerable and the less-favoured as well as the acquisition of real skills. 2-improve every aspect of the quality of education, the internal efficiency and admission conditions at every level. 3-improve the relevance of the contents and adapt them to the national and international needs of the learners and those of the national development programmes. 4-improve upon the management and piloting of the system. 5-promote the education for the culture of peace, the protection of the environment, of democracy and citizenship at every level education. 6-promote sanitary education by giving a great priority to the fight against STD/HIV/AIDS (p. 169).

On the whole, after 50 years of independence, the Togolese education system has registered many upheavals, reforms, National Conference on Education, sector policies for education. While the impact of these different initiatives increased access to education, education quality was undermined.

In fact, at the primary school level there were 472 schools for 87,300 students and almost 3,000 teachers in 1960. In 2010, the numbers increased to 6,049 schools for 1,286,653 students and 31,712 teachers. For the junior secondary school level in 1960, there were 17 schools for 1,930 students and 500 teachers. Fifty years later, these numbers grew to 1,100 schools for 340,103 students and 9,185 teachers. At the secondary school level, just after independence, there were 17 schools for 305 students and about 300 teachers. In 2010, these numbers rose to 264 schools for 119,929 students and 3,929 teachers. Technical education also registered the same increase. From 12 schools for 493 students and less than 100 teachers in 1960, these numbers increased to 116 schools for 26,571 students and 2,011 teachers in 2009. Concerning public higher education (the statistics from the private higher education are not yet available), there was only one university with 845 students and about 100 teachers. The country has now two public universities. In 2010 the two universities registered 50,102 students for about 600 teachers (Gbikpi-Benissan 2012: 169–72)

Nonetheless, the population of Togo has grown from an estimated 1,500,000 inhabitants in 1960 to around 6 million. One can therefore understand the increase in the number of students enroled in schools. It must be noted that if this level of school enrolment has been reached, it is due in part to the different educational policies put in place, even if much remains to be done to reach the required quality in the education system in the country. What are then the prospects?

What prospects for the coming years?

Considering the Jomtien conference in 1990 and the action plan of Dakar, it can be noticed that the government considered the objectives of these conferences as mid-term priority objectives. Apart from the recommendations of Jomtien (1990) and those of Dakar (2000) there are other international institutions which highly recommend countries, especially African countries, to reach the objective of education for all. This is among others the Millennium Development Goals whose second objective consists of ensuring primary education for all. This is also the case of African states with the New Partnership for African Development (NEPAD) which also recommends African states to reach the objective of education for all. To reach this objective not in 2015, as initially planned, but in 2020, following the sector plan for education (2010–20) within which the government in 2010 declared free access to public primary schools in Togo.

In the pursuit of education for all, the education policy in Togo has laid emphasis on some key concepts, namely the management of the system itself, the integration of information and communication technology, education on citizenship, education for democracy and for the culture of peace, education and development, inclusive education, adult education. All these are good intentions. But the question is whether by 2015 or 2020, the government will put sufficient means at the disposal of the education system to help it reach the objectives of these good intentions, especially in the context of the scarcity of resources, and the reduction of budget allocations to the education sector. Another question is whether the government will not succumb to the temptation of sacrificing the quality of education on the altar of quantity in its drive to reach the objective of education for all. The temptation is very high to reproduce the experience of the reform of 1975, whose implementation privileged quantity to the detriment of quality. The task today is to define which kind of citizens Togo would like to have in the coming decades to help it face the challenges of development and globalization.

Conclusion

The analysis of the trends of the education system in Togo reveals some realities. From the time of independence, it has been noticed that the authorities were preoccupied by the need to reform the education system inherited from colonization. It is in this vein that various education initiatives influenced by recommendations of the various conferences in which the country took part were put in place. The analysis of all these policies, underlines the fact that the progression in enrolment rates does not go hand in hand with the quality of education. Furthermore, these policies

> always take into account, the regional and international contexts, which insist on the improvement of access to education, the reduction of the disparities and the pursuit of equity, the improvement of the quality of education in order to reduce school dropouts and the importance of increasing the internal efficiency, the need to adapt the curricula to the socioeconomic needs of the country with the view of improving the external efficiency (Gbikpi-Benissan 2012: 170).

Unfortunately, all these policies have never solved all these problems. One then has the impression that the authorities are beating around the bush.

References

Amegawovo, K. S. (2010). *Les réformes de l'enseignement en Afrique francophone de 1960 à 1990*, mémoire de maîtrise d'histoire, Université de Lomé.

Assima-Kpatcha, E. (2007). 'L'organisation de l'enseignement au Togo indépendant (1960–1992)', in *Revue du C.A.M.E.S.*, Sciences sociales et humaines, Série B, vol. 009, n° 2–2007 (2ème semestre), pp. 77–91.

Assima-Kpatcha, E., Y. Marguerat and P. Sebald. (2005). 'L'éducation sous domination coloniale'. In Gayibor Nicoué Lodjou (dir.), *Histoire des Togolais de 1884 à 1960*, Lomé, Presses de l'UL, Vol. II, Tome 1, pp. 101–59.

Batchodoum, M. (2006). *Structures et infrastructures de l'enseignement au Togo de 1960 à 1990*, mémoire de maîtrise d'histoire, Université de Lomé.

Gayibor, N. L. (ed.). (1997). *Le Togo sous domination coloniale (1884–1960)*, Lomé, PUB.

Gbikpi-Benissan, F. (2012). 'Cinquante ans de politiques éducatives en Afrique francophone: un manque de réalisme. Le cas du Togo', Gayibor Nicoué Lodjou (sous dir.) *Cinquante ans d'indépendance africaine*, Paris, L'Harmattan, pp. 165–80.

Lassey, A. (2011). 'L'école occidentale et la formation de l'intelligentsia au Togo (1884–2009)'. In *Travail et Formations*, n° 001, pp. 111–32.

Ministry of National Education (1975). *La réforme de l'enseignement au Togo (forme condensée)*, Lomé.

Ministère de l'éducation nationale et de la recherche (1998). *Bulletin officiel d'information*.

National Institute of Education (INSE) (1989). *La réforme de l'enseignement de 1975 au Togo: perception de l'INSE quatorze ans après*, Lomé, Université de Lomé.

National Institute of Scientific Research (INRS) (1991). *Economies et sociétés togolaises. Chiffres, tendances et perspectives*, Lomé.

Nyame, J. A. and Y. Nuakey. (2000). 'Réforme des systèmes éducatifs et réformes curriculaires: cas du Togo', commission nationale gabonaise pour l'Unesco, *réforme des systèmes éducatifs et réformes curriculaires: situation dans les Etats africains au sud du Sahara*, Rapport final du séminaire-atelier de Libreville, Gabon, 23 au 28 octobre 2000 'politique de refondation curriculaire, processus de développement curriculaire, réalités locales et défis du XXIe siècle', pp. 71–6.

Occansey, K. S. (1972). 'Contribution à l'histoire de l'enseignement au Togo', Thèse de doctorat d'Etat en droit, Université de Strasbourg.

UNESCO (1961). Rapport final de la conférence d'Etats africains sur le développement de l'éducation en Afrique. Addis-Ababa, 15–25 May.

Unesco-Afrique (1991). 'Spécial MINEDAF VI', *Revue trimestrielle du Bureau régional de Dakar* (BREDA), October.

University of Lomé (2002). 'Direction des affaires académiques et de la scolarité', *Textes fondamentaux de l'Université de Lomé,* Lomé, Presses de l'UL, 3è édition revue et augmentée.

Index

The letter t following an entry indicates a table

Abidjan conference, the 483
Addis Ababa conference, the 481–2
ADEA (Association for the Development of Education in Africa) 13
adult education 112–13
African Charter for Human and People's Rights (ACHPR) 35 n.5
African Development Bank 448
African Union (AU) 227
Afrique de l'Ouest Française (AOF) 334–5
Amin, M. E. 80
AMU (Arab Maghreb Union) 324
Angola 228
AOF (Afrique de l'Ouest Française [French West Africa]) 334–5
Arab Maghreb Union (AMU) 324
Arusha Convention, the 34, 35 n.6, 227
assimilation 249–50, 251
Association for the Development of Education in Africa (ADEA) 13
AU (African Union) 227
AUC Agenda 2063, The 13

Basic Education in Africa Programme (BEAP) 25–6, 35 n.3
BEAP (Basic Education in Africa Programme) 25–6, 35 n.3
Belgium 249
Benin, Republic of 21
   colonialism 22, 23–4, 27
   decentralization and devolution 31–2
   economy 23
   education access 29
   education enrolment 27, 29, 30
   education funding 26–7, 34–5
   education ministries 26
   education policies 27–8, 33
   education quality 29–30
   education system 23–8, 30–1, 34
   education trends 28–34
   employment 30–1
   gender parity 21
   higher education 33
   history 22–3
   human capital 32, 34
   ICT 33
   languages 22
   literacy 32
   National Conference (NC) 22
   population 21–2, 34
   private education 27, 33
   regional integration 33–4
   teachers 32, 34
   trends 28–34
   urban/rural inequalities 30
Berlin Conference 1885, The 446
Boko Haram 365, 372
Brazil 228–9
British Council, the 402
Burkina Faso
   colonialism 38
   culture 44–6
   economy 37, 41–2, 46
   education access 42
   education challenges 44–8
   education enrolment 38–9, 40, 41–2, 44–5, 55–6
   Education for All (EFA) 40–1 45–7, 54–6, 58–60
   education funding 42, 46, 47–8, 61
   education policies 38–44, 47, 54, 56–7, 59–60
   education quality 43, 48, 56–9
   ethnicity 44–5
   gender parity 3, 40, 42, 45, 55–6
   higher education in 60–3
   infrastructure 54, 57–8
   international aid 46
   languages 57, 58

patriarchy 45
PDDEB (Ten-Year Basic Education Development Plan) 41–3, 47, 54, 56–7, 59
population 37
poverty 46
religion 45
State Generals of Education (SGEs) 39–40
student unrest 60–1
teachers 42, 47–8, 54–5, 58–9, 63
universal schooling 59–60
Busan Partnership Agreement 7

Cameroon
bilingualism 70, 77–8, 85–6
colonialism 67, 68–9, 85
decentralization 86, 87–8, 89, 90, 94
education enrolment 70–1, 92, 94
Education for All (EFA) 70, 71
education funding 71, 79, 80
education futures 86, 94–7
education policies 72–4, 87–90
education quality 71, 89–93, 97
education system 67–72, 88
education trends 86–93
futures 86, 94–7
gender parity 80, 96–7
higher education 75–6, 90
history 68–9, 85–6
human capital 94
ICT 76–7, 93, 94
population 86, 94
private education 90, 91
qualifications 92, 95
secondary education 92, 94
students with disabilities 92–3, 95
teachers 71–2, 80, 88, 90–2, 95–6
technical and vocational education and training (TVET) 74–5, 91
trends 86, 87–93
urban/rural inequalities 91–2
youth, the 94
Cape Verde 101
adult education 112–13
basic education 106–7, 115
education challenges 114–15
education enrolment 105, 106, 107, 108, 111, 113–14
education funding 104–5, 109
education levels 102
education policy 102, 110
education quality 106–7, 108–9
education reform 102
education system 102–4, 105–13
employment 101–2, 109
gender parity 111, 112–13
higher education 110–12, 114
infrastructure 110
languages 102
literacy 103, 112–13, 114
non-formal education 112–13
population 101
pre-school education 105–6, 115
private education 104, 111
secondary education 107–8, 115
social support 103
special educational needs 106
teachers 106, 108–9, 111–12, 114, 115
technical and vocational education and training (TVET) 107, 109–10, 114
CEDAW (Convention on the Elimination of All Forms of Discrimination Against Women) 252
Chad 119–20
colonialism 123
conflict 119–20, 123–4
crisis 130
economy 120, 122
education enrolment 127–8
education funding 126, 130, 131
education history 123–4
education policies 124, 130–1
education quality 128–30
education system 124–6
ethnicity 121
higher education 125, 129
infrastructure 129
Interim Strategic Plan for Education and Literacy (SIPEA) 130–2
international aid 122
kindergarten 125, 127
languages 121, 123–4
literacy 129
non-formal education 132
political system 120
population 120–1

poverty 121
pre-school education 125, 127
primary education 125, 127, 128
qualifications 130
religion 121
secondary education 125, 127–8
Strategic Plan for Education and Literacy (SIPEA) 131–2
teachers 129–30
technical and vocational education and training (TVET) 127–9
trends 127–30
China 228
citizenship 283
Collier, P. 229–30
colonialism 247–50 *see also under individual countries*
'common pool' 447
conflict 446–7 *see also under individual countries*
confluence, the 8–11, 14
Convention on the Elimination of All Forms of Discrimination Against Women (CEDAW) 252
corruption 446–8
Côte d'Ivoire *see* Ivory Coast

Dahomey 22
databases 16
Déby, Idriss (President) 120
decentralization 31, 186, 306 *see also under individual countries*
devolution 31–2, 306
Dupont, P. *School Civilization, The* (1990) 333

Economic Community of West African States (ECOWAS) 13, 33–4, 35 n.1, 227–8, 309
economy 14–15 *see also under individual countries*
ECOWAS (Economic Community of West African States) 13, 33–4, 35 n.1, 227–8 309
education 86, 248, 254, 393–4, 407, 451
  higher *see* higher education *under individual countries*
  pre-school *see* pre-school education *under individual countries*
  private *see* private education *under individual countries*
  secondary *see* secondary education *under individual countries*
education development 6–7 *see also* ADEA
education economics, theory of 407 *see also* economy *and* human capital
education enrolment 2–3, 4–5, 481 *see also under individual countries*
Education for All (EFA) 2, 37, 62, 489–90 *see also under individual countries*
education funding 8–9, 183–5, 397t, 481 *see also under individual countries*
education planning 481
education policies 8–9, 13 *see also under individual countries*
education quality 3–4, 183, 413 *see also under individual countries*
education reform 481–2
education systems *see under individual countries*
EFA (Education for All) 2, 37, 62, 489–90 *see also under individual countries*
Eholié, Rose: 'Ivorian Women: Education and Integration in the Economic Development of Côte d'Ivoire' 257
employment *see under individual countries*
'Etas généraux de l'éducation' 24
ethnicity 446–7 *see also under individual countries*
external development partners 6–7 *see also* confluence, the *and* international aid
Ezekwesili, Obiageli 403–4

France 248, 249–52, 333

Gambia, The
  colonialism 137
  curriculum 138
  decentralization 143
  Early Childhood Development (ECD) 144
  economy 148
  education enrolment 139–40
  Education for All (EFA) 138, 143

education funding 139
education history 137–40, 144–8
education policies 135–6, 137–49
education policy reviews 142
education system 142–3, 148–9
employment 145, 146–7
gender parity 141
higher education 138–9, 140
human capital 144–5
international aid 146
Madrassas 143–4
non-formal education 143
population 135
poverty 147–8
primary education 137
qualifications 139, 148
secondary education 137–8
stakeholders 142
teachers 139
technical and vocational education and training (TVET) 136, 144–9
trends 147–8
gender 250
gender parity 3, 4, 260 *see also under individual countries*
Ghana
Amissah Committee 153–4
colonialism 152–3, 170
curriculum 153–4, 155
decentralization 156, 164, 175
education challenges 164, 168
education enrolment 157, 161, 171
Education for All (EFA) 171, 175
education funding 156, 163–4, 171–2, 175–6, 178, 185–95
education history 152–60, 186–8
education policies 153–9
education quality 157, 162–3, 172–3
education reforms 153–9
education system 154–7, 167–9, 178–9
employment 170
gender parity 161–2, 171–2
higher education 168, 177–8, 185, 187, 194
ICT 159–60
infrastructure 155, 158–9, 163, 164
international aid 156, 163, 188–91
languages 168–9

non-formal education 152
Omega Schools 174
perception of education 170
population 170–1
poverty 155, 171
private education 172–5, 194
secondary education 177
social mobility 170, 172, 173
special educational needs 176
teachers 162, 163, 164, 173, 178–9, 192–3
technical and vocational education and training (TVET) 153–4, 178, 192
trends 167–76, 189–92
urban/rural inequalities 174
youth, the 170–1
global contexts 8–11
Global Partnership for Education (GPE) 302, 315, 422
GPE (Global Partnership for Education) 302, 315, 422
Guinea 200
conflict 200
economy 200
education enrolment 201, 202, 204–5, 207
Education for All (EFA) 223–4
education funding 210–11
education history 201–2
education management 203–4
education quality 205–6
employment 202, 207
gender parity 207
higher education curricula 206
higher education policy 203
higher education reforms 201–2
higher education students 207
higher education system 203–5, 211–13
infrastructure 209
opportunities, threats and challenges 212–13
politics 200
population 200
poverty 200
resources 209–10
scientific research 203, 207–8, 211–13
teachers 208–9

technical and vocational education
   and training (TVET) 201
Guinea-Bissau 217–19
   colonialism 219
   conflict and political instability 217,
      218–19, 226, 229–30
   economy 218, 221
   ECOWAS (Economic Community of
      West African States) 227, 228
   education enrolment 221, 222–5
   education equality 222
   education funding 221–2, 226, 228
   education goals 223–4
   education policies 219–21
   education quality 221, 226
   ethnicity 218, 230
   gender parity 223
   higher education 227
   international aid 228–9
   languages 218, 227, 230
   literacy 225–6
   medical training 227–8
   PALOP (Países Africanos de Língua
      Oficial Portuguesa) 227
   population 218, 221
   poverty 218, 229–30
   pre-school education 225
   primary education 223
   regional organization 227–8
   teachers 222
   trends 222–9

Haidara, B. A. 299–300
higher education 5–6, 60, 62, 185–6, 227
   see also under individual countries
Houphouët-Boigny, Denise: 'Women and
   Scientific Education: The Case of
   Higher Education in Côte d'Ivoire'
   257
human capital 6, 13, 185, 254, 407 *see also
   under individual countries*

ICT 14 *see also under individual countries*
infrastructure 482 *see also under
   individual countries*
international aid 6–7, 8–11, 14, 185–6,
   279 *see also under individual
   countries*
'Ivorian Women: Education and
   Integration in the Economic
   Development of Côte d'Ivoire'
   (Eholié) 257
Ivory Coast 235–6
   colonialism 248–52, 255
   community schools 243
   conflict 242–3, 258–9
   decentralization 236
   economy 248, 252–3, 258–9
   education approaches 244
   education enrolment 238–41, 243, 253,
      254–6
   Education for All (EFA) 235, 238, 244
   education funding 235–6, 253, 259
   education history 237, 248, 251–3
   education performance 242
   education policies 259–60
   education staff 241
   education system 236–8, 253
   gender parity 239, 243, 251–2, 253–7,
      259–61
   higher education 238, 241, 256–7
   history 248, 252–3, 258
   literacy 238, 255
      population 235
   poverty 236, 258–9
   pre-school education 237, 239
   primary education 237, 240, 254
   secondary education 237–8, 240–1,
      254
   special educational needs 244
   technical and vocational education
      and training (TVET) 237–8, 241
   urban/rural inequalities 239

'Jomtien, 20 Years: Global Education for All
   Partners Must Renew Commitment
   to Learning' (King) 58–9

Kerekou, Mathieu 22, 23
King, E.: 'Jomtien, 20 Years: Global
   Education for All Partners Must
   Renew Commitment to Learning'
   58–9
Knowledge Aid Sierra Leone 448
Koblavi Mansilla, Frederica: 'Women and
   Scientific Education: The Case of
   Higher Education in Côte d'Ivoire'
   257

languages *see under individual countries*
LDCs (Least Developed Countries) 217–18
Least Developed Countries (LDCs) 217–18
Liberia 280
   Accelerated Learning Programme (ALP) 274–6
   child soldiers 266, 267, 274–6
   citizenship 283–4
   citizenship education 285–94
   conflict 265, 266–9, 272–3, 274, 284–5
   corruption 289
   decentralization 280–1
   democracy 285, 288, 289–92
   development 267–9
   economy 267–8
   education enrolment 269–72, 274–6
   'Education for Peace' programmes 276
   education funding 270, 278–80
   education history 269–70, 285–6
   education policies 274–6, 278–81
   education quality 272–4
   education system 269–71
   employment 268, 269
   equality 270, 278
   ethnicity 270, 283–4, 288
   gender parity 276–8, 293
   global citizenship 292–3, 294
   higher education 272, 280
   history 266, 284–5
   infrastructure 266, 272–3
   international aid 279
   literacy 276
   mortality 266–7
   population 266, 270
   poverty 267–8
   primary education 274–6
   private education 271, 279
   resources 273–4
   secondary education 270
   students 291–2
   teachers 273, 275, 279, 290–1, 294
   technical and vocational education and training (TVET) 272
   urban/rural inequalities 270–1
   youth, the 270, 283–4, 285, 291–2

literacy rates 3, 482 *see also under individual countries*
local solutions 59–60

Madrassas 143–4, 336, 453
Mahama, John (President) 176
Mali 297–9
   colonialism 297–8
   community schools 302–3, 309
   conflict 298
   decentralization 303, 306
   devolution 306
   education enrolment 4, 304, 309
   Education for All (EFA) 307
   education funding 301–2, 309
   education history 299–300
   education policies 300–1, 303, 306–8
   education quality 304–5
   education system 299–303
   employment 305–6
   ethnicity 298
   gender parity 305, 307–8
   higher education 301
   history 298–9
   human capital 307
   ICT 308, 309
   inequalities 305
   international aid 302
   literacy 307–8
   population 298
   pre-school education 300
   primary education 300
   private education 302–3
   regional integration 308–9
   secondary education 300, 308–9
   staff 307
   teachers 307, 309
   technical and vocational education and training (TVET) 300
   Ten-Year Educational Development Plan (PRODEC) 303
   trends 303–9
   urban/rural inequalities 305, 308
Mauritania 311–13
   colonialism 323
   conflict 321–2, 325
   economy 312–13, 315, 322, 325
   education enrolment 318–19, 321, 325
   Education for All (EFA) 317–18

education funding 315, 325
education history 313–14
education policies 314, 315–17, 323
education quality 320
education system 313–17
employment 322, 325
equality 320
ethnicity 312
gender parity 318–19, 321
higher education 316t, 323
history 312
human capital 322–3, 325
ICT 323
international aid 315
languages 312, 313–14, 323–4
literacy 316t, 320–1
population 312, 325
poverty 312, 313, 315–17
Poverty Reduction Strategy Paper (PRSP) 315–17
primary education 316t
regional integration 324
secondary education 316t
student mobility 322–3
technical and vocational education and training (TVET) 316t, 323
trends 317–24
urban/rural inequalities 320
Merrick, Joseph (Reverend) 68
mobile phones 14

Nairobi conference, the 482
Ndoye, Mamadou 4
Nduom, Paa Kwesi (Dr) 176
NEPAD (New Partnership for African Development) 489
Networked Readiness Index (NRI) 76
New Partnership for African Development (NEPAD) 489
NFE (non-formal education) 444 *see also under individual countries*
Niger 329–31
  administration 332
  colonialism 332, 333–5, 343, 346
  community schools 347
  conflict 337
  economy 330, 339
  education access 330–1, 355, 347–50, 351–3

education enrolment 334, 338, 340, 346, 347–9, 351–4
Education for All (EFA) 335, 349, 351
education funding 331, 338–9, 351, 354
education history 333–9, 343–4, 346–
education policies 333–40, 347, 356–9
education quality 350–1, 354, 357
education system 332, 339–40, 343–6
ethnicity 331
future 356–9
gender parity 347, 349, 350t, 351–4, 355–6, 358–9
higher education 338, 345, 354–5
languages 331–2, 335–6, 343, 356–7
literacy 344
Niger Education System Reform Law (LOSEN) 343, 344–5, 349, 356
population 331
poverty 331, 339
pre-school education 344, 347 or pre-school
primary education 335–6, 344, 348–51
private education 347, 355
qualifications 344–5, 354
secondary education 336–7, 344–5, 351–4
teachers 334–5, 338, 348, 354, 357–8
technical and vocational education and training (TVET) 336, 345, 354
Ten-year Program for Education Development (PDDE) 340, 347, 356–9 trends 346–56
urban/rural inequalities 349–50
Nigeria 363–4, 393–4
  Boko Haram 372
  citizenship 372–4
  colonialism 364, 395
  Community Accountability and Transparency Initiative (CATI) 403–4
  conflict 365, 372
  conflict resolution 372–3
  decentralization 367
  economy 364–5, 367, 373
  education access 367–8, 393
  education enrolment 367–8
  education funding 367, 368, 388, 394–404

education history 364, 379, 380, 382–5, 395
education policies 382–5, 394, 399, 403–4
education quality 369, 388–9, 403
education system 385–6,
employment 387, 388
ethnicity 364, 355–6
formal education 379–80
gender parity 370, 388
globalization 389
higher education 370–1, 380, 396, 402–3
human capital 382, 389, 394
ICT 389
Industrial Training Fund (ITF) 386
inequalities 364–5
informal education 79, 379
infrastructure 398, 399
Innovative Enterprises Institutes (IEIs) 386
international aid 402
languages 369–70
literacy 364, 369–70
National Board for Technical Education (NBTE) 385–6
National Business and Technical Examinations Board (NABTEB) 386
National Directorate of Employment (NDE) 386
national identity 366
non-formal education 379
poverty 389
pre-vocational subjects 380
primary education 380, 399
private education 371–2
religion 365, 366, 372
secondary education 380, 399
taxation 401–2
teachers 369, 386, 399–400
technical and vocational education and training (TVET) 377–8, 379–81, 382–90
technical and vocational education graduates 388–9
technical and vocational education institutions 380–1, 385–7
technical and vocational education policies 382–5, 388
technical and vocational education system 385–6
technical and vocational qualifications 383, 386, 387
trends 382–5, 387–90
UNESCO–UNEVOC centres 386
Vocational Enterprises Institutions (VEIs) 386
vocational subjects 380
youth, the 372, 387
non-formal education (NFE) 444 *see also under individual countries*
NRI (Networked Readiness Index) 76

Omega schools 174

Países Africanos de Língua Oficial Portuguesa (PALOP) 227
PALOP (Países Africanos de Língua Oficial Portuguesa) 227
patriarchy 45
population 2 *see also under individual countries*
poverty 15 *see also under individual countries*
pre-school education *see under individual countries*
primary education 482 *see also under individual countries*
private education *see under individual countries*
productivity 14
Psacharopoulos, G. 62
pupil/teacher ratio 3–4

school
  attendance 2–3 *see also* education enrolment
School Civilization, The (1990) (Dupont) 333
secondary education 4, 92, 94, 185 *see also under individual countries*
Senegal 407–8, 421
  basic community schools (ECBs) 427–8
  decentralization 427
  Development Plan for Education and Training (PDEF) 421–2, 429
  economy 408, 409

education access 410–12, 423
education enrolment 408–9, 411–13, 423–4, 428
Education for All (EFA) 408, 413, 422, 427
education funding 413–16, 429
education management 414–16
education policies 416–17, 421–3
education quality 409, 412–13, 416, 424–6, 429
education recommendations 416–17
education system 410–11
gender parity 411, 424
higher education 412, 428–30
human capital 407, 416
inequalities 410
informal education 410–11
infrastructure 414, 415t, 423, 425
kindergarten 411
languages 424–5, 427
literacy 424, 426–7
LMD (Licence-Master-Doctorate) reforms 429–30
non-formal education (NFE) 410–11, 426–8
population 408
poverty 407, 410
pre-school education 411
primary education 411, 412, 413
private education 424
religion 410
secondary education 411–13
teachers 414–15, 425
technical and vocational education and training (TVET) 415
Tostan 428
trends 423–6
West African Economic and Monetary Union (WAEMU) 429–30
SIDS (Small Island Developing States) 218
Sierra Leone 435–6
    2004 Education Act 458
    2010 Education Act 458–9
    adult education 460–1
    agricultural education 455
    American International School 461
    'Athens of West Africa' 456
    Ayoub International School (A.I.S.) 461
    boarding schools 454
    Christianity 453–4
    civil war 457–8, 460
    colonialism 452–3, 454, 455, 456
    conflict 436–7, 448, 457–8
    corruption 446–8
    curricula 453
    economy 436
    education development 448–9
    education enrolment 438, 454, 457–8
    education funding 448, 459
    education history 435, 451, 452–9
    education management 445–6
    education policies 441–2, 444–6, 448, 457–9, 460–1
    education quality 435
    education structure 443t
    education system 457, 458
    employment 436, 437
    ethnicity 436, 446–8
    gender parity 444, 460
    Girls' Education Support Programme, The 460
    higher education 439–40, 456
    history 436
    infrastructure 437, 461
    international aid 448, 461
    Lebanese School 461
    literacy 436, 437, 445
    Madrassas 452–3
    Muslims 453
    National Board of Education, The 445
    National Commission for Basic Education, The 445
    National Council for Science and Technology 446
    National Institute for Education Training and Research, The 445
    non-formal education (NFE) 444–5
    Non-Formal Education Council, The 445–6
    population 436
    poverty 436, 437, 459
    pre-school education 438, 460
    primary education 438, 453–4
    Rehabilitation of Basic Education Project/SABABU Education Project 460
    religion 453

secondary education 438-9, 454-5
special educational needs 460
teachers 437, 440-2, 455-6, 459, 460
Teaching Service Commission, The 445
technical and vocational education and training (TVET) 442-4, 455
Tertiary Education Commission, The 445
trends 452-3
urban/rural inequalities 441
youth, the 437
Sirleaf, Ellen Johnson (President) 268, 276, 281, 285
Small Island Developing States (SIDS) 218
Soglo, Nicéphore 22
sources 16
special educational needs 106, 176, 244, 460
student unrest 60-1
subsidiarity principle, the 31

teachers 4 *see also under individual countries*
technical and vocational education and training (TVET) 5, 378-82, 386 *see also under individual countries*
technical education 378
technology 14 *see also* ICT
tertiary education *see* higher education
Togo
  agricultural education 469, 471
  British education system 468
  colonialism 465, 466-72, 475-6, 479, 480-1
  Declaration of Sector Policy for Education 487
  economy 472, 473, 485
  education access 489
  education enrolment 471, 474-5, 480-1, 485, 489
  Education for All (EFA) 486-90
  education funding 470, 473-4, 485, 486-7, 490
  education history 465-75, 479, 480-9
  education policies 473, 487-91
  education quality 473, 474, 482, 486
  education reform 473-5, 483-7

education system 465, 467-72, 476, 480-7
equality 484
French education system 468-72, 476
gender parity 474, 485
German education system 465, 467-8, 476
higher education 474-5, 477, 483, 489
informal education 465, 466
languages 467, 468, 484
literacy 485
Lome school 468, 469
National Conference on Education 486
population 472, 489
pre-school education 474
primary education 469-71, 472, 474, 476-7, 482, 489
private education 473-4
Project for the Support to the Management of Education (PAGED) 487-8
qualifications 471
religion 467-8
secondary education 471, 472, 474, 482, 489
teachers 471, 472, 473, 475, 483, 484, 485-6
technical and professional education 475, 482-3, 489
trends 483-7
trends 2-6 *see also under individual countries*
TVET (technical and vocational education and training) 5, 378-82, 386 *see also under individual countries*

UNESCO (United Nations Educational, Scientific and Cultural Organization) 381, 386, 448
UNICEF (United Nations Children and Educational Fund) 80, 402, 448
university education *see* higher education

USA 228

vocational education 378-9

WAEMU (West African Economic and Monetary Union) 33–4, 35 n.2, 309, 429
West African Economic and Monetary Union (WAEMU) 33–4, 35 n.2, 309, 429
West African Federation (AOF) 334–5
'Women and Scientific Education: The Case of Higher Education in Côte d'Ivoire' (Houphouët-Boigny and Koblavi Mansilla) 257
World Bank, the 6–7, 8–9, 185–6

Gambia, The 146
Ghana 188
higher education 61–2
Nigeria 395–6, 402

youth, the 2–4, 12, 283
Cameroon 94
Ghana 170–1
Liberia 269–70, 283–4, 285, 291–2
Nigeria 372, 388
Sierra Leone 437